Minnesota Real Estate

PROSOURCE SPECIAL EDITION

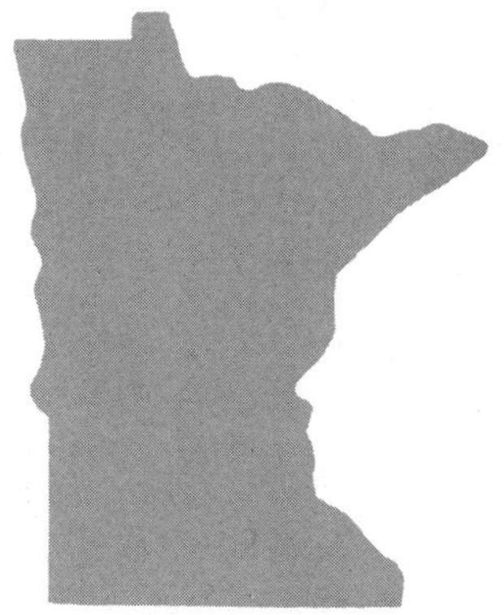

RICHARD LARSON

& BRUCE HARWOOD

Minnesota Real Estate

PROSOURCE SPECIAL EDITION

RESTON PUBLISHING COMPANY, INC.
A Prentice-Hall Company
RESTON, VIRGINIA

Library of Congress Cataloging in Publication Data

Larson, Richard.

Minnesota real estate.
Rev. ed. of: Minnesota real estate/William D. Foster,
Rita E. Lukes, and Bruce Harwood. 1980.
Includes bibliographies and index.
1. Real property—Minnesota. 2. Real estate business--
Licenses—Minnesota. 3. Vendors and purchasers—Minnesota.
I. Harwood, Bruce M. II. Foster, William D.
Minnesota real estate. III. Title.
KFM5512.L37 1984b 346.77604'3 83-24491
ISBN 0-8359-4431-X 347-760643

A Prentice-Hall Company
RESTON, VIRGINIA 22090

1 3 5 7 9 10 8 6 4 2

PRINTED IN THE UNITED STATES OF AMERICA

This book is dedicated
to the reader's success in the field of real estate.

CONTENTS

APPENDICES

MINNESOTA EDUCATION REQUIREMENTS

Course I Reference Guide

COURSE TOPICS *(text location)*	CREDITS *(class hours)*
Introduction to Real Estate:	3
Overview of the Industry (chapter 1)	
Real Estate Licensing Law:	4
Minnesota Statute Chapter 82 (chapter 18)	
Minnesota Statute Chapter 83 (appendix H)	
Law of Agency:	4
Broker-Principal Relationship (chapter 17)	
Duties of the Broker (chapters 17 & 18)	
Listing Contract (chapter 17)	
Responsibilities to the Buyer (chapters 17 & 18)	
Law of Contracts:	5
Essentials of a Valid Contract (chapter 7)	
Purchase Agreements (chapter 8)	
Contract for Deed (chapter 8)	
Property Description (chapter 2)	
Real Estate Financing	6
Buyer Qualifications (chapter 12)	
Lending Documents (chapter 9)	
Sources of Mortgage Funds (chapter 11)	
FHA-VA (chapter 11)	
Usury (chapter 12)	
Foreclosure (chapter 9)	
Types and Classifications of Property:	3
Real and Personal Property (chapter 2)	
Title to Property (chapter 5)	
Estates and Interests (chapter 3)	
Concurrent Ownership (chapter 4)	
Examination of Title:	1
Abstract (chapter 6)	
Title Insurance (chapter 6)	
Title Closing:	6
Methods of Closing (chapter 14)	
Delivery of Deed (chapter 5)	
Responsibilities of the Buyer and Seller (chapter 14)	
Broker Responsibilities (chapter 14)	
Truth in Lending (chapter 11)	

MINNESOTA EDUCATION REQUIREMENTS

Course II Reference Guide

COURSE TOPICS *(text location)*	CREDITS *(class hours)*
Deeds:	3
Parts of a Deed (chapter 5)	
Types of Deeds (chapter 5)	
Delivery and Recording (chapters 5 & 6)	
Search and Examination of Title:	1
Chain of Title (chapter 6)	
Grantor-Grantee Indexing System (chapter 6)	
Residental Appraisal:	6
Principles and Characteristics of Value (chapter 16)	
Highest and Best Use (chapter 16)	
Approaches to Value (chapter 16)	
Appraisal techniques (chapter 16)	
Residential Construction:	2
Construction Methods (appendix B)	
Home Warranties (chapter 20)	
Mechanic's Liens (chapter 3 and appendix I)	
Land Development and Use:	3
City Planing and Zoning (chapter 21)	
Building Codes (chapter 21)	
Subdivision Regulations (appendix H)	
Environmental Impact Statements (chapter 21)	
Platting (chapter 2)	
Condominiums, Cooperatives and PUDs:	3
Concepts of Cluster Ownership (chapter 19)	
Condominiums, Cooperatives and PUDs (chapter 19)	
Taxation:	4
Real Property Taxes (chapter 13)	
Income Taxes on Residential Property (chapter 13)	
Income Taxes on Investment Property (chapter 23)	
Investment and Appraisal:	4
Risks, Leverage and Cash Flow (chapter 23)	
Investment Analysis (chapters 16 & 23)	
Syndication (chapters 4 & 23)	
Appraisal Techniques (chapter 16)	
Real Property Management:	2
Property Management (chapter 15)	
Government Regulations (chapters 15 & 17)	
Leases and Leasing:	2
Contracts (chapters 7 & 15)	
Tenancies (chapters 3 & 15)	
Leases (chapter 15)	
Minnesota Landlord-Tenant Act (chapter 15)	

PREFACE

Minnesota Real Estate, second edition, combines the real estate law, custom and practice of Minnesota with the best and most readable national text, the latest edition of *Real Estate Principles* by Bruce Harwood.

At the beginning of each chapter there is a list of the new "key" terms that will be learned, along with brief definitions. And, at the end of each chapter there are review questions and problems based on the material just studied. Emphasis is placed on an easily readable presentation that combines explanations of "how" things are done in real estate with "why" they are done.

Sketches and diagrams are used to explain and sort out the complex rights and interests that are involved in real property. Warranty deeds, quit claim deeds, contracts for deeds, offers, listings, leases, title insurance policies, promissory notes, and mortgages are among the real estate forms and documents carefully analyzed. Wherever possible, simplified versions of these "key" documents are included and their key elements identified.

The choice of topics included in this book is the result of extensive market research conducted at privately organized real estate schools, at community colleges, and at four-year colleges that offer real estate courses to non-business majors. The topics also include those listed in the outline of real estate principles published by the National Association of Real Estate License Law Officials. In addition, Minnesota Real Estate, second edition, is specifically cross-referenced to the topics included in the first sixty hours of real estate education required in Minnesota. This is shown on the previous two pages.

This book will provide you in a single volume, a complete, efficient resource for developing and increasing your real estate knowledge and practical skills. Between these covers you will find the helpful, concrete information you need regarding Minnesota's Licensing Laws and requirements, Minnesota's Code of Agency, the Minnesota Subdivided Land Sales Act and other areas of Minnesota law, custom and practice.

ACKNOWLEDGMENTS *Special thanks to the following people for their assistance in preparing this book:* Carol Ansolabehere, Patricia Beauchamp, David Beson, Thomas Carey, Joe Coyne, Steve Dalluhn, William Foster, George Halonen, Lance Johnson, Margaret Karsten, Barbara Kivisto, Archie E. Larson, Rita Lukes, James Manke, Paul Matuschek, Kathleen Sullivan McGuiggan, Thomas Musil, Martin Otto, Fran Schoen, James Sexton, Dr. John Stone, Dr. Richard Swanson, Karlin Symons, Michael Symons, Lee Weiss, Lon Williams, and Michael Wollan.

R. L.

B. H.

A SPECIAL NOTE TO READERS

The author anticipates that as many women as men will read this book. However, it would make the sentences in this book harder to read if "he and she" and "his and her" were used on every possible occasion. Therefore, when you read, "he," "his," or "him" in this book, please note that they are being used in their grammatical sense and refer to women as well as men.

* * *

The forms in this text are for information only and are not intended for use as legal documents. In such matters, an attorney should be consulted.

1

Introduction to Real Estate

Welcome!
Real estate is an exciting business. But it is also a demanding one since it requires that one know the ethical and business principles fundamental to the successful selling and buying of real property. There are some who say that the only way to learn these principles is by experience. That can be extremely time-consuming and costly, no matter how good a teacher experience is. A more logical approach is to learn a substantial portion of this complicated body of knowledge from experts already at work in the field. Then personal experience can be acquired. With that combination in mind, this book has been written to provide you with an understanding of the basic principles and business fundamentals of real estate. Emphasis is placed on an easily readable presentation that combines explanations of "how" things are done in real estate with "why" they are done.

HOW TO READ THIS BOOK

At the beginning of each chapter (2 through 23) there is a list of the new "Key Terms" that you will learn, along with brief definitions. Read these before starting the chapter. In the body of the chapter these terms, along with other terms important to real estate, are set in **boldface type** and given a more in-depth discussion. At the end of each chapter is a vocabulary review plus questions and problems. These are designed to help you test yourself on your comprehension of the material in the chapter you've just read. The answers are given in Appendix H in the back of the book.

At the back of this book is a combined index-glossary. This approach was taken to help reinforce your familiarity with the language of real estate. When you use this glossary-index, you will receive a short definition followed by a page reference for more detailed discussion.

A unique feature of this book is its simplified documents. Deeds, mortgages and title policies, for example, are usually written in legal language and small type that defies comprehension by anyone except a lawyer. In the chapters ahead, you will find simplified versions of these documents, written in plain English and set in standard size type. The benefit to you is that you will come away with an understanding as to what is actually inside these important real estate documents.

Another special feature of this book is the wide margin on each page. Besides its eye appeal, it is helpful for locating subject headings, and it provides a handy place for your study notes.

Persons who wish to make a career in real estate may want additional questions, problems and situations in order to test and improve their grasp of the subject. An accompanying workbook by Bruce Harwood and John T. Ellis is designed to fill that need. It is available from bookstores and the publisher of this book and is called *Real Estate Resource Book.*

TRANSACTION OVERVIEW

Figure 1:1 provides a visual summary of the real estate transaction cycle. It is included here to give you an overview of the different steps involved in the sale of real property and to show how the steps are related to each other. The chapter where each step is discussed is also shown. Whether your point of view is that of a real estate agent, owner, buyer, or seller, you will find the chapters which follow to be informative and valuable.

Chapter Organization

Great care has been taken in organizing this text so as to carefully build your knowledge of real estate. For example, land description methods and rights and interests in land are necessary to sales contracts, abstracts, deeds, mortgages and listings and therefore are discussed early in the text.

In Chapter 2, you will find such topics as metes and bounds and tract maps. You will also find a discussion of what is real estate and what is not, and how land is physically and economically different from other commodities. Having described real estate, the next logical step is to look at the various rights and interests that exist in a given parcel of land. In Chapter 3 you will see that there is much more to ownership of land than meets the eye! In Chapter 4 we look at how a given right or interest in land can be held by an individual, by two or more persons, or by a business entity. Included in this chapter are discussions of joint tenancy and tenancy in common.

AN OVERVIEW OF A REAL ESTATE TRANSACTION **Figure 1:1**

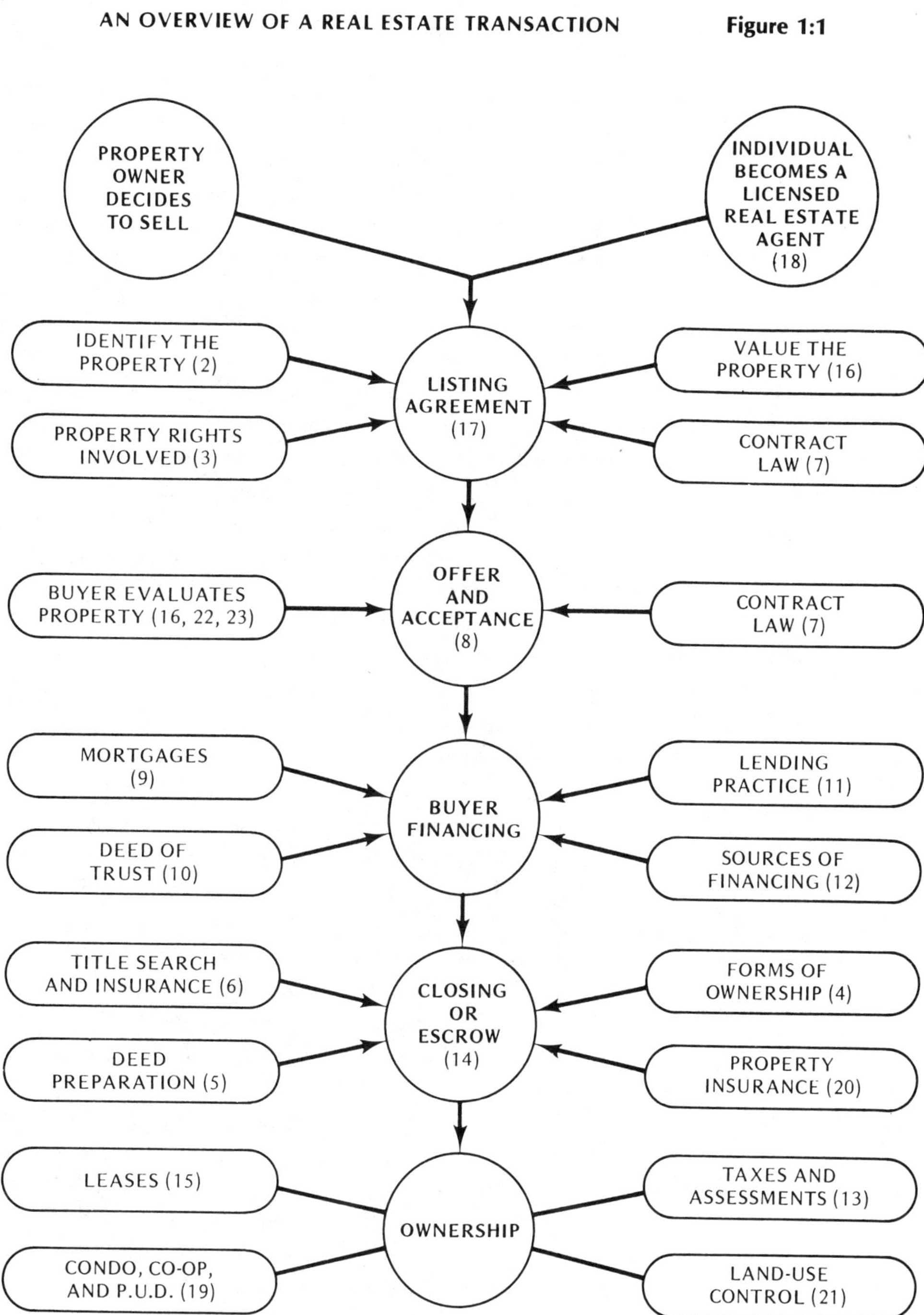

NOTE: Numbers in parentheses refer to Chapter Numbers.

Chapters 5 and 6 deal with the process by which the ownership of real estate is transferred from one person to another. In particular, Chapter 5 discusses deeds and wills, and Chapter 6 deals with how a person gives evidence to the world that he possesses a given right or interest in land. Abstracts and title insurance are among the topics included.

In Chapters 7 and 8, we turn to contract law and its application to offers and acceptances. Because so much of what takes place in real estate is in the form of contracts, you will want to have a solid understanding of what makes a contract legally binding, and what doesn't.

Chapters 9–12 are devoted to real estate finance. In Chapter 9, mortgages and the laws regarding their use are explained. Chapter 10 covers the deed of trust and is intended for readers in those states where the deed of trust is used in place of a mortgage. Amortized loans, points, FHA and VA programs, and mortgage insurance are discussed in Chapter 11. Mortgage lenders, loan approval, interest rates, due-on-sale clauses, adjustable rate mortages, and financing alternatives are covered in Chapter 12.

In Chapter 13, we see how property taxes and assessments are calculated, and Chapter 14 explains title closing and escrow. Chapter 15 deals with leasing real estate and includes a sample lease document with discussion. Chapter 16 presents the language, principles, and techniques of real estate appraisal.

In Chapter 17 we examine the relationship between real estate agents and buyers and sellers. Special emphasis is placed on the duties and obligations of the broker to his clients and on fair housing laws. The chapter following that deals with real estate license law requirements, how a salesperson goes about choosing a broker to affiliate with, and with professional ethics. Included in Chapter 18 are the Minnesota License Law Act and the Minnesota Code of Agency.

The remaining chapters of this book deal with a number of individual and specialized real estate topics. Chapter 19 explores the condominium, cooperative, and planned unit development forms of real estate ownership. Included is a look at how they are created and the various rights and interests in land that are created by them. In Chapter 20 we take a brief and informative look at property insurance. As an owner of real property, you should know how to insure against financial loss due to property damage and public liability.

Zoning, land planning and deed restrictions are covered in Chapter 21. These are important topics because any limitation on a landowner's right to develop and use his land can have a substantial effect on the value of his property. Chapter 22 explores several pertinent and timely relationships between the value of real estate and the condition of the United States economy. The final chapter, Chapter 23, is an introduction to the opportunities available to you as a real estate investor. Topics include tax shelter, equity build-up, what to buy and when to buy.

Following the final chapter are several appendices which you will find useful. There are compound interest, present value and measurement conversion tables. (Amortization and loan balance tables are located in Chapter 11.) There is also an appendix containing over a dozen construction illustrations to help acquaint you with construction terminology. Still another appendix contains sample questions typical of those found on real estate licensing examinations administered by the Educational Testing Service. This firm writes and administers the real estate license exams in Minnesota. You will also find a short real estate math review section plus the answers to the quizzes and problems found at the end of Chapters 2 through 23. Lastly you will see key excerpts from the Minnesota Subdivided Land Sales Act and Minnesota's Mechanic's Lien Law.

CAREER OPPORTUNITIES

The contents and organization of this book are designed for persons who are interested in real estate because they now own or plan to own real estate, and for persons interested in real estate as a career. It is to those who are considering real estate as a profession that the balance of this chapter is devoted.

Most persons who think of real estate from the career standpoint see only the real estate agent who specializes in selling homes. This is quite natural as home selling is the most visible segment of the real estate industry. Selling residential real estate is how most people enter the real estate business, and where most practicing real estate licensees make their living. Moreover, residential sales can be an excellent way to combine what you have learned from this book with first-hand experience. Residential sales is also a good way to experience whether real estate sales appeals to you, or whether residential property is the type of property in which you wish to specialize.

RESIDENTIAL BROKERAGE

Residential brokerage requires a broad knowledge of the community and its neighborhoods, finance, real estate law, economics, and the money market. Working hours will often include nights and weekends as these times are usually most convenient to buyers and sellers. A residential agent must also supply and drive his or her own automobile—one that is suitable for taking clients to see property.

In only a few real estate offices are new residential salespersons given a minimum guaranteed salary or a draw against future commissions. Therefore, a newcomer should have enough capital to survive until the first commissions are earned—and that can take four to six months. Additionally, the salesperson must be capable of developing and handling a personal budget that will withstand the feast and famine cycles that can occur in real estate selling.

A person who is adept at people relations, who can identify clients' buying motives, and who can find property to fit, will probably be quite successful in this business.

COMMERCIAL BROKERAGE

Commercial brokers, also called income property brokers, specialize in income-producing properties such as apartment and office buildings, retail stores, and warehouses. In this specialty, the salesperson is primarily selling monetary benefits. These benefits are the income, appreciation, mortgage reduction and tax shelter that a property can reasonably be expected to produce.

To be successful in income property brokerage, one must be very competent in mathematics, know how to finance transactions, and keep abreast of current tax laws. One must also have a sense for what makes a good investment, what makes an investment salable, and what the growth possibilities are in the neighborhood where a property is located.

Commission income from commercial brokerage is likely to be less frequent, but in larger amounts compared to residential brokerage. Also the time required to break into the business is longer, but once in the business, agent turnover is low. The working hours of a commercial broker are much closer to regular business hours than for those in residential selling.

INDUSTRIAL BROKERAGE

Industrial brokers specialize in finding suitable land and buildings for industrial concerns. This includes leasing and developing industrial property as well as listing and selling it. An industrial broker must be familiar with industry requirements such as proximity to raw materials, water and power, labor supplies, and transportation. He must also know about local building, zoning, and tax laws as they pertain to possible sites, and about the schools, housing, cultural and recreational facilities that would be used by future employees of the plant.

Commissions are irregular, but usually substantial. Working hours are regular business hours and one's sales efforts are primarily aimed at locating facts and figures and presenting them to clients in an orderly fashion. Industrial clients are usually sophisticated business people. Gaining entry to industrial brokerage and acquiring a client list can be slow.

FARM BROKERAGE

With the rapid disappearance of the family farm, the farm broker's role is changing. Today he must be equally capable of handling the 160 acre spread of farmer Jones and the 10,000 acre operation owned by an agribusiness corporation. College training in agriculture is an advantage and on-the-job training is a must. Knowledge of soil types, seeds, fertilizers, production methods, new machinery, government subsidies, and tax laws are vital to success. Farm brokerage offers as many opportunities to earn commissions and fees from leasing and property management as from listing and selling property.

PROPERTY MANAGEMENT

For an investment property, the property manager's job is to supervise every aspect of a property's operation so as to produce the highest possible financial return over the longest period of time. The manager's tasks include renting, tenant relations, building repair and maintenance, accounting, advertising and supervision of personnel and tradesmen.

The current boom in condominiums has resulted in a growing demand for property managers to maintain them. In addition, large businesses that own property for their own use hire property managers. Property managers are usually paid a salary, and if the property is a rental, a bonus for keeping the building fully occupied. To be successful, a property manager should be at ease with tenants, a public relations expert, handy with tools, a good bookkeeper, and knowledgeable about laws applicable to rental units.

RENTAL SERVICES

In recent years, the service of helping tenants to find rental units and helping landlords to find tenants has become increasingly popular. Most rental services are firms that compile lists of available rentals and then sell this information to persons looking for rentals. A few also charge the landlord for listing the property. The objective is to save a person time and gasoline by providing pertinent information on a large number of rentals. Each property on the list is accompanied by information regarding location, size, rent, security deposit, pet policy, and the like.

An offshoot of apartment rental services are roommate locators. These are especially popular in cities with substantial numbers of single persons. Roommate locators are central places where persons looking for other persons who are willing to share living space can meet. The locator maintains files on persons with space to share (such as the second bedroom in a two-bedroom apartment) and those looking for space. The files will contain information on location, rent, male or female, smoking or nonsmoking, and the like. Most rental service and roommate locator services have been started by individual entrepreneurs and are not affiliated with real estate offices. In Minnesota, a real estate license is required if a fee is charged.

REAL ESTATE APPRAISING

The job of the real estate appraiser is to gather and evaluate all available facts affecting a property's value. Appraisal is a real estate career opportunity that does not emphasize property selling, however, it does demand a special set of skills of its own. The job requires practical experience, technical education and good judgment. If you have an analytical mind and like to collect and interpret data, you might consider becoming a real estate appraiser. The job combines office work and field work, and the income of an expert appraiser can match that of a top real estate salesman. One can be an independent appraiser, or there are numerous opportunities to work as a salaried appraiser for local tax authorities or lending institutions.

GOVERNMENT SERVICE

Approximately one-third of the land in the United States is government owned. This includes vacant and forested lands, office buildings, museums, parks, zoos, schools, hospitals, public housing, libraries, fire and police stations, roads and highways, subways, airports and courthouses. All of these are real estate and all of these require government employees who can negotiate purchases and sales, appraise, finance, manage, plan and develop. Cities, counties and state governments all have extensive real estate holdings. At the federal level, the Forest Service, Park Service, Department of Agriculture, Army Corps of Engineers, Bureau of Land Management, and Government Services Administration are all major landholders. In addition to outright real estate ownership, government agencies such as the Federal Housing Administration, Veterans Administration and Federal Home Loan Bank employ thousands of real estate specialists to keep their real estate lending programs operating smoothly.

LAND DEVELOPMENT

Most new homes in the United States are built by developers who in turn sell them to homeowners and investors. Some homes are built by small-scale developers who produce only a few a year. Others are part of 400-home subdivisions and 40-story condominiums that are developed and constructed by large corporations that have their own planning, appraising, financing, construction, and marketing personnel. There is equal opportunity for success in development whether you build 4 houses a year or work for a firm that builds 400 a year.

URBAN PLANNING

Urban planners work with local governments and civic groups for the purpose of anticipating future growth and land-use changes. The urban planner makes recommendations for new streets, highways, sewer and water lines, schools, parks and libraries. The current emphasis on environmental protection and controlled growth has made urban planning one of real estate's most rapidly expanding specialties. An urban planning job is usually a salaried position and does not emphasize sales ability.

MORTGAGE FINANCING

Specialists in mortgage financing have a dual role: (1) to find economically sound properties for lenders, and (2) to locate money for borrowers. A mortgage specialist can work independently, receiving a fee from the borrower for locating a lender, or as a salaried employee of a lending institution. The commission paid to a mortgage specialist on a multi-million dollar loan can be quite substantial.

SYNDICATIONS

Limited partnerships and other forms of real estate syndications that combine the investment capital of a number of investors to buy large properties have become popular over the past 20 years. The investment opportunities and professional management offered by syndications are eagerly sought after by people with money to invest in real estate. As a result, there are a number of job opportunities connected with the creation, promotion and management of real estate syndications.

COUNSELING

Real estate counseling is a new and growing segment of the real estate industry. The work involves giving others advice about real estate for a fee. A counselor must have a very broad knowledge about real estate—including financing, appraising, brokerage, management, development, construction, investing, leasing, zoning, taxes, title, economics and law. To remain in business as a counselor, one must develop a good track record of successful suggestions and advice.

RESEARCH AND EDUCATION

A person interested in real estate research can concentrate on solutions to applied questions such as improved construction materials and management methods or to economic questions such as "What is the demand for homes going to be next year in this community (state, country)?"

Opportunities abound in real estate education. Nearly all states require the completion of specified real estate courses before a real estate license can be issued. A growing number of states also require continued education for license renewal. As a result, persons with experience in the industry and an ability to create understanding in their students are much sought after as instructors.

FULL-TIME INVESTOR

One of the advantages of the free-enterprise system is that you can choose to become a full-time investor solely for yourself. There are a substantial number of people who have quit their jobs to work full time with their investment properties and who have done quite well at it. A popular and successful route for many has been to purchase inexpensively and with a low down payment, a small apartment building that has not been maintained, but is in a good neighborhood. The property is then thoroughly reconditioned and rents are raised. This process increases the value of the property. The increase is parlayed into a larger building—often through a tax-deferred exchange—and the process is repeated. Alternatively, the investor can increase the mortgage loan on the building and take the cash he receives as a "salary" for himself or use it as a down payment on another not-too-well maintained apartment building in a good neighborhood.

Other individual investors have done well financially by searching newspaper ads and regularly visiting real estate brokerage offices looking for underpriced properties which can be sold at a mark-up. A variation of this is to write to out-of-town property owners in a given neighborhood to see if any wish to sell at a bargain price. Another approach is to become a small-scale developer and contractor. Through your own personal efforts you create value in your projects and then hold them as investments. A Minnesota real estate license is not required in order to buy or sell investment property for your own account unless you are involved in 5 or more transactions within a 12-month period where you did not use a real estate broker.

LICENSE REQUIREMENTS

A homeowner selling his or her own home is not required to hold a real estate license. However, any person who for compensation or the promise of compensation lists or offers to list, sells or offers to sell, buys or offers to buy, negotiates or offers to negotiate either directly or indirectly for the purpose of bringing about a sale, purchase or option to purchase, exchange, auction, lease, or rental of real estate, or any interest in real estate, is required to hold a valid real estate license. Minnesota also requires real estate property managers, mortgage bankers and mortgage brokers to hold real estate licenses.

If your real estate plans are such that you may need a license, you should skip ahead to Chapter 18 and read the material there regarding real estate licensing.

ADDITIONAL READINGS

Dodd, Marian. "Coping with a Commission Income." *Real Estate Today,* October, 1977, pages 16–19. Living on a commission income, especially for a new sales associate can be trying, but there are methods of coping explained in this article.

Ellis, John T. *Guide to Real Estate License Examinations,* 3rd ed. Englewood Cliffs, N.J.: Prentice-Hall, 1982, 300 pages. A combination text and workbook designed for real estate salesperson and broker applicants. Provides non-technical coverage of exam subjects plus several hundred practice questions.

Foster, Ray. *Sensible Real Estate Selling Skills.* Reston, Va.: Reston Publishing Co., 1981, 160 pages. Provides an overview of the skills necessary for successful real estate selling. Has examples and suggestions for telephoning, listing, selling, closing, prospecting, and handling objections.

Lyon, Robert, and **Gardner, Gene.** *Real Estate Career Opportunities.* College Station, Texas: Texas Real Estate Research Center, 1979, 96 pages. Looks at job opportunities in real estate with emphasis on job tasks, hours and working conditions, employment prospects, promotion, education requirements, training, and personality traits.

Reilly, John W. *The Language of Real Estate,* 2nd ed. Chicago: Real Estate Education Company, 1982, 550 pages. This single-volume reference book contains over 1,700 of the most frequently encountered real estate terms. Includes basic definitions, examples and cross-references.

Weitzman, Herbert D., and **Eichinger, Robert W.** "The Statistics Behind Success." *Real Estate Today,* April, 1978, pages 11–17. Article looks at one real estate firm's method of judging a beginner's chances of success. Includes 45 character traits, success profiles.

2

Nature and Description of Real Estate

KEY TERMS

Base line: an imaginary latitude line selected as a reference in the rectangular survey system
Fixture: an object that has been attached to land so as to become real estate
Improvements: any form of land development, such as buildings, roads, fences, pipelines, etc.
Meridians: imaginary lines running north and south, used as references in mapping land
Metes and bounds: a method of land description that identifies a parcel by specifying its shape and boundaries
Monument: an iron pipe, stone, tree or other fixed point used in marking a survey
Personal property: a right or interest in things of a temporary or movable nature; anything not classed as real property
Real estate: land and improvements in a physical sense as well as the rights to own or use them
Recorded plat: a subdivison map filed in the county recorder's or registrar of titles office that shows the location and boundaries of individual parcels of land
Riparian right: the right of a landowner whose land borders a river or stream to use and enjoy that water

What is real estate? Real estate is land and the improvements made to land, and the rights to use them. Let us begin in this chapter by looking more closely at what is meant by land and improvements. Then in the next chapter we shall focus our attention on the various rights one may possess in land and improvements.

LAND

Often we think of land as only the surface of the earth. But, it is substantially more than that. As Figure 2:1 illustrates, land starts at the center of the earth, passes through the earth's surface, and continues on into space. An understanding of this concept is important because, given a particular parcel of land, it is possible for one person to own the rights to use its surface **(surface rights),** another to own the rights to drill or dig below its surface **(subsurface rights),** and still another to own the rights to use the airspace above it **(air rights).**

Figure 2:1

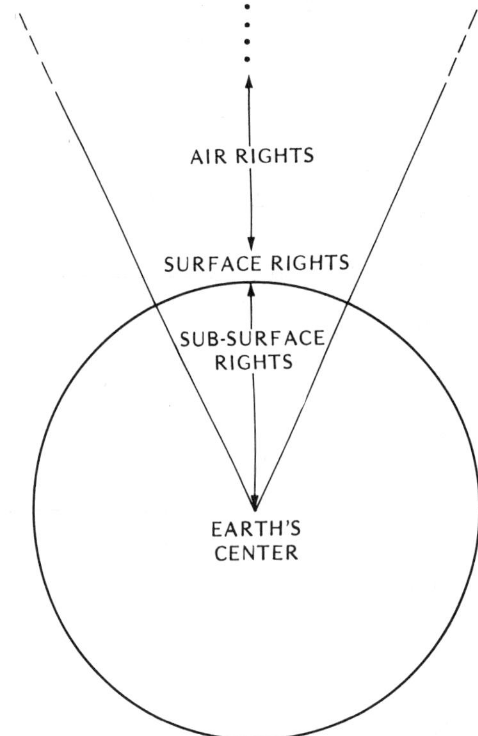

Land includes the surface of the earth and the sky above and everything to the center of the earth.

IMPROVEMENTS

Anything affixed to land with the intent of being permanent is considered to be part of the land and therefore real estate. Thus houses, schools, factories, barns, fences, roads, pipelines and landscaping are real estate. As a group, these are referred to as **improvements** because they improve or develop land.

Being able to identify what is real estate and what is not, is important. For example, in conveying ownership to a house, only the lot is described in the deed. It is not necessary to describe the dwelling unit itself, or the landscaping, driveways, sidewalks, wiring or plumbing. Items that are not a part of the land, such as tables, chairs, beds, desks, automobiles, farm machinery, and the like, are classified as **personal property;** if their ownership is to be transferred to the buyer, there must be a separate **bill of sale** in addition to the deed.

FIXTURES

When an object that was once personal property is attached to land (or a building thereon) so as to become real estate, it is called a **fixture.** As a rule, a fixture is the property of the landowner and when the land is conveyed to a new owner, it is automatically included with the land.

Whether or not an object becomes real estate depends on whether the object was affixed or installed with the apparent intent of permanently improving the land. This in turn is evidenced by these three tests: (1) the manner of attachment, (2) the adaptation of the object, and (3) the existence of an agreement.

Attachment

The first test, **manner of attachment,** refers to how the object is attached to the land. Ordinarily, when an object which was once personal property is attached to land by virtue of its being imbedded in the land or affixed to the land by means of cement, nails, bolts, etc., it becomes a fixture. To illustrate, when asphalt and concrete for driveways and sidewalks are still on the delivery truck, they are movable and therefore personal property. But once they are poured into place, the asphalt and concrete become part of the land. Similarly, lumber, wiring, pipes, doors, toilets, sinks, water heaters, furnaces and other construction materials change from personal property to real estate when they become part of a building. Items brought into the house that do not become permanently affixed to the land remain personal property; for example, furniture, clothing, cooking utensils, radios and television sets.

Adaptation

Historically, the manner of attachment was the only method of classifying an object as personal property or real estate, but as time progressed, this test alone was no longer adequate. For example, how would you classify storm windows, which for a few months of the year are temporarily clipped or hung in position? For the answer, we must apply a second test: **How is the article adapted** to the building? If the storm windows were custom cut for the windows in the building, they are automatically included in the purchase or rental of the building. Storm windows of a general design and suitable for use on other buildings are personal property and are not automatically included with the building. Note the difference: in the first case, the storm windows are specifically adapted to the building; in the second case, they are not.

Agreement

The third test is the **existence of an agreement** between the parties involved. For example, a seller can clarify in advance and in writing to his real estate broker what he considers personal property and thus will take when he leaves, and what he does not consider personal property and thus will leave for the buyer. Likewise, a tenant may obtain an agreement from his landlord that items installed by the tenant will not be considered fixtures by the landlord. When it is not readily clear if an item is real or personal property, the use of an agreement can avoid later argument or a court case.

Trade Fixtures

Normally, when a tenant makes permanent additions to the property that he is renting, the additions belong to the landlord when the lease or rental agreement expires. However, this can work a particular hardship on tenants operating a trade or business. For example, a supermarket moves into a rented building, then buys and bolts to the floor various **trade fixtures** such as display shelves, meat and dairy coolers, frozen-food counters, and checkout stands. When the supermarket later moves out, do these items, by virtue of their attachment, become the property of the building owner? Modern courts rule that tenant-owned trade fixtures do not become the property of the landlord. However, for the tenant to keep the trade fixtures, they must be removed before the expiration of the lease and without seriously damaging the building.

Ownership of Plants, Trees and Crops

Trees, cultivated perennial plants, and uncultivated vegetation of any sort are classed as **fructus naturales** and are considered part of the land. Annual cultivated crops are called **fructus industriales** or **emblements** and most courts of law regard them as personal property even though they are attached to the soil.

WATER RIGHTS

The ownership of land that borders on a river or stream carries with it the right to use that water in common with the other landowners whose land borders the same watercourse. This is known as a **riparian right.** The landowner does not have absolute ownership of the water that flows past his land, but he may use it in a reasonable manner. In some states, but not Minnesota, riparian rights have been modified by the **doctrine of prior appropriation:** the first owner to divert water for his own use may continue to do so, even though it is not equitable to the other landowners along the watercourse. Where land borders on a lake or sea, it is said to carry **littoral rights** rather than riparian rights. Littoral rights allow a landowner to use and enjoy the water touching his land provided he does not alter the water's position by artificial means.

Ownership of land normally includes the right to drill for and remove water found below the surface. Where water is not confined to a defined underground waterway, it is known as **percolating water.** In some states (including Minnesota), a landowner has the right, in conjunction with neighboring owners, to draw his share of percolating water. Other states subscribe to the doctrine of prior appropriation. When speaking of underground water, the term **water table** refers to the upper limit of percolating water below the earth's surface. It is also called the **groundwater level.** This may be only a few feet below the surface or hundreds of feet down.

REALTY, REAL PROPERTY AND PERSONALTY

Realty refers to land and buildings and other improvements from a physical standpoint; **real property** refers to the right to own land and improvements; and **real estate** refers to land and improvements and the rights to own or use them. As a practical matter, however, these three terms are used interchangeably in everyday usage. A similar situation also exists with regard to the terms personal property and personalty. **Personal property** refers to ownership rights to intangibles and to items of a temporary or movable nature, whereas **personalty** refers to the physical object itself. Again, in everyday usage both the object and the right to own it are known as "property." In this book, we shall follow everyday usage because it is standard in the real estate industry and because most people are already familiar with it.

LAND DESCRIPTIONS

There are six commonly used methods of describing the location of land: (1) informal reference, (2) metes and bounds, (3) rectangular survey system, (4) recorded plat, (5) assessor parcel number, and (6) reference to documents other than maps. We shall look at each in detail.

INFORMAL REFERENCES

Street numbers and place names are informal references: the house located at 7216 Maple Street; the apartment identified as Apartment 101, 875 First Street; the office identified as Suite 222, 3570 Oakview Boulevard; or the ranch known as the Rocking K Ranch—in each case followed by the city (or county) and state where it is located—are informal references. The advantage of an informal reference is that it is easily understood. The disadvantage from a real estate standpoint is that it is not a precise method of land description: a street number or place name does not provide the boundaries of the land at that location, and these numbers and names change over the years. Consequently, in real estate the use of informal references is limited to situations in which convenience is more important than precision. Thus, in a rental contract, Apartment 101, 875 First Street, city and state, is sufficient for a tenant to find the apartment unit. The apartment need not be described by one of the following more formal land descriptions.

METES AND BOUNDS

A **metes and bounds** land description is one which identifies a parcel by specifying its shape and boundaries. Early land descriptions in America depended on convenient natural or man-made objects. A stream might serve to mark one side of a parcel, an old oak tree to mark a corner, a road another side, a pile of rocks a second corner, a fence another side, and so forth. This method was handy, but it had two major drawbacks: there might not be a convenient corner or boundary marker where one was needed, and over time, oak trees died, stone heaps were moved, streams and rivers changed course, stumps rotted, fences were removed, and unused roads became overgrown with vegetation. The following description in the Hartford, Connecticut, probate court records for 1812 illustrates what is sometimes encountered:

> Commencing at a heap of stone about a stone's throw from a certain small clump of alders, near a brook running down off from a rather high part of said ridge; thence, by a straight line to a certain marked white birch tree, about two or three times as far from a jog in a fence going around a ledge nearby; thence by another straight line in a different direction, around said ledge and the Great Swamp, so called; thence, in line of said lot in part and in part by another piece of fence which joins on to said line, and by an extension of the general run of said fence

> to a heap of stone near a surface rock; thence, as aforesaid, to the "Horn," so called, and passing around the same as aforesaid, as far as the "Great Bend," so called, and from thence to a squarish sort of a jog in another fence, and so on to a marked black oak tree with stones piled around it; thence, by another straight line in about a contrary direction and somewhere about parallel with the line around by the ledge and the Great Swamp, to a stake and stone bounds not far off from the old Indian trail; thence, by another straight line on a course diagonally parallel, or nearly so, with "Fox Hollow Run," so called, to a certain marked red cedar tree out on a sandy sort of a plain; thence, by another straight line, in a different direction, to a certain marked yellow oak tree on the off side of a knoll with a flat stone laid against it; thence, after turning around in another direction, and by a sloping straight line to a certain heap of stone which is, by pacing, just 18 rods and about one half a rod more from the stump of the big hemlock tree where Philo Blake killed the bear; thence, to the corner begun at by two straight lines of about equal length, which are to be run by some skilled and competent surveyor, so as to include the area and acreage as herein before set forth.*

Permanent Monuments

The drawbacks of the above outmoded method of land description are resolved by setting a permanent man-made **monument** at one corner of the parcel, and then describing the parcel in terms of distance and direction from that point. From the monument, the surveyor runs the parcel's outside lines by compass and distance so as to take in the land area being described. Distances are measured in feet, usually to the nearest tenth or one-hundredth of a foot. Direction is shown in degrees, minutes and seconds. There are 360 degrees (°) in a circle, 60 minutes (′) in each degree and 60 seconds (″) in each minute. The abbreviation 29°14′52″ would be read as 29 degrees, 14 minutes, and 52 seconds. Figure 2:2 illustrates a modern metes and bounds land description.

At the corner where the survey begins, a monument in the form of an iron pipe or bar 1 to 2 inches in diameter is driven into the ground. Alternatively, concrete or stone monuments are sometimes used. To guard against the possibility

* F. H. Moffit and Harry Bouchard, *Surveying,* 6th ed. (New York: Harper and Row, 1975). By permission.

Figure 2:2 **DESCRIBING LAND BY METES AND BOUNDS**

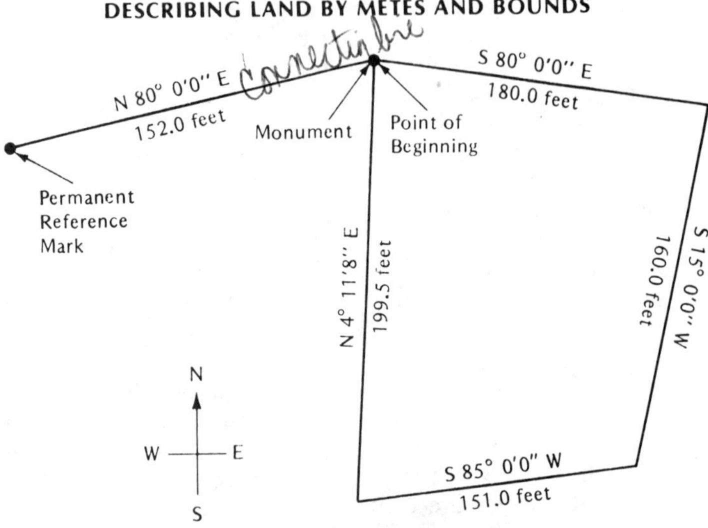

that the monument might later be destroyed or removed, it is referenced by means of a **connection line** to a nearby **permanent reference mark** established by a government survey agency. The corner where the parcel survey begins is called the **point of beginning** or **point of commencement.** From this point in Figure 2:2, we travel clockwise along the parcel's perimeter, reaching the next corner by going in the direction 80 degrees east of south for a distance of 180 feet. We then travel in a direction 15 degrees west of south for 160 feet, thence 85 degrees west of south for 151 feet, and thence 4 degrees, 11 minutes and 18 seconds east of north for 199.5 feet back to the point of beginning. In mapping shorthand, this parcel would be described by first identifying the monument, then the county and state within which it lies, and "thence S80°0′0″E, 180.0′; thence S15°0′0″W, 160.0′; thence S85°0′0″W, 151.0′; thence N4°11′18″E, 199.5′ back to the p.o.b."

Compass Directions

The compass illustrated in Figure 2:3 A shows how the direction of travel along each side of the parcel in Figure 2:2 is determined. Note that the same line can be labeled two ways depending on which direction you are traveling. To illustrate, look at the line from *P* to *Q*. If you are traveling toward *P* on the line, you are going N45°W. But, if you are traveling toward point *Q* on the line, you are going S45°E.

Curved boundary lines are produced by using arcs of a circle. The length of the arc is labeled *L* or *A;* the radius of the circle producing the arc is labeled *R*. The symbol Δ (delta) indicates the angle used to produce the arc (see Figure 2:3 B). Where an arc connects to a straight boundary or another arc the connection is indicated by the symbol —●— or the symbol —⊖—.

Bench marks are commonly used as permanent reference markers. A bench mark is a fixed marker of known location and elevation. It may be as simple as an iron post or as elaborate as an engraved 3¾″ brass disc set into concrete. The mark is usually set in place by a government survey team such as the United States Geological Survey (USGS) or the United States Coast and Geodetic Survey (USCGS). Bench marks are refer-

METES AND BOUNDS MAPPING

Figure 2:3

(A) NAMING DIRECTIONS FOR A METES AND BOUNDS SURVEY

N
P
N 45° W
N 4° E
N 60° E
N 80° W
N 80° E
W
E
S 85° W
S 80° E
S 15° W
S 45° E
Q
S

(B) MAPPING A CURVE

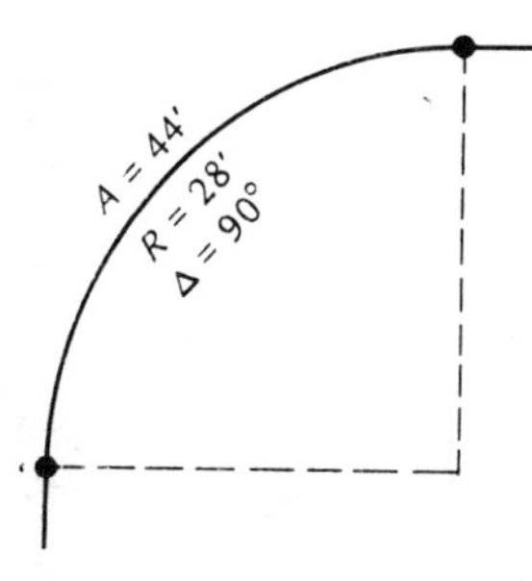

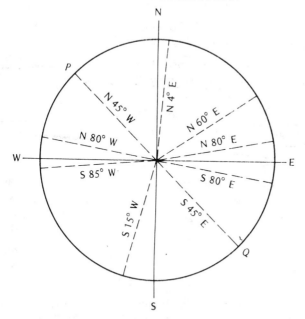

A = Length of the arc. (Some maps use the letter 'L")

R = Radius of the circle necessary to make the required arc (shown here by the broken lines)

Δ = Angle necessary to make the arc, i.e., the angle between the broken lines

Moving in a clockwise direction from the point of beginning, set the center of a circle compass (like the one shown above) on each corner of the parcel to find the direction of travel to the next corner. (*Note:* Minutes and seconds have been omitted above for clarity).

enced to each other by distance and direction. The advantages of this type of reference point, compared to trees, rocks, and the like, are permanence and accuracy to within a fraction of an inch. Additionally, even though it is possible to destroy a reference point or monument, it can be replaced in its exact former position because the location of each is related to other reference points.

It is also possible to describe a parcel using metes and bounds when there is no physical monument set in the ground. This is done by identifying a corner of a parcel of land by using the rectangular survey system or a recorded plat map, and then using that corner as a reference point to begin a metes and bounds description. As long as the starting place for a metes and bounds description can be accurately located by future surveyors, it will serve the purpose.

RECTANGULAR SURVEY SYSTEM

The **rectangular survey system** was established by Congress in May 1785. It was designed to provide a faster and simpler method than metes and bounds for describing land in newly annexed territories and states. Rather than using physical monuments, the rectangular survey system, also known as the **government survey** or **U.S. public lands survey,** is based on imaginary lines. These lines are the east-west **latitude lines** and the north-south **longitude lines** that encircle the globe, as illustrated in Figure 2:4.

Certain longitude lines were selected to act as **principal meridians.** For each of these an intercepting latitude line was selected as a **base line.** Every 24 miles north and south of a base line, **correction lines** or **standard parallels** were established. Every 24 miles east and west of a principal meridian, **guide meridians** were established to run from one standard parallel to the next. These are needed because the earth is a globe, not a flat surface. As one travels north in the United States, longitude (meridian) lines come closer together, that is, they converge. Figure 2:4 shows how guide meridians and correction lines adjust for this problem. Each 24 by 24-mile area created by the guide meridians and correction lines is called a **check** or **tract.**

There are 36 principal meridians and their intersecting base lines in the U.S. public land survey system. Figure 2:5 shows the states in which this system is used and the land area for

SELECTED LATITUDE AND LONGITUDE LINES SERVE AS BASE LINES AND MERIDIANS **Figure 2:4**

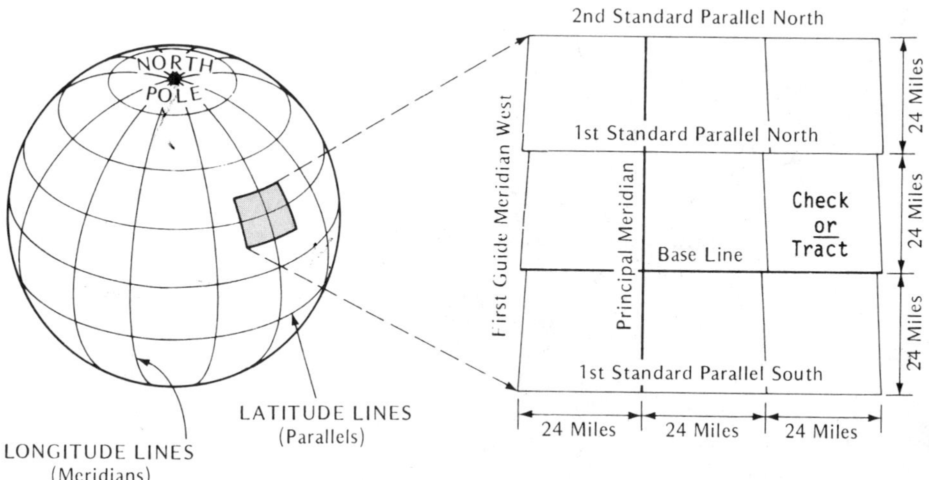

which each principal meridian and base line act as a reference. For example, the Sixth Principal Meridian is the reference point for land surveys in Kansas, Nebraska, and portions of Colorado, Wyoming, and South Dakota. Minnesota measures from the **Fourth** and **Fifth Principal Meridians.** Figure 2:5A shows Minnesota's two principal meridians and the land areas they control.

Figure 2:6 shows how land is referenced to a principal meridian and base line. Every 6 miles east and west of each principal meridian, parallel imaginary lines are drawn. The resulting 6-mile-wide columns are called **ranges** and are numbered consecutively east and west of the principal meridian. For example, the first range west is called Range 1 West and abbreviated R1W. The next range west is R2W, and so forth. The fourth range east is R4E.

Every six miles north and south of a base line, township lines are drawn. They intersect with the range lines and produce 6 by 6-mile imaginary squares called **townships** (not to be confused with the word township as applied to political subdivisions). Each tier or row of townships thus created is numbered with respect to the base line. Townships lying in the first tier north of a base line all carry the designation Township 1 North, abbreviated T1N. Townships lying in the first tier south of

6x6 Townships

Figure 2:5 THE PUBLIC LAND SURVEY SYSTEM OF THE UNITED STATES

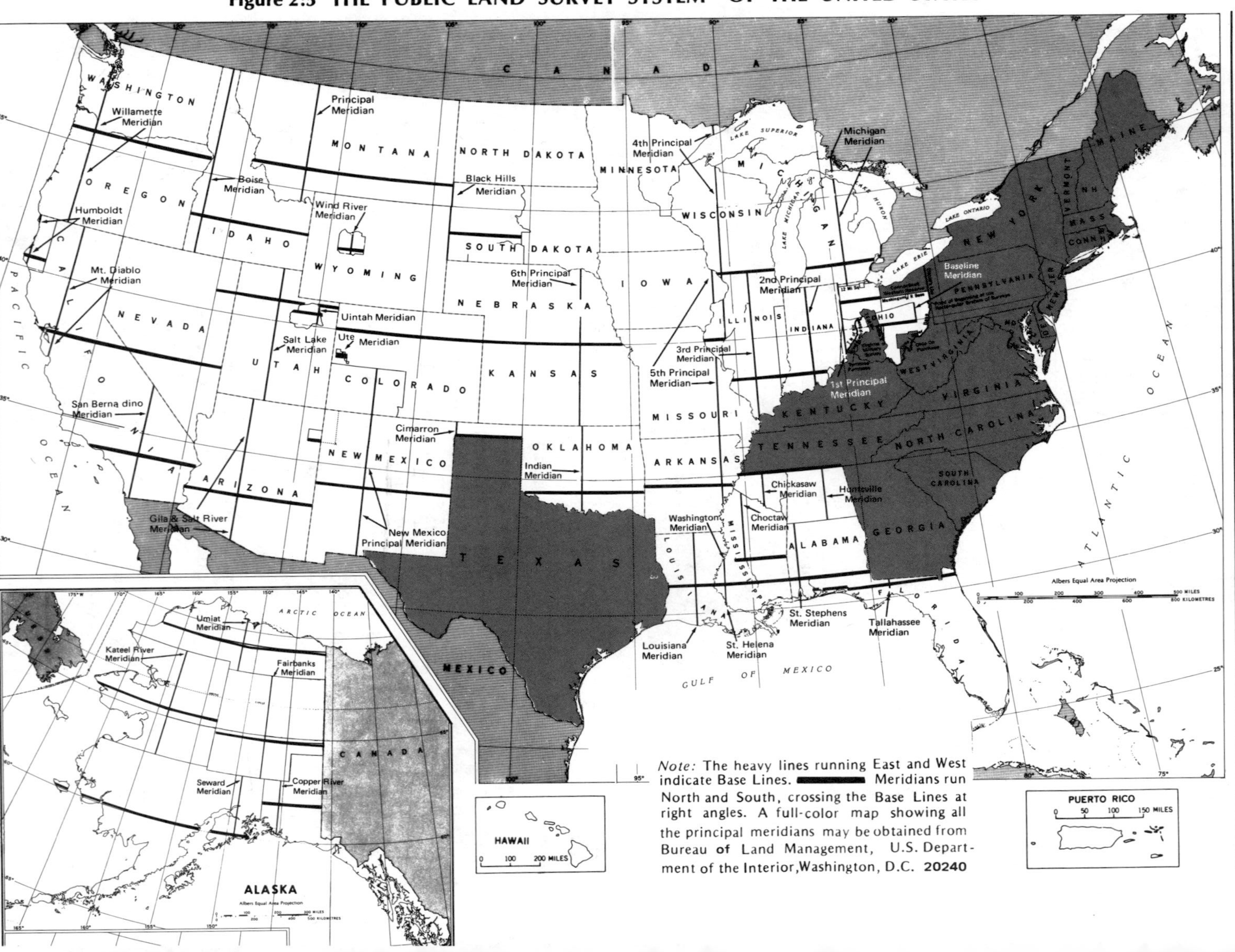

Note: The heavy lines running East and West indicate Base Lines. ▬▬ Meridians run North and South, crossing the Base Lines at right angles. A full-color map showing all the principal meridians may be obtained from Bureau of Land Management, U.S. Department of the Interior, Washington, D.C. 20240

Figure 2:5 A

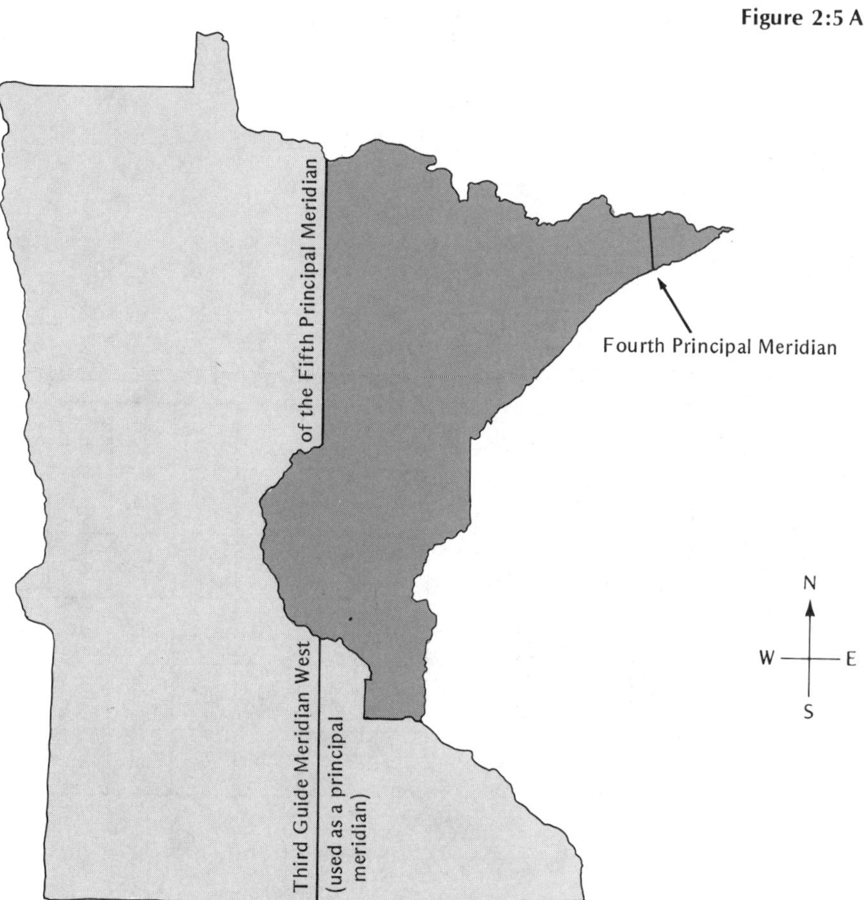

Twenty-fifth Standard Parallel North used as a Base Line for Minnesota

the base line are all designated T1S, and in the second tier south, T2S. By adding a range reference, an individual township can be identified. Thus, T2S, R2W would identify the township lying in the second tier south of the base line and the second range west of the prime meridian. T14N, R52W would be a township 14 tiers north of the base line and 52 ranges west of the principal meridian.

Each 36 square-mile township is divided into 36 one-square-mile units called **sections.** When one flies over farming areas, particularly in the Midwest, the checkerboard pattern of farms and roads that follow section boundaries can be seen.

Figure 2:6 IDENTIFYING TOWNSHIP AND SECTIONS

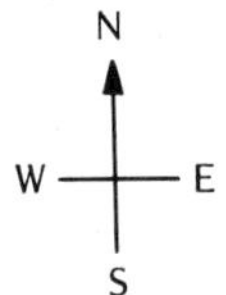

RANGES WEST | RANGES EAST

TOWNSHIPS NORTH	T4N R4W	T4N R3W	T4N R2W	T4N R1W	T4N R1E	T4N R2E	T4N R3E	T4N R4E
	T3N R4W	T3N R3W	T3N R2W	T3N R1W	T3N R1E	T3N R2E	T3N R3E	T3N R4E
	T2N R4W	T2N R3W	T2N R2W	T2N R1W	T2N R1E	T2N R2E	T2N R3E	T2N R4E
	T1N R4W	T1N R3W	T1N R2W	T1N R1W	T1N R1E	T1N R2E	T1N R3E	T1N R4E
Base Line								
TOWNSHIPS SOUTH	T1S R4W	T1S R3W	T1S R2W	T1S R1W	T1S R1E	T1S R2E	T1S R3E	T1S R4E
	T2S R4W	T2S R3W	T2S R2W	T2S R1W	T2S R1E	T2S R2E	T2S R3E	T2S R4E
	T3S R4W	T3S R3W	T3S R2W	T3S R1W	T3S R1E	T3S R2E	T3S R3E	T3S R4E
	T4S R4W	T4S R3W	T4S R2W	T2S R1W	T4S R1E	T4S R2E	6 mi.	6 mi.

Guide Meridian

24 miles

24 miles

Standard Parallel

6th Principal Meridian

IDENTIFYING TOWNSHIPS

T2N R3E

6 MILES

6	5	4	3	2	1
7	8	9	10	11	12
18	17	16	15	14	13
19	20	21	22	23	24
30	29	28	27	26	25
31	32	33	34	35	36

6 MILES

TOWNSHIP DIVIDED INTO SECTIONS

Sections are numbered 1 through 36, starting in the upper-right corner of the township. With this numbering system, any two sections with consecutive numbers share a common boundary. The section numbering system is illustrated in the right half of Figure 2:6 where the shaded section is described as Section 32, T2N, R3E, 6th Principal Meridian.

Each square-mile **section** contains 640 acres, and each **acre** contains 43,560 square feet. Any parcel of land smaller than a full 640-acre section is identified by its position in the section. This is done by dividing the section into quarters and halves as shown in Figure 2:7. For example, the shaded parcel shown at Ⓐ is described by dividing the section into quarters and then dividing the southwest quarter into quarters. Parcel Ⓐ is described as the NW¼ of the SW¼ of Section 32, T2N,

SUBDIVIDING A SECTION **Figure 2:7**

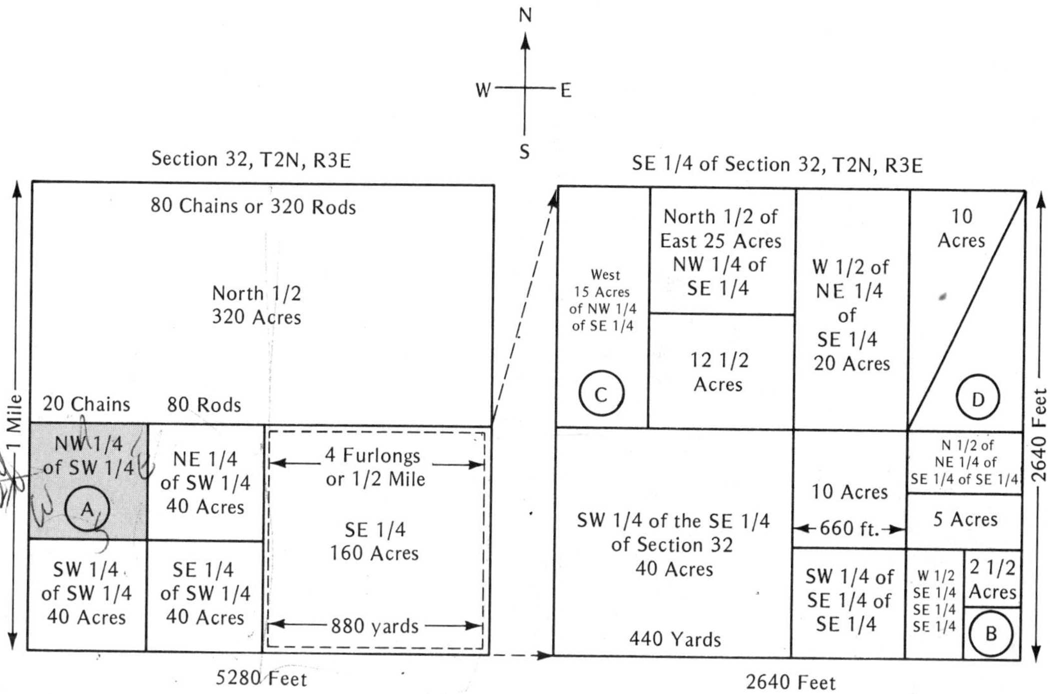

N
W E
S

Section 32, T2N, R3E

80 Chains or 320 Rods

North 1/2
320 Acres

1 Mile

20 Chains 80 Rods

NW 1/4 of SW 1/4 (A)

NE 1/4 of SW 1/4 40 Acres

4 Furlongs or 1/2 Mile

SE 1/4 160 Acres

SW 1/4 of SW 1/4 40 Acres

SE 1/4 of SW 1/4 40 Acres

880 yards

5280 Feet

ONE SECTION (640 Acres) SUBDIVIDED

SE 1/4 of Section 32, T2N, R3E

West 15 Acres of NW 1/4 of SE 1/4 (C)

North 1/2 of East 25 Acres NW 1/4 of SE 1/4

12 1/2 Acres

W 1/2 of NE 1/4 of SE 1/4 20 Acres

10 Acres (D)

N 1/2 of NE 1/4 of SE 1/4 of SE 1/4

10 Acres

660 ft.

5 Acres

SW 1/4 of the SE 1/4 of Section 32 40 Acres

440 Yards

SW 1/4 of SE 1/4 of SE 1/4

W 1/2 SE 1/4 SE 1/4 SE 1/4

2 1/2 Acres (B)

2640 Feet

2640 Feet

SE 1/4 (160 Acres) SUBDIVIDED FURTHER

R3E, 6th P.M. Additionally, it is customary to name the county and state in which the land lies. How much land does the NW¼ of the SW¼ of a section contain? A section contains 640 acres; therefore, a quarter-section contains 160 acres. Dividing a quarter-section again into quarters results in four 40-acre parcels. Thus, the northwest quarter of the southwest quarter contains 40 acres.

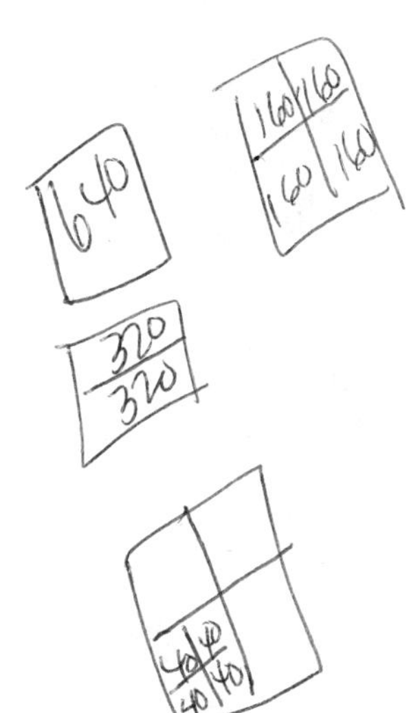

The rectangular survey system is not limited to parcels of 40 or more acres. To demonstrate this point, the SE¼ of section 32 is exploded in the right half of Figure 2:7. Parcel Ⓑ is described as the SE¼ of the SE¼ of the SE¼ of the SE¼ of section 32 and contains 2½ acres. Parcel Ⓒ is described as the west 15 acres of the NW¼ of the SE¼ of section 32. Parcel Ⓓ would be described in metes and bounds using the northeast corner of the SE¼ of section 32 as the starting point.

Not all sections contain exactly 640 acres. Some are smaller because the earth's longitude lines converge toward the North

Pole. Also, a section may be larger or smaller than 640 acres due to historical accommodations or survey errors dating back a hundred years or more. For the same reasons, not all townships contain exactly 36 square miles.

In terms of surface area, more land in the United States is described by the rectangular survey system than by any other survey method. But in terms of number of properties, the recorded plat is the most important survey method.

RECORDED PLAT

When a tract of land is ready for subdividing into lots for homes and businesses, reference by **recorded plat** provides the simplest and most convenient method of land description. A **plat** is a map that shows the location and boundaries of individual properties. Also known as the **lot-block-subdivision system, recorded map,** or **recorded survey,** this method of land description is based on the filing of a surveyor's plat in the public recorder's office of the county where the land is located. Figure 2:8 illustrates a plat. Notice that a metes and bounds survey has been made and a map prepared to show in detail the boundaries of each parcel of land. Each parcel is then assigned a lot number. Each block in the tract is given a block number, and the tract itself is given a name or number. A plat showing all the blocks in the tract is delivered to the county recorder's office, where it is placed in **map books** or **survey books,** along with plats of other subdivisions in the county.

Each plat is given a book and page reference number, and all map books are available for public inspection. From that point on, it is no longer necessary to give a lengthy metes and bounds description to describe a parcel. Instead, one need only provide the lot and block number, tract name, map book reference, county, and state. To find the location and dimensions of a recorded lot, one need only refer to the map book at the county recorder's office.

Note that the plat in Figure 2:8 combines both of the land descriptions just discussed. The boundaries of the numbered lots are in metes and bounds. These, in turn, are referenced to a section corner in the rectangular survey system.

ASSESSOR'S PARCEL NUMBERS

In Minnesota, the county tax assessor assigns an assessor's parcel number to each parcel of land in the county. The primary

Figure 2:8

LAND DESCRIPTION BY RECORDED PLAT

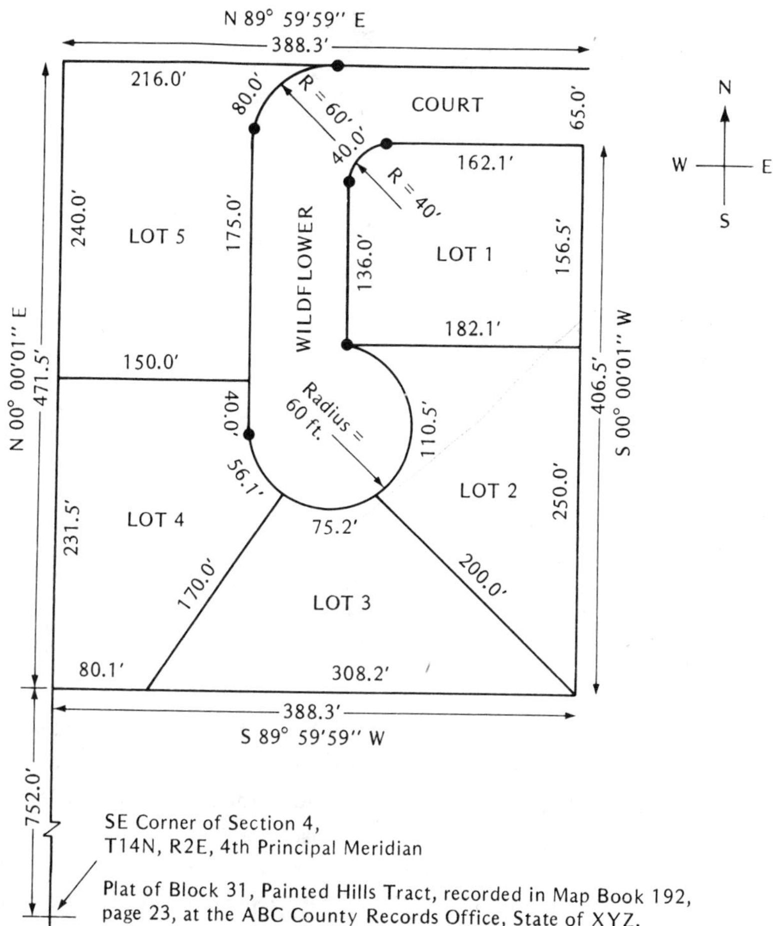

purpose is to aid in the assessment of property for tax collection purposes. However, these parcel numbers are public information and real estate brokers, appraisers, and investors can and do use them extensively to assist in identifying real properties.

In most counties in Minnesota the system is to divide the county into map books. Each book is given a number and covers a given portion of the county. Depending on the size of the county and the number of separate parcels of land in the county, the number of map books necessary to cover a county can range from less than a dozen to several hundred. On each page of the map book are parcel maps, each with

Figure 2:9

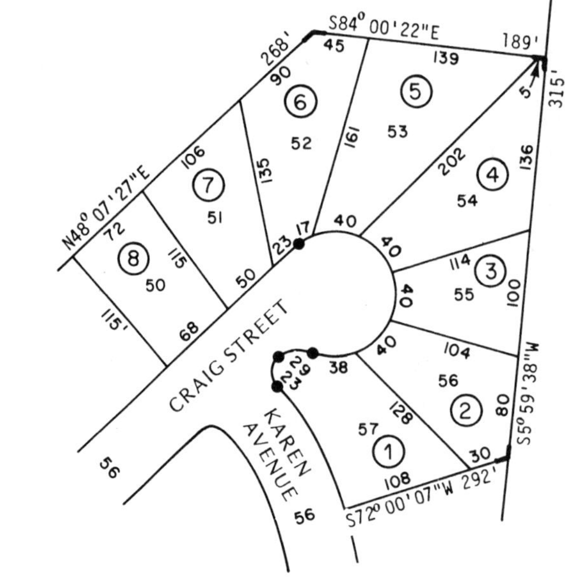

Assessor's Map
Book 34
Page 18

Assessor Parcel Numbers shown in circles

Lots 50 through 57 of Tract 2118, filed in Recorded Maps, Book 63, page 39.

The tax assessor assigns every parcel of land in the county its own parcel number. For example, the westernmost parcel (Lot 50) in the map would carry the number 34-18-8, meaning Book 34, Page 18, Parcel 8.

its own number. For subdivided lots, these maps are based on the plats submitted by the subdivider to the county records office when the subdivision was made. For unsubdivided land, the assessor prepares his own maps.

Each parcel of land on the map is assigned a parcel number by the assessor. In some Minnesota counties this is called a **property identification number** or **PIN.** The PIN may or may not be the same as the lot number assigned by the subdivider. To reduce confusion, the assessor's parcel number is either circled or underlined. Figure 2:9 illustrates a page out of an assessor's map book. The assessor's maps are open to viewing by the public at the assessor's office. They are also available for sale.

Before leaving the topic of assessor's maps, a word of caution is in order. These maps should not be relied upon as the final authority for the legal description of a parcel. That can come only from a title search that will include looking at the current deed to the property and the recorded copy of the subdivider's plat. Note also that an assessor's parcel number is never used as a legal description in a deed.

REFERENCE TO DOCUMENTS OTHER THAN MAPS

Land can also be described by referring to another publicly recorded document, such as a deed or a mortgage, that contains a full legal description of the parcel in question. For example, suppose that several years ago Baker received a deed from Adams which contained a long and complicated metes and bounds description. Baker recorded the deed in the public records office, where a photocopy was placed in Book 1089, page 456. If Baker later wants to deed the same land to Cooper, Baker can describe the parcel in his deed to Cooper by saying, "all the land described in the deed from Adams to Baker recorded in Book 1089, page 456, county of ABC, state of XYZ, at the public recorder's office for said county and state." Since these books are open to the public, Cooper (or anyone else) could go to Book 1089, page 456 and find a detailed description of the parcel's boundaries.

The key test of a land description is: "Can another person, reading what I have written or drawn, understand my description and go out and locate the boundaries of the parcel?"

VERTICAL LAND DESCRIPTION

In addition to surface land descriptions, land may also be described in terms of vertical measurements. This type of measurement is necessary when air rights or subsurface rights need to be described—as for condominiums or oil and mineral rights.

Any point, line, or surface from which a distance, vertical height or depth is measured is called a **datum.** The most commonly used datum plane in Minnesota is mean sea level. Starting from a datum, **bench marks** are set at calculated intervals by government survey teams; thus, a surveyor need not travel to the original datum to determine an elevation. These same bench marks are used as reference points for metes and bounds surveys.

In selling or leasing subsurface drilling or mineral rights, the chosen datum is often the surface of the parcel. For example, an oil lease may permit the extraction of oil and gas from a depth greater than 500 feet beneath the surface of a parcel of land. (Subsurface rights are discussed more in Chapter 3.)

An **air lot** (a space over a given parcel of land) is described by identifying both the parcel of land beneath the air lot and the elevation of the air lot above the parcel (see Figure 2:10 A). Multi-story condominiums use this system of land description.

Contour maps (topographic maps) indicate elevations. On these maps, **contour lines** connect all points having the same

Figure 2:10 AIR LOT AND CONTOUR LINES

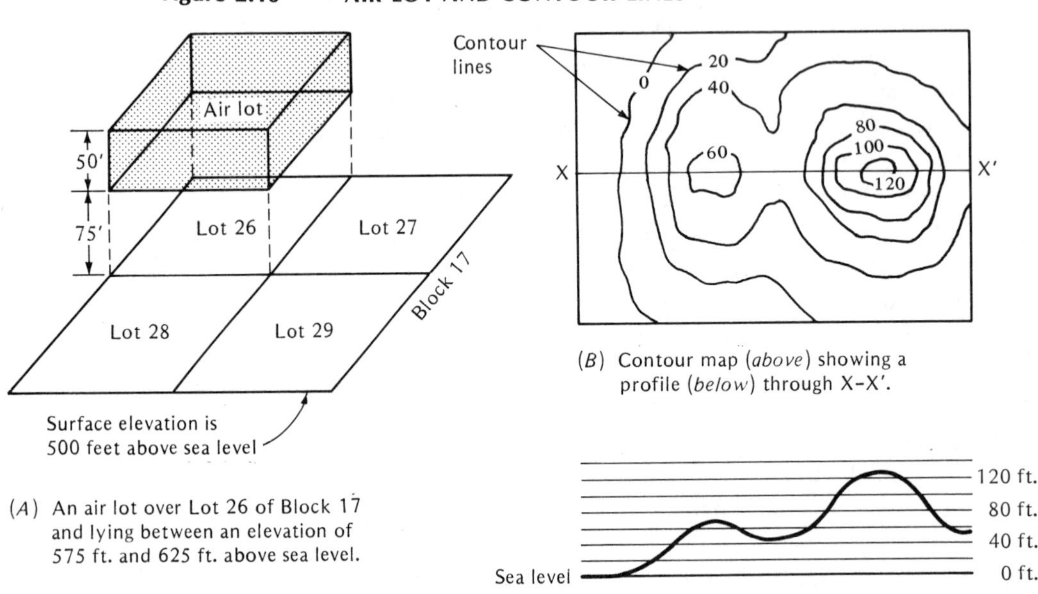

(*A*) An air lot over Lot 26 of Block 17 and lying between an elevation of 575 ft. and 625 ft. above sea level.

(*B*) Contour map (*above*) showing a profile (*below*) through X–X′.

elevation. The purpose is to show hills and valleys, slopes, and water runoff. If the land is to be developed, the map shows where soil will have to be moved to provide level building lots. Figure 2:10 B illustrates how vertical distances are shown using contour lines.

PHYSICAL CHARACTERISTICS OF LAND

The physical characteristics of land are immobility, indestructibility, and nonhomogeneity. This combination of characteristics makes land different from other commodities and directly and indirectly influences man's use of it.

Immobility

A parcel of land cannot be moved. It is true that soil, sand, gravel, and minerals can be moved by the action of nature (erosion) or man (digging); however, the parcel itself still retains its same geographical position on the globe. Because land is **immobile,** a person must go to the land; it cannot be brought to him. When land is sold, the seller cannot physically deliver his land to the buyer. Instead, the seller gives the buyer a document called a deed that transfers to the buyer all right, title, and interest in the property. Because land is immobile, real estate offices nearly always limit their sales activities to nearby properties. Even then a great deal of a salesperson's effort is used in traveling to show properties to clients. Immobility also creates a need for property-management firms, because, unless an owner of rental property lives on it or nearby, neither land nor buildings can be efficiently managed.

Indestructibility

Land is **indestructible,** that is, durable. For example, today one can travel to the Middle East and walk on the same land that was walked on in Biblical days, and most of the land that we use in the United States today is the same land used by the American Indians a thousand years ago.

The characteristic of physical durability encourages many people to buy land as an investment because they feel that paper money, stocks and bonds, and other commodities may come and go, but land will always be here. Although this is true in a physical sense, whether a given parcel has and will have economic value depends on one's ability to protect his ownership and on subsequent demand for that land by other persons. In other words, physical durability must not be confused with economic durability.

Nonhomogeneity

The fact that no two parcels of land are exactly alike because no two parcels can occupy the same position on the globe is known as **nonhomogeneity** (heterogeneity). Courts of law recognize this characteristic of land and consequently treat land as a **nonfungible** (pronounced non·fun′je′ble) commodity; that is, nonsubstitutable. Thus, in a contract involving the sale or rental of land (and any improvements to that land), the courts can be called upon to enforce specific performance of the contract. For example, in a contract to sell a home, if the buyer carries out his obligations and the seller fails to convey ownership to the buyer, generally a court of law will force the seller to convey ownership of *that* specific home to the buyer. The court will not require the buyer to accept a substitute home. This is different than a homogeneous or **fungible** commodity which is freely substitutable in carrying out a contract. For example, one bushel of No. 1 grade winter wheat can be freely replaced by another bushel of the same grade, and one share of United States Steel common stock can be substituted for another as all are identical.

Although land is nonhomogeneous, there can still be a high degree of physical and economic similarity. For example, in a city block containing 20 house lots of identical size and shape, there will be a high degree of similarity even though the lots are still nonhomogeneous. Finding similar properties is, in fact, the basis for the market-comparison approach to appraising real estate.

ECONOMIC CHARACTERISTICS OF LAND

The dividing line between the physical and economic characteristics of land is sometimes difficult to define, because the physical aspects of land greatly influence man's economic behavior toward land. However, four economic characteristics are generally recognized: scarcity, modification, permanence of investment (fixity), and area preference (situs, pronounced sī′tus).

Scarcity

The shortage of land in a given geographical area where there is great demand for land is referred to as **scarcity.** It is a man-made characteristic. For example, land is scarce in Miami Beach, Florida, because a relatively large number of people want to use a relatively small area of land. Another well-known example is 2-mile-wide, 13-mile-long Manhattan Island in New York City, where more than 1,000,000 people live and twice that number work. Yet one need only travel 25 miles west of Miami Beach or into central New York State to find plenty of uncrowded land available for purchase at very reasonable prices. The sheer quantity of undeveloped land in the United States as seen from an airplane on a cross-country flight is staggering.

Land scarcity is also influenced by man's ability to use land more efficiently. To illustrate, in agricultural areas, production per acre of land has more than doubled for many crops since 1940. This is not due to any change in the land, but is the result of improved fertilizers and irrigation systems, better seeds and modern crop management. Likewise, in urban areas, an acre of land that once provided space for five houses can be converted to high-rise apartments to provide homes for 100 or more families.

Thus, although there is a limited physical amount of land on the earth's surface, scarcity is chiefly a function of demand for land in a given geographical area and the ability of man to make land more productive. The persistent notion that all land is scarce has led to periodic land sale booms in undeveloped areas, which are often followed by a collapse in land prices when it becomes apparent that that particular land is not economically scarce.

Modification

Land use and value are greatly influenced by **modification,** that is, improvements made by man to surrounding parcels of land. For example, the construction of an airport will increase the usefulness and value of land parallel to runways but have a negative effect on the use and value of land at the ends of runways because of noise from landings and takeoffs. Similarly, land subject to flooding will become more useful and valuable if government-sponsored flood control dams are built upriver.

One of the most widely publicized cases of land modification occurred near Orlando, Florida, when Disney World was constructed. Nearby land previously used for agricultural purposes suddenly became useful as motel, gas station, restaurant, house, and apartment sites and increased rapidly in value. Another example is the development of property along Highway 494 in the City of Bloomington following the construction of the Minneapolis–St. Paul International Airport and Metropolitan Sports Complex.

Fixity

The fact that land and buildings and other improvements to land require long periods of time to pay for themselves is referred to as **fixity** or **investment permanence.** For example, it may take 20 or 30 years for the income generated by an apartment or office building to repay the cost of the land and building plus interest on the money borrowed to make the purchase. Consequently, real estate investment and land use decisions must consider not only how the land will be used next month or next year, but also the usefulness of the improvements 20 years from now. There is no economic logic in spending money to purchase land and improvements that will require 20 to 30 years to pay for themselves, if their usefulness is expected to last only 5 years.

Fixity also reflects the fact that land cannot be moved from its present location to another location where it will be more valuable. With very few exceptions, improvements to land are also fixed. Even with a house, the cost of moving it, plus building a foundation at the new site, can easily exceed the value of the house after the move. Thus, when an investment is made in real estate, it is regarded as a **fixed** or **sunk cost.**

Situs

Situs or **location preference** refers to location from an economic rather than a geographic standpoint. It has often been said that the single most important word in real estate is "location." What this means is the preference of people for a given area. For a residential area, these preferences are the result of *natural* factors, such as weather, air quality, scenic views, and closeness to natural recreation areas, and *man-made* factors, such as job opportunities, transportation facilities, shopping, and schools. For an industrial area, situs depends on such things as an available labor market, adequate supplies of water and electricity, nearby rail lines, and highway access. In farming areas, situs includes soil and weather conditions, water and labor availability, and transportation facilities.

Situs is the reason that house lots on street corners sell for more than identical-sized lots not on corners. This reflects a preference for open space. The same is true in apartments; corner units usually rent for more than similar-sized noncorner units. In a high-rise apartment building, units on the top floors, if they offer a view, command higher prices than identical units on lower floors. On a street lined with stores, the side of the street that is shaded in the afternoon will attract more shoppers than the unshaded side. Consequently, buildings on the shaded side will generate more sales and as a result be worth more.

It is important to realize that, since situs is a function of people's preferences and preferences can change with time, situs can also change. For example, the freeway and expressway construction boom, that started up in the 1950s, and accelerated during the 1960s, increased the preference for suburban areas. This resulted in declining property values in inner city areas and increasing land values in the suburbs. Today, with higher gasoline prices and transportation costs, people are starting to show a preference for living closer to the centers of cities.

VOCABULARY REVIEW

Match terms **a–r** *with statements* **1–18.**

a. *Acre*
b. *Base line*
c. *Contour lines*
d. *Datum*
e. *Emblements*
f. *Fixity*
g. *Fixture*
h. *Government survey*
i. *Lot–block–subdivision*
j. *Meridian*
k. *Metes and bounds*
l. *Monument*
m. *Quarter-section*
n. *Riparian right*
o. *Section*
p. *Subsurface rights*
q. *Township*
r. *Water table*

1. An object that has been attached to land so as to become real estate.
2. Contains 36 sections of land.
3. The depth below the surface at which water-saturated soil can be found.
4. A survey line running east and west from which townships are established.
5. Contains 640 acres of land.
6. The right of a landowner to use water flowing across his land.
7. An iron pipe or other object set in the ground to establish land boundaries.
8. A survey line that runs north and south in the rectangular survey system.
9. Annual crops produced by man.
10. A horizontal plane from which height and depth are measured.
11. Refers to the permanence of real estate investments.
12. A system of land description that identifies a parcel by specifying its shape and boundaries.
13. A land survey system based on imaginary latitude and longitude lines.
14. Includes the right to mine minerals and drill for oil.
15. Lines on a map that connect points having the same elevation.
16. Land description by reference to a recorded map.
17. 43,560 square feet.
18. Contains 160 acres of land.

QUESTIONS AND PROBLEMS

1. Is the land upon which you make your residence described by metes and bounds, lot–block–subdivision, or the rectangular survey system?
2. On a sheet of paper sketch the following parcels of land in Section 6, T1N, R3E: (a) the NW¼; (b) the SW¼ of the SW¼; (c) the W½ of the SE¼; (d) the N17 acres of the E½ of the NE¼; (e) the SE¼ of the SE¼ of the SE¼ of the NE¼.
3. How many acres are there in each parcel described in number 2?

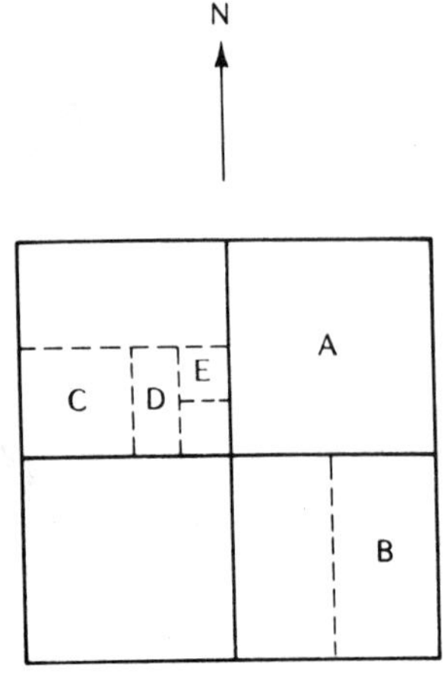

4. Describe the parcels labeled A, B, C, D, and E in the section shown in the margin.
5. Using an ordinary compass and ruler, sketch the following parcel of land: "Beginning at monument M, thence due east for 40 feet, thence south 45° east for 14.1 feet, thence due south for 40 feet, thence north 45° west for 70.7 feet back to the point of beginning."
6. If a landowner owns from the center of the earth to the limits of the sky, are aircraft that pass overhead trespassers?
7. Would you classify the key to the door of a building as personal property or real property?
8. With regard to your own residence, itemize what you consider to be real property and what you consider to be personal property.
9. With regard to riparian rights, does Minnesota follow the doctrine of prior appropriation or the right to a reasonable share?
10. What effects do you think changes in the location of the magnetic north pole would have on surveys over a long period of time? How would earthquakes affect bench marks?

ADDITIONAL READINGS

Boyer, Ralph E. *Survey of the Law of Property,* 3rd ed. St. Paul, Minn.: West Publishing Co., 1981, 716 pages. Chapter 7–14 in Part II deal with the legal aspects of air, surface, and subsurface rights, water rights, fixtures, and emblements.

Clark, Robert Emmet. *Waters and Water Rights.* Indianapolis: The Allen Smith Co., 1978, 7 volumes. This is an historical and legal treatise on the law of waters in the United States.

Herubin, Charles A. *Principles of Surveying,* 3rd ed. Reston, Va.: Reston Publishing Co., 1982, 318 pages. Covers basic surveying theory and techniques, including horizontal and vertical distance measurement, angle measurement, and mapping.

Kratovil, Robert, and **Werner, Raymond J.** *Real Estate Law,* 8th ed. Englewood Cliffs, N.J.: Prentice-Hall, 1983, 650 pages. Chapter 2 discusses land and its elements, Chapter 3 is on fixtures, and Chapter 5 deals with land descriptions.

Levi, Donald R., and **Jacobus, Charles J.** *Real Estate Law.* Reston, Va.: Reston Publishing Co., 1980. Chapter 2 looks at what real property is and what it is not.

McMahan, John. "Land for All: A History of U.S. Real Estate to 1900." *Real Estate Review,* Winter, 1976, page 78 ff. A fascinating four-part history of American real estate speculation and development.

3

Rights and Interests in Land

KEY TERMS

Chattel: an article of personal property

Curtesy: the legal right of a widower to a portion of his deceased wife's real property

Dower: the legal right of a widow to a portion of her deceased husband's real property

Easement: the right or privilege one party has to use land belonging to another for a special purpose not inconsistent with the owner's use of the land

Eminent domain: the right of government to take privately held land for public use, provided fair compensation is paid

Encroachment: the unauthorized intrusion of a building or other improvement onto another person's land

Encumbrance: any impediment to a clear title, such as a lien, lease, or easement

Fee simple: the largest, most complete bundle of rights one can hold in land; land ownership

Lien: a hold or claim which one person has on the property of another to secure payment of a debt or other obligation

Title: the right to or ownership of something; also the evidence of ownership such as a deed or bill of sale

Early man was nomadic and had no concept of real estate. Roaming bands followed game and the seasons, and did not claim the exclusive right to use a given area. When man began to cultivate crops and domesticate animals, the concept of an exclusive right to the use of land became important. This right was claimed for the tribe as a whole, and each family in the tribe was given the right to the exclusive use of a portion of the tribe's land. In turn, each family was obligated to aid in defending the tribe's claim against other tribes.

As time passed, individual tribes allied with each other for mutual protection; eventually these alliances resulted in political states. In the process, land ownership went to the head of the state, usually a king. The king, in turn, gave the right (called a feud) to use large tracts of land to select individuals, called lords. The lords did not receive ownership. They were tenants of the king, and were required to serve and pay duties to the king and to help fight the king's wars. It was customary for the lords to remain tenants for life, subject, of course, to the defeat of their king by another king. This system, wherein all land ownership rested in the name of the king, became known as the **feudal system.**

The lords gave their subjects the right to use small tracts of land. For this, the subjects owed their lord a share of their crops and their allegiance in time of war. The subjects (vassals) were, in effect, tenants of the lord and subtenants of the king. Like the lord, the vassal could not sell his rights nor pass them to his heirs.

Allodial System

The first major change in the feudal system occurred in 1285 when King Edward I of England gave his lords the right to pass their tenancy rights to their heirs. Subsequently, tenant vassals were permitted to convey their tenancy rights to others. By the year 1650, the feudal system had come to an end in England; in France it ended with the French Revolution in 1789. In its place arose the **allodial system** of land ownership under which individuals were given the right to own land. Initially, lords became owners and the peasants remained tenants of the lord. As time passed, the peasants became landowners either by purchase or by gift from the lord.

When the first European explorers reached North American shores, they claimed the land in the name of the king or queen whom they represented. When the first settlers later came to America from England, they claimed the land in the name of their mother country. However, since the feudal system had been abolished in the meantime, the king of England granted the settlers private ownership of the land upon which they settled, while retaining the claim of ownership to the unsettled lands.

Claims by the king of England to land in the 13 colonies were ended with the American Revolution. Subsequently, the U.S. government acquired the ownership right to additional lands by treaty, wars, and purchase, resulting in the borders of the United States as we know them today. The United States adopted the allodial system of ownership, and not only permits but encourages its citizens to own land within its borders.

GOVERNMENT RIGHTS IN LAND

Under the feudal system, the king was responsible for organizing defense against invaders, making decisions on land use, providing services such as roads and bridges, and the general administration of the land and his subjects. An important aspect of the transition from feudal to allodial ownership was that the need for these services did not end. Consequently, even though ownership could now be held by private citizens, it became necessary for the government to retain the rights of taxation, eminent domain, police power, and escheat. Let us look at each of these more closely.

Property Taxes

Under the feudal system, governments financed themselves by requiring lords and vassals to share a portion of the benefits they received from the use of the king's lands. With the change to private ownership, the need to finance governments did not end. Thus, the government retained the right to collect **property taxes** from landowners. Before the advent of income taxes, taxes levied against land were the main source of government revenues. Taxing land was a logical method of raising revenue for two reasons: (1) until the Industrial Revolution, which started in the mid-eighteenth century, land and agriculture were the primary sources of income; the more land one owned, the wealthier one was considered to be and therefore the better able to pay taxes to support the government; (2) land is impossible to hide, making it easily identifiable for taxation. This is not true of other valuables such as gold or money.

The real property tax has endured over the centuries, and today it is still a major source of government revenue. The major change in real estate taxation is that initially it was used to support all levels of government, including defense. Today, defense is supported by the income tax, and real estate taxes are sources of city, county, and, in some places, state revenues. At state and local government levels, the real property tax provides money for such things as schools, fire and police protection, parks, and libraries. To encourage property owners to pay their taxes in full and on time, the right of taxation also enables the government to seize ownership of real estate upon which taxes are delinquent and to sell the property to recover the unpaid taxes.

Eminent Domain

The right of government to take ownership of privately held real estate regardless of the owner's wishes is called **eminent domain.** Land for schools, freeways, streets, parks, urban renewal, public housing, public parking, and other social and public purposes is obtained this way. Quasi-public organizations, such as utility companies and railroads, are also permitted to obtain land needed for utility lines, pipes, and tracks by state law. The legal proceeding involved in eminent domain is a **condemnation proceeding,** and the property owner must be paid the fair market value of the property taken from him. The actual condemnation is usually preceded by negotiations between the property owner and an agent of the public body wanting to acquire ownership. If the agent and the property owner can arrive at a mutually acceptable price, the property is purchased outright. If an agreement cannot be reached, a formal proceeding in eminent domain is filed against the property owner in a court of law. The court hears expert opinions from appraisers brought by both parties, and then sets the price the property owner must accept in return for the loss of ownership.

When only a portion of a parcel of land is being taken, **severance damages** may be awarded in addition to payment for land actually being taken. For example, if a new highway requires a 40-acre strip of land through a 160-acre farm, the farm owner will not only be paid for the 40 acres; he will also receive severance damages to compensate for the fact that his farm will be more difficult to work because it is no longer in one piece.

An **inverse condemnation** is a proceeding brought about by a property owner demanding that his land be purchased from him. In a number of cities, homeowners at the end of airport runways have forced airport authorities to buy their homes because of the deafening noise of jet aircraft during takeoffs. Damage awards may also be made when land itself is not taken but its usefulness is reduced because of a nearby condemnation. These are **consequential damages,** and might be awarded, for instance, when land is taken for a sewage treatment plant, and privately owned land downwind from the plant suffers a loss in value owing to foul odors.

Police Power

The right of government to enact laws and enforce them for the order, safety, health, morals, and general welfare of the public is called **police power.** Examples of police power applied to real estate are zoning laws, planning laws, building, health and fire codes, and rent control. A key difference between police power and eminent domain is that, although police power restricts how real estate may be used, there is no legally recognized "taking" of property. Consequently, there is no payment to an owner who suffers a loss of value through the exercise of police power. A government may not utilize police power in an offhand or capricious manner; any law that restricts how an owner may use his real estate must be deemed in the public interest and applied even handedly to be valid. The breaking of a law based upon police power results in either a civil or criminal penalty rather than in the seizing of real estate, as in the case of unpaid property taxes. Of the various rights government holds in land, police power has the most impact on land value.

Escheat

When a person dies and leaves no heirs and no instructions as to how to dispose of his real and personal property, or when property is abandoned, the ownership of that property reverts to the state. This reversion to the state is called **escheat** from the Anglo-French word meaning to fall back. Escheat solves the problem of property becoming ownerless.

PROTECTING OWNERSHIP

It cannot be overemphasized that, to have real estate, there must be a system or means of protecting rightful claims to the use of land and the improvements thereon. In the United States, the federal government is given the task of organizing a defense system to prevent confiscation of those rights by a foreign power. The federal government, in combination with state and local governments, also establishes laws and courts within the country to protect the ownership rights of one citizen in relation to another citizen. Whereas armed forces protect against a foreign takeover, within a country deeds, public records, contracts, and other documents have replaced the need for brute force to prove and protect ownership of real estate.

FEE SIMPLE

The concept of real estate ownership can be more easily understood when viewed as a collection or bundle of rights. Under the allodial system, the rights of taxation, eminent domain, police power, and escheat are retained by the government. The remaining bundle of rights, called **fee simple**, is available for private ownership. The fee simple bundle of rights

Figure 3:1 THE FEE SIMPLE BUNDLE OF RIGHTS

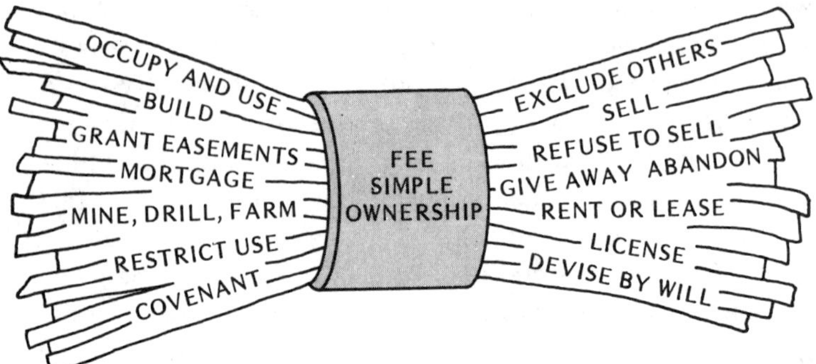

Real estate ownership is, in actuality, the ownership of rights to land. The largest bundle available for private ownership is called "fee simple".

can be held by a person and his heirs forever, or until his government can no longer protect those rights. Figure 3:1 illustrates the fee simple bundle of rights concept.

The term **estate** is synonymous with bundle of rights. Stated another way, estate refers to one's legal interest or rights in land, not the physical quantity of land as shown on a map. A fee simple is the largest estate one can hold in land. Most real estate sales are for the fee simple estate. When a person says he or she "owns" or has "title" to real estate, it is usually the fee simple estate that is being discussed. The word **title** refers to the right or ownership of something. All other lesser estates in land, such as life estates and leaseholds, are created from the fee estate.

Real estate is concerned with the "sticks" in the bundle: how many there are, how useful they are, and who possesses the sticks not in the bundle. With that in mind, let us describe what happens when sticks are removed from the bundle.

ENCUMBRANCES

Whenever a stick is removed from the fee simple bundle, it creates an impediment to the free and clear ownership and use of that property. These impediments to title are called encumbrances. An **encumbrance** is defined as any claim, right, lien, estate, or liability on the fee simple title to property. An encumbrance is, in effect, a stick that has been removed from the bundle. Commonly found encumbrances are easements, encroachments, deed restrictions, liens, leases and air and subsurface rights. In addition, qualified fee estates are encumbered estates, as are life estates.

The party holding a stick from someone else's fee simple bundle is said to hold a claim to or a right or interest in that land. In other words, what is one person's encumbrance is another person's right or interest or claim. For example, a lease

Figure 3:2

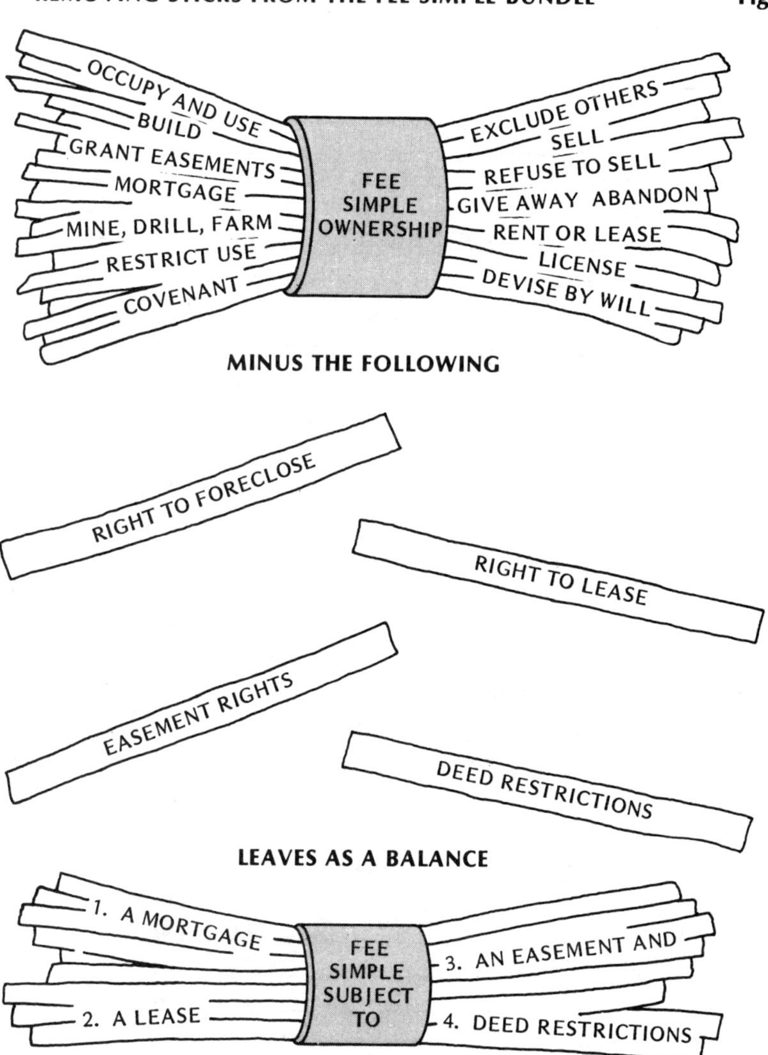

Note that the fee simple bundle shrinks as an owner voluntarily removes rights from it.

is an encumbrance from the standpoint of the fee simple owner. But from the tenant's standpoint, it is an interest in land that gives the tenant the right to the exclusive use of land and buildings. A mortgage is an encumbrance from the fee owner's viewpoint, but a right to foreclose from the lender's viewpoint. A property that is encumbered with a lease and a mortgage is called "a fee simple subject to a lease and a mortgage." Figure 3:2 illustrates how a fee simple bundle shrinks as rights are removed from it. Meanwhile, let us turn our attention to a discussion of individual sticks found in the fee simple bundle.

EASEMENTS

An **easement** is a right or privilege one party has to the use of land of another for a special purpose consistent with the general use of the land. The landowner is not dispossessed from his land, but rather coexists side by side with the holder of the easement. Examples of easements are those given to telephone and electric companies to erect poles and run lines over private property, easements given to people to drive or walk across someone else's land, and easements given to gas and water companies to run pipelines to serve their customers. Figure 3:3 illustrates several examples of easements.

The usual procedure in creating an easement is for the landowner to use a written document to specifically grant an easement to someone else or to reserve an easement to himself in the deed when he sells the property. A land developer may reserve easements for utility lines and then grant them to the utility companies that will service the lots.

It is also possible for an easement to arise without a written document. For example, a parcel of land fronts on a road and the owner sells the back half of the parcel. If the only access to the back half is by crossing over the front half, even if the seller did not expressly grant an easement, the law will generally protect the buyer's right to travel over the front half to get to his land. The buyer cannot be landlocked by the seller. This is known as an **easement by necessity.** Another method of acquiring an easement without a written document is by constant use, or **easement by prescription:** if a person acts as though he owns an easement long enough, he will have a legally recognized easement. Persons using a private

COMMONLY FOUND EASEMENTS **Figure 3:3**

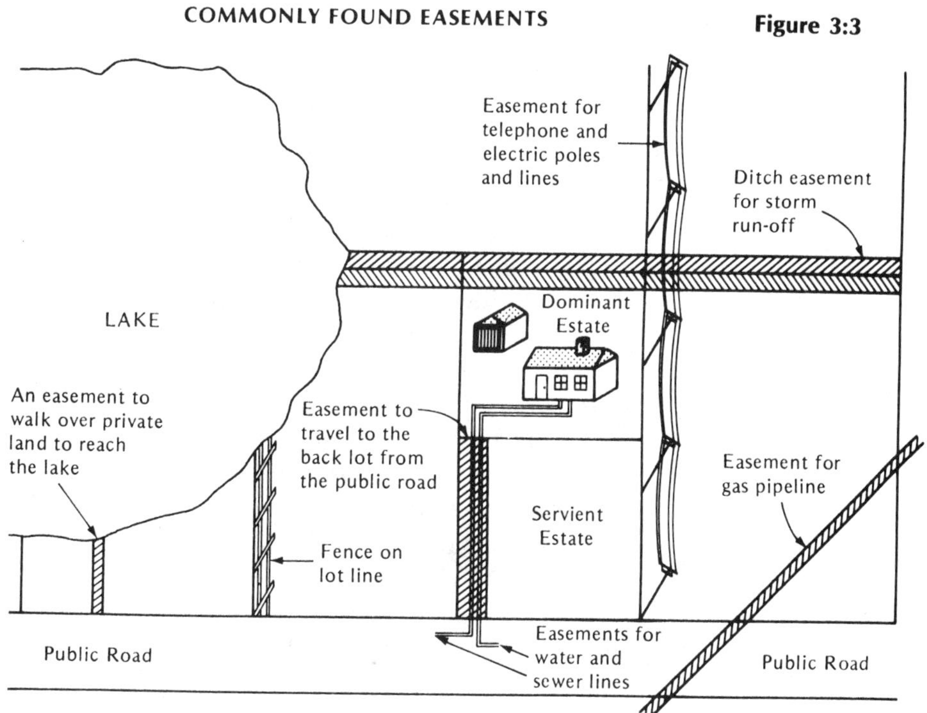

road without permission for a long enough period of time can acquire a legally recognized easement by this method.

Easement Appurtenant

An **easement appurtenant** is one that attaches itself to a parcel of land. When a person sells the back half of his lot, the easement to travel over the front to reach the back attaches to the land in the back and is said to "run with the land." Whenever the back half is sold, the easement to travel over the front automatically goes to the new owner. The back half of the lot is the **dominant estate** (or dominant tenement) because it acquires the easement; the front half is the **servient estate** (or servient tenement) because it gives up the easement.

An **easement in gross** is given to a person or business, and a subsequent sale of the land does not usually affect ownership of the easement. Telephone, electricity, and gas line easements are examples of easements in gross. The holder of a commercial easement usually has the right to sell, assign, or devise it. However, easements in gross for personal use are not transferable and terminate with the death of the person holding the easement. An example of a personal easement in gross would be a landowner giving a friend an easement to travel over his land to reach a choice fishing area.

Party Wall Easement

Party wall easements exist when a single wall straddles the lot line that separates two parcels of land. The wall may be either a fence or the wall of a building. In either case, each lot owner owns that portion of the wall on his land, plus an easement in the other half of the wall for physical support. Party walls are common where stores and office buildings are built right up to the lot line. Such a wall can present an interesting problem when the owner of one lot wants to demolish his building. Since the wall provides support for the building next door, it is usually his responsibility to either leave the wall or provide special supports for the adjacent building during demolition and until another building is constructed on the lot.

Easements may be terminated when the purpose for the easement no longer exists (for example, a public road is built adjacent to the back half of the lot mentioned earlier), or when the dominant and servient estates are combined with the intent of extinguishing the easement, or by release from the owner of the dominant estate to the servient estate, or by lack of use.

ENCROACHMENTS

The unauthorized intrusion of a building or other improvement onto another person's land is called an **encroachment.** A tree that overhangs into a neighbor's yard, or a building or eave of a roof that crosses a property line are examples of encroachments. The owner of the property being encroached upon has the right to force the removal of the encroachment. Failure to do so may eventually injure his title and make his land more difficult to sell. Ultimately, inaction may result in the encroaching neighbor claiming a legal right to continue his use. Figure 3:4 illustrates several commonly found encroachments.

DEED RESTRICTIONS

Private agreements that govern the use of land are known as **deed restrictions** or **deed covenants.** For example, a land subdivider can require that persons who purchase lots from him build only single-family homes containing 1,200 square

COMMONLY FOUND ENCROACHMENTS **Figure 3:4**

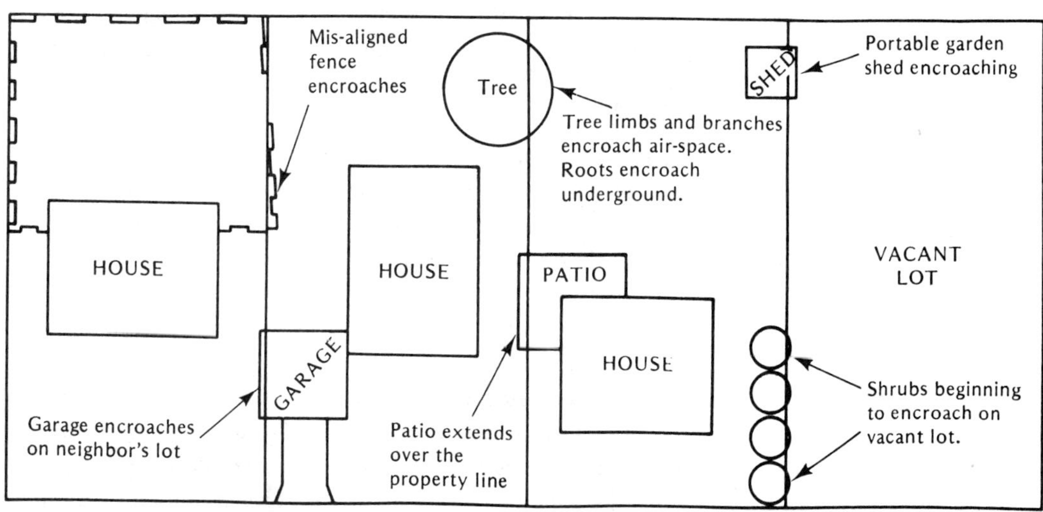

Most commonly found encroachments are not intentional but are due to poor or nonexistent planning. For example, a weekend garden shed, fence, or patio project is built without surveying to find the lot line, or a tree or bush grows so large it encroaches upon a neighbor's land.

feet or more. The purpose would be to protect those who have already built houses from an erosion in property value due to the construction of nearby buildings not compatible with the neighborhood. Where scenic views are important, deed restrictions may limit the height of buildings and trees to 15 feet. A buyer would still obtain fee simple ownership, but at the same time would voluntarily give up some of his rights to do as he pleases. As a buyer, he is said to receive a fee simple title subject to deed restrictions. The right to enforce the restrictions is usually given by the developer to the subdivision's homeowner association. Violation of a deed restriction can result in a civil court action brought by other property owners who are bound by the same deed restriction.

LIENS

A hold or claim that one person has on the property of another to secure payment of a debt or other obligation is called a **lien.** Common examples are property tax liens, mechanics' liens, judgment liens, and mortgage liens. From the standpoint of the property owner, a lien is an encumbrance on his title. Note that a lien does not transfer title to property. The debtor retains title until the lien is foreclosed. When there is more than one lien against a property, the lien which was recorded first has the highest priority in the event of foreclosure. Property tax liens are, however, always superior to other liens.

Property Tax Liens

Property tax liens result from the right of government to collect taxes from property owners. At the beginning of each tax year, a tax lien is placed on taxable property. It is removed if the property taxes are paid. If they are not paid, the lien gives the state the right to force the sale of the property in order to collect the unpaid taxes.

Mechanic's Lien

Mechanic's lien laws give anyone who has furnished labor or materials for the improvement of land lien rights against that land if payment has not been received. A sale of the property can then be forced to recover the money owed. To be entitled to a mechanic's lien, the work or materials must have been provided under contract with the property owner or his representative. For example, if a landowner hires a contractor to build a house or add a room to his existing house, and then fails to pay the contractor, the contractor has a lien against the land and its improvements. Furthermore, if the landowner pays the contractor, but the contractor does not pay his subcontractors, the subcontractors are entitled to file a mechanic's lien against the property. In this situation, the owner may have to pay twice.

The legal theory behind mechanic's lien rights is that the labor and materials supplied enhance the value of the property. Therefore the property should be security for payment. If the property owner does not pay voluntarily, the lien can be enforced with a court-supervised foreclosure sale.

Mechanics (contractors), materialmen, architects, surveyors and engineers are among those who may be entitled to the protection of the mechanics' lien laws in Minnesota. All mechanics' liens attach and take effect at the time the first item of labor or material is furnished, even though no document has been filed with the county recorder. To preserve the lien, a lien statement must be filed in the county where the improved property is located within 90 days after the last item of labor or material has been furnished. This is called **perfecting** the lien.

Under Minnesota law, a homeowner is afforded some protection against unauthorized mechanics' liens because statutory provisions require that contractors and subcontractors give written notice to the owner of the work or services provided to the property. However, this notice need not be given to an owner of a building containing more than four units, nor to certain owners of non-residential property. Whenever improvements are made to the land, all persons (including sellers under a contract for deed and landlords) may be held to have authorized the improvements so as to subject their interest to a mechanic's lien. The owner may protect himself by serving or posting a notice that the improvement is being made without his authority. With respect to Torrens property, the mechanic's lien must be recorded on the certificate of title to be an encumbrance on the property.

In Appendix I of this book is a copy of the notice that must be given the property owner plus additional details regarding mechanics' liens. When you finish reading this chapter, turn to Appendix I. The material there will help your understanding of mechanics' liens.

Judgment Lien

Judgment liens arise from lawsuits for which money damages are awarded. The law permits a hold to be placed against the real and personal property of the debtor until the judgment is paid. Usually the lien created by the judgment covers only property in the county where the judgment was awarded. However, the creditor can extend the lien to property in other counties by filing a **notice of lien** in each of those counties. If the debtor does not repay the lien voluntarily, the creditor can ask the court to issue a **writ of execution** that directs the county sheriff to seize and sell a sufficient amount of the debtor's property to pay the debt and expenses of the sale.

In Minnesota, judgment liens are valid for ten years and are capable of being extended for additional ten-year periods. The priority of a judgment lien under Minnesota law is the date the original judgment against the debtor was docketed (filed) in the district court for the county in which the debtor's property is located. With respect to Torrens property, the judgment lien must be recorded on the certificate of title to be an encumbrance on the property.

Mortgage Lien

A **mortgage lien** is a pledge of property by its owner to secure the repayment of a debt. In contrast to a property tax lien which is imposed by law, a mortgage lien is a voluntary lien created by the property owner. In contrast to a judgment lien which applies to all the debtor's property, a mortgage lien covers only the specific property that its owner elects to pledge. If the debt secured by the mortgage lien is not repaid, the creditor can foreclose and sell the pledged property. If this is insufficient to repay the debt, some states allow the creditor to petition the court for a judgment lien for the balance due. (Mortgage law is covered in more detail in Chapter 9.)

QUALIFIED FEE ESTATE

A **qualified fee estate** is a fee estate that is subject to certain limitations imposed by the person creating the estate. For example, Mr. Smith donates a parcel of land to a church so long as the land is used for religious purposes. The key words are "so long as." So long as the land is used for religious purposes the church has all the rights of fee simple ownership. But, if some other use is made of the land, it reverts back to the grantor (Mr. Smith).

LIFE ESTATE

A **life estate** conveys a fee simple estate for the duration of someone's life. The duration of the estate can be tied to the life of the **life tenant** (the person holding the life estate) or to a third party. In addition, someone must be named to acquire the estate upon its termination. The following example will illustrate the life estate concept. Suppose you have an aunt who needs financial assistance and you have decided to grant her, for the rest of her life, a house to live in. When you create the life estate, she becomes the life tenant. Additionally, you must decide who gets the house upon her death. If you want it back, you would want a **reversionary interest** for yourself. This way the house reverts back to you, or if you predecease her, to your heirs. If you want the house to go to someone else, your son or daughter for example, you could name him or her as the **remainderman.** Alternatively, you could name a friend, relative, or charity as the remainderman.

Since a life estate arrangement is temporary, the life tenant must not commit **waste** by destroying or harming the property. Furthermore, the life tenant is required to keep the property in reasonable repair and to pay any property taxes, assessments, and interest on debt secured by the property.

STATUTORY ESTATES

Statutory estates are created by state law. They include **dower,** which gives a wife rights in her husband's real property; **curtesy,** which gives a husband rights in his wife's real property; and **community property** that gives each spouse a one-half interest in marital property. Additionally there is **homestead protection** which is designed to protect the family's home from certain debts and, upon the death of one spouse, provide the other with a home for life. Both dower and curtesy have been abolished in Minnesota. The rights of spouses in each other's real property is governed in Minnesota by the Probate Code discussed more fully in Chapter 5. Community property ownership is not found in Minnesota.

Dower

Historically **dower** came from old English common law, in which the marriage ceremony was viewed as merging the wife's legal existence into that of her husband's. From this viewpoint, property bought during marriage belonged to the husband, and both husband and wife shared the use of it. Thus the husband could not convey ownership of the family's real estate without the wife's permission.This protected her even if she was left out of her husband's will.

Curtesy

Roughly the opposite of dower, **curtesy** gave the husband benefits in his deceased wife's property as long as he lived. However, unlike dower, the wife could defeat those rights in her will. States with statutory dower and curtesy rights are shown in Table 3:1.

Community Property

Eight states, Arizona, California, Idaho, Louisiana, Nevada, New Mexico, Texas, and Washington, subscribe to the legal theory that during marriage, each spouse has an equal interest in all property acquired by their joint efforts during the marriage. This jointly produced property is called **community property.** Upon the death of one spouse, one-half of the community property passes to his or her heirs. The other one-half is retained by the surviving spouse. When community property is sold or mortgaged, both spouses must sign the document. Community property rights arise upon marriage (either formal or common law) and terminate upon divorce or death.

Table 3:1 DOWER, CURTESY, AND HOMESTEAD PROTECTION BY STATE

	Dower Right for Wife	Curtesy or Dower Right for Husband	Homestead Protection
Alabama	×		×
Alaska			×
Arizona			×
Arkansas	×	×	×
California			×
Colorado			×
Connecticut			
Delaware			
District of Columbia	×	×	
Florida			×
Georgia			×
Hawaii	×	×	
Idaho			×
Illinois			×
Indiana			×
Iowa			×
Kansas			×
Kentucky	×	×	×
Louisiana			×
Maine			×
Maryland			
Massachusetts	×	×	×
Michigan			×
Minnesota			×
Mississippi			×
Missouri			×
Montana			×
Nebraska			×
Nevada			×
New Hampshire			×
New Jersey	×	×	
New Mexico			×
New York			×
North Carolina			×
North Dakota			×
Ohio	×	×	×
Oklahoma			×
Oregon			×
Pennsylvania			
Rhode Island			
South Carolina			×
South Dakota			×
Tennessee			×
Texas			×
Utah			×
Vermont	×	×	×
Virginia	×	×	×
Washington			×
West Virginia	×	×	×
Wisconsin	×	×	×
Wyoming			×

Homestead Protection

Nearly all states (see Table 3:1) have passed **homestead protection laws,** usually with two purposes in mind: (1) to provide some legal protection for the homestead claimants from debts and judgments against them that might result in the forced sale and loss of the home, and (2) to provide a home for a widow, and sometimes a widower, for life. Homestead laws also restrict one spouse from acting without the other when conveying the homestead or using it as collateral for a loan. In Minnesota, the entire value of the homestead is protected from creditors, provided it does not exceed 80 acres in the country or one-half acre in town. However, this protection does not extend to mortgage liens, tax liens, or mechanics' liens on the homestead property. As referred to here, homestead is not the acquiring of title to state or federally owned lands by filing and establishing a residence. Additionally, "homestead protection" should not be confused with the "homestead exemption" Minnesota grants to homeowners in order to reduce their property taxes.

A homeowner is also protected by the Federal Bankruptcy Reform Act of 1979. A person who seeks protection under this Act is entitled to an exemption of up to $7,500 of the equity in his or her residence. Also exempt is any household item that does not exceed $200 in value.

FREEHOLD ESTATES

In a carryover from the old English court system, estates in land are classified as either **freehold estates** or **leasehold estates.** The main difference is that freehold estate cases are tried under real property laws whereas leasehold (also called **non-freehold** or less-than-freehold) estates are tried under personal property laws.

The two distinguishing features of a freehold estate are (1) there must be actual ownership of the land, and (2) the estate must be of unpredictable duration. Fee estates, life estates, and estates created by statute are freehold estates. The distinguishing features of a leasehold estate are (1) although there is possession of the land, there is no ownership, and (2) the estate is of definite duration.

LEASEHOLD ESTATES

As previously noted, the user of a property need not be its owner. Under a leasehold estate, the user is called the **lessee** or **tenant,** and the person from whom he leases is the **lessor** or **landlord.** As long as the tenant has a valid lease, abides by it, and pays the rent on time, the owner, even though he owns the property, cannot occupy it until the lease has expired. During the lease period, the freehold estate owner is said to hold a **reversionary interest.** This is his right to recover possession at the end of the lease period. Meanwhile, the lease is an encumbrance against the property.

There are four categories of leasehold estates: estate for years, periodic estate, estate at will, and tenancy at sufferance. Note that in this chapter, we will be examining leases primarily from the standpoint of estates in land. Leases as financing tools are discussed in Chapter 12 and lease contracts are covered in Chapter 15.

Estate for Years

Also called a tenancy for years, the **estate for years** is somewhat misleadingly named as it implies that a lease for a number of years has been created. Actually, the key criterion is that the lease have a specific starting time and a specific ending time. It can be for any length of time, ranging from less than a day to many years. An estate for years does not automatically renew itself. Neither the landlord nor the tenant must act to terminate it, as the lease agreement itself specifies a termination date.

Usually the lessor is the freehold estate owner. However, the lessor could be a lessee himself. To illustrate, a fee owner leases his property to a lessee, who in turn leases his right to still another person. By doing this, the first lessee has become a **sublessor** and is said to hold a **sandwich lease.** The person who leases from him is a **sublessee.** It is important to realize that in no case can a sublessee acquire from the lessee any more rights than the lessee has under his lease. Thus, if a lessee has a 5-year lease with 3 years remaining, he can assign to a sublessee only the remaining 3 years or a portion of that.

Periodic Estate

Also called an estate from year to year or a periodic tenancy, a **periodic estate** has an original lease period with fixed length; when it runs out, unless the tenant or his landlord acts to terminate it, renewal is automatic for another like period of time. A month-to-month apartment rental is an example of this arrangement. To avoid last minute confusion, rental agreements usually require that advance notice be given if either the landlord or the tenant wishes to terminate the tenancy.

Estate at Will

Also called a tenancy at will, an **estate at will** is a landlord–tenant relationship with all the normal rights and duties of a lessor–lessee relationship, except that the estate may be terminated by either the lessor or the lessee at anytime. However, most states recognize the inconvenience a literal interpretation of "anytime" can cause and require that reasonable advance notice be given.

In Minnesota, periodic estates and estates at will have been merged under the name **estates at will.** By statute, a Minnesota estate at will can be terminated by either party giving three months written advance notice, or one full rental period of advance notice, whichever is less.

Tenancy at Sufferance

A **tenancy at sufferance** occurs when a tenant stays beyond his legal tenancy without the consent of the landlord. In other words, the tenant wrongfully holds the property against the owner's wishes. In a tenancy at sufferance, the tenant is commonly called a **holdover tenant,** although once he stays beyond his legal tenancy he is not actually a tenant in the normal landlord–tenant sense. The landlord is entitled to evict him and recover possession of his property, provided he does so in a timely manner. A tenant at sufferance differs from a trespasser only in that his original entry was rightful. If during the holdover period, the landlord and tenant express their agreement to allow the tenant to remain, Minnesota views the tenancy at sufferance as converted to an estate at will.

Overview

Figure 3:5 provides an overview of the various rights and interests in land that are discussed in this chapter and the previous chapter. This chart is designed to give you an overall perspective of what the term real estate includes.

LICENSE

A **license** is not a right or an estate in land, but a personal privilege given to someone to use land. It is nonassignable and can be canceled by the person who issues it. A license to park is typically what an automobile parking lot operator provides for persons parking in his lot. The contract creating the license is usually written on the stub that the lot attendant gives the driver, or it is posted on a sign on the lot. Tickets to theaters and sporting events also fall into this category. Because it is a personal privilege, a license is not an encumbrance against land.

CHATTELS

A chattel is an article of personal property. Chattels are divided into two categories: chattels personal and chattels real. Examples of **chattels personal** are automobiles, clothes, food,

Figure 3:5 **RIGHTS AND INTERESTS IN LAND**

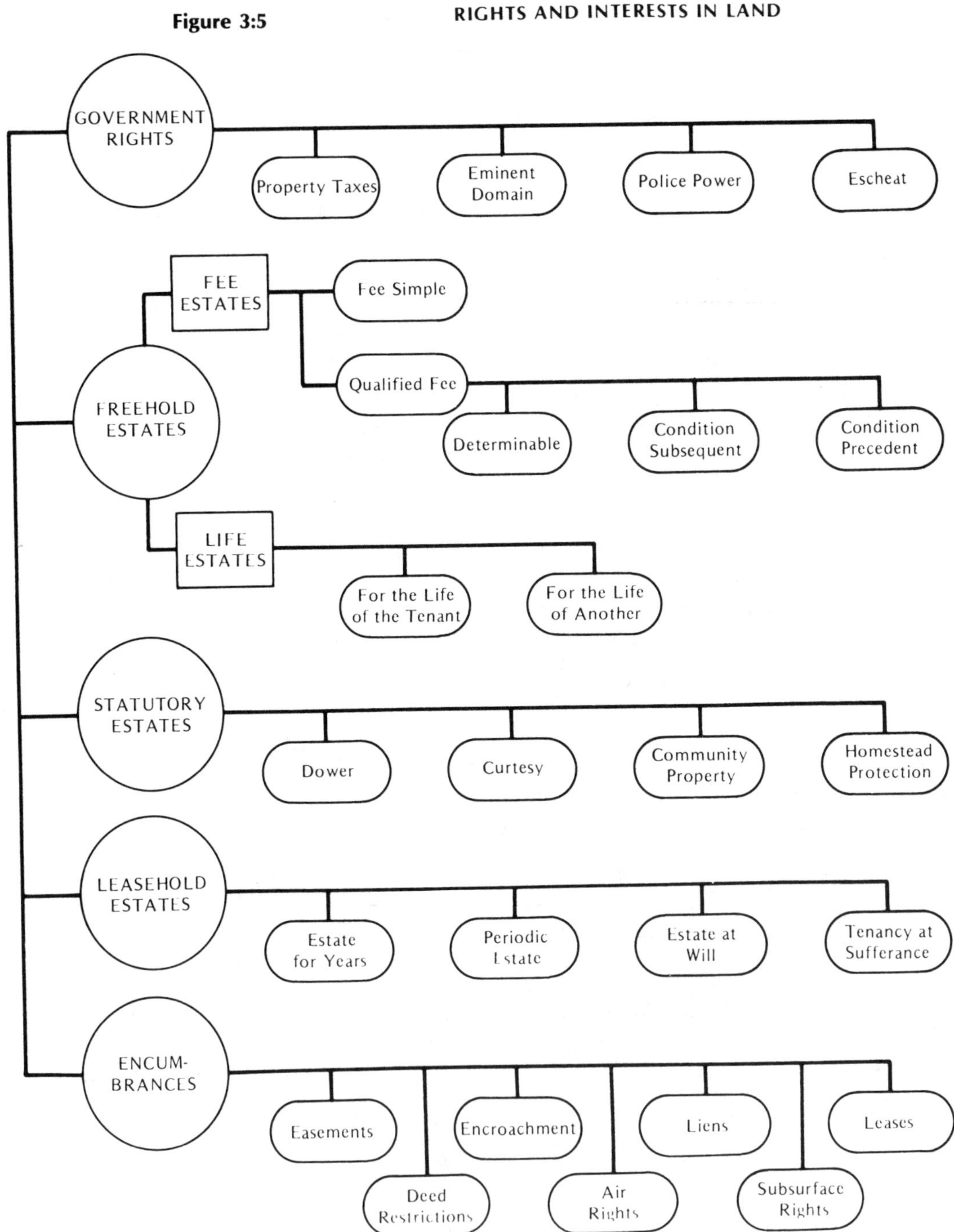

and furniture. **Chattels real** are interests in real estate that remain personal property; for example, a contract for the purchase of real estate or a leasehold estate. In the United States, chattels are governed by personal property laws. Freehold estates are governed by real property laws.

PICTORIAL SUMMARY

Let us conclude this chapter by combining what has been discussed in Chapter 2 regarding the physical nature of land with what has been covered in this chapter regarding estates and rights in land. The results, diagrammed in Figures 3:6 and 3:7, show why real estate is both complicated and exciting at the same time. A single parcel of land can be divided into subsurface, surface, and air-space components, and each of these carries its own fee simple bundle of rights, which can be divided into the various estates and rights discussed in this chapter.

To more clearly convey this idea, let us turn our attention to Figure 3:6. In parcel A, the fee landowner has leased the bulk of his surface and air rights, plus the right to draw water from his wells, to a farmer for the production of crops and livestock. This leaves the fee owner with the right to lease or sell subterranean rights for mineral, oil, and gas extraction. With a single parcel of land, the fee owner has created two estates, one for farming and another for oil and gas production. With the minor exception of the placement of the well plat-

CROSS SECTION OF ESTATES AND RIGHTS IN LAND **Figure 3:6**

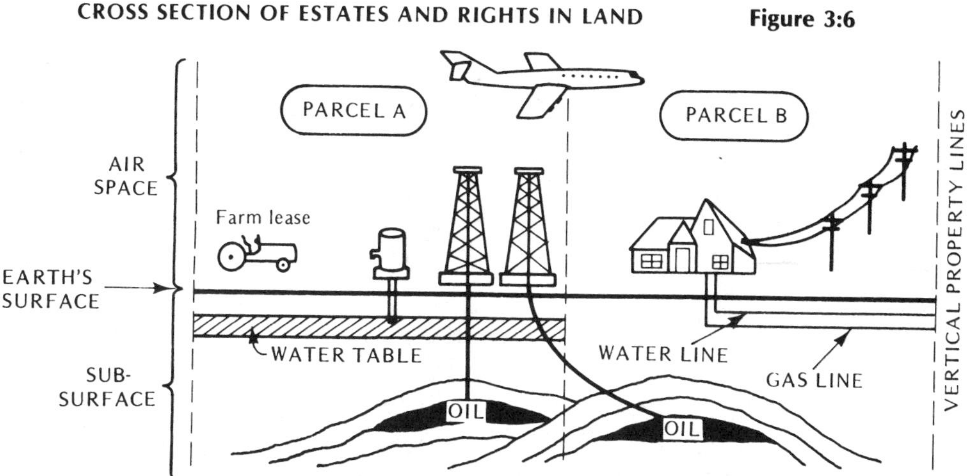

forms, pumps, and pipes, neither use interferes with the other and both bring income to the landowner. The farmer, in turn, can personally utilize the leasehold estate he possesses or he can sublease it to another farmer. The oil company, if it has leased its rights, can sublease them; if it has purchased them, it can sell or lease them. A variation would be for an oil company to buy the land in fee, conduct its drilling operations, and lease the remainder to a farmer. In the public interest, the government has claimed the right to allow aircraft to fly over the land. Although technically a landowner owns from the center of the earth out to the heavens, the right given aircraft to fly overhead creates a practical limit on that ownership.

Surface Right of Entry

In parcel B, the fee simple landowner has leased or sold the right to extract oil and gas from beneath his land. However, no surface right for the purpose of entering and drilling has been leased or sold. Thus, the oil company must slant drill from a nearby property where it does have a **surface right of entry.** The remaining rights amount to a full fee estate in the surface and air space. However, use of those rights is subject to zoning laws and building codes that restrict what can be built. Deed restrictions may include additional limitations on the type of structure that can be built. Also, the government claims air-space rights for passing aircraft, as it does over all land within its borders. Just above and beneath the surface, easement rights have been granted to utility companies for electric, telephone, water, and gas lines.

Despite the fact that this homeowner's bundle of rights is not complete, what he does have is quite suitable for a home site. Recognizing this, lenders will accept the owner's offer to pledge this house and lot as collateral for a loan. This might not be the case if the oil company had a surface right of entry. The noise, odor, and fire hazard of a working oil well next to a house would considerably reduce its value as a residence.

Land Lease

In parcel C shown in Figure 3:7, the fee owner has created an estate for years by a long-term lease of his land to an investor, who has subsequently constructed an apartment building on the land. This estate gives the building owner the right to occupy and use the land for a fixed period of time, most often between 55 and 99 years. In turn, the building owner

CROSS SECTION OF ESTATES AND RIGHTS IN LAND—Continued **Figure 3:7**

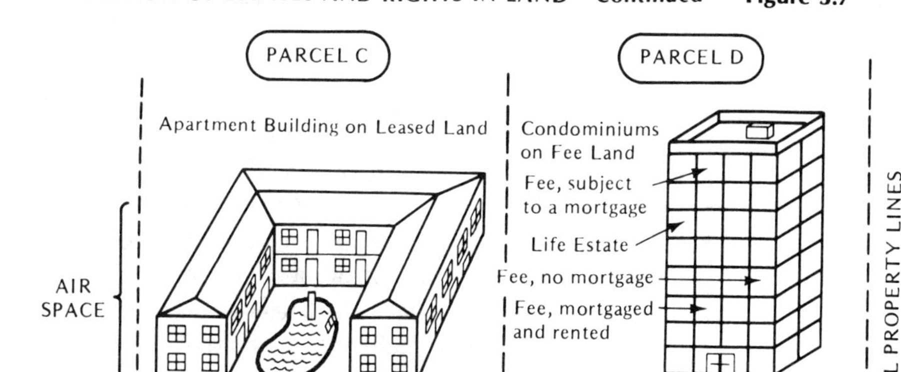

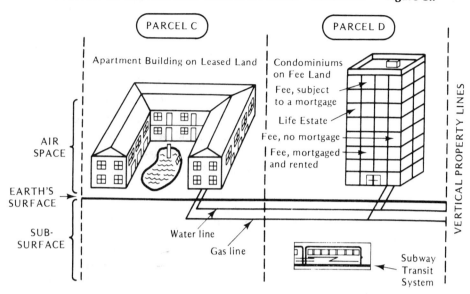

rents out apartment units on a monthly or yearly basis. The rights to any mineral, oil, or gas deposits can either be included in the lease or reserved by the landowner. At the end of the lease period, the reversionary interest held by the owner of the fee estate entitles him to retake possession of his land, including the buildings and other improvements thereon.

Condominium Lots

In parcel D, fee simple air lots have been sold to individual apartment owners in a condominium apartment building. The owner of each air lot has a fee simple bundle of rights with respect to his air lot and is free to dispense the bundle as he pleases. For example, he can mortgage his apartment, taking the foreclosure "stick" out of his bundle of rights and giving it to a lender in exchange for a loan. Also, he can lease his unit to a tenant, thereby creating a leasehold estate and a reversionary right.

Condominium owners as a group usually own the surface of the land upon which the building rests, any air space not used as air lots, and the subsurface. In parcel D, the owners have either sold, leased, or granted to a transit authority the right to build a subway line under this parcel. Underground rights of this type are very important in cities with subsurface transportation networks and will continue to be so as more cities open underground mass transit systems, such as Washington, D.C., did in 1976.

An alternative to fee owners granting a subsurface right for underground transportation lines is for the line owner to own the fee interest in the entire parcel, use the subsurface portion for its tracks, and sell or lease the use of the surface and air space above. In Chicago and New York City, for instance, railroads have sold or leased surface and air rights above their downtown tracks for the purpose of constructing office buildings and convention halls. Passenger trains run just below the surface, while new buildings occupy the space above.

VOCABULARY REVIEW

Match terms **a–t** *with statements* **1–20.**

a. *Allodial*
b. *Bundle of rights*
c. *Chattel*
d. *Curtesy*
e. *Dower*
f. *Easement*
g. *Eminent domain*
h. *Encroachment*
i. *Escheat*
j. *Estate*
k. *Estate for years*
l. *Holdover tenant*
m. *Inverse condemnation*
n. *Lessee*
o. *Lessor*
p. *Lien*
q. *Periodic tenancy*
r. *Police power*
s. *Reversionary interest*
t. *Waste*

1. A lease with a specific starting and ending date and no automatic renewal provision.
2. A charge or hold against property to use it as security for a debt.
3. A leasehold estate that automatically renews itself unless cancelled.
4. An article of personal property.
5. The unauthorized intrusion of a building or other improvement upon the land of another.
6. A tenant who wrongfully remains in possession of leased property after his lease expires.
7. The right of government to take property from private owners, who in turn must be compensated.
8. A real property ownership system that allows land to be owned by individuals.
9. The right of government to enact laws and enforce them for the order, safety, health, morals, and general welfare of the public.
10. A lawsuit by a property owner demanding that a public agency purchase his property.
11. The abuse or destructive use of property.
12. Real estate ownership viewed as a collection of many rights.
13. The reversion of property to the state when the owner dies without leaving a will or heirs.

14. The extent of interest which a person has in real property. Also used to describe all the real and personal property owned by a person.
15. One who holds title and leases out his property; the landlord.
16. One who holds the right to use property but does not own it; the tenant.
17. The right that a wife has in her husband's estate at his death.
18. The right that a husband has in his wife's estate at her death.
19. A right or privilege one party has in the use of land belonging to another.
20. The right to the future enjoyment of property presently in the possession of another.

QUESTIONS AND PROBLEMS

1. Distinguish between freehold and leasehold estates in land.
2. Under what conditions is it possible for an easement to be created without there being specific mention of it in writing?
3. Why are dower, curtesy, and homestead protection sometimes referred to as statutory estates?
4. From the standpoint of possession, what is the key difference between an easement and a lease?
5. What is an encumbrance? Give three examples.
6. In your community, name specific examples of the application of police power to the rights of landowners.
7. What homestead protection does Minnesota offer and what must a person do to qualify?
8. Technically speaking, a 99-year lease on a parcel of land is personal property. However, from a practical standpoint, the exclusive right to use a parcel of land for such a long period of time seems more like real property. Do the laws of your state treat a 99-year lease as real or personal property?

ADDITIONAL READINGS

Boyer, Ralph E. *Survey of the Law of Property,* 3rd ed. St. Paul, Minn.: West Publishing Co., 1981, 718 pages. Part I discusses freehold estates, concurrent estates, less than freehold estates, dower, curtesy, and future interests.

Conser, Eugene P. *Real Estate—European Style.* New York: Exposition Press, 1976, 634 pages. Book provides a fascinating and informative look at real estate ownership in 32 countries. Includes local ownership laws, customs, and government regulation.

Harrison, Henry, and **Leonard, Margery B.** *Home Buying.* Chicago: Realtors National Marketing Institute, 1980, 620 pages. A practical guide to buying a home. Includes calculating how much home you can afford, how to compare houses and their features, steps in buying a home, and 62 tear-out checklists to help compare homes. Useful for buyer and agent alike.

Kusnet, Jack. "Air Rights: The Third Dimension," *Real Estate Today,* Aug. 1974, pages 12–15. Explains the concept of air space rights and discusses how these rights can be used for real estate development in crowded downtown areas.

Lawrence, Glenn. *Condemnation—Your Rights When Government Acquires Your Property.* Dobbs Ferry, N.Y.: Oceana Publications, 1967, 123 pages. A short nontechnical book about the legal rights of a property owner whose property is being taken in an eminent domain action.

Powell, Richard R. *The Law of Property.* New York: Matthew Bender, 1975, 7 volumes. Volume 1, Chapters 6–8, deal with the right of a person to own land; Volume 2, Chapters 12, 13, 15, 17 and 18A deal with classification and historical evolution of estates in land, life estates, leaseholds, and air rights; Volume 6, Chapter 79, deals with police powers as they effect the rights of land owners.

4

Forms of Ownership

KEY TERMS

Association: a not-for-profit organization that can own property and transact business in its own name

Estate in severalty: owned by one person; sole ownership

Financial liability: the amount of money one can lose; one's risk exposure

Joint tenancy: a form of property co-ownership that features the right of survivorship

Joint venture: an association of two or more persons or firms in order to carry out a single business project

Right of survivorship: A feature of joint tenancy whereby the surviving joint tenants automatically acquire all the right, title and interest of the deceased joint tenant

Tenancy by the entirety: a form of joint ownership reserved for married persons; right of survivorship exists and neither spouse has a disposable interest during the lifetime of the other

Tenants in common: shared ownership of a single property among two or more persons; interests need not be equal and no right of survivorship exists

Undivided interest: ownership by two or more persons that gives each the right to use the entire property

In Chapter 2 we looked at land from a physical standpoint: the size and shape of a parcel, where it is located and what was affixed to it. In Chapter 3 we explored various legal rights and interests that can be held in land. In this chapter, we shall look at how a given right or interest in land can be held by one or more individuals.

SOLE OWNERSHIP

When title to property is held by one person, it is called an **estate in severalty** or **sole ownership.** Although the word "severalty" seems to imply that several persons own a single property, the correct meaning can be easily remembered by thinking of "severed" ownership. Sole ownership is available to single and married persons. However, in the case of married persons, most states require one spouse to waive community property, dower, or curtesy rights in writing. In Minnesota both spouses join in any conveyance of an interest in real estate. Businesses usually hold title to property in severalty.

It is from the estate in severalty that all other tenancies are carved.

The major advantage of sole ownership for an individual is flexibility. As a sole owner you can make all the decisions regarding a property without having to get the agreement of co-owners. You can decide what property or properties to buy, when to buy, and how much to offer. You can decide whether to pay all cash or to seek a loan by using the property as collateral. Once bought, you control (within the bounds of the law) how the property will be used, how much will be charged if it is rented, and how it will be managed. If you decide to sell, you alone decide when to offer the property for sale and at what price and terms.

But freedom and responsibility go together. For example, if you purchase a rental property you must determine the prevailing rents, find tenants, prepare contracts, collect the rent, and keep the property in repair; or you must hire and pay someone else to manage the property. Another deterrent to sole ownership is the high entry cost. This form of real estate ownership is not possible for someone with only a few hundred dollars to invest.

TENANTS IN COMMON

When two or more persons wish to share the ownership of a single property, they may do so as **tenants in common.** As tenants in common, each owns an **undivided interest** in the whole property. This means that each owner has a right to possession of the entire property. None can exclude the others nor claim any specific portion for himself. In a tenancy in common, these interests need not be the same size, and each owner can independently sell, mortgage, give away, or devise his individual interest. This independence is possible because each tenant in common has a separate legal title to his undivided interest.

Suppose that you invest $20,000 along with two of your friends, who invest $30,000 and $50,000, respectively; together you buy 100 acres of land as tenants in common. Presuming that everyone's ownership interest is proportional to his or her cash investment, you will hold a 20% interest in the entire 100 acres and your two friends will hold 30% and 50%. You cannot pick out 20 acres and exclude the other co-owners from them, nor can you pick out 20 acres and say, "These are mine and I'm going to sell them"; nor can they do that to you. You do, however, have the legal right to sell or otherwise dispose of your 20% interest (or a portion of it) without the permission of your two friends. Your friends have the same right. If one of you sells, the purchaser becomes a new tenant in common with the remaining co-owners.

Wording of Conveyance

As a rule, a tenancy in common is indicated by naming the co-owners in the conveyance and adding the words "as tenants in common." For example, a deed might read, "Samuel Smith, John Jones, and Robert Miller, as tenants in common." If nothing is said regarding the size of each co-owner's interest in the property, the law presumes that all interests are equal. Therefore, if the co-owners intend their interests to be unequal, the size of each co-owner's undivided interest must be stated as a percent or a fraction such as 60% and 40% or one-third and two-thirds.

In nearly all states, including Minnesota, if two or more persons are named as owners, and there is no specific indication as to how they are taking title, they are presumed to be tenants in common with equal interests. Thus, if a deed is made out to "Donna Adams and Barbara Kelly," the law would consider them to be tenants in common, each holding an undivided one-half interest in the property.

When a tenancy in common exists, if a co-owner dies his interest passes to his heirs or devisees, who then become tenants in common with the remaining co-owners. There is no **right of survivorship;** that is, the remaining co-owners do not acquire the deceased's interest unless they are named in the deceased's last will and testament to do so. When a creditor has a claim on a co-owner's interest and forces its sale to satisfy the debt, the new buyer becomes a tenant in common with the remaining co-owners. If one co-owner wants to sell (or give away) only a portion of his undivided interest, he may; the new owner becomes a tenant in common with the other co-owners.

Any income generated by the property belongs to the tenants in common in proportion to the size of their interests. Similarly, each co-owner is responsible for paying his proportionate share of property taxes, repairs, upkeep, and so on, plus interest and debt repayment, if any. If any co-owner fails to contribute his proportionate share, the other co-owners can pay on his behalf and then sue him for that amount. If co-owners find that they cannot agree as to how the property is to be run and cannot agree on a plan for dividing or selling it, it is possible to request a court-ordered partition. A **partition** divides the property into distinct portions so that each person can hold his proportionate interest in severalty. If this is physically impossible, such as when three co-owners each have a one-third interest in a house, the court will order the property sold and the proceeds divided between the co-owners.

The major advantage of tenancy in common is that it allows two or more persons to achieve goals that one person could not accomplish alone. However, prospective co-owners should give advance thought to what they will do (short of going to court) if (1) a co-owner fails to pay his share of ownership expenses, (2) differences arise regarding how the property is to be operated, (3) agreement cannot be reached as to when to sell, for how much, and on what terms, and (4) what happens if a co-owner dies and those who inherit his interest have little in common with the surviving co-owners. The counsel of an attorney experienced in property ownership can be very helpful when considering the co-ownership of property.

JOINT TENANCY

Another form of multiple-person ownership is joint tenancy. The most distinguishing characteristic of joint tenancy is the right of survivorship. Upon the death of a joint tenant, his interest does not descend to his heirs or pass by his will. Rather, the entire ownership remains in the surviving joint tenant(s).

Four Unities

Historically, to create a joint tenancy, **four unities** must be present. They are the unities of time, title, interest, and possession.

Unity of time means that each joint tenant must acquire his or her ownership interest at the same moment. Once a joint tenancy is formed, it is not possible to add new joint tenants later unless an entirely new joint tenancy is formed among the existing co-owners and the new co-owner. To illustrate, suppose that *A*, *B*, and *C* own a parcel of land as joint tenants. If *A* sells his interest to *D* then *B*, *C*, and *D* must sign documents to create a new joint tenancy among them.

If this is not done, *D* automatically becomes a tenant in common with *B* and *C* who, between themselves, remain joint tenants. *D* will then own an undivided one-third interest in common with *B* and *C* who will own an undivided two-thirds interest as joint tenants.

Unity of title means that the joint tenants acquire their interests from the same source, i.e., the same deed or will. (Some states allow a property owner to create a valid joint tenancy by conveying to himself, or herself, and another without going through a third party.)

Unity of interest means that the joint tenants own one interest together and each joint tenant has exactly the same right in that interest. (This, by the way, is the foundation upon which the survivorship feature rests.) If the joint tenants list individual interests, they lack unity of interest and will be treated as tenants in common. Unity of interest also means that, if one joint tenant holds a fee simple interest in the property, the others cannot hold anything but a fee simple interest.

Unity of possession means that the joint tenants must enjoy the same undivided possession of the whole property. All joint tenants have the use of the entire property, and no individual owns a particular portion of it. By way of contrast, unity of possession is the only unity essential to a tenancy in common.

The common law requirements for unities of time, title, interest and possession (the four unities) to create a joint tenancy have been abolished by statute in Minnesota as of August 1, 1979. A valid joint tenancy is created in Minnesota by a conveyance to the grantees "as joint tenants, and not as tenants in common."

Right of Survivorship

The feature of joint tenancy ownership that is most widely recognized is its **right of survivorship.** Upon the death of a joint tenant, that interest in the property is extinguished. In a two-person joint tenancy, when one person dies, the other immediately becomes the sole owner. With more than two persons as joint tenants, when one dies the remaining joint tenants are automatically left as owners. Ultimately, the last survivor becomes the sole owner. The legal philosophy is that the joint tenants constitute a single owning unit. The death of one joint tenant does not destroy that unit—it only reduces the number of persons owning the unit. For the public record, a copy of the death certificate and an affidavit of survivorship of the joint tenant(s) is recorded in the county where the property is located. The property must also be released from any Minnesota or federal estate tax liens.

It is the right of survivorship that has made joint tenancy a popular form of ownership among married couples. Married couples often want the surviving spouse to have sole ownership of the marital property. Any property held in joint tenancy goes to the surviving spouse without the delay of probate and usually with less legal expense.

"Poor Man's Will"

Because of the survivorship feature, joint tenancy has been loosely labeled a "poor man's will." However, it cannot replace a properly drawn will as it affects only that property held in joint tenancy. Moreover, a will can be changed if the persons named therein are no longer in one's favor. But once a joint tenancy is formed, title is permanently conveyed and there is no further opportunity for change. A joint tenant cannot name someone in his will to receive his joint tenant interest because his interest ends upon his death. One should also be aware of the possibility that ownership in joint tenancy may result in additional estate taxes.

There is a popular misconception that a debtor can protect himself from creditors' claims by taking title to property as a joint tenant. It is true that in a joint tenancy, the surviving joint tenant(s) acquire(s) the property free and clear of any liens against the deceased. However, this can happen only if the debtor dies before the creditor seizes his interest.

Only a human being can be a joint tenant. A corporation cannot be a joint tenant. This is because a corporation is an artificial legal being and can exist in perpetuity, i.e., never die. Joint tenancy ownership is not limited to the ownership of land: any estate in land and any chattel interest (such as an automobile or bank account) may be held in joint tenancy.

TENANCY BY THE ENTIRETY

Tenancy by the entirety (also called tenancy by the entireties) is a form of joint tenancy specifically for married persons. To the four unities of a joint tenancy is added a fifth: **unity of person.** The basis for this is the legal premise that a husband and wife are an indivisible legal unit. Two key characteristics of a tenancy by the entirety are (1) the surviving spouse becomes the sole owner of the property upon the death of the other, and (2) neither spouse has a disposable interest in the property during the lifetime of the other. Thus, while both are alive and married to each other, both signatures are necessary to convey title to the property. With respect to the first characteristic, tenancy by the entirety is similar to joint tenancy because both feature the right of survivorship. They are quite different, however, with respect to the second characteristic. A joint tenancy can be terminated by one tenant's conveyance of his or her interest, but a tenancy by the entirety can be terminated only by joint action of husband and wife.

Minnesota does not recognize tenancy by the entirety. States that do are listed in Table 4:1. Note that severalty, tenancy in common, joint tenancy, and tenancy by the entirety are called English common law estates because of their English origin.

COMMUNITY PROPERTY

Laws and customs acquired from Spain and France when vast areas of the United States were under their control are the basis for the **community property** system of ownership for married persons. Table 4:1 identifies the eight community property states. Minnesota is not one of those states. The laws of each community property state vary slightly, but the underlying concept is that the husband and wife contribute jointly and equally to their marriage and thus should share equally in any property purchased during marriage. Whereas English law is based on the merging of husband and wife upon marriage, community property law treats husband and wife as equal partners, with each owning a one-half interest.

Separate Property

Property owned before marriage, and property acquired after marriage by gift, inheritance, or purchase with separate funds, can be exempted from the couple's community property. Such property is called **separate property** and can be conveyed or mortgaged without the signature of the owner's spouse. All other property acquired by the husband or wife during marriage is considered community property and requires the signature of both spouses before it can be conveyed or mortgaged. Under community property ownership, each spouse can devise his or her one-half interest as he or she pleases. It does

Table 4:1 **CONCURRENT OWNERSHIP BY STATES**

	Tenancy in Common	Joint Tenancy	Tenancy by the Entirety	Community Property
Alabama	×	×		
Alaska	×	×	×	
Arizona	×	×		×
Arkansas	×	×	×	
California	×	×		×
Colorado	×	×		
Connecticut	×	×		
Delaware	×	×	×	
District of Columbia	×	×	×	
Florida	×	×	×	
Georgia	×	×		
Hawaii	×	×	×	
Idaho	×	×		×
Illinois	×	×		
Indiana	×	×	×	
Iowa	×	×		
Kansas	×	×		
Kentucky	×	×	×	
Louisiana				×
Maine	×	×		
Maryland	×	×	×	
Massachusetts	×	×	×	
Michigan	×	×	×	
Minnesota	×	×		
Mississippi	×	×	×	
Missouri	×	×	×	
Montana	×	×		
Nebraska	×	×		
Nevada	×	×		×
New Hampshire	×	×		
New Jersey	×	×	×	
New Mexico	×	×		×
New York	×	×	×	
North Carolina	×	×	×	
North Dakota	×	×		
Ohio	×		×	
Oklahoma	×	×	×	
Oregon	×		×	
Pennsylvania	×	×	×	
Rhode Island	×	×	×	
South Carolina	×	×		
South Dakota	×	×		
Tennessee	×	×	×	
Texas	×	×		×
Utah	×	×	×	
Vermont	×	×	×	
Virginia	×	×	×	
Washington	×	×		×
West Virginia	×	×	×	
Wisconsin	×	×		
Wyoming	×	×	×	

not have to go to the surviving spouse. If death occurs without a will, in five states (California, Idaho, Nevada, New Mexico, and Washington) the deceased spouse's interest goes to the surviving spouse. In Arizona, Louisiana, and Texas, the descendents of the deceased spouse are the prime recipients. Neither dower nor curtesy exist in community property states.

The major advantage of the community property system

is found in its philosophy: it treats the spouses as equal partners in property acquired through their mutual efforts during marriage. Even if the wife elects to be a full-time homemaker and all the money brought into the household is the result of her husband's job (or vice versa), the law treats them as equal co-owners in any property bought with that money. This is true even if only one spouse is named as the owner.

In the event of divorce, if the parting couple cannot amicably decide how to divide their community property, the courts will usually do so. If the courts do not, the ex-spouses will become tenants in common with each other. If it later becomes necessary, either can file suit for partition.

PARTNERSHIP

A **partnership** exists when two or more persons, as partners, unite their property, labor, and skill as a business to share the profits created by it. The agreement between the partners may be oral or written. The partners may hold the partnership property either in their own names (as tenants in common or as joint tenants) or in the name of the partnership (which would hold title in severalty). When property is held in the name of the partnership, it is called a **tenancy in partnership.** In that case the name of the partnership and a list of the partners must be published in the public records of each county and state where the partnership owns property. From then on, business may be transacted in the name of the partnership. For convenience, especially in a large partnership, the partners may designate two or three of their group to make contracts and sign documents on behalf of the entire partnership. There are two types of partnerships: general partnerships made up entirely of general partners and limited partnerships composed of general and limited partners.

General Partnership

The **general partnership** is an outgrowth of common law. However, to introduce clarity and uniformity into general partnership laws across the United States, 48 states and the District of Columbia have adopted the **Uniform Partnership Act** either in total or with local modifications. (The two exceptions are Georgia and Louisiana.) Briefly, the highlights of the Act are that (1) title to partnership property may be held in the partnership's name, (2) each partner has an equal right of possession of partnership property—but only for partnership purposes,

(3) upon the death of one partner his rights in the partnership property vest in the surviving partners—but the decedent's estate must be reimbursed for the value of his interest in the partnership, (4) a partner's right to specific partnership property is not subject to dower or curtesy, and (5) partnership property can only be attached by creditors for debts of the partnership, not for debts of a partner.

As a form of property ownership, the partnership is a method of combining the capital and expertise of two or more persons. It is equally important to note that the profits and losses of the partnership are taxable directly to each individual partner in proportion to his or her interest in the partnership. Although the partnership files a tax return, it is only for informational purposes. The partnership itself does not pay taxes. Negative aspects of this form of ownership center around financial liability, illiquidity, and in some cases, management.

Financial liability means each partner is personally responsible for all the debts of the partnership. Thus, each general partner can lose not only what he has invested in the partnership, but more, up to the full extent of his personal financial worth. If one partner makes a commitment on behalf of the partnership, all partners are responsible for making good on that commitment. If the partnership is sued, each partner is fully responsible. **Illiquidity** refers to the possibility that it may be very difficult to sell one's partnership interest on short notice in order to raise cash. **Management** means that each general partner is expected to take an active part in the operation of the partnership.

Limited Partnership

Because of unlimited financial liability and management responsibility an alternative partnership form, the **limited partnership,** has developed. Forty-nine states, plus the District of Columbia, have adopted the **Uniform Limited Partnership Act.** (The exception is Louisiana, which has its own general and limited partnership laws.) This act recognizes the legality of limited partnerships and requires that a limited partnership be formed by a written document.

A limited partnership is composed of general and limited partners. The general partners organize and operate the partnership, contribute some capital, and agree to accept the full financial liability of the partnership. The **limited partners** provide the bulk of the investment capital, have little say in the day-to-day management of the partnership, share in the profits and losses, and contract with their general partners to limit the financial liability of each limited partner to the amount he or she invests. Additionally, a well-written partnership agreement will allow for the continuity of the partnership in the event of the death of a general or limited partner.

The advantages of limited liability, minimum management responsibility, and direct pass-through of profits and losses for taxation purposes have made this form of ownership popular. However, being free of management responsibility is only advantageous to the investors if the general partners are capable and honest. If they are not, the only control open to the limited partners is to vote to replace the general partners.

Before investing in a limited partnership, one should investigate the past record of the general partners, for this is usually a good indication of how the new partnership will be managed. The investigation should include their previous investments, talking to past investors, and checking court records for any legal complaints brought against them. Additionally, the prospective partner should be prepared to stay in for the duration of the partnership as the resale market for limited partnership interests is small.

JOINT VENTURE

A **joint venture** is an association of two or more persons or firms to carry out a single business project. A joint venture is similar to a partnership and is treated as a partnership for tax purposes. However, whereas a general partner can bind his partnership to a contract, a joint venturer cannot bind the other joint venturers to a contract. Examples of joint ventures in real estate are the purchase of land by two or more persons with the intent of grading it and selling it as lots, the association of a landowner and builder to build and sell, and the association of a lender and builder to purchase land and develop buildings on it to sell to investors. Each member of the joint venture makes a contribution in the form of capital or talent, and all have a strong incentive to make the joint venture succeed. If more than one project is undertaken, the relationship becomes more like a partnership than a joint venture.

SYNDICATION

A **syndication** (or **syndicate**) is not a form of ownership; rather, it refers to individuals or firms combining to pursue an investment enterprise too large for any of them to undertake individually. The form of ownership might be a tenancy in common, joint tenancy, general or limited partnership, or a corporation. Applied to real estate investing, the term "syndicate" usually refers to a limited partnership in which the limited partners provide the investment capital and the general partners provide the organizational talent and ongoing management services. The general partners receive compensation for purchasing, managing, and reselling the properties. The limited partners receive a return on and a return of their investment if the syndicate is successful. Most states require that real estate syndicates be registered with the state before they can be sold to investors. Federal registration may also be necessary. Registration does not relieve an interested investor from investigating carefully and seeking experienced legal direction.

CORPORATIONS

Each state has passed laws to permit groups of people to create **corporations** that can buy, sell, own, and operate in the name of the corporation. The corporation, in turn, is owned by stockholders, who possess shares of stock as evidence of their ownership.

Because the corporation is an entity (or legal being) in the eyes of the law, the corporation must pay income taxes on its profits. What remains after taxes can be used to pay dividends to the stockholders, who in turn pay personal income taxes on their dividend income. This double taxation of profits is the most important negative factor in the corporate form of ownership. On the positive side, the entity aspect shields the investor from unlimited liability. Even if the corporation falls on the hardest of financial times and owes more than it owns, the worst that can happen to the stockholder is that the value of his stock will drop to zero. Another advantage is that shares of stock are much more liquid than any previously discussed form of real estate ownership, even sole ownership. Stockbrokers and stock exchanges who specialize in the purchase and sale of corporate stock usually complete a sale in a week or less. Furthermore, shares of stock in most corporations sell for less than $100, thus enabling an investor to operate with small amounts of capital. In a corporation, the stockholders elect a board of directors, who in turn hire the management needed to run the day-to-day operations of the company. As a practical matter, however, unless a person is a major shareholder in a corporation, he will have little control over management. His alternative is to buy stock in firms where he likes the management and sell where he does not.

ASSOCIATIONS

An **association** is a not-for-profit organization that can own property and transact business in its own name. Examples of associations are the homeowner associations found in condominiums and planned unit developments, and the National Association of Realtors. If properly incorporated, an association will shield its members from personal liability in the event of lawsuits against the association.

REAL ESTATE INVESTMENT TRUSTS

The idea of creating a trust that in turn carries out the investment objectives of its investors is not new. What has changed is that in 1961 Congress passed a law allowing trusts that specialize in real estate investments to avoid double taxation by following strict rules. These **real estate investment trusts (REITs)** pool the money of many investors for the purchase of real estate, much like mutual funds do with stocks and bonds. Investors in a REIT are called **beneficiaries** and they purchase **beneficial interests** somewhat similar to shares of corporate stock. The trust officers, with the aid of paid advisors, buy, sell, mortgage, and operate real estate investments on behalf of the beneficiaries. If a REIT confines its activities to real estate investments, and if the REIT has at least 100 beneficiaries and distributes at least 90% of its net income every year, then the Internal Revenue Service will collect tax on the distributed income only once—at the beneficiaries' level. Failure to follow the rules results in double taxation.

The REIT is an attempt to combine the advantages of the corporate form of ownership with single taxation status. Like stock, the beneficial interests are freely transferable and usually sell for $100 each or less, a distinct advantage for the investor with a small amount of money to invest in real estate. Beneficial interests in the larger REITs are sold on a national basis, thus enabling a REIT to have thousands of beneficiaries and millions of dollars of capital for real estate purchases.

INTER VIVOS AND TESTAMENTARY TRUSTS

In all states, the trust form of ownership can be used to provide for the well-being of another person. Basically, this is an arrangement whereby title to real and/or personal property is transferred by its owner (the **trustor**) to a trustee. The **trustee** holds title and manages the property for the benefit of another (the **beneficiary**) in accordance with instructions given by the trustor. Two popular trust forms are the inter vivos trust also called a living trust, and the testamentary trust.

An **inter vivos trust** takes effect during the life of its creator. For example, you can transfer property to a trustee with instructions that it be managed and that income from the trust assets be paid to your children, spouse, relatives, or a charity.

Figure 4:1

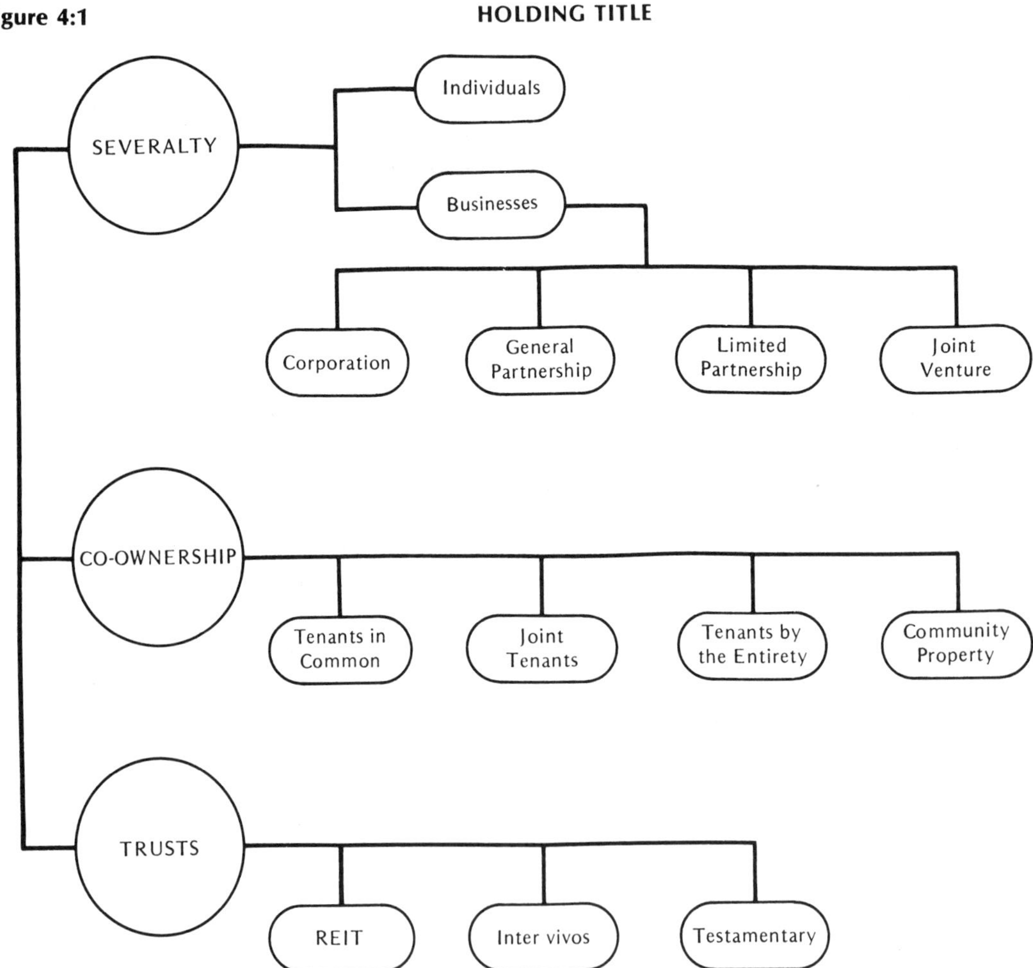

A visual summary of the various methods of holding title to real estate discussed in this chapter.

A **testamentary trust** takes effect after death. For example, you could place instructions in your will that upon your death, your property is to be placed into a trust. You can name whomever you want as trustee (a bank or trust company or friend, for example) and whom you want as beneficiaries. You can also give instructions as to how the assets are to be managed and how much (and how often) to pay the beneficiaries. Because trusts provide property management and financial control as well as a number of tax and estate planning advantages, this form of property ownership is growing in popularity.

CAVEAT

The purpose of this chapter has been to acquaint you with the fundamental aspects of the most commonly used forms of real estate ownership in the United States. You undoubtedly saw instances where you could apply these. Unfortunately, it is not possible in a real estate principles book to discuss each detail of each state's law (many of which change frequently), nor to take into consideration the specific characteristics of a particular transaction. In applying the principles in this book to a particular transaction, you should add competent legal advice regarding your state's legal interpretation of these principles.

VOCABULARY REVIEW

Match terms **a–q** *with statements* **1–17.**

a. *Community property*
b. *Estate in severalty*
c. *Financial liability*
d. *General partnership*
e. *Joint tenancy*
f. *Joint venture*
g. *Limited partner*
h. *Partition*
i. *Real estate investment trust*
j. *Right of survivorship*
k. *Separate property*
l. *Syndication*
m. *Tenancy by the entirety*
n. *Tenants in common*
o. *Undivided interest*
p. *Unity of interest*
q. *Unity of time*

1. Owned by one person only. Sole ownership.
2. Each owner has a right to use the entire property.
3. Undivided ownership by two or more persons without right of survivorship; interests need not be equal.
4. The remaining co-owners automatically acquire the deceased's undivided interest.
5. A form of co-ownership in which the most widely recognized feature is the right of survivorship.
6. All co-owners have an identical interest in the property. A common law requirement for joint tenancy.
7. All co-owners acquired their ownership interests at the same time. A common law requirement for joint tenancy.
8. Spouses are treated as equal partners with each owning a one-half interest. French and Spanish law origin.
9. An English law form of ownership reserved for married persons. Right of survivorship exists and neither spouse has a disposable interest during the lifetime of the other.
10. Each partner is fully liable for all the debts and obligations of the partnership.
11. A member of a limited partnership whose financial liability is limited to the amount invested.
12. Two or more persons joining together on a single project as partners.
13. Property acquired before marriage in a community property state.
14. A type of mutual fund for real estate investment and ownership wherein a trustee holds property for the benefit of the beneficiaries.
15. A general term that refers to a group of persons who organize to pool their money.
16. Refers to the amount of money a person can lose.
17. To divide jointly held property so that each owner can hold a sole ownership.

QUESTIONS AND PROBLEMS

1. What is the key advantage of sole ownership? What is the major disadvantage?
2. Explain what is meant by the term "undivided interest" as it applies to co-ownership of real estate.

3. Name the four unities of a common law joint tenancy. What does each mean to the property owner?
4. What does the term "right of survivorship" mean in real estate ownership?
5. Suppose that a deed was made out to "John and Mary Smith, husband and wife" with no mention as to how they were taking title. Which would Minnesota assume: joint tenancy, tenancy in common, tenancy by the entirety, or community property?
6. Does Minnesota permit the right of survivorship among persons who are not married?
7. If a deed is made out to three women as follows, "Susan Miller, Rhoda Wells, and Angela Lincoln," with no mention as to the form of ownership or the interest held by each, what can we presume regarding the form of ownership and the size of each woman's ownership interest?
8. In a community property state, if a deed names only the husband (or the wife) as the owner, can we assume that only that person's signature is necessary to convey title? Why or why not?
9. List two ways in which a general partnership differs from a limited partnership.
10. What advantages does a real estate investment trust offer a person who wants to invest in real estate?

ADDITIONAL READINGS

Cartwright, John M. *Glossary of Real Estate Law.* Rochester, N.Y.: The Lawyer's Cooperative Publishing Company, 1972, 1,027 pages. Contains definitions of legal terms and concepts frequently encountered in real estate transactions.

Powell, Richard R. *The Law of Property.* New York: Matthew Bender, 1975. Chapter 4 in Volume 1 reviews the history of American property law and includes a short discussion of how the property laws of each state developed. Chapters 49–53 in Volume 4A cover in detail the legal aspects of tenancy in common, joint tenancy, tenancy by the entirety, community property, and partnerships.

Rabkin, Jacob, and **Johnson, Mark H.** *Current Legal Forms with Tax Analysis,* Volume 8. New York: Matthew Bender, 1976. Deals with the advantages and disadvantages of the following forms of real estate ownership: tenancy in common, partnership, corporation, trust, cooperative and condominium. Special emphasis is placed on legal implications and income tax considerations.

Reader's Digest. *You and the Law,* 3rd ed. Pleasantville, N.Y.: Reader's Digest Association, 1981, 863 pages. Presents in nontechnical language one's legal rights and obligations under the law. Contains sections on contract law, landlord–tenant law, home purchase, mortgages, real estate taxes, and rights and interests of spouses. Charts show how laws vary from state to state.

Ross, Martin J. *Handbook of Everyday Law,* 4th ed. New York: Harper & Row, 1977, 361 pages. Written for the layman; describes his legal rights and shows how to protect them. Includes sections on purchasing real estate, contracts, agency, joint ownership, and taxes. With glossary.

5

Transferring Title

KEY TERMS

Adverse possession: acquisition of real property through prolonged and unauthorized occupation
Bargain and sale deed: a deed that contains no covenants, but does imply the grantor owns the property being conveyed
Cloud on the title: any claim, lien or encumbrance that impairs title to property
Color of title: some plausible, but not completely clear-cut indication of ownership rights
Consideration: anything of value given to induce another to enter into a contract
Covenant: a written agreement or promise
Deed: a written document that when properly executed and delivered conveys title to land
Grantee: the person named in a deed who acquires ownership
Grantor: the person named in a deed who conveys ownership
Quitclaim deed: a legal instrument used to convey whatever title the grantor has; it contains no covenants, warranties, nor implication of the grantor's ownership
Warranty: an assurance or guarantee that something is true as stated

The previous three chapters emphasized how real estate is described, the rights and interests available for ownership, and how title can be held. In this chapter we shall discuss how ownership of real estate is conveyed from one owner to another. We begin with the voluntary conveyance of real estate by deed, and then continue with conveyance after death, and conveyance by occupancy, accession, public grant, dedication, and forfeiture.

DEEDS

A **deed** is a written legal document by which ownership of real property is conveyed from one party to another. Deeds were not always used to transfer real estate. In early England, when land was sold its title was conveyed by inviting the purchaser onto the land. In the presence of witnesses, the seller picked up a clod of earth and handed it to the purchaser. Simultaneously, the seller stated that he was delivering ownership of the land to the purchaser. In times when land sales were rare, because ownership usually passed from generation to generation, and when witnesses seldom moved from the towns or farms where they were born, this method worked well. However, as transactions became more common and people more mobile, this method of title transfer became less reliable. Furthermore, it was susceptible to fraud if enough persons could be bribed or forced to make false statements. In 1677, England passed a law known as the **Statute of Frauds.** This law, subsequently adopted by each of the American states, requires that transfers of real estate ownership be in writing and signed in order to be enforceable in a court of law. Thus, the need for a deed was created.

ESSENTIAL ELEMENTS OF A DEED

What makes a written document a deed? What special phrases, statements and actions are necessary to convey the ownership rights one has in land and buildings? First, a deed must identify the **grantor,** who is the person giving up ownership, and the **grantee,** the person who is acquiring that ownership. The actual act of conveying ownership is known as a **grant.** To be legally enforceable, the grantor must be of legal age (18 years in Minnesota) and of sound mind.

Second, the deed must state that **consideration** was given by the grantee to the grantor. In Minnesota, it is common to use the phrase, "For one dollar ($1.00) and other good and valuable consideration," or the phrase, "For valuable consideration." These meet the legal requirement that consideration be shown, but retain privacy regarding the exact amount paid. If the conveyance is a gift, the phrase, "For natural love and affection," may be used, provided the gift is not for the purpose of defrauding the grantor's creditors.

Third, the deed must contain **words of conveyance.** With these words the grantor clearly states that he is making a grant of real property to the grantee, and identifies the quantity of the estate being granted. Usually, this is the fee simple estate, but it may also be a lesser estate (such as a life estate) or an easement.

A land **description** that cannot possibly be misunderstood is the fourth requirement. Acceptable legal descriptions are made by the metes and bounds method, by the government survey system, by recorded plat, or by reference to another recorded document that in turn uses one of these methods. Street names and numbers are not used as they do not identify the exact boundaries of the land and because street names and numbers can and do change over time. Assessor parcel numbers are not used either. If the deed conveys only an easement or air right, the deed states that fact along with the legal description of the land. The key point is that a deed must clearly specify what the grantor is granting to the grantee.

Fifth, the grantor must **sign** his name on the deed. Eight states also require that the grantor's signature be witnessed and that the witnesses sign the deed. If the grantor is unable to write his name, he may make a mark, usually an X, in the presence of witnesses. They in turn print his name next to the X and sign as witnesses. If the grantor is a corporation, the corporation's seal is affixed to the deed and an officer of the corporation with the proper authority signs it. Minnesota requires witnesses only if the grantor is unable to sign his name.

Figure 5:1

Witnesseth, John Stanley, grantor, for valuable consideration given by Robert Brenn, grantee, does hereby grant and release unto the grantee, his heirs and assigns to have and to hold forever, the following described land: [insert legal description here].

John Stanley
Grantor's signature

Figure 5:1 illustrates the essential elements that combine to form a deed. Notice that the example includes an identification of the grantor and grantee, fulfills the requirement for consideration, has words of conveyance, a legal description of the land involved, and the grantor's signature. The words of conveyance are "grant and release" and the phrase, "to have and to hold forever," says that the grantor is conveying all future benefits, not just a life estate or a tenancy for years. Ordinarily, the grantee does not sign the deed.

Delivery and Acceptance

For a deed to convey ownership, there must also be **delivery and acceptance.** Although a deed may be completed and signed, it does not transfer title to the grantee until the grantor voluntarily delivers it to the grantee and the grantee willingly accepts it. At that moment title passes.

COVENANTS AND WARRANTIES

Although legally adequate, a deed meeting the preceding requirements can still leave a very important question unanswered in the grantee's mind: "Does the grantor possess all the right, title, and interest he is purporting to convey by this deed?" As a protective measure, the grantee can ask the grantor to include certain covenants and warranties in the deed. These are written promises by the grantor that the condition of title is as stated in the deed together with the grantor's guarantee that if title is not as stated he will compensate the grantee for any loss suffered. Five covenants and warranties have evolved over the centuries for use in deeds, and a deed may contain none, some, or all of them, in addition to the essential elements already discussed. They are seizin, quiet enjoyment, encumbrances, further assurance, and warranty forever.

Under the **covenant of seizin** (sometimes spelled seisin), the grantor warrants (guarantees) that he is the owner and possessor of the property being conveyed and that he has the right to convey it. Under the **covenant of quiet enjoyment,** the grantor warrants to the grantee that the grantee will not be disturbed, after he takes possession, by someone else claiming an interest in the property.

In the **covenant against encumbrances,** the grantor guarantees to the grantee that the title is not encumbered with easements, restrictions, or any unpaid property taxes, assessments, mortgages, judgments, or the like, except as stated in the deed. If the grantee later discovers an undisclosed encumbrance, he can sue the grantor for the cost of removing it. The **covenant of further assurance** requires the grantor to procure and deliver to the grantee any subsequent documents that might be necessary to make good the grantee's title. **Warranty forever** is a guarantee to the grantee that the grantor will bear the expense of defending the grantee's title. If at any time in the future someone else can prove that he is the rightful owner, the grantee can sue the grantor for damages up to the value of the property at the time of the sale.

Date and Acknowledgment

Although it is customary to show on the deed the **date** it was executed by the grantor, it is not essential to the deed's validity. Remember that title passes upon **delivery** of the deed to the grantee, and that this may not necessarily be the date it was signed.

It is standard practice to have the grantor appear before a notary public or other public officer and formally declare that he signed the deed as a voluntary act. This is known as an **acknowledgment.** Minnesota and most states consider a deed to be valid even though it is not witnessed or acknowledged. However, it must be acknowledged to be placed in the public records. Acknowledgments and the importance of recording deeds will be covered in more detail in Chapter 6. Meanwhile, let us turn our attention to examples of the most commonly used deeds in Minnesota.

GENERAL WARRANTY DEED

The **general warranty deed,** also known as the **full covenant and warranty deed** or **warranty deed,** contains all five covenants and warranties. It is thus considered to be the best deed a grantee can receive, and is used extensively in most states.

Figure 5:2 illustrates in plain language the essential parts of a warranty deed. Beginning at ①, it is customary to identify at the top of the document that it is a warranty deed. At ② the wording begins with "This deed. . . ." These words are introductory in purpose. The fact that this is a deed depends on what it contains, not on what it is labeled. A commonly found variation starts with "This indenture" (meaning this agreement or contract) and is equally acceptable. The place the deed was made ③ and the date it was signed ④ are customarily included, but are not necessary to make the deed valid.

At numbers ⑤ and ⑥ the grantor is identified by name and, to avoid confusion with other persons having the same name, by address. Marital status is also stated: husband and wife, single man, single woman, widow, widower, divorced and not remarried. To avoid the inconvenience of repeating the grantor's name each time it is needed, the wording at ⑦ states that in the balance of the deed the word "Grantor" (plural, "Grantors") will be used instead. A common variation of this is to call the first party named "the party of the first part." Next appears the name and marital status of the "Grantee" ⑧ (plural, "Grantees") and the method by which title is being taken (severalty, tenants in common, joint tenants, etc.). The grantee's address appears at ⑨, and the wording at ⑩ states that the word "Grantee" will now be used instead

Figure 5:2

WARRANTY DEED ①

②

THIS DEED, made in the city of ______③______ *, state of* __________ *, on the* __④__ *day of* __________ *, 19* __ *, between* ______⑤______ *, residing at* ______⑥______ *, herein called the GRANTOR,* ⑦ *and* ______⑧______ *residing at* ______⑨______ *, herein called the GRANTEE:* ⑩

WITNESSETH that in consideration ⑪ *of one dollar ($1.00) and other valuable consideration, paid by the Grantee to the Grantor, the Grantor does hereby grant* ⑫ *and convey unto the Grantee, the Grantee's* ⑬ *heirs and assigns forever, the following described parcel of land:*

[legal description of land] ⑭

together with the buildings ⑮ *and improvements thereon and all the estate* ⑯ *and rights pertaining thereto,*

⑰ *TO HAVE AND TO HOLD the premises herein granted unto the Grantee, the Grantee's heirs* ⑱ *and assigns forever.*

The premises are free from encumbrances except as stated herein: ⑲

[note exceptions here]

The Grantee shall not: ⑳

[list restrictions imposed by Grantor on the Grantee]

The Grantor is lawfully seized ㉑ *of a good, absolute, and indefeasible estate in fee simple and has good right, full power, and lawful authority to convey the same by this deed.*

The Grantee, the Grantee's heirs and assigns, shall peaceably ㉒ *and quietly have, hold, use, occupy, possess, and enjoy the said premises.*

The Grantor shall execute or procure any further ㉓ *necessary assurance of the title to said premises, and the Grantor will forever* ㉔ *warrant and defend the title to said premises.*

IN WITNESS WHEREOF, the Grantor has duly executed this deed the day and year first written above. ㉕

㉖

____
(Grantor's signature) ㉗

[location of the acknowledgment: see Chapter 6] ㉘ (SEAL)

of the grantee's name. The alternative method is to call him "the party of the second part."

The legal requirement that consideration be shown is fulfilled at ⑪. Next we come to the **granting clause** at ⑫. Here the grantor states that the intent of this document is to pass ownership to the grantee, and at ⑬ the grantor describes the extent of the estate being granted. The phrase, "The grantee's heirs and assigns forever," indicates a fee simple estate. The word **assigns** refers to anyone the grantee may later convey the property to, such as by sale or gift.

The legal description of the land involved is then shown at ⑭. When a grantor is unable or does not wish to convey certain rights of ownership, he can list the exceptions here. For example, a grantor either not having or wishing to hold back oil and gas rights for himself may convey to the grantee the land described, "except for the right to explore and recover oil and gas at a depth below 500 feet beneath the surface." The separate mention at numbers ⑮ and ⑯ of buildings, estate, and rights is not an essential requirement as the definition of land already includes these items.

The **habendum clause,** sometimes called the "To have and to hold clause," begins at ⑰ and continues through ⑱. This clause, together with the statements at ⑫ and ⑬, forms the deed's words of conveyance. For this reason, the words at ⑱ must match those at ⑬. Number ⑲ identifies the covenant against encumbrances. The grantor warrants that there are no encumbrances on the property except as listed here. The most common exceptions are property taxes, mortgages, and assessment (improvement district) bonds. For instance, a deed may recite, "Subject to an existing mortgage . . . ," and name the mortgage holder and the original amount of the loan, or "Subject to a city sewer improvement district bond in the amount of $1,500."

At ⑳ the grantor may impose restrictions as to how the grantee may use the property. For example, "The grantee shall not build upon this land a home with less than 1,500 square feet of living space."

Special Wording

The covenants of seizin and quiet enjoyment are located at ㉑ and ㉒, respectively. Number ㉓ identifies the covenant of further assurance, and at ㉔ the grantor agrees to warrant and defend forever the title he is granting. The order of grouping of the five covenants is not critical, and in Minnesota there are laws that permit the use of the words "grant, bargain, sell, and convey" or "convey and warrant" to imply the presence of all five covenants.

At ㉕ the grantor states that he signed this deed on the date noted at ④. This is the **testimony clause;** although customarily included in deeds, it is redundant and could be left out as long as the grantor signs the deed at ㉖. Historically, a seal made with hot wax was essential to the validity of a deed. Today, those few states that require a seal ㉗ accept a hot wax seal, a glued paper seal, an embossed seal, the word "seal," or "L.S." The letters "L.S." are an abbreviation for the Latin words "locus sigilli" (place of the seal). Minnesota does not require a seal. The acknowledgment is placed at ㉘, the full wording of which is given in Chapter 6.

The exact style or form of a deed is not critical as long as it contains all the essentials clearly stated and is in conformity with state law. For example, one commonly used warranty deed format begins with the words "Know all men by these presents," is written in the first person, and has the date at the end. Although a person may prepare his own deed, the writing of deeds should be left to experts in the field. Even the preparation of preprinted deeds from stationery stores and title companies should be left to knowledgeable persons. Preprinted deeds contain several pitfalls for the unwary. First, the form may have been prepared and printed in another state and, as a result, may not meet the laws of your state. Second, if the blanks are incorrectly filled in, the deed will not be legally recognized. This is a particularly difficult problem when neither the grantor nor grantee realizes it until several years after the deed's delivery. Third, the use of a form deed presumes that the grantor's situation can be fitted to the form and that the grantor will be knowledgeable enough to select the correct form.

GRANT DEED

Some states, notably California, Idaho, and North Dakota, use a grant deed instead of a warranty deed. In a **grant deed** the grantor covenants and warrants that (1) he has not previously conveyed the estate being granted to another party, (2) he has not encumbered the property except as noted in the deed, and (3) he will convey to the grantee any title to the property he may later acquire. These covenants are fewer in number and narrower in coverage than those found in a warranty deed, particularly the covenant regarding encumbrances. In the warranty deed, the grantor makes himself responsible for the encumbrances of prior owners as well as his own. The grant deed limits the grantor's responsibility to the period of time he owned the property. Figure 5:3 summarizes the key elements of a California grant deed.

Figure 5:3

GRANT DEED①

*For a valuable*② *consideration, receipt of which is hereby acknowledged,* ③ *hereby*
(name of the grantor)
*GRANT(S)*④ *to* ⑤ *the*
(name of the grantee)
following described real property in the ⑥ ,
(city, town, etc.)
County of ______, *State of California:*

*[legal description of land here]*⑦

Subject to:

*[note exceptions and restrictions here]*⑧

Dated ⑨ ⑩
(Grantor's signature)

⑪[location of the acknowledgment]

Referring to the circled numbers in Figure 5:3, ① labels the document, ② fulfills the requirement that consideration be shown, and ③ is for the name and marital status of the grantor. By California statutory law, the single word GRANT(S) at ④ is both the granting clause *and* habendum, *and* it implies the covenants and warranties of possession, prior encumbrances, and further title. Thus, they need not be individually listed.

Number ⑤ is for the name and marital status of the grantee and the method by which title is being taken. Numbers ⑥ and ⑦ identify the property being conveyed. Easements, property taxes, conditions, reservations, restrictions, and the like, are noted at ⑧. The deed is dated at ⑨, signed at ⑩, and acknowledged at ⑪.

Why have grantees, in states with more than one-tenth of the total U.S. population, been willing to accept a deed with fewer covenants than a warranty deed? The primary reason is the early development and extensive use of title insurance in these states, whereby the grantor and grantee acquire an insurance policy to protect themselves if a flaw in ownership is later discovered. Title insurance is now available in nearly all parts of the United States and is explained in Chapter 6.

SPECIAL WARRANTY DEED

The **special warranty deed** (also called a **limited warranty deed**) contains only one covenant, wherein the grantor covenants and warrants he has not encumbered the property except as stated in the deed under the exceptions and restrictions section. Except for containing just one covenant instead of all five, it is identical to the deed shown in Figure 5:2.

QUITCLAIM DEED

A **quitclaim deed** has no covenants or warranties (see Figure 5:4). Moreover, the grantor makes no statement, nor does he even imply that he owns the property he is quitclaiming to the grantee. Whatever rights the grantor possesses at the time the deed is delivered are conveyed to the grantee. If the grantor has no interest, right, or title to the property described in the deed, none is conveyed to the grantee. However, if the grantor possesses fee simple title, fee simple title will be conveyed to the grantee.

The critical wording in a quitclaim deed is the grantor's statement that he "does hereby remise, release, and quitclaim forever." The word **quitclaim** means to renounce all possession, right, or interest. **Remise** means to give up any existing claim one may have, as does the word **release** in this usage. If the grantor subsequently acquires any right or interest in the property, he is not obligated to convey it to the grantee.

At first glance it may seem strange that such a deed should even exist, but it does serve a very useful purpose. Situations often arise in real estate transactions when a person claims to have a partial or incomplete right or interest in a parcel of land. Such a right or interest, known as a **cloud on the title,** may have been due to an inheritance, a dower, curtesy, or

Figure 5:4

QUITCLAIM DEED

THIS DEED, made the ____ day of ________, 19___, BETWEEN ____________ of ____________________, party of the first part, and ____________________ of ______________, party of the second part.

WITNESSETH, that the party of the first part, in consideration of one dollar ($1.00) and other valuable consideration, paid by the party of the second part, does hereby remise, release, and quitclaim unto the party of the second part, the heirs, successors and assigns of the party of the second part forever,

ALL that certain parcel of land, with the buildings and improvements thereon, described as follows,

[insert legal description here]

TOGETHER WITH the appurtenances and all the estate and rights of the Grantor in and to said property.

TO HAVE AND TO HOLD the premises herein granted unto the party of the second part, the heirs or successors and assigns of the party of the second part, forever.

IN WITNESS WHEREOF, the party of the first part has duly executed this deed the day and year first above written.

____
(Grantor)

[location of the acknowledgment]

community property right, or to a mortgage or right of redemption due to a court-ordered foreclosure sale. By releasing that claim to the fee simple owner through the use of a quitclaim deed, the cloud on the fee owner's title is removed. A quitclaim deed is also the standard deed format for granting an easement.

OTHER TYPES OF DEEDS

A **gift deed** is created by simply replacing the recitation of money and other valuable consideration with the statement, "in consideration of his [her, their] natural love and affection."

This phrase may be used in a warranty, special warranty, or grant deed. However, it is most often used in a quitclaim deed as it permits the grantor to avoid committing himself to any warranties regarding the property.

A **guardian's deed** is used to convey a minor's interest in real property. It usually contains only one covenant, that the guardian and minor have not encumbered the property. The deed must state the legal authority (usually a court order) that permits the guardian to convey the minor's property.

Sheriff's deeds and **referee's deeds in foreclosure** are issued to the new buyer when a person's real estate is sold as the result of a mortgage or other court-ordered foreclosure sale. The deed should state the source of the sheriff's or referee's authority and the amount of consideration paid. Such a deed conveys only the foreclosed party's title, and, at the most, carries only one covenant: that the sheriff or referee has not damaged the property's title.

A **correction deed,** also called a deed of confirmation, is used to correct an error in a previously executed and delivered deed. For example, a name may have been misspelled or an error found in the property description. A quitclaim deed containing a statement regarding the error is used for this purpose. A **cession deed** is a form of a quitclaim deed wherein a property owner conveys street rights to a county or municipality. A **tax deed** is used to convey title to property that has been sold by the government because of the non-payment of taxes.

DESCENT OF PROPERTY

If a person dies without leaving a last will and testament (or leaves one that is subsequently ruled void by the courts because it was improperly prepared), he is said to have died **intestate,** which means without a testament. When this happens, state law directs how the deceased's assets shall be distributed. This is known as **title by descent** or **intestate succession.** The surviving spouse and children are the dominant recipients of the deceased's assets. The deceased's grandchildren receive the next largest share, followed by the deceased's parents, brothers and sisters, and their children. These are known as the deceased's **heirs** or **distributees.** The amount each heir receives, if anything, depends on individual state law and on how many persons with superior positions in the succession are alive. If no heirs can be found, the deceased's property escheats (reverts) to the state.

Generally, under Minnesota's Probate Code and assuming the property was not held in joint tenancy, descent would be as follows: (1) If the property was the homestead of the deceased, the surviving spouse receives a life estate and any children have a remainder interest in fee simple. If there were no children, the spouse receives a fee simple. (2) If the property was not the homestead, the surviving spouse is entitled to a minimum interest of one-third. If the deceased had two or more children, the surviving spouse receives one-third and the children divide the remaining two-thirds equally. If there was only one child, the spouse and child each take one-half. If no children were born of the marriage, the surviving spouse receives 100%. Note, that if a child has died before his parent but after producing offspring, the deceased child's offspring share his interest equally by right of representation. If there are children but no surviving spouse, the children share equally. If there are neither spouse nor children surviving, the property would go first to the parents of the deceased if either is still living, and if not, to brothers and sisters of the deceased or more distant relatives if necessary.

Testate, Intestate

A person who dies and leaves a valid will is said to have died **testate,** which means that he died leaving behind a testament telling how his property shall be distributed. The person who made the will, now deceased, is known as the **testator.** In the will, the testator names the persons or organizations who are to receive his real and personal property after he dies. Real property that is willed is known as a **devise** and the recipient, a **devisee.** Personal property that is willed is known as a **bequest** or **legacy,** and the recipient, a **legatee.** The will usually names an **executor** to carry out its instructions. If one is not named, the court will appoint an **administrator.**

Notice an important difference between the transfer of real estate ownership by deed and by will: once a deed is made and delivered, the ownership transfer is permanent, the grantor cannot change his mind and take back the property. With respect to a will, the devisees, although named, have no rights to the testator's property until he dies. Until that time the testator can change his mind and his will.

Probate Court

Upon death, the deceased's will is submitted to probate. Minnesota has, with some modifications, adopted major portions of the **Uniform Probate Code** which provides substantial flexibility in the administration of estates and transfer of real estate. If the testator owned real property, its ownership is conveyed by Decree of Distribution of the Probate Court or by an **executor's deed** prepared and signed by the executor. A Decree of Distribution may be used to transfer title to a devisee. The executor's deed is used to convey property during administration, and also may be used to transfer title to a devisee. These documents do not contain warranties.

Protecting the Deceased's Intentions

Because the deceased is not present to protect his assets, state laws attempt to ensure that fair market value is received for the deceased's real estate by requiring court approval of proposed sales. To protect his interests, a purchaser should ascertain that the executor has the authority to convey title.

For a will to be valid, and subsequently bind the executor to carry out the instructions, it must meet specific legal requirements. All states recognize the **formal or witnessed** will, a written document prepared, in most cases, by an attorney. The testator must declare it to be his will and sign it in the presence of two witnesses who, at the testator's request and in his presence, sign the will as witnesses. A formal will prepared by an attorney is the preferred method, as the will then conforms explicitly to the law. This greatly reduces the likelihood of its being contested after the testator's death. Additionally, an attorney may offer valuable advice on how to word the will to reduce inheritance taxes.

Holographic Wills

Holographic wills are wills that are entirely handwritten, dated, and signed by the testator; but there are no witnesses. Nineteen states recognize holographic wills as legally binding. Minnesota is not one of these. Persons selecting this form of will generally do so because it saves the time and expense of seeking professional legal aid, and because it is entirely private. Besides the fact that holographic wills are considered to have no effect in 31 states, they often result in much legal argument in states that do accept them. This can occur when the testator is not fully aware of the law as it pertains to the making of wills. Many otherwise happy families have been torn apart by dissension when a relative dies and the will is opened—only to find that there is a question as to whether or not it was properly prepared and hence valid. Unfortunately, what follows is not what the deceased intended; those who would receive more from intestate succession will contest that the will be declared void and of no effect. Those with more to gain if the will stands as written will muster legal forces to argue for its acceptance by the probate court.

Oral Will

An **oral will,** more properly known as a **noncupative will,** is a will spoken by a person who is very near death. The witness must promptly put what he has heard in writing and submit it to probate. An oral will can only be used to dispose of personal property. Any real estate belonging to the deceased would be disposed of by intestate succession.

Codicil

A **codicil** is a written supplement or amendment made to a previously existing will. It is used to change some aspect of the will or to add a new instruction, without the work of rewriting the entire will. The codicil must be dated, signed, and witnessed in the same manner as the original will. The only way to change a will is with a codicil or by writing a complete new will. The law will not recognize cross-outs, notations, or other alterations made on the will itself.

ADVERSE POSSESSION

Through the unauthorized occupation of another person's land for a long enough period of time, it is possible under certain conditions to acquire ownership by **adverse possession.** The historical roots of adverse possession go back many centuries to a time before written deeds were used as evidence of ownership. At that time, in the absence of any claims to the contrary, a person who occupied a parcel of land was presumed to be its owner. Today, adverse possession is, in effect, a statute of limitations that bars a legal owner from claiming title to land when he has done nothing to oust an adverse occupant during the statutory period. From the adverse occupant's standpoint, adverse possession is a method of acquiring title by possessing land for a specified period of time under certain conditions.

Minnesota courts are quite demanding of proof before they will issue a new deed to a person claiming title by virtue of adverse possession. The claimant must have maintained actual, open, continuous, hostile, notorious and exclusive possession under a claim of right. (**Claim of right** is also called **color of title** in some other states). These requirements mean that the claimant's use must have been visible and obvious to the legal owner, continuous and not just occasional, and exclusive enough to give notice of the claimant's individual claim. Furthermore, the use must have been without permission and the claimant must have acted as though he were the owner, even in the presence of the actual owner. Finally, the adverse claimant must be able to prove that he has met these requirements for a period ranging from 3 to 30 years, as shown in Table 5:1. In Minnesota the requirement is 15 years.

Taxes and Tacking

In accumulating the required number of years, an adverse claimant may **tack on** his period of possession to that of a prior adverse occupant. This could be done through the purchase of that right. The current adverse occupant could in turn sell his claim to a still later adverse occupant until enough years were accumulated to present a claim in court.

Although the concept of adverse possession often creates the mental picture of a trespasser moving onto someone else's land and living there long enough to acquire title in fee, this is not the usual application. More often, adverse possession is used to extinguish weak or questionable claims to title and to settle boundary line disputes. For example, if a farmer builds a fence which extends onto his neighbor's property and maintains all of the property up to the fence for 15 years, adverse possession could permit the fence to become the actual property line. Another source of successful adverse possession claims arises from building encroachments. If a building extends over a property line and nothing is said about it for a long enough period of time, the building will be permitted to stay.

In addition to the requirements set out above, Minnesota requires that the adverse claimant pay the property taxes on the adversely possessed property for five consecutive years, except in the case of boundary disputes. Finally, Minnesota courts will not recognize any adverse possession of property registered under the Torrens system.

EASEMENT BY PRESCRIPTION

An easement can also be acquired by prolonged adverse use. This is known as acquiring an **easement by prescription.** Like adverse possession, the laws are strict: the usage must

ADVERSE POSSESSION: NUMBER OF YEARS OF OCCUPANCY REQUIRED TO CLAIM TITLE* **Table 5:1**

	Adverse Occupant Lacks Color of Title & Does Not Pay the Property Taxes	Adverse Occupant Has Color of Title &/or Pays the Property Taxes
Alabama	20	3–10
Alaska	10	7
Arizona	10	3
Arkansas	15	2–7
California		5
Colorado	18	7
Connecticut	15	15
Delaware	20	20
District of Columbia	15	15
Florida		7
Georgia	20	7
Hawaii	20	20
Idaho	5	5
Illinois	20	7
Indiana		10
Iowa	10	10
Kansas	15	15
Kentucky	15	7
Louisiana	30	10
Maine	20	20
Maryland	20	20
Massachusetts	20	20
Michigan	15	5–10
Minnesota	15	15
Mississippi	10	10
Missouri	10	10
Montana		5
Nebraska	10	10
Nevada		5
New Hampshire	20	20
New Jersey	30–60	20–30
New Mexico	10	10
New York	10	10
North Carolina	20–30	7–21
North Dakota	20	10
Ohio	21	21
Oklahoma	15	15
Oregon	10	10
Pennsylvania	21	21
Rhode Island	10	10
South Carolina	10–20	10
South Dakota	20	10
Tennessee	20	7
Texas	10–25	3–5
Utah		7
Vermont	15	15
Virginia	15	15
Washington	10	7
West Virginia	10	10
Wisconsin	20	10
Wyoming	10	10

* As may be seen, in a substantial number of states, the waiting period for title by adverse possession is shortened if the adverse occupant has color of title and/or pays the property taxes. In California, Florida, Indiana, Montana, Nevada, and Utah, the property taxes must be paid to obtain the title. Generally speaking, adverse possession does not work against minors and other legal incompetents. However, when the owner becomes legally competent, the adverse possession must be broken within the time limit set by each state's law (the range is one to 10 years). In the states of Louisiana, Oklahoma, and Tennessee, adverse possession is referred to as title by prescription.

be openly visible, continuous and exclusive, as well as hostile and adverse to the owner. Additionally the use must have occurred over a period of 5 to 20 years, depending on the state. Fifteen years are required in Minnesota. All these facts must be proved in a court of law before the court will issue the claimant a document legally recognizing his ownership of the easement. As an easement is a right to use land for a specific purpose, and not ownership of the land itself, courts rarely require the payment of property taxes to acquire a prescriptive easement.

As may be seen from the foregoing discussion, a landowner must be given obvious notification *at the location* of his land that someone is attempting to claim ownership or an easement. Since an adverse claim must be continuous and hostile, an owner can break it by ejecting the trespassers or by preventing them from trespassing, or by having them pay $1.00 per year. Any of these actions would demonstrate the landowner's superior title. Owners of stores and office buildings with private sidewalks or streets used by the public can take action to break any possible claims to a public easement by either periodically barricading the sidewalk or street or by posting signs giving permission to pass. These signs are often seen in the form of brass plaques embedded in the sidewalk or street. Federal, state, and local governments protect themselves against adverse claims to their lands by passing laws making them immune.

OWNERSHIP BY ACCESSION

The extent of one's ownership of land can be altered by **accession.** This can result from natural or man-made causes. With regard to natural causes, the owner of land fronting on a lake, river, or ocean may acquire additional land due to the gradual accumulation of rock, sand, and soil. This process is called **accretion** and the results are referred to as alluvion and reliction. **Alluvion** is the increase of land that results when waterborne soil is gradually deposited to produce firm dry ground. **Reliction** (or dereliction) results when a lake, sea or river permanently recedes, exposing dry land. When land is rapidly washed away by the action of water, it is known as **avulsion.** Man-made accession occurs when man attaches personal property to land. For example, when lumber, nails, and cement are used to build a house, they alter the extent of one's land ownership.

PUBLIC GRANT

A transfer of land by a government body to a private individual is called a **public grant.** The Homestead Act passed by the U.S. Congress in 1862 permits persons wishing to settle on otherwise unappropriated federal land to acquire fee simple ownership by paying a small filing charge and occupying and cultivating the land for 5 years. Similarly, for only a few dollars, a person may file a mining claim to federal land for the purpose of extracting whatever valuable minerals he can find. To retain the claim, a certain amount of work must be performed on the land each year. Otherwise, the government will consider the claim abandoned and another person may claim it. If the claim is worked long enough, a public grant can be sought and fee simple title obtained. In the case of both the homestead settler and the mining claim, the conveyance document that passes fee title from the government to the grantee is known as a **land patent.**

DEDICATION

When an owner makes a voluntary gift of his land to the public, it is known as **dedication.** To illustrate, a land developer buys a large parcel of vacant land and develops it into streets and lots. The lots are sold to private buyers, but what about the streets? In all probability they will be dedicated to the town, city, or county. By doing this, the developer, and later the lot buyers, will not have to pay taxes on the streets, and the public will be responsible for maintaining them. The fastest way to accomplish the transfer is by either statutory dedication or dedication by deed. In **statutory dedication,** the developer prepares a map showing the streets, has the map approved by local government officials, and then records it as a public document. In **dedication by deed** the developer prepares a deed that identifies the streets and grants them to the city.

Common law dedication takes place when a landowner, by his acts or words, shows that he intends part of his land to be dedicated even though he has never officially made a written dedication. For example, a landowner may encourage the public to travel on his roads in an attempt to convince a local road department to take over maintenance.

FORFEITURE

Forfeiture can occur when a deed contains a condition or limitation. For example, a grantor states in his deed that the land conveyed may be used for residential purposes only.

If the grantee constructs commercial buildings, the grantor can reacquire title on the grounds that the grantee forfeited his interest by not using the land for the required purpose. Similarly, a deed may prohibit certain uses of land. If the land is used for a prohibited purpose, the grantor can claim forfeiture has occurred.

ALIENATION

A change in ownership of any kind is known as an **alienation.** In addition to the forms of alienation discussed in this chapter, alienation can result from court action in connection with escheat, eminent domain, partition, foreclosure, execution sales, quiet title suits, and marriage. These topics are discussed in other chapters.

VOCABULARY REVIEW

Match terms **a–t** *with statements* **1–20.**

a. *Adverse possession*
b. *Alienation*
c. *Alluvion*
d. *Cloud on the title*
e. *Codicil*
f. *Color of title*
g. *Consideration*
h. *Covenants and warranties*
i. *Dedication*
j. *Deed*
k. *Easement by prescription*
l. *Grantee*
m. *Grantor*
n. *Holographic will*
o. *Intestate*
p. *Land patent*
q. *Probate*
r. *Quitclaim deed*
s. *Statute of Frauds*
t. *Warranty deed*

1. A written document that, when properly executed and delivered, conveys title to land.
2. Requires that transfers of real estate be in writing to be enforceable.
3. Person named in a deed who conveys ownership.
4. Person named in a deed who acquires ownership.
5. Anything of value given to produce a contract. It may be personal or real property, or love and affection.
6. Promises and guarantees found in a deed.
7. Any claim, lien or encumbrance that impairs title to property.
8. A deed that contains the covenants of seizin, quiet enjoyment, encumbrances, further assurance, and warranty forever.
9. Any change in the ownership of property.
10. A deed with no covenants and no implication that the grantor owns the property he is deeding to the grantee.
11. To die without a last will and testament.
12. A will written entirely in one's own handwriting and signed but not witnessed.

13. The process of verifying the legality of a will and carrying out its instructions.
14. A supplement or amendment to a previous will.
15. Acquisition of real property through prolonged and unauthorized occupation.
16. Some plausible, but not completely clear-cut, indication of ownership rights.
17. Acquisition of an easement by prolonged use.
18. Waterborne soil deposited to produce firm, dry ground.
19. A document for conveying government land in fee to settlers and miners.
20. Private land voluntarily conveyed to the government.

QUESTIONS AND PROBLEMS

1. Is it possible for a document to convey fee title to land even though it does not contain the word "deed"? If so, why?
2. In the process of conveying real property from one person to another, at what instant in time does title actually pass from the grantor to the grantee?
3. What legal protections does a full covenant and warranty deed offer a grantee?
4. As a real estate purchaser, which deed would you prefer to receive: warranty, special warranty, bargain and sale? Why?
5. Does Minnesota require a seal on deeds?
6. What are the hazards of preparing your own deeds?
7. Name five examples of title clouds.
8. What is meant by the term "intestate succession"?
9. With regard to probate, what is the key difference between an executor and an administrator?
10. Does Minnesota consider holographic wills to be legal? How many witnesses are required by your state for a formal will?
11. Can a person who has rented the same building for 30 years claim ownership by virtue of adverse possession? Why or why not?
12. Cite examples from your own community or state where land ownership has been altered by alluvion, reliction, or avulsion.

ADDITIONAL READINGS

Gross, Jerome S. *Encyclopedia of Real Estate Forms.* Englewood Cliffs, N.J.: Prentice-Hall, 1973, 458 pages. Chapter 10 contains examples of deeds including executor's deed, life estate deed, correction deed, cession deed, referee's deed in foreclosure, and referee's deed in partition.

Holzman, Robert S. *Estate Planning: The New Golden Opportunities.* New York: Boardroom Books, 1983, 230 pages. Provides suggestions on how to write a will in order to reduce legal hassles and estate taxes. Topics include wills, trusts, marital deduction, gifts, joint tenancy, life insurance, annuities, executor powers and estate tax return preparation.

Kratovil, Robert, and **Werner, Raymond J.** *Real Estate Law,* 8th ed. Englewood Cliffs, N.J.: Prentice-Hall, 1983, 650 pages. Chapter 7 is devoted to the legal aspects of deeds.

Petersen, Kristelle L. *The Single Person's Home-Buying Handbook.* New York: Hawthorn, 1980, 275 pages. This book looks at the special needs, concerns and discriminatory pitfalls that single home-buyers encounter. Includes shopping, evaluation, negotiation, buying together as singles, and advice for the single-again.

Quinlan, Elsie M. "Adverse Possession," *Real Estate Review,* Winter 1974, pages 128–30. This article recounts three adverse possession cases that reached the courts in 1973: 13 acres of oceanfront land in Delaware, a logging road in Vermont, and a sewer line in Colorado.

Semenow, Robert W. *Questions and Answers on Real Estate,* 9th ed. Englewood Cliffs, N.J.: Prentice-Hall, 1978, 762 pages. Chapter 3 contains text and questions on title transfer, parts of a deed, kinds of deeds, and adverse possession.

6

Recordation, Abstracts, and Title Insurance

KEY TERMS

Abstract: a summary of all recorded documents affecting title to a given parcel of land
Acknowledgment: a formal declaration by a person signing a document that he or she, in fact, did sign the document
Actual notice: knowledge gained from what one has seen, heard, read, or observed
Chain of title: the linkage of property ownership that connects the present owner to the original source of title
Constructive notice: notice given by the public records and by visible possession, and the legal presumption that all persons are thereby notified
Marketable title: title that is free from reasonable doubt as to who the owner is
Mechanic's lien: a lien placed against real property by unpaid workmen and materials suppliers
Quiet title suit: court ordered hearings held to determine land ownership
Title insurance: an insurance policy against defects in title not listed in the title report or abstract
Torrens system: a state-sponsored method of registering land titles

In this chapter we shall focus on (1) the need for a method of determining real property ownership, (2) the process by which current and past ownership is determined from public records, (3) the availability of insurance against errors made in determining ownership, (4) the Torrens system of land title registration, and (5) the Uniform Marketable Title Act.

NEED FOR PUBLIC RECORDS

Until the enactment of the Statute of Frauds in England in 1677, determining who owned a parcel of land was primarily a matter of observing who was in physical possession. A landowner gave notice to the world of his claim to ownership by visibly occupying his land. After 1677 written deeds were required to show transfers of ownership. The problem then became one of finding the person holding the most current deed to the land. This was easy if the deedholder also occupied the land, but was more difficult if he did not. The solution was to create a government-sponsored public recording service where a person could record his deed. These records would then be open free of charge to anyone. In this fashion, an owner could post notice to all that he claimed ownership of a parcel of land.

Constructive Notice, Actual Notice

When a person records a document in the public records, he gives **constructive notice** to the world at large as to the document's existence and its contents. A person also gives constructive notice that he is claiming a right or interest by being visibly in possession of the property. Constructive notice is also called **legal notice** because the public is charged with the responsibility of looking in the public records and at the property itself so as to have knowledge of all who are claiming a right or interest.

Actual notice is knowledge that one has actually gained based on what he has seen, heard, read, or observed. For example, if you read a deed from Jones to Smith, you have actual notice of the deed and Smith's claim to the property. If you go to the property and you see someone in possession, you have actual notice of his/her claim to be there.

Inquiry notice is notice the law presumes you to have where circumstances, appearances, or rumors warrant further inquiry. For example, suppose you are considering the purchase of vacant acreage and upon inspecting it see a dirt road cutting across the land that is not mentioned in the public records. The law expects you to make further inquiry. The road may be a legal easement across the property. Another example is that anytime you buy rental property, you are expected to make inquiry as to the rights of the occupants. They may hold substantial rights you would not know about without asking them.

Remember that anyone claiming an interest or right is expected to make it known either by recorded claim or visible use of the property. Anyone acquiring a right or interest is expected to look in the public records and go to the property and make a visual inspection for claims.

Recording Acts

All states have passed **recording acts** to provide for the recording of every instrument (i.e., document) by which an estate, interest, or right in land is created, transferred, or encumbered. Within Minnesota, each county has a **public recorder's office,** known as the County Recorder's Office for abstract property or the Registrar of Titles Office for Torrens (registered) property. The person in charge is called the recorder or registrar. Located at the seat of county government, each public recorder's office will record documents submitted to it that pertain to real property in that county. Thus a deed to property in XYZ County is recorded with the public recorder in XYZ County. Similarly, anyone seeking information regarding ownership of land in XYZ County would go to the recorder's office in XYZ County. Some cities also maintain record rooms where deeds are recorded. The recording process itself involves photocopying the documents and filing them for future reference.

To encourage people to use public recording facilities, laws in each state decree that (1) a deed, mortgage, or other instrument affecting real estate is not effective as far as subsequent purchasers and lenders without actual notice are concerned if it is not recorded, and (2) prospective purchasers, mortgage lenders, and the public at large are presumed notified when a document is recorded. Figure 6:1 illustrates the concept of public recording.

Figure 6:1

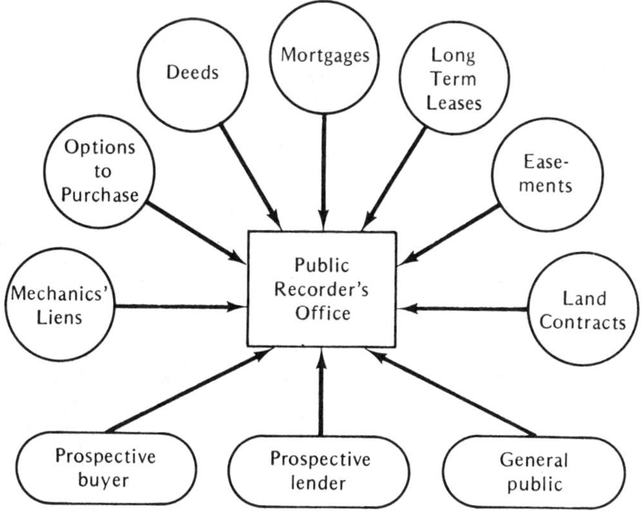

The public recorder's office serves as a central information station for changes in rights, estates, and interests in land.

Example of Notice Laws

To illustrate the effect of constructive and actual notice laws, suppose that Brown offers to sell his land to Carver. Carver then inspects both the land and the public records and finds Brown to be the owner. Satisfied as to Brown's ownership, Carver pays Brown and receives a deed in return. Suppose that Carver does not occupy the land, but he does record his deed with the public recorder's office in the county where the land is located. If Brown now approaches Dawson and attempts to sell the same land, Dawson will find, upon visiting the public records office, that Brown has already conveyed title to Carver.

But what if Dawson assumes that Brown is telling the truth and does not trouble himself to inspect the land or the records? Even though Dawson pays for the land and receives a deed from Brown, the law will not regard Dawson as the owner, even if Dawson records his deed. When Dawson discovers that Carver is the true owner, the only recourse open to Dawson is to sue Brown for the return of his money, presuming he can still locate Brown.

What would the result be if Carver did not record the deed he received and did not occupy the land? If Dawson became interested in buying the land and inspected the public records, he would find Brown to be the owner of record. Upon inspecting the land, Dawson would find no notice of Carver's ownership either. Having satisfied the law and himself regarding the land's ownership, Dawson would pay Brown and receive a deed to the land. If Dawson records his deed before Carver does, the law will consider Dawson to be the new owner. At this point, the only recourse open to Carver is to try to get his money back from Brown. Even if Carver later records his deed and claims that the date on his deed is earlier than the date on Dawson's deed, it is of no avail. Priority is established by the date of recording, not by the date written on the deed. Failure to record does not invalidate the deed itself; it is still binding between the parties who made it. But it is not valid with respect to the rest of the world.

If Carver does not record the deed he receives, but does occupy the land, the law holds Dawson responsible for visiting the land and asking Carver what his rights are. At that point Dawson would learn of Brown's deed to Carver. Any time a person buys property knowing that it has been sold before to another and the deed has not been recorded, he will not receive good title.

Although recording acts permit the recording of any estate, right, or interest in land, many lesser rights are rarely recorded because of the cost and effort involved. Month-to-month rentals and leases for a year or less fall into this category. Consequently, only an on-site inspection would reveal their existence, or the existence of any developing adverse possession or prescriptive easement claim.

With respect to actual and constructive notice, we can draw two important conclusions. First, a prospective purchaser (or lessee or lender) is presumed by law to have inspected both the land itself and the public records to determine the present rights and interests of others. Second, upon receiving a deed, mortgage, or other document relating to an estate, right, or interest in land, one should have it *immediately* recorded in the county in which the land is located.

REQUIREMENTS FOR RECORDING

Nearly all states, including Minnesota, require that a document be **acknowledged** before it is eligible to be recorded. A few states other than Minnesota will permit **proper witnessing** as a substitute. Some states require both. The objective of these requirements is to make certain that the person who signs the document is the same person named in the document and that the signing was a free and voluntary act. This is done to ensure the accuracy of the public records and to eliminate the possibility of forgery and fraud. To illustrate, suppose that you own 50 acres of vacant land and someone is intent on stealing it from you. Since the physical removal of your land is an impossibility, an attempt could be made to change the public records. A deed would be typed and the forger would sign your name to it. If he were successful in recording the deed, and then attempted to sell the land, the buyer would, upon searching the records, find a deed conveying the land from you to the forger. A visual inspection of the vacant 50 acres would not show you in actual possession. Although innocent of any wrongdoing and buying in good faith, the buyer would be left with only a worthless piece of paper, as there was no intent on your part to convey title to him.

Witnesses

In states that accept witnesses, the person executing the document signs in the presence of at least two witnesses, who in turn sign the document indicating that they were witnesses. To protect themselves, witnesses should not sign unless they know that the person named in the document is the person signing. In the event the witnessed signature is contested, the witnesses would be summoned to a court of law and under

Figure 6:2

IN WITNESS whereof, the grantor has duly executed this deed in the presence of:

________________ Witness   ________________ Grantor

________________ Witness

oath testify to the authenticity of the signature. An example of a witness statement is shown in Figure 6:2.

Acknowledgment

An **acknowledgment** is a formal declaration by a person signing a document that he or she, in fact, did sign the document. Persons authorized to take acknowledgments include notaries public, recording office clerks, commissioners of deeds, judges of courts of record, justices of the peace, and certain others as authorized by state law. Commissioned military officers are authorized to take the acknowledgments of persons in the military; foreign ministers and consular agents can take acknowledgments abroad. If an acknowledgment is taken outside the state where the document will be recorded, either the recording county must already recognize the out-of-state official's authority or the out-of-state official must provide certification that he or she is qualified to take acknowledgments. The official seal or stamp of the notary on the acknowledgment normally fulfills this requirement.

The acknowledgment illustrated in Figure 6:3 is typical of those used by an individual. Notice that the person signing the document must personally appear before the notary, and that the notary states that he or she knows that person to be the person described in the document. If they are strangers, the notary will require proof of identity. The person executing the document states that he or she acknowledges executing the document by signing it in the presence of the notary. Note that it is the signer who does the acknowledging, not the notary.

PUBLIC RECORDS ORGANIZATION

Each document brought to a public recorder's office for recordation is photocopied and then returned to its owner. The photocopy is arranged in chronological order with photocopies of other documents and bound into a book. These books

Figure 6:3

ACKNOWLEDGMENT FOR AN INDIVIDUAL

STATE OF ________________
COUNTY OF ________________ *ss*

On this ________ *day of* ________, *19*__, *before me, the undersigned, a Notary Public in and for said State, personally appeared* [name of person executing document] *known to me to be the person whose name is subscribed to the within instrument and acknowledged that he (she) executed the same. Witness my hand and official seal.*

[space for seal or stamp of the notary public]

____
Signature of notary public

[On some Minnesota forms, the words "by his (her) free act and deed" are added here]

My commission expires __________
Date

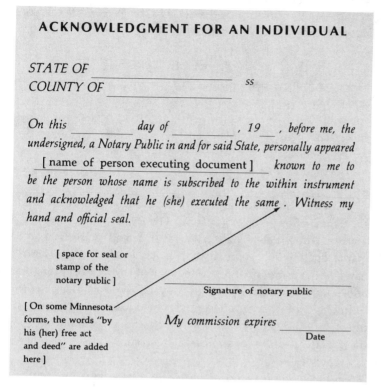

are placed in chronological order on shelves that are open to the public for inspection. Documents are referenced by **book and page** location. In some Minnesota counties they are given consecutive document reference numbers.

Filing incoming documents in chronological order makes sense for the recorder's office, but it does not provide an easy means for a person to locate all the documents relevant to a given parcel of land. To illustrate, suppose that you are planning to purchase a parcel of land and want to make certain that the person selling it is the legally recognized owner. Without an index to guide you, you would have to inspect every document in every volume, starting with the most recent book, until you located the current owner's deed. In a heavily populated county, your search might require you to look through hundreds of books, each containing up to 1,000 pages of documents. Consequently, recording offices have developed systems of indexing. The two most commonly used are the grantor and grantee indexes, used by all states, and the tract index, used by nine states. In Minnesota, tract indexes are frequently maintained by the public recorder. However, they are not considered official.

Tract Indexes

Of the two indexing systems, the **tract index** is the simplest to use. In it, one page is allocated to either a single parcel of land or to a group of parcels, called a tract. On that page you will find a reference to all the recorded deeds, mortgages, and other documents at the recorder's office that relate to that parcel. Each reference gives the book and page where the original document is recorded.

Grantor and Grantee Indexes

Grantor and grantee indexes are alphabetical indexes and are usually bound in book form. For each calendar year, the **grantor index** lists in alphabetical order all grantors named in the documents recorded that year. Next to each grantor's name is the name of the grantee named in the document, the book and page where a photocopy of the document can be found, and a few words describing the document. The **grantee index** is arranged by grantee names and gives the name of the grantor and the location and description of the document.

Example of Title Search

As an example of the application of the grantor and grantee indexes to a title search, suppose Robert T. Davis states that he is the owner of Lot 2, Block 2, in the Hilldale Tract in your county, and you would like to verify that statement in the public records. You begin by looking in the grantee index for his name, starting with this year's index and working backward in time. The purpose of this first step is to determine if the property was ever granted to Davis. If it was, you will find his name in the grantee index and, next to his name, a book and page reference to a photocopy of his deed to that parcel.

The next step is to look through the grantor index for the period of time starting from the moment he received his deed up to the present. If he has granted the property to someone else, Davis's name will be noted in the grantor index with a reference to the book and page where you can see a copy of the deed. (Davis could have reduced your efforts by showing you the actual deed conveying the lot to him. However, you would still have to inspect the grantor index for all dates subsequent to his taking title to see if he had conveyed title to a new grantee. If you do not have the name of the property owner, you would first have to go to the property tax office.)

Suppose your search shows that on July 1, 1974, in Book 2324, page 335, a warranty deed from John S. Miller to Davis, for Lot 2, Block 2 of the Hilldale Tract was recorded. Furthermore, you find that no subsequent deed showing Davis as grantor of this land has been recorded. Based on this, it would appear that Davis is the fee owner. However, you must inquire further to determine if Miller was the legally recognized owner of the property when he conveyed it to Davis. In other words, on what basis did Miller claim his right of ownership and, subsequently, the right to convey that ownership to Davis? The answer is that Miller based his claim to ownership on the deed he received from the previous owner.

CHAIN OF TITLE

By looking for Miller's name in the 1974 grantee index and then working backward in time through the yearly indexes, you will eventually find his name and a reference to Lot 2, Block 2 in the Hilldale Tract. Next to Miller's name you will find the name of the grantor and a reference to the book and page where the deed was recorded.

By looking for that name in the grantee index, you will locate the next previous deed. By continuing this process you can construct a chain of title. A **chain of title** shows the linkage of property ownership that connects the present owner to the original source of title. In most cases it starts with the original sale or grant of the land from the government to a private citizen. It is used to prove how title came to be **vested** in (i.e., possessed by) the current owner. Figure 6:4 illustrates the chain-of-title concept.

Sometimes, while tracing (running) a chain of title back through time, an apparent break or dead end will occur. This can happen because the grantor is an administrator, executor, sheriff, or judge, or because the owner died or because a mortgage against the land was foreclosed. To regain the title sequence, one must search outside the recorder's office by checking probate court records in the case of a death, or by checking civil court actions in the case of a foreclosure.

In addition to looking for grantors and grantees, a search must be made for any outstanding mortgages, judgments, actions pending, liens, and unpaid taxes that may affect the title.

Figure 6:4 CHAIN OF TITLE

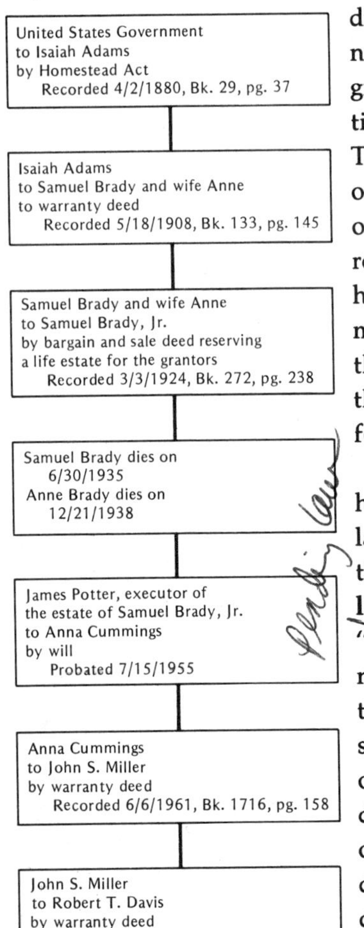

With regard to searching for mortgages, Minnesota counties differ slightly. Some place mortgages in the general document numbering system, listing the borrower (mortgagor) as the grantor and the lender (mortgagee) as the grantee. Other counties have separate index books for mortgagors and mortgagees. The process involves looking for the name of the property owner in each annual **mortgagor index** published while he owned the land. If a mortgage is found, a further check will reveal whether or not it has been satisfied and released. If it has been released, the recorder's office will have noted on the margin of the recorded mortgage the book and page where the release is located. When one knows the lender's name, the mortgage location and its subsequent release can also be found by searching the **mortgagee index.**

Public records must also be checked to learn if any lawsuits have resulted in judgments against recent owners, or if any lawsuits are pending that might later affect title. This information is found, respectively, on the **judgment rolls** and in the **lis pendens index** at the office of the county clerk. The term "lis pendens" is Latin for pending lawsuits. A separate search must also be made for **mechanics' liens** against the property that may have been filed by unpaid workmen and material suppliers. This step should also include an on-site inspection of the land for any recent construction activity or material deliveries. A visit must also be made to the local tax assessor's office to check the tax rolls for unpaid property taxes. This does not exhaust all possible places that must be visited to do a thorough title search. A title searcher may also find himself researching birth, marriage, divorce, and adoption records, probate records, military files, and federal tax liens in an effort to identify all the parties with an interest or potential interest in a given parcel of land and its improvements.

ABSTRACT

Although it is useful for the real estate practitioner to be able to find a name or document in the public records, full-scale title searching should be left to professionals. In a sparsely populated county, title searching is usually done on a part-time basis by an attorney. In more heavily populated counties, a full-time **conveyancer** or **abstracter** will search the records. These persons are experts in the field of title search, and for a fee they will prepare an abstract for a parcel of land.

An **abstract** is a complete historical summary of all recorded documents affecting the title of a property. It recites all recorded grants and conveyances as well as identifies and summarizes recorded easements, mortgages, wills, tax liens, judgments, pending lawsuits, marriages, divorces, etc., that might affect title. The abstract also includes a list of the public records searched, and not searched, in preparing the abstract.

The abstract is next sent to an attorney. Based on his knowledge of law and the abstract he is reading, he renders an **opinion** as to who the fee owner is and names anyone else he feels has a legitimate right or interest in the property. Alternatively, the abstract can be sent to a title company for an opinion and a commitment to insure.

TITLE INSURANCE

Despite the diligent efforts of conveyancers, abstracters, and attorneys to give as accurate a picture of land ownership as possible, there is no guarantee that the finished abstract is completely accurate. Persons preparing abstracts and opinions are liable for mistakes due to their own negligence, and they can be sued if that negligence results in a loss to a client. But what if a recorded deed in the title chain is a forgery? Or what if a married person represented himself on a deed as a single person, thus resulting in unextinguished dower rights? Or what if a deed was executed by a minor or an otherwise legally incompetent person? Or what if a document was misfiled, or there were undisclosed heirs, or a missing will later came to light, or there was confusion because of similar names on documents? These situations can result in substantial losses to a property owner, yet the fault may not lie with the conveyancer, abstracter, or attorney. The solution has been the organization of private companies to sell insurance against losses arising from title defects such as these as well as from errors in title examination.

Efforts to insure titles date back to the last century and were primarily organized by and for the benefit of attorneys who wanted protection from errors that they might make in the interpretation of abstracts. As time passed, **title insurance** (also called **title guarantee**) became available to anyone wishing to purchase it. The basic principle of title insurance is similar to any form of insurance: many persons pay a small amount into an insurance pool that is then available if any one of them should suffer a loss.

Commitment for Title Insurance

When a title company receives a request for a title insurance policy, the first step is an examination of the public records. This is done either by an independent abstracter or attorney, or by an employee of the title company. A company attorney then reviews the findings and renders an opinion as to who the fee owner is and lists anyone else he feels has a legitimate right or interest in the property such as a mortgage lender or easement holder. This information is typed up and becomes the commitment for title insurance. An example is illustrated in plain language in Figure 6:5.

Notice how a commitment differs from an abstract. Whereas an abstract is a summary of all recorded events that have affected the title to a given parcel of land; a commitment is more like a snapshot that shows the condition of title at a specific moment in time. A commitment does not tell who the previous owners were; it only tells who the current owner is. A commitment does not list all mortgage loans ever made against the land, but only those that have not been removed. The commitment in Figure 6:5 states that a search of the public records shows Barbara Baker to be the fee owner of Lot 17, Block M, at the time the search was conducted.

In Part I, the commitment lists all recorded objections that could be found to Baker's fee estate, in this case, county property taxes, a mortgage and two easements. In Part II, the title company states that there may be certain unrecorded matters that either could not be or were not researched in preparing the report. Note in particular that the title company does not make a visual inspection of the land for signs of actual notice nor does it make a boundary survey. The owner is responsible for making his own inspection and for hiring a surveyor if he is not certain as to the land's boundaries.

Although an owner may purchase a title insurance policy on his property at any time, it is most often purchased when land is sold. In connection with a sale, the commitment is used to verify that the seller is indeed the owner. Additionally, the commitment alerts the buyer and seller as to what needs to be done to bring title to the condition called for in the sales contract. For example, referring to Figure 6:5, the present owner (Barbara Baker) may have agreed to remove the existing mortgage so that the buyer can get a new and larger loan. Once this is done and the seller has delivered her deed to

Figure 6:5

COMMITMENT FOR TITLE INSURANCE

The following is a report of the title to the land described in your application for a policy of title insurance.

LAND DESCRIPTION: Lot 17, Block M, Atwater's Addition, Jefferson County, State of __________________.

DATE AND TIME OF SEARCH: March 3, 19xx at 9:00am

VESTEE: Barbara Baker, a single woman

ESTATE OR INTEREST: Fee simple

EXCEPTIONS:

PART I:

1. *A lien in favor of Jefferson County for property taxes, in the amount of $645.00, due on or before April 30, 19xx.*
2. *A mortgage in favor of the First National Bank in the amount of $30,000.00, recorded June 2, 1974, in Book 2975, Page 245 of the Official County Records.*
3. *An easement in favor of the Northern Telephone Company along the eastern five feet of said land for telephone poles and conduits. Recorded on June 15, 1946, in Book 1210, Page 113 of the Official County Records.*
4. *An easement in favor of Midwest Gas and Electric Company along the north ten feet of said land for underground pipes. Recorded on June 16, 1946, in Book 1210, Page 137 of the Official County Records.*

PART II:

1. *Taxes or assessments not shown by the records of any taxing authority or by the public records.*
2. *Any facts, rights, interests, or claims that, although not shown by the public records, could be determined by inspection of the land and inquiry of persons in possession.*
3. *Discrepancies or conflicts in boundary lines or area or encroachments that would be shown by a survey, but which are not shown by the public records.*
4. *Easements, liens, or encumbrances not shown by the public records.*
5. *Unpatented mining claims and water rights or claims.*

the buyer, the title company issues a policy that deletes the old mortgage, adds the new mortgage, and shows the buyer as the owner.

Policy Premium

In some parts of the United States it is customary for the seller to pay the cost of both the title search and the insurance. In Minnesota, the practice is for the seller to bring his abstract up to date and leave the buyer responsible for securing an opinion or a title policy. If a property is insured, customarily it is for an amount equal to the purchase price. This insurance remains effective as long as the buyer (owner) or his heirs have an interest in the property.

The insurance premium consists of a single payment. On the average-priced home, the charge for title insurance amounts to about ½ of 1% of the amount of insurance purchased. Each time the property is sold, a new policy must be purchased. The old policy cannot be assigned to the new owner.

Some title insurance companies offer reduced **reissue rates** if the previous owner's policy is available for updating, because the time period that must be searched is shorter.

Mortgagee's Policy

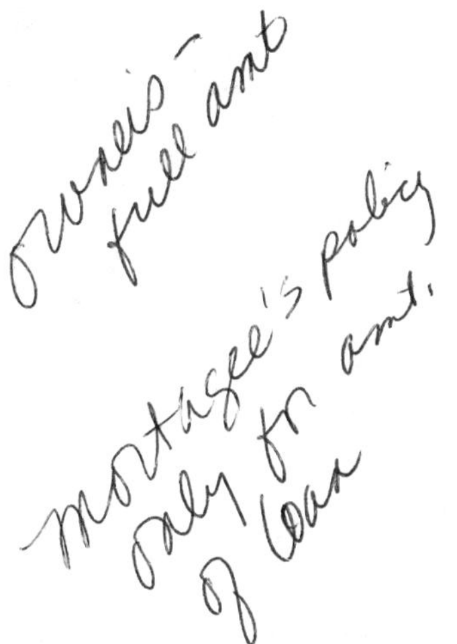

Thus far our discussion of title insurance has centered on what is called an **owner's policy.** In addition, title insurance companies also offer what is called a **mortgagee's policy.** This protects a lender who has taken real estate as collateral for a loan. There are three significant differences between an owner's and a mortgagee's policy. First, the owner's policy is good for the full amount of coverage stated on the policy for as long as the insured or his heirs have an interest in the property. In contrast, the mortgagee's policy protects only for the amount owed on the mortgage loan. Thus, the coverage on a mortgagee's policy declines and finally terminates when the loan is fully repaid. The second difference is that the mortgagee's policy does not make exceptions for claims to ownership that could have been determined by physically inspecting the property. The third difference is that the mortgagee's title policy is assignable to subsequent holders of the same mortgage loan.

The cost of a mortgagee's policy (also known as a lender's policy or loan policy) is similar to an owner's policy. Although the insurance company takes added risks by eliminating some exceptions found in the owner's policy, this is balanced by the fact that the liability decreases as the loan is repaid. When an owner's and a mortgagee's policy are purchased at the same time, as in the case of a sale with new financing, the combined cost is only a few dollars more than the cost of the owner's policy alone.

Claims for Losses

The last item in a title policy is a statement as to how the company will handle claims. Although this "Conditions and Stipulations Section" is too lengthy to reproduce here, its key aspects can be summarized as follows. When an insured defect arises, the title insurance company reserves the right to either pay the loss or fight the claim in court. If it elects to fight, any legal costs the company incurs are in addition to the amount of coverage stated in the policy. If a loss is paid, the amount of coverage is reduced by that amount and any unused coverage is still in effect. If the company pays a loss, it acquires the right to collect from the party who caused the loss.

In comparing title insurance to other forms of insurance (e.g., life, fire, automobile), note that title insurance protects against something that has already happened but has not been discovered. A forged deed may result in a disagreement over ownership: the forgery is a fact of history, the insurance is in the event of its discovery. But in some cases the problem will never be discovered. For example, a married couple may be totally unaware of dower and curtesy rights and fail to extinguish them when they sell their property. If neither later claims them, when they die, the rights extinguish themselves, and the intervening property owners will have been unaffected.

Only a small part of the premiums collected by title insurance companies are used to pay claims, largely because they take great pains to maintain on their own premises complete photographic copies of the public records for each county in which they do business. These are called **title plants;** in many cases they are actually more complete and better organized than those available at the public recorder's office. The philosophy is that the better the quality of the title search, the fewer the claims that must be paid.

Marketable Title

In nearly all real estate transactions the seller agrees to deliver **marketable title** to the buyer. Marketable title is title that is free from reasonable doubt as to who the owner is. Even when the seller makes no mention of the quality of the title, courts ordinarily require that marketable title be conveyed. To illustrate, a seller orders an abstract prepared, and it is read by the buyer's attorney who feels that certain technical defects in the title chain contradict certification as marketable. He advises the buyer to refuse to complete the sale. The line between what is and what is not marketable title can be exceedingly thin, and differences of legal opinion are quite possible. One means of breaking the stalemate is to locate a title insurance company that will insure the title as being marketable. If the defect is not serious, the insurance company will accept the risk. If it is a serious risk, the company may either accept the risk and increase the insurance fee or recommend a quiet title suit.

QUIET TITLE SUIT

When a title defect (or **title cloud**) must be removed, it is logical to remove it by using the path of least resistance. For example, if an abstract or title report shows unpaid property taxes, the buyer may require the seller to pay them in full before the deal is completed. A cloud on the title due to pending foreclosure proceedings can be halted by either bringing the loan payments up to date or negotiating with the lender for a new loan repayment schedule. Similarly, a distant relative with ownership rights might be willing, upon negotiation, to quitclaim them for a price.

Sometimes a stronger means is necessary to remove title defects. For example, the distant relative may refuse to negotiate, or the lender may refuse to remove a mortgage lien despite pleas from the borrower that it has been paid. The solution is a **quiet title suit** (also called a quiet title action). Forty-seven states, including Minnesota, have enacted legislation that permits a property owner to ask the courts to hold hearings on the ownership of his land. At these hearings anyone claiming to have an interest or right to the land in question may present verbal or written evidence of that claim. A judge, acting on the evidence presented and the laws of his state, rules on the validity of each claim. The result is to legally recognize those with a genuine right or interest and to "quiet" those without.

THE TORRENS SYSTEM

Over a century ago, Sir Robert Torrens, a British administrator in Australia, devised an improved system of identifying land ownership. He was impressed by the relative simplicity of the British system of sailing-ship registration. The government maintained an official ships' registry that listed on a single page a ship's name, its owner, and any liens or encumbrances against it. Torrens felt land titles might be registered in a similar manner. The system he designed, known as the **Torrens system** of land title registration, starts with a land-owner's application for registration and the preparation of an abstract. This is followed by a court hearing at which all parties named in the abstract and anyone else claiming a right or interest to the land in question may attend and present proof of their claim.

Torrens Certificate of Title

Based on the outcome of the action, a government-appointed **registrar of titles** prepares a **certificate of title.** This certificate names the legally recognized fee owner and lists any legally recognized exceptions to that ownership, such as mortgages, easements, long-term leases, or life estates. The registrar keeps the original certificate of title and issues a duplicate to the fee owner.

Once a title is registered, any subsequent liens or encumbrances against it must be entered on the registrar's copy of the certificate of title in order to give constructive notice. When a lien or encumbrance is removed, its notation on the certificate is canceled. In this manner, the entire concept of constructive notice for a given parcel of land is reduced to a single-page document open to public view at the registrar's office. This, Torrens argued, would make the whole process of title transfer much simpler and cheaper.

When the owner of registered land wishes to convey that land, the owner has an abstracter prepare a **registered property abstract** (RPA). This summarizes the information on the certificate of title and reports any unpaid taxes and special assessments or other liens of record. The buyer's attorney reads the RPA to determine if the condition of title is acceptable to the buyer. If it is acceptable, the grantor gives the grantee a deed and the owner's duplicate certificate. The grantee takes these to the registrar of titles, who transfers the title by canceling the grantor's certificate and filing a new certificate in the name of the grantee. Any liens or other encumbrances not removed at the same time are carried over from the old to the new certificate. The deed and certificate are kept by the registrar; the grantee receives a duplicate of the certificate. If the conveyance is accompanied by a new mortgage, it is noted on the new certificate, and a copy of the mortgage is retained by the registrar. Except for the quiet title action aspect, the concept of land title registration is quite similar to that used in the United States for registering ownership of motor vehicles.

Adoption

In the United States, the first state to have a land registration act was Illinois in 1895. Other states slowly followed, but often their laws were vague and cumbersome to the point of being useless. At one point, 20 states had land title registration acts, but since then 9 states have repealed their acts and only 11 remain. They are Hawaii, Illinois, Massachusetts, Minnesota, New York, Colorado, Georgia, North Carolina, Ohio, Virginia, and Washington.

MARKETABLE TITLE ACTS

At least 11 states have a **Marketable Title Act.** This is *not* a system of title registration. Rather, it is legislation aimed at making abstracts easier to prepare and less prone to error. This is done by cutting off claims to rights or interests in land that have been inactive for longer than the act's statutory period. In Connecticut, Michigan, Minnesota, Utah, Vermont, and Wisconsin, this is 40 years. Thus, in these states, a person who has an unbroken chain of title with no defects for at least 40 years is regarded by the law as having marketable title. Generally, any defects more than 40 years old are outlawed. The result is to concentrate the title search process on the immediate past 40 years. Thus, abstracts can be produced with less effort and expense, and the chance for an error either by the abstracter or in the documents themselves is greatly reduced. This is particularly true in view of the fact that record-keeping procedures in the past were not as sophisticated as they are today.

The philosophy of a marketable title act is that a person has 40 years to come forward and make his claim known; if he does not, then he apparently does not consider it worth pursuing. As protection for a person actively pursuing a claim that is about to become more than 40 years old, the claim can be renewed for another 40 years by again recording notice of the claim in the public records. In certain situations, a title must be searched back more than 40 years (e.g., when there is a lease of more than 40-year duration or when no document affecting ownership has been recorded in over 40 years). In Nebraska the statutory period is 22 years; in Florida, North Carolina, and Oklahoma it is 30 years; in Indiana, 50 years.

Marketable title acts do not eliminate the need for legal notice nor do they eliminate the role of adverse possession.

VOCABULARY REVIEW

Match terms **a–q** *with statements* **1–17.**

a. *Abstract*
b. *Acknowledgment*
c. *Actual notice*
d. *Chain of title*
e. *Constructive notice*
f. *Grantor index*
g. *Lis pendens index*
h. *Marketable title*
i. *Marketable title acts*
j. *Mechanic's lien*
k. *Mortgagee's title policy*
l. *Notary public*
m. *Owner's title policy*
n. *Public recorder's office*
o. *Quiet title suit*
p. *Title opinion*
q. *Torrens system*

1. Knowledge gained from what one has seen, heard, read, or observed.
2. Notice given by means of a document placed into the public records.
3. A formal declaration, made in the presence of a notary public or other authorized individual, by a person affirming that he or she signed a document.
4. A person authorized to take acknowledgments.
5. A place where a person can inform the world as to his land ownership by recording his deed.
6. A book at the public recorder's office that lists grantors alphabetically by name.
7. The linkage of ownership that connects the present owner to the original source of title.
8. A publicly available index whereby a person can learn of any pending lawsuits that may affect title.
9. A lien placed against real property by unpaid workmen and material suppliers.
10. A complete summary of all recorded documents affecting title to a given parcel of land.
11. Insurance to protect a property owner against monetary loss if his title is found to be imperfect.
12. An opinion prepared by an attorney showing current title condition.
13. A title policy written to protect a real estate lender.

14. Title that is free from reasonable doubt as to who the owner is.
15. Court-ordered hearings held to determine land ownership.
16. Laws that automatically cut off inactive claims to rights or interests in land.
17. A method of registering land titles that is similar to that of automobile ownership registration.

QUESTIONS AND PROBLEMS

1. Explain in your own words the concepts of actual and constructive notice and the roles that they play in real estate ownership.
2. Where is the public recorder's office for your community located?
3. How much does your public recorder's office charge to record a deed? A mortgage? What requirements must a document meet before it will be accepted for recording?
4. What is the purpose of grantor and grantee indexes?
5. Why is it important that a title search be carried out in more places than just the county recorder's office?
6. What is the difference between a title opinion issued by an attorney and a Torrens certificate of title?
7. How does a title opinion differ from an abstract?
8. What is the purpose of title insurance?
9. Thorsen sells his house to Williams. Williams moves in but for some reason does not record his deed. Thorsen discovers this and sells the house to an out-of-state investor who orders a title search, purchases an owner's title policy, and records his deed. Thorsen then disappears with the money he received from both sales. Who is the loser when this scheme is discovered: Williams, the out-of-state investor, or the title company? Why?
10. If you are located near the public recorder's office for your county, examine the records for a parcel of land (such as your home) and trace its ownership back through three owners.

ADDITIONAL READINGS

Fusilier, H. L. *Real Estate Law.* Boulder, Colo.: Business Research Division of the Graduate School of Business Administration, University of Colorado, 1977, 444 pages. A very readable real estate law text. Chapter 4 deals with evidence of title, and Chapter 5 discusses the conveyance of title.

Gross, Jerome S. *Illustrated Encyclopedic Dictionary of Real Estate,* 2nd ed. Englewood Cliffs, N.J.: Prentice-Hall, 1978, 418 pages. Contains definitions of an extensive list of real estate terms. Also has 150 pages of reproductions of real estate forms. Cross-referenced.

Levi, Donald R., and **Jacobus, Charles J.** *Real Estate Law.* Reston, Va.: Reston Publishing Co., 1980, 416 pages. Chapter 8 deals with conveyancing, Chapter 9 with recording, and Chapter 12 with title insurance.

Perspective: America's Land Title Industry. Washington, D.C.: American Land Title Association, n.d., 32 pages. A group of six articles that first appeared in the *National Capital Area Realtor.* Included are articles about title plants, abstracting, title lawyers, title insurance, and title losses.

Thau, William A. "Protecting the Real Estate Buyer's Title," *Real Estate Review,* Winter 1974, pages 71–83. A discussion of the role of title insurance in protecting the real estate buyer's title. Explains the standardized American Land Title Association insurance forms, title policy exceptions, title company liability, claim recovery, and policy cost.

Title Insurance. Los Angeles: Title Insurance and Trust Company, 1975, 24 pages. This pamphlet, which is available free from Ticor Title offices across the United States, provides a brief explanation of how title insurance works.

7

Contract Law

KEY TERMS

Breach of contract: failure without legal excuse to perform as required by a contract

Competent parties: persons considered legally capable of entering into a binding contract

Contract: a legally enforceable agreement to do (or not to do) a particular thing

Duress: the application of force to obtain an agreement

Fraud: an act or omission which misrepresents a material fact and is made with the intention of inducing another to give up something of value

Liquidated damages: an amount of money specified in a contract as compensation to be paid if the contract is not satisfactorily completed

Minor, Infant: a person under the age of legal competence; in most states, under 18 years

Specific performance: contract performance according to the precise terms agreed upon

Void contract: a contract that has no binding effect on the parties who made it

Voidable contract: a contract that binds one party but gives the other the right to withdraw

A **contract** is a legally enforceable agreement to do (or not to do) a specific thing. In this chapter we shall see how a contract is created and what makes it legally binding. Topics covered include offer and acceptance, fraud, mistake, lawful objective, consideration, performance, and breach of contract. In Chapter 8 we will turn our attention to the purchase contract, trade agreement, and installment contract as they relate to the buying and selling of real estate.

HOW A CONTRACT IS CREATED

A contract may be either expressed or implied. An **expressed contract** occurs when the parties to the contract declare their intentions either orally or in writing. (The word **party** [plural, **parties**] is a legal term that refers to a person or group involved in a legal proceeding.) A lease or rental agreement, for example, is an expressed contract. The lessor (landlord) expresses his intent to permit the lessee (tenant) to use the premises, and the lessee agrees to pay the rent. A contract to purchase real estate is also an expressed contract.

An **implied contract** is created by neither words nor writing but rather by actions of the parties indicating that they intend to create a contract. For example, when you step into a taxicab, you imply that you will pay the fare. The cab driver, by allowing you in the cab, implies that he will take you where you want to go. The same thing occurs at a restaurant. The presence of tables, silverware, menus, waiters, and waitresses implies that you will be served food. When you order, you imply that you are going to pay when the bill is presented.

Bilateral Contract

A contract may be either bilateral or unilateral. A **bilateral contract** results when a promise is exchanged for a promise. For example, in the typical real estate sale, the buyer promises to pay the agreed price, and the seller promises to deliver title to the buyer. A bilaterial contract is basically an "I will do this *and* you will do that" arrangement.

Unilateral Contract

A **unilateral contract** results when a promise is exchanged for performance. For instance, during a campaign to get more listings, a real estate office manager announces to the firm's sales staff that an extra $100 bonus will be paid for each saleable new listing. No promises or agreements are necessary from the salespersons. However, each time a salesperson performs by bringing in a saleable listing, he or she is entitled to the promised $100 bonus. A unilateral contract is basically an "I will do this *if* you will do that" arrangement.

Forbearance

Most contract agreements are based on promises by the parties involved to act in some manner (pay money, provide services, or deliver title). However, a contract can contain a promise to **forbear** (not to act) by one or more of its parties. For example, a lender may agree not to foreclose on a delinquent mortgage loan if the borrower agrees to a new payment schedule.

Valid, Void, Voidable

A **valid contract** is one that meets all the requirements of law. It is binding upon its parties and legally enforceable in a court of law. A **void contract** has no legal effect and, in fact, is not a contract at all. Even though the parties may have gone through the motions of attempting to make a contract, no legal rights are created and any party thereto may ignore it at his pleasure. A **voidable contract** binds one party but not the other. Let us now turn our attention to the requirements of a valid contract.

ESSENTIALS OF A VALID CONTRACT

For a contract to be **legally valid,** and hence binding and enforceable, the following five requirements must be met:

1. Legally competent parties.
2. Mutual agreement.
3. Lawful objective.
4. Consideration or cause.
5. Contract in writing when required by law.

If these conditions are met, any party to the contract may, if the need arises, call upon a court of law to either enforce the contract as written or award money damages for nonperformance. In reality, a properly written contract seldom ends in court because each party knows it will be enforced as written. It is the poorly written contract or the contract that borders between enforceable and unenforceable that ends in court. A judge must then decide if a contract actually exists and the obligations of each party. Using the courts, however, is an expensive and time-consuming method of interpreting an agreement. It is much better if the contract is correctly prepared in the first place. Let us look more closely at the five requirements of an enforceable contract.

COMPETENT PARTIES

For a contract to be legally enforceable, all parties entering into it must be legally competent. In deciding competency, the law provides a mixture of objective and subjective standards. The most objective standard is that of age. A person must reach the age of **majority** to be legally capable of entering into a contract. **Minors** do not have contractual capability. Until the voting age in national elections was reduced from 21 to 18 years by Congress, persons were considered to be minors by most states until the age of 21. Since then most state legislatures (including Minnesota's) have lowered the age for entering into legally binding contracts to 18 years. The purpose of majority laws is to protect minors (also known as "infants" in legal terminology) from entering into contracts that they may not be old enough to understand. Depending on the circumstances, a contract entered into by a minor may be void or voidable. For example, the adult might be bound but the minor could withdraw. If a contract with a minor is required, it is still possible to obtain a binding contract by working through the minor's legal guardian.

Persons of unsound mind who have been declared incompetent by a judge may not make a valid contract, and any attempt to do so results in a void contract. The solution is to contract through the person appointed to act on behalf of the incompetent. If a person has not been judged legally incompetent but nonetheless appears incapable of understanding the transaction in question, he has no legal power to contract. In some states persons convicted of felonies may not enter into valid contracts without the prior approval of the parole board.

Regarding intoxicated persons, if there was a deliberate attempt to intoxicate a person for the purpose of approving a contract, the intoxicated person, upon sobering up, can call upon the courts to void the contract. If the contracting party was voluntarily drunk to the point of incompetence, when he is sober he may ratify or deny the contract if he does so promptly. However, some courts look at the matter strictly from the standpoint of whether the intoxicated person had the capability of formulating the intent to enter into a contract. Obviously, there are some fine and subjective distinctions among these three categories, and a judge may interpret them differently than the parties to the contract.

Power of Attorney

An individual can give another person the power to act on his behalf: for example to buy or sell land, or to sign lease documents. This is called a **power of attorney.** The person holding the power of attorney is called an **attorney-in-fact.** With regard to real estate, a power of attorney must be stated in writing because the real estate documents to be signed must be in writing. Any document signed with a power of attorney should be executed as follows: "Paul Jones, principal, by Samuel Smith, agent, his attorney-in-fact." If the agent has power to convey title to land, then the document granting him power of attorney should be acknowledged by the principal and recorded. The agent is legally competent to the extent of the powers granted to him by the principal as long as the principal remains legally competent, and as long as both of them are alive. The power of attorney can, of course, be terminated by the principal at any time. A recorded notice of revocation is needed to revoke a recorded power of attorney.

Corporations

Corporations are considered legally competent parties. However, the individual contracting on behalf of the corporation must have authority from the board of directors. Some states also require that the corporate seal be affixed to contracts. A partnership can contract either in the name of the partnership or in the name of any of its general partners. Also, executors and administrators can legally contract on behalf of trusts and estates.

MUTUAL AGREEMENT

The requirement of **mutual agreement** (also called **mutual consent,** or **mutual assent,** or **meeting of the minds**) means that there must be agreement to the provisions of the contract by the parties involved. In other words, there must be a mutual willingness to enter into a contract. The existence of mutual agreement is evidenced by the words and acts of the parties indicating that there is a valid offer and an unqualified acceptance. In addition, there must be no fraud, misrepresentation, or mistake, and the agreement must be genuine and freely given. Let us consider each of these points in more detail.

Offer and Acceptance

Offer and acceptance requires that one party (the **offeror**) make an offer to another party (the **offeree**). The offeree must then communicate to the offeror that he accepts. The means of communication may be spoken or written or an action that implies acceptance. To illustrate, suppose that you own an apartment and want to rent it. You tell a prospective tenant that he can rent it for $350 per month beginning today, and inform him of the house rules, when the rent is due, how much the deposit is, and under what conditions it will be returned. This is the offer, and you, the offeror, have just communicated it to the offeree. One requirement of a valid contract is that the offer be specific in its terms. Mutual agreement cannot exist if the terms of the offer are vague or undisclosed and/or the offer does not clearly state the obligations of each party involved. If you were to say to a prospective tenant, "Do you want to rent this apartment?" without stating the price, and the prospective tenant said "Yes," the law would not consider this to be a contract.

Counteroffer

Upon receiving an offer, the offeree has three options: to agree to it, to reject it, or to make a counteroffer. If he agrees, he must agree to every item in the offer. An offer is considered by law to be rejected if the offeree either rejects it outright or makes a change in the terms. If he makes any changes, it is a **counteroffer** and, although it would appear the offeree is only amending the offer before he will accept it, in reality the offeree has rejected it and is making an offer of his own. This now makes him the offeror. To illustrate, suppose that the prospective tenant for your apartment states that he would like to rent the apartment on the terms you offered, but instead of paying $350 per month, he wants to pay $330 per month. This is a rejection of your offer and the making of a counteroffer. You now have the right to accept or reject his offer. If you counter at $340 per month, this rejects his offer and you are again the offeror. If $340 is agreeable with the offeree, he must communicate his acceptance to you. In this case, a spoken "Yes, I'll take it" would be legally adequate.

If the offeree does not wish to accept the offer nor make a counteroffer, how is the offer terminated? Certainly he can simply say "No." However, if he says nothing, the passage of time can also terminate the offer. This can happen in two ways. The offeror can state how long the offer is to remain open; for example, "You have until 8:00 P.M. tonight to decide if you want the apartment." If nothing is heard by 8:00 P.M., the offer terminates. When nothing is said as to how long the offer is to remain open, the courts will permit a reasonable amount of time, depending on the situation. To illustrate, it is reasonable to presume that if the prospective tenant left without accepting your offer or arranging for time to think about it, your offer terminates with his departure. This frees you to look for another tenant and make another offer without still being committed to the first offeree. When the offer is for the purchase of real estate and no termination date is given, law courts have ruled that a reasonable period of time might be several days or a week.

The best policy is to state the length of time an offer is open to avoid the problem of receiving two acceptances. Selecting a time period depends on the amount of time the offeror feels the offeree needs to decide and the length of time the offeror is willing to tie up his property.

Fraud

Mutual agreement requires that there be no fraud, misrepresentation, or mistake in the contract if it is to be valid.

Under Minnesota law, there are 11 requirements to a charge for **fraud** or **misrepresentation.** First, there must be a representation (or a nondisclosure). Second, the representation must be false. Third it must have to do with a past or present fact. Fourth, that fact must be material. Fifth, the fact must be something one would be able to know. Sixth, the representer must know it to be false, or must assert it as of his own knowledge without knowing whether it is true or false. Seventh, the representer must intend to have the other person act upon it or realize the other person would be justified in acting upon it. Eighth, that person must be so induced to act or so justified in acting. Ninth, that person's action must be in reliance on the representation. Tenth, that person must suffer damage. And, eleventh, the damage must be attributable to the misrepresentation.

Note that Minnesota does not require an intent to deceive or injure. For example, a real estate broker may have been told by the seller that there have never been water problems in the home. The broker may firmly believe that statement, and repeat it to a prospective purchaser. However, if the property has been affected by leaking or seepage and the buyer suffers damage after purchasing the property, the broker is liable for fraud despite his own "innocence." Because mutual agreement was lacking, the purchaser can **rescind** (cancel) the contract and get his money back. This creates a greater burden and standard of care not only for brokers in Minnesota, but to all parties to a contract as well.

Although the law will permit the aggrieved party to rescind the contract, the purchaser is not required to do so. If he likes the other features of the home enough, he can elect to live with the problems and sue for damages. However, if a real estate agent commits a fraud to make a sale and the deceived party later does rescind the sales contract, not only is the commission lost, but explanations will be necessary to the other parties of the contract. Moreover, state license laws provide for suspension or revocation of a real estate license for fraudulent acts.

Mistake

Mistake as applied in contract law has a very narrow meaning. It does not include misrepresentation nor does it include ignorance, inability, or poor judgment. If a person enters into a contract that he later regrets because he did not investigate it thoroughly enough, or because it did not turn out to be beneficial, the law will not grant relief to him on the grounds of mistake, even though he may now consider it was a "mistake" to have made the contract in the first place. Mistake as used in contract law arises from ambiguity in negotiations and mistake of material fact. For example, you offer to sell your mountain cabin to an acquaintance. He has never seen your cabin, and you give him instructions on how to get there to look at it. He returns and accepts your offer. However, he made a wrong turn and the cabin he looked at was not your cabin. A week later he discovers his error. The law considers this ambiguity in negotiations. In this case the buyer, in his mind, was purchasing a different cabin than the seller was selling; therefore, there is no mutual agreement and any contract signed is void.

To illustrate a mistake of fact, suppose that you show your apartment to a prospective tenant and tell him that he must let you know by tomorrow if he wants to rent it. The next day he visits you and together you enter into a rental contract. Although neither of you is aware of it, there has just been a serious fire in the apartment. Since a fire-gutted apartment is not what the two of you had in mind when the rental contract was signed, there is no mutual agreement.

Occasionally, "mistake of law" will be claimed as grounds for relief from a contract. However, mistake as to one's legal rights in a contract is not generally accepted by courts of law unless it is coupled with a mistake of fact. Ignorance of the law is not considered a mistake.

Contractual Intent

Mutual agreement also requires that the parties express **contractual intent.** This means that their intention is to be bound by the agreement, thus precluding jokes or jests from becoming valid contracts.

Duress

The last requirement of mutual agreement is that the offer and acceptance be genuine and freely given. **Duress** (use of force), **menace** (threat of violence), or **undue influence** (unfair advantage) cannot be used to obtain agreement. The law permits a contract made under any of these conditions to be revoked by the aggrieved party.

LAWFUL OBJECTIVE

To be enforceable, a contract cannot call for the breaking of laws. The reason is that a court of law cannot be called upon to enforce a contract that requires that a law be broken. Such a contract is void, or if already in operation, it is unenforceable in a court of law. For example, a debt contract requiring interest rates in excess of those allowed by state law would be void. If the borrower had started repaying the debt and then later stopped, the lender would not be able to look to the courts to enforce collection of the balance. Contracts contrary to good morals and general public policy are also unenforceable.

CONSIDERATION

For an agreement to be enforceable it must be supported by **consideration.** Money is usually thought of as meeting this requirement. Yet in the vast majority of contracts, the consideration requirement is met by a promise for a promise. For example, in selling real estate the promise of a purchaser to buy and the promise of an owner to sell constitute sufficient consideration to support their agreement. No deposit money is necessary.

The purpose of requiring consideration is to demonstrate that a bargain has been struck between the parties to the contract. The size, quantity, nature, or amount of what is being exchanged is irrelevant as long as it is present. Consideration can be a promise to do something, for money, property, or personal services. For example, there can be an exchange of a promise for a promise, money for a promise, money for property, goods for services, etc. Forbearance also qualifies as consideration.

In a typical offer to purchase a home, the consideration is the mutual exchange of promises by the buyer and seller to obligate themselves to do something they were not previously required to do. In other words, the seller agrees to sell on the terms agreed and the buyer agrees to buy the property on those same terms. The earnest money the buyer may put down is not the consideration necessary to make the contract valid. Rather, earnest money is a tangible indication of the buyer's intent and may become a source of compensation (damages) to the seller in the event the buyer does not carry out his promises.

In a deed, which is evidence of a contract, the consideration requirement is usually met with a statement such as "For ten dollars and other good and valuable consideration." In a lease, the periodic payment of rent is the consideration for the use of the premises.

A contract fails to be legally binding if consideration is lacking from any party to the contract. The legal philosophy is that a person cannot promise to do something of value for someone else without receiving in turn some form of consideration. Stated another way, each party must give up something, i.e., each must suffer a detriment. For example, if I promise to give you my car, the consideration requirement is not met because you promise nothing in return. But if I promise to give you my car when you quit smoking, that meets the consideration requirement.

As a group, money, plus promises, property, legal rights, services, and forbearance, if they are worth money, are classified as **valuable consideration.** There is one exception to the requirement that each party must provide valuable consideration. That is the case of a gift. If a person wishes to give something of value to a friend or loved one, courts have ruled that "love and affection" will meet the consideration requirement. From time to time you will come across deeds and contracts that recite "love and affection" as the consideration. Although this not valuable consideration, it is nonetheless **good consideration** and as such fulfills the legal requirement that consideration be present. The law generally will not inquire as to the adequacy of the consideration unless there is evidence of fraud, mistake, duress, threat, or undue influence. For instance, if a man gave away his property or sold it very cheaply to keep it from his creditors, the creditors could ask the courts to set aside those transfers.

If the word consideration continues to be confusing to you, it is because the word has three meanings in real estate. The first is consideration from the standpoint of a legal requirement for a valid contract. You may wish to think of this form of consideration as **legal consideration** or **cause.** The second meaning is money. For example, the consideration upon which deed stamps are charged is the amount of money exchanged in the transaction. The third meaning is acknowledgment. Thus the phrase "in consideration of ten dollars" means "in acknowledgment of" or "in receipt of."

CONTRACT IN WRITING

In Minnesota there is a law that is commonly known as the **statute of frauds.** The purpose of this law is to prevent frauds by requiring that all contracts for the sale of land, or an interest in land, be in writing to be enforceable in a court of law. This includes such things as offers, acceptances, binders, land contracts, deeds, escrows, and options to purchase. Mortgages and trust deeds (and their accompanying bonds and notes) and leases for more than one year must also be in writing to be enforceable. In addition, Minnesota has adopted the **Uniform Commercial Code** which requires, among other things, that the sale of personal property with value in excess of $500 be in writing. Most states also require that real estate listing contracts be expressed in writing.

The purpose of requiring that a contract be written and signed is to prevent perjury and fraudulent attempts to seek legal enforcement of a contract that never existed. It is not necessary that a contract be a single formal document. It can consist of a series of signed letters or memorandums as long as the essentials of a valid contract are present. Note that the requirement for a written contract relates only to the enforceability of the contract. Thus if Mr. X orally agrees to sell his land to Mr. Y and they carry out the deal, neither can come back after the contract was peformed and ask a court to rescind the deal because the agreement to sell was oral.

The most common real estate contract that does not need to be in writing to be enforceable is a month-to-month rental agreement that can be terminated by either landlord or tenant on 1-month notice. Nonetheless, most are in writing, because people tend to forget oral promises. While the unhappy party can go to court, the judge may have a difficult time determining what oral promises were made, particularly if there were no witnesses other than the parties to the agreement. Hence, it is advisable to put all important contracts in writing and for each party to recognize the agreement by signing it. It is also customary to date written contracts, although most can be enforced without showing the date the agreement was reached.

A written contract will supersede an oral one. Thus, if two parties orally promise one thing and then write and sign something else, the written contract will prevail. This fact has been the basis for many complaints against overzealous real estate agents who make oral promises that do not appear anywhere in the written sales contract.

Under certain circumstances the **parol evidence rule** permits oral evidence to complete an otherwise incomplete or ambiguous written contract. However, the application of this rule is quite narrow. If a contract is complete and clear in its intent, the courts presume that what the parties put into writing is what they agreed upon.

PERFORMANCE AND DISCHARGE OF CONTRACTS

Having made a valid contract, the parties involved are expected to carry out their respective contractual duties. While the contract is in the process of being completed, it is called **executory.** When all contract duties are completed, the contract is said to be **executed.**

Most contracts are discharged by being fully performed by the contracting parties in accordance with the contract terms. However, alternatives are open to the parties of the contract. One is to sell or otherwise **assign** the contract to another party. Unless prohibited by the contract, rights, benefits, and obligations under a contract can be assigned to someone else. The original party to the contract, however, still remains ultimately liable for its performance. Note, too, that an assignment is a contract in itself and must meet all the essential contract requirements to be enforceable. A common example of an assignment occurs when a lessee wants to move out and sells his lease to another party. When a contract creates a personal obligation, such as a listing agreement with a broker, an assignment may not be made.

A contract can also be performed by **novation.** Novation is the substitution of a new contract between the same or new parties. For example, novation occurs when a buyer assumes a seller's loan, *and* the lender releases the seller from the loan contract. With novation the departing party is released from the obligation to complete the contract.

If the objective of a contract becomes legally impossible to accomplish, the law will consider the contract discharged. For example, a new legislative statute may forbid what the contract originally intended. If the parties mutually agree to cancel their contract before it is executed, this too is a form of discharge. For instance, you sign a 5-year lease to pay $500 per month for an office. Three years later you find a better location and want to move. Meanwhile, rents for similar offices in your building have increased to $575 per month. Under these conditions the landlord might be happy to agree to cancel your lease.

If one of the contracting parties dies, a contract is considered discharged if it calls for some specific act that only the dead person could have performed. For example, if you hired a free-lance gardener to tend your landscaping and he died, the contract would be discharged. However, if your contract is with a firm that employs other gardeners who can do the job, the contract would still be valid.

Damage to the premises may also discharge the agreement. Under the **Uniform Vendor and Purchaser Risk Act,** if neither possession nor title has passed and there is material destruction to the property, the seller cannot enforce the contract and the purchaser is entitled to his money back. If damage is minor and promptly repaired by the seller, the contract would still be enforceable. If either title or possession has passed and destruction occurs, the purchaser is not relieved of his duty to pay the price, nor is he entitled to a refund of money already paid.

BREACH OF CONTRACT

When one party fails to perform as required by a contract and the law does not recognize the reason for failure to be a valid excuse, there is a **breach of contract.** The wronged or innocent party has six alternatives: (1) accept partial performance, (2) rescind the contract unilaterally, (3) sue for specific performance, (4) sue for money damages, (5) accept liquidated money damages, or (6) mutually rescind the contract. Let us consider each of these.

Partial Performance

Partial performance may be acceptable to the innocent party because there may not be a great deal at stake or because the innocent party feels that the time and effort to sue would not be worth the rewards. Suppose that you contracted with a roofing repairman to fix your roof for $400. When he was finished you paid him. But a week later you discover a spot that he had agreed to fix, but missed. After many futile phone calls, you accept the breach and consider the contract discharged, because it is easier to fix the spot yourself than to keep pursuing the repairman.

Unilateral Rescission

Under certain circumstances, the innocent party can **unilaterally rescind** a contract. That is, the innocent party can take the position that if the other party is not going to perform his obligations, then the innocent party will not either. An example would be a rent strike in retaliation to a landlord who fails to keep the premises habitable. Unilateral rescission should be resorted to only after consulting an attorney.

Specific Performance

The innocent party may sue in a court of equity to force the breaching party to carry out the remainder of the contract according to the precise terms, price, and conditions agreed upon. For example, you make an offer to purchase a parcel of land and the seller accepts. A written contract is prepared and signed by both of you. If you carry out all your obligations under the contract, but the seller changes his mind and refuses to deliver title to you, you may bring a lawsuit against the seller for **specific performance.** In reviewing your suit, the court will determine if the contract is valid and legal, if you have carried out your duties under the contract, and if the contract is just and reasonable. If you win your lawsuit, the court will force the seller to deliver title to you as specified in the contract.

Money Damages

If the damages to the innocent party can be reasonably expressed in terms of money, the innocent party can sue for **money damages.** For example, you rent an apartment to a tenant. As part of the rental contract you furnish the refrigerator and freezer unit. While the tenant is on vacation, the unit breaks down and $200 worth of frozen meat and other perishables spoil. Since your obligation under the contract is to provide the tenant with a working refrigerator–freezer, the tenant can sue you for $200 in money damages. He can also recover interest on the money awarded to him.

Comparison

Note the difference between suing for money damages and suing for specific performance. When money can be used to restore one's position (such as the tenant who can buy $200 worth of fresh food), a suit for money damages is appropriate. In situations where money cannot provide an adequate remedy, and this is often the case in real estate because no two properties are exactly alike, specific performance is appropriate. Notice, too, that the mere existence of the legal rights of the wronged party is often enough to gain cooperation. In the case of the spoiled food, you would give the tenant the value of the lost food before spending time and money in court to hear a judge tell you to do the same thing. A threat of a lawsuit will often bring the desired results if the defendant knows that the law will side with the wronged party. The cases that do go to court are usually those in which the identity of the wronged party and/or the extent of the damages is not clear.

Liquidated Damages

The parties to a contract may decide in advance the amount of damages to be paid in the event either party breaches the contract. An example is an offer to purchase real estate that includes a statement to the effect that, once the seller accepts the offer, if the buyer fails to complete the purchase, the seller may keep the buyer's deposit (earnest money) as **liquidated damages.** If a broker is involved, the seller and broker may agree to divide the damages, thus compensating the seller for damages and the broker for his time and effort. Another case of liquidated damages occurs when a builder promises to finish a building by a certain date or pay the party that hired him a certain number of dollars per day until it is completed. This impresses upon the builder the need for prompt completion and compensates the property owner for losses due to the delay.

Mutual Rescission

Specific performance, money damages, and liquidated damages are all designed to aid the innocent party in the event of a breach of contract. However, as a practical matter the time and cost of pursuing a remedy in a court of law may sometimes exceed the benefits to be derived. Moreover, there is the possibility the judge for your case may not agree with your point of view. Therefore, even though you are the innocent party and you feel you have a legitimate case that can be pursued in the courts, you may find it more practical to agree with the other party (or parties) to simply cancel (i.e., rescind or annul) the contract. To properly protect everyone involved, the agreement to cancel must be in writing and signed by the parties to the original contract. Properly executed, mutual rescission relieves the parties to the contract from their obligations to each other.

An alternative to mutual rescission is novation. As noted

earlier, this is the substitution of a new contract for an existing one. Novation provides a middle ground between suing and rescinding. Thus the breaching party may be willing to complete the contract provided the innocent party will voluntarily make certain changes in it. If this is acceptable, the changes should be put into writing (or the contract redrafted) and then signed by the parties involved.

STATUTE OF LIMITATIONS

The **statute of limitations** limits by law the amount of time a wronged party has to seek the aid of a court in obtaining justice. The aggrieved party must start legal proceedings within a certain period of time or the courts will not help him. The amount of time varies from state to state and by type of legal action involved. However, time limits of 3 to 7 years are typical for breach of contract. Minnesota generally permits a person 6 years to bring such an action.

IMPLIED OBLIGATIONS

As was pointed out at the beginning of this chapter, one can incur contractual obligations by implication as well as by oral or written contracts. Home builders and real estate agents provide two timely examples. For many years, if a homeowner discovered poor design or workmanship after he had bought a new home, it was his problem. The philosophy was **caveat emptor,** let the buyer beware *before* he buys. Today in Minnesota, a builder or contractor involved in the construction of a dwelling unit implies that it is free from structural and material defects even though this has not been stated orally or in writing to the buyer. Thus, when a builder installs a toilet in a bathroom, the implication is that it will work. Likewise, a new roof should keep the house dry.

Similarly, real estate agent trade organizations, such as the National Association of Realtors and state and local Realtor associations, are constantly working to elevate the status of real estate brokers and salesmen to that of a competent professional in the public's mind. But as professional status is gained, there is an implied obligation to dispense professional-quality service. Thus, an individual agent is not only responsible for acting in accordance with written laws, but will also be held responsible for being competent and knowledgeable. Once recognized as a professional by the public, the real estate agent will not be able to plead ignorance.

In view of the present trend towards consumer protection,

the concept of "Let the buyer beware" is being replaced with "Let the seller (and the seller's agent) beware."

VOCABULARY REVIEW

Match terms **a–q** *with statements* **1–17.**

a. *Assign*
b. *Breach*
c. *Competent party*
d. *Contract*
e. *Counteroffer*
f. *Duress*
g. *Forbear*
h. *Fraud*
i. *Liquidated damages*
j. *Minor*
k. *Money damages*
l. *Offeror*
m. *Rescind*
n. *Specific performance*
o. *Statute of limitations*
p. *Unilateral contract*
q. *Void contract*

1. A legally enforceable agreement to do (or not to do) something.
2. A contract in which one party makes a promise or begins performance without first receiving any promise to perform from the other.
3. An act or omission which misrepresents a material fact and is made with the intention of inducing another to part with something of value.
4. A person who is considered legally capable of entering into a contract.
5. A person who is not old enough to enter into legally binding contracts.
6. A contract that is not legally binding on any of the parties that made it.
7. The party who makes an offer.
8. An offer made in response to an offer.
9. To cancel a contract and restore the parties involved to their respective positions before the contract was made.
10. Use of force to obtain contract agreement.
11. Not to act.
12. To transfer one's rights in a contract to another person.
13. Damages that can be measured in and compensated by money.
14. Failure, without legal excuse, to perform any promise called for in a contract.
15. Contract performance according to the precise terms agreed upon.
16. A sum of money called for in a contract that is to be paid if the contract is breached.
17. Laws that set forth the period of time within which a lawsuit must be filed.

QUESTIONS AND PROBLEMS

1. What is the difference between an expressed contract and an implied contract? Give an example of each.
2. Name the five requirements of a legally valid contract.

3. What is the difference between a void contract and a voidable contract?
4. Give four examples of persons not considered legally competent to enter into contracts.
5. How can an offer be terminated prior to its acceptance?
6. What does the word "mistake" mean when applied to contract law?
7. Why must consideration be present for a legally binding contract to exist? Give examples of three types of consideration.
8. If a contract is legally unenforceable, are the parties to the contract stopped from performing it? Why or why not?
9. If a breach of contract occurs, what alternatives are open to the parties to the contract?
10. Assume that a breach of contract has occurred and the wronged party intends to file a lawsuit over the matter. What factors would he consider in deciding whether to sue for money damages or for specific performance?

ADDITIONAL READINGS

Atteberry, William L., Pearson, Karl G., and **Litka, Michael P.** *Real Estate Law,* 2nd ed. Columbus, Ohio: Grid, Inc., 1978, 365 pages. Chapter 1 provides an introduction to real estate law, case law, the courts, administrative law, and constitutional law. Chapter 11 deals with contract law.

Deming, Richard. *Man Against Man.* New York: Hawthorn Books, 1974, 210 pages. Written to explain in as clear and interesting terms as possible how civil law works in the United States. Includes the role of civil courts, steps in litigation, and procedures to enforce judgments.

Fisher, Frederick. *Broker Beware: Selling Real Estate Within the Law.* Reston, Va.: Reston Publishing Co., 1981, 220 pages. Examines the real estate professional's duties and obligations of practicing within the law. Covers misrepresentation, malpractice, and case law.

Fusilier, H. L. *Real Estate Law.* Boulder, Colo.: Business Research Division of the Graduate School of Business Administration, University of Colorado, 1977, 444 pages. A very readable real estate law text. Chapters 16 through 22 pertain to real estate contracts. Includes both discussion and cases.

Hogue, Arthur R. *Origins of the Common Law.* Bloomington: Indiana University Press, 1966, 276 pages. Provides a fascinating historical review of the origins of common law in England and how it became transplanted to the United States to serve as the basis for so many U.S. laws.

Martindale-Hubble Law Directory. Summit, N.J.: Martindale-Hubble Inc., 1983, 4,518 pages. Contains summaries of law for each of the United States and various foreign countries. Excellent reference work. Published annually.

Real Estate Sales Contracts

KEY TERMS

Binder: a short purchase contract used to secure a real estate transaction until a more formal contract can be signed
Closing: the act of finalizing a transaction; the day on which title is conveyed
Contract for deed: a method of selling and financing property whereby the seller retains title but the buyer takes possession while he makes his payments
Counteroffer: an offer made in response to an offer
Default: failure to perform a legal duty; such as failure to carry out the terms of a contract
Deposit receipt: a receipt given for a deposit that accompanies an offer to purchase; also refers to a purchase contract that includes a deposit receipt
Earnest money deposit: money that accompanies an offer to purchase as evidence of good faith
Prorate: to apportion ongoing income and expense items when a property is sold
Purchase agreement (earnest money contract): a contract for the purchase and sale of real estate
"Time is of the essence": a phrase that means that the time limits of a contract must be faithfully observed or the contract is voidable

The present chapter focuses on contracts used to initiate the sale of real estate. Chiefly we will look at the purchase contract and the installment contract. There will also be a brief discussion of a real estate binder, letter of intent, and exchange.

PURPOSE OF SALES CONTRACTS

What is the purpose of a real estate sales contract? If a buyer and a seller agree on a price, why can't the buyer hand the seller the necessary money and the seller simultaneously hand the buyer a deed? The main reason is that the buyer needs time to ascertain that the seller is, in fact, legally capable of conveying title. To protect himself, the buyer will enter into a written and signed contract with the seller, promising that the purchase price will be paid only after title has been searched and found to be in satisfactory condition. The seller in turn promises to deliver a deed to the buyer when the buyer has paid his money. This exchange of promises forms the legal consideration of the contract. A contract also gives the buyer time to arrange financing and to specify how such matters as taxes, mortgage debts, existing leases, and fire insurance on the property will be discharged.

A properly prepared contract commits each party to its terms. Once a sales contract is in writing and signed, the seller cannot suddenly change his mind and sell his property to another person. He is obligated to convey title to the buyer when the buyer has performed everything required of him by the contract. Likewise, the buyer must carry out his promises, including paying for the property, provided the seller has done everything required by the contract.

PURCHASE AGREEMENTS

Variously known as a purchase contract, earnest money contract, offer and acceptance, purchase offer, or purchase and sales agreement, these preprinted forms contain three key parts: (1) provision for the buyer's earnest money deposit, (2) the buyer's offer to purchase, and (3) the acceptance of the offer by the seller.

Figure 8:1 illustrates in simplified language the highlights of a real estate purchase agreement.* The contract begins at ① and ② by identifying the location and date of the deposit and offer. At ③, the name of the buyer is written, and at ④, the name of the property owner (seller). At ⑤, the property for which the buyer is making his offer is described. Although the street address and type of property (in this case a house) are not necessary to the validity of the contract, this information is often included for convenience in locating the property. The legal description that follows is crucial. Care must be taken to make certain that it is correct.

Earnest Money Deposit

The price that the buyer is willing to pay, along with the manner in which he proposes to pay it, is inserted at ⑥. Of particular importance in this paragraph is the **earnest money deposit** that the buyer submits with his offer. With the exception of court-ordered sales, no laws govern the size of the deposit or even the need for one. Generally speaking though, the seller and his agent will want a reasonably substantial de-

* This illustration has been prepared for discussion purposes only and not as a form to copy and use in a real estate sale. For that purpose, you must use a contract specifically legal in your state.

Figure 8:1

REAL ESTATE PURCHASE AGREEMENT

(1)

City of Riverdale *, State of* ______________,
October 10, 19xx (2).

(3)Samson Byers *(herein called the Buyer) agrees to purchase and* (4)William and Sarah Ohner *(herein called the Seller) agree to sell the following described real property located in the City of* (5)Riverdale *, County of* Lakeside *, State of* ______________, a single-family dwelling commonly known as 1704 Main Street *, and legally described as* Lot 21, Block C of Madison's Subdivision as per map in Survey Book 10, page 51, in the Office of the County Recorder of said County.

(6)*The total purchase price is* ninety thousand *Dollars* ($90,000.00), *payable as follows:* Three thousand dollars ($3,000.00) is given today as an earnest money deposit, receipt of which is hereby acknowledged. An additional $15,000.00 is to be paid by the Buyer on the closing date. The remaining $72,000.00 is to be by way of a new mortgage on said property.

(7)*Seller will deliver to the Buyer a* warranty *deed to said property. Seller will furnish to the Buyer an abstract of title or registered property abstract. Seller will deliver marketable title to the buyer.*

(8)*The closing date will be* November 25, 19xx *. The delivery of all papers and money shall be at the office of* ______________.

(9)*Property taxes due, property insurance, mortgage interest, income, and expense items shall be prorated as of* the closing date.

(10)*Any outstanding assessments on the property shall be* paid by the Seller.

(11)*Any existing mortgage indebtedness against the property is to be* paid by the Seller.

(12)*Buyer acknowledges receipt of a copy of the truth-in-sale-of-housing disclosure report.*

Figure 8:1 *continued*

(13) *Possession of the property is to be delivered to the Buyer* on closing date.

(14) *Closing expenses shall be* paid by the Seller.

(15) *Conveyance tax to be paid by* Seller.

(16) *The earnest money deposit is to be held* in trust.

(17) *All attached floor coverings, attached television antenna, window screens, screen doors, storm windows, storm doors, plumbing and lighting fixtures (except floor, standing, and swag lamps), curtain rods, shades, venetian blinds, bathroom fixtures, trees, plants, shrubbery, water heaters, awnings, built-in heating, ventilating, and cooling systems, built-in stoves and ranges, and fences now on the premises shall be included unless otherwise noted. Any leased fixtures on the premises are not included unless specifically stated.*

(18) *Other provisions:* The purchase of this property is subject to the Buyer obtaining a mortgage loan on this property in the amount of $72,000.00 or more, with a maturity date of at least 25 years, at an interest rate no higher than 11½% per year and loan fees not to exceed two points. Purchase price to include the refrigerator currently on the premises. Purchase is subject to buyer's approval of a qualified building inspector's report. Said report to be obtained within 7 days at Buyer's expense.

(19) *If the improvements on the property are destroyed or materially damaged prior to the closing, or if the Buyer is unable to obtain financing as stated herein, or if the Seller is unable to deliver title as promised, then the Buyer, at his option, may terminate this agreement and the deposit made by him shall be returned to him in full. If the Seller fails to fulfill any of the other agreements made herein, the Buyer may terminate this agreement with full refund of deposit, accept lesser performance, or sue for specific performance.*

(20) *If this purchase is not completed by reason of the Buyer's default, the seller is released from his obligation to sell to the Buyer and shall retain the deposit money as his sole right to damages.*

(21) *Upon the signature of the Buyer, this document becomes an offer to the Seller to purchase the property described herein. The Seller has until* 11:00 p.m., October 13, 19xx *to indicate*

acceptance of this offer by signing and delivering it to the Buyer. If acceptance is not received by that time, this offer shall be deemed revoked and the deposit shall be returned in full to the Buyer.

㉒ *Time is of the essence in this contract.*

Real Estate Broker Riverdale Realty Company

By ㉓ *Ima D. Salesman*

Address 1234 Riverdale Blvd. *Telephone* 555-1234

㉔ *The undersigned offers and agrees to buy the above described property on the terms and conditions stated herein and acknowledges receipt of a copy hereof.*

Buyer *Samson Byers*

Address 2323 Cedar Ave., Riverdale

Telephone 666-2468

Acceptance

㉕ *The undersigned accepts the foregoing offer and agrees to sell the property described above on the terms and conditions set forth.*

㉖ *The undersigned acknowledges receipt of a copy hereof.*

Seller *Sarah Ohner*

Seller *William Ohner*

Address 1704 Tenth St., Riverdale

Telephone 555-3579 *Date* 10/10/xx

Notification of Acceptance

㉗ *Receipt of a copy of the foregoing agreement is hereby acknowledged.*

Buyer *Samson Byers* *Date* 10/11/xx

Figure 8:1 *continued*

posit to show the buyer's earnest intentions and to have something for their trouble if the seller accepts and the buyer fails to follow through. The buyer will prefer to make as small a deposit as possible, as a deposit ties up his capital and there is the possibility of losing it. However, the buyer also recognizes that the seller may refuse to even consider the offer unless accompanied by a reasonable deposit. In most parts of Minnesota, a deposit of $2,000 to $5,000 on a $90,000 offer would be considered acceptable. In court-ordered sales, the required deposit is usually 10% of the offering price.

Deed and Condition of Title

At ⑦, the buyer requests that the seller convey title by means of a warranty deed and provide and pay for an abstract of title or registered property abstract. The buyer assumes that the seller is the owner of the property. However, the buyer has no way of verifying that until the title is actually searched. To protect himself, the buyer requests that the seller convey marketable title to the property. If title is not presently marketable, the seller is required by the contract to make it marketable by the closing date.

Closing Agent

Number ⑧ sets the closing date for the transaction. It is on that date that the seller will receive his money and the buyer, his deed. The selection of a closing date is based on the estimated length of time necessary to carry out the conditions of the purchase contract. Normally, the most time consuming item is finding a lender to make the necessary mortgage loan. Typically, this takes from 30 to 60 days, depending on the lender and the availability of loan money. The other conditions of the contract, such as the title search and arrangements to pay off any existing liens, take less time and can be done while arranging for a new mortgage loan. Once a satisfactory loan source is found, the lender makes a commitment to the buyer that the needed loan money will be available on the closing date.

Prorating

Number ⑨ deals with the question of how certain ongoing expenses, such as property taxes, insurance, and mortgage interest, will be divided between the buyer and the seller. For example, if the seller pays $220 in advance for a 1-year fire insurance policy and then sells his house halfway through the policy year, what happens to the remaining 6 months of coverage that the seller paid for but will not use? One solution is to transfer the remaining six months of coverage to the buyer for $110. Income items are also prorated. Suppose that the seller has been renting the basement of his house to a college student for $90 per month. The student pays the $90 rent in advance on the first of each month. If the property is sold partway through the month, the buyer is entitled to the portion of the month's rent that is earned while he owns the property. This process of dividing ongoing expenses and income items is known as **prorating.** More information and examples regarding the prorating process are included in Chapter 14.

At ⑩, the buyer states that, if there are any unpaid assessments currently against the property, the seller shall pay them as a condition of the sale. Alternatively, the buyer could agree to assume responsibility for paying them off. Since the buyer wants the property free of mortgages so that he can arrange for his own loan, at ⑪ he asks the seller to remove any existing indebtedness. On the closing date, part of the money received from the buyer is used to clear the seller's debts against the property. Alternatively, the buyer could agree to assume responsibility for paying off the existing debt against the property as part of the purchase price.

Disclosure Report

At ⑫, the buyer acknowledges the receipt of a housing disclosure report. This document is required by some cities in Minnesota. Its purpose is to provide the buyer with a list of material defects in the property prior to the time of sale.

Possession

The day on which possession of the property will be turned over to the buyer is inserted at ⑬. As a rule, this is the same day as the closing. If the buyer needs possession sooner or the seller wants possession after the closing, the usual procedure is to arrange for a separate rental agreement (move-in agreement) between the buyer and seller. Such an agreement produces fewer problems if the closing date is later changed or if the transaction falls through and the closing never occurs.

At ⑭, the purchase agreement calls for the seller to pay the closing expenses. The buyer and seller could divide them differently if they mutually agreed. At ⑮, the seller is to pay for the documentary tax stamps placed on the deed that he delivers to the buyer. At ⑯, the buyer and seller agree as to where the buyer's deposit money is to be held pending the close of the transaction. It could be held by the escrow agent, the broker, the seller, or an attorney.

The paragraph at ⑰ is not absolutely essential to a valid real estate purchase contract, since what is considered real estate (and is therefore included in the price) and what is personal property (and is not included in the price) is a matter of law.

However, because the buyer and seller may not be familiar with the legal definitions of realty and personalty, this statement is often included to avoid misunderstandings. Moreover, such a statement can clarify whether or not an item like a storm window or trash compactor, which may or may not be real property depending on its design, is included in the purchase price. If it is not the intention of the buyer and seller that an item mentioned here be included, that item is crossed out and initialed by both of them.

Loan Conditions

At ⑱, space is left to add conditions and agreements not provided for elsewhere in the preprinted contract. To complete his purchase of this property the buyer must obtain a $72,000 loan. However, what if he agrees to the purchase but cannot get a loan? Rather than risk losing his deposit money, the buyer makes his offer subject to obtaining a $72,000 loan on the property. To further protect himself against having to accept a loan "at any price," he states the terms on which he must be able to borrow. The seller, of course, takes certain risks in accepting an offer subject to obtaining financing. If the buyer is unable to obtain financing on these terms, the seller will have to return the buyer's deposit and begin searching for another buyer. Meanwhile, the seller may have lost anywhere from a few days to a few weeks of selling time. But without such a condition a buyer may hesitate to make an offer at all. The solution is for the seller to accept only those loan conditions that are reasonable in the light of current loan availability. For example, if lenders are currently quoting 12½% interest for loans on similar-type properties, the seller would not want to accept an offer subject to the buyer obtaining a 10% loan. The possibility is too remote. If the buyer's offer is subject to obtaining a loan at current interest rates, the probability of the transaction collapsing on this condition is greatly reduced. The same principle applies to the amount of loan needed, the number of years to maturity, and loan fees: they must be reasonable in light of current market conditions.

Additional Conditions

In the paragraph at ⑱, we also find that the buyer is asking the seller to include an item of personal property in the selling price. While technically a bill of sale is used for the sale of personal property, such items are often included in the real estate purchase contract if the list is not long. If the refrigerator was real property rather than personal, no mention would be required, as all real property falling within the descriptions at ⑤ and ⑰ is automatically included in the price. The third item in the paragraph at ⑱ gives the buyer an opportunity to have the property inspected by a professional building inspector. Most home buyers do not know what to look for in the way of structural deterioration or defects that may soon require expensive repairs. Consequently, in the past several years property inspection clauses in purchase contracts have become more common. The cost of this inspection is borne by the buyer. The inspector's report should be completed as soon as possible so that the property can be returned to the market if the buyer does not approve the findings.

Property damage

The paragraph at ⑲ sets forth conditions under which the buyer can free himself of his obligations under this contract and recover his deposit in full. It begins by addressing the question of property destruction between the contract signing and the closing date. Fire, wind, rain, earthquake, or other damage does occasionally occur during that period of time. Whose responsibility would it be to repair the damage, and could the buyer point to the damage as a legitimate reason for breaking the contract? It is reasonable for the buyer to expect that the property will be delivered to him in as good a condition as when he offered to buy it. Consequently, if there is major damage or destruction, the wording here gives the buyer the option of rescinding the contract and recovering his deposit in full. Note, however, that this clause does not prevent the buyer from accepting the damaged property or the seller from negotiating with the buyer to repair any damage in order to preserve the transaction.

Paragraph ⑲ also states that, if the buyer is unable to obtain financing as outlined at ⑱ or the seller is unable to convey title as stated at ⑦, the buyer can rescind the contract and have his deposit refunded. However, if the buyer is ready to close the transaction and the seller decides he does not want to sell, perhaps because the value of the property has increased between the signing of the contract and the closing date, the buyer can force the seller to convey title through use of a lawsuit for specific performance.

Buyer Default

Once the contract is signed by all parties involved, if the buyer fails to carry out his obligations, the standard choices for the seller are to (1) release the buyer and return his deposit in full, (2) sue the buyer for specific performance, or (3) sue the buyer for damages suffered. Returning the deposit does not compensate for the time and effort the seller and his broker spent with the buyer, nor for the possibility that, while the seller was committed to the buyer, the real estate market turned sour. Yet the time, effort, and cost of suing for specific performance or damages may be uneconomical. A solution is to insert a clause in the purchase contract whereby the buyer agrees in advance to forfeit his deposit if he defaults on the contract, and the seller agrees to accept the deposit as his sole right to damages. Thus, the seller gives up the right to sue the buyer and accepts instead the buyer's deposit. The buyer knows in advance how much it will cost if he defaults, and the cost of default is limited to that amount. This is the purpose of paragraph ⑳.

Time Limits

At ㉑, the buyer clearly states that he is making an offer to buy and gives the seller a certain amount of time to accept. If the seller does not accept the offer within the time allotted, the offer is void. This feature is automatic: the buyer does not have to contact the seller to tell him that the offer is no longer open. The offer must be open long enough for the seller to physically receive it, make a decision, sign it, and return it to the buyer. If the seller lives nearby, the transaction is not complicated, and the offer can be delivered in person, 3 days is reasonable. If the offer must be mailed to an out-of-town seller, 7 to 10 days is appropriate.

If the buyer has another property in mind that he wants to make an offer on if the first offer is not accepted, he may make his offer valid for only a day, or even a few hours. A short offer life also limits the amount of time the seller has to hold out for a better offer. If a property is highly marketable, a buyer will want his offer accepted before someone else makes a better offer. Some experienced real estate buyers argue that a purposely short offer life has a psychological value. It motivates the seller to accept before the offer expires. Note too, a buyer can withdraw and cancel his offer at any time before the seller has accepted and the buyer is aware of that acceptance.

"Time is of the essence" at ㉒ means that the time limits set by the contract must be faithfully observed or the contract is voidable by the non-defaulting party. Moreover, lateness may give cause for an action for damages. Neither buyer nor seller should expect extensions of time to complete their obligations. This clause does not prohibit the buyer or seller from voluntarily giving the other an extension. But, extensions are neither automatic nor mandatory.

Signatures

The real estate agency and salesperson responsible for producing this offer to buy are identified at ㉓. At ㉔, the buyer clearly states that this is an offer to purchase. If the buyer has any doubts or questions regarding the legal effect of the offer, he should take it to an attorney for counsel before signing it. After he signs, the buyer retains one copy and the rest are delivered to the seller for his decision. By retaining one copy, the buyer has a written record to remind him of his obligations under the offer. Equally important, the seller cannot forge a change on the offer, as he does not have all the copies. Regarding delivery, the standard procedure is for the salesperson who obtained the offer to make an appointment with the agent who obtained the listing, and together they call upon the seller and present the offer.

Acceptance

For an offer to become binding, the seller must accept everything in it. The rejection of even the smallest portion of the offer is a rejection of the entire offer. If the seller wishes to reject the offer but keep negotiations alive, he can make a counteroffer. This is a written offer to sell to the buyer at a new price or with terms that are closer to the buyer's offer than the seller's original asking price and terms. The agent prepares the counteroffer by either filling out a fresh purchase contract identical in all ways to the buyer's offer except for these changes, or by writing on the back of the offer (or on another sheet of paper) that the seller offers to sell at the terms the buyer had offered except for the stated changes. The counteroffer is then dated and signed by the seller, and a time limit is given to the buyer to accept. The seller keeps a copy, and the counteroffer is delivered to the buyer for his decision. If the counteroffer is acceptable to the buyer, he signs and dates it, and the contract is complete. Another commonly used but less desirable practice is to take the buyer's offer, cross out each item unacceptable to the seller, and write above or below it what the seller will accept. Each change is then initialed by the seller and buyer.

Returning to Figure 8:1, suppose that the sellers accept the offer as presented to them. At ㉕, they indicate acceptance and at ㉖ they sign and date the contract and acknowledge receipt of a copy. The last step is to notify the buyer that his offer has been accepted, give him a copy of the completed agreement, and at ㉗ have him acknowledge receipt of it. If the offer is rejected, it is good practice to have the sellers write the word "rejected" on the offer, followed by their signatures.

Federal Clauses

In two instances, the government requires that specific clauses be included in real estate sales contracts. First, a **buyer's escape clause** must be included whenever a sales contract is signed by a purchaser prior to the receipt of an FHA Appraised Value or a VA Certificate of Reasonable Value on the property. The purpose is to assure that the purchaser may terminate the contract without loss when it appears that the agreed purchase price may be significantly above appraised value. The specific clauses, which must be used verbatim, are available from FHA and VA approved lenders. Second, the Federal Trade Commission (FTC) requires, beginning September 29, 1980, that **insulation disclosures** be included in all contracts by builders or sellers of new homes. Disclosures, which may be based upon manufacturer claims, must cite the type, thickness, and R-value of the insulation installed in the home. The exact clause will be provided by the builder or seller of the home based on model clauses provided by the National Association of Homebuilders as modified by local laws.

Foam Insulation

In some homes, offices and schools, **urea-formaldehyde foam insulation (UFFI)** has been used as thermal insulation. It gained popularity during the energy crises of the 1970s because it could be applied to existing buildings that were not originally built with insulation in the walls. UFFI, which resembles foamy shaving cream, was pumped into walls where it hardened to form a layer of insulation. In some new buildings the foam was troweled into place before the interior walls were set in place. Although UFFI has excellent insulation qualities, the Consumer Product Safety Commission (CPSC) of the

United States banned the further use of UFFI effective August 9, 1982. The CPSC stated that UFFI "presents an unreasonable risk of injury from irritation, sensitization and cancer because of the release of formaldehyde gas from the product after it is installed." On April 7, 1983, that ban was overturned by a United States Court of Appeals. The Court considered the health complaints of people exposed to UFFI but felt the use of the word "unreasonable" was not supported by enough evidence.

The final chapter of the UFFI issue is yet to come as the CPSC may successfully appeal the case to the U.S. Supreme Court. Meanwhile the National Association of Realtors recommends that real estate agents continue to disclose the presence of UFFI. There are two notable reasons for this. First, the Appeals Court did not give UFFI a clean bill of health. And second, the UFFI issue has not ceased to be an issue with homeowners. There are currently an estimated 700 individual lawsuits in the country seeking to recover damages from UFFI manufacturers, distributors and installers.

Negotiation

One of the most important principles of purchase contracts (and real estate contracts in general) is that nearly everything is negotiable and nearly everything has a price. In preparing or analyzing any contract, consider what the advantages and disadvantages of each condition are to each party to the contract. A solid contract results when the buyer and seller each feel that they have gained more than they have given up. The prime example is the sales price of the property itself. The seller prefers the money over the property, while the buyer prefers the property over the money. Each small negotiable item in the purchase contract has its price too. For example, the seller may agree to include the refrigerator for $200 more. Equally important in negotiating is the relative bargaining power of the buyer and seller. If the seller is confident he will have plenty of buyers at his asking price, he can elect to refuse offers for less money, and reject those with numerous conditions or insufficient earnest money. However, if the owner is anxious to sell and has received only one offer in several months, he may be quite willing to accept a lower price and numerous conditions.

Note that it is the law in this state that any written offer

Figure 8:2

No. 1517
Earnest Money Contract
Revised 1971
MILLER-DAVIS Co.
Minneapolis

PURCHASE AGREEMENT

..........(1)..........Minn., ...(2).........., 19......

RECEIVED OF ....(3)..........

the sum of .... ($..........) DOLLARS

.... as earnest money and in part payment for the purchase of property at
(Check, Cash or Note — State Which)

.....(5).......... situated in the

County of.....(5)........., State of Minnesota, and legally described as follows, to-wit:

(5) Legal Description —

17 including all garden bulbs, plants, shrubs and trees, all storm sash, storm doors, detachable vestibules, screens, awnings, window shades, blinds (including venetian blinds), curtain rods, traverse rods, drapery rods, lighting fixtures and bulbs, plumbing fixtures, hot water tanks and heating plant (with any burners, tanks, stokers and other equipment used in connection therewith), water softener and liquid gas tank and controls (if the property of seller), sump pump, television antenna, incinerator, built-in dishwasher, garbage disposal, ovens, cook top stoves and central air conditioning equipment, if any, used and located on said premises and including also the following personal property: fixtures

all of which property the undersigned has this day sold to the buyer for the sum of:

.....(6).......... ($..........) DOLLARS,

which the buyer agrees to pay in the following manner:

Earnest money herein paid $.......... and $.........., cash, on ....(8).........., the date of closing.

(18)

(7) Subject to performance by the buyer the seller agrees to execute and deliver a .... Warranty Deed (to be joined in by spouse, if any) conveying marketable title to said premises subject only to the following exceptions:

(a) Building and zoning laws, ordinances, State and Federal regulations.
(b) Restrictions relating to use or improvement of premises without effective forfeiture provision.
(c) Reservation of any minerals or mineral rights to the State of Minnesota.
(d) Utility and drainage easements which do not interfere with present improvements.
(e) Rights of tenants as follows: (unless specified, not subject to tenancies)

(10) The buyer shall pay the real estate taxes due in the year 19...... and any unpaid installments of special assessments payable therewith

(9) and thereafter. Seller warrants that real estate taxes due in the year 19...... will be .... homestead classification
(full, partial or non-homestead — state which)

Neither the seller nor the seller's agent make any representation or warranty whatsoever concerning the amount of real estate taxes which shall be assessed against the property subsequent to the date of purchase.

Seller covenants that buildings, if any, are entirely within the boundary lines of the property and agrees to remove all personal property not included herein and all debris from the premises prior to possession date. SELLER WARRANTS ALL APPLIANCES, HEATING, AIR CONDITIONING, WIRING AND PLUMBING USED AND LOCATED ON SAID PREMISES ARE IN PROPER WORKING ORDER AT DATE OF CLOSING.

The seller further agrees to deliver possession not later than (13) .... provided that all conditions of this agreement have been complied with. Unless otherwise specified this sale shall be closed on or before 60 days from the date hereof.

(19) In the event this property is destroyed or substantially damaged by fire or any other cause before the closing date, this agreement shall become null and void, at the purchaser's option, and all monies paid hereunder shall be refunded to him.

(9) The buyer and seller also mutually agree that pro rata adjustments of rents, interest insurance and city water, and, in the case of income property, current operating expenses, shall be made as of ....

The seller shall, within a reasonable time after approval of this agreement, furnish an abstract of title, or a Registered Property Abstract certified to date to include proper searches covering bankruptcies, and State and Federal judgments and liens. The buyer shall be (7) allowed 10 days after receipt thereof for examination of said title and the making of any objections thereto, said objections to be made in writing or deemed to be waived. If any objections are so made the seller shall be allowed 120 days to make such title marketable. Pending correction of title the payments hereunder required shall be postponed, but upon correction of title and within 10 days after written notice to the buyer, the parties shall perform this agreement according to its terms.

If said title is not marketable and is not made so within 120 days from the date of written objections thereto as above provided, this (19) agreement shall be null and void, at option of the buyer, and neither principal shall be liable for damages hereunder to the other principal. All money theretofore paid by the buyer shall be refunded. If the title to said property be found marketable or be so made within said time, and said buyer shall default in any of the agreements and continue in default for a period of 10 days, then and in that case the seller may (20) terminate this contract and on such termination all the payments made upon this contract shall be retained by said seller and said agent, as their respective interests may appear, as liquidated damages, time being of the essence hereof. This provision shall not deprive either party of the right of enforcing the specific performance of this contract provided such contract shall not be terminated as aforesaid, and provided action to enforce such specific performance shall be commenced within six months after such right of action shall arise.

It is understood and agreed that this sale is made subject to the approval by the owner of said premises in writing and that the undersigned agent is in no manner liable or responsible on account of this agreement, except to return or account for the earnest money paid under this contract. (22)

The delivery of all papers and monies shall be made at the office of: ....

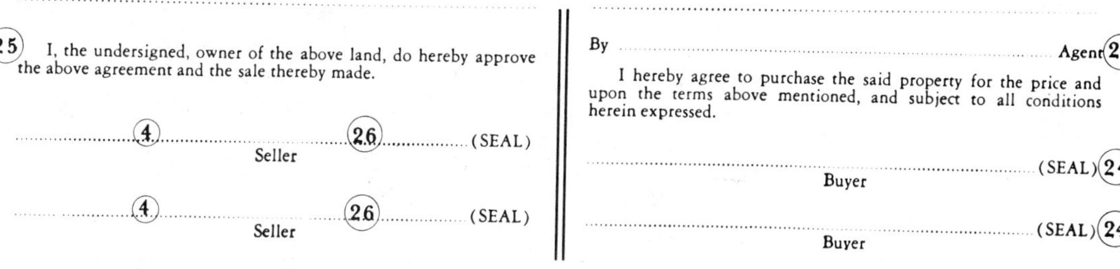

(25) I, the undersigned, owner of the above land, do hereby approve the above agreement and the sale thereby made.

..........(4)..........(26)..........(SEAL)
Seller

..........(4)..........(26)..........(SEAL)
Seller

By .... Agent (23)

I hereby agree to purchase the said property for the price and upon the terms above mentioned, and subject to all conditions herein expressed.

.... (SEAL) (24)
Buyer

.... (SEAL) (24)
Buyer

an agent receives must be presented to the seller promptly. It is not up to the salesperson to decide, for example, that an offer is "much too low to bother presenting." That decision belongs to the seller. Minnesota agents are also under an obligation not to disclose the terms of an offer to anyone else until it is presented to the seller. The purpose of this is to prevent an agent from taking a buyer's offer, and then informing another prospective buyer of the offer—usually with the intent of getting a higher offer—all before the offer has even been presented to the seller.

Minnesota Form

Figure 8:2 illustrates a widely used Minnesota purchase agreement form. Its circled numbers correspond to the foregoing discussion of the same matters in Figure 8:1.

THE BINDER

Throughout most of the United States, the real estate agent prepares the purchase contract as soon as he feels he is about to (or has) put a deal together. Using preprinted forms available from real estate trade associations, title companies and stationery stores, the agent fills in the purchase price, down payment and other details of the transaction and has the buyer and seller sign it as soon as they reach agreement.

In a few communities, however, the practice is for the real estate agent to prepare a short-form contract called a **binder.** The purpose of a binder is to hold a deal together until a more formal purchase contract can be drawn by an attorney and signed by the buyer and seller. In the binder the buyer and seller agree to the purchase price, the down payment and how the balance will be financed. The brokerage commission (to whom and how much) is stated along with an agreement to meet again to draw up a more formal contract that will contain all the remaining details of the sale. The agent then arranges a meeting at the office of the seller's attorney. In attendance are the seller and his attorney, the buyer and his attorney, and the real estate agents responsible for bringing about the sale. Together they prepare a written contract which the buyer and seller sign. Note that when the seller's attorney writes the formal contract, the contract will favor the seller. This is because the seller's attorney is expected to protect the seller's best interests at all times. The purchaser, to protect his interests, should not rely on the seller's attorney for advice, but should bring his own attorney.

While it is easy to play down the binder because it is to be replaced by another contract, it does, nonetheless, meet all the requirements of a legally binding contract. In the absence of another contract, it can be used to enforce completion of a sale by a buyer or seller. The major weakness of a binder is in what it *does not say*. For example, the binder will likely make no mention of a termite inspection, the type of deed the seller is expected to use, or the closing date. Unless the buyer and seller can agree on these matters at the formal contract meeting, a dilemma results. Certainly, the buyer will wonder if his refusal to meet all the seller's demands at the contract meeting will result in the loss of his deposit money. If a stalemate develops, the courts may be asked to decide the termite question, deed type, closing date, and any other unresolved points. However, because this is costly and time consuming for all involved, there is give-and-take negotiation at the contract meeting. If a completely unnegotiable impasse is reached, as a practical matter the binder is usually rescinded by the buyer and seller and the buyer's deposit returned. The use of binders is not common practice in Minnesota and their use is discouraged.

LETTER OF INTENT

If two or more parties want to express their mutual intention to buy, sell, lease, develop or invest, and wish to do so without creating any firm, legal obligation, they may use a **letter of intent.** Generally, such a letter contains an outline of the proposal and concludes with language to the effect that the letter is only an expression of mutual intent and that no liability or obligation is created by it. In other words, a letter of intent is neither a contract nor an agreement to enter into a contract. However, it is expected, and usually stipulated in the letter, that the parties signing the letter will proceed promptly and in good faith to conclude the deal proposed in the letter. The letter of intent is usually found in connection with commercial leases, real estate development and construction projects, and with multi-million dollar real estate sales.

PRACTICING LAW

Historically in the United States, the sale of real estate was primarily a legal service. Lawyers matched buyers with sellers, wrote the sales contract and prepared the mortgage and deed. When persons other than lawyers began to specialize in real estate brokerage, the question of who should write the sales contract became important. The lawyer was more qualified in matters of contract law, but the broker wanted something that could be signed the moment the buyer and seller were in agreement. For many years the solution was a compromise. The broker had the buyer and seller sign a binder and they agreed to meet again in the presence of a lawyer to draw up and sign a more formal contract. The trend today, however, is for the real estate agent to prepare a complete purchase contract as soon as there is a meeting of the minds.

The preparation of contracts by real estate agents for their clients has not gone unnoticed by lawyers. The legal profession maintains that preparing contracts for clients is practicing law, and state laws restrict the practice of law to lawyers. This has been, and continues to be, a controversial issue between brokers and lawyers. Resolution of the matter has come in the form of **accords** between the real estate brokerage industry and the legal profession. In nearly all states, including Minnesota, courts have ruled that a real estate agent is permitted to prepare purchase, installment, and rental contracts provided the agent uses a pre-printed form approved by a lawyer and provided the agent limits himself to filling in only the blank spaces on the form. (Figures 8:1 and 8:2 illustrate this concept.) If the pre-printed form requires extensive cross-outs, changes, and riders, the contract should be drafted by a lawyer. Real estate agents are *not* permitted to practice law.

CONTRACT FOR DEED

A **contract for deed,** also known as an installment contract or land contract, is used to sell property in situations where the seller does not wish to convey title until all, or at least a substantial portion, of the purchase price is paid by the buyer. This is different from the purchase contract shown in Figure 8:1 or 8:2 wherein the buyer receives possession and a deed at the closing. With a contract for deed, the buyer is given the right to use the property, but he does not acquire title. Instead, he receives a contract promising that a deed will be delivered at a later date.

The widest use of the contract for deed occurs when the buyer does not have the full purchase price in cash or he cannot borrow it from a lender. Under these conditions, the seller must be willing to accept a down payment plus installment payments until the property is paid for. Delivering title after payment is advantageous to the seller because if the buyer fails to make his payments, the title to the property is still in the name of the seller. This makes it easier to clear title in the event of default.

Sample Contract

Figure 8:3 (p.164) illustrates a typical Minnesota contract for deed. At the beginning of the contract the seller and buyer are identified. Note that in some contracts for deed, the buyer is referred to as the **vendee** and the seller as the **vendor.** Next, the legal description is inserted at ① and at ② the seller warrants against encumbrances. At ③ the seller promises to deliver both a deed and proper evidence of good title when the buyer has made all payments. At ④ the buyer agrees to the amount and terms of payment, including the amount of each installment. Next, at ⑤ the seller gives the right to prepay without penalty. At ⑥ the buyer agrees to pay taxes and assessments as agreed with the seller.

Continuing, at ⑦ the buyer agrees to protect all improvements on the property and maintain sufficient hazard insurance for the benefit of the seller. This insurance must be in an amount at least equal to the outstanding debt owed the seller. The two paragraphs at ⑧ describe how insurance proceeds will be distributed in the event of fire or other damage to the property. At ⑨ the buyer agrees to free the seller from liability due to injury on the property and promises to maintain liability insurance to protect the seller. At ⑩ the buyer promises that all hazard and liability insurance will be obtained from insurance companies licensed in Minnesota.

Next, at ⑪ the buyer promises that if all or part of the property is taken by eminent domain, all money received, up to the amount still owed, will be paid to the seller. At ⑫ the buyer agrees to keep the property in good repair and to protect the seller from liens or claims. At ⑬ the seller agrees to pay the state deed tax when the deed is delivered. At ⑭ both parties agree to send a copy of any assignment to the other party.

At ⑮ the seller has the right to pay any insurance premiums or tax installments and add them to the payments due from the buyer. At ⑯ the buyer and seller agree that time is of the essence, and at ⑰ bind their heirs and successors to the contract. Note that paragraph ⑯ permits the seller to retain all payments made under the contract *and* to retake possession if any default is made by the buyer. The buyer is, to some extent, protected by the provisions of the Minnesota cancellation statute, a summary of which follows. However, if the buyer fails to remedy his default within the time permitted by the statute, his entire interest in the property is forfeited. Item ⑱ is for clarification purposes only.

If the property is a condominium, then at ⑲ the buyer agrees to pay all owners' association assessments. Additional terms can be inserted at ⑳. Lastly, the parties sign the contract at ㉑ and acknowledge their signatures at ㉒.

Cancellation Statute Summary

As noted above, the seller may regain possession if the buyer, after having been served notice, fails to remedy any default "within the time permitted by the statute." This period varies from 30 to 90 days depending on the date the contract was executed and the amount of money already paid by the buyer at the time of default. The notice required to cancel a contract for deed must be served personally on the buyer or

Figure 8:3

CONTRACT FOR DEED Form No. 55-M Minnesota Uniform Conveyancing Blanks (1978) Miller-Davis Co., Minneapolis

Individual(s) to Joint Tenants

No delinquent taxes and transfer entered;
Certificate of Real Estate Value
( )filed ( )not required
____________, 19___.

____
County Auditor

By ____________
Deputy

(reserved for mortgage registry tax payment data)

(reserved for recording data)

MORTGAGE REGISTRY TAX DUE HEREON:

$ 73.50

Date: February 1, 1984

THIS CONTRACT FOR DEED is made on the above date by Charles M. Johnson and Jayne Y. Johnson, husband and wife, (marital status)

Seller (whether one or more), and Harold W. Gordon and Nancy P. Gordon, husband and wife, Purchasers, as joint tenants.

Seller and Purchasers agree to the following terms:

1. PROPERTY DESCRIPTION. Seller hereby sells, and Purchasers hereby buy, real property in Sunrise County, Minnesota, described as follows:

Lot 17, Block B-1, Sunrise Lakes Tract

together with all hereditaments and appurtenances belonging thereto (the Property).

(2) TITLE. Seller warrants that title to the Property is, on the date of this contract, subject only to the following exceptions:

(a) Covenants, conditions, restrictions, declarations and easements of record, if any;
(b) Reservations of minerals or mineral rights by the State of Minnesota, if any;
(c) Building, zoning and subdivision laws and regulations;
(d) The lien of real estate taxes and installments of special assessments which are payable by Purchasers pursuant to paragraph 6 of this contract; and
(e) The following liens or encumbrances:

First mortgage held in favor of Last National Bank of Minnesota dated December 1, 1971, and filed of record December 2, 1971, as Document Number 1973461, in the original amount of thirty-five thousand and no/100 ($35,000.00) dollars.

(3) DELIVERY OF DEED AND EVIDENCE OF TITLE. Upon Purchasers' prompt and full performance of this contract, Seller shall:

(a) Execute, acknowledge and deliver to Purchasers a Warranty Deed, in recordable form, conveying marketable title to the Property to Purchasers, subject only to the following exceptions:

(i) Those exceptions referred to in paragraph 2(a), (b), (c) and (d) of this contract;
(ii) Liens, encumbrances, adverse claims or other matters which Purchasers have created, suffered or permitted to accrue after the date of this contract; and
(iii) The following liens or encumbrances:

; and

(b) Deliver to Purchasers the abstract of title to the Property or, if the title is registered, the owner's duplicate certificate of title.

(4) PURCHASE PRICE. Purchasers shall pay to Seller, at 3215 Main Street, Biwabik, Minnesota, 56301, the sum of Ninety Thousand and no/100 Dollars ($ 90,000.00), as and for the purchase price for the Property, payable as follows:

Ten thousand and no/100 ($10,000.00) dollars cash, in hand paid, receipt and sufficiently of which are hereby acknowledged,

and

thirty-one thousand and no/100 ($31,000.00) dollars by assuming and agreeing to pay that certain mortgage now of record against the premises in favor of Last National Bank of Minnesota dated December 1, 1971, in the original amount of thirty-five thousand and no/100 ($35,000.00) dollars,

and

the remaining balance in the amount of forty-nine thousand and no/100 ($49,000.00) dollars in the following manner: four hundred ninety and no/100 ($490.00) dollars on the 1st day of March, 1984 and four hundred ninety and no/100 ($490.00) dollars on the 1st day of each month thereafter until the 1st day of February, 1989, which is five (5) years from the date thereof, at which time the entire remaining balance due hereunder together with accrued interest shall be due and payable in full. Interest on the unpaid principal balance shall be at the rate of nine percent (9%) per annum. Payments when made shall be credited first to the payment of accrued interest and the balance to the reduction of principal.

w/o penalty

(5.) PREPAYMENT. Unless otherwise provided in this contract, Purchasers shall have the right to fully or partially prepay this contract at any time without penalty. Any partial prepayment shall be applied first to payment of amounts then due under this contract, including unpaid accrued interest, and the balance shall be applied to the principal installments to be paid in the inverse order of their maturity. Partial prepayment shall not postpone the due date of the installments to be paid pursuant to this contract or change the amount of such installments.

(6.) REAL ESTATE TAXES AND ASSESSMENTS. Purchasers shall pay, before penalty accrues, all real estate taxes and installments of special assessments assessed against the Property which are due and payable in the year 19 85 and in all subsequent years. Real estate taxes and installments of special assessments which are due and payable in the year in which this contract is dated shall be paid as follows:

Sellers herein shall pay $100.00 and Buyers herein shall pay $1,100.00.

Seller warrants that the real estate taxes and installments of special assessments which were due and payable in the years preceding the year in which this contract is dated are paid in full.

(7.) PROPERTY INSURANCE.

(a) INSURED RISKS AND AMOUNT. Purchasers shall keep all buildings, improvements and fixtures now or later located on or a part of the Property insured against loss by fire, extended coverage perils, vandalism, malicious mischief and, if applicable, steam boiler explosion for at least the amount of Eighty thousand and no/100 ($80,000.00) . If any of the buildings, improvements or fixtures are located in a federally designated flood prone area, and if flood insurance is available for that area, Purchasers shall procure and maintain flood insurance in amounts reasonably satisfactory to Seller.

(b) OTHER TERMS. The insurance policy shall contain a loss payable clause in favor of Seller which provides that Seller's right to recover under the insurance shall not be impaired by any acts or omissions of Purchasers or Seller, and that Seller shall otherwise be afforded all rights and privileges customarily provided a mortgagee under the so-called standard mortgage clause.

(c) NOTICE OF DAMAGE. In the event of damage to the Property by fire or other casualty, Purchasers shall promptly give notice of such damage to Seller and the insurance company.

(8.) DAMAGE TO THE PROPERTY.

(a) APPLICATION OF INSURANCE PROCEEDS. If the Property is damaged by fire or other casualty, the insurance proceeds paid on account of such damage shall be applied to payment of the amounts payable by Purchasers under this contract, even if such amounts are not then due to be paid, unless Purchasers make a permitted election described in the next paragraph. Such amounts shall be first applied to unpaid accrued interest and next to the installments to be paid as provided in this contract in the inverse order of their maturity. Such payment shall not postpone the due date of the installments to be paid pursuant to this contract or change the amount of such installments. The balance of insurance proceeds, if any, shall be the property of Purchasers.

(b) PURCHASERS' ELECTION TO REBUILD. If Purchasers are not in default under this contract, or after curing any such default, and if the mortgagees in any prior mortgages and sellers in any prior contracts for deed do not require otherwise, Purchasers may elect to have that portion of such insurance proceeds necessary to repair, replace or restore the damaged Property (the repair work) deposited in escrow with a bank or title insurance company qualified to do business in the State of Minnesota, or such other party as may be mutually agreeable to Seller and Purchasers. The election may only be made by written notice to Seller within sixty days after the damage occurs. Also, the election will only be permitted if the plans and specifications and contracts for the repair work are approved by Seller, which approval Seller shall not unreasonably withhold or delay. If such a permitted election is made by Purchasers, Seller and Purchasers shall jointly deposit, when paid, such insurance proceeds into such escrow. If such insurance proceeds are insufficient for the repair work, Purchasers shall, before the commencement of the repair work, deposit into such escrow sufficient additional money to insure the full payment for the repair work. Even if the insurance proceeds are unavailable or are insuffficient to pay the cost of the repair work,

Purchasers shall at all times be responsible to pay the full cost of the repair work. All escrowed funds shall be disbursed by the escrowee in accordance with generally accepted sound construction disbursement procedures. The costs incurred or to be incurred on account of such escrow shall be deposited by Purchasers into such escrow before the commencement of the repair work. Purchasers shall complete the repair work as soon as reasonably possible and in a good and workmanlike manner, and in any event the repair work shall be completed by Purchasers within one year after the damage occurs. If, following the completion of and payment for the repair work, there remain any undisbursed escrow funds, such funds shall be applied to payment of the amounts payable by Purchasers under this contract in accordance with paragraph 8 (a) above.

9. INJURY OR DAMAGE OCCURRING ON THE PROPERTY.

(a) LIABILITY. Seller shall be free from liability and claims for damages by reason of injuries occurring on or after the date of this contract to any person or persons or property while on or about the Property. Purchasers shall defend and indemnify Seller from all liability, loss, costs and obligations, including reasonable attorneys' fees, on account of or arising out of any such injuries. However, Purchasers shall have no liability or obligation to Seller for such injuries which are caused by the negligence or intentional wrongful acts or omissions of Seller.

(b) LIABILITY INSURANCE. Purchasers shall, at their own expense, procure and maintain liability insurance against claims for bodily injury, death and property damage occurring on or about the Property in amounts reasonably satisfactory to Seller and naming Seller as an additional insured.

10. INSURANCE, GENERALLY. The insurance which Purchasers are required to procure and maintain pursuant to paragraphs 7 and 9 of this contract shall be issued by an insurance company or companies licensed to do business in the State of Minnesota and acceptable to Seller. The insurance shall be maintained by Purchasers at all times while any amount remains unpaid under this contract. The insurance policies shall provide for not less than ten days written notice to Seller before cancellation, non-renewal, termination or change in coverage, and Purchasers shall deliver to Seller a duplicate original or certificate of such insurance policy or policies.

11. CONDEMNATION. If all or any part of the Property is taken in condemnation proceedings instituted under power of eminent domain or is conveyed in lieu thereof under threat of condemnation, the money paid pursuant to such condemnation or conveyance in lieu thereof shall be applied to payment of the amounts payable by Purchasers under this contract, even if such amounts are not then due to be paid. Such amounts shall be applied first to unpaid accrued interest and next to the installments to be paid as provided in this contract in the inverse order of their maturity. Such payment shall not postpone the due date of the installments to be paid pursuant to this contract or change the amount of such installments. The balance, if any, shall be the property of Purchasers.

12. WASTE, REPAIR AND LIENS. Purchasers shall not remove or demolish any buildings, improvements or fixtures now or later located on or a part of the Property, nor shall Purchasers commit or allow waste of the Property. Purchasers shall maintain the Property in good condition and repair. Purchasers shall not create or permit to accrue liens or adverse claims against the Property which constitute a lien or claim against Seller's interest in the Property. Purchasers shall pay to Seller all amounts, costs and expenses, including reasonable attorneys' fees, incurred by Seller to remove any such liens or adverse claims.

13. DEED AND MORTGAGE REGISTRY TAXES. Seller shall, upon Purchasers' full performance of this contract, pay the deed tax due upon the recording or filing of the deed to be delivered by Seller to Purchasers. The mortgage registry tax due upon the recording or filing of this contract shall be paid by the party who records or files this contract; however, this provision shall not impair the right of Seller to collect from Purchasers the amount of such tax actually paid by Seller as provided in the applicable law governing default and service of notice of termination of this contract.

14. NOTICE OF ASSIGNMENT. If either Seller or Purchasers assign their interest in the Property, a copy of such assignment shall promptly be furnished to the non-assigning party.

15. PROTECTION OF INTERESTS. If Purchasers fail to pay any sum of money required under the terms of this contract or fail to perform any of their obligations as set forth in this contract, Seller may, at Seller's option, pay the same or cause the same to be performed, or both, and the amounts so paid by Seller and the cost of such performance shall be payable at once, with interest at the rate stated in paragraph 4 of this contract, as an additional amount due Seller under this contract.

If there now exists, or if Seller hereafter creates, suffers or permits to accrue, any mortgage, contract for deed, lien or encumbrance against the Property which is not herein expressly assumed by Purchasers, and provided Purchasers are not in default under this contract, Seller shall timely pay all amounts due thereon, and if Seller fails to do so, Purchasers may, at their option, pay any such delinquent amounts and deduct the amounts paid from the installment(s) next coming due under this contract.

(16) DEFAULT. The time of performance by Purchasers of the terms of this contract is an essential part of this contract. Should Purchasers fail to timely perform any of the terms of this contract, Seller may, at Seller's option, elect to declare this contract cancelled and terminated by notice to Purchasers in accordance with applicable law. All right, title and interest acquired under this contract by Purchasers shall then cease and terminate, and all improvements made upon the Property and all payments made by Purchasers pursuant to this contract shall belong to Seller as liquidated damages for breach of this contract. Neither the extension of the time for payment of any sum of money to be paid hereunder nor any waiver by Seller of Seller's rights to declare this contract forfeited by reason of any breach shall in any manner affect Seller's right to cancel this contract because of defaults subsequently occurring, and no extension of time shall be valid unless agreed to in writing. After service of notice of default and failure to cure such default within the period allowed by law, Purchasers shall, upon demand, surrender possession of the Property to Seller, but Purchasers shall be entitled to possession of the Property until the expiration of such period.

(17) BINDING EFFECT. The terms of this contract shall run with the land and bind the parties hereto and their successors in interest.

(18) HEADINGS. Headings of the paragraphs of this contract are for convenience only and do not define, limit or construe the contents of such paragraphs.

(19) ASSESSMENTS BY OWNERS' ASSOCIATION. If the Property is subject to a recorded declaration providing for assessments to be levied against the Property by any owners' association, which assessments may become a lien against the Property if not paid, then:

(a) Purchasers shall promptly pay, when due, all assessments imposed by the owners' association or other governing body as required by the provisions of the declaration or other related documents; and

(b) So long as the owners' association maintains a master or blanket policy of insurance against fire, extended coverage perils and such other hazards and in such amounts as are required by this contract, then:

(i) Purchasers' obligation in this contract to maintain hazard insurance coverage on the Property is satisfied; and

(ii) The provisions in paragraph 8 of this contract regarding application of insurance proceeds shall be superceded by the provisions of the declaration or other related documents; and

(iii) In the event of a distribution of insurance proceeds in lieu of restoration or repair following an insured casualty loss to the Property, any such proceeds payable to Purchasers are hereby assigned and shall be paid to Seller for application to the sum secured by this contract, with the excess, if any, paid to Purchasers.

(20) ADDITIONAL TERMS:

SELLER(S)	PURCHASERS
Charles M. Johnson	*Harold W. Gordon*
Jayne Y. Johnson	*Nancy P. Gordon*
______________________	______________________
______________________	______________________

State of Minnesota } ss.

County of Sunrise

The foregoing instrument was acknowledged before me this 1st day of February, 1984, by Charles M. Johnson and Jayne Y. Johnson, husband and wife, and Harold W. Gordon and Nancy P. Gordon, husband and wife.

NOTARIAL STAMP OR SEAL (OR OTHER TITLE OR RANK)

Heather Hagen

SIGNATURE OF NOTARY PUBLIC OR OTHER OFFICIAL

State of Minnesota
County of ______ } ss.

The foregoing instrument was acknowledged before me this ____ day of ______, 19__, by ______.

NOTARIAL STAMP OR SEAL (OR OTHER TITLE OR RANK)

SIGNATURE OF NOTARY PUBLIC OR OTHER OFFICIAL

Tax Statements for the real property described in this instrument should be sent to:

Harold W. Gordon and Nancy P. Gordon
8314 7 Avenue
Sunrise City, Minnesota 55501

THIS INSTRUMENT WAS DRAFTED BY (NAME AND ADDRESS)

John James, Attorney at Law
761 East Main Plaza
Sunrise City, Minnesota 55501

FAILURE TO RECORD OR FILE THIS CONTRACT FOR DEED MAY GIVE OTHER PARTIES PRIORITY OVER PURCHASERS' INTEREST IN THE PROPERTY.

his representative. However, if the buyer cannot be found, the seller is allowed to publish his notice in a legal newspaper in the county in which the property is located. If the buyer fails to redeem within the time specified by the statute, he loses all interest in the property and has no recourse for any monies paid prior to the contract's termination.

In the case of contracts for deed executed prior to May 1, 1980, the buyer must pay the *defaulted* amount within the following time period after receiving notice:

30 days if he has paid 0%–29% of the purchase price excluding interest and assumed mortgages or contracts for deed.
45 days if he has paid 30%–49% of the purchase price excluding interest and assumed mortgages or contracts for deed.
60 days if he has paid 50% or more of the purchase price excluding interest and assumed mortgages or contracts for deed.

In the case of contracts for deed executed on or after May 1, 1980, the buyer must bring *all payments current* within the following time period after receiving notice:

30 days if the purchaser has paid 0%–9% of the purchase price excluding interest and assumed mortgages or contracts for deed.
60 days if the purchaser has paid 10%–24% of the purchase price excluding interest and assumed mortgages or contracts for deed.
90 days if the purchaser has paid 25% or more of the purchase price excluding interest and assumed mortgages or contracts for deed.

A key weak point in the contract for deed concept is that the seller does not deed ownership to the buyer until some later date. Thus, it is possible for a buyer to make payments for several years only to find that the seller cannot deliver title as promised. Generally, in Minnesota this problem can be avoided if the buyer has the title to the premises examined before entering into the contract for deed. In addition, the buyer should record his contract for deed to establish his priority and to give notice of his interest to the public.

EXCHANGE AGREEMENTS

Most real estate transactions involve the exchange of real estate for monetary consideration. However, among sophisticated real estate investors, exchanging real property for real property has become popular for two important reasons. First, real estate trades can be accomplished without large amounts of cash by trading a property you presently own for one you want. This sidesteps the intermediate step of converting real estate to cash and then converting cash back to real estate. Second, by using an exchange, you can dispose of one property and acquire another without paying income taxes on the profit in the first property at the time of the transaction. As a result, the phrase "tax-free exchange" is often used when talking about trading.

To illustrate, suppose that you own, as an investment, an apartment building. The value on your accounting books is $150,000, but its market value today is $250,000. If you sell for cash, you will have to pay income taxes on the difference between the value of the property on your accounting books and the amount you receive for it. If instead of selling for cash, you find another building that you want and can arrange a trade, then for income tax purposes the new building acquires the accounting book value of the old and no income taxes are due at the time of the trade. Taxes will be due, however, if and when you finally sell rather than trade. Owner-occupied dwellings are treated differently. The Internal Revenue Service permits a homeowner to sell and still postpone paying taxes on the gain provided another home of equal or greater value is purchased within 24 months.

Trading Up

Real estate exchanges need not involve properties of equal value. For example, if you own a small office building worth $100,000 that is free of debt, you could trade it for a building worth $500,000 that has $400,000 of mortgage debt against it. Alternatively, if the building you wanted was priced at $600,000 with $400,000 in debt against it, you could offer your building plus $100,000 in cash.

When a simple two-way trade does not leave each party satisfied, exchanges involving several parties can be arranged. In the four-way trade in Figure 8:4A, Fisher would like to own Garcia's property but cannot arrange a trade because Garcia does not want Fisher's property. Fisher then looks for a property Garcia would like to own. He finds one that belongs to Hayden. However, Hayden does not want Fisher's property, and the search must continue to find someone who will take Fisher's property and who has something acceptable to Hayden. Ingram fills this gap, and the four-way trade is possible. Fisher

Figure 8:4 **POSSIBLE TRADING COMBINATIONS**

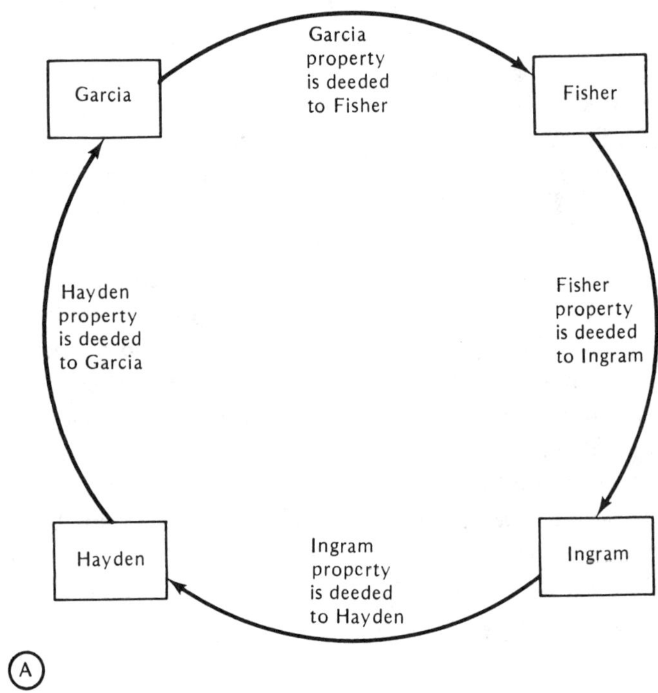

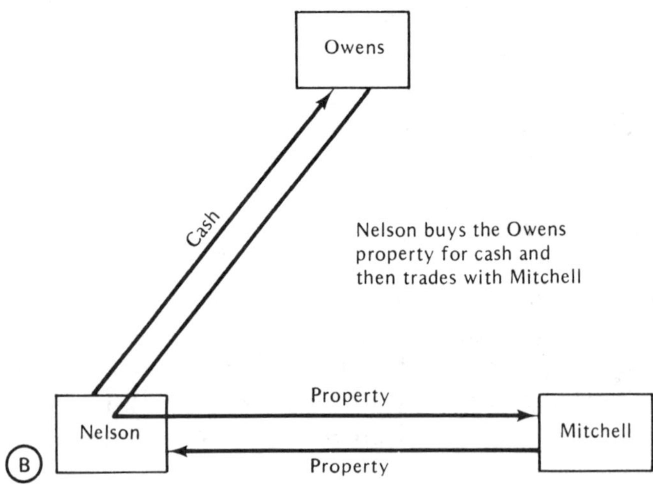

gets Garcia's property, who in turn gets Hayden's property, who in turn acquires Ingram's property, who in turn takes Fisher's property.*

In Figure 8:4B, a combination trade and cash sale is shown. Nelson wants Mitchell's property and is willing to pay cash for it. Mitchell refuses to sell for cash because of the income taxes he would have to pay; he will only trade. Owens has a property for sale that Mitchell would like to have. To make the deal, Nelson buys it and gives it to Mitchell, receiving Mitchell's property in return. The combination trade and cash sale has become very popular in recent years among sophisticated real estate investors. Correctly applied in an appreciating real estate market, an investor can pyramid his or her wealth with it.

Although trading is a a complicated business, it is also very lucrative for real estate agents. Whereas an ordinary sale results in one brokerage commission, a two-party exchange results in two commissions, and a four-party exchange in four commissions.

DELAYED EXCHANGES

For many years it was presumed that in order to qualify as a tax-free exchange, it was necessary for the properties to be exchanged simultaneously. Then came the *Starker* case. On April 1, 1967, T. J. Starker and his son and daughter-in-law entered into an exchange agreement with the Crown Zellerbach Corporation by which the Starkers agreed to convey timberland to Crown that was valued by the parties at $1,500,000. In return, Crown agreed to transfer property of equal value to the Starkers over a five-year period. The Starkers deeded their timberland to Crown and during the next 2½ years, the Starkers designated sufficient properties of equal value to conclude the transaction.

For their 1967 income tax returns, all three Starkers reported the transaction as a tax-deferred exchange. The Internal Revenue Service disagreed and required the Starkers to pay income taxes as if the transaction was an outright sale. The

---

* Although recent tax developments indicate a "wheel" type exchange can be carried out tax-free exactly as shown in Figure 8:4A, a few tax experts feel that they are on safer ground by working the trade as a series of two-party exchanges.

Starkers paid the taxes and filed for refunds in the U.S. District Court. This case was not fully decided until 1979 at which time the key outcome was that simultaneous conveyance is not a requirement for a tax-free exchange.

The Court's decision to allow delayed exchanges to be tax-free will have far-reaching effects on real estate investments. A major hindrance in organizing tax-deferred exchanges has been the difficulty of arranging a simultaneous closing for two or more complex transactions. The Starker decision means that investors will now have more flexibility in arranging trades.

Typical Trade Contract

Space does not permit a detailed review of a trade contract. However, very briefly, a typical trade contract identifies the traders involved and their respective properties; names the type of deed and quality of title that will be conveyed; names the real estate brokers involved and how much they are to be paid; discusses prorations, personal property, rights of tenants, and damage to the property; provides a receipt for the deposit that each trader makes; requires each trader to provide an abstract of title; and sets forth the consequences of defaulting on the contract. If the same broker represents more than one trader, he must disclose this to each trader whom he represents.

VOCABULARY REVIEW

Match terms **a–k** *with statements* **1–11.**

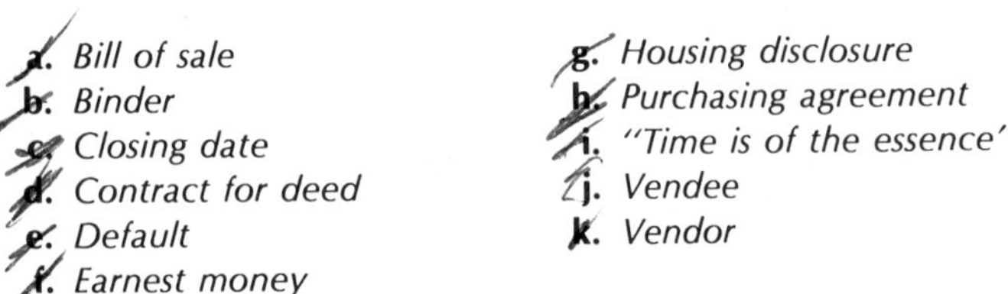

a. *Bill of sale*
b. *Binder*
c. *Closing date*
d. *Contract for deed*
e. *Default*
f. *Earnest money*
g. *Housing disclosure*
h. *Purchasing agreement*
i. *"Time is of the essence"*
j. *Vendee*
k. *Vendor*

1. A written and signed agreement specifying the terms at which a buyer will purchase and an owner will sell.
2. A short-form purchase contract to hold a real estate transaction together until a more formal contract can be prepared and signed.
3. Money that accompanies an offer to purchase as evidence of good faith.
4. The vendee's failure to perform a contractual obligation.
5. An inspection report required by certain Minnesota municipalities to be given to the buyer prior to the time of sale.
6. The day on which the buyer pays his money and the seller delivers title.

7. Written evidence of the sale of personal property.
8. A phrase meaning that all parties to a contract are expected to perform on time as a condition of the contract.
9. Also known as a installment contract or land contract.
10. The buyer under a contract for deed.
11. A seller under a contract for deed.

QUESTIONS AND PROBLEMS

1. Why is it necessary to include the extra step of preparing and signing a purchase agreement when it would seem much easier if the buyer simply paid the seller the purchase price and the seller handed the buyer a deed?
2. Why is it preferable to prepare a purchase agreement that contains all the terms and conditions of sale at the outset rather than to leave some items to be "ironed out" later?
3. What are the advantages and the disadvantages of using preprinted real estate purchase agreement forms?
4. Is it legal for a seller to accept an offer that is not accompanied by a deposit? Why or why not?
5. If a purchase agreement for real property describes the land, is it also necessary to mention the fixtures? Why or why not?
6. How will the relative bargaining strengths and weaknesses of the buyer and seller affect the contract negotiation process?
7. Under a contract for deed, what is the advantage to the seller if he does not have to deliver title to the buyer until all required payments are made?
8. What position does Minnesota take toward payment forfeiture clauses in contracts for deed?
9. What are the advantages of trading real estate rather than selling it? What do you consider the disadvantages to be?
10. What is a letter of intent?

ADDITIONAL READINGS

Halper, Emanuel B. *The Wonderful World of Real Estate.* Boston: Warren, Gorham, and Lamont, 1975, 203 pages. A delightful and highly readable collection of 17 stories designed to educate you as well as entertain you.

Jacobus, Charles, and Levi, Donald. *Real Estate Law.* Reston, Va.: Reston Publishing Co., 1980, 416 pages. An up-to-date guide to the legal aspects of real estate. Identifies a variety of legal problems and points out methods for avoiding them.

Kling, Samuel G. *The Complete Guide to Everyday Law,* 3rd ed. Chicago: Follett, 1973, 709 pages. A law book written for the nonlawyer. Includes explanations of legal words and phrases and has chapters on real estate law. Contains sample legal forms and a glossary.

Kratovil, Robert, and **Werner, Raymond J.** *Real Estate Law,* 8th ed. Englewood Cliffs, N.J.: Prentice-Hall, 1983, 650 pages. Chapter 11 discusses sales contracts, deposits, installment contracts, possession, rescission, and fraud. Contains suggestions on how to draft real estate sales contracts.

Levine, Mark Lee. *Real Estate Exchanges.* Chicago: Realtors National Marketing Institute, 1981, 600 pages. This is a thorough and sophisticated look at the economics, mechanics, and tax consequences of real estate exchanges. Includes cases, court decisions, tax codes, and IRS rulings.

Mortgage Theory and Law

KEY TERMS

Acceleration clause: allows the lender to demand immediate payment of the balance owed

Deficiency judgment: a judgment against a borrower if the sale of pledged property at foreclosure does not bring in enough to pay the balance owed

Foreclosure: the procedure by which a person's property can be taken and sold to satisfy an unpaid debt

Hypothecate: to pledge property to secure a debt but without giving up possession of it

Junior mortgage: any mortgage on a property that is subordinate to the first mortgage in priority

Mortgage: a pledge of property to secure the repayment of a debt

Mortgagee: the party receiving the mortgage; the lender

Mortgagor: the person who gives a mortgage pledging his property; the borrower

Power of sale: allows a mortgagee to conduct a foreclosure sale without first going to court

Subordination: voluntary acceptance of a lower mortgage priority than one would otherwise be entitled to

A mortgage is a pledge of property to secure the repayment of a debt. If the debt is not repaid as agreed between the lender and borrower, the lender can force the sale of the pledged property and apply the proceeds to repayment of the debt. To better understand present-day mortgage laws, it is helpful to first look at their history.

EARLY MORTGAGES

The concept of pledging property as collateral for a loan is not new. According to historians, the mortgage was in use when the pharaohs ruled Egypt and during the time of the Roman Empire. According to Roman laws, loans could be secured by mortgages on either personal or real property. In the early years of the Empire, nonpayment of a mortgage loan entitled the lender to make the borrower his slave. In the year 326 B.C. Roman law was modified to allow the debtor his freedom while working off his debt. Later, Roman law was again changed, this time to permit an unpaid debt to be satisfied by the sale of the mortgaged property.

Hypothecation

Mortgages were also an important part of English law and, as a result of the English colonization of America, ultimately were incorporated into the laws of each state. In England, the concept of pledging real estate by temporarily conveying its title to a lender as security for a debt was in regular use by the eleventh century. However, the Christian church at that time did not allow its members to charge interest. Because of this, the Christian lender took possession of the mortgaged property and collected the rents it produced instead of charging interest. In contrast, Jewish lenders in England charged interest and left the borrower in possession. It was not until the fourteenth century that charging interest, rather than taking possession, became universal. Leaving the borrower in possession of the pledged property is known as **hypothecation.** The borrower conveyed his title to the lender, but he still had the use of the property. This conveyance of title in the mortgage agreement was conditional. The mortgage stated that, if the debt it secured was paid on time, the mortgage was defeated and title returned to the borrower. This was and still is known as a **defeasance clause.**

LIEN THEORY VERSUS TITLE THEORY

Although the United States inherited the whole of English mortgage law, it began to be modified following independence. In 1791 in South Carolina, lawmakers asked the question, "Should a mortgage actually convey title to the lender subject only to the borrower's default? Or does the mortgage, despite its wording, simply create a lien with a right to acquire title only after proper foreclosure?" Their decision was that a mortgage was a lien rather than a conveyance, and South Carolina became the first **lien theory** state in regard to mortgages. Today, 32 states (including Minnesota) have adopted this viewpoint.*

Fifteen jurisdictions adhere to the older idea that a mortgage is a conveyance of title subject to defeat when the debt

* Alaska, Arizona, California, Colorado, Delaware, Florida, Georgia, Hawaii, Idaho, Indiana, Iowa, Kansas, Kentucky, Louisiana, Michigan, Minnesota, Missouri, Montana, Nebraska, Nevada, New Mexico, New York, North Dakota, Oklahoma, Oregon, South Carolina, South Dakota, Texas, Utah, Washington, Wisconsin, and Wyoming.

it secures is paid. They are classified as **title theory** states.† Four states are classified as **intermediate theory** states because they take a position midway between the lien and title theories.‡ In the intermediate states, title does not pass to the lender with the mortgage, but only upon default. In real estate practice, as long as default does not occur, the differences among the three theories are more technical than real.

PLEDGE METHODS

A person can pledge his real estate as collateral for a loan by using any of four methods: the regular mortgage, the equitable mortgage, the deed as security, and the deed of trust.

Regular Mortgage

The **standard** or **regular mortgage** is the mortgage handed down from England and the one commonly found and used in the United States today. In it, the borrower conveys his title to the lender as security for his debt. The mortgage also contains a statement that it will become void if the debt it secures is paid in full and on time. In title theory states, the conveyance feature of the mortgage stands. In lien theory states, such a mortgage is considered to be only a lien against the borrower's property despite its wording.

Equitable Mortgage

An **equitable mortgage** is a written agreement that, although it does not follow the form of a regular mortgage, is considered by the courts to be one. For example, Black sells his land to Green, with Green paying part of the price now in cash and promising to pay the balance later. Normally, Black would ask Green to execute a regular mortgage as security for the balance due. However, instead of doing this, Black makes a note of the balance due him on the deed before handing it to Green. The laws of most states, including Minnesota, would regard this notation as an equitable mortgage. For all intents and purposes, it is a mortgage, although not specifically called one. Another example of an equitable mortgage can arise

---

† Alabama, Arkansas, Connecticut, Maine, Maryland, Massachusetts, New Hampshire, North Carolina, Pennsylvania, Rhode Island, Tennessee, Vermont, Virginia, West Virginia, and the District of Columbia.

‡ Illinois, Mississippi, New Jersey, and Ohio.

from the money deposit accompanying an offer to purchase property. If the seller refuses the offer and refuses to return the deposit, the courts will hold that the purchaser has an equitable mortgage in the amount of the deposit against the seller's property.

Deed of Trust

In some states, but not Minnesota, debts are often secured by trust deeds. Whereas a mortgage is a two-party arrangement with a borrower and a lender, the **trust deed,** also known as a **deed of trust,** is a three-party arrangement consisting of the borrower (the trustor), the lender (the beneficiary), and a neutral third party (a trustee). The key aspect of this system is that the borrower executes a deed to the trustee rather than to the lender. If the borrower pays the debt in full and on time, the trustee reconveys title back to the borrower. If the borrower defaults on the loan, the lender asks the trustee to sell the property to pay off the debt. Trust deeds are covered in more detail in Chapter 10.

Chattel Mortgage

A mortgage can also be used to pledge personal property as security for a debt. This is a **chattel mortgage.** The word chattel is a legal term for personal property and originated from the Old English word for cattle. As with real property mortgages, a chattel mortgage permits the borrower to use his mortgaged personal property as long as the loan payments are made. If the borrower defaults, the lender is permitted to take possession and sell the mortgaged goods. In a growing number of states, including Minnesota, the use of chattel mortgages is being replaced by security agreements under the Uniform Commercial Code.

PROMISSORY NOTE

Two documents are involved in a standard mortgage loan, a promissory note and the mortgage itself; both are contracts. The **promissory note** establishes who the borrower and lender are, the amount of the debt, the terms of repayment, and the interest rate. A sample promissory note, usually referred to simply as a **note,** is shown in Figure 9:1.

To be valid as evidence of debt, a note must (1) be in writing, (2) be between a borrower and lender who both have contractual capacity, (3) state the borrower's promise to pay a certain sum of money, (4) show the terms of payment, (5)

Figure 9:1

PROMISSORY NOTE SECURED BY MORTGAGE①

② City, State March 31, 19xx

③ *For value received, I promise to pay to* ④ Pennywise Mortgage Company , ⑤ *or order at* 2242 National Blvd., [City, State] , *the sum of* ⑥ Sixty thousand and no/100- - - - - - - - - - - - - - - *Dollars, with interest from* March 31, 19xx , *on unpaid principal at the rate of* ⑦ ten *percent per annum; principal and interest payable in installments of* ⑧ five hundred twenty-six and 55/100- - - - - - - - - - - - *Dollars on the* first *day of each month beginning* ⑨ May 1, 19xx , *and continuing until said principal and interest have been paid.*

⑩ *This note may be prepaid in whole or in part at any time without penalty.*

⑪ *There shall be a ten-day grace period for each monthly payment. A late fee of $12.50 will be added to each payment made after its grace period.*

⑫ *Each payment shall be credited first on interest then due and the remainder on principal.*

⑬ *Should default be made in payment of any installment when due, the entire principal plus accrued interest shall immediately become due at the option of the holder of the note.*

⑭ *If legal action is necessary to collect this note, I promise to pay such sum as the court may fix.*

⑮ *This note is secured by a mortgage bearing the same date as this note and made in favor of* Pennywise Mortgage Company.

⑯ *Hap P. Toborrow*
Borrower

be signed by the borrower, and (6) be voluntarily delivered by the borrower and accepted by the lender. If the note is secured by a mortgage or trust deed, it must say so. Otherwise, it is solely a personal obligation of the borrower. Although interest is not required to make the note valid, most loans do carry an interest charge; when they do, the rate of interest must be stated in the note. In Minnesota, it is not required that the borrower's signature on the note be acknowledged or witnessed.

Obligor-Obligee

Referring to Figure 9:1, number ① identifies the document as a promissory note and ② gives the location and date of the note's execution (signing). At ③, the borrower states that he has received something of value and in turn promises to pay the debt described in the note. Typically, the "value received" is a loan of money in the amount described in the note; it could, however, be services or goods or anything else of value.

The section of the note at ④ identifies to whom the obligation is owed, sometimes referred to as the **obligee,** and where the payments are to be sent. The words "or order" at ⑤ mean that the lender can direct the borrower (the **obligor**) to make his payments to someone else, if the lender sells the right to collect the note.

The Principal

The **principal** or amount of the obligation, $60,000, is shown at ⑥. Number ⑦ gives the rate of interest on the debt and the date from which it will be charged. The amount of the periodic payment at ⑧ is calculated from the loan tables discussed in Chapter 11. In this case, $526.55 each month for 30 years will return the lender's $60,000 plus interest at the rate of 10% per year on the unpaid portion of the principal. Number ⑨ outlines when payments will begin and when subsequent payments will be due. In this example, they are due on the first day of each month until the full $60,000 and interest have been paid. The clause at ⑩ is a **prepayment privilege** for the borrower. It allows the borrower to pay more than the required $526.55 per month and to pay the loan off early without penalty. Without this very important privilege, the note requires the borrower to pay $526.55 per month, no more and no less, until the $60,000 plus interest has been paid. On some note forms, the prepayment privilege is created by inserting the words "or more" after the word "dollars" where it appears between ⑧ and ⑨. The note would then read "five hundred twenty-six and 55/100 dollars or more. . . ." The "or more" can be any amount from $526.56 up to and including the entire balance remaining.

Acceleration Clause

At ⑪, the lender gives the borrower a 10-day grace period to accommodate late payments. For payments made after that, the borrower agrees to pay a late charge of $12.50. The clause at ⑫ states that, whenever a payment is made, any interest due on the loan is first deducted, and then the remainder is applied to reducing the loan balance. The provision at ⑬ allows the lender to demand immediate payment of the entire balance remaining on the note if the borrower misses any of the individual payments. This is called an **acceleration clause**, as it "speeds up" the remaining payments due on the note. Without this clause, the lender can only foreclose on the payments that have come due and not been paid. In this example, that could take as long as 30 years. This clause also has a certain psychological value: knowing that the lender has the option of calling the entire loan balance due upon default makes the borrower think twice about being late with his payments.

Signature

At ⑭, the borrower agrees to pay any collection costs incurred by the lender if the borrower falls behind in his payments. At ⑮, the promissory note is tied to the mortgage that secures it, making it a mortgage loan. Without this reference, it would be a personal loan. At ⑯, the borrower signs the note. A person who signs a note is sometimes referred to as a **maker** of the note. If two or more persons sign the note, it is common to include a statement in the note that the borrowers are "jointly and severally liable" for all provisions in the note. Thus, the terms of the note and the obligations it creates are enforceable upon the makers as a group and upon each maker individually. If the borrower is married, lenders generally require both husband and wife to sign.

THE MORTGAGE INSTRUMENT

The mortgage is a separate agreement from the promissory note. Whereas the note is evidence of a debt and a promise to pay, the mortgage pledges collateral that the lender can sell if the note is not paid. The sample mortgage in Figure 9:2 illustrates in simplified language the key provisions most commonly found in real estate mortgages used in the United States. Let us look at these provisions.

Figure 9:2

MORTGAGE

①*THIS MORTGAGE is made this* 31st *day of* March, 19xx, *between* Hap P. Toborrow *hereinafter called the Mortgagor, and* Pennywise Mortgage Company *hereinafter called the Mortgagee.*

②*WHEREAS, the Mortgagor is indebted to the Mortgagee in the principal sum of* Sixty thousand and no/100 - - - - - *Dollars, payable* $526.55, including 10% interest per annum, on the first day of each month starting May 1, 19xx, and continuing until paid *, as evidenced by the Mortgagor's note of the same date as this mortgage, hereinafter called the Note.*

③*TO SECURE the Mortgagee the repayment of the indebtedness evidenced by said Note, with interest thereon, the Mortgagor does hereby mortgage, grant, and convey to the Mortgagee the following described property in the County of* Evans *, State of* ________ *.*

④*Lot 39, Block 17, Harrison's Subdivision, as shown on Page 19 of Map Book 25, filed with the County Recorder of said County and State.*

⑤*FURTHERMORE, the Mortgagor fully warrants the title to said land and will defend the same against the lawful claims of all persons.*

⑥*IF THE MORTGAGOR, his heirs, legal representatives, or assigns pay unto the Mortgagee, his legal representatives or assigns, all sums due by said Note, then this mortgage and the estate created hereby SHALL CEASE AND BE NULL AND VOID.*

⑦*UNTIL SAID NOTE is fully paid:*

⑧*A. The Mortgagor agrees to pay all taxes on said land.*

⑨*B. The Mortgagor agrees not to remove or demolish buildings or other improvements on the mortgaged land without the approval of the lender.*

Figure 9:2 *continued*

⑩C. The Mortgagor agrees to carry adequate insurance to protect the lender in the event of damage or destruction of the mortgaged property.

⑪D. The Mortgagor agrees to keep the mortgaged property in good repair and not permit waste or deterioration.

IT IS FURTHER AGREED THAT:

⑫E. The Mortgagee shall have the right to inspect the mortgaged property as may be necessary for the security of the Note.

⑬F. If the Mortgagor does not abide by this mortgage or the accompanying Note, the Mortgagee may declare the entire unpaid balance on the Note immediately due and payable.

⑭G. If the Mortgagor sells or otherwise conveys title to the mortgaged property, the Mortgagee may declare the entire unpaid balance on the Note immediately due and payable.

⑮H. If all or part of the mortgaged property is taken by action of eminent domain, any sums of money received shall be applied to the Note.

⑯IN WITNESS WHEREOF, the Mortgagor has executed this mortgage.

⑰ [this space for the acknowledgment]

Hap P. Toborrow (SEAL)
Mortgagor

The mortgage begins at ① with the date of its making and the names of the parties involved. In mortgage agreements, the person or party who pledges his property and gives the mortgage is the **mortgagor.** The person or party who receives the mortgage (the lender) is the **mortgagee.** For the reader's convenience, we shall refer to the mortgagor as the borrower and the mortgagee as the lender.

At ②, the debt for which this mortgage acts as security is identified. This mortgage does not act as security for any other debts of the borrower. The key wording in the mortgage occurs at ③, where the borrower conveys to the lender the property described at ④. The pledged property is most often the property that the borrower purchased with the loan money, but this is not a requirement. The mortgaged property need only be something of sufficient value in the eyes of the lender; it could just as easily be some other property the borrower owns. At ⑤, the borrower states that the pledged property is his and that he will defend its ownership. The lender will, of course, verify this with a title search before making the loan.

As you may have already noticed, the wording of ③, ④, and ⑤ is strikingly similar to that found in a warranty deed. In states taking the title theory position toward mortgages, this wording is interpreted to mean that the borrower is deeding his property to the lender. In lien theory states, such as Minnesota, this wording gives only a lien right to the lender, and the borrower (mortgagor) retains title. In either case, the borrower is allowed to remain in physical possession of the mortgaged property as long as he abides by the terms of the note and mortgage.

Provisions for the defeat of the mortgage are given at ⑥. The key words here state that the "mortgage and the estate created hereby shall cease and be null and void" when the note is paid in full. This is the **defeasance clause.**

Covenants

After ⑦, there is a list of covenants (promises) that the borrower makes to the lender. They are the covenants of taxes, removal, insurance and repair. These covenants protect the security for the loan.

In the **covenant to pay taxes** at ⑧, the borrower agrees to pay the taxes on the mortgaged property. This is important to the lender, because if the taxes are not paid on time they become a lien on the property that is superior to the lender's mortgage.

In the **covenant against removal** at ⑨, the borrower promises not to remove or demolish any buildings or improvements. To do so may reduce the value of the property as security for the lender.

The **covenant of insurance** at ⑩ requires the borrower to carry adequate insurance against damage or destruction of the mortgaged property. This protects the value of the collateral for the loan, for without insurance, if buildings or other improvements on the mortgaged property are damaged or destroyed, the value of the property might fall below the amount owed on the debt. With insurance, the buildings can be repaired or replaced, thus restoring the value of the collateral.

The **covenant of good repair** at ⑪, also referred to as the covenant of preservation and maintenance, requires the borrower to keep the mortgaged property in good condition. The clause at ⑫ gives the lender permission to inspect the property to make sure that it is being kept in good repair and has not been damaged or demolished.

If the borrower breaks any of the mortgage covenants or note agreements, the lender wants the right to terminate the loan. Thus, an **acceleration clause** at ⑬ is included to permit the lender to demand the balance be paid in full immediately. If the borrower cannot pay, foreclosure takes place and the property is sold.

Alienation Clause

When used in a mortgage, an **alienation clause** (also called a **due-on-sale clause**) gives the lender the right to call the entire loan balance due if the mortgaged property is sold or otherwise conveyed (alienated) by the borrower. An example is shown at ⑭. The purpose of an alienation clause is twofold. If the mortgaged property is put up for sale and a buyer proposes to assume the existing loan, the lender can refuse to accept that buyer as a substitute borrower if the buyer's credit is not good. But, more importantly, does it give the lender an opportunity to eliminate old loans with low rates of interest? Minnesota regards as unenforceable the use of an alienation clause for the purpose of raising interest rates during the life of a mortgage loan. In Minnesota the lender takes the risk of changing interest rates when making the loan and only if the new buyer is a poor credit risk can the loan be called due. However, this is now changing. A 1982 U.S. Supreme Court decision allows due-on-sale clauses to be enforced by federally-chartered savings and loan associations. Also from Washington, D.C., the 1982 Garn–St Germain Act extends the enforceability of these clauses to individual lenders, banks, and state-chartered savings and loans. (The issue of due-on-sale clauses from both the borrower and lender perspectives is discussed more in Chapter 12.)

Condemnation Clause

Number ⑮ is a **condemnation clause.** If all or part of the property is taken by action of eminent domain, any money so received is used to reduce the balance owing on the note.

At ⑯, the mortgagor states that he has made this mortgage. Actually, the execution statement is more a formality than a requirement; the mortgagor's signature alone indicates his execution of the mortgage and agreement to its provisions. At ⑰, the mortgage is acknowledged as required by state law for placement in the public records. Like deeds, mortgages must be recorded if they are to be effective against any subsequent purchaser, mortgagee, or lessee. The reason the mortgage is recorded, but not the promissory note, is that the mortgage deals with rights and interests in real property, whereas the note represents a personal obligation.

MORTGAGE SATISFACTION

By far, most mortgage loans are paid in full either on or ahead of schedule. When the loan is paid, the standard practice is for the lender to cancel the promissory note and to issue to the borrower a document called a **satisfaction of mortgage.** Issued by the lender, this certificate states that the promissory note has been paid in full and the accompanying mortgage may be discharged from the public records. It is extremely important that this document be promptly recorded by the public recorder in the same county where the mortgage is recorded. Otherwise, the records will continue to indicate that the property is mortgaged. When a satisfaction is recorded, a recording office employee makes a note of its book and page location on the margin of the recorded mortgage. This is done to assist title searchers and is called a **marginal release.**

Partial Release

Occasionally, the situation arises where the borrower wants the lender to release a portion of the mortgaged property from the mortgage after part of the loan has been repaid. This is known as asking for a **partial release.** For example, a land developer purchases 40 acres of land for a total price of $500,000 and finances his purchase with $100,000 in cash plus a mortgage and note for $400,000 to the seller. In the mortgage agreement he might ask that the seller release 10 acres free and clear of the mortgage encumbrance for each $100,000 paid against the loan.

"SUBJECT TO" VERSUS "ASSUMPTION"

Often, when mortgaged real estate is sold, the existing mortgage debt against the property is not paid off as part of the transaction. In this case, the buyer can either purchase the property "subject to" the existing loan or he can "assume" the loan. When the buyer purchases **subject to the existing loan,** he states that he is aware of the existence of the loan and the mortgage that secures it, but takes no personal liability for it. Although the buyer pays the remaining loan payments as they come due, the seller continues to be personally liable to the lender for the loan. As long as the buyer faithfully continues to make the loan payments, which he would normally do as long as the property is worth more than the debts against it, this arrangement presents no problem to the seller. However, if the buyer stops making payments before the loan is fully paid, even though it may be years later, in most states the lender can require the seller to pay the balance due plus interest. This is true even though the seller thought he was free of the loan because he sold the property.

The seller is on safer ground if he requires the buyer to **assume the loan.** Under this arrangement, the buyer promises in writing to the seller that he will pay the loan, thus personally obligating himself. In the event of default on the loan or a breach of the mortgage agreement, the lender will first expect the buyer to remedy the problem. If the buyer does not pay, the lender will look to the seller, because the seller's name is still on the original promissory note. The safest arrangement for the seller is to ask the lender to **substitute** the buyer's liability for his. This releases the seller from the personal obligation created by his promissory note, and the lender can now require only the buyer to repay the loan. The seller is also on safe ground if the mortgage agreement or state law prohibits deficiency judgments, a topic that will be explained shortly.

When a buyer is to continue making payments on an existing loan, he will want to know exactly how much is still owing. A **certificate of reduction** is prepared by the lender to show how much of the loan remains to be paid. If a recorded mortgage states that it secures a loan for $35,000, but the borrower has reduced the amount owed to $25,000, the certificate of reduction will show that $25,000 remains to be paid. Somewhat related to a certificate of reduction is the **estoppel certificate.**

This is used when the holder of a mortgage loan sells it to another investor. In it, the borrower is asked to verify the amount still owed and the rate of interest.

DEBT PRIORITIES

The same property can usually be pledged as collateral for more than one mortgage. This presents no problems to the lenders involved as long as the borrower makes the required payments on each note secured by the property. The difficulty arises when a default occurs on one or more of the loans, and the price the property brings at its foreclosure sale does not cover all the loans against it. As a result, a priority system is necessary. The debt with the highest priority is satisfied first from the foreclosure sale proceeds, and then the next highest priority debt is satisfied, then the next, until either the foreclosure sale proceeds are exhausted or all debts secured by the property are satisfied.

First Mortgage

In many foreclosures, the sale proceeds are not sufficient to pay all the outstanding debt against the property; thus, it becomes extremely important that a lender know his priority position before making a loan. Unless there is a compelling reason otherwise, a lender will want to be in the most senior position possible. This is normally accomplished by being the first lender to record a mortgage against a property that is otherwise free and clear of mortgage debt; this lender is said to hold a **first mortgage** on the property. If the same property is later used to secure another note before the first is fully satisfied, the new mortgage is a **second mortgage,** and so on. The first mortgage is also known as the **senior mortgage.** Any mortgage with a lower priority is a **junior mortgage.** As time passes and higher priority mortgages are satisfied, the lower priority mortgages move up in priority. Thus, if a property is secured by a first and a second mortgage and the first is paid off, the second becomes a first mortgage.

Subordination

Sometimes a lender will voluntarily take a lower priority position than he would otherwise be entitled to by virtue of his recording date. This is known as **subordination** and it allows a junior loan to move up in priority. For example, the holder of a first mortgage can volunteer to become a second mortgagee and allow the second mortgage to move into the first position. Although it seems irrational that a lender would actually volunteer to lower his priority position, it is sometimes done by landowners to encourage developers to buy their land.

Chattel Liens

An interesting situation regarding priority occurs when chattels are bought on credit and then affixed to land that is already mortgaged. If the chattels are not paid for, can the chattel lienholder come onto the land and remove them? If there is default on the mortgage loan against the land, are the chattels sold as fixtures? The solution is for the chattel lienholder to record a **chattel mortgage** or a **financing statement.** This protects his interest even though the chattel becomes a fixture when it is affixed to land.

THE FORECLOSURE PROCESS

Although relatively few mortgages are foreclosed, it is important to have a basic understanding of what happens when foreclosure takes place. First, knowledge of what causes foreclosure can help in avoiding it; and, second, if foreclosure does occur, one should know the rights of the parties involved.

Although noncompliance with any part of the mortgage agreement by the borrower can result in the lender calling the entire balance immediately due, in most cases foreclosure occurs because the note is not being repaid on time. When a borrower is behind in his payments, the loan is said to be **delinquent** or **nonconforming.** At this stage, rather than presume foreclosure is automatically the next step, the borrower and lender usually meet and attempt to work out an alternative payment program. Contrary to early motion picture plots in which lenders seemed anxious to foreclose their mortgages, today's lender considers foreclosure to be the last resort. This is because the foreclosure process is time consuming, expensive, and unprofitable. The lender would much rather have the borrower make regular payments. Consequently, if a borrower is behind in his loan payments, the lender prefers to arrange a new, stretched-out, payment schedule rather than immediately to declare the acceleration clause in effect and move toward foreclosing the borrower's rights to the property.

If a borrower realizes that stretching out payments is not going to solve his financial problem, instead of presuming foreclosure to be inevitable, he can seek a buyer for the property who can make the payments. More than any other reason, this is why relatively few real estate mortgages are foreclosed. The borrower, realizing he is in, or is about to be in, financial trouble, sells his property. It is only when the borrower cannot find a buyer and when the lender sees no further sense in stretching the payments that the acceleration clause is invoked and the path toward foreclosure taken. Let us look at a summary of the foreclosure process for a standard mortgage. (See Chapter 10 for deed of trust foreclosures.)

The Lawsuit

The mortgage foreclosure process begins with a title search. Next, the lender files a **lawsuit** naming as defendants the borrower and anyone who acquired a right or interest in the property after the lender recorded his mortgage. In the lawsuit the lender identifies the debt and the mortgage securing it, and states that it is in default. The lender then asks the court for a judgment directing that (1) the defendants' interests in the property be cut off in order to return the condition of title to what it was when the loan was made, (2) the property be sold at a public auction, and (3) the lender's claim be paid from the sale proceeds.

Surplus Money Action

A copy of the complaint along with a summons is delivered to the defendants. This officially notifies them of the pending legal action against their interests. A junior mortgage holder who has been named as a defendant has basically two choices; he will choose the one that he feels will leave him less worse off. One choice is to allow the foreclosure to proceed and file his own **surplus money action.** By doing this, he hopes that the property will sell at the foreclosure sale for enough money to pay all claims senior to him as well as his own claim against the borrower. The other choice is to halt the foreclosure process by making the delinquent payments on behalf of the borrower and then adding them to the amount the borrower owes him. To do this, the junior mortgage holder must use cash out of his own pocket and decide whether this is a case of "good money chasing bad." It is true that he can add these sums to the amount owed him, but he must also consider whether he will have any better luck being paid than did the holder of the senior mortgage.

Notice of Lis Pendens

At the same time that the lawsuit to foreclose is filed with the court, a **notice of lis pendens** is filed with the county recorder's office where the property is located. This notice informs the public that a legal action is pending against the property. If the borrower attempts to sell the property at this time, the prospective buyer, upon making his title search, would learn of the pending litigation. He can still proceed to purchase the property if he wants, but he is now informed that he is buying under the cloud of an unsettled lawsuit.

Public Auction

The borrower, or any other defendant named in the lawsuit, may now reply to the suit by presenting his side of the issue to the court judge. If no reply is made, or if the issues raised by the reply are found in favor of the lender, the judge will order that the interests of the borrower and other defendants in the property be foreclosed (terminated) and the property sold. The sale is usually a **public auction.** The objective is to obtain the best possible price for the property by inviting competitive bidding and conducting the sale in full view of the public. To announce the sale, the judge orders a notice to be posted on the courthouse door and published once a week for six weeks in a newspaper of general circulation in the Minnesota county in which the property is located.

The sale is conducted by the **county sheriff.** At the sale, which is held at either the property or at the courthouse, the lender and all parties interested in purchasing the property are present. If the borrower should suddenly locate sufficient funds to pay the judgment against him, he can, up to the minute the property goes on sale, step forward and redeem his property. This privilege to redeem property anytime between the first sign of delinquency and the moment of foreclosure sale is the borrower's **equity of redemption.** If no redemption is made, the bidding begins. Anyone with adequate funds can bid.

While the lender and borrower hope that someone at the auction will bid more than the amount owed on the defaulted loan, the probability is not high. If the borrower was unable to find a buyer at a price equal to or higher than the loan balance, the best cash bid will probably be less than the balance owed. If this happens, the lender usually enters a bid of his own. The lender is in a unique position as he can "bid his loan." That is, he can bid up to the amount owed him without having to pay cash. All other bidders must pay cash, as the purpose of the sale is to obtain cash to pay the defaulted loan.

In the event the borrower bids at the sale and is successful in buying back his property, the junior liens against the property are not eliminated. Note however, that no matter who the successful bidder is, the foreclosure does not cut off property tax liens against the property. They remain.

Deficiency Judgment

If the property sells for more than the claims against it, the borrower receives the surplus. For example, if a property with $50,000 in claims against it sells for $55,000, the borrower will receive the $5,000 difference, less unpaid property taxes and expenses of the sale. However, if the highest bid is only $40,000, how is the $10,000 deficiency treated? The laws of the various states differ on this question. Most (including Minnesota) allow the lender to request a **deficiency judgment** for the $10,000, with which the lender can proceed against the borrower's other unsecured assets. In other words, the borrower is still personally obligated to the lender for $10,000 and the lender is entitled to collect it. This may require the borrower to sell other assets.

Several states (for example, California, Montana, North Dakota and North Carolina) have outlawed deficiency judgments in most foreclosure situations so that a lender cannot reach beyond the pledged property for debt satisfaction. In these states the lender would have to stand the $10,000 deficiency loss. Also, there can be no deficiency judgment in a strict foreclosure case. In many states where deficiency judgments are permitted, if the property sells for an obviously depressed price at its foreclosure sale, a deficiency judgment will be allowed only for the difference between the court's estimate of the property's fair market value and the amount still owing against it.

In states that allow deficiency judgments, if the borrower is in a strong enough bargaining position, he can place in the promissory note language to the effect that the note is "without recourse." This generally prohibits the lender from seeking a deficiency judgment.

Statutory Redemption

In Minnesota, the foreclosed borrower has 6 months or 12 months after the foreclosure sale to pay in full the judgment against him and retake title. This leaves the high bidder at the foreclosure auction in a dilemma: he does not know for certain whether he will get the property he bid on until the statutory redemption period has run out. Meanwhile, he receives a **certificate of sale** which is a conveyance of title subject to defeasance by redemption. In Minnesota the purchaser will not get possession until the statutory redemption period has expired. This discourages prospective bidders. In this respect, statutory redemption works against the borrower as well as the lender. This problem can be made less severe if the court appoints a **receiver** (manager) to take charge of the property during the redemption period.

In choosing between a 6 or 12 month redemption period, if the lender wants a deficiency judgment the redemption period must be 12 months. If the lender will forego a deficiency judgment, the redemption period is 6 months.

POWER OF SALE

Forty-two states (including Minnesota) permit the use of **power of sale,** also known as **foreclosure by advertisement,** as a means of simplifying and shortening the foreclosure proceeding itself. If it is necessary to foreclose, this clause in the mortgage gives the lender the power to conduct the foreclosure and sell the mortgaged property without taking the issue to court. The period between default and sale is the borrower's equity of redemption. The property is then advertised and sold at an auction held by the sheriff and open to the public. The precise procedures the lender must follow are set by state statutes. After the auction, the borrower can still redeem the property in Minnesota because of statutory redemption. When a lender uses foreclosure by advertisement in Minnesota, the statutory redemption period is 6 months and the lender cannot obtain a deficiency judgment. If the lender wants a deficiency judgment, the lender must foreclose in court. A major weak point with power of sale is that in many states junior claimants need not be personally notified of a pending sale. Thus, conceivably, a junior claimant could have his rights cut off without being aware of it.

DEED IN LIEU OF FORECLOSURE

To avoid the hassle of foreclosure proceedings, a borrower may voluntarily deed his property to the lender. In turn, the borrower should demand cancellation of the unpaid debt and a letter to that effect from the lender. This method relieves the lender of foreclosing and waiting out any required redemption periods, but it also presents the lender with a sensitive situation. With the borrower in financial distress and about to be foreclosed, it is quite easy for the lender to take advantage of the borrower. As a result, courts of law will usually side with the borrower if he complains of any unfair dealings. Thus, the lender must be prepared to prove conclusively that the borrower received a fair deal by deeding his property voluntarily to the lender in return for cancellation of his debt. If the property is worth more than the balance due on the debt, the lender must pay the borrower the difference in cash. A deed in lieu of foreclosure is a voluntary act by both borrower and lender; if either feels he will fare better in regular foreclosure proceedings, he need not agree to it. Note also that a deed in lieu of foreclosure will not cut off the rights of junior mortgage holders.

VOCABULARY REVIEW

Match terms **a–t** *with statements* **1–20.**

a. *Alienation clause*
b. *Assumption*
c. *Chattel mortgage*
d. *Covenant of insurance*
e. *Defeasance clause*
f. *Deficiency judgment*
g. *Equitable mortgage*
h. *Equity of redemption*
i. *Foreclosure suit*
j. *Junior mortgage*
k. *Mortgage*
l. *Mortgagor*
m. *Nonconforming*
n. *Partial release*
o. *Power of sale*
p. *Promissory note*
q. *Satisfaction*
r. *Statutory redemption*
s. *Subject to*
t. *Subordination*

1. A pledge of property to secure the repayment of a debt.
2. A clause in a mortgage stating that the mortgage is defeated if the borrower repays the accompanying note on time.
3. The borrower's right, prior to the day of foreclosure, to repay the balance due on a delinquent loan.
4. A lawsuit filed by a lender that asks a court to set a time limit on how long a borrower has to redeem his property.
5. An agreement that is considered to be a mortgage in its intent even though it may not follow the usual mortgage wording.
6. A pledge of personal property as security for a promissory note.
7. The evidence of debt; contains amount owed, interest rate, repayment schedule, and a promise to repay.
8. One who gives a mortgage pledging his property; the borrower.
9. A clause in a mortgage that permits the lender to demand full pay-

ment of the loan if the property changes ownership. Also called a due-on-sale clause.

10. A clause in a mortgage whereby the mortgagor agrees to keep mortgaged property adequately insured against destruction.
11. Discharge of a mortgage upon payment of the debt owed.
12. Release of a portion of a property from a mortgage.
13. The buyer personally obligates himself to repay an existing mortgage loan as a condition of the sale.
14. The buyer of an already mortgaged property makes the payments but does not take personal responsibility for the loan.
15. Any mortgage lower than a first mortgage in priority.
16. A loan on which the borrower is behind in his payments.
17. A clause in a mortgage that gives the mortgagee the right to conduct a foreclosure sale without first going to court.
18. A judgment against a borrower if the sale of pledged property at foreclosure does not bring in enough to pay the balance owing.
19. The right of a borrower, after a foreclosure sale, to reclaim his property by repaying his defaulted loan.
20. Voluntary acceptance of a lower mortgage priority position than one would otherwise be entitled to.

QUESTIONS AND PROBLEMS

1. Is a prepayment privilege to the advantage of the borrower or the lender?
2. What are the legal differences between lien theory and title theory?
3. How does strict foreclosure differ from foreclosure by sale? Which system does Minnesota use?
4. A large apartment complex serves as security for a first, a second, and a third mortgage. Which of these are considered junior mortgage(s)? Senior mortgage(s)?
5. Describe the procedure in Minnesota that is used in foreclosing a mortgage.
6. What do the laws of Minnesota allow real estate borrowers in the way of equitable and statutory redemption?
7. Do the laws of Minnesota allow a delinquent borrower adequate opportunity to recover his mortgaged real estate? Do you advocate more or less borrower protection than is presently available?
8. In a promissory note, who is the obligor? Who is the obligee?
9. Why does a mortgage lender insist on including covenants pertaining to insurance, property taxes and removal, in the mortgage?
10. What roles do a certificate of reduction and an estoppel certificate play in mortgage lending?

ADDITIONAL READINGS

Brueggeman, William B. and **Leo D. Stone.** *Real Estate Finance,* 6th ed. Homewood, Ill.: Richard D. Irwin, 1977. Chapters 2–6 deal with the legal nature of mortgages, kinds of mortgages, default, foreclosure, alternatives to default, and junior liens.

Dennis, Marshall. *Mortgage Lending Fundamentals and Practices.* Reston, Va.: Reston Publishing Co., 1980, 350 pages. Contains history, law, and practices of mortgage lending plus numerous reproductions of actual mortgage lending documents.

Kratovil, Robert and **Werner, Raymond.** *Modern Mortgage Law and Practice.* 2nd ed. Englewood Cliffs, N.J.: Prentice-Hall, 1981, 651 pages. Includes the history of mortgage law, types of mortgages, contents of a mortgage, subordination, foreclosure, redemption, and other mortgage topics.

Powell, Richard R. *The Law of Property.* New York: Matthew Bender, 1975, 7 volumes. Volume 3, Chapter 37, discusses in detail the history of mortgages, the creation of a mortgage, equitable mortgages, rights of the mortgagor and the mortgagee, foreclosure, deed in lieu of foreclosure, and statutory redemption.

Roberts, Paul E. "Deeds in Lieu of Foreclosure." *Real Estate Review,* Winter, 1979, pages 27–48. Author suggests that this alternative to foreclosure may involve a venture into uncharted legal areas. Discussion includes benefits, negotiation, title problems, insolvency problems, fraudulent transfers, and consideration.

Semenow, Robert W. *Questions and Answers on Real Estate,* 9th ed. Englewood Cliffs, N.J.: Prentice-Hall, 1978, 762 pages. Chapter 5 contains discussion and questions on the history of mortgages, various types of mortgages, rights of the mortgagee and mortgagor, and foreclosure.

Deed of Trust

KEY TERMS

Assignment of rents clause: wording that establishes the right to collect the rents from a property in the event the borrower does not repay the note
Beneficiary: one for whose benefit a trust is created; the lender in a deed of trust arrangement
Naked title: title that lacks the rights and privileges usually associated with ownership
Reconveyance: the return to the borrower of legal title to his property upon repayment of the debt against it
Release deed: a document used to reconvey title from the trustee back to the property owner once the debt has been paid
Deed of trust: a document resembling a mortgage that conveys legal title to a neutral third party as security for a debt
Trustee: one who holds property in trust for another
Trustor: one who creates a trust; the borrower in a deed of trust arrangement

The basic purpose of a **deed of trust,** also referred to as a **trust deed** or **deed in trust,** is the same as a mortgage. Real property is used as security for a debt; if the debt is not repaid, the property is sold and the proceeds are applied to the balance owed. In a few states (Georgia, for example), a security deed that is similar to a deed of trust is used for this purpose. The main legal difference between a deed of trust and a mortgage is diagrammed in Figure 10:1.Minnesota does not use the deed of trust. However because of its importance in other states in which you may have transactions, the topic is included here.

PARTIES TO A DEED OF TRUST

Figure 10:1A shows that when a debt is secured by a mortgage the borrower delivers his promissory note and mortgage to the lender, who keeps them until the debt is paid. But when a note is secured by a deed of trust, three parties are involved: the borrower (the **trustor**), the lender (the **beneficiary**), and a neutral third party (the **trustee**). The lender makes a loan to the borrower, and the borrower gives the lender a promissory note (like the one shown in Chapter 9) and a deed of trust. In the deed of trust document, the borrower conveys title to the trustee, to be held in trust until the note is paid in full.

The deed of trust is recorded in the county where the property is located and then is usually given to the lender for safekeeping. A variation used in some areas of the country is to deliver the recorded deed of trust to the trustee to be held in a long-term escrow until the note is paid in full. Anyone searching the title records on the borrower's property would find the deed of trust conveying title to the trustee. This would alert the title searcher to the existence of a debt against the property.

The title that the borrower grants to the trustee is sometimes referred to as a "naked" or "bare" title, because the borrower still retains the usual rights of an owner such as the right to occupy and use the property, and the right to sell it. The title held by the trustee is limited only to what is necessary to carry out the terms of the trust. In fact, as long as the note is not in default, the trustee's title lies dormant. The lender does not receive title, but only a right that allows him to request the trustee to act.

RECONVEYANCE

Referring to Figure 10:1B, we see that when the note is repaid in full under a regular mortgage, the lender cancels the note and issues the borrower a mortgage satisfaction or release. Upon recordation, this document informs the world at large that the mortgage is nullified and no longer encumbers the property. Under the deed of trust arrangement, the lender sends to the trustee the note, the deed of trust, and a **request for reconveyance.** The trustee cancels the note and issues to the borrower a **reconveyance deed,** or a **release deed,** which reconveys title back to the borrower. The borrower records this document to inform the world that the trustee no longer has title. At the recorder's office, a marginal note is made on the record copy of the original deed of trust to show it has been discharged.

If a borrower defaults under a deed of trust, the lender delivers the deed of trust to the trustee and instructs him to sell the property and pay the balance due on the note. The trustee can do this because of two important features found in the deed of trust. First, by virtue of signing the deed of trust, the borrower has already conveyed title to the trustee. Second, the power of sale clause found in a deed of trust gives the trustee the authority to sell the pledged property without having to go through a court-ordered foreclosure proceeding.

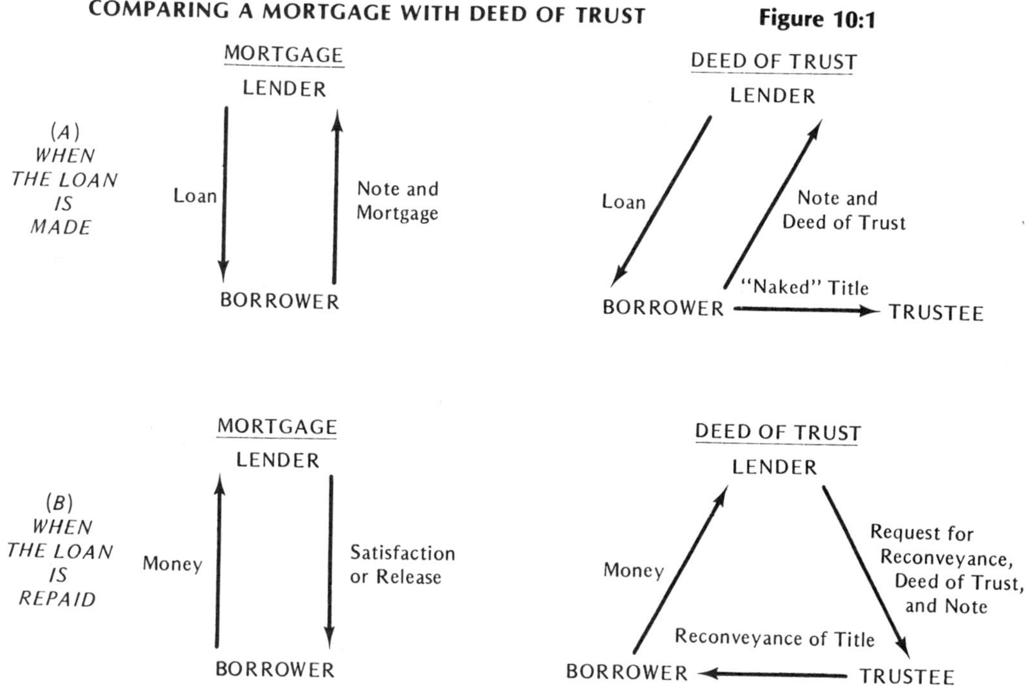

In nearly all states, a title, trust, or escrow company or the trust department of a bank, may act as trustee. An individual can be named as a trustee in most jurisdictions. However, this can present a problem if the person dies before reconveyance is made. Therefore, a corporate trustee is preferred because its life span is not limited by the human life span. In a few jurisdictions, Colorado for example, the role of trustee is performed by a government official known as a **public trustee.** Whether public or private, the trustee is expected to be neutral and fair to both the borrower and lender. To accomplish this, the trustee carefully abides by the agreements found in the deed of trust.

THE DOCUMENT

Figure 10:2 is a simplified example of a deed of trust that shows the agreements between the borrower and lender and states the responsibilities of the trustee. Beginning at ①, the document is identified as a deed of trust. This is followed by the date of its execution and the names of the trustor, beneficiary, and trustee. For discussion purposes, this chapter will continue to refer to them as the borrower, lender, and trustee, respectively.

At ②, the promissory note that accompanies this deed of trust is identified, and, it is clearly stated that the purpose of this deed is to provide security for that note. In other words, although this deed grants and conveys title to the trustee at ③, it is understood that the quantity of title the trustee receives is only that which is necessary to protect the note. This permits the borrower to continue to possess and enjoy the use of the property as long as the promissory note is not in default.

Figure 10:2

DEED OF TRUST WITH POWER OF SALE

①*This Deed of Trust, made this* 15th *day of* April *, 19* xx *, between* Fred and Mary Olsen, Husband and Wife *, herein called the Trustor, and* Blue Sky Mortgage Company, *herein called the Beneficiary, and* Safety Title and Trust Co., Inc. *herein called the Trustee.*

② *WITNESSETH: To secure the repayment of one promissory note in the principal sum of $* 70,000 *executed by the Trustor in favor of the Beneficiary and bearing the same date as this Deed, and to secure the agreements shown below, the Trustor irrevocably* ③ *grants and conveys to the Trustee, in trust, with* ④ *power of sale, the following described real property in the County of* San Juan *, State of* ________________.

⑤*Lot 21, Block "A," of Tract 2468, as shown in Map Book 29, Page 17, filed in the Public Records Office of the above County and State.*

⑥*FURTHERMORE: The trustor warrants the title to said property and will defend the same against all claims.*

⑦*UPON WRITTEN REQUEST by the Beneficiary to the Trustee stating that all sums secured hereby have been paid, and upon surrender of this Deed and said Note to the Trustee for cancellation, the Trustee shall reconvey the above described property to the Trustor.*

⑧*THIS DEED BINDS all parties hereto, their successors, assigns, heirs, devisees, administrators, and executors.*

Figure 10:2 *continued*

⑨UNTIL SAID NOTE IS PAID IN FULL:

A. The Trustor agrees to pay all taxes on said property.

B. The Trustor agrees not to remove or demolish any buildings or other improvements on said property without the approval of the Beneficiary.

C. The Trustor agrees to carry adequate insurance to protect the Beneficiary in the event of damage or destruction of said property.

D. The Trustor agrees to keep the mortgaged property in good repair and not permit waste or deterioration.

E. The Beneficiary shall have the right to inspect said property as may be necessary for the security of the Note.

F. If all or part of said property is taken by eminent domain, any money received shall be applied to the Note.

UPON DEFAULT BY THE TRUSTOR in payment of the debt secured hereby, or the nonperformance of any agreement hereby made, the Beneficiary:

G. May declare all sums secured hereby immediately due and payable.

⑩H. May enter and take possession of said property and collect the rents and profits thereof.

⑪I. May demand the Trustee sell said property in accordance with state law, apply the proceeds to the unpaid portion of the Note, and deliver to the purchaser a Trustee's Deed conveying title to said property.

⑫THE TRUSTEE ACCEPTS THIS TRUST when this Deed, properly executed and acknowledged, is made a public record. The Beneficiary may substitute a successor to the Trustee named herein by recording such change in the public records of the county where said property is located.

⑬ *Mary Olsen*
Trustor

Fred Olsen
Trustor

⑭ [acknowledgment of trustor's signature is placed here.]

POWER OF SALE

Under the power of sale clause shown at ④, if the borrower defaults, the trustee has the right to foreclose and sell the pledged property and convey ownership to the purchaser. If the borrower does not default, this power lies dormant. The presence of a power of sale right does not prohibit the trustee from using a court-ordered foreclosure. If the rights of the parties involved, including junior debt holders and other claimants, are not clear, the trustee can request a court-ordered foreclosure.

At ⑤, the property being conveyed to the trustee is described, and at ⑥ the borrower states that he has title to the property and he will defend that title against the claims of others. At ⑦, the procedure that must be followed to reconvey the title is described. Note that state laws provide that, when the note is paid, the lender must deliver a request for reconveyance to the trustee. The lender must also deliver the promissory note and deed of trust to the trustee. Upon receiving these three items, the trustee reconveys title to the borrower and the trust arrangement is terminated. (A sample reconveyance request is illustrated in Figure 10:3.)

Figure 10:3

REQUEST FOR FULL RECONVEYANCE

To: Safety Title and Trust Company, Inc., *trustee.*
The undersigned is the owner of the debt secured by the above Deed of Trust. This debt has been fully paid and you are requested to reconvey to the parties designated in the Deed of Trust, the estate now held by you under same.

____
Beneficiary

Date ____________

[as a matter of convenience, this form is often printed at the bottom or on the reverse of the trust deed itself]

Continuing in Figure 10:2, the sections identified at ⑧ and ⑨ (paragraphs A through G) are similar to those found in a regular mortgage. They were discussed in Chapter 9 and will not be repeated here. At ⑩, the lender reserves the right to take physical possession of the pledged property, operate it, and collect any rents or income generated by it. The right to collect rents in the event of default is called an **assignment of rents** clause. The lender would only exercise this right if the borrower continued to collect rental income from the property without paying on the note. The right to take physical possession in the event of default is important because it gives the lender the opportunity to preserve the value of the property until the foreclosure sale takes place. Very likely, if the borrower has defaulted on the note, his financial condition is such that he is no longer maintaining the property. If this continues, the property will be less valuable by the time the foreclosure sale occurs.

FORECLOSURE

At ⑪, the lender establishes his right to instruct the trustee to sell the pledged property in the event of the borrower's default on the note or nonperformance of the agreements in the deed of trust. This section also sets forth the rules which the trustee is to follow if he conducts the foreclosure sale. Either appropriate state laws are referred to or each step of the process is listed in the deed at this point. Generally, state laws regarding power of sale foreclosure require that (1) the lender demonstrate conclusively to the trustee that there is reason to cut off the borrower's interest in the property, (2) a notice of default be filed with the public recorder, (3) the notice of default be followed by a 90- to 120-day waiting period before sale advertising begins, (4) advertising of the proposed foreclosure sale occur for at least 3 weeks in public places and a local newspaper, (5) the sale itself be a public auction held in the county where the property is located, and (6) the purchaser at the sale be given a trustee's deed conveying all title held by the trustee. This is all the right, title, and interest the borrower had at the time he deeded his property, in trust, to the trustee. Proceeds from the sale are used to pay (1) the expenses of the sale and any unpaid property taxes, (2) the lender, (3) any junior claims, and (4) the borrower, in that order. Once the sale is held, the borrower's equitable right of redemption is ended. In some states, statutory redemption may still exist. Anyone can bid at the sale, including the borrower. However, junior claims that would normally be cut off by the sale are not extinguished if the borrower is the successful bidder.

Trusteeship

The wording at ⑫ reflects what is called the **automatic form** of trusteeship. The trustee is named in the deed of trust, but is not personally notified of the appointment. In fact, the trustee is not usually aware of the appointment until called upon to either reconvey or proceed under the power of sale provision. The alternative method is called the **accepted form:** the trustee is notified in advance and either accepts or rejects the appointment. Its primary advantage is that it provides positive acceptance of appointment. The main advantage of the automatic form is that it is faster and easier. In the event the trustee cannot or will not perform when called upon by the lender, the wording at ⑫ permits the lender to name a substitute trustee. This would be necessary if an individual appointed as a trustee had died, or a corporate trustee was dissolved, or an appointed trustee refused to perform. Finally, the borrowers sign at ⑬, their signatures are acknowledged at ⑭, and the deed of trust is recorded in the county where the property is located.

JURISDICTIONS USING DEEDS OF TRUST

The deed of trust is used almost exclusively in place of regular mortgages in California, the District of Columbia, Mississippi, Missouri, Tennessee, Texas, and West Virginia. They are also used to a certain extent in Alabama, Alaska, Colorado, Delaware, Illinois, Montana, Nevada, New Mexico, North Carolina, Oregon, Utah, Virginia, Washington, and a few other states. The extent of their use in a state is governed by that state's attitude toward conveyance of title to the trustee, power of sale, and statutory redemption privileges. Many states not listed here allow the use of a deed of trust, but consider it to be a lien. As such it is treated no differently than a mortgage with a power of sale clause.

A few states recognize some, but not all, of the provisions of a deed of trust. For example, a state may allow a power of sale clause in a deed of trust, but not in a regular mortgage. Or it may rule that a foreclosed mortgage must have a statutory redemption period while a deed of trust does not. In those states that allow all the provisions of a deed of trust to function without hindrance, the deed of trust has flourished. In California, for example, where it is well established legally that a trust deed does convey title to the trustee, that the trustee has the power of sale, and that there is no statutory redemption on trust deeds, trust deed recordings outnumber regular mortgages by a ratio of more than 500 to 1.

ADVANTAGES OF THE DEED OF TRUST

The popularity of the deed of trust can be traced to the following attributes: (1) if a borrower defaults, the lender can take possession of the pledged property to protect it and collect the rents; (2) the time between default and foreclosure is relatively short, on the order of 90 to 180 days; (3) the foreclosure process under the power of sale provision is far less expensive and complex than a court-ordered foreclosure; (4) title is already in the name of the trustee, thus permitting him to grant title to the purchaser after the foreclosure sale; and (5) once the foreclosure sale takes place, there is usually no statutory redemption. These are primarily advantages to the lender, but such advantages have attracted lenders and made real estate loans easier for borrowers to obtain and less expensive. Some states prohibit deficiency judgments against borrowers when a deed of trust is used.

Property can be purchased "subject to" an existing deed of trust or it can be "assumed," just as with a regular mortgage. Debt priorities are established as for mortgages: there are first and second, senior and junior trust deeds. Deeds of trust can be subordinated and partial releases are possible.

VOCABULARY REVIEW

Match terms **a–f** *with statements* **1–6.**

a. *Beneficiary*
b. *Public trustee*
c. *Reconveyance*
d. *Deed of trust*
e. *Trustee*
f. *Trustor*

1. A document that conveys legal title to a neutral third party as security for a loan.
2. One who creates a trust; the borrower under a deed of trust.
3. The lender.
4. One who holds property in trust for another.
5. Transfer of title from the trustee to the trustor.
6. A publicly appointed official who acts as a trustee in some states.

QUESTIONS AND PROBLEMS

1. How does a deed of trust differ from a mortgage?
2. Does possession of a deed of trust give the trustee any rights of entry or use of the property in question as long as the promissory note is not in default? Explain.
3. What role does a request for reconveyance play?
4. What is the purpose of a power of sale clause in a deed of trust?
5. Explain the purpose of an assignment of rents clause.
6. How does the automatic form of trusteeship differ from the accepted form?
7. What is Minnesota's attitude toward trust deeds, power of sale, statutory redemption, and deficiency judgments?

ADDITIONAL READINGS

California Department of Real Estate. *Reference Book*. Sacramento: Department of Real Estate, 1979. Contains a section where trust deeds are discussed and compared to mortgages.

Case, Frederick E., and **Clapp, John M.** *Real Estate Financing.* New York: John Wiley & Sons, 1978, 417 pages. Book is designed as a college text, as a reference for practitioners, and as a guide for real estate borrowers. Topics include financing risks, sources of funds, tax law influences, borrower analysis, property analysis, finance law, forecasting, etc.

Powell, Richard R. *The Law of Property.* New York: Matthew Bender, 1975, 7 volumes. Volume 3, Section 439, and Volume 4A, Section 574, explain the deed of trust and its use and application from a legal point of view.

Thompson, George W. *Commentaries on the Modern Law of Real Property.* Indianapolis: Bobbs-Merrill, 1963 (plus 1979 supplement), 13 volumes. Volume 9, Chapter 59, discusses the use of trust deeds in place of mortgages. Volume 10, Chapters 73 and 74, deal with enforcing trust deeds and mortgages.

Unger, Maurice A., and **Melicher, Ronald W.** *Real Estate Finance.* Cincinnati: South-Western Publishing Co., 1978, 391 pages. Book provides the reader with a basic understanding of the institutions and instruments important to financing real estate. Topics include debt instruments, seller financing, interest rates, special purpose financing, sources of funds, loan application, foreclosure, etc. Two finance cases are included.

11

Lending Practices

KEY TERMS

Amortized loan: a loan requiring periodic payments that include both interest and partial repayment of principal

Balloon loan: any loan in which the final payment is larger than the preceding payments

Conventional loans: real estate loans that are not insured by the FHA or guaranteed by the VA

Equity: the market value of a property less the debt against it

Impound or reserve account: an account into which the lender places monthly tax and insurance payments

PITI payment: a loan payment that combines principal, interest, taxes, and insurance

Point: one percent of the loan amount; one-hundredth of the total amount of a mortgage loan

Principal: the balance owing on a loan

Purchase money mortgage: a loan used to purchase the real property that serves as the loan collateral

Take-out loan: a permanent loan arranged to replace a construction loan

The previous two chapters were primarily devoted to the legal aspects of mortgages and trust deeds. In this and the following chapter we focus on the financial side of real estate lending. Let us begin by looking at the three basic patterns that mortgage loan repayments can follow: (1) term, (2) amortized, or (3) partially amortized.

TERM LOANS

A loan that requires only interest payments until the last day of its life, at which time the full amount borrowed is due, is called a **term loan** (or straight loan). Until 1930, the term loan was the standard method of financing real estate in the United States. These loans were typically made for a period of 3 to 5 years. The borrower signed a note or bond agreeing (1) to pay the lender interest on the loan every 6 months and (2) to repay the entire amount of the loan upon **maturity**; that is, at the end of the life of the loan. As security, the borrower mortgaged his property to the lender.

Loan Renewal

In practice, most real estate term loans were not paid off when they matured. Instead, the borrower asked the lender, typically a bank prior to the 1930s, to renew the loan for another 3 to 5 years. The major flaw in this approach to lending was that the borrower might never own his property free and clear of debt. This left him continuously at the mercy of the lender for renewals. As long as the lender was not pressed for funds, the borrower's renewal request was granted. However, if the lender was short of funds, no renewal was granted and the borrower was expected to pay in full. The borrower might then go to another lender. But there have been periods during America's economic history when loans have been difficult to obtain from any source. If the borrower's loan came due during one of these periods, going to other lenders did not solve the borrower's problem. With the borrower unable to repay, the lender foreclosed and applied the sale proceeds to the amount due on the loan.

The inability to renew a term loan was the cause of hardship to thousands of property owners during the first 155 years of U.S. history, but at no time were the consequences so harsh as during the Great Depression that began in 1930 and lasted most of the decade. Banks were unable to accommodate requests for loan renewals and at the same time satisfy unemployed depositors who needed to withdraw their savings to live. As a result, owners of homes, farms, office buildings, factories, and vacant land lost their property as foreclosures reached into the millions. So glutted was the market with properties being offered for sale to satisfy unpaid mortgage loans that real estate prices fell at a sickening pace.

AMORTIZED LOANS

In 1933, a congressionally legislated Home Owner's Loan Corporation (HOLC) was created to assist financially distressed homeowners by acquiring mortgages that were about to be foreclosed. The HOLC then offered monthly repayment plans tailored to fit the homeowner's budget and aimed at repaying the loan in full by its maturity date without the need for a balloon payment. The HOLC was terminated in 1951 after rescuing over 1 million mortgages in its 18-year life. However, the use of this stretched-out repayment plan, known as an **amortized loan,** took hold in American real estate, and today it is the accepted method of loan repayment.

Repayment Methods

The amortized loan requires regular equal payments during the life of the loan, of sufficient size and number, to pay all

Figure 11:1

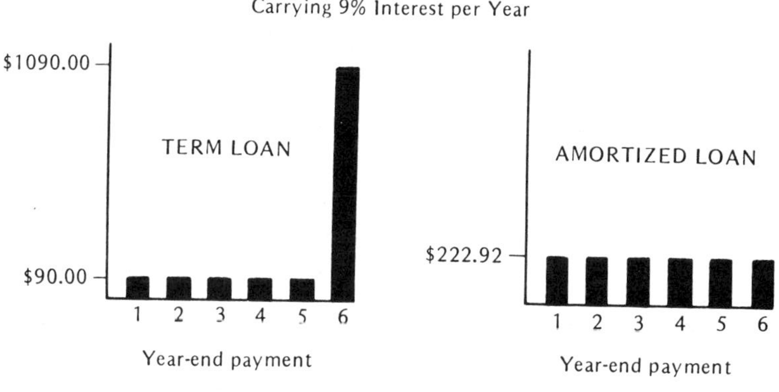

(A) Total payments = $1,540.00 (B) Total payments = $1,337.52

interest due on the loan and reduce the amount owed to zero by the loan's maturity date. Figure 11:1 illustrates the contrast between an amortized and a term loan. Figure 11:1A shows a 6-year, $1,000 term loan with interest of $90 due each year of its life. At the end of the sixth year the entire **principal** (the amount owed) is due in one lump sum payment along with the final interest payment. In Figure 11:1B, the same $1,000 loan is fully amortized by making six equal annual payments of $222.92. From the borrower's standpoint, $222.92 once each year is easier to budget than $90 for 5 years and $1,090 in the sixth year.

Furthermore, the amortized loan shown in Figure 11:1 actually costs the borrower less than the term loan. The total payments made under the term loan are $90 + $90 + $90 + $90 + $90 + $1,090 = $1,540. Amortizing the same loan requires total payments of 6 × $222.92 = $1,337.52. The difference is due to the fact that under the amortized loan the borrower begins to pay back part of the $1,000 principal with his first payment. In the first year, $90 of the $222.92 payment goes to interest and the remaining $132.92 reduces the principal owed. Thus, the borrower starts the second year owing only $867.08. At 9% interest per year, the interest on $867.08 is $78.04; therefore, when the borrower makes his second payment of $222.92, only $78.04 goes to interest. The remaining $144.88 is applied to reduce the loan balance, and the borrower starts the third year owing $722.20.

Figure 11:2 charts this repayment program. Notice that

Figure 11:2 **REPAYING A 6-YEAR $1,000 AMORTIZED LOAN**

Carrying 9% Interest per Year

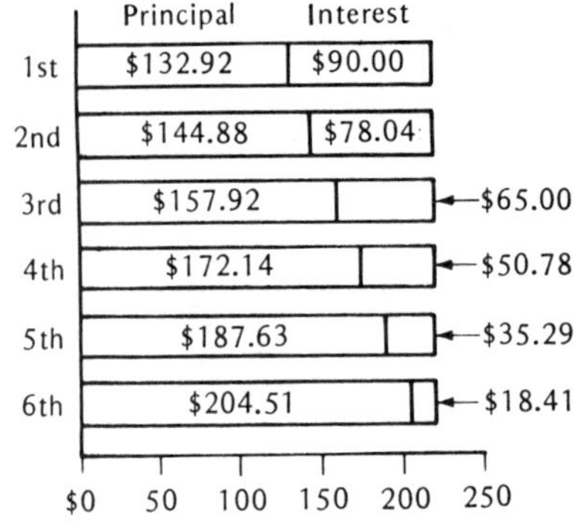

(A) Allocation of each annual payment to principal and interest

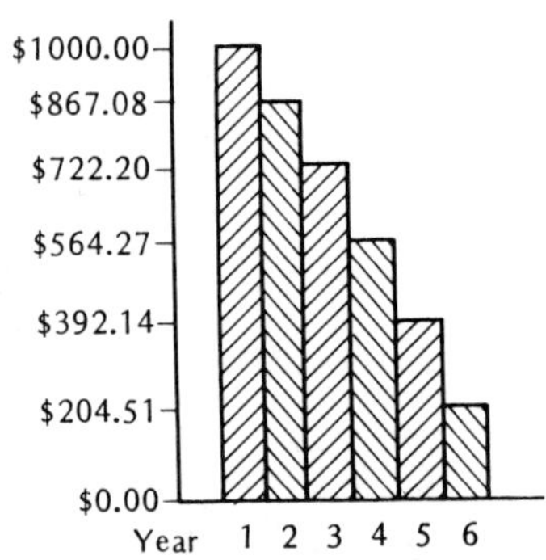

(B) Balance owed during each year of the loan.

as the loan balance is reduced, the interest that must be paid is reduced, thus allowing a larger and larger portion of each successive payment to be used to reduce the loan balance. As a result, the balance owed drops faster as the loan becomes older; that is, matures.

Monthly Payments

As you can see, calculating the payments on a term loan is relatively simple compared to calculating amortized loan payments. As a result, amortization payment tables are published and used throughout the real estate industry. Table 11:1 shows the monthly payments per $1,000 of loan for interest rates from 5% to 25% for periods ranging from 5 to 40 years. (Amortization tables are also published for quarterly, semiannual, and annual payments.) When you use an amortization table, notice that there are five variables: (1) frequency of payment, (2) interest rate, (3) maturity, (4) amount of the loan, and (5) amount of the periodic payment. If you know any four of these, you can obtain the fifth variable from the tables. For example, suppose that you want to know the monthly payment necessary to amortize a $60,000 loan over 30 years at 10½% interest. The first step is to look in Table 11:1 for the 10½% line. Then locate the 30-year column. Where they cross, you will find the necessary monthly payment per $1,000: $9.15. Next multiply $9.15 by 60 to get the monthly payment for a

$60,000 loan: $549. If the loan is to be $67,500, then multiply $9.15 by 67.5 to get the monthly payment: $617.63.

Suppose the interest rate is 12%, the maturity is 35 years, and the amount of the loan is $100,000. Table 11:1 shows the monthly payment per $1,000 to be $10.16. Multiply this by 100 for a $100,000 loan and you get $1,016 as the monthly payment. At 13% interest this loan would cost $1,096 per month; at 14% it would cost $1,176 per month, and at 15% it would cost $1,257 per month.

Loan Size

Amortization tables are most often used to find the payments needed to repay a loan. However, they can also be used in a number of other ways. Suppose that a prospective home buyer can afford monthly principal and interest payments of $650 and lenders are making 30-year loans at 10¾%. How large a loan can this buyer afford? In Table 11:1 find where the 10¾% line and the 30-year column meet. You will see 9.34 there. This means that every $9.34 of monthly payment will support $1,000 of loan. To find how many thousands of dollars $650 per month will support, just divide $650 by $9.34. The answer is 69.593 thousands or $69,593. By adding the buyer's down payment, you know what price property he can afford to purchase.

Maturity

With amortization tables you can find the number of years necessary to repay a loan when you know the interest, loan amount, and the periodic payment. For example, if the amount to be borrowed is $200,000, the interest rate is 11½% and the monthly payments are $2,034, how long will it take to repay the loan? Divide $2,034 by $200 to get the rate per thousand: $10.17. Then look for $10.17 on the 11½% line. You will see that it falls in the 25-year column. So your answer is 25 years.

Interest Rates

An amortization table can also help you find the interest rate when you know the length of the loan, the loan amount, and the monthly payment. Again, the first thing you do is to find the monthly payment per thousand by dividing the loan payment by the loan size in thousands. Given a 20-year, $50,000 loan with monthly payments of $450, you first divide

Table 11:1

AMORTIZATION TABLE
MONTHLY PAYMENT PER $1,000 OF LOAN

Interest Rate per Year	Life of the Loan							
	5 years	10 years	15 years	20 years	25 years	30 years	35 years	40 years
5%	$18.88	$10.61	$ 7.91	$ 6.60	$ 5.85	$ 5.37	$ 5.05	$ 4.83
5½	19.11	10.86	8.18	6.88	6.15	5.68	5.38	5.16
6	19.34	11.11	8.44	7.17	6.45	6.00	5.71	5.51
6½	19.57	11.36	8.72	7.46	6.76	6.32	6.05	5.86
7	19.81	11.62	8.99	7.76	7.07	6.66	6.39	6.22
7½	20.04	11.88	9.28	8.06	7.39	7.00	6.75	6.59
8	20.28	12.14	9.56	8.37	7.72	7.34	7.11	6.96
8½	20.52	12.40	9.85	8.68	8.06	7.69	7.47	7.34
9	20.76	12.67	10.15	9.00	8.40	8.05	7.84	7.72
9½	21.01	12.94	10.45	9.33	8.74	8.41	8.22	8.11
10	21.25	13.22	10.75	9.66	9.09	8.78	8.60	8.50
10½	21.50	13.50	11.06	9.99	9.45	9.15	8.99	8.89
11	21.75	13.78	11.37	10.33	9.81	9.53	9.37	9.29
11½	22.00	14.06	11.69	10.67	10.17	9.91	9.77	9.69
12	22.25	14.35	12.01	11.02	10.54	10.29	10.16	10.09
12½	22.50	14.64	12.33	11.37	10.91	10.68	10.56	10.49
13	22.76	14.94	12.66	11.72	11.28	11.07	10.96	10.90
13½	23.01	15.23	12.99	12.08	11.66	11.46	11.36	11.31
14	23.27	15.53	13.32	12.44	12.04	11.85	11.76	11.72
14½	23.53	15.83	13.66	12.80	12.43	12.25	12.17	12.13
15	23.79	16.14	14.00	13.17	12.81	12.65	12.57	12.54
15½	24.06	16.45	14.34	13.54	13.20	13.05	12.98	12.95
16	24.32	16.76	14.69	13.92	13.59	13.45	13.39	13.36
16½	24.59	17.07	15.04	14.29	13.99	13.85	13.80	13.77
17	24.86	17.38	15.39	14.67	14.38	14.26	14.21	14.19
17½	25.13	17.70	15.75	15.05	14.78	14.67	14.62	14.60
18	25.40	18.02	16.11	15.44	15.18	15.08	15.03	15.02
18½	25.67	18.35	16.47	15.82	15.58	15.48	15.45	15.43
19	25.95	18.67	16.83	16.21	15.98	15.89	15.86	15.85
19½	26.22	19.00	17.20	16.60	16.38	16.30	16.27	16.26
20	26.50	19.33	17.57	16.99	16.79	16.72	16.69	16.68
20½	26.78	19.66	17.94	17.39	17.19	17.13	17.10	17.09
21	27.06	20.00	18.31	17.78	17.60	17.54	17.52	17.51
21½	27.34	20.34	18.69	18.18	18.01	17.95	17.93	17.92
22	27.62	20.67	19.06	18.57	18.42	18.36	18.35	18.34
22½	27.91	21.02	19.44	18.97	18.83	18.78	18.76	18.75
23	28.20	21.36	19.82	19.37	19.24	19.19	19.18	19.17
23½	28.48	21.70	20.20	19.78	19.65	19.61	19.59	19.59
24	28.77	22.05	20.59	20.18	20.06	20.02	20.01	20.01
24½	29.06	22.40	20.97	20.58	20.47	20.43	20.42	20.42
25	29.36	22.75	21.36	20.99	20.88	20.85	20.84	20.84

$450 by 50 to get the monthly payment per thousand: $9.00. In the 20 year column, this is opposite 9% interest.

As you have noticed, everything in Table 11:1 is on a monthly payment per thousand basis. With a full book of amortization tables rather than one page, it is possible to check on monthly payments for loans from $100 to $100,000, to determine loan maturities for each year from 1 to 40 years, and to calculate many more interest rates. Books of this type are available from most real estate lenders and from the Financial Publishing Company in Boston.

Change in Maturity Date

An amortization table also shows the impact on the size of the monthly payment when the life of a loan is extended. For example, at 11% interest, a 10-year loan requires a monthly payment of $13.78 per thousand of loan. Increasing the life of the loan to 20 years drops the monthly payment to $10.33 per $1,000. Extending the loan payback to 30 years reduces the monthly payment to $9.53 per thousand. The smaller monthly payment is why 30 years is a popular loan with borrowers. Note, however, that going beyond 30 years does not significantly reduce the monthly payment. Going from 30 to 35 years reduces the monthly payment by only 16¢ per thousand but adds 5 years of monthly payments. Extending the payback period from 35 to 40 years reduces the monthly payment by just 8¢ per $1,000 ($4 per month on a $50,000 loan) and adds another 60 months of payments at $464.50 per month.

At still higher interest rates the reduction is even less impressive: at 12% interest, a $100,000 loan for 30 years requires monthly payments of $1,029; at 35 years it is $1,016; and at 40 years it is $1,009. Since the interest on this loan amounts to $1,000 per month, you can readily see why there is a limit as to how far the monthly payment can be reduced by extending its maturity. As a practical matter, amortized real estate loans are seldom made for more than 30 years. This practical limit is also affected by the life span of the property being mortgaged. As a rule of thumb, lenders do not like to lend for longer than three-quarters of the remaining useful life of a building. This permits a 30-year loan on a property with 40 remaining useful years and a 15-year loan on a property with only 20 remaining years.

BUDGET MORTGAGE

The **budget mortgage** takes the amortized loan one step further. In addition to collecting the monthly principal and interest payment (often called P + I), the lender collects one-twelfth of the estimated cost of the annual property taxes and hazard insurance on the mortgaged property. The money for tax and insurance payments is placed in an **escrow account** (also called an **impound** or **reserve account**). When taxes and insurance payments are due, the lender pays them. Thus, the lender makes certain that the value of the pledged property will not be undermined by unpaid property taxes or by uninsured fire or weather damage. This form of mortgage also helps the borrower to budget for property taxes and insurance on a monthly basis. To illustrate, if insurance is $240 per year and property taxes are $1800 per year, the lender collects an additional $20 and $150 each month along with the regular principal and interest payments. This combined principal, interest, taxes, and insurance payment is often referred to as a **PITI payment.**

BALLOON LOAN

A **balloon loan** is any loan which has a final payment that is larger than any of the previous payments on the loan. The final payment is called a **balloon payment.** The term loan described at the beginning of this chapter is a type of balloon loan. Partially amortized loans, discussed next, are also a type of balloon loan. In the tight money markets of recent years, the use of balloon loans has increased considerably. Balloon loans with maturities as short as 3 to 5 years have been commonplace. This, in effect, gives the buyer (borrower) 3 to 5 years to find cheaper and longer-term financing elsewhere. If such financing does not materialize and the loan is not repaid on time, the lender, usually the seller, has the right to foreclose. The alternative is for the lender and borrower to agree to an extension of the loan, usually at prevailing interest rates.

PARTIALLY AMORTIZED LOANS

When the repayment schedule of a loan calls for a series of amortized payments followed by a balloon payment at maturity, it is called a **partially amortized loan.** For example, a lender might agree to a 30-year amortization schedule with a provision that at the end of the tenth year all the remaining principal be paid in a single balloon payment. The advantage to the borrower is that for 10 years his monthly payments

Table 11:2 **BALANCE OWING ON A $1,000 AMORTIZED LOAN**

9½% Annual Interest

Age of loan (years)	Original Life (years) 10	15	20	25	30	35
2	$868	$934	$963	$978	$987	$992
4	708	853	918	952	971	983
6	515	756	864	921	953	971
8	282	639	799	883	930	957
10		497	720	837	902	940
12		326	625	781	869	920
14		119	510	714	828	896
16			371	633	780	866
18			203	535	721	830
20				416	650	787
22				273	564	735
24				100	460	671
26					335	595
28					183	503
30						391
32						256
34						94

11½% Annual Interest

Age of loan (years)	Original Life (years) 10	15	20	25	30	35
2	$880	$944	$971	$984	$991	$995
4	729	873	935	965	981	989
6	539	784	889	940	967	982
8	300	672	831	909	950	972
10		531	759	870	929	960
12		354	667	821	902	945
14		132	553	759	868	926
16			409	682	825	903
18			228	585	772	873
20				462	704	836
22				308	620	789
24				115	513	729
26					380	655
28					211	561
30						444
32						296
34						110

13½% Annual Interest

Age of loan (years)	Original Life (years) 10	15	20	25	30	35
2	$891	$953	$977	$989	$994	$997
4	749	890	948	974	987	993
6	562	809	909	955	978	989
8	319	703	859	930	965	982
10		564	793	898	949	974
12		383	707	855	927	963
14		145	593	799	899	949
16			446	727	862	930
18			253	631	815	906
20				507	752	874
22				343	670	833
24				130	563	779
26					423	708
28					240	615
30						493
32						335
34						127

15½% Annual Interest

Age of loan (years)	Original Life (years) 10	15	20	25	30	35
2	$902	$960	$983	$992	$996	$998
4	768	906	959	981	992	996
6	585	833	927	967	985	993
8	337	732	883	947	976	989
10		596	823	920	964	983
12		411	742	884	947	975
14		158	632	834	924	965
16			482	766	893	951
18			278	674	850	931
20				549	793	905
22				378	715	869
24				146	609	820
26					464	753
28					268	663
30						539
32						372
34						143

will be smaller than if he completely amortized his loan in 10 years. (You can verify this in Table 11:1.) However, the disadvantage is that the balloon payment due at the end of the tenth year might be his financial downfall. Just how large that balloon payment will be can be determined in advance by using a **loan progress chart.** Presuming an interest rate of 15½% and a 30-year loan, at the end of 10 years the loan progress chart in Table 11:2 shows that for each $1,000 originally loaned, $964 would still be owed. If the original loan was for $100,000, at the end of 10 years 100 × $964 = $96,400 would be due as one payment. This qualifies it as a balloon loan.

A loan progress chart is not only useful for determining in advance the amount of the final payment in a partially amortized loan, but also for determining what portion of a fully amortized loan remains to be paid at any given moment in time. For example, a $10,000 amortized loan originally made for 30 years at 9½% interest is 6 years old. How much of the loan has been paid off and how much remains to be paid? In Table 11:2, enter the column marked "30" under the heading "original life in years." Then under "age of loan" find the 6-year line. Where they intersect you will find the number $953. This means that for each $1,000 of original loan, $953 remains to be paid. For a $10,000 loan, multiply by 10 and you will find that $9,530 remains to be paid. As you can see, on amortized loans with long maturities, relatively little of the debt is paid off during the initial years of the loan's life. Nearly all the early payments go for interest, so that little remains for principal reduction. For example, the loan progress chart shows that even after 16 years of payments on a 30-year, 11½% loan, 82½% of the loan is still unpaid. Not until this loan is about 6 years from maturity will half of it have been repaid.

PACKAGE MORTGAGE

Normally, we think of real estate mortgage loans as being secured solely by real estate. However, it is possible to include items classed as personal property in a real estate mortgage, thus creating a **package mortgage.** In residential loans, such items as the refrigerator, clothes washer and dryer can be pledged along with the house and land in a single mortgage. The purpose is to raise the value of the collateral in order to raise the amount a lender is willing to loan. For the borrower, it offers the opportunity of financing major appliances at the same rate of interest as the real estate itself. This rate is usually lower than if the borrower finances the appliances separately. Once an item of personal property is included in a package mortgage, it is a violation of the mortgage to sell it without the prior consent of the lender.

BLANKET MORTGAGE

A mortgage secured by two or more properties is called a **blanket mortgage.** Suppose you want to buy a house plus the vacant lot next door, financing the purchase with a single mortgage that covers both properties. The cost of preparing one mortgage instead of two is a savings. Also, by combining the house and lot, the lot can be financed on better terms than if it were financed separately, as lenders more readily loan on a house and land than on land alone. Note, however, if the vacant lot is later sold separately from the house before the mortgage loan is fully repaid, it will be necessary to have it released from the blanket mortgage. This is usually accomplished by including a release clause in the original mortgage agreement that specifies how much of the loan must be repaid before the lot can be released.

REFINANCING

When a mortgage allows a borrower to obtain further money advances at a later date, it is called an **open-end mortgage.** The amount of the advance is usually limited to the difference between the original loan amount and the current amount owing. Terms of repayment will depend on prevailing interest rates and the condition and value of the pledged property at the time of the advance.

The alternative is to **refinance** by obtaining a new loan that is large enough to pay off the existing loan and leave cash left over. Refinancing is a popular way of taking cash out of a property that has appreciated in value. For example, suppose you bought a house in 1970 for $40,000 using $10,000 cash down and a mortgage for $30,000. Today the house is worth $100,000 and the mortgage balance is $25,000. If you can qualify financially, you can get a new loan on the house for $75,000. This would pay off the $25,000 existing loan and leave $50,000 in your pocket. Your new payments would, however, be much larger and would be at current interest rates.

REVERSE MORTGAGE

With a regular mortgage, the lender makes a lump sum payment to the borrower, who in turn repays it through monthly payments to the lender. With a **reverse mortgage,** the lender makes a monthly payment to the homeowner who later repays in a lump sum. The reverse mortgage can be particularly valuable for an elderly homeowner who does not want to sell, but whose retirement income is not quite enough for comfortable living. The homeowner receives a monthly check, has full use of the property, and is not required to repay until he sells or dies. If he sells his home, money from the sale is taken to repay the loan. If he dies first, his property is sold through the estate and the loan repaid.

CONSTRUCTION LOANS

Under a **construction loan,** also called an interim loan, money is advanced as construction takes place. For example, a vacant lot owner arranges to borrow $60,000 to build a house. The lender does not advance all $60,000 at once because the value of the collateral is insufficient to warrant that amount until the house is finished. Instead, the lender will parcel out the loan as the building is being constructed, always holding a portion until the property is ready for occupancy, or in some cases actually occupied. Some lenders specialize only in construction loans and do not want to wait 20 or 30 years to be repaid. If so, it will be necessary to obtain a permanent long-term mortgage from another source for the purpose of repaying the construction loan. This is known as a permanent commitment or a **take-out loan,** since it takes the construction lender out of the financial picture when construction is completed and allows him to recycle his money into new construction projects.

PURCHASE MONEY MORTGAGES

A loan used to purchase the real property that serves as its collateral is called a **purchase money mortgage** or, in trust deed states, a **purchase money deed of trust.** Most real estate loans made in connection with a sale fall into this category. For example, an investor buys a $2 million apartment building with a cash down payment of $400,000 and the cash he receives from a $1.6 million mortgage loan for which he pledges the building as security. The $1.6 million loan is called a purchase money mortgage.

A purchase money mortgage or deed of trust is also created

when a seller agrees to accept part of the purchase price in the form of a promissory note or bond accompanied by a mortgage or deed of trust. For instance, suppose that you are interested in buying a $100,000 farm. The seller owns the property free and clear of all debt and offers to deed title to you if you give him $20,000 in cash and your promissory note for the remaining $80,000, secured by a mortgage against the farm.

LOAN-TO-VALUE RATIO

The relationship between the amount of money a lender is willing to loan and the lender's estimate of the fair market value of the property that will be pledged as security is called the **loan-to-value ratio** (often abbreviated **L/V ratio**). For example, a prospective home buyer wants to purchase a house priced at $80,000. A local lender appraises the house, finds it has a fair market value of $80,000, and agrees to make an 80% L/V loan. This means that the lender will loan up to 80% of the $80,000 and the buyer must provide at least 20% in cash. In dollars, the lender will loan up to $64,000 and the buyer must make a cash down payment of at least $16,000. If the lender appraises the home for more than $80,000, the loan will still be $64,000. If the appraisal is for $80,000 and the buyer is paying $85,000, the loan will be 80% of the appraised value and the buyer must pay the balance of $21,000 in cash. The rule is that price or value, whichever is lower, is applied to the L/V ratio.

EQUITY

The difference between the market value of a property and the debt owed against it is called the owner's **equity.** On a newly purchased $80,000 home with a $16,000 cash down payment, the buyer's equity is $16,000. As the value of the property rises or falls and as the mortgage loan is paid down, equity changes. For example, if the value of the home rises to $90,000 and the loan is paid down to $62,000, the owner's equity will be $28,000. If the owner pays the loan off so that there is no debt against the home, his equity will be equal to the market value of the property.

FHA INSURANCE PROGRAMS

The Great Depression caused a major change in the attitude of the federal government toward home mortgage financing in the United States. In 1934, one year after the Home Owners Loan Corporation was established, Congress passed the Na-

tional Housing Act. The Act's most far-reaching provision was to establish the Federal Housing Administration (FHA) for the purpose of encouraging new construction as a means of creating jobs. To accomplish this goal, the FHA offered to insure lenders against losses due to nonrepayment when they made loans on both new and existing homes. In turn, the lender had to grant up to 20-year amortized loan terms and loan-to-value ratios of up to 80% rather than the 3- to 5-year, 50% to 60% term loans common up to that time. Lenders were at first skeptical regarding the change, but finally reasoned that, if the U.S. Government would insure against losses, they would make the loans.

Meanwhile, the FHA did its best to keep from becoming a continuous burden to the American taxpayer. When a prospective borrower approached a lender for an FHA-secured home loan, the FHA reviewed the borrower's income, expenses, assets, and debts. The objective was to determine if there was adequate room in the borrower's budget for the proposed loan payments. The FHA also sent inspectors to the property to make certain that it was of acceptable construction quality and to determine its fair market value. To offset losses that would still inevitably occur, the FHA charged the borrower an annual insurance fee of ½ of 1% of the balance owed on his loan. The FHA was immensely successful in its task. Not only did it create construction jobs, but it raised the level of housing quality in the nation and, in a pleasant surprise to taxpayers, actually returned annual profits to the U.S. Treasury. In response to its success, in 1946 Congress changed its status from temporary to permanent.

Current FHA Coverage

Although the FHA insures only a portion of the home loans in the United States (presently about one home loan in five is FHA insured), it has had a marked influence on lending policies and construction techniques throughout the real estate industry. Foremost among these is the widespread acceptance of the high loan-to-value, amortized loan. In the 1930s, lenders required FHA insurance before making 80% L/V loans. By the 1960s, lenders were readily making 80% L/V loans without FHA insurance. Meanwhile, the FHA insurance program was working so well that the FHA raised the portion it was willing to insure. By 1983, for a fee of ½ of 1% per year, the FHA offered to insure a lender for 97% of the first $25,000 of appraised value and 95% above that to a maximum loan of $90,000. To illustrate, on a $60,000 home the FHA would insure 97% of the first $25,000 and 95% of the remaining $35,000, for a total of $57,500. This means a cash down payment of only $2,500 for the buyer.

The borrower is not permitted to use a second mortgage to raise his down payment money. The FHA requires some down payment; otherwise, it is too easy for the borrower to walk away from his debt obligation and leave the FHA to pay the lender's insurance claim. A strong argument can be made that even if a buyer places 3% to 5% cash down he still owes more than he owns the moment he takes title. This is because it would cost about 6% in brokerage fees plus another 1% to 2% in closing costs to resell the home. Inflation in home prices since the 1940s has kept the FHA's insurance losses relatively low.

The FHA led the way in other respects. Once 20-year amortized mortgage loans were shown to be successful investments for lenders, loans without FHA insurance were made for 20 years. Later, when the FHA successfully went to 30 years, non-FHA-insured loans followed. The FHA also established loan application review techniques that have been widely accepted and copied throughout the real estate industry. The biggest step in this direction was to analyze a borrower's loan application in terms of his earning power. Prior to 1933, emphasis had been placed on how large the borrower's assets were, a measurement that tended to exclude all but the already financially well-to-do from home ownership. Since 1933, the emphasis has shifted primarily to the borrower's ability to meet monthly PITI payments. The rule of thumb today is that no more than 38% of a person's gross monthly income should go to the repayment of fixed monthly obligations including monthly PITI payments.

Construction Requirements

The FHA has also been very influential in improving construction techniques. When the property for which FHA insurance is requested is of new construction, the FHA imposes minimum construction requirements regarding the quantity and quality of materials to be used. Lot size, street access, landscaping, and general house design must also fall within the broad guidelines set by the FHA. During construction, an FHA inspector comes to the property several times to check if the work is being done correctly. A home that was not FHA inspected during construction can still qualify for an FHA-insured loan if it has been occupied for 1 year and meets certain FHA requirements.

The establishment of construction standards is a two-edged sword. The FHA recognizes that if a building is defective either from a design or construction standpoint, the borrower is more likely to default on his loan and create an insurance claim against the FHA. Furthermore, the same defects will lower the price the property will bring at its foreclosure sale, thus increasing losses to the FHA. An important side effect has been to establish certain national standards in housing construction that have raised the quality of construction in regions where FHA standards are more stringent than local building codes.

Other FHA Programs

Thus far, our discussion of the FHA has centered on insuring home mortgage loans under **Section 203(b)** of Title II of the National Housing Act. This FHA program has insured over 11 million home loans and is the program for which the FHA is most widely known. However, the FHA administers a number of other real estate programs. Several of the better known programs will be briefly discussed.

Under **Title I** of the National Housing Act, the FHA will insure lenders against losses on loans made to finance repairs, improvements, alterations, or conversions of existing residences. Under **Title II, Section 207** provides for insuring mortgage loans on rental housing projects of eight or more family units and on mobile home parks. **Section 213** provides for insuring mortgages on cooperative housing projects of eight or more family units. **Section 220** insures financing used to rehabilitate salvageable housing and to replace slums with new housing. **Section 221(d)(2)** operates similarly to 203(b), but permits 100% insured financing for low- and moderate-income family housing. **Section 221(d)(3)** provides mortgage insurance to finance nonprofit rental and cooperative multifamily housing for low- and moderate-income households. Under **Section 223(e),** the FHA insures mortgages used to purchase or rehabilitate housing in older, declining urban areas. **Section 223(f)** offers mortgage insurance to purchase or refinance existing multifamily rental housing. Under **Section 234,** the FHA insures individual housing units in a multifamily building of five or more units operated on a condominium basis.

Section 235 offers a single-family residence interest subsidy program. However, **Section 236** which subsidized owners of low-rent apartment buildings has not been reactivated since it was suspended in 1973. As an alternative the FHA now administers a **Title II, Section 8** housing assistance program. Under this program, low- and moderate-income families, including single, elderly, disabled, or handicapped persons, can obtain FHA certificates that permit them to negotiate for suitable rental dwellings. Aided families then contribute between 15% and 25% of their total family income to the dwelling unit's rent. The difference between that amount and the actual rent is subsidized by the U.S. Government through the Department of Housing and Urban Development (HUD).

Section 237 deals with special credit risks. A low- or moderate-income applicant with a poor credit history must agree to accept budget advice and debt counseling before the FHA will insure his or her loan. Under **Section 245,** FHA mortgage insurance is available for graduated payment mortgages. This mortgage format allows the borrower to make smaller payments initially and to increase their size gradually over time. The idea is to parallel the borrower's rising earning capacity.

In addition to the above FHA programs, the FHA offers mortgage insurance on rental projects on or near military bases, land purchases for new town developments, nursing homes, hospitals, mobile homes, mobile home parks, and college housing.

VETERANS ADMINISTRATION

To show its appreciation to servicemen returning from World War II, in 1944 Congress passed far-reaching legislation to aid veterans in education, hospitalization, employment training, and housing. In housing, the popularly named G.I. Bill of Rights empowered the comptroller general of the United States to guarantee the repayment of a portion of first mortgage real estate loans made to veterans. For this guarantee, no fee would be charged to the veteran. Rather, the government itself would stand the losses. The original 1944 law provided that lenders would be guaranteed against losses up to 50% of the amount of the loan, but in no case more than $2,000.

No Down Payment

The objective was to make it possible for a veteran to buy a home with no cash down payment. Thus, on a house offered for sale at $5,000 (houses were much cheaper in 1944) this guarantee enabled a veteran to borrow the entire $5,000. From the lender's standpoint, having the top $2,000 of the loan guaranteed by the U.S. government offered the same asset protection as a $2,000 cash down payment. If the veteran defaulted and the property went into foreclosure, the lender had to net less than $3,000 before suffering a loss.

In 1945, Congress increased the guarantee amount to $4,000 and 60% of the loan and turned the entire operation over to the Veterans Administration (VA). The VA was quick to honor claims and the program rapidly became popular with lenders. Furthermore, the veterans turned out to be excellent credit risks, bettering, in fact, the good record of FHA-insured home owners. (The FHA recognizes this and gives higher insurance limits to FHA borrowers who have served in the Armed Forces. The limits are 100% of the first $25,000, and 95% above that to a maximum loan of $90,000.) The program blossomed, and to date over 9 million home loans have been guaranteed by the VA, over two-thirds of them with no down payment.

To keep up with the increased cost of homes, the guarantee has been increased several times and in mid-1983 was at $27,500. Generally, a $27,500 guarantee means a veteran can purchase up to a $110,000 home with no down payment, provided, of course, that the veteran has enough income to support the monthly PITI payments. Some lenders will go higher if the borrower makes a down payment. Whether or not a lender will make a no-down-payment VA loan is entirely up to the lender. Some lenders feel the borrower should make at least a token down payment so as to have a sense of ownership. However, the majority of lenders, if they have the funds available, require none.

In the original G.I. Bill of 1944, eligibility was limited to World War II veterans. However, subsequent legislation has broadened eligibility to include any veteran who served for a period of at least 90 days in the armed forces of the United

States, or an ally, between September 16, 1940, and July 25, 1947, or between June 27, 1950, and January 31, 1955. Any veteran of the United States who has served 180 days or more since January 31, 1955, to the present is also eligible. If service was during the Viet Nam conflict period (August 5, 1964 to May 7, 1975) 90 days is sufficient to qualify. The veteran's discharge must be on conditions other than dishonorable and the guarantee entitlement is good until used. Spouses of veterans who died as a result of service can also obtain housing guarantees, if not remarried. Active duty personnel can also qualify.

VA Certificates

To find out what his benefits are, a veteran should make application to the Veterans Administration for a **certificate of eligibility.** This shows if the veteran is qualified and the amount of guarantee available. It is also one of the documents necessary to obtain a VA-guaranteed loan.

The VA works diligently to protect veterans and reduce foreclosure losses. When a veteran applies for a VA guarantee, the property is appraised and the VA issues a **certificate of reasonable value.** Often abbreviated **CRV,** it informs the veteran of the appraised value of the property and the maximum VA guaranteed loan a private lender may make. Similarly, the VA establishes income guidelines to make certain that the veteran can comfortably meet the proposed loan payments. It makes no sense, for the veteran or the VA, to approve a loan that the veteran will have trouble repaying.

The VA will guarantee loans for periods of up to 30 years on homes, and there is no prepayment penalty if the borrower wishes to pay sooner. The VA will also guarantee loans for the purchase of farms and farm equipment, farm buildings, and farm capital, to buy or establish a business, or to purchase a mobile home as a residence. A veteran wishing to refinance his existing home or farm can also obtain a VA-guaranteed loan. The VA will also make direct loans to veterans if there are no private lending institutions nearby.

No matter what loan guarantee program is elected, the veteran should know that in the event of default and subsequent foreclosure he is required to eventually make good any losses suffered by the VA on his loan. (This is not the case with FHA-insured loans. There the borrower pays for protection against foreclosure losses that may result from his loan.) Even if the veteran sells his property and the buyer assumes the VA loan, the veteran is still financially responsible if the buyer later defaults. To avoid this, the veteran must arrange with the VA to be released from liability.

Legislation that took effect in 1975 permits a veteran a full new guarantee entitlement if he has completely repaid a previous VA-guaranteed loan. Even if the veteran has sold his home and let the buyer assume the VA loan, the 1975 law change is still valuable. For example, if a veteran has used $15,000 of his entitlement to date, he still has $12,500 available to him.

As Congress frequently changes eligibility and benefits, a person contemplating a VA or FHA loan should make inquiry to the field offices of these two agencies and to mortgage lenders to ascertain the current status and details of the law, as well as the availability of loan money.* One should also query lenders as to the availability of state veteran benefits. A number of states offer special advantages, including mortgage loan assistance, to residents who have served in the armed forces.

PRIVATE MORTGAGE INSURANCE

The financial success of the FHA's Section 203(b) loan insurance program was not lost on private industry. In 1957, the Mortgage Guaranty Insurance Corporation (MGIC) was formed in Milwaukee, Wisconsin, as a privately owned business venture to compete with the FHA in insuring home mortgage loans. Growth was slow but steady for the first 10 years. However, in the late 1960s several things happened that allowed MGIC to enjoy a sudden burst of growth. The first was a red-tape snarl at the FHA that resulted in loan insurance applications taking 4 to 8 weeks to process, much too long a wait for sellers, buyers, brokers, and lenders who were anxious to close. In contrast, MGIC offered 3-day service. Then, too, FHA terms were not keeping up with the times; moderately priced homes required larger down payments with FHA insurance than with private insurance, and the FHA-imposed inter-

* Consult the telephone directory white pages under United States Government for Veterans Administration and Housing and Urban Development—FHA headings—and the yellow pages for Real Estate Loans.

est rate ceiling hindered rather than helped many borrowers. Also, private mortgage insurance (PMI) was priced at less than the FHA was charging. Then in 1971 the Federal Home Loan Bank Board, overseer of savings and loan institutions, approved the use of private mortgage insurers. By 1972 private insurers in the United States were regularly insuring more new mortgages than the FHA.

PMI Coverage

Success spawns competition, and by 1983, 13 private mortgage insurance companies were insuring loans. MGIC, however, is still the dominant force in the industry. Like FHA insurance, the object of PMI is to insure lenders against losses due to nonrepayment of low down-payment mortgage loans. But unlike the FHA, PMI insures only the top 20% to 25% of a loan, not the whole loan. This allows a lender to make 90% and 95% L/V loans with about the same exposure to foreclosure losses as a 72% L/V loan.* The borrower, meanwhile, can purchase a home with a cash down payment of either 10% or 5%. Under the 10% down payment program, the borrower pays a mortgage insurance fee ½ of 1% the first year and ¼ of 1% thereafter. The 5%-down program costs the borrower ¾ of 1% the first year and ¼ of 1% annually thereafter. When the loan is partially repaid (for example, to a 70% L/V), the premiums and coverage can be terminated at the lender's option. PMI is also available on apartment buildings, offices, stores, warehouses, and leaseholds but at higher rates than on homes.

Private mortgage insurers work to keep their losses to a minimum by first approving the lenders with whom they will do business. Particular emphasis is placed on the lender's operating policy, appraisal procedure, and degree of government regulation. Once approved, a lender simply sends the borrower's loan application, credit report, and property appraisal to the insurer. Based on these documents, the insurer either agrees

* The arithmetic of this statement is as follows: On 90% L/V loans, the borrower, by placing 10% cash down, takes the top 10% of risk exposure to falling real estate prices. PMI takes 20% of the next 90%, that is, 18%, and the lender takes the remaining 72%. On 95% L/V loans, the borrower takes the top 5% of risk exposure with his 5% down payment. PMI takes 25% of the next 95%, that is, 23.75%, and the lender takes the remaining 71.25%.

or refuses to issue a policy. Although the insurer relies on the appraisal prepared by the lender, on a random basis the insurer sends its own appraiser to verify the quality of the information being submitted. When an insured loan goes into default, the insurer has the option of either buying the property from the lender for the balance due or letting the lender foreclose and then paying the lender's losses up to the amount of the insurance. As a rule, insurers take the first option because it is more popular with the lenders and it leaves the lender with immediate cash to re-lend. The insurer now has the task of foreclosing.

LOAN POINTS

Probably no single term in real estate finance causes as much confusion and consternation as the word **points.** In finance, the word **point** means one percent of the loan amount. Thus, on a $60,000 loan, one point is $600. On a $40,000 loan, three points is $1,200. On a $100,000 loan, eight points is $8,000.

The use of points in real estate mortgage finance can be split into two categories: (1) loan origination fees expressed in terms of points and (2) the use of points to change the effective yield of a mortgage loan to a lender. Let us look at these two uses in more detail.

Origination Fee

When a borrower asks for a mortgage loan, the lender incurs a number of expenses, including such things as the time its loan officer spends interviewing the borrower, office overhead, the purchase and review of credit reports on the borrower, an on-site appraisal of the property to be pledged, title searches and review, legal and recording fees, and so on. For these, some lenders make an itemized billing, charging so many dollars for the appraisal, credit report, title search, and so on. The total becomes the **loan origination fee,** which the borrower pays to get his loan. Other lenders do not make an itemized bill, but instead simply state the origination fee in terms of a percentage of the loan amount, for example, one point. Thus, a lender quoting a loan origination fee of one point is saying that, for a $65,000 loan, its fee to originate the loan will be $650.

Discount Points

Points charged to raise the lender's monetary return on a loan are known as **discount points.** A simplified example will illustrate their use and effect. If you are a lender and agree to make a term loan of $100 to a borrower for 1 year at 10% interest, you would normally expect to give the borrower $100 now (disregard loan origination fees for a moment), and 1 year later the borrower would give you $110. In percentage terms, the **effective yield** on your loan is 10% per annum (year) because you received $10 for your 1-year, $100 loan. Now suppose that, instead of handing the borrower $100, you handed him $99 but still required him to repay $100 plus $10 in interest at the end of the year. This is a charge of one point ($1 in this case), and the borrower paid it out of his loan funds. The effect of this financial maneuver is to raise the effective yield (yield to maturity) to you without raising the interest rate itself. Therefore, if you loan out $99 and receive $110 at the end of the year, you effectively have a return of $11 for a $99 loan. This gives you an effective yield of $11 ÷ $99 or 11.1%, rather than 10%.

Calculating the effective yield on a discounted 20- or 30-year mortgage loan is more difficult because the amount owed drops over the life of the loan, and because the majority are paid in full ahead of schedule due to refinancing. However, a useful rule of thumb states that on the typical home loan each point of discount raises the effective yield by ⅛ of 1%. Thus, four discount points would raise the effective yield by approximately ½ of 1% and eight points would raise it by 1%. Discount points are most often charged during periods of **tight money,** that is, when mortgage money is in short supply. During periods of **loose money,** when lenders have adequate funds to lend and are actively seeking borrowers, discount points disappear.

Rate Ceilings

The use of discount points is an important part of FHA and VA loans, because the FHA and VA set interest-rate ceilings on loans they insure or guarantee. With only two exceptions since 1950, the FHA and VA ceilings have been below the prevailing rates on **conventional loans** (non-FHA or non-VA loans). Thus, if the prevailing open-market interest rate on conventional loans is 10½% and the FHA and VA ceilings are at 10%, a borrower will not be able to obtain an FHA or VA loan without offering the lender enough discount points to raise the effective yield to 10½%. If conventional loans can be made at 10½% interest, it is illogical for the lender to accept 10%. To obtain a 10% loan, the borrower must pay the lender four discount points.

However, the FHA and VA limit the number of points that the borrower is allowed to pay to 1 point for existing homes and 2½ points for homes under construction, and these are usually consumed by loan origination costs. These are called **borrower's points** or **service points.**

Any additional points charged by the lender must be paid by someone other than the buyer. That usually means the seller. For example, on a $60,000 loan, when the market rate is ½% above the FHA and VA ceilings, this amounts to $2,400 in **seller's points.** In other words, out of the proceeds from the sale, the seller would have to pay the lender $2,400 so the buyer could enjoy the privilege of obtaining a loan with an interest rate ½% below the market.

By placing yourself in the seller's position, you can see the situation this creates. A buyer making an offer under the above conditions is in effect asking you to take a $2,400 cut in price. If you were planning on reducing your price $2,400 anyway, you would accept the offer. However, if you felt you could readily sell at your price to a buyer not requiring seller's points, you would refuse the offer. The alternative is to price the property high enough to allow for anticipated points. However, this is an effective solution only if your price does not exceed the FHA appraisal or VA certificate of reasonable value. If it does, the FHA or VA buyer is either prohibited from buying or must make a larger cash down payment. One reason for the success of private mortgage insurers is that they impose no restrictions on either interest rates or discount points.

TRUTH IN LENDING

Regulation Z

The **Federal Consumer Credit Protection Act,** popularly known as the **Truth in Lending Act,** went into effect in 1969. The Act, implemented by Federal Reserve Board **Regulation Z,** requires that a borrower be clearly shown how much he is paying for credit in both dollar terms and percentage terms before committing himself. The borrower is also given the right to rescind (cancel) the transaction in certain instances. The

Act came into being because it was not uncommon to see loans advertised for rates lower than the borrower actually wound up paying. This was possible because most people are unable to calculate interest rates for themselves. Therefore, a key provision of the Act was to devise a standardized yardstick by which a prospective borrower could measure and compare various credit terms available.

Once put into use, several weaknesses and ambiguities of the Act and Regulation Z became apparent. Thus, the **Truth in Lending Simplification and Reform Act** (TILSRA) was passed by Congress and became effective October 1, 1982. Concurrently, the Federal Reserve Board issued a **Revised Regulation Z** (RRZ) which details rules and regulations for TILSRA. Since real estate transactions are affected, let us explore these further. First we will talk about who is required to comply with these laws. Second, we will talk about what types of financing are exempt from disclosure. Third, we will talk about what financing disclosures must be made including the disclosures that must be made if a real estate advertisement contains the mention of credit. Fourth, we will discuss the penalties for not complying with the law and learn about a borrower's right to cancel a credit transaction.

Who Must Comply?

If you extend credit to others, you must comply with the rules and regulations of TILSRA and RRZ if you meet both of the following requirements. The first is that you regularly extend consumer credit which is either subject to a finance charge (such as interest) or is payable by written agreement in more than four installments. This includes not only persons and firms in the business of extending credit (such as banks, savings and loan associations, credit unions, etc.) but also private individuals who extend credit secured by dwellings more than 5 times a year.

The second requirement is that you be initially payable. Once your name is on the note as a creditor, you meet this requirement even though you plan to sell the note to another person.

A key difference between TILSRA and the old 1969 Act is that TILSRA does not include mortgage brokers or real estate agents as creditors just because they brokered a deal containing financing. This is because they do not appear as creditors on the note. But if a broker takes back a note for part of the commission on a deal, that is the extension of credit.

What Transactions are Exempt?

If you meet the requirements above and must comply, the next question is whether the particular transaction is exempt from the law. The first exemption is for credit extended primarily for business, commercial or agricultural purposes. This exemption includes dwelling units purchased for rental purposes (unless the property contains 4 or less units and the owner occupies one of them in which case special rules apply).

The second exemption applies to credit over $25,000 secured by personal property unless the property is the principal residence of the borrower. For example, a mobile home that secures a loan over $25,000 qualifies under this exemption if it is used as a vacation home. But it is not exempt if it is used as a principal residence.

What Must be Disclosed?

If you qualify as a creditor and your transaction is not exempt, there are 18 disclosures you must make. Of these, the four that must be most prominently displayed on the papers the borrower signs are (1) the amount financed, (2) the finance charge, (3) the annual percentage rate, and (4) the total payments.

The **amount financed** is the amount of credit provided to the borrower. The **finance charge** is the total dollar amount the credit will cost the borrower over the life of the loan. This includes such things as interest, borrower-paid discount points, loan fees, loan finder's fees, loan service fees, required life insurance, and mortgage guarantee premiums. On a long-term mortgage loan, the total finance charge can easily exceed the amount of money being borrowed. For example, the total amount of interest on an 11%, 30-year, $60,000 loan is just over $145,000.

The **annual percentage rate** (APR) combines the interest rate with the other costs of the loan into a single figure that shows the true annual cost of borrowing. This is one of the most helpful features of the law as it gives the prospective borrower a standardized yardstick by which to compare financing from different sources. The **total payments** is the amount in dollars the borrower will have paid after making all the payments as scheduled. In the previous 11%, 30-year loan it would be the interest of $145,000 plus the principal of $60,000 for a total of $205,000.

The other 14 disclosures that a lender must make are as follows. (1) The identity of the lender. (2) The payment schedule. (3) Prepayment penalties and rebates. (4) Late payment charges. (5) Any insurance required. (6) Any filing fees. (7) Any collateral required. (8) Any required deposits. (9) Whether the loan can be assumed. (10) The demand feature, if the note has one. (11) The total sales price of the item being purchased if the seller is also the creditor. (12) Any variable rate features of the loan. (13) Any itemization of the amount financed. (14) A reference to any terms not shown on the disclosure statement but which are shown on the loan contract.

These disclosures must be delivered or mailed to the credit applicant within three business days after the creditor receives the applicant's written request for credit. The applicant must have this information before the transaction can take place, e.g., before the closing can take place.

Advertising Requirements

Although as a real estate agent or a property owner you will only occasionally come under TILSRA and RRZ as an extender of credit, you will regularly do so when you write real estate advertising. This is because anyone (business or personal) who advertises must comply with truth in lending advertising regulations. As with the extension of credit, TILSRA also requires that advertising of credit must be meaningfully and accurately disclosed. The provisions are simple. If an advertisement contains any one of the Act's list of financing terms (called **trigger terms**), the ad must also include other required terms. For example, an advertisement that reads: "Bargain! Bargain! Bargain! New 3 bedroom townhouses only $499 per month" may or may not be a bargain depending on other financing information missing from the ad.

Trigger Terms

The type of financing information required in an ad depends on the type of transaction proposed. Therefore we shall concentrate on the advertisement of real estate. If an ad contains any of the following trigger terms, five specific disclosures must be included in the ad. Here are the trigger terms. The amount of down payment (for example, nothing down, 10% down, $4995 down, 95% financing). The amount of any payment (for example, monthly payments only $499, buy for less than $650 a month, payments only 1% per month). The number of payments (for example, only 36 monthly payments and you own it, all paid up in 10 annual payments). The period of repayment (for example, 30-year financing available, owner will carry for five years, 10-year second available). The dollar amount of finance charge (finance this for only $999) or the statement that there is no charge for credit (pay no interest for three years).

If any of the above trigger terms is used, then the following five disclosures must appear in the ad. They are (1) the cash price or the amount of the loan; (2) the amount of down payment or a statement that none is required; (3) the number, amount and frequency of repayments; (4) the annual percentage rate; and (5) the deferred payment price or total payments. Item (5) is not a requirement in the case of the sale of a dwelling or a loan secured by a first lien on a dwelling to purchase that dwelling.

If the annual percentage rate being offered is subject to increase after the transaction takes place (such as with a variable rate mortgage), that fact must be stated. For example, "12% annual percentage rate subject to increase after settlement." If the loan has interest rate changes that will follow a predetermined schedule, those terms must be stated. For example, "8% first year, 10% second year, 12% third year, 14% remainder of loan, 13.5% annual percentage rate." Note too, that whereas under the 1969 Act, the words annual percentage rate could be abbreviated to APR, under TILSRA the words must be spelled out in the ad.

If you wish to say something about financing and avoid triggering full disclosure, you may use general statements. The following would be acceptable: "assumable loan," "financing available," "owner will carry," "terms to fit your budget," "easy monthly payments," or "FHA and VA financing available."

Failure to Disclose

If the Federal Trade Commission (FTC) determines that an advertiser has broken the law, the FTC can order the advertiser to cease from further violations. Each violation of that order can result in a $10,000 civil penalty each day the violation continues.

Failure to properly disclose when credit is extended can result in a penalty of twice the amount of the finance charge with a minimum of $100 and a maximum of $1,000 plus court costs, attorney fees, and actual damages. In addition the FTC can add a fine of up to $5,000 and/or one year imprisonment. If the required disclosures are not made or the borrower not given the required 3 days to cancel (see below), the borrower can cancel the transaction at anytime within 3 years following the date of the transaction. In that event the creditor must return all money paid by the borrower and the borrower returns the property to the creditor.

Right to Cancel

A borrower has a limited right to rescind (cancel) a credit transaction. The borrower has 3 business days (counting Saturdays) to back out after signing the loan papers. This aspect of the law was inserted primarily to protect a homeowner from unscrupulous sellers of various home improvements and appliances where the credit to purchase is secured by a lien on the home. Vacant lots for sale on credit to buyers who expect to use them for principal residences are also subject to cancellation privileges.

The right to rescind does not apply to credit that is used for the acquisition or initial construction of one's principal dwelling.

Summary

TILSRA and Regulation Z are complex and only the highlights have been presented here. If you are involved in transactions that require disclosure, you should seek more information from your local real estate board, lender, attorney, or the FTC. Note that the whole topic of truth in lending deals only with disclosure—who must disclose, in what types of situations, what must be disclosed, etc. Truth in lending legislation does not set the price a lender can charge for a loan. That is determined by supply and demand for funds in the marketplace and, to a lesser degree, by usury laws.

VOCABULARY REVIEW

Match terms **a–p** *with statements* **1–16.**

a. *Annual percentage rate*	**i.** *PITI*
b. *Blanket mortgage*	**j.** *PMI*
c. *Conventional loan*	**k.** *Point*
d. *CRV*	**l.** *Principal*
e. *Discount points*	**m.** *Purchase money mortgage*
f. *Impound account*	**n.** *Take-out*
g. *Loose money*	**o.** *Term loan*
h. *L/V ratio*	**p.** *Tight money*

1. Balance owing on a loan.
2. A loan that requires the borrower to pay interest only until maturity, at which time the full amount of the loan must be repaid.
3. Refers to a monthly loan payment that includes principal, interest, property taxes, and property insurance.
4. An escrow or reserve account into which the lender places the borrower's monthly tax and insurance payments.
5. A mortgage secured by more than one property.
6. A permanent loan used to repay a construction loan.
7. A mortgage given by the buyer as part or all of the purchase price of a property.
8. The amount a lender will loan on a property divided by the valuation the lender places on the property.
9. A document issued by the Veterans Administration showing the VA's estimate of a property's value.
10. Mortgage guaranty insurance sold by privately owned companies.
11. One hundredth of the total amount; 1 percent of a loan.
12. Used by lenders to adjust the effective interest rate on a loan so that it is equal to the prevailing market interest rate.
13. Refers to periods when mortgage loan money is in short supply and loans are hard to get.
14. Lenders have adequate funds to lend and are actively seeking borrowers.
15. A real estate loan made without FHA insurance or a VA guarantee.
16. A uniform measure of the annual cost of credit.

QUESTIONS AND PROBLEMS

1. What is the major risk that the borrower takes when he agrees to a term loan or a balloon loan?
2. Explain how an amortized loan works.
3. Using the amortization tables in Table 11:1, calculate the monthly payment necessary to completely amortize a $65,000, 30-year loan at 11½% interest.

4. A prospective home buyer has a $10,000 down payment and can afford $420 per month for principal and interest payments. If 30-year, 9½% amortized loans are available, what price home can the buyer afford?
5. Same problem as in Number 4 except that the interest rate has risen to 10½%. What price home can the buyer afford now?
6. Using the loan progress chart shown in Table 11:2, calculate the balance still owing on a $90,000, 9½% interest, 30-year amortized loan that is 10 years old.
7. Explain the purpose and operation of the FHA 203(b) home mortgage insurance program.
8. What advantage does the Veterans Administration offer veterans who wish to purchase a home?
9. Explain "points" and their application to real estate lending.
10. What is the basic purpose of truth in lending legislation?
11. How does a reverse mortgage work?

ADDITIONAL READINGS

Ballard, James M. "Financing Multi-Family Housing Through the FHA." *Real Estate Today,* March, 1977, pages 16–22. FHA mortgage insurance is one method of financing frequently overlooked by brokers involved in sales of multi-family structures.

Dennis, Marshall W. *Mortgage Lending Fundamentals and Practices.* Reston, Va.: Reston Publishing Co., 1980, 350 pages. Book traces mortgage lending from ancient times through the depression years to the present and discusses the importance of mortgage lending to the economy. Topics include lending institutions, security instruments, secondary markets, mortgage insurance, loan appraisal, and loan administration.

Golden, Edward John. "Loan Points: Understanding and Using Them." *Real Estate Today,* February, 1979, pages 8–12. Article explains in detail the arithmetic used to calculate points for mortgage loans. Includes numerous examples.

Hines, Mary Alice. *Real Estate Finance.* Englewood Cliffs, N.J.: Prentice-Hall, 1978, 514 pages. A comprehensive text and reference for college, professional, and personal use. Coverage includes interest rates, lenders, legal aspects, risk, return, default, and specialized properties.

To the Home-Buying Veteran, VA Pamphlet 26–6, revised. Washington, D.C.: Veterans Administration, 34 pages. This free booklet discusses such topics as house selection, costs of home ownership, the purchase contract, VA loans, and closing procedures.

Wiedemer, John P. *Real Estate Finance, 3rd ed.* Reston, Va.: Reston Publishing Co., 1980, 356 pages. Chapter 1 provides a historical background of real estate lending in the United States. Chapter 7 deals with federal government mortgage loan programs. Chapter 14 discusses loan closing procedures. Contains a glossary of real estate finance terms.

12

Sources of Financing

KEY TERMS

Adjustable rate mortgage: a mortgage on which the interest rate rises and falls with changes in prevailing interest rates

Alienation clause: a provision in a loan contract that a loan against a property must be paid in full if ownership is transferred

Contract for deed: a method of selling and financing property whereby the buyer obtains possession but the seller retains the title

Fannie Mae: a real estate industry nickname for the Federal National Mortgage Association

Mortgage banker: a person or firm that makes mortgage loans and then sells them to investors

Option: a right to buy, sell, or lease property at specified price and terms for a certain length of time

Participation loans: real estate loans that require interest plus a percentage of the profits from rentals

Usury: the charging of a rate of interest higher than that permitted by law

Wraparound Mortgage: a mortgage that encompasses any existing mortgages and is subordinate to them

Chapters 9–11 dealt with mortgage and deed of trust law, amortized loans, and FHA and VA mortgage programs. In this chapter we turn our attention to the lenders themselves, secondary mortgage markets, and alternatives to lending institutions. It is important to realize that real estate profits and commissions would be hard to come by if buyers were unable to borrow.

SAVINGS AND LOAN ASSOCIATIONS

As a group, the nation's 4,500 savings and loan associations are the single most important source of loan money for residential real estate. Historically, their origin can be traced to early building societies in England and Germany. These were cooperative lending associations whose members pooled their money to make home loans to each other.

S&L Growth

Savings and loan associations (S&Ls) are now found in all 50 states (in Louisiana they are called Homestead Associations and in Massachusetts, Cooperative Banks). As may be seen in Figure 12:1, their importance to mortgage lending is

Figure 12:1

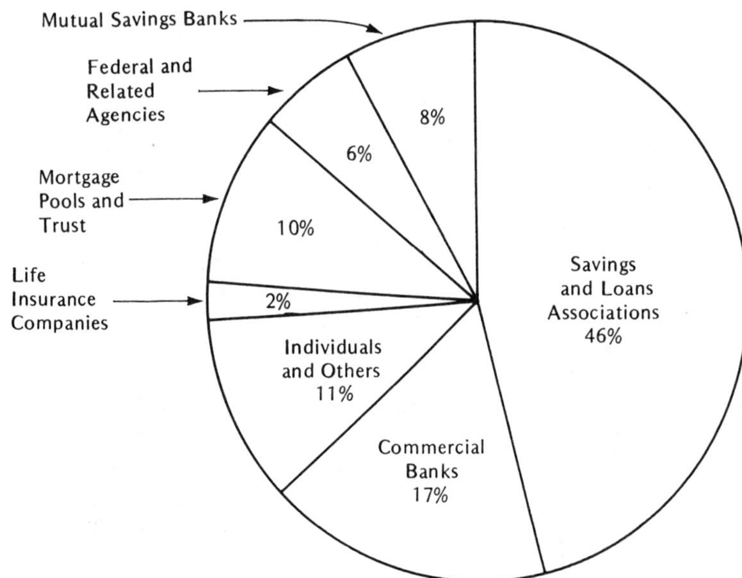

Distribution of One- to Four-Family Nonfarm, Home Mortgage Loans, by Type of Lender in 1979.

Source: Federal Reserve Board.

tremendous. In 1983 mortgage loans held by S&Ls numbered 19 million and amounted to $525 billion. Of this vast amount, 78% was for loans on single-family homes, 4% for loans on two-to-four family buildings, 9% for apartment buildings, and 9% for commercial real estate. Additionally, S&Ls held $20 billion worth of mobile home, home improvement, and educational loans.

Regulation and Deposit Insurance

A savings and loan association may be either state or federally chartered. In the latter case, the word "Federal" appears in its name. A charter is an association's permit to operate. Federal charters are issued by the Federal Home Loan Bank Board (FHLBB). A federally-chartered association must be a member of the Federal Home Loan Bank System (FHLBS), and carry Federal Savings and Loan Insurance Corporation (FSLIC) insurance. (The FHLBB is the governing body of the FHLBS.) Until new federal legislation in 1981, federally-chartered S&Ls were required to be mutually owned (owned by their depositors). Today, a federally-chartered S&L can be either mutually owned or owned by stockholders.

An outgrowth of the 1930 depression, the FSLIC is an agency of the U.S. Government that insures savers' deposits against the possibility they will not be available whenever the savers wish to withdraw them. For this insurance, which is $100,000 per account, the S&L pays an insurance premium to the FSLIC of 1/12 of 1% per year times its savings deposits. The FHLBS was also a product of the Great Depression; it was formed to bring order to chaotic and often weak state banking and savings laws. Today the FHLBS regulates the geographic area a federally-chartered S&L can lend in, maximum loan size, maximum loan-to-value ratios, and the ratio of home loans to other types of loans. The FHLBS also provides S&Ls with access to the nation's capital markets, as we will see later.

State-chartered associations can be mutually owned by depositors or by corporations owned by stockholders. FHLBS membership and FSLIC insurance are optional. Whether federal or state in origin, to be chartered an association must be financially healthy, have a sound lending policy, and maintain adequate amounts of cash and other liquid assets to meet depositors' withdrawal demands. The FHLBB and the FSLIC periodically audit the accounting books of members to assure compliance with regulations and sound lending practices. Minnesota-chartered associations are subject to audit by the Office of the Commissioner of Banking.

Savings Accounts

As of October, 1983, savings and loan associations were offering several types of accounts to attract savers. These included regular passbook savings accounts, checking accounts, fixed rate certificates, market rate passbook and checking accounts, and various retirement accounts.

The standard passbook pays savers 5½% per year interest and allows the flexibility of depositing or withdrawing without penalty and requires a minimum balance of as little as $1. Higher interest is available to passbook savers willing to keep a balance of $2,500 or more. Checking accounts, introduced in 1981, allow the payment of interest on funds held in a checking account. The rate of interest paid is 5¼% and checking services are usually free if a minimum balance of $500 is maintained in the account. Higher interest is available with a $2,500 minimum.

Money Market Certificates

To compete with yields offered on bills, notes and bonds offered by the U.S. Treasury, S&Ls offer a variety of **money market certificates.** These are **savings certificates,** also called **certificates of deposit,** wherein the saver agrees to leave money on deposit for a fixed period of time. In return, the S&L agrees to pay the saver a rate of interest which is higher than that offered on passbook accounts. These certificates range from as short as 32 days in length up to 10 years and sometimes 20 years.

Generally speaking, the longer a saver agrees to leave money on deposit, the higher the rate of interest the S&L will pay the saver. Each S&L sets its own rate, and it is usually based on current yields available on the above listed Treasury securities. Also, each S&L can change its rates in response to current interest rates in the marketplace. The minimum account balance for a certificate is typically $1,000 to $2,500. If a saver wants a certificate of $100,000 or more, sometimes called a "jumbo" certificate, most S&Ls will negotiate a higher interest rate on an individual account basis. S&Ls also offer various types of tax-deferred retirement accounts at attractive rates of interest.

A key point to remember is that a savings and loan is an intermediary between savers and borrowers. S&Ls borrow from savers and then lend those dollars to borrowers. Because the bulk of S&L loans tend to be long-term, S&Ls pay higher interest rates to savers who are willing to commit to leaving their savings on deposit for longer periods of time.

Disintermediation

The purpose of offering savings certificates that pay interest similar to what is available from Treasury securities is to prevent disintermediation. **Disintermediation** results when depositors take money out of their savings accounts and invest directly in Treasury securities. In the past, when Treasury securities, in particular 3-month and 6-month Treasury bills, paid more than S&L accounts, money would flow out of savings accounts with the result that S&Ls had less money to lend.

Without loan money, the real estate market would go into the doldrums. Today, S&Ls can offer high enough returns to attract money.

COMMERCIAL BANKS

The nation's 14,400 commerical banks store far more of the country's money than the S&Ls. However, only one bank dollar in six goes to real estate lending. As a result, in total number of dollars, commercial banks rank second behind S&Ls in importance in real estate lending.

Of the loans made by banks on real estate, the tendency is to emphasize short-term maturities since the bulk of a bank's deposit money comes from demand deposits (checking accounts) and a much smaller portion from savings and time deposits. Consequently, banks are particularly active in making loans to finance real estate construction as these loans have maturities of 6 months to 3 years. They are less inclined to offer long-term real estate loans. When they do, maturities are usually 5 to 15 years rather than 25 to 30 years. There are, however, two exceptions to this. In rural areas where longer-term savings deposits make up a larger portion of a bank's money sources, the town bank is a major source of long-term real estate loans. The other exception is the bank that makes 20- and 30-year loans but afterwards sells them, rather than keeping them in its own investment portfolio.

Commercial banks operate under state or national charters, the latter being identified by the word "National" in the bank's name. National banks are chartered and supervised by the U.S. Comptroller of the Currency, and are required to be members of the Federal Reserve System (FRS) and the Federal Deposit Insurance Corporation (FDIC). The Federal Reserve System is the "nation's bank," and the FDIC provides insurance to checking and savings depositors. As of mid-1983, FDIC insurance was $100,000 per account. State-chartered banks are controlled by state banking regulatory agencies, usually in a manner similar to the national banks. State banks can voluntarily join the FRS and the FDIC. Banks offer depositors a choice of accounts similar to those offered by S&Ls.

MUTUAL SAVINGS BANKS

Important contributors to real estate credit in several states are the nation's 500 mutual savings banks. Started in Philadelphia in 1816 and in Boston in 1817 these banks historically provided a place where a person of limited financial means could save money for any purpose. Today, mutual savings banks are found primarily in the northeastern United States, where they compete aggressively for the savings dollar. The states of Massachusetts, New York, and Connecticut account for 75% of the nation's total. There are only a handful in Minnesota.

As the word "mutual" implies, the depositors are the owners, and the "interest" they receive is the result of the bank's success or failure in lending. Mutual savings banks offer accounts similar to those offered by S&Ls. To protect depositors, laws require mutual savings banks to place deposits in high-quality investments. This includes sound real estate mortgage loans. Loan-to-value ratios can be 70% to 80% (higher for FHA and VA loans), maturities are of 20 to 30 years, and as a rule, loans are made within a 100-mile radius of the bank. Presently, real estate loans account for two out of every three loan dollars at mutual savings banks. Mutual savings banks are chartered and controlled by state regulatory agencies. Membership in the FDIC is available and optional.

LIFE INSURANCE COMPANIES

As a group, the nation's 1,800 life insurance companies have long been active investors in real estate, as developers, owners and long-term lenders. Their source of money is the premiums paid by policyholders. These premiums are invested and ultimately returned to the policyholders. Because premiums are collected in regular amounts on regular dates and because policy payoffs can be calculated from actuarial tables, life insurers are in ideal positions to commit money to long-term investments.

Life insurance companies are state chartered and state regulated. Requirements regarding investments vary from state to state, but generally speaking, states allow insurers to place their funds wherever sound investments can be found that will protect policyholder money. Within these guidelines, life insurers channel their funds primarily into government and corporate bonds and real estate. The dollars allocated to real estate are used for purchases of land and buildings, which are leased to users, and to real estate loans on commercial, industrial, and residential property. Generally, life insurers specialize in large-scale projects and mortgage packages such as shopping centers, office and apartment buildings, and million dollar blocks of home mortgage loans.

Participation

Repayment terms on loans for shopping centers, office buildings, and apartment complexes sometimes call for interest and a percentage of any profits from rentals over a certain level. This **participation** feature, or "piece of the action," is intended to provide the insurance company with more inflation protection than a fixed rate of interest.

Few insurers maintain their own loan offices. Most purchase loans were originated by commercial banks and mortgage bankers. As a result, the lending activity of life insurers is often not as visible as savings and loan associations, mutual savings banks, or commercial banks.

MORTGAGE BANKERS AND BROKERS

A **mortgage banker** makes a mortgage loan and then sells it to a long-term investor. The process begins with locating borrowers, next qualifying them, then preparing the necessary loan papers, and finally making the loans. Once the loan is made, it is sold for cash to a life insurance company, pension or trust fund, savings institution, or government agency. The mortgage banker is usually retained by the mortgage purchaser to **service the loan,** that is, to collect the monthly payments and to handle such matters as insurance and property tax impounds, delinquencies, early payoffs, and mortgage releases.

Mortgage bankers often take the form of **mortgage companies,** that vary in size from one or two persons up to several dozen. As a rule, they are locally oriented, finding and making loans within 25 or 50 miles of their offices. This gives them a feel for their market, greatly aids in identifying sound loans, and makes loan servicing much easier. For their efforts, mortgage bankers typically receive 1% to 2% of the amount of the loan when it is originated, and from ¼ to ½ of 1% of the outstanding balance each year thereafter for servicing. On very large loans, such as a major shopping center or a large office building, the servicing fee drops to 1/10 of 1%.

Mortgage banking is not limited to mortgage companies. Commercial banks, savings and loan associations, and mutual savings banks in active real estate areas often originate more real estate loans than they can hold themselves, and these are sold to other investors. Mortgage bankers are important sources of FHA and VA loans.

Mortgage brokers, in contrast to mortgage bankers, specialize in bringing together borrowers and lenders, just as real estate brokers bring together buyers and sellers. The mortgage broker does not lend his own money, nor does he usually service the loans he has arranged. The mortgage broker's fee is expressed in points and is usually paid by the borrower.

MUNICIPAL BOND PROGRAMS

In some cities, municipal bond issues are providing a new source of mortgage money for home buyers. The special advantage to borrowers is that municipal bonds pay interest that is tax-free from federal income taxes. Knowing this, bond investors will accept a lower rate of interest than they would if the interest were taxable—as it normally is on mortgage loans. This savings is passed on to the home buyer. Those who qualify will typically pay about 3% less than if they had borrowed through conventional channels.

The objective of such programs is to make home ownership more affordable for low and middle income households. Also, some cities stipulate that loans must be used in neighborhoods that local officials want to revitalize. The bonds themselves are not backed by the full faith and credit of the municipality sponsoring them, but the mortgages made with them do carry mortgage insurance. Loans are made by local lenders who are paid a fee for originating and servicing these loans. Although popular with the real estate industry, the U.S. Treasury has been less than enthusiastic about the concept because it bears the cost in lost tax revenues. As a result, legislation has been passed that limits the future use of this source of money.

OTHER LENDERS

Pension funds and trust funds traditionally have channeled their money to high-grade government and corporate bonds and stocks. However, the trend now is to place more money into real estate loans. Since their rapid growth is projected, pension and trust funds will likely become a major source of real estate financing in the future. At present, pension and trust funds either buy mortgages through mortgage bankers or on the open market. In some localities, pension fund members can tap their own pension funds for home mortgages at very reasonable rates.

Finance companies that specialize in making business and consumer loans also provide limited financing for real estate. As a rule, finance companies seek second mortgages at interest rates 2 to 5 percent higher than the rates prevailing on first mortgages. First mortgages are also taken as collateral; however, the lenders already discussed usually charge lower interest rates for these loans and thus are more competitive.

Credit unions normally specialize in consumer loans. However, some of the country's 23,000 credit unions have recently branched out into first and second mortgage loans on real estate. Credit unions are an often overlooked, but excellent source of home loan money.

Individuals are sometimes a source of cash loans for real estate, with the bulk of these loans made between relatives or friends. Generally, loan maturities are shorter than those obtainable from the institutional lenders already described. In some cities, persons can be found who specialize in making or buying second and third mortgage loans of up to 10-year maturities.

SECONDARY MORTGAGE MARKET

The secondary mortgage market provides a way for a lender to sell a loan. It also permits investment in real estate loans without the need for loan origination and servicing facilities. Although apparently remote to real estate buyers, sellers, and agents alike, the secondary mortgage market plays an important role in getting money from those who want to lend to those who want to borrow. In other words think of the secondary mortgage market as a pipeline for loan money.

Federal National Mortgage Association

The best known secondary mortgage market operation in the United States is run by the Federal National Mortgage Association (FNMA), fondly known in the real estate business as **"Fannie Mae."** Originally organized by the federal government and later converted to a part public, part private corporation, Fannie Mae buys and sells FHA, VA, and conventional mortgage loans. Purchases are made, usually every 2 weeks, by inviting mortgage holders to offer their loans for sale to the FNMA. Funds for FNMA purchases come from the issue of corporate stock (which is currently traded on the New York

Stock Exchange) and the sale of FNMA bonds and notes. Funds are also generated by selling FNMA loan holdings to insurance companies, pension funds, savings associations, and other mortgage investors on a competitive basis. Whether FNMA holds a loan or resells it, the actual month-to-month servicing remains with the loan originator.

FNMA currently holds in excess of $39 billion of FHA and VA loans and $35 billion of conventional loans. This is about 5% of the total residential mortgage debt in the nation. By purchasing mortgage loans from lenders, FNMA provides lenders with more money to make more loans. This is an invaluable aid to the real estate industry, especially during periods of tight money.

In 1980, FNMA added two important financing programs: a home-seller loan program and a home refinance program. The home-seller program is actually a purchase money first mortgage accepted by a home seller. The loan is originated by an FNMA-approved lender using standard FNMA loan qualification procedures. The mortgage may then be kept by the home seller as an investment, or it may be sold to the FNMA-approved lender for possible resale to FNMA. The home refinance program permits any creditworthy buyer or owner of any home on which FNMA holds the mortgage to obtain a new conventional FNMA loan that reflects the property's current value. Existing FHA, VA, and conventional mortgages held by FNMA are eligible for the program.

Government National Mortgage Association

Known as **"Ginnie Mae,"** the Government National Mortgage Association (GNMA) was split off from FNMA in 1968 and established as a part of the U.S. Department of Housing and Urban Development (HUD). GNMA is known for its Tandem Plan and mortgage-backed securities program. Both of these are secondary market operations.

The **Tandem Plan** is a United States Government subsidy program whereby GNMA is authorized to purchase both federally insured and conventional mortgages at below-market interest rates in order to stimulate housing production in areas with special housing needs. These mortgages are then resold at current market prices with the government absorbing the loss as a subsidy. For example, a real estate loan made at an interest rate two percent below the market is attractive to a borrower but is not attractive to a lender. But, under the Tandem Plan, GNMA agrees to buy such a mortgage from the lender at full value, then resell it on the open market at a price low enough to be attractive to investors. The discount on the sale is absorbed by GNMA. Because of its cost the Tandem Plan is being phased out and only previously made commitments are being honored.

Under its **mortgage-backed securities program,** Ginnie Mae guarantees the timely payment of principal and interest to holders of securities issued by private lenders and backed by pools of HUD-insured and VA-guaranteed mortgages. The guarantee is backed by the full faith and credit of the United States Government. The **mortgage pools** are for similar types of property (for example, all single-family houses or all apartment buildings) at similar interest rates. Investors in these pools receive the monthly payments of principal and interest due on the mortgage loans in the pool regardless of whether or not they are collected from the borrowers. All prepayments and claims settlements are also passed through to the investors. This GNMA program has been very successful (currently over $150 billion in 70,000 pools) in attracting pension funds, trust funds, and individual investors to real estate lending.

Federal Home Loan Mortgage Corporation

The Federal Home Loan Mortgage Corporation (FHLMC), known as **"Freddie Mac,"** was established by an act of Congress in 1970 to provide a secondary market facility for savings and loan associations and other approved lenders. Freddie Mac has the authority to buy and sell FHA, VA, and conventional loans, enter into mortgage participations, and issue its own mortgage investment certificates. Under its loan purchase program (the **whole loan program**), the FHLMC will buy individual mortgages from banks and from savings and loan associations that meet FHLMC requirements as to loan application, appraisal methods, promissory note, and mortgage format. These loans are in turn packaged into lots of several million dollars each and resold to investors.

The FHLMC also markets **participation certificates** wherein an investor can purchase an undivided interest in a pool of mortgages rather than in individual loans. Designed to attract pension and trust fund money into home mortgages, these certificates are backed by residential mortgages held by

Freddie Mac. Principal and interest are paid monthly. This program has been very successful in moving money from investors to borrowers. From time-to-time the FHLMC also markets a **guaranteed mortgage certificate** that pays interest semiannually to investors.

During the 1970 decade, the Federal Home Loan Mortgage Corporation focused on finding buyers for fixed-rate loans. However, by 1980, rapidly rising interest rates made fixed-rate loans increasingly unpopular with lenders and investors. In response, a pilot program was introduced in 1982 wherein Freddie Mac would buy adjustable rate mortgages and resell them to investors as whole loans or as participation certificates. This program, if successful, will go a long way toward keeping money flowing from investors to home buyers.

A by-product of buying and selling loans has been the tremendously influential role of the FHLMC in standardizing loan documents. Prior to 1970, nearly every bank and savings and loan association in the country used a slightly different loan application form, appraisal form, mortgage form, promissory note, and loan approval procedure for its conventional mortgage loans. Part of the task of creating a nationwide secondary market for conventional loans was to develop standardized forms. Today, when you walk into a bank or savings and loan or mortgage company and apply for a home loan, the loan application that you fill out will be the same FHLMC form wherever you go. Similarly, the appraisal form will be the same FHLMC form as will be the mortgage form, the promissory note, and the loan approval procedure.

MGIC Investment Corporation

In 1972, the MGIC Investment Corporation, originators of the Mortgage Guaranty Insurance Corporation, formed a buying and selling unit to provide the first nonfederal secondary market for conventional mortgages. Promptly nicknamed **"Maggie Mae,"** it provides an outlet where a lender can sell MGIC-insured mortgages to other investors. Maggie Mae accepts loans on consignment from sellers and turns them into a single mortgage-backed security. MGIC has also developed mortgage certificates whereby a number of different investors can participate in the same pool of mortgages. MGIC provides the standard mortgage guaranty coverage plus a policy on the mortgage pool itself that guarantees the monthly pass-through of principal and interest to the investor. As with FNMA, GNMA, and FHLMC, the purpose is to attract investors who might not otherwise invest in mortgage loans.

AVAILABILITY AND PRICE OF MORTGAGE MONEY

Thus far we have been concerned with the money pipelines between lenders and borrowers. Ultimately though, the money a lender has available for loans must have a source. There are two basic sources: (1) savings generated by individuals and businesses as a result of their spending less than they earn **(real savings),** and (2) government-created money, commonly referred to as **fiat money** or "printing press money." This second source does not represent unconsumed labor and materials; instead it competes for available goods and services alongside the savings of individuals and businesses.

In the arena of money and capital, real estate borrowers must compete with the needs of government, business, and consumers. Governments, particularly the federal government, compete the hardest when they borrow to finance a deficit. Not to borrow would mean bankruptcy and the inability to pay government employees and provide government programs and services. Strong competition also comes from business and consumer credit sectors. In the face of strong competition for loan funds, home buyers must either pay higher interest or be outbid.

One "solution" to this problem is for the federal government to create more money, thus making competition for funds easier and interest rates lower. Unfortunately, the net result is often "too much money chasing too few goods" and prices are pulled upward by the demand caused by the newly created money. This is followed by rising interest rates as savers demand higher returns to compensate for losses in purchasing power. Many economists feel that the higher price levels and interest rates of the 1970s were due to applying too much of this "solution" to the economy since 1965.

The alternative solution, from the standpoint of residential loans, is to increase real savings or decrease competing demands for available money. A number of plans and ideas have been put forth by civic, business, and political leaders. They include proposals to balance the federal budget, incentives to increase productive output from available manpower and machines, incentives to increase savings by exempting savings deposit interest from income taxes, and proposals to decrease competition for funds through a credit allocation (rationing) system.

USURY

An old idea that has been tried, but is currently of dubious value for holding down interest rates, is legislation to impose interest rate ceilings. Known as **usury laws** and found in nearly all states, these laws were originally enacted to prohibit lenders from overcharging interest on loans to individuals. However, since the end of World War II, the ceilings in some states have failed to keep in step with rising interest rates. For example, a state with a 10% ceiling would have presented no problem to a home buyer in 1965, as home loans then carried interest rates around 6%. However, 14 years later, when home loan rates were 11%, if the ceiling was not increased, the home buyer would be denied a loan. To charge 11%, even if it is the current fair market rate for a home loan, is usury if the state-set ceiling is less than 11%. In states where that has happened, lenders have found it necessary to divert their funds to out-of-state borrowers, usually through a mortgage banker or the facilities of the FNMA, GNMA, FHLMC, and MGIC.

In response to this problem, Minnesota has established a flexible or floating interest ceiling based on a figure established monthly by the State Commissioner of Banking. Generally, Minnesota home mortgage lenders may charge 2% over the interest rate established on long-term U.S. Treasury bonds. Exempted from usury regulations are FHA and VA loans, loans to corporations, and loans in excess of $100,000.

Price to the Borrower

Ultimately, the rate of interest the borrower must pay to obtain a loan is dependent on the cost of money to the lender, reserves for default, loan servicing costs, and available investment alternatives. For example, in mid-1983 savings and loan associations were paying savers an average of 10% interest. To this must be added the cost of maintaining cash in the tills, office space, personnel, advertising, free gifts for depositors, FSLIC insurance, and loan servicing, plus loan reserves for defaults and a ¼% profit margin. This adds another 1¾%. Therefore, an association must charge 11¾% just to break even.

Life insurance companies do not have to "pay" for their money because it comes from policyholder premiums. Nonetheless, they do want to earn the highest possible yields, with safety, on the money in their custody in order to meet policy claims. Thus, if a real estate buyer wants to borrow from a life insurance company, he must compete successfully with the other investment opportunities available to the company. For example, if high-grade corporate bonds with maturities similar to mortgages are yielding 11¼% interest, to be competitive, real estate mortgage loans must offer 11¼%. As mortgage servicing costs of about ⅜ of 1% must be added to that, the borrower must pay 11⅝% to be equally attractive and 11¾% to be more attractive than corporate bonds. The same holds true when one wants to borrow from pension or trust funds.

ALIENATION AND PREPAYMENT CLAUSES

From an investment-risk standpoint, when a lender makes a loan with a fixed interest rate, the lender recognizes that, during the life of the loan, interest rates may rise or fall. When they rise, the lender remains locked into a lower rate. Most old loans contain an **alienation clause** (also called a **due-on-sale clause** or a **call clause**). In the past, these were inserted by lenders so that if the borrower sold the property to someone considered uncreditworthy by the lender, the lender could call the loan balance due. Today lenders are attempting to use these clauses to increase the rate of interest on the loan when the property changes hands. Sellers feel this to be an unfair use of the due-on-sale clause and have gone to court on the matter.

In the case of *Wellenkamp* v. *Bank of America* (21 Cal. 3d 943), Cynthia Wellenkamp purchased a home by paying the seller cash for the equity and assuming the existing loan. Shortly after the sale, the lender, Bank of America, attempted to enforce its alienation clause. Ms. Wellenkamp objected, and filed a lawsuit to stop the pending foreclosure. In a landmark decision made in 1978, the Supreme Court of California held that in order to enforce a due-on-sale clause the lender must demonstrate that enforcement is necessary to protect repayment of the loan. This decision effectively stopped most lenders in the state from raising the interest rate on a loan when the property securing it was sold. By 1981, 17 states, including Minnesota, had taken the position that a due-on-sale clause cannot be used to increase the interest rate on a loan.

In June of 1982 the U.S. Supreme Court decided the *Fidelity Federal Savings and Loan* v. *de la Cuesta* case. The Court found in favor of Fidelity Federal, ruling that federally-chartered savings and loan associations have the right to enforce due-on-sale clauses. Although this ruling does not apply to individuals, banks or state-chartered savings and loans, it is reasonable to expect new legislation and court rulings that will allow these lenders to enforce their due-on-sale clauses. One such law, the Garn-St Germain Depository Institutions Act of 1982 passed by the federal government, overrules Minnesota Statutes that restrict enforcement of due-on-sale clauses unless the lender's security is impaired. There are certain exceptions in Minnesota under which the due-on-sale clause is not enforceable until October 15, 1985. After that time, however, all lenders, whether an individual, bank or state-chartered savings and loan, may enforce their due-on-sale clauses.

Due-on-sale clauses are an important issue because in periods of high interest rates, it is advantageous to the seller to be able to pass along to the buyer an existing low-interest rate loan. In fact, often it is the only way a property can be sold. A lender, however, takes a financial loss whenever the lender receives less interest on a loan than it is paying to borrow from savers. With enough loans like this a lender can go bankrupt. And if enough lenders go bankrupt, loans will be harder to find. So there is no simple solution. Meanwhile, lenders are placing due-on-sale clauses in new loan contracts that specifically allow for interest rate increases upon conveyance of a property. FNMA goes one step further by requiring a 7-year call provision that allows the loan to be called after 7 years, and the interest rate changed, even though the property has not changed ownership.

Prepayment Penalty

If loan rates drop it becomes worthwhile for a borrower to shop for a new loan and repay the existing one in full. To discourage this, loan contracts sometimes call for a **prepayment penalty** in return for giving the borrower the right to repay his loan early. Typically, a prepayment penalty amounts to the equivalent of 3 to 6 months interest on the amount that is being paid early. Minnesota does not now permit prepayment penalties on residential mortgage loans. By federal law, prepayment penalties are not allowed on FHA, VA, and FNMA standardized loans.

VARIABLE RATE MORTGAGES

As we have already seen, a major problem for savings institutions is that they are locked into long-term loans while being dependent on relatively short-term savings deposits. Because of their experience of rising interest rates paid to savers in the 1970s and early 1980s, many savings institutions and banks prefer to make mortgage loans that allow the interest rate to rise and fall during the life of the loan.

The first step in this direction was the **variable rate mortgage (VRM)** introduced in the late 1970s. It was a mortgage loan with an interest rate that could be adjusted up or down during the life of the loan to reflect the rising or falling cost of funds to the lender. The Federal Home Loan Bank Board (FHLBB) limited adjustments to no more than ½ of 1% per year and a total upward adjustment of no more than 2½% during the life of the loan. Rate adjustments are based on an index of borrowing costs for savings and loan associations published by the FHLBB. The rules specify that if the index falls, the lender must reduce the interest rate. If the index rises, the lender may increase the rate. Additionally, the lender was required to offer the prospective borrower the choice of a fixed-rate loan or a VRM and to disclose to the borrower what would happen to the monthly payments if interest rates increased. Despite these safeguards and the fact that VRMs usually carry lower initial interest rates than fixed-rate loans, there was skepticism from the public. After all, long-term fixed-rate loans had been the standard method of real estate lending for more than a generation.

RENEGOTIABLE RATE MORTGAGES

On April 3, 1980, another type of variable interest rate mortgage loan was approved by the FHLBB. This was the **renegotiable rate mortgage** or **RRM.** This mortgage is amortized over 30 years but must be renewed at 3-, 4-, or 5-year intervals. At renewal time, the interest rate can be increased no more than ½ of 1% for each year of the initial term. Thus on a three-year RRM, the maximum rate adjustment allowed is 1½%. On a five-year term it is 2½%. There is a 5% limit on upward adjustments during the life of the loan. Downward adjustments must be made if the lender's borrowing costs decline.

Rules regarding VRMs also were changed when it became

apparent that they were not flexible enough to keep pace with rapidly rising interest rates. As a result, banks can now make VRMs that may be adjusted by as much as 1% every six months with no cap on how much the rate can rise over the life of the loan. The borrower must be given 30 days advance notice of any change in rate and the opportunity to repay the loan early without penalty.

ADJUSTABLE RATE MORTGAGES

On March 30, 1981, savings and loan associations were authorized to make a new type of adjustable interest rate mortgage. This is the **adjustable rate mortgage (ARM),** sometimes called an adjustable mortgage loan (AML). More flexible than the VRM or RRM, there is no limit on how far and how often the interest rate on an ARM can fluctuate. The main requirement is that the rate on the loan be tied to some publicly available index that is mutually acceptable to the lender and the borrower. For example, yields on Treasury bills or the average cost of funds to S&Ls as published by the FHLBB could be used as an index. The lender must also carefully explain to the borrower what will happen if and when rates rise and fall over the life of the loan and give the borrower the privilege of repaying the loan early without a prepayment penalty.

Rate Changes

There are three ways to accommodate a change in the interest rate on an existing loan. The first is to raise or lower the monthly payment by the amount of the change. The second is to keep the monthly payment constant but shorten or lengthen the maturity. The third is to keep the monthly payment and maturity constant but change the amount owed. In response to consumer concern that a loan with no limits on interest rate increases could produce unlimited increases in monthly payments, ARM regulations allow lenders to set interest rate and monthly payment caps. An interest rate cap would be, for example, an agreement by the lender to limit interest rate increases (or decreases) to 2% per year even though the index being used called for a change greater than that. With a payment-capped loan, the monthly payment remains constant even though the index rises. If the payment does not cover the new interest rate, the excess is added to the amount owed on the loan. In other words, there will be **negative amortization** of the loan. To keep the loan from growing too large, a payment adjustment is scheduled from time to time as agreed to in the lending contract. This might be as often as every six months or as infrequent as every five years. At that time the monthly payment is adjusted to fully amortize the loan over the remaining term.

The other alternative, extending the maturity, is only effective if the interest rate change is a small one. For example, extending a maturity from 25 to 40 years will accommodate an interest increase of less than 1%. Moreover, a lender may not be willing to extend a maturity to 40 years due to the age of the mortgaged structure. Because of these problems, maturity changes are little used.

Some have called unlimited interest rate increases and negative amortization legalized gambling. Others point out that as long as banks and savings and loans must rely on short-term deposits, they must have equal flexibility in the rates they charge their borrowers or they will go out of business. Ultimately the borrower must decide whether or not the need to borrow outweighs the risks of rising monthly payments. The alternative to a variable loan is a fixed-rate loan. However, these may be scarcer and more expensive.

SHARED APPRECIATION MORTGAGES

The basic concept of a **shared appreciation mortgage (SAM)** is that the borrower gives the lender a portion of the property's appreciation in return for a lower rate of interest. To illustrate, a lender who would otherwise charge 15% interest might agree to take 10% interest plus one-third of the appreciation of the property. The lender is accepting what amounts to a speculative investment in the property in return for a reduced interest rate. The borrower is able to buy and occupy a home that he or she might not otherwise be able to afford, but gives up part of any future price appreciation. In August, 1980, $2½ million of SAM loan money was offered by a Florida S&L. The prevailing market rate at the time was 12% and the loans were offered at 8% with one-third of the appreciation going to the lender. All loans were taken by the end of the next business day.

Despite the apparent advantages of the SAM, there are some major pitfalls. For example, at what point in the future is the gain recognized and the lender paid off? If the home is sold, the profits can be split in accordance with the agreement.

However, what if the lender feels the home is being sold at too low a price? What if the home is not sold for cash? What if the borrower does not want to sell? One answer to the last situation is that the lender may set a time limit of 10 years on the loan. If the home has not been sold by that time, the home is appraised and the borrower pays the lender the lender's share of the appreciation. At a 10% appreciation rate, a $93,750 house would be worth $243,164 ten years later. If the lender was entitled to one-third of the $149,414 appreciation, the borrower would owe the lender $49,805 in appreciation plus the remaining $70,000 balance on the loan. Unless the borrower can pay cash, this would have to be refinanced at then current rates of interest. On the other hand, if the property experiences no appreciation in value, the borrower will have enjoyed a below-market-rate loan for 10 years and be responsible only for refinancing the remaining loan balance at that time.

GRADUATED PAYMENT MORTGAGE

The objective of a **graduated payment mortgage** is to help borrowers qualify for loans by basing repayment schedules on salary expectations. With this type of mortgage, the interest rate and maturity are fixed but the monthly payment varies. For example, a 10%, $60,000, 30-year loan normally requires monthly payments of $527 for complete amortization. Under the graduated payment mortgage, payments could start out as low as $437 per month the first year, then gradually increase to $590 in the eleventh year and then remain at that level until the thirtieth year.

Since the interest alone on this $60,000 loan is $500 per month, the amount owed on the loan actually increases every month. Only when the monthly payment exceeds the monthly interest does the balance owed on the loan decrease.

The graduated payment mortgage was created by the U.S. Department of Housing and Urban Development. The FHA insures graduated payment mortgages under Section 245 and offers five repayment plans, each designed to fit a different buyer's particular needs. It is expected that this program will likely appeal most to first-time home buyers in the $15,000 to $25,000 income range because it enables them to tailor their installment payments to their expanding incomes, and thus buy a home sooner than under regular mortgage financing. Note, however, that the down payment required will be somewhat larger than the 3% to 5% required on standard FHA 203(b) mortgages. This is because the FHA stipulates that the mortgage cannot exceed 97% of the house value, including deferred interest. To be more attractive to lenders, an **adjustable graduated payment mortgage** is now available. It combines variable interest provisions with graduated payment features.

BLENDED-RATE LOAN

Most real estate lenders still hold loans that were made at interest rates below the current market. One way of raising the return on these loans is to offer borrowers who have them a **blended-rate loan.** Suppose you owe $50,000 on your home loan and the interest rate on it is 7%. Suppose further that the current rate on home loans is 12%. Your lender might offer to refinance your home for $70,000 at 9%, or $100,000 at 10½%, presuming the property will appraise high enough and you have the income to qualify. The $70,000 refinance offer would put $20,000 in your pocket (less loan fees), but would increase the interest you pay from 7% to 9% on the original $50,000. This actually makes the cost of the $20,000 14% per year.

With the $100,000 loan, you would be giving up the 7%, $50,000 loan you now have. This makes the cost of the extra $50,000 14% per year. That is the figure you should use in comparing other sources of financing (such as a second mortgage) or deciding whether you even want to borrow.

A blended-rate loan can be very attractive in a situation where you want to sell your home and you do not want to help finance the buyer. Suppose your home is worth $125,000 and you have the above described $50,000, 7% loan. A buyer would normally expect to make a down payment of $25,000 and pay up to 12% interest on a new $100,000 loan. But with a blended loan your lender could offer the buyer the needed $100,000 financing at 10½%, a far more attractive rate and one that requires less income in order to qualify. Blended loans are available on FHA, VA, and conventional loans held by the FNMA. Other lenders also offer them on fixed-rate loans they hold.

BUY-DOWNS

Buy-downs are used to reduce the rate of interest a buyer must pay on a new mortgage loan. They have been used extensively in recent years by builders with new homes to sell.

For example, suppose a builder has a tract of homes for sale and the interest rate on home loans is 16½%, as they were in 1982. At that interest rate, he is finding few buyers. What he can do is to arrange with a lender to pay the lender enough money so that the lender can offer the loan at a lower interest to the buyer. This could take the form of a 12½% interest rate for the first 3 years of the loan. Not only is 12½% more attractive than 16½%, but more buyers can qualify for loans at 12½% than at 16½%. Although the buy-down is costly to the builder, it will help sell homes that might otherwise go unsold. Moreover, a buy-down will usually boost sales more than a price reduction of like amount. Hopefully, loan rates will drop before the three years expire and the buyer can refinance. If not, at least the buyer has a loan.

GROWING EQUITY MORTGAGE

The **growing equity mortgage (GEM)** is rapidly gaining acceptance by lenders and borrowers alike. The GEM combines the low initial payment of a 30-year mortgage loan with the lower interest rate obtainable for a much shorter term mortgage. In the GEM, the borrower agrees to raise his monthly payment by some fixed percentage each year over the life of the loan. The extra money generated by each payment after the initial year is applied entirely to principal. Thus, a GEM calling for an annual increase in monthly payments of 3% would be completely paid out in approximately 15 years. It is a fixed-interest-rate, adjustable-payment loan and is sometimes described as a **fixed-rate-adjustable-mortgage (FRAM).**

EQUITY MORTGAGES

The rapid price increases of houses in the late 1970s combined with an FHLBB rule change that now allows S&Ls to make second mortgage loans has opened a potentially large loan market. Prior to 1979, S&Ls were not permitted to make second mortgage loans. Thus, a homeowner who wanted to borrow against the equity in his or her home would either refinance with a new and larger first mortgage or leave the existing first and obtain a second mortgage loan from a specialty lender or mortgage broker. Today, an S&L can make a second provided the amount of the first and the second combined does not exceed 80% of the appraised value of the property. Thus a home worth $100,000 with a $30,000 mortgage balance would be eligible for a $50,000 **equity mortgage.**

OTHER MORTGAGE PLANS

In addition to the fixed-rate, adjustable rate, and graduated payment mortgages described thus far, there have been other loan payment variations and there will be more in the future. Exactly what evolves will depend on the problem to be solved. For example, the long-term fixed-rate amortized mortgage was a solution for loan foreclosures in the 1930s and it served well as long as interest rates did not fluctuate greatly. Graduated payment mortgages came into being when housing prices were rising faster than incomes and a means of lowering monthly payments was needed. VRMs, RRMs, and ARMs came into existence so that lenders could more closely align the interest they receive from borrowers with the interest they pay their savers. Extensive use of loan assumptions and seller financing (discussed later in this chapter) became necessary in the early 1980s because borrowers could not qualify for 16% and 18% mortgage loans.

With regard to the future, if mortgage money remains expensive or is in short supply, assumptions and seller financing will be major sources of real estate finance. With the experience of rapidly increasing interest rates still fresh in people's memories, loans with adjustable interest rates will prevail at lending institutions. Fixed-rate loans will either carry short maturities or carry a premium to compensate the lender for being locked into a fixed rate. In periods of falling interest rates, borrowers with adjustable mortgages will benefit from lower monthly payments. If rates stay down long enough, fixed-rate loans will become more plentiful.

LOAN APPLICATION AND APPROVAL

When a mortgage lender reviews a real estate loan application, the primary concern for both applicant and lender is to approve loan requests that show a high probability of being repaid in full and on time, and to disapprove requests that are likely to result in default and eventual foreclosure. How is this decision made? Figure 12:2 summarizes the key items that a loan officer considers when making a decision regarding a loan request. Let us review these items and observe how they affect the acceptability of a loan to a lender.

In section ①, the lender begins the loan analysis procedure by looking at the property and the proposed financing. Using the property address and legal description, an appraiser is assigned to prepare an appraisal of the property and a title search

Figure 12:2

RESIDENTIAL MORTGAGE LOAN ANALYSIS

(1)

Property address __________
Legal description __________
Appraised value $ __________ *Purchase price $* __________ *Year Built* __________
Down payment $ __________ *Total cash required for settlement $* __________
Amount of this mortgage loan $ __________ *Other financing $* __________
Loan to value ratio: This mortgage loan __________ *% All financing for the property* __________ *%*
Source of settlement funds? __________
Purpose of loan? __________ *Occupancy of property?* __________
Attitude of borrower __________

(2) Borrower

Name __________ *Age* __________
Dependents other than co-borrower
Number __________ *Ages* __________
Employer __________
Years with current employer __________
Years this line of work __________
Position/Title __________
Type of business __________
Self-employed? __________
Previous employer __________
Position __________ *Years* __________

(3) Co-Borrower

Name __________ *Age* __________
Dependents other than co-borrower
Number __________ *Ages* __________
Employer __________
Years with current employer __________
Years this line of work __________
Position/Title __________
Type of business __________
Self-employed? __________
Previous employer __________
Position __________ *Years* __________

(4) Gross Monthly Income

	Borrower	Co-borrower
Base income	$	$
Overtime		
Bonuses		
Commissions		
Interest/Dividends		
Rental income		
Other		
Other		
Total	$	$

(5) Monthly Housing Expense

	Previous	Proposed
Rent	$	
First loan (P+I)		$
Other loans (P+I)		
Mortgage insurance		
Hazard insurance		
Real estate taxes		
Assessments		
Owners' Assn.		
Total	$	$

Ratio of monthly housing expense to gross monthly income ________ % (6)

(7) Assets

Cash toward purchase	$
Checking and savings	
Stocks and bonds	
Life insurance cash value	
(Face amount $ ________)	
Sub-total liquid assets	$
Real estate owned	
Retirement fund	
Net worth of business	
Automobiles	
Furniture	
Other assets	
Total Assets	$

(8) Liabilities

Installment debts	Mo. Pymt/Mos.	Balance
	$ /	$
	/	
	/	
Auto loan	/	
Real estate loans		
	/	
	/	
Other debts		
	/	
Alimony/Child support	/	
Total Mo. Payments	$	
Total Debts		$

(10)

Net Worth: *Total assets minus total debts equals $* ________ (9)

Report from credit bureau ________

Any bankruptcies? ________ *Any pending lawsuits?* ________

Is either applicant a co-maker or endorser on any other loans? ________

Do applicants have health insurance? ________ *Disability insurance?* ________

is ordered. These steps are taken to determine the fair market value of the property and the condition of title. In the event of default, this is the collateral the lender must fall back upon to recover the loan. If the loan request is in connection with a purchase, rather than the refinancing of an existing property, the lender will know the purchase price. As a rule, loans are made on the basis of the appraised value or purchase price, whichever is lower. If the appraised value is lower than the purchase price, the usual procedure is to require the buyer to make a larger cash down payment. The lender does not want to overloan simply because the buyer overpaid for the property.

Continuing in section ①, the year the home was built is useful in setting the loan's maturity date. The idea is that the length of the loan should not outlast the remaining economic life of the structure serving as collateral. Note however, chronological age is only part of this decision because age must be considered in light of the upkeep and repair of the structure and its construction quality.

Redlining

In the past, it was not uncommon for lenders to refuse to make loans in certain neighborhoods regardless of the quality of the structure or the ability of the borrower to repay. This was known as **redlining** and it effectively shut off mortgage loans in many older or so-called "bad risk" neighborhoods across the country. Today, a lender cannot deny a loan application solely because of the age of a building or because of neighborhood income level or racial composition. To assure compliance, the federal government requires lenders who make federally-related loans to disclose the number of loans made in various sections of their service area.

A lender can refuse to lend on a structure intended for demolition, a property in a known geological hazard area, a property that is in violation of zoning laws, deed covenants, conditions, or restrictions, or significant health, safety, or building codes, or upon a single family dwelling in an area devoted to industrial or commercial use.

Loan-to-Value Ratios

The lender next looks at the amount of down payment the borrower proposes to make, the size of the loan being requested and the amount of other financing the borrower plans to use. This information is then converted into loan-to-value ratios. As a rule, the more money the borrower places into the deal, the safer the loan is for the lender. On an uninsured loan, the ideal loan-to-value (L/V) ratio for a lender on owner-occupied residential property is 70% or less. This means the value of the property would have to fall more than 30% before the debt owed would exceed the property's value, thus encouraging the borrower to stop making loan payments. Because of the nearly constant inflation in housing prices since the 1940s, very few residential properties have fallen 30% or more in value.

Loan-to-value ratios from 70% through 80% are considered acceptable but do expose the lender to more risk. Lenders sometimes compensate by charging slightly higher interest rates. Loan-to-value ratios above 80% present even more risk of default to the lender, and the lender will either increase the interest rate charged on these loans or require that an outside insurer, such as the FHA or a private mortgage insurer, be supplied by the borrower.

Settlement Funds

Next in section ①, the lender wants to know if the borrower has adequate funds for settlement (the closing). Are these funds presently in a checking or savings account, or are they coming from the sale of the borrower's present property? In the latter case, the lender knows the present loan is contingent on another closing. If the down payment and settlement funds are to be borrowed, then the lender will want to be extra cautious as experience has shown that the less of his own money a borrower puts into a purchase, the higher the probability of default and foreclosure.

Purpose of Loan

The lender is also interested in the proposed use of the property. Lenders feel most comfortable when a loan is for the purchase or improvement of a property the loan applicant will actually occupy. This is because owner-occupants usually have pride-of-ownership in maintaining their property and even during bad economic conditions will continue to make the monthly payments. An owner-occupant also realizes that if he stops paying, he will have to vacate and pay for shelter elsewhere.

If the loan applicant intends to purchase a dwelling to

rent out as an investment, the lender will be more cautious. This is because during periods of high vacancy, the property may not generate enough income to meet the loan payments. At that point, a strapped-for-cash borrower is likely to default. Note too, that lenders generally avoid loans secured by purely speculative real estate. If the value of the property drops below the amount owed, the borrower may see no further logic in making the loan payments.

Lastly in this section, the lender assesses the borrower's attitude toward the proposed loan. A casual attitude, such as "I'm buying because real estate always goes up," or an applicant who does not appear to understand the obligation he is undertaking would bring a low rating here. Much more welcome is the applicant who shows a mature attitude and understanding of the loan obligation and who exhibits a strong and logical desire for ownership.

Borrower Analysis

In sections ② and ③ the lender begins an analysis of the borrower, and if there is one, the co-borrower. At one time, age, sex and marital status played an important role in the lender's decision to lend or not to lend. Often the young and the old had trouble getting loans, as did women and persons who were single, divorced, or widowed. Today, the Federal Equal Credit Opportunity Act prohibits discrimination based on age, sex, race and marital status. Lenders are no longer permitted to discount income earned by women even if it is from part-time jobs or because the woman is of child-bearing age. If the applicant chooses to disclose it, alimony, separate maintenance, and child support must be counted in full. Young adults and single persons cannot be turned down because the lender feels they have not "put down roots." Seniors cannot be turned down as long as life expectancy exceeds the early risk period of the loan and collateral is adequate. In other words, the emphasis in borrower analysis is now focused on job stability, income adequacy, net worth and credit rating.

Thus in sections ② and ③ we see questions directed at how long the applicants have held their present jobs and the stability of those jobs themselves. The lender recognizes that loan repayment will be a regular monthly requirement and wishes to make certain the applicants have a regular monthly inflow of cash in a large enough quantity to meet the loan payment as well as their other living expenses. Thus, an applicant who possesses marketable job skills and has been regularly employed with a stable employer is considered the ideal risk. Persons whose income can rise and fall erratically, such as commissioned salespersons, present greater risks. Persons whose skills (or lack of skills) or lack of job seniority result in frequent unemployment are more likely to have difficulty repaying a loan. In these sections the lender also inquires as to the number of dependents the applicant must support out of his or her income. This information provides some insight as to how much will be left for monthly house payments.

Monthly Income

In section ④ the lender looks at the amount and sources of the applicants' income. Sheer quantity alone is not enough for loan approval; the income sources must be stable too. Thus a lender will look carefully at overtime, bonus and commission income in order to estimate the levels at which these may reasonably be expected to continue. Interest, dividend and rental income would be considered in light of the stability of their sources also. Under the "other" category, income from alimony, child support, social security, retirement pensions, public assistance, etc. is entered and added to the totals for the applicants.

In section ⑤ the lender compares what the applicants have been paying for housing with what they will be paying if the loan is approved. Included in the proposed housing expense total are principal, interest, taxes and insurance along with any assessments or homeowner association dues (such as in a condominium). Some lenders add the monthly cost of utilities to this list.

At ⑥, proposed monthly housing expense is compared to gross monthly income. A general rule of thumb is that monthly housing expense (PITI) should not exceed 25% to 30% of gross monthly income. A second guideline is that total fixed monthly expenses should not exceed 33% to 38% of income. This includes housing payments plus automobile payments, installment loan payments, alimony, child support, and investments with negative cash flows. These are general guidelines, but lenders recognize that food, health care, clothing, transportation, entertainment and income taxes must also come from the applicants' income.

Assets and Liabilities

In section ⑦ the lender is interested in the applicants' sources of funds for closing and whether, once the loan is granted, the applicants have assets to fall back upon in the event of an income decrease (a job lay-off) or unexpected expenses (hospital bills). Of particular interest is the portion of those assets that are in cash or are readily convertible into cash in a few days. These are called **liquid assets.** If income drops, they are much more useful in meeting living expenses and loan payments than assets that may require months to sell and convert to cash; that is, assets which are **illiquid.**

Note in section ⑦ that two values are shown for life insurance. **Cash value** is the amount of money the policyholder would receive if he surrendered his policy or, alternatively, the amount he could borrow against the policy. **Face amount** is the amount that would be paid in the event of the insured's death. Lenders feel most comfortable if the face amount of the policy equals or exceeds the amount of the proposed loan. Less satisfactory are amounts less than the proposed loan or none at all. Obviously a borrower's death is not anticipated before the loan is repaid, but lenders recognize that its possibility increases the probability of default. The likelihood of foreclosure is lessened considerably if the survivors receive life insurance benefits.

In section ⑧, the lender is interested in the applicants' existing debts and liabilities for two reasons. First, these items will compete each month against housing expenses for available monthly income. Thus high monthly payments in this section may reduce the size of the loan the lender calculates that the applicants will be able to repay. The presence of monthly liabilities is not all negative: it can also show the lender that the applicants are capable of repaying their debts. Second, the applicants' total debts are subtracted from their total assets to obtain their net worth, reported at ⑨. If the result is negative (more owed than owned), the loan request will probably be turned down as too risky. In contrast, a substantial net worth can often offset weaknesses elsewhere in the application, such as too little monthly income in relation to monthly housing expense.

Past Credit Record

At number ⑩, lenders examine the applicants' past record of debt repayment as an indicator of the future. A credit report that shows no derogatory information is most desirable. Applicants with no previous credit experience will have more weight placed on income and employment history. Applicants with a history of collections, adverse judgments or bankruptcy within the past three years will have to convince the lender that this loan will be repaid on time. Additionally, the applicants may be considered poorer risks if they have guaranteed the repayment of someone else's debt by acting as a co-maker or endorser. Lastly, the lender may take into consideration whether the applicants have adequate insurance protection in the event of major medical expenses or a disability that prevents returning to work.

ALTERNATIVES TO INSTITUTIONAL LENDERS

When institutional lenders, such as those already described in this chapter, will not loan on a property, one must seek alternative sources of financing or lose the sale. Let us briefly review some of the more commonly available alternatives.

PURCHASE MONEY MORTGAGE

When a seller is willing to accept part of the purchase price owed him in the form of the buyer's promissory note accompanied by a mortgage or deed of trust, it is called a **purchase money mortgage** or **purchase money deed of trust.** This allows the buyer to substitute a promissory note for cash and the seller is said to be "taking back paper." Purchase money financing is popular for land sales (where lenders rarely loan), on property where an existing mortgage is being assumed by the buyer, and on property where the seller prefers to receive his money spread out over a period of time, with interest, instead of lump-sum cash. For example, a retired couple moves out of a large home into a smaller one. The large home is worth $120,000, and they owe $20,000. If they need only $60,000 to make their move, they might be more than happy to take $60,000 down, let the buyer assume the existing mortgage and accept the remaining $40,000 as $400 per month payments at current interest rates. Alternatively, the buyer and seller can agree to structure the $40,000 as a VRM, RRM, ARM, GPM, partially amortized loan or interest-only term loan.

If the seller receives the sales price spread out over two or more years, the seller can use the installment reporting method for calculating income taxes as discussed in Chapter 13. Being able to spread out the taxes on a gain is a major incentive to use seller financing, especially for investment property.

The seller should be aware, however, that he may not be able to convert his "paper" to cash without a long wait or without having to sell it at a substantial discount to an investor. Additionally, the seller is responsible for servicing the loan and is subject to losses due to default and foreclosure. Nonetheless, in a tight money market a purchase money mortgage, or one of the financing alternatives discussed next, may be the only way he will be able to sell.

WRAPAROUND MORTGAGES

An alternative method of financing a real estate sale such as the one just reviewed is to use a **wraparound mortgage** or **wraparound deed of trust.** A "wraparound" encompasses existing mortgages and is subordinate (junior) to them. The existing mortgages stay on the property and the new mortgage wraps around them.

To illustrate, presume the existing mortgage in the previous example carries an interest rate of 7% and that there are 15 years remaining on the loan. Presume further that current interest rates are 11%. With a wraparound it is possible for the buyer to pay less than 11% and at the same time for the seller to receive more than 11% on the money owed him. This is done by taking the buyer's $60,000 down payment and then creating a new junior mortgage that includes not only the $20,000 owed on the existing first mortgage, but also the $40,000 the buyer owes the seller. In other words, the wraparound mortgage will be for $60,000, and the seller continues to remain liable for payment of the first mortgage. If the interest rate on the wraparound is set at 10%, the buyer saves by not having to pay 11% as he would on an entirely new loan. The advantage to the seller is that he is earning 10% not only on his $40,000 equity, but also on the $20,000 loan for which he is paying 7% interest. This gives the seller an actual yield of 11½% on his $40,000. (The calculation is as follows. The seller receives 10% on $60,000, which amounts to $6,000. He pays 7% on $20,000, which is $1,400. The difference, $4,600, is divided by $40,000 to get the seller's actual yield of 11½%.)

Wraparounds are not limited to seller financing. If the seller in the above example did not want to finance the sale, a third party lender could provide the needed $40,000 and take a wraparound mortgage. The wraparound concept will not work when the mortgage debt to be "wrapped" contains an enforceable alienation clause.

SUBORDINATION

Another financing alternative is **subordination.** For example, a person owns a $20,000 vacant lot suitable for building, and a builder wants to build an $80,000 building on the lot. The builder has only $10,000 cash and the largest construction loan available is $80,000. If the builder can convince the seller to take $10,000 in cash and $10,000 later, he would have the $100,000 total. Note, however, that the lender making the $80,000 loan will want to be the first mortgagee to protect its position in the event of foreclosure. The lot owner must be willing to take a subordinate position, in this case a second mortgage. If the project is successful, the lot owner will receive $10,000, plus interest, either in cash after the building is built and sold or as monthly payments. If the project goes into foreclosure, the lot seller can be paid only if the $80,000 first mortgage claim is satisfied in full from the sale proceeds.

CONTRACT FOR DEED

A **contract for deed,** also called an **installment contract** or **land contract,** enables the seller to finance a buyer by permitting him to make a down payment followed by monthly payments. However, title remains in the name of the seller. In addition to its wide use in financing land sales, it has also been a very effective financing tool in several states as a means of selling homes during periods of tight money. For example, a homeowner owes $25,000 on his home and wants to sell it for $85,000. A buyer is found but does not have the $60,000 down payment necessary to assume the existing loan. The buyer does have $8,000, but for one reason or another money is not available from institutional lenders. If the seller is agreeable, the buyer can pay $8,000 and enter into an installment contract for the remaining $77,000. The contract will call for monthly payments by the buyer to the seller that are large enough to allow the seller to meet the payments on the $25,000 loan plus repay the $52,000 owed to the seller, with interest. Unless property taxes and insurance are billed to the buyer, the seller will also collect for these and pay them. When loan money is later available from institutional lenders, the installment contract and existing loan are paid in full and title is conveyed to the buyer. Meanwhile the seller continues to hold title and is responsible for paying the mortgage. In addition to wrapping around a mortgage, an installment contract can also be used to wrap around another installment contract, provided it does not contain an enforceable alienation clause.

Because title is not conveyed until some later date, the buyer is in a vulnerable position. It is possible that the buyer could make all the required payments only to find that the title cannot be delivered because the seller died or became legally incompetent, or because the seller did not pay the existing mortgage payments as agreed, or because the property has become encumbered with new liens against the seller. Commonly used safeguards are to (1) record the contract, (2) have a neutral third party (escrow) collect the buyer's payments and disburse them to existing lienholders and the seller, and (3) have the seller sign a deed now and place it into escrow for delivery later.

Recording the contract puts the public on notice that the buyer has an equitable interest in the property that is superior to subsequent encumbrances. The use of a disbursing agent gives the buyer confidence that existing liens are being paid. Holding the deed in escrow avoids death and incompetence complications, but it does place a major responsibility on the escrow agent to make certain the contract has been properly fulfilled before releasing the deed to the buyer.

OPTION

When viewed as a financing tool, an **option** provides a method by which the need to immediately finance the full price of a property can be postponed. For example, a builder is offered 100 acres of land for a house subdivision, but is not sure the market will absorb that many houses. The solution is to buy 25 acres outright and take three 25-acre options at set prices on the remainder. If the houses on the first 25 acres sell promptly, the builder can exercise the options to buy the remaining land. If sales are not good, the builder can let the remaining options expire and avoid being stuck with unwanted acreage.

A useful variation on the option idea is the lease-option combination. Under it an owner leases to a tenant who, in addition to paying rent and using the property, also obtains the right for 6 months or 1 year to purchase it at a set price.

Homes are often sold this way, particularly when the resale market is sluggish.

The option can also provide speculative opportunities to persons with limited amounts of capital. If prices do not rise, the optionee loses only the cost of the option; if prices do rise, the optionee finds a buyer and simultaneously exercises the option, thereby realizing a nice profit.

RENTAL

Even though tenants do not acquire fee ownership, **rentals and leases** are a means of financing real estate. Whether the tenant is a bachelor receiving the use of a $20,000 apartment for which he pays $250 rent per month, or a large corporation leasing a warehouse for 20 years, leasing is an ideal method of financing when the tenant does not want to buy, cannot raise the funds to buy, or perfers to invest available funds elsewhere. Similarly, **farming leases** provide for the use of land without the need to purchase it. Although some farm leases call for fixed rental payments, the more common arrangement is for the farmer to pay the landowner a share of the value of the crop that is actually produced—say 25%. Thus, the landowner shares with the farmer the risks of weather, crop output, and prices.

Under a **sale and leaseback** arrangement, an owner-occupant sells the property and then remains as a tenant. Thus, the buyer acquires an investment and the seller obtains capital for other purposes while retaining the use of the property. A variation is for the tenant to order a building constructed, sell it to a prearranged buyer, and lease it back upon completion.

OVERENCUMBERED PROPERTY

The decade of the 1980s started with a shortage of money for real estate loans and an abundance of financing ideas. Many of these involved seller-assisted financing. In fact, by 1982 it was estimated that 80% of home mortgage financing was by way of assumptions and seller financing.

One seller-financing arrangement that deserves special attention because of its traps for the unwary is the **overencumbered property.** Institutional lenders are closely regulated regarding the amount of money they can loan against the appraised value of the property. Individuals are not regulated. The following example will illustrate the potential problem. Suppose you own a house that is worth, realistically, $100,000, and the mortgage balance is $10,000. A buyer offers to purchase the property with the condition that he be allowed to obtain an $80,000 loan on the property from a lender. The $80,000 is used to pay off the existing $10,000 loan and to pay the broker's commission, loan fees and closing costs. The remaining $62,000 is split $30,000 to the seller and $32,000 to the buyer. The buyer also gives the seller a note, secured by a second mortgage against the property, for $80,000. The seller may feel good about getting $30,000 in cash and an $80,000 mortgage, for this is more than the property is worth, or so it seems.

But the $80,000 second stands junior to the $80,000 first. That's $160,000 of debt against a $100,000 property. The buyer might be trying to resell the property for $160,000 or more, but the chances of this are slim. More likely the buyer will wind up walking away from the property. This leaves the seller the choice of taking over the payments on the first mortgage or losing the property completely to the holder of the first.

INVESTING IN MORTGAGES

The opportunity for individuals to invest their money in mortgages has been available for many years. But it was not until money became increasingly tight in 1979 and the early 1980s that the idea caught on with the public. Although it is possible for individuals to purchase GNMA mortgage-backed securities through stockbrokers, many individuals prefer to invest in junior mortgages that offer yields 3% to 15% above rates offered on bank and S&L savings certificates. These are second, third, and fourth mortgages offered by mortgage brokers. The reason these mortgages offer higher yields than savings certificates is that they are riskier and more illiquid. Whereas bank and S&L deposits are insured by the FDIC and FSLIC, if a borrower stops making payments on a mortgage, the investor has to foreclose. Foreclosing is time-consuming, expensive, and usually results in a financial loss to the investor. Furthermore, it may be difficult to resell a mortgage if the investor does not want to wait for all of the borrower's payments. Banks and S&L certificates usually provide a means by which a saver can borrow against the certificate or cash it in.

The above-market yields offered by junior mortgages are very attractive. However, one must also realize that when a borrower offers to pay a substantial premium over the best loan rates available from banks and savings and loan associations, it is because the borrower and/or the property probably does not qualify for the best rates. Before investing, a mortgage investor should have the title to the property searched. This is the only way to know for certain what priority the mortgage will have in the event of foreclosure. There have been cases where investors have purchased what they were told to be first and second mortgages only to find in foreclosure that they were actually holding third and fourth mortgages on overencumbered property.

And how does one recognize an overencumbered property? By having it appraised by a professional appraiser who is independent of the party making or selling the mortgage investment. This is compared to the existing and proposed debt against the property. The investor should also run a credit check on the borrower. The investor's final protection is, however, in making certain that the market value of the property is well in excess of the loans against it and that the property is well-constructed, well-located, and functional.

LAND LEASES

Although **leased land** arrangements are common throughout the United States for both commercial and industrial users and for farmers, anything other than fee ownership of residential land is unthinkable in many areas. Yet in some parts of the United States (for example, Baltimore, Maryland; Orange County, California; throughout Hawaii; and in parts of Florida) homes with long-term land leases are an accepted practice. Typically, these leases are from 55 to 99 years in length and, barring an agreement to the contrary, the improvements to the land become the property of the fee owner at the end of the lease. Rents may be fixed in advance for the life of the lease, renegotiated at preset points during the life of the lease, or a combination of both.

To hedge against inflation, when fixed rents are used in a long-term lease, it is common practice to use **step-up rentals.** For example, under a 55-year house-lot lease, the rent may be set at $400 per year for the first 15 years, $600 per year for the next 10 years, $800 for the next 10 years, and so forth. An alternative is to renegotiate the rent at various points during the life of a lease so that the effects of land value changes are more closely equalized between the lessor and the lessee.

For example, a 60-year lease may contain renegotiation points at the fifteenth, thirtieth, and forty-fifth years. At those points the property would be reappraised and the lease rent adjusted to reflect any changes in the value of the property. Finally, if the lessor is responsible for paying the property taxes on the land, he will include an escalation clause in the lease contract that permits him to raise the lease rent by the amount of any property tax increase. The alternative is for the lessee to assume direct responsibility for paying property taxes.

VOCABULARY REVIEW

Match terms **a–m** *with statements* **1–13.**

a. *Contract for deed*
b. *Fannie Mae*
c. *Ginnie Mae*
d. *Graduated payment mortgage*
e. *Money market certificate*
f. *Mortgage banker*
g. *Mortgage broker*
h. *Mortgage pool*
i. *Participation*
j. *Savings certificate*
k. *Usury*
l. *Variable-rate mortgage*
m. *Wraparound mortgage*

1. A collection of mortgages of similar maturity and yield in which a person can invest.
2. A deposit that the saver agrees not to withdraw for a specified period of time.
3. Real estate loans that require interest plus a percentage of the profits from rentals.
4. A person or firm that makes mortgage loans and then sells them to investors.
5. A person or firm that brings borrowers and lenders together much as real estate brokers bring buyers and sellers together.
6. A method of selling and financing property whereby the buyer obtains possession but the seller retains the title.
7. A lending industry name for the Federal National Mortgage Association.
8. A lending industry name for the Government National Mortgage Association.
9. Charging a rate of interest higher than that permitted by state law.
10. A mortgage loan on which the rate of interest can rise and fall with changes in prevailing interest rates.
11. A mortgage repayment plan that allows the borrower to make smaller monthly payments at first and larger ones later. Interest rate and maturity are fixed.

12. Six-month savings certificates that offer yields comparable to prevailing 6-month treasury bills.
13. A debt instrument that encompasses existing mortgages.

QUESTIONS AND PROBLEMS

1. How have the FSLIC and FDIC helped to make mortgage money more readily available to borrowers?
2. Compared to passbook savings accounts, what advantages do savings certificates offer savers and savings institutions?
3. What is meant by the term "loan servicing"?
4. What is an adjustable rate mortgage?
5. Why does a lender feel more comfortable lending on an owner-occupied home than on a property being purchased as a rental investment?
6. Why is the monthly income of a loan applicant more important to a lender than the sheer size of the applicant's assets?
7. By what financing methods do FNMA and GNMA provide money for real estate loans?
8. If a dollar is a dollar no matter where it comes from, what difference does it make if the source of a real estate loan was real savings or fiat money?
9. Regarding variable-rate mortgage loans, what are the advantages and disadvantages to the borrower and lender?
10. Explain why rentals and leases are considered forms of real estate financing.
11. What is the single most important precaution an investor should take before buying a junior mortgage?

ADDITIONAL READINGS

Historical Chart Book. Washington, D.C.: Board of Governors of the Federal Reserve Board. Published annually, this book contains easy to read graphs and charts of money, finance, price, real estate, production and labor statistics. Most go back 50 years or more to give the reader an excellent historical perspective.

Plant, Kenneth M. "For Sale: Mortgages." *Real Estate Today,* October, 1978, pages 42–45. Author shows how the secondary mortgage market helps salespersons complete their residential transactions with more certainty.

Rose, Daniel. "The Redlining Controversy: One Viewpoint." *Real Estate Review,* Winter, 1978, pages 94–97. Author reviews current redlining rules and points out that to be successful any new program must work with market forces, not against them.

Savings and Loan Fact Book. Chicago: United States League of Savings Associations. Published annually, this handbook provides an excellent reference source for statistics on savings, home ownership, residential construction and financing.

Sirota David. *Creative Real Estate Finance: A Survival Manual for the 80s.* Reston, Va.: Reston Publishing Co., 1982, 320 pages. Covers innovative finance methods for today's markets. Includes concepts and mathematics of real estate finance.

Sklar, Stanley P. "Signposts to the Second Mortgage." *Real Estate Today,* May, 1979, pages 26–29. Article discusses the role of the second mortgage in putting a transaction together. Includes impact of usury laws.

13

Taxes and Assessments

KEY TERMS

Adjusted sales price: the sales price of a property less commissions, fix-up, and closing costs
Ad valorem taxes: taxes charged according to the value of a property
Assessed value: a value placed on a property for the purpose of taxation
Assessment appeal board: local governmental body which hears and rules on property owner complaints of overassessment
Basis: the price paid for property; used in calculating income taxes
Capital gain: the gain (profit) on the sale of an appreciated asset
Documentary tax: a fee or tax on deeds and other documents payable at the time of recordation
Mill rate: property tax rate that is expressed in tenths of a cent per dollar of assessed valuation
Tax certificate: a document issued at a tax sale that entitles the purchaser to a deed at a later date if the property is not redeemed
Tax lien: a charge or hold by the government against property to insure the payment of taxes

PROPERTY TAXES

The largest single source of income in America for local government programs and services is the property tax. Schools (from kindergarten through two-year colleges), fire and police departments, local welfare programs, public libraries, street maintenance, parks, and public hospital facilities are mainly supported by property taxes.

Property taxes are **ad valorem** taxes. This means that they are levied according to the value of one's property; the more valuable the property, the higher the tax, and vice versa. The underlying theory of ad valorem taxation is that those owning the more valuable properties are wealthier and hence able to pay more taxes.

Determining how much tax a property owner will be charged involves three basic steps: (1) local government budget determination and appropriation, (2) appraisal of all taxable property within the taxation district, and (3) allocation among individual property owners of the revenue that needs to be collected.

Appropriation

Each taxing body with the authority to tax prepares its budget for the coming year. Taxing bodies include counties, cities, boroughs, towns, and villages and, in some states, school boards, sanitation districts, and county road departments. In Minnesota, only counties have the power to tax property. Each budget along with a list of sources from which the money will be derived is enacted into law. This is the **appropriation process.** Then estimated sales taxes, state and federal revenue sharing, business licenses, and city income taxes are subtracted from the budget. The balance must come from property taxes.

Assessment

Next, the valuation of the taxable property within each county must be determined. A county assessor's office appraises each taxable parcel of land and the improvements thereon. In Minnesota, the appraised value is the estimated fair market cash value of the property. This is the cash price one would expect a buyer and a seller to agree upon in a normal open market transaction.

In addition to each county having its own assessors, municipalities also employ assessors who work under the authority of the county. Major cities in Minnesota (population over 30,000) have local assessors whose authority and responsibility are co-equal with county assessors.

Every parcel of land in Minnesota is reassessed at least every four years to determine its estimated market value as of January 2. The assessed value will depend on the property's classification as agricultural, homestead residential, non-homestead residential, etc. In order to avoid a sudden and possibly burdensome increase in property taxes when a parcel is reassessed, Minnesota uses a figure between market value and assessed value. This intermediate figure is known as **limited market value (LMV).** LMV can increase by only 10% of the preceding year's estimated market value, or by 25% of the actual increase in market value, whichever is greater. Anything over this is added to limited market value in the years remaining before the next reassessment of the property.

Tax Rate Calculation

Certain types of property are exempt from taxation. The assessed values of the remaining taxable properties are then added together in order to calculate the tax rate. To explain this process, suppose that a building lies within the taxation districts of the Westside School District, the city of Rostin, and the county of Pearl River. The school district's budget for the coming year requires $800,000 from property taxes, and the assessed value of taxable property within the district is $20,000,000. By dividing $800,000 by $20,000,000, we see that the school district must collect a tax of 4 cents for every dollar of assessed valuation. This levy can be expressed three ways: (1) as a mill rate, (2) as dollars per hundred, or (3) as dollars per thousand. All three rating methods are found in the United States. Minnesota uses a mill rate.

As a **mill rate,** this tax rate is expressed as mills per dollar of assessed valuation. Since 1 mill equals one-tenth of a cent, a 4-cent tax rate is the same as 40 mills. Expressed as **dollars per hundred,** the same rate would be $4 per hundred of assessed valuation. As **dollars per thousand,** it would be $40 per thousand.

The city of Rostin also calculates its tax rate by dividing its property tax requirements by the assessed value of the property within its boundaries. Suppose that its needs are $300,000 and the city limits enclose property totaling $10,000,000 in assessed valuation. (In this example, the city covers a smaller geographical area than the school district.) Thus the city must collect 3 cents for each dollar of assessed valuation in order to balance its budget.

The county government's budget requires $2,000,000 from property taxes and the county contains $200,000,000 in assessed valuation. This makes the county tax rate 1 cent per dollar of assessed valuation. Table 13:1 shows the school district, city, and county tax rates expressed as mills, dollars per hundred, and dollars per thousand.

The final step is to apply the tax rate to each property. So applying the mill rate to a home with an assessed value of $20,000, is simply a matter of multiplying the 80 mills (the equivalent of 8 cents) by the assessed valuation to arrive at

EXPRESSING PROPERTY TAX RATES **Table 13:1**

	Mill rate	Dollars per hundred	Dollars per thousand
School district	40 mills	$4.00	$40.00
City	30	3.00	30.00
County	10	1.00	10.00
Total	80 mills	$8.00	$80.00

property taxes of $1,600 per year. On a dollars per hundred basis, divide the $20,000 assessed valuation by $100 and multiply by $8. The result is $1,600. To insure collection, a lien for this amount is placed against the property. It is removed when the tax is paid. Property tax liens are superior to other types of liens. Also, a mortgage foreclosure does not clear property tax liens; they still must be paid.

Minnesota's tax year runs from January 1 to December 31. Once assessed, these taxes may be paid in two installments on May 31 and October 31 of the year *following* the assessment of the tax. Minnesota also provides for the charging of penalties and interest for late payments. All tax payments are made at the office of the county assessor.

UNPAID PROPERTY TAXES

If a property owner fails to pay his taxes, the property is sold to the State subject to redemption by the owner. The redemption period is five years for homestead property and generally three years for other classifications of land. If within the time provided the owner has not redeemed, the county will remove him from possession, establish a minimum value for the property and offer it for public sale. While the county is responsible for handling the sale, it is the State of Minnesota that issues the tax deed to the purchaser. The tax deed is the equivalent of a quitclaim deed and conveys the State's entire interest in the land with the exception of mineral rights. Because of the priority of tax liens, other lienholders should pay careful attention to tax delinquencies on the property securing their liens.

The right of government to divorce a property owner from his land for nonpayment of property taxes is well established by law. However, if the sale procedure is not properly followed, the purchaser may find his title later successfully challenged in court. Thus, it behooves the purchaser to obtain a title search and title insurance and, if necessary, to conduct a quiet title suit or file a suit to foreclose the rights of anyone previously having a right to the property.

ASSESSMENT APPEAL

By law, assessment procedures must be uniformly applied to all properties within a taxing jurisdiction. To this end, the assessed values of all lands and buildings, as determined by the assessors, are made available for public inspection. These are the **assessment rolls.** They permit a property owner to compare the assessed valuation on his property with assessed valuations on similar properties. If an owner feels he is overassessed, he can file an appeal before his city **board of equalization and review.** If the property owner remains dissatisfied with his assessment, he may appeal to his county board of equalization and review. If still dissatisfied he may appeal to the Minnesota Tax Court. Note that the appeal process deals only with the method of assessment and taxation, not with the tax rate or the amount of tax. Note also that an appeal to a city or county board may result in an increased assessment for the property and/or neighboring properties.

PROPERTY TAX EXEMPTIONS

More than half the land in many cities and counties is exempt from real property taxation. This is because governments and their agencies do not tax themselves or each other. Thus, goverment-owned offices of all types, public roads and parks, schools, military bases, and government-owned utilities are exempt from property taxes. Also exempted are most properties owned by religious and charitable organizations (so long as they are used for religious or charitable purposes), hospitals, and cemeteries. In rural areas of many states, large tracts of land are owned by federal and state governments, and these too are exempt from taxation. In Minnesota, agricultural land within city limits is taxed at special low rates.

Property tax exemptions are also used to attract industries and to appease voters. In the first instance, a local government agency buys industrial land and buildings, and leases them to industries at a price lower than would be possible if they were privately owned and hence taxed. Alternatively, outright property tax reductions can be granted for a certain length of time to newly established or relocating firms. The rationale is that the cost to the public is outweighed by the economic boost that the new industry brings to the community. In the second instance, a number of states grant assessment reductions to homeowners. This increases the tax burden for households that rent and for commercial properties.

In Minnesota, the assessed value of a non-agricultural homestead is lower than it would be if the same property was not the owner's homestead. For example, assume that a house has an estimated market value of $75,000 and a LMV of $68,000. If the owner resides in the house and has filed his homestead declaration form with the county, the assessed value of the property would be figured by first learning the homestead base value. A statewide homestead base value figure is established each year for all homesteaded property under a statutory formula. For 1979 property taxes, which in Minnesota would be due and payable the following year, the homestead base value was $21,000. Only 22% of the homestead base value will be included in assessed value, or in our example, $4,620. The homestead base value is then subtracted from LMV, leaving $47,000. Only 36% of this figure will be included in the assessed value, or $16,920. Therefore, $21,540 will be the assessed value of our homesteaded $75,000 house. Figure 13:1 summarizes the calculation.

Figure 13:1 **HOMESTEAD CALCULATION**

LMV =	$68,000	
homestead base value =	−21,000 × 22% =	$ 4,620
	47,000 × 36% =	16,920
assessed value of the homestead =		$21,540

If a property is not homesteaded, such as would be the case of a non-owner-occupied house, the assessed value is 40% of the limited market value. If the LMV is $68,000, then the assessed value would be $68,000 × 40% = $27,200. The amount of tax is then calculated by multiplying the assessed value by the mill rate.

From his property tax bill, the owner-resident of a Minnesota homestead is entitled to a maximum state-paid tax credit of $500. Depending on the owner's income, this amount can be increased to as much as $1,000. Additionally, Minnesota law provides for extensive property tax reductions for the elderly. These property tax reductions are a result of the State of Minnesota sharing its revenue with Minnesota counties.

TAX LIMITATION MEASURES

In June 1978, California voters approved Proposition 13 by a 2 to 1 margin. This amendment to the State Constitution rolled back annual real property taxes to 1% of the market value of a property in fiscal year 1975–76 and limits property tax increases to 2% per year as long as ownership remains unchanged. If a property is sold, the new tax will be 1% of the sales price. Also, bonded indebtedness repayment can add another ¼ of 1% per year. The effect of Proposition 13 was to reduce property taxes by some 57% and property tax revenues by $7 billion. To date this gap in revenues has been bridged by dropping some government services, charging user fees for others, and obtaining money from state government surpluses.

Anti-tax sentiment flickered briefly in various states during the early 1970s. But sparked in part by the success of Proposition 13, nearly every state has since considered or is considering some form of tax limitation. In some states a limitation is being placed on the amount of taxes that can be collected either by local property tax officials or by the state government itself. The supporting philosophy is that what the government does not collect, it cannot spend.

In other states the limit is being placed on how much government can spend. Here the philosophy is that what government is not allowed to spend, it won't have to collect. The following examples are indicative of the general mood in the United States: Tennessee voters overwhelmingly approved a constitutional amendment specifying that the state may not tax or spend at a rate greater than the state's actual economic growth; Colorado legislation places a 7% ceiling on the rate at which state spending can grow; Utah's new formula ties state and local spending to the state's growth in population and personal income; and Kentucky limits the growth of property taxes in the state to no more than 4% a year. In Massachusetts property taxes are limited to 2½% of property value, and in Michigan the state budget cannot exceed 2% of personal income.

SPECIAL ASSESSMENTS

Often the need arises to make local municipal improvements that will benefit property owners within a limited area, such as the paving of a street, the installation of street lights, curbs, storm drains, and sanitary sewer lines, or the construction of irrigation and drainage ditches. Such improvements can be provided through special assessments on property.

The theory underlying special assessments is that the improvements must benefit the land against which the cost will be charged, and the value of the benefits must exceed the cost. The area receiving the benefit of an improvement is the **improvement district** or **assessment district,** and the property within that district bears the cost of the improvement. This is different from a **public improvement.** A public improvement, such as reconstruction of the city's sewage plant, benefits the general public and is financed through the general (ad valorem) property tax. A local improvement, such as extending a sewer line into a street of homes presently using septic tanks or cesspools, does not benefit the public at large and should properly be charged only to those who directly benefit. Similarly, when streets are widened, owners of homes lining a 20-foot-wide street in a strictly residential neighborhood would be expected to bear the cost of widening it to 30 or 40 feet and to donate the needed land from their frontyards. But a street widening from two lanes to four to accommodate traffic not generated by the homes on the street is a different situation, as the widening benefits the public at large. In this case the street widening is funded from public monies and the homeowners are paid for any land taken from them.

Forming an Improvement District

An improvement district can be formed by the action of a group of concerned citizens who want and are willing to pay for an improvement. Property owners desiring the improvement take their proposal to the city council or township board. A public notice showing the proposed improvements, the extent of the improvement district, and the anticipated costs is prepared. This notice is mailed to landowners in the proposed improvement district, posted conspicuously in the district, and published in a local newspaper. The notice also contains the date and place of public hearings on the matter at which property owners within the proposed district are invited to voice their comments and objections.

Confirmation

If the hearings result in a decision to proceed, then under the authority granted by state laws regarding special improvements, a local government ordinance is passed that describes the project and its costs and the improvement district boundaries. An assessment roll is also prepared that shows the cost to each parcel in the district. Hearings are held regarding the assessment roll. When everything is in order, the roll is **confirmed** (approved). Then the contract to construct the improvements is let and work is started.

The proposal to create an improvement district can also come from a city council, township board, or county commission. When this happens, notices are distributed and hearings held to hear objections from affected parties. Objections are ruled upon by a court of law and if found to have merit, the assessment plans must be revised or dropped. Once approved, assessment rolls are prepared, more hearings held, the roll confirmed, and the contract let.

Bond Issues

Upon completion of the improvement, each landowner receives a bill for his portion of the cost. If the cost to a landowner is less than $100, the landowner either pays the amount in full to the contractor directly or to a designated public official who, in turn, pays the contractor. If the assessment is larger, the landowner can immediately pay it in full or let it **go to bond.** If he lets it go to bond, local government officials prepare a bond issue that totals all the unpaid assessments in the improvement district. These bonds are sold to the public through a securities dealer and the proceeds are used to pay the contractor. The collateral for the bonds is the land in the district upon which assessments have not been paid.

The bonds spread the cost of the improvements over a period of 5 to 10 years and are payable in equal annual (or semiannual) installments plus accumulated interest. Thus, a $2,000 sewer and street-widening assessment on a 10-year bond would be charged to a property owner at the rate of $200 per year (or $100 each 6 months) plus interest. As the bond is gradually retired, the amount of interest added to the regular principal payment declines.

Like property taxes, special assessments are a lien against the property. Consequently, if a property owner fails to pay his assessment, the assessed property can be sold in the same manner as when property taxes are delinquent.

Apportionment

Special assessments are apportioned according to benefits received, rather than by the value of the land and buildings being assessed. In fact, the presence of buildings in an improvement district is not usually considered in preparing the assessment roll; the theory is that the land receives all the benefit of the improvement. Several illustrations can best explain how assessments are apportioned. In a residential neighborhood, the assessment for installation of storm drains, curbs, and gutters is made on a **front-foot basis.** A property owner is charged for each foot of his lot that abuts the street being improved. A square-foot basis can also be used.

In the case of a sanitary sewer line assessment, the charge per lot can either be based on front footage or on a simple count of the lots in the district. In the latter case, if there are 100 lots on the new sewer line, each would pay 1% of the cost. In the case of a park or playground, lots nearest the new facility are deemed to benefit more and thus are assessed more than lots located farther away. This form of allocation is very subjective, and usually results in spirited objections at public hearings from those who do not feel they will use the facility in proportion to the assessment that their lots will bear.

INCOME TAXES ON THE SALE OF A RESIDENCE

We now turn to the income taxes that are due if a home is sold for more than it cost. Income taxes are levied by the federal government, by 44 states (the exceptions are Florida, Nevada, South Dakota, Texas, Washington, and Wyoming), and by 48 cities, including New York City, Baltimore, Pittsburgh, Philadelphia, Cincinnati, Cleveland, and Detroit. The discussion here centers on the federal income tax. Minnesota income tax laws generally follow the pattern of federal tax laws.

Calculating a Home's Basis

The first step in determining the amount of taxable gain upon the sale of an owner-occupied residence is to calculate the home's **basis.** This is the price originally paid for the home plus any fees paid for closing services and legal counsel, and any fee or commission paid to help find the property. If the home was built rather than purchased, the basis is the cost of the land plus the cost of construction, such as the cost of materials and construction labor, architect's fees, building permit fees, planning and zoning commission approval costs, utility connection charges, and legal fees. The value of labor contributed by the homeowner and free labor from friends and relatives cannot be added. If the home was received as compensation, a gift, an inheritance, or in a trade, or if a portion of the home was depreciated for business purposes, special rules apply that will not be covered here and the seller should consult the Internal Revenue Service (IRS).

Assessments for local improvements and any improvements made by the seller during his occupancy are added to the original cost of the home. An improvement is a permanent betterment that materially adds to the value of a home, prolongs its life, or changes its use. For example, finishing an unfinished basement or upper floor, building a swimming pool, adding a bedroom or bathroom, installing new plumbing or wiring, installing a new roof, erecting a new fence, and paving a new driveway are classed as improvements and are added to the home's basis. Maintenance and repairs are not added as they merely maintain the property in ordinary operating condition. Fixing gutters, mending leaks in plumbing, replacing broken windowpanes, and painting the inside or outside of the home are considered maintenance and repair items. However, repairs, when done as part of an extensive remodeling or restoration job, may be added to the basis.

Calculating the Amount Realized

The next step in determining taxable gain is to calculate the **amount realized** from the sale. This is the selling price of the home less selling expenses. Selling expenses include brokerage commissions, advertising, legal fees, title services, escrow or closing fees, and mortgage points paid by the seller. If the sale includes furnishings, the value of those furnishings is deducted from the selling price and reported separately as personal property. If the seller takes back a purchase money mortgage which is immediately sold at a discount, the discounted value of the mortgage is used, not the face amount.

Calculating Gain on the Sale

The **gain on the sale** is the difference between the amount realized and the basis. Table 13:2 illustrates this with an example. Unless the seller qualifies for tax postponement or tax exclusion as discussed next, this is the amount he reports as gain on his annual income tax forms.

Income Tax Postponement

The income tax law of the United States provides that if a seller purchases another home, the gain on the sale of the first home shall be postponed. To qualify for this postponement, the seller must meet two conditions. One deals with time and the other deals with purchase price. With regard to time, another home must be purchased and occupied within the time period beginning 24 months before the closing date

Table 13:2 **CALCULATION OF GAIN**

May 1, 1976	*Buy home for $50,000, closing costs are $500*	Basis is	$50,500
July 1, 1976	*Add landscaping and fencing for $3,000*	Basis is	$53,500
Dec. 1, 1977	*Add extra bedroom and bathroom for $10,000*	Basis is	$63,500
June 1, 1983	*Sell home for $85,000; sales commissions and closing costs are $6,000*	Amount realized is	$79,000
	Calculation of gain:	Amount realized	$79,000
		Less basis	−63,500
		Equals gain	$15,500

of the old home and ending 24 months after the closing date of the old home. A seller who decides to build his/her next home has 24 months to finish and occupy the home.

The second requirement for postponement is that in order to postpone all the gain, the next home must cost more than the adjusted sales price of the previous home. **Adjusted sales price** is the selling price of the old home less selling expenses and fix-up expenses. Fix-up expenses are expenditures for fix-up and repair work performed on the home to make it more salable. For fix-up and repair work to be deductible the work must be performed during the 90-day period ending on the day the contract to sell is signed, and it must be paid for before another 30 days elapses after that date. Table 13:3 illustrates the method for calculating adjusted sales price. As long as the cost of the next home, plus closing costs, exceeds the adjusted sales price of the previous home, the gain from the previous home is postponed. The homeowner does not have a choice as to postponing his gain or not. He must postpone his gain if he meets the time and purchase price conditions.

If the new home costs less than the adjusted sales price of the old, there will be a taxable gain. For example, if the old home had a basis of $50,000 and an adjusted sales price of $78,000, and the new home cost $75,000, then there would be a taxable gain of $3,000 and a postponed gain of $25,000. The basis of the new home is $75,000 minus the postponed gain of $25,000, i.e., $50,000.

Postponement of gain is continued from one home to the next as long as the cost of each subsequent home exceeds

Table 13:3

ADJUSTED SALES PRICE

Selling price of old home	$85,000
Less selling expenses	−6,000
Less fix-up costs	−1,000
Equals adjusted sales price	$78,000

the adjusted sales price of the previous home, and as long as 24 months elapses between sales. (An exemption to the 24-month requirement is usually made for work-related moves.) The basis of the first home is simply carried forward and included in the basis of the second home, which in turn is carried forward to the third home, and so on. Note that it is not the amount of cash one puts into a home or the size of the mortgage that counts, but the sales price. Thus it is possible to move from a home with a small mortgage to a slightly more expensive home with a large mortgage, and finish the transaction with cash in the pocket and postponed taxes. Additionally, the law does not restrict the type of home one may own and occupy. Thus the seller of a single family residence can buy another house, or a condominium, or a cooperative (or vice versa) and still qualify for postponement.

LIFETIME EXCLUSION

The postponement of taxes on gains as one moves from one home to the next works well as long as consistently more expensive homes are purchased. However, there may come a time in the homeowner's life when a smaller and presumably less expensive home is needed. To soften the tax burden that such a move usually causes, Congress has enacted legislation that allows a once-in-a-lifetime election to avoid tax on up to $125,000 of gain on the sale of one's residence. To qualify for this, one must be 55 years of age or older on the date of sale and have owned and occupied the residence for at least 3 of the 5 years preceding the sale. Any profit over $125,000 is taxable, but may be postponed if another residence is purchased in accordance with the rules previously described. For example, a person owning a $225,000 home with a basis of $50,000 could sell and move to a $100,000 home with no taxable gain. A person owning a $175,000 home with a $50,000 basis could sell and rent an apartment and have no taxable gain. By combining postponement with this $125,000 exclusion it is quite possible to eliminate the taxable gain from a lifetime of homeownership.

CAPITAL GAIN

The gain on the sale of an appreciated investment asset is called a **capital gain.** Capital gains are divided into two categories: long-term and short-term. A **short-term capital gain** results when a gain is realized on the sale of a capital asset, such as real estate, which has been owned for one year or less. A **long-term capital gain** results when a gain is realized on the sale of a capital asset which has been owned for more than a year. The significance of the distinction is that the tax rate on long-term capital gains is considerably less than on short-term capital gains. Short-term gains are taxed at ordinary income tax rates, in other words, at the same rate as ordinary income. Long-term gains are subject to a 60% exclusion which in effect means they are taxed at only 40% of ordinary income tax rates. Therefore, unless there is a strong reason not to, it is beneficial from a tax standpoint to wait a year and a day before selling an appreciated asset that is subject to taxation.

Losses from the sale of capital assets are also classified as long-term (over a year) and short-term (a year or less). Because the same 60% exclusion applies, short-term losses are more valuable at tax time than long-term losses. Note that with regard to the owner-occupied residences, any gain not postponed or excluded is taxed as a capital gain—either long-term or short-term depending on the holding period. However, if there is a loss on the sale of a personal residence, it cannot be used as a deduction against other income the taxpayer may have.

With regard to real estate other than an owner-occupied residence, capital losses are deductible against the taxpayer's other capital gains and income. However, it is important to note that no real estate other than owner-occupied residences qualifies for postponement of gains upon sale and for the $125,000 lifetime exclusion. For real estate other than one's personal residence, the choices are to pay the taxes due on the sale, effect a tax-free exchange (discussed in Chapter 8), or elect the installment method of reporting the gain, a topic we consider next.

INSTALLMENT SALE

When a gain cannot be postponed or excluded, a popular method of reducing income taxes is to use the **installment method** of reporting the gain. This can be applied to any kind of real estate, including vacant land and income producing property, and homeowner gains that do not qualify for postponement or exclusion.

Suppose that your property, which is free and clear of debt, is sold for $100,000. The real estate commission and closing costs are $7,500 and your basis is $40,000. As a result, the gain on this sale is $52,500. Ordinarily you are required to pay all the income taxes due on that gain in the year of sale, a situation that will undoubtedly force you into a higher tax bracket. A solution is to sell to the buyer on terms rather than to send him to a lender to obtain a loan.

For example, if the buyer pays you $20,000 down and gives you a promissory note calling for payments of $5,000 and interest this year, and $25,000 plus interest in each of the next 3 years, your gains would be calculated and reported as follows. Of each dollar of sales price received, 52½¢ would be reported gain. Thus, $13,125 would be reported this year and in each of the next 3 years. The interest you earn on the promissory note is reported and taxed separately as interest income.

If there was a $30,000 mortgage on the property that the buyer agreed to assume, the $100,000 sales price would be reduced by $30,000 to $70,000 for tax-calculating purposes. The portion of each dollar paid to you by the buyer that must be reported as gain is $52,500 divided by $70,000, or 75%. If the down payment is $20,000 followed by $10,000 per year for 5 years, you would report 75% of $20,000, or $15,000 this year and $7,500 in each of the next 5 years. The gain is taxed at the capital gains rates in effect at the time the installment is received.

Prior to 1980 there was a 30% limit on the amount of principal that you could receive in the year of the sale and still qualify for installment reporting treatment. However, a 1980 federal law change repealed that limit for all sales made after January 1, 1980. Now there is no maximum or minimum payment due in the year of sale in order to qualify. At the same time, the old two-payment rule was abolished for sales after January 1, 1980. Thus it is now possible to sell a property for no down payment and still qualify for installment sale treatment. Also changed was the old law requirement that you must make an election on your tax return if you want to report your gain on an installment basis. Effective October 20, 1980, the installment-sale treatment is automatic unless you elect to pay in full.

ENERGY CREDITS

A taxpayer may take a credit of 15% of the first $2,000 spent on items to save energy in the taxpayer's home. Items that qualify include insulation, fuel-reducing furnace burners, storm or thermal windows or doors, caulking and weatherstripping, and meters that show the cost of energy usage.The full $2,000 of energy-saving items does not have to be installed in a single tax year and a new $2,000 limit applies each time the taxpayer moves to another home. Thus the fact that a previous owner claimed an energy credit does not stop the next owner from adding more energy-saving items and taking a 15% credit.

A taxpayer may also take a credit for 40% of the first $10,000 spent on renewable energy sources. This refers to solar or wind or geothermal energy equipment for heating or cooling the home and/or for providing hot water or electricity for use in the home. As with the 15% conservation credit, the equipment does not have to be installed all at once and a new limit applied to each subsequent residence owned by the taxpayer.

Note that a tax credit differs from a tax deduction in that a tax credit is deducted dollar for dollar from income taxes due. A tax deduction is made from income before taxes are computed.

PROPERTY TAX AND INTEREST DEDUCTIONS

Since the federal income tax began in 1913, owners of single-family residences have been permitted to claim as itemized personal deductions money paid out for state and local realty taxes, as well as interest on debt secured by their homes. Subsequently, this deduction was extended to condominium and cooperative apartment owners. The deduction allowed for property taxes does not extend to special assessment taxes for improvement districts. However, if the assessment goes to bond, that portion of each payment attributable to interest is deductible. With regard to mortgages, the IRS also permits the deduction of loan prepayment penalties, and the deduction of points on new loans that are clearly distinguishable as interest and not service fees for making the loan. Loan points paid by a seller to help a buyer obtain an FHA or VA loan are not deductible as interest (it is not the seller's debt), but can be deducted from the home's selling price in computing a gain or loss on the sale. FHA mortgage insurance premiums are not deductible, nor are those paid to private mortgage insurers.

From an individual taxpayer's standpoint, the ability to deduct property taxes and mortgage interest on a personal residence becomes more valuable in successively higher tax brackets. At the 50% bracket, every dollar spent for something tax-deductible costs the taxpayer only 50¢ in after-tax money. Or seen from another viewpoint, the taxpayer obtains the full enjoyment of the money he spends on interest and property taxes without having to first pay income taxes on it. Although progressively less dramatic, the same argument applies to persons in the 40%, 30%, and 20% tax brackets. As viewed from a national standpoint, the deductibility of interest and property taxes encourages widespread ownership of the country's land and buildings.

INCOME TAXES ON INVESTMENT PROPERTY

When a person owns real estate for investment purposes, the rental income from that property is fully taxable. However, from this income one can deduct all expenses incurred in earning it, such as property taxes, interest, maintenance, repairs, management, utilities, insurance, and depreciation. In contrast, a homeowner can deduct only property taxes and interest. Money spent on improvements is not immediately deductible from rental income, but must be added to the basis of the property and depreciated when the property is ultimately sold. Long-term capital gains tax treatment is possible if the property is owned more than 12 months. Also an investor can structure the sale on an installment basis so as to use the installment method to report the gain. Tax treatment of investment property is covered in more detail in Chapter 23, where the ability of investment property to "shelter" the owner's other sources of income from taxation is discussed.

Finally, it should be pointed out that if a property owner fails to pay his income taxes, the government may place a lien against his property by issuing a tax warrant. When properly filed, this lien makes the property security for payment of the delinquent taxes.

CONVEYANCE TAXES

Minnesota charges a conveyance tax (deed tax) on the difference between the purchase price and any assumed mortgage. If there is no mortgage being assumed, the tax is based on the purchase price. The tax rate is $1.10 per $500, or fractional part thereof, with a minimum tax of $2.20. This is known as the **State deed tax.** For example, on the sale of a home for $75,000 with the buyer assuming a $50,000 mortgage, the tax would be based on $25,000 and would equal $55. The seller is responsible for the payment of this tax.

In addition to the State deed tax, Minnesota also charges a **mortgage registration tax** on all new debt arising out of the transaction. This tax is $.15 per $100 of the value shown on the recorded instrument and is levied on contracts for deed not recorded within six months of their execution, and on all new mortgages. This tax must be paid by the borrower. Both the mortgage registration tax and the State deed tax are paid to the county treasurer prior to recording and are in addition to the charge for recording the document itself.

VOCABULARY REVIEW

Match terms **a–l** *with statements* **1–12.**

a. *Adjusted sales price*
b. *Ad valorem*
c. *Appropriation process*
d. *Assessed valuation*
e. *Assessment roll*
f. *Long-term capital gain*
g. *Front-foot basis*
h. *Installment reporting*
i. *Mill rate*
j. *Special assessments*
k. *State deed tax*
l. *Tax deed*

1. A tax rate expressed in tenths of a cent per dollar of assessed valuation.
2. According to value.
3. The tax levied on the new money in a transaction.
4. The enactment of a taxing body's budget and sources of money into law.
5. A book that contains the assessed valuation of each property in the county or taxing district.
6. A document conveying title to property purchased at a tax sale.
7. A value placed on a property for the purpose of taxation.
8. Assessments levied to provide publicly built improvements that will primarily benefit property owners within a small geographical area.

9. A charge or levy based directly on the measured distance that a parcel of land abuts a street.
10. Sales price of a property less fix-up costs and sales commissions, closing and other selling costs.
11. Income tax treatment on the sale of an appreciated asset held more than 12 months.
12. Sale of an appreciated property structured to spread out the payment of income taxes on the gain.

QUESTIONS AND PROBLEMS

1. Explain the process for calculating the property tax rate for a county.
2. Southside County contains property totalling $120,000,000 in assessed valuation. If the county's budget is $960,000, what will the mill rate be?
3. Continuing with Problem 2 above, if a vacant lot situated in Southside County carries an assessed valuation of $40,000, how much will the owner be required to pay to support the county this year?
4. The Lakeview Mosquito Abatement District needs 5 mills to pay for a mosquito-control program. How much does that amount to for a property in the district with an assessed valuation of $10,000?
5. In your county, if a property owner wishes to appeal an assessment, what procedure must he follow?
6. If the assessment on your home were to rise 90% in 1 year, where would you go to protest the increase: to the board of equalization and review, to the city council, or to the county government? Explain.
7. How does the amount of tax-exempt real estate in a community affect nonexempt property owners?
8. What methods and techniques are used by your assessor's office to keep up to date with changing real estate prices?
9. The Smiths bought a house in 1963 for $21,000, including closing costs. Five years later they made improvements costing $2,000 and 5 years after that more improvements that cost $5,000. Today they sell the house; the sales price is $68,000 and commissions and closing costs total $5,000. For income tax purposes, what is their gain?
10. Continuing with Problem 9, a month after selling, the Smiths purchase a two-bedroom condominium for $58,000, including closing costs. What is their taxable gain now? Will it be taxed as a short-term or a long-term capital gain? (Assume that the Smiths are less than 55 years of age.)
11. What is the current documentary transfer tax in Minnesota?

ADDITIONAL READINGS

Case, Karl E. *Property Taxation: The Need for Reform.* Cambridge, Mass.: Ballinger Publishing Co., 1978, 124 pages. Book explores inequities in present systems of property taxation and makes suggestions for improvements.

Internal Revenue Service. "Tax Information for Homeowners," Publication 530. Washington, D.C.: U.S. Government Printing Office, 1982, 8 pages. Discusses income tax aspects of settlement costs, itemized deductions, rental and business use, repairs, improvements, buying, selling, record keeping, casualty losses, etc., for owners of houses, condominiums, and cooperatives. Published annually. Available free from the IRS.

Internal Revenue Service. "Tax Information on Selling Your Home," Publication 523. Washington, D.C.: U.S. Government Printing Office, 1982, 12 pages. Provides instructions on how to report taxable income from the sale of one's residence. Published annually. Available free from the IRS.

International Association of Assessing Officers, *Assessing and the Appraisal Process,* 5th ed. Chicago: International Association of Assessing Officers, 1974, 167 pages. Book sets forth principles and practices of appraising real estate for assessment purposes.

Jeddeloh, James B. and **Perkins, Cheryl G.** *Real Estate Taxation.* Reston, Va.: Reston Publishing Co., 1982, 240 pages. Includes income tax aspects of home ownership, vacation homes, investment properties plus information on tax deductions and credits that real estate professionals may take.

Johnson, Robert G. *Lower Your Real Estate Taxes.* New York: Walker & Co., 1977, 163 pages. In simple language, the book explains the various systems of property taxation in use in the United States and shows how to reduce the taxes on your home.

14

Title Closing and Escrow

KEY TERMS

Affidavit: a sworn statement by a seller or a buyer that he knows of no matters that would encumber title

Closing: a meeting at which the seller delivers his deed to the buyer, the buyer pays for the property, and all other matters pertaining to the sale are concluded

Closing statement: an accounting of funds to the buyer and the seller at the completion of a real estate transaction

Escrow closing: the deposit of documents and funds with a neutral third party along with instructions as to how to conduct the closing

Escrow agent: the person placed in charge of an escrow

Prorating: the division of ongoing expenses and income items between the buyer and the seller

RESPA, Real Estate Settlement Procedures Act: a federal law that deals with procedures to be followed in certain types of real estate closings

Title closing: the process of consummating a real estate transaction

Title search: a search of publicly available records and documents to determine the current ownership and title condition of a property

Numerous details must be dealt with between the time a buyer and a seller sign a real estate sales contract and the day title is conveyed to the buyer. The seller's title must be searched, loans must be arranged, insurance and property taxes must be prorated, and a deed must be prepared. Finally, when everything is in order, the buyer pays for the property and the seller delivers a deed. This is the **title closing** process; and the day on which the deed is delivered to the buyer is called the **closing day.** Depending on where one resides in the United States, the title closing process is referred to as a **closing, settlement,** or **escrow.** In Minnesota it is called a closing.

In some parts of the United States, particularly in the East, and to a certain extent in the Mountain states, the Midwest, and the South, the title closing process is concluded at a meeting at which each party to the transaction, or his/her representative, is present. Elsewhere, title closing is conducted by an escrow agent, who is a neutral third party mutually selected by the buyer and seller to carry out the closing. With an escrow, there is no closing meeting; in fact, most of the closing process is conducted by mail. Let us look at the operation of each method.

CLOSING MEETING

When a meeting is used to close a real estate transaction, the seller (or his representative) meets in person with the buyer and delivers the deed. At the same time, the buyer pays the seller for the property. To ascertain that everything promised in the sales contract has been properly carried out, it is customary for the buyer and seller to each have an attorney present. The real estate agents who brought the buyer and seller together are also present. If a new loan is being made at the closing, a representative of the lender will be present.

The location of the meeting and the selection of the person responsible for conducting the closing will depend on local custom and the nature of the closing.

If a real estate transaction is brokeraged in Minnesota, the listing broker is responsible for the closing. The broker orders the abstract, notifies the parties involved as to where and when to meet, prepares the closing documents, and conducts the closing meeting. If the transaction involves a new lender, the closing meeting is held at the lender's office or title company's office. If a new loan is not involved, the closing meeting is held at the listing broker's office. There is usually a closing specialist in the broker's office who handles closings or the broker can hire an independent closer to do the work.

If a Minnesota transaction does not involve a broker, the closing is conducted by the seller's attorney or by an independent closer. If there is a new loan, the closing is held at the lender's or title company's office. If a new loan is not involved, the closing is held at the attorney's or closer's office.

Seller's Responsibilities at Closing

To assure a smooth closing, each person attending is responsible for bringing certain documents. The seller and his attorney are responsible for preparing and bringing the deed together with the most recent property tax bill (and receipt if it has been paid). If required by the sales contract, they also bring the insurance policy for the property, abstract, affidavit, Torrens documents, deeds or documents showing the removal of unacceptable liens and encumbrances, bill of sale for personal property, survey map, documentary tax stamps for the deed, and statement showing the remaining balance on any loan that the buyer will assume. The loan payment booklet, keys to the property, garage door opener and the like are also brought to the meeting. If the property produces income, existing leases, rent schedules, current expenditures, and letters advising the tenants of the new owner must also be furnished.

Buyer's Responsibilities at Closing

The buyer's responsibilities include having adequate settlement funds ready, making certain his attorney is present to protect his interests, and, if borrowing, obtaining the loan commitment and advising the lender of the meeting's time and place. The real estate agent is present because the agent is responsible for the closing and the proration calculations. The agent also receives a commission check at that time and, as a matter of good business, will make certain that all goes well.

If a new loan is involved, the lender (or the lender's representative) brings a check for the amount of the loan along with a note and mortgage for the borrower to sign. If an existing loan is to be paid off as part of the transaction, the closer is responsible for withholding funds sufficient to pay off the loan and for receiving a mortgage satisfaction.

Agent's Duties

It is customary for the agent who listed the property to order and follow-up on the truth in housing report and home energy audit, if required, and to deliver these at the closing. The listing agent also sees that the deed is prepared for the seller in the event that the seller has not engaged an attorney for this purpose. The agent who found the buyer follows through on the financing process and helps the buyer find an insurance agent, an attorney, and a title company. When an agent lists and sells the same property, that agent assists both the buyer and seller. If more than one agent is involved in the transaction, each should keep the other(s) fully informed so the transaction will go as well as possible. At all times the buyer and seller are to be kept informed as to the status of the closing. If the agent becomes aware that one of the parties is not performing as required by the contract, the agent must immediately disclose this fact to the other party(ies). An agent should provide them with a preview of all actions that will take place, explain the amounts of money involved and the purpose served by each payment or receipt, and in general prepare the parties for informed participation in the closing meeting.

The Transaction

When everyone concerned has arrived at the meeting place, the closing begins. The various documents called for by the sales contract are exchanged for inspection. The buyer and his attorney inspect the deed the seller is offering, the title search and/or title policy, the mortgage papers, survey, leases, removals of encumbrances, and proration calculations. The lender also inspects the deed, survey, title search, and title policy. This continues until each party has a chance to inspect each document of interest.

As the title search will usually have been prepared a day or more before the meeting, the buyer and lender both want protection against any changes in title condition since then. One solution is for the seller to sign a **seller's affidavit.** In this affidavit, the seller states that he is the true owner of the property, that there are no judgments, bankruptcy, or divorce proceedings currently against him, and that he has done nothing to damage the quality of title since the title search. If a defect caused by the seller later appears, he may be sued for damages. Furthermore, he may be liable for criminal charges if it can be shown that he was attempting to obtain money under false pretenses by signing the affidavit.

A settlement statement (discussed in detail later) is given to the buyer and seller to summarize the financial aspects of their transaction. It is prepared by the person in charge of the closing either just prior to or at the meeting. It provides a clear picture of where the buyer's and seller's money is going at the closing by identifying each party to whom money is being paid.

Disagreements

In a closing conducted by professionals, disagreements should be extremely rare. If all concerned have properly carried out their responsibilities, any major problems will have been identified and worked out prior to the closing meeting. If any questions or disagreements arise, they are usually resolved at the meeting, possibly with more negotiating. But, if an impasse is reached, the parties can agree to adjourn the closing to a later date. For example, if the seller does not bring all the documents required by the buyer, or if there is a cloud on the title unacceptable to the buyer and the seller feels it can be removed, an adjournment is appropriate. However, if the impasse is major, such as a cloud on the title that will be difficult to clear, a lender who will not make the needed loan, or a title insurance company which refuses to insure, it may be necessary to cancel the entire transaction.

Dry Closing

Occasionally an unavoidable circumstance can cause delays. Perhaps an important document, known to be in the mails, has not arrived. Yet the seller needs to catch an airplane to meet his responsibility in a new location. In such a situation, the parties concerned may agree to a **dry closing.** In a dry closing, all parties sign their documents and entrust them to the closing attorney for safekeeping. No money is disbursed and the deed is not delivered until the missing paperwork has arrived. When it does, the closing attorney completes the transaction and delivers the money and documents by mail or messenger.

If everyone involved in the closing has done his or her homework and comes prepared to the meeting, the closing usually goes smoothly. Should an error be discovered in the figures or in the documentation, a quiet request to confer separately with the closing attorney or even a short note passed to him will do much to preserve the confidence of the seller and the buyer. When everything is in order, the seller delivers a completed deed to the buyer. The buyer gives a check to the closer that combines his down payment and closing costs. The lender has the buyer sign the mortgage and note. The closer hands a check to the seller and to the existing lender if one is involved. The closer also pays the broker, the abstracter, and any other closing expenses. The deed, new mortgage, and release of the old mortgage are then recorded, and the transaction is complete.

Post-Closing

After the closing meeting is finished, the closing attorney mails payments to persons who have provided service to the closing, e.g., the surveyor, pest control company, etc. The closing attorney also is responsible for paying revenue stamp fees, recording the deed, and delivering the completed loan package to the lender.

ESCROWS

The use of escrow to close a real estate transaction involves a neutral third party, called an **escrow agent,** escrow holder, or escrowee, who acts as a trusted stakeholder for all the parties to the transaction. Instead of delivering his deed directly to the buyer at a closing meeting, the seller gives the deed to the escrow agent with instructions that it be delivered only after the buyer has completed all his promises in the sales contract. Similarly, the buyer hands the escrow agent the money for the purchase price plus instructions that it be given to the seller only after fulfillment of the seller's promises. Let us look closer at this arrangement.

A typical real estate escrow closing starts when a sales contract is signed by the buyer and seller. They select a neutral escrow agent to handle the closing. This may be the escrow department of a bank or savings and loan or other lending agency, an independent escrow company, an attorney, or the escrow department of a title insurance company. Sometimes real estate brokers offer escrow services. However, if the broker is earning a sales commission in the transaction, the broker cannot be classed as neutral and disinterested. Because escrow agents are entrusted with valuable documents and large sums of money, most states have licensing and bonding requirements that escrow agents must meet. Escrows are used only occasionally in Minnesota and then only in connection with commercial transactions.

Escrow Agent's Duties

The escrow agent's task begins with the deposit of the buyer's earnest money in a special bank trust account and the preparation of a set of escrow instructions based on the signed sales contract. These must be promptly signed by the buyer and seller. The instructions establish an agency relationship between the escrow agent and the buyer, and the escrow agent and the seller. The instructions also detail in writing everything that each party to the sale must do before the deed is finally delivered to the buyer. In a typical transaction, the escrow instructions will tell the escrow agent to order a title search and obtain title insurance.

If an existing loan against the property is to be repaid as part of the sale, the escrow agent is asked to contact the lender to request a statement of the amount of money necessary to repay the loan and to request a mortgage release. The lender then enters into an agreement with the escrow agent wherein the lender is to give the completed release papers to the escrow agent; but the agent may not deliver them to the seller until the agent has remitted the amount demanded by the lender. If the existing loan is to be assumed, the escrow agent asks the lender for the current balance and any documents that the buyer must sign.

When the title search is completed, the escrow agent forwards it to the buyer or his attorney for approval. The property insurance and tax papers the seller would otherwise bring to the closing meeting are sent to the escrow agent for proration. Leases, service contracts, and notices to tenants are also sent to the escrow agent for proration and delivery to the buyer. The deed conveying title to the buyer is prepared by the seller's attorney (in some states by the escrow agent), signed by the seller, and given to the escrow agent. Once delivered into escrow, even if the seller dies, marries, or is declared legally incompetent before the close of escrow, the deed will still pass title to the buyer.

The Closing

As the closing date draws near, if all the instructions are otherwise complete, the escrow agent requests any additional money the buyer and lender must deposit in order to close. The day before closing the escrow agent calls the title company and orders a last minute check on the title. If no changes have occurred since the first (preliminary) title search, the deed, mortgage, mortgage release, and other documents to be recorded as part of the transaction are recorded first thing the following morning. As soon as the recording is confirmed, the escrow agent hands or mails a check to every party to whom funds are due from the escrow (usually the seller, real estate broker, and previous lender), along with any papers or documents which must be delivered through escrow (such as the fire insurance policy, copy of the property tax bill, and tenant leases). Several days later the buyer and lender will receive a title insurance policy in the mail from the title company. The public recorder's office also mails the documents it recorded to each party. The deed is sent to the buyer, the mortgage release to the seller, and the new mortgage to the lender.

In the escrow closing method, the closing, delivery of title, and recordation usually all take place at the same moment. Technically, the seller does not physically hand a deed to the buyer on the closing day. However, once all the conditions of the escrow are met, the escrow agent becomes an agent of the seller as to the money in the transaction, and an agent of the buyer as to the deed. Thus, a buyer, through an agent, receives the deed, and the law regarding delivery is fulfilled.

It is not necessary for the buyer and seller to meet face-to-face during the escrow period or at the closing. This can eliminate personality conflicts that might be detrimental to an otherwise sound transaction. The escrow agent, having previously accumulated all the documents, approvals, deeds, and monies prior to the closing date, does the closing alone.

In a brokeraged transaction, the real estate agent is usually the only person who actually meets the escrow agent. All communication can be handled through the broker, by mail, or by telephone. If a real estate agent is not involved, the buyer and/or seller can open the escrow, either in person or by mail. The use of an escrow agent does not eliminate the need for an attorney. Although there is no closing meeting for the attorneys to attend, they play a vital role in advising the buyer and seller on each document sent by the escrow agent for approval and signature.

Loan Escrows

Escrows can be used for purposes other than real estate or sales transactions. For example, a homeowner who is refinancing his property could enter into an escrow with the lender. The conditions of the escrow would be that the homeowner deliver a properly executed note and mortgage to the escrow agent and that the lender deposit the loan money. Upon closing, the escrow agent delivers the documents to the lender and the money to the homeowner. Or, in reverse, an escrow could be used to pay off the balance of a loan. The conditions would be the borrower's deposit of the balance due and the lender's deposit of the mortgage release and note. Even the weekly office sports pool is an escrow—with the person holding the pool money acting as escrow agent for the participants.

PRORATING AT THE CLOSING

Ongoing expenses and income items must be prorated between the seller and buyer when property ownership changes hands. Items subject to proration include property insurance premiums, property taxes, accrued interest on assumed loans, and rents and operating expenses if the property produces income. If heating is done by oil and the oil tank is partially filled when title transfers, that oil can be prorated, as can utility bills when service is not shut off between owners. The prorating process has long been a source of considerable mystery to real estate newcomers. Several sample prorations common to most closings will help to clarify the process.

Hazard Insurance

Hazard insurance policies for such things as fire, wind, storm, and flood damage are paid for in advance. At the beginning of each year of the policy's life, the premium for that year's coverage must be paid. When real estate is sold, the buyer may ask the seller to transfer the remaining coverage to him. The seller usually agrees if the buyer reimburses him for the value of the remaining coverage on a prorated basis.

The first step in prorating hazard insurance is to find out how often the premium is paid, how much it is, and what period of time it covers. Suppose that the seller has a 1-year policy that cost $180 and started on January 1 of the current year. If the property is sold and the closing date is July 1, the policy is half used up. Therefore, if the buyer wants the policy transferred to him, he must pay the seller $90 for the remaining 6 months of coverage.

Because closing dates do not always occur on neat, evenly divided portions of the year, nor do most items that need prorating, it is usually necessary to break the year into months and the months into days to make proration calculations. Suppose, in the previous hazard insurance example, that prorations are to be made on June 30 instead of July 1. This would give the buyer 6 months and 1 day of coverage. How much does he owe the seller? The first step is to calculate the monthly and daily rates for the policy: $180 divided by 12 is $15 per month. Dividing the monthly rate of $15 by 30 days gives a daily rate of 50¢. The second step is to add 6 months at $15 and 1 day at 50¢. Thus, the buyer owes the seller $90.50 for the unused portion of the policy.

Loan Interest

When a buyer agrees to assume an existing loan from the seller, an interest proration is necessary. For example, a sales contract calls for the buyer to assume a 9% mortgage loan with a principal balance of $31,111 at the time of closing. Loan payments are due the 10th of each month, and the sales contract calls for a July 3 closing date, with interest on the loan to be prorated through July 2. How much is to be prorated and to whom?

First, we must recognize that interest is normally paid in arrears. On a loan that is payable monthly, the borrower pays interest for the use of the loan at the end of each month he has had the loan. Thus, the July 10 monthly loan payment includes the interest due for the use of $31,111 from June 10 through July 9. However, the seller owned the property through July 2, and from June 10 through July 2 is 23 days. At the closing the seller must give the buyer enough money to pay for 23 days interest on the $31,111. If the annual interest rate is 9%, one day's interest is $31,111 times 9% divided by 365, which is $7.67. Multiply the daily rate by 23 to obtain the interest for 23 days, $176.41.

30-Day Month

In many parts of the country, it is the custom when prorating interest, property taxes, water bills, and insurance to use a 30-day month because it simplifies proration calculations. Naturally, using a 30-day month produces some inaccuracy when dealing with months that do not have 30 days. If this inaccuracy is significant to the buyer and seller, they can agree to prorate either by using the exact number of days in the closing month or by dividing the yearly rate by 365 to find a daily rate. Dividing the yearly rate by 365 is the preferred method in Minnesota. Both methods are demonstrated in this chapter.

Rents

It is the custom throughout the country to prorate rents on the basis of the actual number of days in the month. Using the July 3 closing date again, if the property is currently rented for $450 per month, paid in advance on the first of each month, what would the proration be? If the seller has already collected the rent for the month of July, he is obligated to hand over to the buyer that portion of the rent earned between July 3 and July 31, inclusive, a period of 29 days. To determine how many dollars this is, divide $450 by the number of days in July. This gives $14.516 as the rent per day. Then multiply the daily rate by 29 days to get $420.96, the portion of the July rent that the seller must hand over to the buyer. If the renter has not paid the July rent by the July 3 closing date, no proration is made. If the buyer later collects the July rent, he must return 2 days rent to the seller.

Property Taxes

Prorated property taxes are common to nearly all real estate transactions. The amount of proration depends on when the property taxes are due, what portion has already been paid, and what period of time they cover. Property taxes are levied on a calendar year basis in Minnesota and are due the following year in two equal installments on May 31 and October 31.

If a transaction calls for property taxes to be prorated to September 5, how is the calculation made? Suppose the amount of taxes due are $1095 for the year and that the first half has been paid. The proration would be from July 1 through September 4, a period of 66 days. Dividing $1095 by 365 gives a daily rate of $3. If you take 66 days at $3 each, then the seller must pay the buyer $198 because he owned the property through September 4; yet the buyer will later pay for the period starting July 1.

Let us work one more property tax proration example. Presume that the annual property taxes are $1460, and the closing and proration date is December 28. First, determine how much of the annual property tax bill has been paid by the seller. If the seller has paid the taxes for the year, the buyer must reimburse the seller for the taxes from December 28 through December 31, a period of 4 days. The amount is calculated by dividing $1460 by 365 and multiplying by 4 days. This is $16, the amount that the buyer must give the seller.

Proration Date

Prorations need not be calculated as of the closing date. In the sales contract, the buyer and seller can mutually agree to a different proration date if they wish. If nothing is said, local law and custom will prevail. In Minnesota, closing practices vary. Some closers charge the day of closing to the buyer. Some charge the day of closing to the seller. Both methods are demonstrated in this chapter. If the difference of 1 day is important to the buyer or seller, they should not rely on local custom, but agree in writing on a proration day of their own choosing.

Special assessments for such things as street improvements, water mains, and sewer lines are not usually prorated. As a rule, the selling price of the property reflects the added value of the improvements, and the seller pays any assessments in full before closing. This is not an ironclad rule, however; the buyer and seller in their sales contract can usually agree to do whatever they want about the assessment.

Proration Summary

Table 14:1 summarizes the most commonly found proration situations found in real estate closings. The table also shows who is to be charged and who is to be credited and whether the proration is to be worked forward from the closing date or backward. As a rule, items that are paid in advance by the seller are prorated forward from the closing date; for example, prepaid fire insurance. Items that are paid in arrears, such as interest on an existing loan, are prorated backward from the closing date.

SAMPLE CLOSING

To illustrate the arithmetic involved, let us work through a residential closing situation. Note that this example is not particular to any region of Minnesota, but is rather a composite that shows you how the most commonly encountered residential closing items are handled.

Homer Leavitt has listed his home for sale with List-Rite Realty for $130,000, and the sales commission is to be 6% of the selling price. A salesperson from Quick-Sale Realty learns about the property through the multiple listing service and produces a buyer willing to pay $125,000 with $35,000 down. The offer is conditioned on the seller paying off the existing $48,000, 10% interest mortgage loan and the buyer obtaining a new loan for $90,000. Property taxes, hazard insurance, and heating oil in the home's oil tank are to be prorated as of the closing date. The buyer also asks the seller to pay for a continuation of abstract and the deed stamps. The seller accepts this offer on August 1, and they agree to close on September 15.

The property tax year is the calendar year and the first half of the taxes due this year have been paid in full. The second half of the taxes have not yet been paid. Taxes are

SUMMARY OF COMMON PRORATIONS **Table 14:1**

Accumulated interest on existing loan assumed by buyer	Charge seller	Credit buyer	*Prorate backward*
Insurance premium paid in advance	Charge buyer	Credit seller	*Prorate forward*
Property taxes paid in advance	Charge buyer	Credit seller	*Prorate forward*
Property taxes in arrears	Charge seller	Credit buyer	*Prorate backward*
Rent paid in advance	Charge seller	Credit buyer	*Prorate forward*
Interest on a new loan	Charge buyer	Credit lender	*Prorate forward*
Interest on a loan to be paid off at the closing	Charge seller	Credit lender	*Prorate backward*

$1,680 for the year and $840 are due on October 31. The hazard insurance policy (fire, windstorm, etc.) that the buyer wishes to assume was purchased by the seller for $240 and covers the period June 15 through the following June 14. The Old-Line Abstract Company will charge the seller $70 for a continuation of abstract. The Safety Title Insurance Company will charge the buyer $300 for a combined owner's and mortgagee's title policy.

The buyer obtains a loan commitment from the Ajax National Bank for $90,000. To make this loan, the bank will charge a $900 loan origination fee, $100 for an appraisal, and $25 for a credit report on the buyer. The bank also requires 6 months of property tax reserves, and 4 months of hazard insurance reserves. The loan is to be repaid in equal monthly installments beginning November 1. The recording fees are $5 each for deeds and mortgage releases and $10 for mortgages. The real estate agent will conduct the sale closing as a part of the brokerage fee. The bank will charge the buyer $60 to close the mortgage. The state levies a tax on deeds of $1.10 per

Table 14:2 **TRANSACTION SUMMARY**

	Amount	Comments
Sale Price	$125,000	
Down Payment	$ 35,000	
Deposit (Earnest Money)	$ 3,000	Credit to buyer's down payment.
Existing Mortgage	$ 48,000	Seller to pay off through settlement. Interest rate is 10%.
New Mortgage	$ 90,000	Monthly payments begin Nov. 1. Interest rate is 11.2% per annum.
Loan Fee	$ 900	Paid by buyer in connection with obtaining $90,000 loan.
Appraisal Fee	$ 100	
Credit Report	$ 25	
Title Policy	$ 300	Buyer pays Safety Title Insurance Company.
Property Taxes	$ 1,680/yr	Second half, due Oct. 31, is not yet paid.
Hazard Insurance	$ 240/yr	Remaining 9 months coverage to be transferred to buyer.
Fuel Oil	$ 130	Remaining heating oil in tank.
Abstract fee	$ 70	Seller pays Old-Line Abstract Co.
Property Tax Reserves	$ 840	6 months at $140 for lender.
Hazard Insurance Reserves	$ 80	4 months at $20 for lender.
Lender's Closing Fee	$ 60	Charge by Ajax National Bank to buyer.
Mortgage registration tax	$ 135	Buyer pays.
Deed Stamps	$ 275	Seller pays.
Record Deed	$ 5	Buyer pays.
Record Mortgage Release	$ 5	Seller pays.
Record Mortgage	$ 10	Buyer pays.
Brokerage Commission	$ 7,500	Seller pays to List-Rite Realty.

Settlement and Proration date is September 15. Charge seller with day of closing. All prorations are to be based on a 30-day banker's month.

$500 of new money and 15¢ per $100 on new debt. The seller is leaving $130 worth of fuel oil for the buyer.

The sales commission is $7,500 and is to be paid to List-Rite Realty. (List-Rite then pays Quick-Sale Realty its share). Finally, the $3,000 earnest money deposit that the buyer made with the offer is to be credited toward the down payment. Using this information, which is summarized in Table 14:2 for your convenience, let us see exactly how a settlement statement is prepared.

PURCHASER'S CLOSING STATEMENT

The purchaser's (buyer's) closing statement is divided into two columns: debits (charges) and credits. The debits column lists everything the purchaser must pay. The credits column lists the cash and mortgages the purchaser is using to pay for the property plus any credits that result from the prorating.

Figure 14:1 shows the purchaser's closing statement for the transaction outlined in Table 14:2. Let us work through this statement line by line. On line 1, the purchaser is debited

Figure 14:1

PURCHASER'S CLOSING STATEMENT

Line		Debits	Credits
1	Purchase price	$125,000	$
2	Earnest money deposit		3,000
3	New mortgage loan		90,000
4	Loan origination fee	900	
5	Appraisal fee for mortgage loan	100	
6	Credit report fee	25	
7	Interest for Sept. 15–30	420	
8	Propery tax reserves for new loan	840	
9	Hazard insurance reserves for new loan	80	
10	Title policy	300	
11	Lender's closing fee	60	
12	Mortgage registration tax	135	
13	Record mortgage	10	
14	Record deed	5	
15	Hazard insurance proration	180	
16	Fuel oil left in tank	130	
17	Property tax proration		350
18		128,185	93,350
19	Money due from purchaser at closing		34,835
20		$128,185	$128,185

(charged) for the $125,000 purchase price of the house. On line 2 he is credited for the amount of the earnest money deposit made with the offer. On the following line is a credit for the money coming from the new $90,000 mortgage loan.

Lines 4 through 16 deal with debits to the purchaser. On line 4 is the $900 loan origination fee that will be paid to the lender and on line 5 the $100 appraisal fee. Line 6 shows the credit report fee of $25. On line 7 is the interest on the new $90,000 loan calculated from the date of closing to the end of September. This brings the loan up to the first of the next month and simplifies future bookkeeping for the monthly loan payments; at 11.2% annual interest, it comes to $420. The first monthly payment on the new loan will be due November 1 and include interest for the month of October.

As we saw earlier in Chapter 9, mortgage lenders prefer to pay such items as property taxes, hazard insurance, and property assessment payments on behalf of the borrower. To do this, the lender collects, along with each monthly principal and interest payment, one-twelfth of the amount needed each year.

In our example, property taxes are currently $1,680 per year. On a monthly basis, $140 must be added to each monthly loan payment. However, the lender will not have collected any loan payments by the time the second-half taxes fall due on October 31. Consequently, the lender requires that the borrower place $840 into a tax reserve account at settlement (line 8). Once past October 31, $140 per month will accumulate for payment of future taxes.

The same concept also applies to the payment of insurance. In our example, hazard insurance costs $240 per year, and on June 15 of the following year the lender must have that amount available in the borrower's reserve account. However, collecting one-twelfth of $240 each month until June 15 will leave the lender $80 short. Therefore, the lender asks that $80 from the borrower's closing funds be placed into a reserve at the closing date. This is shown on line 9.

On line 10 the buyer is charged for his title policy. On lines 11 through 14, the buyer is debited for the lender's closing fee, the mortgage registration tax, and his two recording fees. The person responsible for conducting the closing is responsible for seeing that each of these is actually paid.

The next three lines deal with prorations between the buyer and the seller. Line 15 shows that the buyer is assuming the remaining nine months of hazard insurance coverage. The seller paid $240 for the one-year policy. This works out to $20 per month, or $180 for the remaining 9 months of coverage, and is a debit to the buyer. Also charged to the buyer (line 16) is the fuel oil left in the home's heating system tank. The value of this is determined by looking at the tank gauge or dipstick to see how many gallons are left and then multiplying that total by the current price per gallon. In this example, the seller leaves $130 of oil in the tank for the buyer. On line 17 the property tax proration is a credit to the buyer. This is because $840 in property taxes are due on October 31 for the period July 1 through December 31. As the buyer will be the owner on October 31, he will be responsible for paying them. However, the seller has owned the property from July 1 to September 15, a period of 2½ months. At the rate of $140 per month, this means the seller must give the buyer $350 at the closing.

Money Due From Purchaser

The next step in preparing the purchaser's settlement statement is to add all the debits in the debits column and then all the credits in the credits column. If the debits exceed the credits, the difference is the amount of money due from the purchaser at the closing. In the example, line 19 shows that $34,835 is due from the purchaser in order to close. This is the usual situation where a settlement meeting is used to close the transaction.

In an escrow closing, the purchaser will have already deposited the rest of his money with the escrow agent a day or two before the closing. This will show as a credit to the purchaser in the settlement statement. In an escrow closing, the escrow agent will ask for a few dollars more than necessary, then return the excess to the purchaser after closing. This is done because the escrow agent can closely approximate the closing statement amounts in advance, but will not know the precise figures until the closing actually takes place. The excess to be returned to the purchaser will show in the debit column on line 19.

Lastly, on line 20, the total of the debits must equal the total of the credits. If they do not, then an error was made in the closing statement.

SELLER'S CLOSING STATEMENT

Figure 14:2 shows the closing statement the seller receives. Like the purchaser's closing statement, it also has two columns, one for debits and one for credits. In the debits column, the seller is charged his expenses of the sale, any prorated items that are paid in arrears, and any mortgage payoffs. In the credits column the seller is credited for the sales price of the property plus any prepaid items he is passing along to the buyer. Let us look more closely at a seller's closing statement.

On line 1 of the seller's closing statement, the seller is credited with the $125,000 purchase price. This is the same amount as shown on the purchaser's statement except that for the purchaser it was a debit item. On line 2 of the seller's statement, the seller is debited (charged) for the $48,000 existing loan that is to be paid off at the closing. (The new lender will write the check to the old lender. If the settlement is through escrow, the escrow agent will make the payment.) On line 3, the accrued interest on the existing loan for the period September 1 through September 15 is charged to the seller. At 10% interest, $48,000 for 15 days comes to $200. On line 4, the seller is charged for recording the mortgage release.

Deed stamps, i.e., conveyance taxes or fees, are listed on line 5. The abstract continuation fee is itemized on line 6, and the sales commission on line 7.

Lines 8, 9, and 10 deal with prorations. These mirror the

Figure 14:2

SELLER'S CLOSING STATEMENT

Line		Debits	Credits
1	Sales price		$125,000
2	Mortgage loan payoff	$ 48,000	
3	Accrued interest Sept. 1–15	200	
4	Record mortgage release	5	
5	Deed stamps	275	
6	Abstract fee	70	
7	Sales commission	7,500	
8	Property tax proration	350	
9	Hazard insurance proration		180
10	Fuel oil left in tank		130
11		56,400	125,310
12	Money due seller at closing	68,910	
		$125,310	$125,310

prorations made in lines 15, 16, and 17 on the purchaser's closing statement (Figure 14:1). The $350 property tax proration that was a credit to the purchaser on line 17 of his statement is a debit in the same amount to the seller on line 8 of the seller's statement. The $180 of hazard insurance the purchaser is taking from the seller shows on line 9 as a credit. The value of the fuel oil being left for the buyer is credited to the seller on line 10.

At line 11, the debit column and the credit column are each totaled. The debit total is subtracted from the credit total and the difference (line 12) is the money payable to the seller at the closing. At line 13 the total of the debits must equal the total of the credits; if not, an error was made in the closing statement.

REAL ESTATE SETTLEMENT PROCEDURES ACT

In response to consumer complaints regarding real estate closing costs and procedures, Congress passed the Real Estate Settlement Procedures Act (RESPA) of 1974. This act became effective June 20, 1975 throughout the United States. However, because RESPA generated considerable criticism from real estate brokers, mortgage lenders, and home buyers, Congress enacted some changes that went into effect on June 30, 1976.

The purpose of RESPA, as amended, is to regulate and standardize real estate settlement practices when "federally related" first mortgage loans are made on one- to four-family residences, condominiums and cooperatives. Federally related is defined to include FHA or VA or other government-backed or assisted loans, loans from lenders with federally insured deposits, loans that are to be purchased by FNMA, GNMA, FHLMC or other federally controlled secondary mortgage market institutions, and loans made by lenders who make or invest more than $1 million per year in residential loans. As the bulk of all home loans now made fall into one of these categories, the impact of this law is far-reaching.

Restrictions

RESPA prohibits kickbacks and fees for services not performed during the closing process. For example, in some regions of the United States prior to this act, it was common practice for attorneys and closing agents to channel title business to certain title companies in return for a fee. This increased settlement costs without adding services. Now there must be a justifiable service rendered for each closing fee charge. The act also prohibits the seller from requiring that the buyer purchase title insurance from a particular title company.

The Real Estate Settlement Procedures Act also contains restrictions on the amount of advance property tax and insurance payments that a lender can collect and place in an impound or reserve account. The amount is limited to the property owner's share of taxes and insurance accrued prior to settlement, plus one-sixth of the estimated amount that will come due for these items in the twelve-month period beginning at settlement. This requirement assures that the lender has an adequate but not excessive amount of money impounded when taxes and insurance payments fall due. If the amount in the reserve account is not sufficient to pay an item when it comes due, the lender must temporarily use its own funds to make up the difference. Then the lender bills the borrower or increases the monthly reserve payment. If there is a drop in the amount the lender must pay out, then the monthly reserve requirement can be reduced.

Considerable criticism and debate have raged over the topic of reserves. Traditionally, lenders have not paid interest to borrowers on money held as reserves, effectively creating an interest-free loan to themselves. This has tempted many lenders to require overly adequate reserves. HUD's RESPA sets a reasonable limit on reserve requirements and some states now require that interest be paid on reserves. Although not always required to do so, some lenders now voluntarily pay interest on reserves.

Benefits

To the typical homebuyer who is applying for a first mortgage loan the most obvious benefits of RESPA are that (1) he will receive from the lender a special HUD information booklet explaining RESPA, (2) he will receive a good faith estimate of closing costs from the lender, (3) the lender will use the HUD Uniform Settlement Statement, and (4) the borrower has the right to inspect the Uniform Settlement Statement one business day before the day of closing.

The primary reason lenders are required to promptly give loan applicants an estimate of closing costs is to allow the loan applicant an opportunity to compare prices for the various services his transaction will require. Additionally, these esti-

GOOD FAITH ESTIMATES OF CLOSING COSTS **Figure 14:3**

The charges listed below are our Good Faith Estimate of some of the settlement charges you will need to pay at settlement of the loan for which you have applied. These charges will be paid to the title or escrow company that conducts the settlement. This form does not cover all items you will be required to pay in cash at settlement, for example, deposit in escrow for real estate taxes and insurance. You may wish to inquire as to the amounts of such other items. You may be required to pay other additional amounts at settlement. This is not a commitment to make a loan.

Services			Estimated Fees
801.	Loan Origination Fee _____% + $ __________		$
802.	Loan Discount %		$
803.	Appraisal Fee		$
804.	Credit Report		$
806.	Mortgage Insurance Application Fee		$
807.	Assumption Fee		$
808.	Tax Service Fee		$
901.	Interest		$
902.	Mortgage Insurance Premium		$
1106.	Notary Fees		$
1109.	Title Insurance Lender's	List only those items Buyer will pay	$
1110.	Title Insurance Owner's		$
1111.	Escrow Fee		$
1201.	Recording Fees		$
1202.	County Tax/Stamps		$
1203.	City Tax/Stamps		$
1302.	Pest Inspection		$
1303.	Building Inspection		$
↑			$
These numbers correspond to the HUD Settlement Statement		TOTAL	$

mates help the borrower calculate how much his total closing costs will be. Figure 14:3 illustrates a good faith estimate form. Note that it is primarily concerned with settlement services.

RESPA does not require estimates of escrow impounds for property taxes and insurance, although the lender can vol-

Form Approved
OMB NO. 63-R-1501

Figure 14:4

A.

U. S. DEPARTMENT OF HOUSING AND URBAN DEVELOPMENT

SETTLEMENT STATEMENT

B. TYPE OF LOAN

1. ☐ FHA 2. ☐ FmHA 3. ☐ CONV. UNINS.
4. ☐ VA 5. ☐ CONV. INS.

6. File Number:

7. Loan Number:

8. Mortgage Insurance Case Number:

C. NOTE: *This form is furnished to give you a statement of actual settlement costs. Amounts paid to and by the settlement agent are shown. Items marked "(p.o.c.)" were paid outside the closing; they are shown here for informational purposes and are not included in the totals.*

D. NAME OF BORROWER:	E. NAME OF SELLER:	F. NAME OF LENDER:
Neidi d'Moni 2724 East 22nd Street City, State 00000	Homer Leavitt 1654 West 12th Street City, State 00000	Ajax National Bank 1111 West 1st Street City, State 00000

G. PROPERTY LOCATION:	H. SETTLEMENT AGENT:	I. SETTLEMENT DATE:
1654 West 12th Street City, State 00000	Safety Title Insurance Company PLACE OF SETTLEMENT: Ajax National Bank	Sept. 15, 19xx

J. SUMMARY OF BORROWER'S TRANSACTION	
100. GROSS AMOUNT DUE FROM BORROWER:	
101. Contract sales price	$125,000
102. Personal property	
103. Settlement charges to borrower *(line 1400)*	2,875
104.	
105.	
Adjustments for items paid by seller in advance	
106. City/town taxes to	
107. County taxes to	
108. Assessments to	
109. Hazard insurance 9/15 to 6/15	180
110. Fuel oil	130
111.	
112.	
120. GROSS AMOUNT DUE FROM BORROWER	$128,185
200. AMOUNTS PAID BY OR IN BEHALF OF BORROWER:	
201. Deposit or earnest money	$ 3,000
202. Principal amount of new loan(s)	90,000
203. Existing loan(s) taken subject to	
204.	
205.	
206.	
207.	
208.	
209.	
Adjustments for items unpaid by seller	
210. City/town taxes to	
211. County taxes 7/1 to 9/15	350
212. Assessments to	
213.	
214.	
215.	
216.	
217.	
218.	
219.	
220. TOTAL PAID BY/FOR BORROWER	$ 93,350
300. CASH AT SETTLEMENT FROM/TO BORROWER	
301. Gross amount due from borrower *(line 120)*	$128,185
302. Less amounts paid by/for borrower *(line 220)*	(93,350)
303. CASH (☑ FROM) (☐ TO) BORROWER	$ 34,835

K. SUMMARY OF SELLER'S TRANSACTION	
400. GROSS AMOUNT DUE TO SELLER:	
401. Contract sales price	$125,000
402. Personal property	
403.	
404.	
405.	
Adjustments for items paid by seller in advance	
406. City/town taxes to	
407. County taxes to	
408. Assessments to	
409. Hazard insurance 9/15 to 6/15	180
410. Fuel oil	130
411.	
412.	
420. GROSS AMOUNT DUE TO SELLER	$125,310
500. REDUCTIONS IN AMOUNT DUE TO SELLER:	
501. Excess deposit *(see instructions)*	
502. Settlement charges to seller *(line 1400)*	7,850
503. Existing loan(s) taken subject to	
504. Payoff of first mortgage loan	48,000
505. Payoff of second mortgage loan	
506. Accrued interest 9/1 to 9/15	200
507.	
508.	
509.	
Adjustments for items unpaid by seller	
510. City/town taxes to	
511. County taxes 7/1 to 9/15	350
512. Assessments to	
513.	
514.	
515.	
516.	
517.	
518.	
519.	
520. TOTAL REDUCTION AMOUNT DUE SELLER	$ 56,400
600. CASH AT SETTLEMENT TO/FROM SELLER	
601. Gross amount due to seller *(line 420)*	$125,310
602. Less reductions in amount due seller *(line 520)*	(56,400)
603. CASH (☑ TO) (☐ FROM) SELLER	$ 68,910

Previous Edition is Obsolete

HUD-1 (5-76)

Figure 14:4 *continued*

–2–

L. SETTLEMENT CHARGES	PAID FROM BORROWER'S FUNDS AT SETTLEMENT	PAID FROM SELLER'S FUNDS AT SETTLEMENT
700. TOTAL SALES/BROKER'S COMMISSION based on price $125,000 @ 6 % = $7,500		
Division of Commission (line 700) as follows:		
701. $7,500 to List-Rite Realty		
702. $ to		
703. Commission paid at Settlement		$ 7,500
704.		
800. ITEMS PAYABLE IN CONNECTION WITH LOAN		
801. Loan Origination Fee %	$ 900	
802. Loan Discount %		
803. Appraisal Fee to	100	
804. Credit Report to	25	
805. Lender's Inspection Fee		
806. Mortgage Insurance Application Fee to		
807. Assumption Fee		
808. Lender's Closing Fee	60	
809.		
810.		
811.		
900. ITEMS REQUIRED BY LENDER TO BE PAID IN ADVANCE		
901. Interest from Sept. 15 to Sept. 30 @ $28.00 /day	420	
902. Mortgage Insurance Premium for months to		
903. Hazard Insurance Premium for years to		
904. years to		
905.		
1000. RESERVES DEPOSITED WITH LENDER		
1001. Hazard insurance 4 months @ $ 20 per month	80	
1002. Mortgage insurance months @ $ per month		
1003. City property taxes months @ $ per month		
1004. County property taxes 6 months @ $ 140 per month	840	
1005. Annual assessments months @ $ per month		
1006. months @ $ per month		
1007. months @ $ per month		
1008. months @ $ per month		
1100. TITLE CHARGES		
1101. Settlement or closing fee to		
1102. Abstract or title search $70 to Old-Line Abstract Company		70
1103. Title examination to		
1104. Title insurance binder to		
1105. Document preparation to		
1106. Notary fees to		
1107. Attorney's fees to		
(includes above items numbers;)		
1108. Title insurance to Safety Title Insurance Company	300	
(includes above items numbers;)		
1109. Lender's coverage $ 90,000		
1110. Owner's coverage $ 125,000		
1111.		
1112.		
1113.		
1200. GOVERNMENT RECORDING AND TRANSFER CHARGES		
1201. Recording fees: Deed $ 5 ; Mortgage $ 10 ; Releases $ 5	15	5
1202. City/county tax/stamps: Deed $; Mortgage $		
1203. State tax/stamps: Deed $ 275 ; Mortgage $ 135	135	275
1204.		
1205.		
1300. ADDITIONAL SETTLEMENT CHARGES		
1301. Survey to		
1302. Pest inspection to		
1303.		
1304.		
1305.		
1400. TOTAL SETTLEMENT CHARGES (enter on lines 103, Section J and 502, Section K)	$ 2,875	$ 7,850

HUD-1 (5-76)

untarily add these items to the form. Note also that RESPA allows lenders to make estimates in terms of ranges. For example, escrow fees may be stated as $110 to $140 to reflect the range of rates being charged by local escrow companies for that service.

HUD SETTLEMENT STATEMENT

The HUD Settlement Statement is used by the person conducting the settlement. It includes a summary of all charges to be paid by the borrower (buyer) and the seller in connection with the settlement. A sample HUD settlement, filled out to reflect the same transaction illustrated in Figures 14:1 and 14:2 is shown as Figure 14:4. The HUD format must be used in any settlement covered by RESPA. This includes nearly all real estate transactions where a loan is being made by an institutional lender. In closings that require the HUD settlement statement, the closing agent may use his own closing statement format in addition to the HUD form. In transactions not covered by RESPA, any suitable format may be used.

More information on the Real Estate Settlement Procedures Act can be obtained in a free HUD booklet available from lenders and titled "Settlement Costs and You."

VOCABULARY REVIEW

Match terms **a–g** *with statements* **1–7.**

a. *Closing*
b. *Closing statement*
c. *Deed delivery*
d. *Documentary transfer tax*
e. *Prorate*
f. *Seller's affidavit*
g. *RESPA*

1. An accounting of funds to the buyer and seller at the completion of a real estate transaction. B
2. The act of finalizing a transaction. A
3. A source of state and local revenue derived from taxing conveyance documents. D
4. A document provided by the seller at a closing meeting stating that he has done nothing to encumber title since the title search was made for this sale. F
5. The moment at which title passes from the seller to the buyer. C
6. To divide the ongoing income and expenses of a property between the buyer and seller. E
7. A federal law that deals with procedures to be followed in certain types of real estate closings. G

QUESTIONS AND PROBLEMS

1. What are the duties of a closer?
2. As a means of closing a real estate transaction, how does an escrow differ from a closing?
3. Is an escrow agent the agent of the buyer or the seller? Explain.
4. The buyer agrees to accept the seller's fire insurance policy as part of the purchase agreement. The policy cost $180, covers the period January 16 through the following January 15, and the settlement date is March 12. How much does the buyer owe the seller (closest whole dollar)?
5. A buyer agrees to assume an existing 8% mortgage on which $45,000 is still owed; the last monthly payment was made on March 1 and the next payment is due April 1. Settlement date is March 12. Local custom is to use a 30-day month and charge the buyer interest beginning with the settlement day. Calculate the interest proration. To whom is it credited? To whom is it charged?
6. In real estate closing, does the buyer or seller normally pay for the following items: deed stamps, deed preparation, lender's title policy, loan appraisal fee, mortgage recording, and mortgage release?

ADDITIONAL READINGS

A General Discussion of Escrows. Los Angeles, Calif.: Title Insurance and Trust Company, n.d., 32 pages. Explains the duties and obligations of an escrow officer in a real estate transaction. Available free from the publisher. (Most title companies in the United States have similar booklets available at no charge.)

Gardner, Phil. "Avoiding the Settlement Shakes." *Real Estate Today,* August, 1978, pages 14–18. Article points out that the keys to a smooth settlement are a well-informed buyer and a confident seller. Sample pre-closing forms are shown.

Kratovil, Robert and **Werner, Raymond J.** *Real Estate Law,* 8th ed. Englewood Cliffs, N.J.: Prentice-Hall, 1983, 650 pages. Chapters 12 and 13 deal with the legal aspects of closing a real estate deal and escrows.

Pace, Peter. *Complete Handbook of Real Estate Math.* Reston, Va.: Reston Publishing Co., 1982. Covers every mathematical problem the real estate agent encounters in daily business. A hands-on book for the beginner and a reference tool for the experienced agent.

U.S. Department of Housing and Urban Development. *Settlement Costs and You.* Washington, D.C.: U.S. Government Printing Office, 1977, 31 pages. Explains homebuyer rights under the 1976 RESPA revision. Demonstrates sample closings using the HUD Settlement forms. Available free.

Weber, Fred R. *Real Estate Math: Using the Handheld Calculator.* Reston, Va.: Reston Publishing Co., 1979, 150 pages. Explains how to use pocket calculators to figure interest, yield, depreciation, monthly payments, commissions, loan payoffs, investment return, and other real estate math problems. Shows what numbers to enter and what buttons to press to get the answers.

Real Estate Leases

KEY TERMS

Escalator clause: provision in a lease for upward and downward rent adjustments
Ground rent: rent paid to occupy a plot of land
Lessee: the tenant
Lessor: the landlord
Option clause: the right at some future time to purchase or lease a property at a predetermined price
Quiet enjoyment: the right of possession and use of property without undue disturbance by others
Reversionary interest: the right to retake possession at some future time
Sandwich lease: a leasehold interest lying between the owner of a property and its actual user
Sublease: a lease that is given by a lessee
Sublessee: a lessee who rents from another lessee
Sublessor: a lessee who rents to another lessee

Earlier in this text, we talked about leases both as estates in land (Chapter 3) and as a means of financing (Chapter 12). Our purpose now is to explore further the rights of the landlord and tenant, various types of leases, lease termination, and a sample lease form.

THE LEASEHOLD ESTATE

A lease conveys to the **lessee** (tenant) the right to possess and use another's property for a period of time. During this time, the **lessor** (the landlord or fee owner) possesses a **reversion** that entitles him to retake possession at the end of the lease period. This is also called a **reversionary right** or **reversionary interest.**

The tenant's right to occupy land is called a leasehold estate. There are four categories of leasehold estates: estate for years, periodic estate, estate at will, and tenancy at sufferance. An **estate for years** must have a specific starting time and a specific ending time. It can be for any length of time, and it does not automatically renew itself. A **periodic estate** has an original lease period of fixed length that continually renews itself for like periods of time until the tenant or landlord acts to terminate it. A month-to-month lease is an example. In an **estate at will** all the normal landlord-tenant rights and duties exist except that the estate can be terminated by either party at any time. Minnesota has merged the periodic estate and the estate at will under the name estate at will. This type of tenancy can be terminated by either the landlord or the tenant upon giving one full rental period of notice or three months of notice, whichever is less. A **tenancy at sufferance** occurs when a tenant stays beyond his legal tenancy without the consent of the landlord. The tenant is commonly called a **holdover tenant** and no advance notice is required for eviction. He differs from a trespasser only in that his original entry onto the property was legal.

CREATING A VALID LEASE

In addition to conveying the right to use property, a lease also contains provisions for the payment of rent and any other obligations the landlord and tenant have to each other. Since

Figure 15:1

LEASE

This lease agreement is entered into the 10th *day of* April *, 19* xx *between* John and Sally Landlord ① *(hereinafter called the Lessor) and* Gary and Barbara Tenant ② *(hereinafter called the Lessee). The Lessor hereby leases to the Lessee* ③ *and the Lessee hereby leases from the Lessor the premises known as* Apartment 24, 1234 Maple St., City, State ④ *for the term of* one ⑤ *year beginning 12:00 noon on* April 15, 19xx *and ending 12:00 noon on* April 15, 19xx *unless sooner terminated as herein set forth.*

The rent for the term of this lease is $ 3,600.00 ⑥ *payable in equal monthly installments of $* 300.00 ⑦ *on the* 15th *day of each month beginning on* April 15, 19xx. *Receipt of the first monthly installment and $* 300.00 ⑧ *as a security, damage and cleanup deposit is hereby acknowledged. It is furthermore agreed that:*

⑨ *The use of the premises shall be as a residential dwelling for the above named Lessee only.*

⑩ *The Lessee may not assign this lease or sublet any portion of the premises without written permission from the Lessor.*

Figure 15:1 *continued*

(11) *The Lessee agrees to abide by the house rules as posted. A current copy is attached to this lease.*

(12) *The Lessor shall furnish water, sewer and heat as part of the rent. Electricity and telephone shall be paid for by the Lessee.*

(13) *The Lessor agrees to keep the premises structure maintained and in habitable condition.*

(14) *The Lessee agrees to maintain the interior of said premises and at the termination of this lease to return said premises to the Lessor in as good condition as it is now except for ordinary wear and tear.*

(15) *The Lessee shall not make any alterations or improvements to the premises without the Lessor's prior written consent. Any alterations or improvements become the property of the Lessor at the end of this lease.*

(16) *If the premises are not ready for occupancy on the date herein provided, the Lessee may cancel this agreement and the Lessor shall return in full all money paid by the Lessee.*

(17) *If the Lessee defaults on this lease agreement, the Lessor may give the Lessee three days notice of intention to terminate the lease. At the end of those three days the lease shall terminate and the Lessee shall vacate and surrender the premises to the Lessor.*

(18) *If the Lessee holds over after the expiration of this lease without the Lessor's consent, the tenancy shall be month-to-month at twice the monthly rate indicated herein.*

(19) *If the premises are destroyed or rendered uninhabitable by fire or other cause, this lease shall terminate as of the date of the casualty.*

(20) *The Lessor shall have access to the premises for the purpose of inspecting for damage, making repairs, and showing to prospective tenants or buyers.*

(21)	(22)
John Landlord	*Gary Tenant*
Lessor	Lessee
Sally Landlord	*Barbara Tenant*
Lessor	Lessee

a lease is both a conveyance and a contract, it must meet the usual requirements of a valid contract. That is to say, the parties involved must be legally competent, and there must be mutual agreement, lawful objective, and sufficient consideration. The main elements of a lease are (1) the names of the lessee and lessor, (2) a description of the premises, (3) an agreement to convey (let) the premises by the lessor and to accept possession by the lessee, (4) provisions for the payment of rent, (5) the starting date and duration of the lease, and (6) signatures of the parties to the lease.

In most states, a lease longer than one year must be in writing to be enforceable in court. A lease for one year or less or a month-to-month lease could be oral and still be valid, but as a matter of good business practice, they should be put in writing and signed. This gives all parties involved a written reminder of their obligations under the lease and reduces chances for dispute.

THE LEASE DOCUMENT

Figure 15:1 illustrates a lease document that contains a typical cross-section of residential lease provisions. These provisions are presented in simplified language to help you more easily grasp the rights and responsibilities created by a lease. Figure 15:2 is a popular Minnesota lease form. Although it is more difficult to read than Figure 15:1, it does follow closely the Minnesota statutes and gives an accurate indication of Minnesota's landlord-tenant legislation. The circled numbers in both figures correspond to the discussion which follows.

The first paragraph is the conveyance portion of the lease. At ① and ② the lessor and lessee are identified. At ③, the lessor conveys to the lessee and the lessee accepts the property. A description of the property follows at ④, and the term of the conveyance at ⑤. The property must be described so that there is no question as to the extent of the premises the lessee is renting. If the lease illustrated here was a month-to-month lease, the term of the lease would be changed to read, "commencing April 15, 19xx and continuing on a month-to-month basis until terminated by either the lessee or the lessor." During his tenancy, the lessee is entitled to **quiet enjoyment** of the property. This means uninterrupted use of the property without interference from the owner, lessor or other third party.

A month-to-month rental is the most flexible arrangement.

It allows the owner to recover possession of the property on one-month notice and the tenant to leave on one-month notice with no further obligation to the owner. In rental agreements for longer periods of time, each party gives up some flexibility to gain commitment from the other. Under a one-year lease, a tenant has the property committed to him for a year. This means that the tenant is committed to paying rent for a full year, even though he may want to move out before the year is over. Similarly, the owner has the tenant's commitment to pay rent for a year, but loses the flexibility of being able to regain possession of the property until the year is over.

The balance of the lease document is concerned with contract aspects of the lease. At number ⑥, the amount of rent that the lessee will pay for the use of the property is set forth. In a lease for years it is the usual practice to state the total rent for the entire lease period. This is the total number of dollars the lessee is obligated to pay to the lessor. If the lessee wants to leave the premises before the lease period expires, he is still liable for the full amount of the contract. The method of payment of the obligation is shown at number ⑦. Unless the contract calls for rent to be paid in advance, under common law it is not due until the end of the rental period. At number ⑧, the lessor has taken a deposit in the form of the first monthly installment and acknowledges receipt of it. The lessor has also taken additional money as security against the possibility of uncollected rent or damage to the premises and for clean-up expenses. (The tenant is supposed to leave the premises clean.) The deposit is refunded, less legitimate charges, when the tenant leaves.

Items ⑨ through ⑳ summarize commonly found lease clauses. At ⑨ and ⑩, the lessor wants to maintain control over the use and occupancy of the premises. Without this he might find the premises used for an entirely different purpose by people he did not rent to. At ⑪, the tenant agrees to abide by the house rules. These normally cover such things as use of laundry and trash facilities, swimming pool rules, noise rules, etc. Number ⑫ states the responsibility of the lessee and lessor with regard to the payment of utilities.

The strict legal interpretation of a lease as a conveyance means the lessee is responsible for upkeep and repairs during his tenancy unless the lessor promises to do so in the lease

Figure 15:2

No. 1533 – House Lease (Revised 1977) Miller-Davis Co., Minneapolis

By This Lease Agreement, *Made and entered into on* ______________ *19*____,

between ___ (1) ______________________________,

herein referred to as Lessor , *and* ___ (2) ______________________________,

herein referred to as Lessee , *Lessor leases and lets to Lessee the premises situated at* ______________

______________ (3) ___ *in the City of* ______________, *and County*

of ______________, *State of Minnesota, and more particularly described as follows:*

(4)

together with all appurtenances, for a term of ________ (5) ____________ to commence on

______________, 19____, and to end on ______________, 19____, at

______________ o'clock ____m, on the following terms and conditions:

Lessee agrees to pay, without demand, to Lessor as rent for the demised premises the sum of ___ (6) ____

______________ Dollars ($____________) per month in advance on the ________ day

7 of each calendar month beginning ______________, 19____, at ______________

______________, City of ______________, State of Minnesota, or at such other place as Lessor may designate, PROVIDED HOWEVER, that in case said premises, without fault or neglect on the part of said Lessee is destroyed or is so injured by the elements or any other cause as to be untenantable or unfit for occupancy, Lessee is not liable thereafter to pay rent to said Lessor ; and the Lessee shall thereupon quit and surrender possession of said premises.

8 SECURITY DEPOSIT: On execution of this lease, Lessee deposits with Lessor ______________ ______________Dollars ($______________), receipt of which is acknowledged by Lessor as security for the faithful performance by Lessee of the terms herein. Said security deposit shall bear simple interest at the rate of five percent (5%) per annum noncompounded, computed from the first day of the next month following the full payment of such deposit to the last day of the month of termination of the tenancy. In compliance with M. S. A. 504.20, Subd. 3, Lessor shall refund said security deposit or furnish to Lessee vacating the demised premises a statement showing the reason for the withholding of the security deposit or any portion thereof within three weeks after termination of the tenancy and receipt of Lessee's mailing address or delivery instructions.

QUIET ENJOYMENT: Lessor covenants that on paying the rent and performing the covenants herein contained, Lessee shall peacefully and quietly have, hold, and enjoy the demised premises for the agreed term.

9 USE OF PREMISES: The demised premises shall be used and occupied by Lessee exclusively as a private single family residence. Neither the premises nor any part thereof shall be used at any time during the term of this lease by Lessee for the purpose of carrying on any business, profession, or trade of any kind, or for any purpose other than as a private single family residence.

15 ALTERATIONS AND IMPROVEMENTS: Lessee shall make no alterations to the buildings on the demised premises or construct any building or make other improvements on the demised premises without the prior written consent of Lessor. All alterations, changes, and improvements built, constructed, or placed on the demised premises by Lessee with the exception of fixtures removable without damage to the premises and movable personal property, shall, unless otherwise provided by written agreement between Lessor and Lessee be the property of Lessor, and remain on the demised premises at the expiration or sooner termination of this lease.

MAINTENANCE AND REPAIR: Lessor covenants (a) that the premises and all common areas are fit for the use intended by the parties; (b) to keep the premises in reasonable repair during the term of the lease; and (c) to maintain the premises in compliance with the applicable health and safety laws of the state and of the local units of government where the demised premises are located during the term of this lease. Lessee will, at Lessee's sole expense, make all required repairs of the premises and eliminate any violation of the applicable health and safety laws which exist on the premises whenever such disrepair and conditions shall have resulted from Lessee's negligence, willful, malicious, or irresponsible conduct or that of his employee, family, agent, or visitor. Lessor
13 further covenants that at the commencement and at all times during the continuation of the term that the demised premises and the building are not and shall not be in such condition as to constitute a violation of any state, county or city health, housing, building, fire prevention, or housing maintenance code applicable to the building which materially endangers the health or safety of the tenants of the building. In any action against Lessor for breach of this covenant, it shall be a sufficient defense that: (a) the violation or violations alleged do not in fact exist or that such violation or violations have been removed or remedied; or (b) such violations have been caused
14 by the willful, malicious, negligent or irresponsible conduct of a complaining tenant or anyone under his direction or control; or (c) any tenant of the building has unreasonably refused entry to the Lessor or Lessor's agent to a portion of the premises for the purpose of correcting such violation, and such effort to correct was made in good faith; or (d) such violation or violations alleged in the complaint do not materially endanger the health or safety of the tenants of the dwelling. Lessee shall comply with all the sanitary laws, ordinances, rules, and orders of appropriate governmental authorities affecting the cleanliness, occupancy, and preservation of the demised prem-

Figure 15:2 *continued*

ises during the term of this lease, and any renewal thereof, except where such compliance is the duty of the Lessor under M. S. A. 504.18 (c) and the covenants contained herein.

Lessee shall perform the following specified repairs and maintenance not required of Lessor by other provisions of this lease:

Lessee agrees that no signs shall be placed or painting done on or about the demised premises by Lessee or at Lessee's direction without the prior written consent of Lessor .

DAMAGE TO PREMISES: If the demised premises, or any part thereof, shall be partially damaged by fire or other casualty not due to Lessee's negligence or willful act or that of lessee's employee, family, agent or visitor,
(19) the premises shall be promptly repaired by Lessor and there shall be an abatement of rent corresponding with the time during which, and the extent to which, the leased premises may have been untenantable; but, if the leased premises should be damaged other than by Lessee's negligence or willful act or that of Lessee's employee, family, agent, or visitor to the extent that Lessor shall, in good faith, decide not to rebuild or repair, the term of this lease shall end and the rent shall be prorated up to the time of the damage.

(12) UTILITIES: Lessee shall be responsible for paying for all utility services required on the premises, except that ________________________________ shall be provided by Lessor.

(20) RIGHT OF ENTRY: Lessor and Lessor's agents reserve the right to enter the demised premises at all reasonable hours during the term of this lease, and any renewal thereof, for the purpose of inspecting the premises and all building improvements thereon, and whenever necessary to make repairs and alterations to the demised premises. Lessee hereby grants permission to Lessor to show the demised premises to new rental applicants at reasonable hours of the day, within ____________ days of the expiration of the tenancy.

(10) ASSIGNMENT AND SUBLETTING: Without prior written consent of Lessor , Lessee shall not assign this lease, or sublet or grant any concession or license to use the premises or any part thereof. A consent by Lessor to one assignment, subletting, concession, or license shall not be deemed to be a consent to any subsequent assignment, subletting, concession, or license. An assignment, subletting, concession, or license without the prior written consent of Lessor , or an assignment or subletting by operation of law, shall be void and the lease shall, at Lessor's option, be terminated in compliance with the default provision contained herein.

TERMINATION: Lessee agrees to give Lessor thirty (30) days written notice before the expiration of this lease of Lessee's intention to vacate at the end of this lease, otherwise Lessor will have the option of continuing
(18) this lease for ____________________ from such expiration, and any subsequent expirations. This renewal provision shall be valid only if Lessor or Lessor's agent, within fifteen (15) days prior to the time that Lessee is required to furnish notice of Lessee's intention to quit, but not more than thirty (30) days prior thereto, has given to Lessee written notice, served personally or by registered mail, directing Lessee's attention to this renewal provision.

(14) SURRENDER OF PREMISES: At the expiration of the lease term, Lessee shall quit and surrender the premises hereby demised in as good state and condition as they were at the commencement of this lease, reasonable use and wear thereof and damages by the elements excepted.

ABANDONMENT: If at any time during the term of this lease Lessee abandons the demised premises, or any part thereof, Lessor may, at Lessor's option, bring an action to recover possession of the demised premises and such action is equivalent to a demand for the rent and a reentry upon the property. Lessor may, at Lessor's option, hold Lessee liable for any difference between the rent that would have been payable under this lease during the balance of the unexpired term, if this lease had continued in force, and the net rent for such period realized by Lessor by means of reletting the premises. If Lessor recovers possession of the demised premises following abandonment of the premises by Lessee then Lessor may consider any personal property belonging to Lessee and left on the premises to also have been abandoned, in which case Lessor may dispose of all such property in any manner Lessor shall deem proper and Lessee is hereby relieved of all liability for doing so.

(17) DEFAULT: If any default is made in payment of rent, or any part thereof, at the times herein before specified, or if any default is made in performance of or compliance with any other term or condition hereof, the lease, at the option of Lessor may be terminated.

HEIRS AND ASSIGNS: The covenants and conditions herein contained shall apply to and bind the heirs, legal representatives, and assigns of the parties hereto, and all covenants are to be construed as conditions of this lease.

IN WITNESS WHEREOF, the parties hereto have executed this lease this ________________ day of ____________________, 19____.

(21) ______________________________

____

(22) ______________________________

____

contract. The paragraph at number ⑬ is that promise. Note however that with regard to residential properties, courts and legislatures are now taking the position that the landlord is obligated to keep the property repaired and habitable even though this is not specifically stated in the contract.

Number ⑭ is the lessee's promise to maintain the interior of the dwelling. If the lessee damages the property, he is to repair it. Normal wear and tear are considered to be part of the rent. At paragraph ⑮, the lessor protects himself against unauthorized alterations and improvements and then goes on to point out that anything the tenant affixes to the building becomes realty. As realty it remains a part of the building when the tenant leaves.

Paragraphs ⑯ through ⑲ deal with the rights of both parties if the premises are not ready for occupancy, if the lessee defaults after moving in, if the lessee holds over, or if the premises are destroyed. The lessor also retains the right (paragraph ⑳) to enter the leased premises from time to time for business purposes.

Finally, at ㉑ and ㉒, the lessor and lessee sign. It is not necessary to have these signatures acknowledged. That is done only if the lease is to be recorded and then only the lessor's signature is acknowledged. The purpose of recording is to give constructive notice that the lessee has an estate in the property. Recording is usually done only when the lessee's rights are not apparent from inspection of the property for actual notice or where the lease is to run many years. From the property owner's standpoint, the lease is an encumbrance on the property. If the owner should subsequently sell the property or mortgage it, the lessee's tenancy remains undisturbed. The buyer or lender must accept the property subject to the lease.

LANDLORD-TENANT LAWS

Traditionally, a lease was enforceable in court based solely on what it contained. This philosophy still prevails with regard to leases on commercial property. However, with regard to residential rental property, the trend today is for state legislatures to establish special landlord-tenant laws. The intent is to strike a reasonable balance between the responsibilities of landlords to tenants and vice versa. Typically these laws limit the amount of security deposit a landlord can require, tell the tenant how many days notice he has to give before vacating a periodic tenancy, and require the landlord to deliver possession on the date agreed. The landlord must maintain the premises in a fit condition for living and the tenant is to keep his unit clean and not damage it. The tenant is to obey the house rules and the landlord must give advance notice before entering an apartment except in legitimate emergencies. Additionally the laws set forth such things as the procedure for accounting for any deposit money not returned, the right of the landlord to file court actions for unpaid rent, and the proper procedure for evicting a tenant. In addition to Minnesota's landlord-tenant law reflected in Figure 15:2, tenants must provide three days written notice of vacating any residence during the winter months. Failure to give such notice is a misdemeanor and exposes the tenant to liability for any damage suffered by the landlord as the result of freezing pipes and water damage.

Interest on Deposits

A new trend among states is the requirement that interest be paid to tenants on their security (damage) deposits. The **Minnesota Landlord-Tenant Act** requires that these deposits must be returned, along with 5% non-compounded interest, within 21 days of termination. The landlord may retain from the security deposit money necessary to restore the rented property to its original condition (except for normal wear and tear) and any rents or other money due the landlord. The landlord is not required to return the deposit if the tenant does not leave a forwarding address and does not return to claim the deposit.

Habitability, Death

In Minnesota, a tenant cannot be forced to pay rent during the time that the rented property is uninhabitable due to the landlord's inaction. Moreover, a tenant has a right to vacate and be relieved of rent liability under these conditions. If a tenant dies, the Act provides that death does not automatically terminate an estate for years or a periodic estate. However, the deceased's personal representative may terminate the lease by giving two months written notice to the lessor. If the lease provides for a shorter termination notice, such as a month-to-month tenancy, that shorter notice would apply. An estate at will is automatically terminated by death.

SETTING RENTS

There are several methods for setting rents. The first is the **fixed rental fee,** also called a **flat rent** or **gross lease.** The tenant agrees to pay a specified amount of money for the use of the premises. A tenant paying $300 per month on a month-to-month apartment lease or a dentist paying $5,000 per year for office space are both examples of fixed rents. A second method of setting rents is called the **step-up** or **graduated rental.** For example, a five-year office lease might call for monthly rents of 70¢ per square foot of floor space the first year, 73¢ the second year, 77¢ the third year, 81¢ the fourth year, and 85¢ the fifth.

Because of inflation, some lessors (particularly in office buildings) add an **escalator** or **participation clause.** This allows the landlord to pass along to the tenant increases in such items as property taxes, utility charges or janitorial fees. Another variation is to have the tenant pay for all property taxes, insurance, repairs, utilities, etc. This arrangement is called a **net lease** and it is commonly used when an entire building is being leased. Long-term ground leases are usually net leases.

Another system for setting rents is the **percentage basis** wherein the owner receives a percentage of the tenant's gross receipts as rent. For example, a farmer who leases land may give the landowner 20% of the value of the crop when it is sold. The monthly rent for a small hardware store might be $600 plus 6% of gross sales above $10,000. A supermarket may pay $7,500 plus 1½% of gross above $50,000 per month. By setting rents this way, the tenant shares some of his business risk with the property owner. Also, there is a built-in inflation hedge to the extent that inflation causes the tenant's receipts to increase.

OPTION CLAUSES

Option clauses in long-term leases can be used to give a tenant more flexibility. For example, suppose that you are starting a new business and are not certain how successful it will be. Therefore, in looking for space to rent, you want a lease that will allow you an "out" if the new venture does not succeed, but will permit you to stay if your venture is successful. The solution is a lease with options. Thus, you might arrange for a 1-year lease, plus an option to stay for 2 more years at a higher rent, and a second option for an additional 5 years at a still higher rent. If your venture is not successful, you are obligated for only 1 year. But if you are successful, you have the option of staying 2 more years, and if still successful, for 5 years after that.

ASSIGNMENT & SUBLETTING

Unless otherwise provided in the lease contract, the tenant may assign his lease or he may sublet. An **assignment** is the total transfer of the tenant's rights to another person. These parties are referred to as the **assignor** and the **assignee,** respectively. The assignee acquires all the right, title and interest of the assignor, no more and no less. However, the assignor remains liable for the performance of the contract unless he is released by the landlord. To **sublet** means to transfer only a portion of the rights held under a lease. The sublease thereby created may be for a portion of the premises, or part of the lease term. The party acquiring those rights is called the **sublessee.** The original lessee is the **sublessor** with respect to the sublessee. The sublessee pays rent to the lessee who in turn remains liable to the landlord for rent on the entire premises. When a sublease is created, the middle lease position is called a **sandwich lease.**

GROUND LEASE

A **ground lease** is a lease of land alone. The lessor is the fee simple owner of the land. He conveys to the lessee an estate for years typically lasting from 55 to 99 years. The lessee pays for and owns the improvements. Thus a ground lease separates the ownership of land from the ownership of buildings on that land. The lease rent, called the **ground rent,** is on a net lease basis. As a hedge against inflation, the rent is usually increased every 10 to 25 years. This is done either by a graduated lease or by requiring a reappraisal of the land and then charging a new rent based on that valuation.

A lease need not be restricted to the use of the earth's surface. In Chapter 2 it was shown that land extends from the center of the earth skyward. Consequently it is possible for one person to own the mineral rights, another the surface rights, and a third the air rights. This can also be done with leases. A landowner can lease to another person the right to explore and extract minerals, oil and gas below his land. In Chicago and New York City, railroads have leased surface and air rights above their downtown tracks for the purpose of constructing office buildings.

CONTRACT RENT, ECONOMIC RENT

The amount of rent that the tenant must pay the landlord for the use of the premises is called the **contract rent.** The rent which a property can command in the competitive open market is called the **economic rent.** When a lease contract is negotiated the contract rent and economic rent are nearly always the same. However as time passes, the market value of the right to use the premises may increase while the contract rent stays the same. When this occurs the lease itself becomes valuable. That value is determined by the difference between the contract rent and the economic rent, and how long the lease has to run. An example would be a 5 year lease with 3 years left at a contract rent of $300 per month where the current rental value of the premises is now $400 per month. If the lease is assignable, the fact that it offers a $100 per month savings for 3 years makes it valuable. Similarly, an oil lease obtained for $50 per acre before oil was discovered might be worth millions after its discovery. Conversely, when contract rent exceeds economic rent, the lease takes on a negative value.

LEASE TERMINATION

Most leases terminate because of the expiration of the term of the lease. The tenant has received the use of the premises and the landlord has received rent in return. However, a lease can be terminated if the landlord and the tenant mutually agree. The tenant surrenders the premises and the landlord releases him from the contract. Under certain conditions, destruction of the premises is cause for lease termination. Abandonment of the premises by the tenant can be grounds for lease termination provided the tenant's intention to do so is clear.

If either the tenant or the landlord fails to live up to the lease contract, termination can occur. Where the tenant is at fault, the landlord can evict him and recover possession of the premises. If the premises are unfit for occupancy, the tenant can claim **constructive eviction** as his reason for leaving. The government under its right of eminent domain can also terminate a lease, but must provide just compensation. An example of this would be construction of a new highway that requires the demolition of a building rented to tenants. The property owner and the tenants would be entitled to compensation.

FAIR HOUSING

There are two federal laws that deal with discrimination in housing. They are (1) the Civil Rights Act of 1866 which prohibits discrimination on the basis of race only, and (2) the Fair Housing Act of 1968 which prohibits discrimination based on race, color, religion, sex, or national origin.

So far as real estate licensees are concerned, these laws specify that they are not to accept sale or rental listings where they are asked to discriminate, nor are they permitted to make, print, or publish any statement or advertisement with respect to a sale or rental of a dwelling which suggests discrimination because of race, color, religion, or national origin.

So far as owners are concerned, the 1968 Act made two potentially significant exceptions. One is that a homeowner who does not use discriminatory advertising and who does not use a broker's services is permitted to discriminate in the sale or rental of his home. The other is that the owner of a building with four or less apartment units, and who lived in one of the units, could discriminate in renting to others. However, in the 1968 case of *Jones* v. *Mayer,* the Supreme Court of the United States disallowed these two exceptions if the discrimination is based on racial grounds.

Minnesota Human Rights Act

The Minnesota Human Rights Act prohibits discrimination on the additional grounds of sex, marital status, children, disability and public assistance. Landlords can no longer arbitrarily set "adults only" rental policies. However, a landlord is not required to make any structural modification on behalf of a disabled tenant. Minnesota does permit a nonprofit organization to discriminate on the basis of sex. For example, the YWCA can restrict lodging to women. It is also permissible for the resident of a single-family unit to discriminate on the grounds of sex, marital status, children, disability or public assistance when renting a room or rooms within that unit. No discrimination is permitted in the leasing of a duplex or other multifamily dwelling even if one of the units is owner-occupied.

If a person thinks that he/she has been discriminated against in the sale or rental of housing, the case may be taken directly to Federal Court for enforcement of the 1866 Act or to the Department of Housing and Urban Development, a U.S. District Court, or the Attorney General for enforcement of the 1968 Act. Complaints under the Minnesota Act should be directed to the Department of Human Rights.

A lengthier discussion of fair housing can be found in Chapter 17 of this book.

RENT CONTROL

For the most part, until 1970, the concept of residential rent control was reserved for wartime use in the United States. During World War I, six states and several major cities and, in World War II, the federal government imposed limits on how much rent an owner could charge for the use of his real property. The purpose was twofold: (1) to discourage the construction of new housing so that the resources could be channeled to war needs, and (2) to set ceilings so that American householders would not drive up prices by bidding against each other for available rental housing. With limits on rents, but no price controls on the cost of construction materials and labor, the construction of new housing was slowed without the need for a direct government order to stop building.

Within a few years after World War I, and again after World War II, rent controls disappeared in nearly all parts of the country. The notable exception was New York City, where they have survived since the end of World War II and are still in use. However, beginning in the 1970s a number of other cities have enacted rent control laws. This time the major attraction is inflation protection.

Although it is true that since 1956 residential rents in the United States have not risen as rapidly as the general level of consumer prices, any relief from rent increases would nonetheless be welcomed by the 36% of American households that rent. Most tenants recognize that newly constructed properties must command higher rents to meet higher construction, land, and interest costs. However, in existing buildings they resent rent increases that have nothing to do with the original cost of the building or the cost of operating it. The argument of rent control supporters is that only increases in such things as property taxes, utilities, and maintenance should be passed on to tenants. The tenant's assumption in this argument is that rent alone is enough to attract dollars into housing investments. In reality, rents would have to be even higher if the investor could not also look forward to price appreciation of his property.

Rent Control Experience

Experience to date strongly suggests that rent control creates more problems than it solves. In New York City, for example, it is generally agreed that controlled rents have discouraged new residential construction and have taken existing dwelling units out of circulation. Despite relatively low vacancy rates (about 3%), thousands of dwelling units are abandoned each year by their owners at a cost of millions of dollars in lost property taxes to the city. These abandonments are primarily due to rent control levels that do not rise fast enough to allow for increases in property taxes, maintenance, and utilities. As a result, in some parts of the city, property owners are actually better off abandoning their properties than operating them. In other parts of the city, where rents are artificially low but the building continues to operate, black markets occur. For example, a tenant vacating a controlled apartment may demand a substantial cash payment from a tenant who wants to move in. Although this is illegal, the vacating tenant may attempt to circumvent the law by requiring the incoming tenant to purchase his furniture for several times its actual worth. This places the actual cost of the controlled apartment much closer to the value of the unit on the open market, and the advantage of low, controlled rents is lost to the incoming tenant.

Other Side-Effects

In Washington, D.C., a side effect of rent control has been a surge of conversions of existing rental apartments to condominiums, as there are no controls, as yet, on prices of dwelling units offered for sale. Because this removed rental apartments from the market, laws were enacted to restrict conversions. This encouraged owners to demolish and build new condominiums; however, laws were then enacted to restrict demolition permits.

Los Angeles has also opted for rent control on apartment units in that city. Annual rent increases may not exceed 7%. The only time an owner can raise rents more than that is when a tenant moves out. This is a strong incentive for a tenant to stay where he is even though he might want to move elsewhere.

Other side effects of rent control in the United States are that lenders prefer not to lend on rent-controlled buildings, or if they do, are very conservative in their lending practices. This is because lenders do not like to loan unless the investor is assured of reasonable returns. Developers find it hard to attract tenants to new rental units from rent-controlled buildings where they are enjoying below market rents. The beneficiaries of rent control are middle and upper-income tenants, not just the poor and the elderly on fixed incomes. Some cities have attempted to limit the annual return investors can earn on rentals to 8%. Yet an investor can earn more than that with savings certificates and bonds and with much less hassle. Owner-occupied properties and non-controlled properties are charged higher property taxes to make up for the falling values of controlled properties. Also there is a significant cost to the public to operate the government offices that administer the controls.

One of the ironies of rent control is that although controlled rents are very attractive to the tenant, he soon finds that the number of people like himself who want to buy at controlled prices exceeds the number who want to sell. Consequently a shortage develops. A better solution is to pursue public policies that encourage the construction of housing rather than discourage it.

PROPERTY MANAGEMENT

The first step in successful property management is to have a property that will merchandise itself. In residential management, this means offering an apartment unit that is designed for living. As more and more families are priced out of the single-family-house market, the demand for rental apartments suitable for permanent residency increases. In the past, many apartment dwellers considered renting to be a stepping-stone to home ownership. Today renting is becoming a permanent way of life. As a result, the trend in apartment construction (and the remodeling of existing apartments) is toward such features and amenities as wall-to-wall carpeting, dishwashers, self-cleaning ovens, large closets, decorator-designed kitchens, sunken living rooms, extra bathrooms, more attractive landscaping, recreation centers, and enclosed parking facilities. Moreover, these features must be installed and visible to the prospective tenant before he rents. Unlike the house buyer who can install a dishwasher or plant a tree after he moves in, the prospective tenant must assume that what is there is what he gets; if it is not presently there, it never will be.

Advertising Methods

The traditional search pattern for the prospective apartment tenant is to drive through the neighborhoods he or she is interested in and to read the newspaper classified advertisements for rentals in that area. Thus, advertising money is most effectively spent on classified newspaper advertisements, plus signs and arrows placed on nearby roads and highways. Even for large apartment complexes, full-page ads are not necessary; quarter-page or smaller ads cost less and are usually sufficient to catch the interest of the person looking for an apartment to rent.

TENANT SELECTION

Programs to fill buildings should be accompanied by a sound tenant selection system. Decisions must be made on an individual basis as prospective tenants apply to rent space. An extensive application form, a seasoned manager, and a substantial security deposit are valuable screening tools for identifying tenants who have a high probability of being compatible with the other tenants in a project and of paying their rent on time. If it appears that a prospect, once moved in, will not pay his rent or will be obnoxious to the neighbors, the time to avoid the problem is before he moves in.

A lengthy application form acts to discourage prospects who themselves feel only marginally qualified or who prefer not to divulge the information requested. It also provides a basis for checking the tenant's references. This includes talking with his former landlords to ask why he left, checking with the local credit bureau to learn if he pays his bills on time, and, in some cities, checking with a landlord's reference bureau to find out if he left a previous apartment without paying his rent.

The purpose of the interview is to determine if the prospect has the income to support the rental he wants and if he will be compatible with the other tenants. For example, if the project does not allow children or pets, the manager will want to be sure the prospect understands this. Finally, the security deposit (against which the manager can deduct for unpaid rent or damage to the building) also serves as a screening device. If, for example, a prospect wants to rent a $400 per month apartment but does not have the money for a $200 security deposit, it is doubtful that he will be able to pay $400 rent each month.

In some communities, there are firms that specialize in referring prospective tenants to apartment managers. However, the usefulness of this source depends on the level of prescreening provided. If the firm simply channels all its apartment inquiries directly to the apartment manager without any prescreening, the service loses its usefulness; the manager may be better off relying on less costly newspaper advertising to draw prospects.

Rent Concessions

When a building owner is trying to attract tenants in an otherwise soft rental market, he can either keep rents the same and increase the quality of services offered to tenants, or he can provide a monetary inducement. If he selects the latter, he has two choices: (1) reduce the monthly rent, or (2) offer a rent concession. With a **rent concession,** the property owner keeps the rents at the same level, but offers a premium to a prospective tenant to entice him to move in. Often this takes the form of giving a free month's rent to prospects who will sign a 1-year lease. Other concessions include offering the tenant a cash moving allowance or giving him a free weekend vacation at a nearby resort. The philosophy behind using concessions rather than outright rent reductions is that, when the rental market firms up, it is easier to quietly stop offering concessions than it is to raise rents.

TENANT RETENTION

Tenant retention begins with selecting tenants who can pay the rent and who will be compatible with existing tenants. Having once found good tenants, the property manager's most important task is to keep them as long as possible. Besides the rent lost while the apartment is empty, the costs of apartment clean-up and finding a new tenant are high.

Statistically, about one-third of the units in a typical apartment project must be rerented each year. Certainly, many moves are due to job relocation or the need for larger or smaller quarters. But some moves occur because tenants find something they dislike about the way their apartments are managed. For example, if a building is poorly kept up or the manager gives the impression that he does not care about his tenants or the owner increases the rent with no apparent justification, people will move out. To retain tenants, the property owner and manager should think of them as permanent residents, even though turnover is expected. This begins with using a rental contract that an average tenant can read and understand. A complicated and legalistic contract may be seen by the tenant as the first step in a sparring match with management that will last as long as he resides there. The tenant also expects the property to be clean and properly maintained, and if repairs become necessary to his unit that they will be made promptly.

Communications

Good communications between management and tenants is also crucial to tenant retention. If the swimming pool is closed or the electricity shut off to the building with no announcement or no apparent reason, tenants become disgusted and add it to their private lists of reasons for ultimately leaving. As a minimum, tenants expect management to keep them informed through bulletin board announcements or notices placed under their doors. In many larger apartment projects, managers publish newsletters to keep tenants informed about how the project is being managed, and to provide an avenue by which tenants can communicate with each other. For example, one page can explain why rents must go up because of rising property taxes, maintenance, and utility costs, while another page announces the formation of a bowling league among project dwellers.

Leases

A very straightforward approach to improving tenant retention is to use leases. Once signed to a 1-year lease, a tenant is much less likely to leave after a few months if he has a minor complaint than he would be on a month-to-month agreement. Similarly, leases for longer than 1 year will reduce tenant turnover even more, although residential tenants are often wary about committing themselves that far into the future. A tenant can also be encouraged to stay by offering him a renewal lease at a slightly lower rate than that being offered to new tenants. Another technique is to offer long-time tenants free carpet shampooing, drape cleaning, and wall painting, all things normally done if the tenant leaves and the apartment must be rerented.

Recreation Facilities

Recreation centers may aid in tenant retention. However, to effectively do that, they must be useful. To a first-time renter, a flashy recreation center may be one of the reasons he chooses a particular apartment building. However, if after he moves in he finds the gym equipment inadequate, the swimming pool too small, and the billiard tables overcrowded, he soon thinks about another place to live.

COLLECTING RENTS

Ultimately, the success of a rental building depends on the ability of management to collect the rents due from tenants. In accomplishing this, it is generally agreed among property managers that a firm and consistent collection policy, handled in a businesslike manner, is the best approach. Monthly rent statements can be mailed to each tenant, but more often, the tenant is told in his rental contract when his rent is due each month, and he is expected to pay it on time. Rents can be collected door-to-door, but most managers prefer that rent checks be mailed or brought to their office when due.

Late Rents

When a tenant's rent is not received on time, the manager must decide what to do. Is the lateness simply a matter of delayed mail or temporary but honest forgetfulness, or is the delay an early sign of a much deeper problem, one that may cost the property owner lost rent and ultimately lead to eviction? The accepted procedure is to wait 5 days before sending the tenant a reminder. This avoids generating a negative feeling when the problem was only due to a minor delay, for it is a fact that the vast majority of tenants do pay their rent on time. However, if payment is not received by the tenth day after it was due, a second reminder goes out requesting that the tenant personally call on the manager. By meeting with the delinquent tenant, the manager may obtain an indication as to what the underlying problem is. If the tenant is suffering from a temporary financial setback, the manager can weigh the humanitarian side and the cost of rerenting the apartment against the possibility that payment will never be received.

Eviction Problems

When it is apparent that a delinquent tenant will never bring his rent up to date, it is time to ask the tenant to leave and to rerent the space. What happens if the tenant will neither leave nor pay his rent? Years ago, it was not uncommon for an owner to enter a tenant's unit, remove all his belongings, and lock them up. The key to the apartment door was changed and the apartment rerented; if the delinquent tenant wanted his belongings back, he had to pay the back rent. Minnesota's laws provide more protection for the tenant, and he may sue his landlord for removing his belongings and locking him out. Under current Minnesota law, a manager can bring a forcible entry and unlawful detainer action to get a court order compelling the tenant to leave. He may even call upon a sheriff to enforce it. Nevertheless, a nonpaying tenant who is well versed in the law can remain for several rent-free weeks. This is possible because of the time required to go through the legal procedures of eviction. When the delinquent tenant finally leaves a month or two later, he may owe several hundred dollars in back rent. The legal cost of forcing payment may be more than what is owed. The tenant knows this and hopes he will not be pursued.

Manager Remedies

More and more tenants are learning that if they are brash enough they can use the method just described to live rent-free and then move on. Others stop just short of the sheriff knocking on their door and leave on their own. Called "skipping out," the delinquent tenant moves out without paying his back rent, hoping the manager or owner will not go to the trouble of pursuing the issue. Tenants are also learning to use the small claims courts as an inexpensive way to legally pursue all sorts of real and fancied complaints against management, and managers are learning that judges often favor the tenant in these cases. What can owners and managers do about this? The best defense is careful tenant selection, substantial security deposits, good service, and a businesslike policy on rent collection. In other words, the old idea of filling up a building as fast as possible and later weeding out the problem tenants is no longer practical. Beyond that, the presence of a full-time manager means tenants are likely to take better care of the premises and are less likely to leave without paying the rent.

Managers can also make more effective use of the law by using the small claims courts to obtain judgments for unpaid rent claims against delinquents, skips, and those who write bad checks for rent payments. Although a tenant may have left the area and it may not be worth the effort of locating him, the fact that a manager does take a firm stand serves as a deterrent to those planning the same tactics. For the nonpaying tenant, the judgment against him becomes a part of his credit record and a warning to the next manager he approaches for an apartment. Small claims cases that go against managers can often be appealed to a municipal court, where lawyers are permitted and more weight is given to contracts.

Security Deposits

A useful protection against future delinquency is to require a security deposit from the tenant before moving in. This is in addition to the first month's rent and can be applied to unpaid rent and/or to damages to the property caused by the tenant. A security deposit is shown in Figures 15:1 and 15:2 at ⑧. Additionally, a security deposit requirement is a useful screening device in that a tenant who has the money to post a deposit will probably be a better financial risk than a tenant who can't.

OPPORTUNITIES IN PROPERTY MANAGEMENT

Property management responsibilities can be divided into two categories: off-site and on-site. **Off-site management** consists of those duties that can be accomplished without actually having to be on the premises, for example, accounting for rents collected, handling payrolls, attending to legal matters, and paying bills. Minnesota requires that off-site property managers be licensed as brokers. **On-site management** refers to such matters as showing vacant space to prospective tenants, maintaining the premises, supervising repairs, handling tenant complaints, and in general looking after the building and the welfare of the tenants.

Management Qualifications

Commercial and industrial property management positions tend to be filled by persons who have had prior property management experience and who have a good understanding of how business and industry make use of real estate. Residential properties are managed by persons with a wider variety of experience backgrounds. The most successful apartment managers seem to be those who have had previous experience in managing people and money and who are handy with tools. Those with prior military experience or experience as owners or managers of small businesses are eagerly sought after. Least successful as on-site property managers are those who see it as a quiet, peaceful retirement job, those who are unable to work with and understand people, those who cannot organize or make decisions, those without a few handyman skills, and those looking for strictly an 8-to-5, Monday-to-Friday job. The last item is particularly critical as the manager who lives on the property is on call 24 hours a day, in addition to regular working hours that may stretch from early morning janitorial supervision to late night security checks of the premises.

Management-Unit Ratios

The rule of thumb in apartment management is that one on-site manager can handle 50 or 60 units by himself. Between 60 and 100 units, the manager needs an assistant to help with management chores and to make it possible to have someone on the property at all times. In projects over 100 units, an approach that is gaining popularity is to hire husband–wife teams, placing both on the payroll and adding assistants in proportion to project size. For example, a 150-unit apartment building would be managed by a husband–wife team and one assistant (usually a full-time custodian). A 200-unit building would have a husband–wife team plus two fulltime assistants, and so on, adding an additional employee for each additional 50 to 60 apartment units. Larger projects also mean assistants can specialize. For example, in a 625-unit complex with a husband–wife team and nine assistants, two assistants might run the leasing office, two specialize in cleaning apartments when tenants leave, one act as a gardener, one as a repairman, one as a custodian, one as a rent collector and bookkeeper, and one as a recreational facilities director.

Training Programs

Finding experienced and capable property managers is not an easy task. There is little formal education in property management available in the United States. Instead, most managers learn their profession almost entirely by experience. An individual property owner can place an advertisement in the newspaper and attract a manager from another project, but most professional management firms have found it necessary to develop their own internal training programs. With such a program, a management firm can start a person with no previous property management experience as an assistant manager on a large project. If he or she learns the job and enjoys the work, there is a promotion to manager of a 50- or 60-unit building and an increase in salary. If this works well, the manager is moved to a larger complex, with an assistant and another increase in salary. Each step brings more responsibility and more pay. This system provides a steady stream of qualified managers for the management firm.

The dominant professional organization in the property management field is the Institute of Real Estate Management (IREM). Established in 1933, the Institute is a division within the National Association of Realtors. Its primary purposes are to serve as an exchange medium for management ideas and to recognize specialists in the field. The Institute awards the designation Certified Property Manager (CPM) to members who successfully complete required educational courses in property management.

VOCABULARY REVIEW

Match terms **a–l** *with statements* **1–12.**

a. *Assignment*
b. *Ground rent*
c. *Holdover tenant*
d. *Lessee*
e. *Lessor*
f. *Month-to-month rental*
g. *Option clause*
h. *Participation clause*
i. *Percentage lease*
j. *Reversionary interest*
k. *Step-up rent*
l. *Sublet*

1. The landlord.
2. The tenant.
3. Partial transfer of rights held under a lease.
4. Complete transfer of rights held under a lease.
5. One who holds a tenancy at sufferance.
6. Example of a periodic estate.
7. The right of the landowner to retake possession at the end of the lease.
8. Rent charged for the use of land.
9. A lease that calls for specified rent increases at various points in time during the life of the lease.
10. A lease clause that allows the landlord to add to the tenant's rent any increases in property taxes, maintenance, and utilities during the life of the lease.
11. A lease clause that gives a tenant the opportunity of renewing his lease at a predetermined rental, but does not obligate him to do so.
12. A lease where the amount of rent paid is related to the income the lessee obtains from the use of the premises.

QUESTIONS AND PROBLEMS

1. From the standpoint of the tenant, what are the advantages and disadvantages of a lease versus a month-to-month rental?
2. What remedies does a property manager in Minnesota have when a tenant does not pay his rent and/or refuses to move out?
3. Does Minnesota have a landlord-tenant law? What are its major provisions?
4. What is the difference between contract rent and economic rent?
5. On what basis could a tenant claim constructive eviction? What would the tenant's purpose be in doing this?

6. Is an option to renew a lease to the advantage of the lessor or the lessee?
7. What effects do the Civil Rights Act of 1866 and the Fair Housing Act of 1968 have on real estate licensees who handle rentals?
8. Is rent control currently in effect in your community? If so, what effects have these controls had on the sales of investment properties and on the construction of new rental buildings in your community?
9. If you were an apartment building manager interviewing prospective tenants, what questions would you ask?

ADDITIONAL READINGS

Downs, James C., Jr. *Principles of Real Estate Management,* 12th ed. Chicago: Institute of Real Estate Management, 1980, 488 pages. Considered by many to be *the* authoritative text in real property management, it covers a wide range of property management topics.

Glassman, Sidney. *A Guide to Residential Management,* 3rd ed. Washington, D.C.: National Association of Homebuilders, 1978, 260 pages. Topics include renting procedures, rent collections, delinquent rent, security deposits, tenant–management relations, maintenance, personnel policy, and computer use, with an appendix of sample forms and documents used in property management.

Kelly, Edward N. *Practical Apartment Management,* 2nd ed. Chicago: National Association of Realtors, 1981, 360 pages. Contains practical ideas and suggestions to help a person succeed as a property manager. Emphasis is on properties containing 50 units or more.

Selesnick, Herbert L. *Rent Control.* Lexington, Mass.: D. C. Heath, 1976, 118 pages. Author makes a case for rent control based on a rent-control study in Massachusetts.

Shenkel, William M. *Modern Real Estate Management.* New York: McGraw-Hill, 1980, 436 pages. Includes management operations, management office organization, leasing policies, energy conservation, and federal laws affecting management. Includes sample management forms.

Utt, Ron. "Rent Control: History's Unlearned Lesson." *Real Estate Review,* Spring, 1978, pages 87–90. Despite past negative experiences, author finds pressures for rent control still exist. Results of rent control in Paris, Great Britain, and New York are cited.

16

Real Estate Appraisal

KEY TERMS

Capitalize: to convert future income to current value

Comparables: properties similar to the subject property that are used to estimate the value of the subject property

Cost approach: property valuation based on land value plus current construction costs minus depreciation

Gross rent multiplier (GRM): a number, that when multiplied by a property's gross rents, produces an estimate of the property's worth

Highest and best use: that use of a parcel of land which will produce the greatest current value

Income approach: a method of valuing property based on the monetary returns that a property can be expected to produce

Market approach: a method of valuing a property based on the prices of recent sales of similar properties

Market value: the cash price that a willing buyer and a willing seller would agree upon, given reasonable exposure of the property to the marketplace, full information as to the potential uses of the property, and no undue compulsion to act

Net operating income (NOI): gross income less operating expenses, vacancies, and collection losses

Operating expenses: expenditures necessary to maintain the production of income

Scheduled gross, Projected gross: the estimated rent that a fully-occupied property can be expected to produce on an annual basis

To appraise real estate means to estimate its value. There are three approaches to making this estimate. The first is to compare similar properties that have sold recently, and use them as a guide to estimate the value of the property that you are appraising. This is the **market approach.** The second approach is to add together the cost of the individual components that make up the property being appraised. This is the **cost approach;** it starts with the cost of a similar parcel of vacant land, and adds the cost of the lumber, concrete, plumbing, wiring, and so on, necessary to build a similar building. Depreciation is then subtracted. The third approach is to consider only the amount of net income that the property can reasonably be expected to produce for its owner, plus any anticipated price increase or decrease. This is the **income approach.** For the person who owns or plans to own real estate, knowing how much a property is worth is a crucial part of the buying or selling decision. For the real estate agent, being able to appraise a property is an essential part of taking a listing.

MARKET VALUE

The purpose of this chapter is to show you how the market, cost, and income approaches are used in determining market value. **Market value,** also called **fair market value,** is the highest price in terms of money that a property will bring if (1) payment is made in cash or its equivalent, (2) the property is exposed on the open market for a reasonable length of time, (3) the buyer and seller are fully informed as to market conditions and the uses to which the property may be put, (4) neither is under abnormal pressure to conclude a transaction, and (5) the seller is capable of conveying marketable title. Market value is at the heart of nearly all real estate transactions.

MARKET COMPARISON APPROACH

Let us begin by demonstrating the application of the market comparison approach to a single-family residence. The residence to be appraised is called the **subject property** and is described as follows:

> The subject property is a one-story, wood-frame house of 1,520 square feet containing three bedrooms, two bathrooms, a living room, dining room, kitchen, and utility room. There is a two-car garage with concrete driveway to the street, a 300-square-foot concrete patio in the backyard, and an average amount of landscaping. The house is located on a 10,200-square-foot, level lot that measures 85 by 120 feet. The house is 12 years old, in good repair, and is located in a well-maintained neighborhood of houses of similar construction and age.

Comparables

After becoming familiar with the physical features and amenities of the subject property, the next step in the market approach is to locate houses with similar physical features and amenities that have sold recently under market value conditions. These are known as **comparables** or "comps." The more similar they are to the subject property, the fewer and smaller the adjustments that must be made in the comparison process and hence the less room for error. As a rule of thumb, it is best to use comparable sales no more than 6 months old. During periods of relatively stable prices, this can be extended to 1 year. However, during periods of rapidly changing prices, even a sale 6 months old may be out of date.

Sales Records

To apply the market comparison approach, the following information must be collected for each comparable sale: date of sale, sales price, financing terms, location of the property, and a description of its physical characteristics and amenities. Recorded deeds at public records offices can provide dates and locations of recent sales. Although a deed seldom states the purchase price, nearly all states levy a deed transfer fee or conveyance tax, the amount of which is shown on the recorded deed. This tax can sometimes provide a clue as to the purchase price. However in Minnesota, unless one knows the amount of assumed financing in the transaction, the tax amount is of little value.

Records of past sales can often be obtained from title and abstract companies. Property tax assessors keep records on changes in ownership as well as property values. Where these records are kept up to date and are available to the public, they can provide information on what has sold recently and for how much. Assessors also keep detailed records of improvements made to land. This can be quite helpful in making adjustments between the subject property and the comparables. Each Minnesota county assessor's office keeps on file a Certificate of Real Estate Value. The state requires that this document be filed when a deed is recorded. It contains, among other things, the date of sale, purchase price, mortgage assumed, and information as to whether the transaction was made at "arm's length." For real estate salespeople, locally-operated multiple listing services provide asking prices and descriptions of properties currently offered for sale by member brokers, along with descriptions, sales prices, and dates for properties that have been sold.

Verification

To produce the most accurate appraisal possible, one should call upon the new owner of each comparable to verify the purchase price, obtain information on the terms of the sale, and inspect the premises. One will also want to know the date the buyer and seller signed their sales contract, for it was on that date, not on the date the deed was recorded, that a meeting of minds took place regarding the price and terms of the sale. Failure to verify sales data invites errors.

Number of Comparables

As a rule of thumb, from three to five comparables need be used. To use only one or two comparables invites too much error. Above five, the additional accuracy must be weighed against the extra effort involved. When the supply of comparable sales is more than adequate, one should choose the sales that require the fewest adjustments.

It is also important that the comparables selected represent current market conditions. Sales between relatives or close friends may result in an advantageous price to the buyer or seller, and sales prices that for some other reason appear to be out of line with the general market should not be used. Listings and offers to buy should not be used in place of actual sales. They do not represent a meeting of minds between a buyer and a seller. Listing prices are, however, useful in establishing the upper limit on prices, whereas offers to buy set lower limits. Thus, if a property is listed for sale at $80,000 and there have been offers as high as $76,000, it is reasonable to presume the market price lies somewhere between $76,000 and $80,000.

Adjustment Process

Let us now work through the example shown in Table 16:1 to demonstrate the application of the market comparison approach to a house. We begin at lines 1 and 2 by entering the address and sale price of each comparable property. For convenience, we shall refer to these as comparables A, B, and C. On lines 3 through 10, we make time adjustments to the sale price of each comparable to make it equivalent to the subject property today. Adjustments are made for price changes since each comparable was sold, as well as for differences in physical features, amenities, and financial terms. The result indicates the market value of the subject property.

Time Adjustments

Returning to line 3 in Table 16:1, let us assume that house prices in the neighborhood where the subject property and comparables are located have risen 5% during the 6 months that have elapsed since comparable A was sold. If comparable A were for sale today, it would bring 5% or $4,590 more.

VALUING A HOUSE BY THE MARKET COMPARISON APPROACH **Table 16:1**

Line	Item	Comparable Sale A		Comparable Sale B		Comparable Sale C	
1	**Address of comparable house**	1702 Brookside Ave.		1912 Brookside Ave.		1501 18th St.	
2	**Sales price of comparable house**		$91,800		$88,000		$89,000
3	**Time adjustment**	*sold 6 mos. ago, add 5%*	+4,590	*sold 3 mos. ago, add 2½%*	+2,200	*just sold*	0
4	**House size**	*160 sq ft larger at $40 per sq ft*	−6,400	*20 sq ft smaller at $40/sq ft*	+ 800	*same size*	0
5	**Garage/carport**	*carport*	+4,000	*3-car garage*	− 2,000	*2-car garage*	0
6	**Other**	*larger patio*	− 300	*no patio*	+ 600	*built-in bookcases*	− 500
7	**Age, upkeep, & overall quality of house**	*superior*	− 2,000	*inferior*	+ 400	*equal*	0
8	**Landscaping**	*inferior*	+ 1,000	*equal*	0	*superior*	− 700
9	**Lot size, features, & location**	*superior*	− 3,890	*inferior*	+ 900	*equal*	0
10	**Terms & conditions of sale**	*equal*	0	*special financing*	−1,500	*equal*	0
11	**Total adjustments**		− 3,000		+1,400		−1,200
12	**ADJUSTED MARKET PRICE**		$88,800		$89,400		$87,800

Line				
13	**Correlation process:**			
	Comparable A	$88,800 × 20%	=	$17,760
	Comparable B	$89,400 × 30%	=	$26,820
	Comparable C	$87,800 × 50%	=	$43,900
14		**INDICATED VALUE**		$88,480
		Round to		$88,500

Therefore, we must add $4,590 to bring comparable A up to the present. Comparable B was sold 3 months ago, and to bring it up to the present we need to add 2½% or $2,200 to its sales price. Comparable C was just sold and needs no time correction, as its price reflects today's market.

When using the market comparison approach, all adjustments are made to the comparable properties, not to the subject property. This is because we cannot adjust the price of something for which we do not yet have the price. We do, however, have the selling price and date of sale for each comparable and can adjust these prices to make them similar to the subject property in today's market.

House Size

Because house A is 160 square feet larger than the subject house, it is logical to expect that the subject property would sell for less money. Hence a deduction is made from the sales price of comparable A on line 4. The amount of this deduction is based on the difference in floor area and the current cost of similar construction, minus an allowance for depreciation. If we value the extra 160 square feet at $40 per square foot, we must subtract $6,400. For comparable B, the house is 20 square feet smaller than the subject house. At $40 per square foot, we add $800 to comparable B, as it is reasonable to expect that the subject property would sell for that much more because it is that much larger. Comparable C is the same sized house as the subject property, so no adjustment is needed.

Garage and Patio Adjustments

Next, the parking facilities (line 5) are adjusted. We first look at the current cost of garage and carport construction and the condition of these structures. Assume that the value of a carport is $2,000; a one-car garage, $4,000; a two-car garage, $6,000; and a three-car garage, $8,000. Adjustments would be made as follows. The subject property has a two-car garage worth $6,000 and comparable A has a carport worth $2,000. Therefore, based on the difference in garage facilities, we can reasonably expect the subject property to command $4,000 more than comparable A. By adding $4,000 to comparable A, we effectively equalize this difference. Comparable B has a garage worth $2,000 more than the subject property's garage. Therefore, $2,000 must be subtracted from comparable B to equalize it with the subject property. For comparable C, no adjustment is required, as comparable C and the subject property have similar garage facilities.

At line 6, the subject property has a 300-square-foot patio in the backyard worth $600. Comparable A has a patio worth $900; therefore, $300 is deducted from comparable A's selling price. Comparable B has no patio. As it would have sold for

$600 more if it had one, a +$600 adjustment is required. The patio at comparable C is the same as the subject property's; however, comparable C has custom built-in bookcases in the living room worth $500 that the subject property does not have. Therefore, $500 is subtracted from comparable C's sales price. Any other differences between the comparables and the subject property such as swimming pools, fireplaces, carpeting, drapes, roofing materials, and kitchen appliances would be adjusted in a similar manner.

Building Age, Condition, and Quality

On line 7 we recognize differences in building age, wear and tear, construction quality, and design usefulness. Where the difference between the subject property and a comparable can be measured in terms of material and labor, the adjustment is the cost of that material and labor. For example, the $400 adjustment for comparable B reflects the cost of needed roof repair at the time B was sold. The adjustment of $2,000 for comparable A reflects the fact it has better-quality plumbing and electrical fixtures than the subject property. Differences that cannot be quantified in terms of labor and materials are usually dealt with as lump-sum judgments. Thus, one might allow $1,000 for each year of age difference between the subject and a comparable, or make a lump-sum adjustment of $2,000 for an inconvenient kitchen design.

Keep in mind that adjustments are made on the basis of what each comparable property was like on the day it was sold. Thus, if an extra bedroom was added or the house was painted after its sale date, these items are not included in the adjustment process.

Landscaping

Line 8 shows the landscaping at comparable A to be inferior to the subject property. A positive correction is necessary here to equalize it with the subject. The landscaping at comparable B is similar and requires no correction; that at comparable C is better and thus requires a negative adjustment. The dollar amount of each adjustment is based on the market value of lawn, bushes, trees and the like.

Lot Features and Location

Line 9 deals with any differences in lot size, slope, view, and neighborhood. In this example, all comparables are in the same neighborhood as the subject property, thus eliminating the need to judge, in dollar terms, the relative merit of one neighborhood over another. However, comparable A has a slightly larger lot and a better view than the subject property. Based on recent lot sales in the area, the difference is judged to be $890 for the larger lot and $3,000 for the better view. Comparable B has a slightly smaller lot judged to be worth $900 less, and comparable C is similar in all respects.

Terms and Conditions of Sale

Line 10 in Table 16:1 accounts for differences in financing. As a rule, the more accommodating the terms of the sale to the buyer, the higher the sales price, and vice versa. We are looking for the highest cash price the subject property may reasonably be expected to bring, given adequate exposure to the marketplace and a knowledgeable buyer and seller not under undue pressure. If the comparables were sold under these conditions, no corrections would be needed in this category. However, if it can be determined that a comparable was sold under different conditions, an adjustment is necessary. For example, if the going rate of interest on home mortgages is 11% per year and the seller offers to finance the buyer at 9% interest, it is reasonable to expect that the seller can charge a higher selling price. Similarly, the seller can get a higher price if he has a low-interest loan that can be assumed by the buyer. Favorable financing terms offered by the seller of comparable B enabled him to obtain an extra $1,500 in selling price. Therefore, we must subtract $1,500 from comparable B. Another situation that requires an adjustment on line 10 is if a comparable was sold on a rush basis. If a seller is in a hurry to sell, he must usually accept a lower selling price than if he can give his property longer exposure in the marketplace.

Adjusted Market Price

Adjustments for each comparable are totaled and either added or subtracted from its sales price. The result is the **adjusted market price** shown at line 12. This is the dollar value of each comparable sale after it has gone through an adjustment process to make it the same as the subject property. If it were possible to precisely evaluate every adjustment, and if the buyers of comparables A, B, and C had paid exactly what their properties were worth at the time they purchased them, the three prices shown on line 12 would be the same. However, buyers are not that precise, particularly in purchasing a home where amenity value influences price and varies considerably from one person to the next.

Correlation Process

While comparing the properties, it will usually become apparent that some comparables are more like the subject property than others. The **correlation** step gives the appraiser the opportunity to assign more weight to the more similar comparables and less to the others. At 13, comparable C is given a weight of 50% since it is more like the subject and required fewer adjustments. Moreover, this sameness is in areas where adjustments tend to be the hardest to estimate accurately: time, age, quality, location, view, and financial conditions. Of the remaining two comparables, comparable B is weighted slightly higher than comparable A because it is a more recent sale and overall required fewer adjustments.

In the correlation process, the adjusted market price of each comparable is multiplied by its weighting factor and totaled at line 14. The result is the **indicated value** of the subject property. It is customary to round it off to the nearest $50 or $100 for properties under $10,000, to the nearest $250 or $500 for properties between $10,000 and $100,000, to the nearest $1,000 or $2,500 for properties between $100,000 and $250,000, and to the nearest $2,500 or $5,000 above that.

CONDOMINIUM, TOWNHOUSE, AND COOPERATIVE APPRAISAL

The process for estimating the market value of a condominium, townhouse, or cooperative living unit by the market approach is similar to the process for houses except that fewer steps are involved. For example, in a condominium complex with a large number of two-bedroom units of identical floor plan, data on a sufficient number of comparable sales may be available within the building. This would eliminate adjustments for differences in unit floor plan, neighborhood, lot size and features, age and upkeep of the building, and landscaping. The only corrections needed would be those that make one unit different from another. This would include the location of the individual unit within the building (end units and units with better views sell for more), the upkeep and interior decoration of the unit, a time adjustment, and an adjustment for terms and conditions of the sale.

When there are not enough comparable sales of the same floor plan within the same building and it is necessary to use different-sized units, an adjustment must be made for floor area. If the number of comparables is still inadequate and units in different condominium buildings must be used, adjustments will be necessary for neighborhood, lot features, management, upkeep, age, and overall condition of the building.

MARKET APPROACH TO VACANT LAND VALUATION

When using the market approach, the main difference between appraising homes and appraising land is that a home is treated as a single unit. This is possible when the property as a whole is basically similar to its comparables. However, such similarity often does not exist in vacant land. For example, how would one establish a value for 21 acres of vacant land when the only comparables available are 16 acre and 25 acre sales? The usual method is to establish a per acre value from comparables and apply it to the subject land. Thus, if 16- and 25-acre parcels sold for $32,000 and $50,000, respectively, and are similar in all other respects to the 21-acre subject property, it would be reasonable to conclude that land is selling for $2,000 per acre. Therefore, the subject property is worth $42,000.

Subdivided lots zoned for commercial, industrial or apartment buildings are usually appraised and sold on a square foot basis. Thus, if apartment land is currently selling for $3.00 per square foot, a 100,000 square-foot parcel of comparable zoning and usefulness would be appraised at $300,000. Another method is to value on a front-foot basis. For example, if a lot has 70 feet of street frontage and if similar lots are selling for $300 per front foot, that lot would be appraised at $21,000. Storefront land is often sold this way. House lots can be valued either by the square foot, front foot, or lot method. The lot method is useful when one is comparing lots of similar size and zoning in the same neighborhood. For example, recent sales of 100-foot by 100-foot house lots in the $18,000 to $20,000 range would establish the value of similar lots in the same neighborhood.

COMPETITIVE MARKET ANALYSIS

A method of valuing homes that is very popular with real estate agents is the competitive market analysis (CMA). This method is based on the principle that value can be estimated by looking at similar homes that have sold recently. In addition the CMA method considers homes presently on the market plus homes that were listed for sale but did not sell. The CMA approach is usually simpler to work than the standard market comparison approach because it requires no dollar adjustments. Most importantly, a CMA is more than a market appraisal; it is a listing tool that a sales agent prepares in order to show a seller what his or her home will likely sell for, and it helps the agent decide whether or not to accept the listing.

Figure 16:1 shows a competitive market analysis form published by the National Association of Realtors. The procedure in preparing a CMA is to select homes that are comparable to the subject property. The greater the similarity, the more accurate the appraisal will be and the more likely the client will accept the agent's estimate of value and counsel. It is usually best to use only properties in the same neighborhood; this is easier for the seller to relate to and removes the need to compensate for neighborhood differences. The comparables should also be similar in size, age, and quality.

In section ① of the CMA shown in Figure 16:1, similar homes presently offered for sale are listed. This information is usually taken directly from the agent's multiple listing book and hopefully the agent will already have toured these properties and have first-hand knowledge of their appearance. These are the homes the seller's property will compete against in the marketplace.

In section ② the agent lists similar properties that have sold in the past several months. These are prices sellers agreed to accept and buyers agreed to pay. Section ③ is for listing homes that were offered for sale, but did not sell. In other words, buyers were unwilling to take these homes at the prices offered.

In section ④ recent FHA and VA appraisals of comparable homes can be included if it is felt that they will be useful in determining the price at which to list. Two words of caution are in order here. First, using someone else's opinion of value is risky. It is better to determine your own opinion based on actual facts. Second, FHA and VA appraisals often tend to lag behind the market. In a rising market, this means they will be too low, in a declining market, they will be too high.

In section ⑤ buyer appeal, and in section ⑥ market position, the agent evaluates the subject property from the stand-

Figure 16:1

Competitive Market Analysis

Property Address ______________________ Date ______

For Sale Now: (1)	Bed-rms.	Baths	Den	Sq. Ft.	1st Loan	List Price	Days on Market	Terms

Sold Past 12 Mos. (2)	Bed-rms.	Baths	Den	Sq. Ft.	1st Loan	List Price	Days on Market	Date Sold	Sale Price	Terms

Expired Past 12 Mos. (3)	Bed-rms.	Baths	Den	Sq. Ft.	1st Loan	List Price	Days on Market	Terms

(4) F.H.A — V.A. Appraisals

Address	Appraisal	Address	Appraisal

(5) Buyer Appeal **(6) Marketing Position**

(Grade each item 0 to 20% on the basis of desirability or urgency)

1 Fine Location ______ %
2 Exciting Extras ______ %
3 Extra Special Financing ______ %
4 Exceptional Appeal ______ %
5 Under Market Price ______ Yes ____ No ____ %

Rating Total ______ %

1 Why Are They Selling ______ %
2 How Soon Must They Sell ______ %
3 Will They Help Finance .... Yes ____ No ____ %
4 Will They List at Competitive Market Value ... Yes ____ No ____ %
5 Will They Pay for Appraisal .... Yes ____ No ____ %

Rating Total ______ %

(7)
Assets ______
Drawbacks ______
Area Market Conditions ______

Recommended Terms ______

(8) Selling Costs

Brokerage	$
Loan Payoff	$
Prepayment Privilege	$
FHA — VA Points	$
Title and Escrow Fees: IRS Stamps. Recons. Recording	$
Termite Clearance	$
Misc. Payoffs: 2nd T.D., Pool, Patio, Water Softener, Fence, Improvement Bond.	$
	$
	$
Total	$

Top Competitive Market Value $ ______

(9)
Probable Final Sales Price $ ______

Total Selling Costs $ ______

Net Proceeds $ ______ Plus or Minus $ ______

10-75-F606

The statements and figures presented herein, while not guaranteed, are secured from sources we believe authoritative.

Prepared by ______

BY PERMISSION

point of whether or not it will sell if placed on the market. It is important to make the right decision to take or not to take a listing. Once taken, the agent knows that valuable time and money must be committed to get it sold. Factors which make a property more appealing to a buyer include good location, extra features, small down payment, low interest, meticulous maintenance, and a price below market. Similarly, a property is more salable if the sellers are motivated to sell and want to do so soon, will help with financing, and will list at or below market. A busy agent will want to avoid spending time on overpriced listings, listings for which no financing is available and listings where the sellers have no motivation to sell. With the rating systems in section ⑤ and ⑥, the closer the total is to zero, the less desirable the listing; the closer to 100%, the more desirable the listing.

Section ⑦ provides space to list the property's high and low points, current market conditions, and recommended terms of sale. Section ⑧ shows the seller how much to expect in selling costs. Section ⑨ shows the seller what to expect in the way of a sales price and the amount of cash he can reasonably expect from the sale.

The emphasis in CMA is on a visual/organic inspection of available sales data to arrive at market value directly. No pencil and paper adjustments are made. Instead adjustments are made in a generalized fashion in the minds of the agent and the seller. In addition to its application to single-family houses, CMA can also be used on condominiums, cooperative apartments, townhouses, and vacant lots—provided sufficient comparables are available.

GROSS RENT MULTIPLIERS

A popular market comparison method that is used when a property produces income is the **gross rent multiplier,** or **GRM.** The GRM is an economic comparison factor that relates the gross rent a property can produce to its purchase price. For apartment buildings and commercial and industrial properties the GRM is computed by dividing the sales price of the property by its gross annual rent. For example, if an apartment building grosses $10,000 per year in rents and has just sold for $70,000, it is said to have a GRM of 7. The use of a GRM to value single-family houses is questionable since they are usually sold as owner-occupied residences, rather than as income properties.

Table 16:2

CALCULATING GROSS RENT MULTIPLIERS

Building	Sales Price		Gross Annual Rents		Gross Rent Multiplier
No. 1	$245,000	÷	$ 34,900	=	7.02
No. 2	$160,000	÷	$ 22,988	=	6.96
No. 3	$204,000	÷	$ 29,352	=	6.95
No. 4	$196,000	÷	$ 27,762	=	7.06
As a Group:	$805,000	÷	$115,002	=	7.00

Where comparable properties have been sold at fairly consistent gross rent multiples, the GRM technique presumes the subject property can be valued by multiplying its gross rent by that multiplier. To illustrate, suppose that apartment buildings were recently sold in your community as shown in Table 16:2. These sales indicate that the market is currently paying seven times gross. Therefore, to find the value of a similar apartment building that grosses $24,000 per year, $24,000 is multiplied by 7.00 to give an indicated value of $168,000.

The GRM method is popular because it is simple to apply. Having once established what multiplier the market is paying, one need only know the gross rents of a building to set a value. However, this simplicity is also the weakness of the GRM method, because the GRM takes into account only the gross rent that a property produces. Gross rent does not allow for variations in vacancies, uncollectable rents, property taxes, maintenance, management, insurance, utilities, or reserves for replacements.

Weakness of GRM

To illustrate the problem, suppose that two apartment buildings each gross $100,000 per year. However, the first has expenses amounting to $40,000 per year and the second, expenses of $50,000 per year. Using the same GRM, the buildings would be valued the same. This is illogical since the first produces $10,000 more in net income for its owner. The GRM also overlooks the expected economic life span of a property. For example, a building with an expected remaining life span of 30 years would be valued exactly the same as one expected to last 20 years, if both currently produce the same rents. One method of partially offsetting these errors is to use different

GRMs under different circumstances. Thus, a property with low operating expenses and a long expected economic life span might call for a GRM of 7 or more, whereas a property with high operating expenses or a shorter expected life span would be valued using a GRM of 6 or 5 or even less.

COST APPROACH

In the cost approach to value, land is valued as though vacant and then added to the depreciated cost of all improvements. Table 16:3 demonstrates the basic procedure. Step 1 is to estimate the value of the land upon which the building is located. The land is valued as though vacant using the market comparison approach described earlier. In Step 2, the cost of constructing a similar building at today's costs is estimated. These costs include the current prices of building materials, construction wages, architect fees, contractor's services, building permits, utility hookups, and the like, plus the cost of financing during the construction stage and the cost of construction equipment used at the project site. Step 3 is the calculation of the amount of money that represents the subject building's wear and tear, lack of usefulness, and obsolescence when compared to the new building of Step 2. In Step 4, depreciation is subtracted from today's construction cost to give the current value of the subject building on a used basis. Step 5 is to add this amount to the land value. Let us work through these steps.

Table 16:3

COST APPROACH TO VALUE

Step 1:	Estimate land as though vacant		$18,000
Step 2:	Estimate new construction cost of similar building	$68,000	
Step 3:	Less depreciation	−12,000	
Step 4:	Indicated value of building		56,000
Step 5:	Appraised property value by the cost approach		$74,000

Estimating New Construction Costs

To choose a method of estimating construction costs, one must decide whether cost will be approached on a reproduction or on a replacement basis. **Reproduction cost** is the cost at today's prices of constructing an exact replica of the subject improvements using the same or very similar materials. **Replacement cost** is the cost, at today's prices and using today's methods of construction, for an improvement having the same or equivalent usefulness as the subject property. Replacement cost is the more practical choice of the two as it eliminates nonessential or obsolete features and takes full advantage of current construction materials and techniques. It is the approach that will be described here.

Square-Foot Method

The most widely used approach for estimating construction costs is the **square-foot method.** It provides reasonably accurate estimates that are fast and simple to prepare.

The basis of the square-foot method is to find a newly constructed building that is similar to the subject building in terms of size, type of occupancy, design, materials, and construction quality. This becomes the base or standard building. The cost of the base building is converted to cost per square foot by dividing its current construction cost by the number of square feet in the building.

One source is to go into the field and locate similar buildings that have just been completed and inquire as to their construction costs. Another source is from published construction cost handbooks. Most appraisers use both: the handbooks are the most convenient to use but they should be verified with actual local construction costs. Using a handbook starts with selecting a cost handbook appropriate to the type of building being appraised. From photographs of houses included in a residential handbook along with brief descriptions of the buildings' features, the appraiser finds a house that most nearly fits the description of the subject house. Next to the pictures is the current cost per square foot to construct it. If the subject house has a better quality roof, floor covering, heating system, greater or fewer built-in appliances, plumbing fixtures, or has a garage, basement, porch, or swimming pool, the handbook provides costs for each of these. Figure 16:2 illustrates the calculations involved in the square-foot method.

Estimating Depreciation

Having estimated the current cost of constructing the subject improvements, the next step in the cost approach is to estimate the loss in value due to depreciation since they were built. In making this estimate, we look for three kinds of depre-

SQUARE-FOOT METHOD OF COST ESTIMATING

Figure 16:2

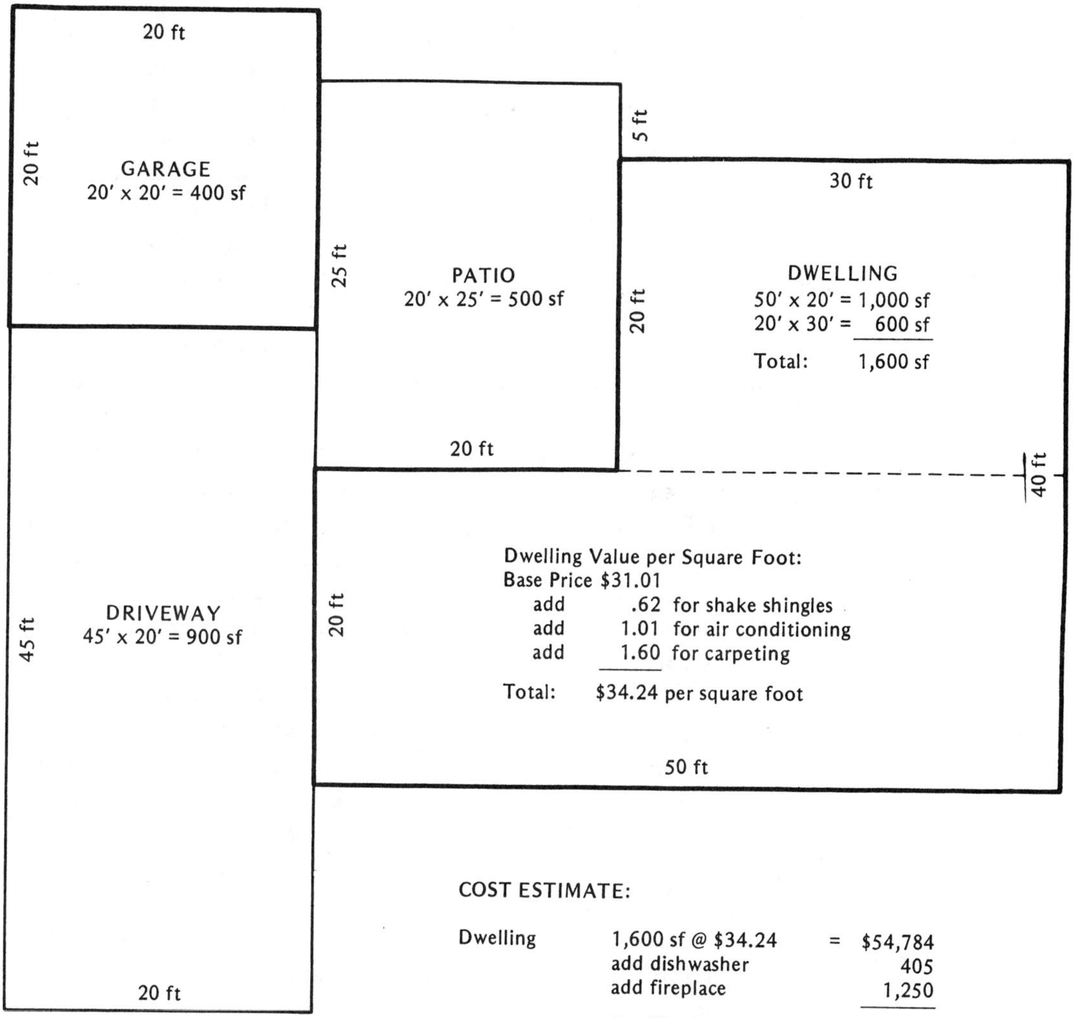

COST ESTIMATE:

Dwelling	1,600 sf @ $34.24	=	$54,784
	add dishwasher		405
	add fireplace		1,250
	Dwelling total		$56,439
Garage	400 sf @ $15.00	=	6,000
Driveway	900 sf @ $2.00	=	1,800
Patio	500 sf @ $2.00	=	1,500
Landscaping		=	2,000
	Subtotal		$67,739
Construction financing, real estate taxes and title policy, add 8%			5,419
	GRAND TOTAL		$73,158

ciation: physical deterioration, functional obsolescence, and economic obsolescence.

Physical deterioration results from wear and tear through use, such as wall-to-wall carpet that has been worn thin, or a dishwasher, garbage disposal, or water heater that must be replaced. Physical deterioration also results from the action of nature in the form of sun, rain, heat, cold, and wind, and from damage due to plants and animal life, such as tree roots breaking sidewalks and termites eating wood. Physical deterioration can also result from neglect (an overflowing bathtub) and from vandalism.

Functional obsolescence results from outmoded equipment (old-fashioned plumbing fixtures in the bathrooms and kitchen), faulty or outdated design (a single bathroom in a three- or four-bedroom house or an illogical room layout), inadequate structural facilities (inadequate wiring to handle today's household appliance loads), and overadequate structural facilities (high ceilings in a home). Functional obsolescence can be summarized as loss of value to the improvements because they are inadequate, overly adequate, or improperly designed for today's needs.

Economic obsolescence is the loss of value due to external forces or events. The effect can be on the improvements or the land or both. For example, if a home costing $160,000 is built in a neighborhood of $80,000 homes, the surrounding homes will detract from the value of the more expensive home. The more expensive home is an overimprovement of the neighborhood, and the structure suffers depreciation because of that. Economic obsolescence can also occur if a once-popular neighborhood becomes undesirable because of air or noise pollution, or because surrounding property owners fail to maintain their properties. In these cases the adverse effect is usually picked up in the land valuation.

Final Steps in the Cost Approach

After calculating the current construction cost of the subject improvements and estimating the amount of depreciation, the next step is to subtract the amount of depreciation from the current construction cost to get the depreciated value of the improvements. This is added to the value of the land upon which the subject improvements rest. The total is the value of the property by the cost approach.

INCOME APPROACH

The income approach to real estate appraisal considers expected monetary returns from a property in the light of return on investment currently being demanded by investors. To illustrate, suppose that an available investment promises to return $900 per year in net income to an investor, and at any time the investor wants to withdraw, the money he originally invested will be returned to him in full. The value of this investment depends on the rate of return that must be paid to attract investors. If an investor is willing to accept a 9% per year return on his invested dollars, he would pay $10,000 for this investment opportunity. The calculation is as follows:

$$\frac{\text{Income}}{\text{Rate}} = \text{Value} \qquad \frac{\$900}{0.09} = \$10{,}000$$

This is called capitalizing the income stream. To **capitalize** means to convert future income to current value. In this example, the capitalized value of $900 per year is $10,000, because for each 9 cents of anticipated annual income, $1 will have to be invested.

The capitalized value of $900 per year changes as the return per dollar invested changes. If a rate of 10% per year is necessary to attract investors, the present value of $900 per year is $9,000. This is because a $900 return per year on a $9,000 investment yields the investor a 10% return per year. On the other hand, if investors are willing to accept 8% per year, we divide the $900 annual income by 8% and obtain $11,250, as the value of this investment.

In applying the income approach to real property, the appraiser is concerned with three questions: (1) how much income the property will provide for its owners, (2) how long the income will last, and (3) what rate of return on investment must be paid to attract investors.

Income and Expense Forecasting

The goal of income and expense forecasting is to project the probable net income that may be expected from a property. Not only does the net income provide the underlying basis on which value is determined; it is also a critical process, because each $1 error in annual net income can make a difference of from $5 to $10 in the market value of the property.

The best starting point in projecting gross income and expenses is the actual record of income and expenses for the subject property over the past 3 to 5 years. Although the future will not be an exact repetition of the past, the past record of a property is usually the best guide to future performance. These historical data are blended with the current operating experience of similar buildings and the appraiser's estimates as to what the future will bring. The result is a projected operating statement, such as the one shown in Table 16:4, which begins with the estimated rents that the property can be expected to produce on an annual basis. This is the **projected gross,** or **scheduled gross,** and represents expected rentals from the subject property on a fully occupied basis.

Vacancy and collection loss projections are based partly on the building's past experience and partly on the appraiser's best judgment as to what may be expected, based on his familiarity with the operating experience of similar buildings. For example, if the subject property has unusually low vacancy rates, the appraiser may be justified in using a higher vacancy factor in his forecast if a higher rate is more typical. This would definitely be the case if the low vacancy rate could be traced to below-market rents or to superior management. This is because the appraiser is attempting to forecast under normal conditions—that is, with rents at market levels and with competent, but not necessarily superior, management. Similarly, if the subject property is experiencing higher than normal vacancies, the problem may be curable by lowering rents, changing managements, or refurbishing the property. Under these circumstances, the appraiser would base his forecast on these problems being corrected.

Operating Expenses

The next step is to itemize anticipated **operating expenses** for the subject property. These are expenses necessary to maintain the production of income. For an apartment building without recreational facilities or an elevator, the list in Table 16:4 is typical. Again, the appraiser considers both the property's past operating expenses and what he expects those expenses to be in the future. For example, even though the property is currently being managed by the owner and no management fee is being paid, the appraiser will include a typical fee, say 6% of the gross rents.

Not included as operating expenses are outlays for capital

PROJECTED ANNUAL OPERATING STATEMENT
(Also called a Pro Forma Statement)

Table 16:4

Scheduled gross annual income	$84,000	
Vacancy allowance and collection losses	4,200	
Effective Gross Income		$79,800
Operating Expenses		
Property taxes	9,600	
Hazard and liability insurance	1,240	
Property management	5,040	
Janitorial services	1,500	
Gardener	1,200	
Utilities	3,940	
Trash pickup	600	
Repairs and maintenance	5,000	
Other	1,330	
Reserves for replacement		
Furniture & furnishings	1,200	
Stoves & refrigerators	600	
Furnace &/or air-conditioning system	700	
Plumbing & electrical	800	
Roof	750	
Exterior painting	900	
Total Operating Expenses		$34,400
Net Operating Income		$45,400

OPERATING EXPENSE RATIO: $34,400 ÷ $79,800 = 43.1%

improvements, such as the construction of a new swimming pool, the expansion of parking facilities, and assessments for street improvements. Improvements are not classified as expenses because they increase the usefulness of the property, which increases the rent the property will generate and therefore the property's value.

Reserves

Reserves for replacement are established for items that do not require an expenditure of cash each year. To illustrate, lobby furniture (and furniture in apartments rented as "furnished") wears out a little each year, eventually requiring replacement. Suppose that these items cost $7,200 and are expected to last 6 years, at which time they must be replaced. An annual $1,200 reserve for replacement not only reflects a cost for that portion of the furniture that was used up during the year, but also reminds us that, to avoid having to meet the entire furniture and furnishings replacement cost out of one year's income, money should be set aside each year. In a similar manner, reserves are established for other items that must be replaced or repaired more than once during the life of the building, but not yearly. Depreciation of the building itself is not included here; it will be accounted for later.

Operating Expense Ratio

At this point, the **operating expense ratio** can be calculated. It is obtained by dividing the total operating expenses by the effective gross income. The resulting ratio provides a handy yardstick against which similar properties can be compared. If the operating expense ratio is out of step compared to similar properties, it signals the need for further investigation.

Net Operating Income

The operating expense total is then subtracted from the effective gross income. The balance that remains is the **net operating income.** From the net operating income the property owner receives both a return *on* and a return *of* his investment. The return *on* his investment is the interest he receives for investing his money in the property. The return *of* investment is to compensate him for the fact that the building is wearing out.

Capitalizing Income

The final step in the income approach is to capitalize the net operating income. In other words, what price should an investor offer to pay for a property that produces a given net income per year? The solution is: income ÷ rate = value. If the annual net operating income is $45,400 and if the investor intends to pay all cash, expects to receive a 12% return on his investment, and anticipates no change in the value of the property while he owns it, the solution is to divide $45,400 by 12%. However, most investors today borrow much of the purchase price and usually expect an increase in property value. Under these conditions, how much should the investor pay?

The best known method for solving this type of investment question involves using the Ellwood Tables, published in 1959 by L. W. Ellwood, MAI. However, for the person who does not use these tables regularly, the arithmetic involved can prove

OVERALL RATES—10-YEAR HOLDING PERIOD **Table 16:5**

25-Year Loan for 75% of the Purchase Price, 18% Investor Return

Appreciation, Depreciation	**Loan Interest Rate**			
	9%	**10%**	**11%**	**12%**
+100%	.07251	.07935	.08631	.09338
+ 50%	.09376	.10060	**.10756**	.11463
+ 25%	.10439	.11123	.11819	.12526
+ 15%	.10864	.11548	.12244	.12951
+ 10%	.11077	.11761	.12457	.13164
+ 5%	.11289	.11973	.12669	.13376
0	.11502	.12186	.12882	.13589
− 5%	.11715	.12399	.13095	.13802
− 10%	.11927	.12611	.13307	.14014
− 15%	.12140	.12824	.13520	.14227
− 25%	.12565	.13249	.13945	.14652
− 50%	.13628	.14312	.15008	.15715
−100%	.15753	.16437	.17133	.17840

Source: *Financial Capitalization Rate Tables,* Publication No. 73, page 103, copyright 1974, Financial Publishing Company, Boston, Mass. By permission.

confusing. As a result, Irvin Johnson, in 1972,* and the Financial Publishing Company, in 1974, published **mortgage-equity tables** that allow the user to look up a single number, called an **overall rate,** and divide it into the net operating income to find a value for the property.

For example, suppose an investor who is interested in buying the above property can obtain an 11%, fully-amortized 25-year mortgage loan for 75% of the purchase price. He wants an 18% return on his investment (his equity) in the property, plans to hold it 10 years, and expects it will increase 50% in value (after selling costs) during that time. How much should he offer to pay the seller? In Table 16:5, we look for an interest rate of 11% and for appreciation of 50%. This gives an overall rate of .10756 and the solution is:

---

* Irvin E. Johnson, *The Instant Mortgage-Equity Technique,* copyright 1972, by Lexington Books, D. C. Heath & Company, Lexington, Mass.

$$\frac{\text{Income}}{\text{Overall Rate}} = \text{Value} \quad \frac{\$45{,}400}{.10756} = \$422{,}090$$

Further exploration of the numbers in Table 16:5 shows that as loan money becomes more costly, the overall rate rises, and as interest rates fall, so does the overall rate. If the investor can anticipate appreciation in value, the overall rate drops; if he can't, the overall rate climbs. You can experiment by dividing some of the other overall rates in this table into $45,400 to see how the value of this property changes under different circumstances.

CHOICE OF APPROACHES

Whenever possible, all three appraisal methods discussed in this chapter should be used to provide an indication, as well as a crosscheck, of a property's value. If the marketplace is acting rationally and is not restricted in any way, all three approaches will produce the same value. If one approach is out of line with the others, it may indicate an error in the appraiser's work or a problem in the market itself. It is not unusual to find individual sales that seem out of line with prevailing market prices. Similarly, there are times when buyers will temporarily bid the market price of a property above its replacement cost.

For certain types of real property, some approaches are more suitable than others. This is especially true for single-family residences. Here the appraiser must rely almost entirely on the market and cost approaches, as very few houses are sold on their ability to generate cash rent. Unless the appraiser can develop a measure of the "psychic income" in home ownership, relying heavily on rental value will lead to a property value below the market and cost approaches. Applying all three approaches to special-purpose buildings may also prove to be impractical. For example, in valuing a church, bridge, or courthouse, the income and market approaches have only limited applicability.

RECONCILIATION

The appraiser's final step is to **reconcile** the market, cost, and income approaches for the subject property. The appraiser does this by assigning each approach a weighting factor based on his judgment as to which of the approaches are the most relevant in valuing the property. To demonstrate, he might reconcile a single-family house in the following manner:

Market approach	$88,000 × 75% =	$66,000
Cost approach	$87,000 × 20% =	$17,400
Income approach	$80,000 × 5% =	$ 4,000
FINAL INDICATED VALUE		$87,400

What the appraiser is telling us here is that recent sales of comparable properties have the most influence on today's sales prices. He also points out that we must not overlook the fact that the same house can be built for $1,000 less. However, by weighting the cost approach at only 20%, the appraiser is saying that most house buyers want to move in quickly and not wait until a house can be built from scratch. By weighting the income approach by only 5%, the appraiser is recognizing that houses in the area are rarely purchased for rental purposes.

Appraiser's Best Estimate

It is important to realize that the appraised value is the appraiser's best *estimate* of the subject property's worth. Thus, no matter how painstakingly it is done, property valuation requires the appraiser to make many subjective judgments as he develops his estimate of a property's worth. Because of this, it is not unusual for three highly qualified appraisers to look at the same property and produce three substantially different appraised values. It is also important to recognize that an appraisal is made as of a specific date. It is not a certificate of value, good forever until used. If a property was valued at $78,500 on January 5th of this year, the more time that has elapsed since that date, the less accurate that value is as an indication of the property's current worth.

An appraisal does not take into consideration the financial condition of the owner, his health, sentimental attachment or any other personal matter. An appraisal does not guarantee the property will sell for the appraised market value. (The buyer and the seller determine the actual selling price.) Nor does buying at the appraised market value guarantee a future profit for the purchaser. (The real estate market can change.) An appraisal is not a guarantee that the roof will not leak, that there are no termites, or that everything in the building works. An appraisal is not an offer to buy although it can serve as the basis for one. An appraisal is neither a loan commitment nor does it insure that a lender will never have to foreclose.

THE APPRAISAL REPORT

There are four methods by which one can report his appraisal findings and conclusions: oral, letter, form and narrative.

Oral Report

The **oral report** is most often used by a real estate agent who is meeting with a seller for the purpose of listing a property. After inspecting the property and considering market conditions, the agent tells the owner what he feels the property can reasonably be expected to sell for. The advantage of the oral report is that it is fast and easy. The disadvantage is that there is no written evidence of what was said. Because of this disadvantage, professional appraisers avoid making oral appraisal reports. There is too much chance of being misquoted—intentionally or unintentionally.

Appraisal Letter

An **appraisal letter** is a report in the form of a business letter. In it the appraiser identifies the property and the rights being appraised, states his value conclusion and provides highlights of the facts used in drawing that conclusion. An appraisal letter is usually one or two pages long and seldom over 10 pages.

Form Appraisal

A **form appraisal** report is an appraisal made on a preprinted form. The best examples of form appraisals are those used by real estate lenders in connection with residential mortgage loans. The objective is to reduce the amount of time the appraiser must spend on reporting his findings and conclusions and to standardize the information the lender is asking for. The development of standardized appraisal forms has been an important factor in the success of the secondary mortgage market.

Narrative Appraisal

A **narrative appraisal** is a complete report by the appraiser and typically runs 10 to 100 pages and sometimes longer. In it the appraiser reports on everything pertinent to the property and the market for the property. This thoroughness allows the reader to follow in detail the appraiser's reasoning. In addition to identifying the property, the rights being appraised, and giving the value conclusion, a narrative report will include detailed information on the objective of the appraisal assignment; the definition of value as used in the report; regional, city, and neighborhood influences on value; economic trends; the physical characteristics of the land and its improvements; the condition of title; the zoning; a survey or map; photographs of the property; and a statement as to the property's highest and best use.

All three approaches to value (market data, cost and income) are used where possible. Each comparable sale is reported with its sale details and all facts used are identified as to their sources. The appraiser concludes by showing how he analyzed the information in order to arrive at his value estimate. The entire report is prefaced with a cover letter wherein the appraiser states his value conclusion and certifies that he has no financial interest in the property and that the report was prepared in accordance with accepted appraisal practices.

Format Choice

The appraisal format one would choose will depend on the amount of information needed and the amount of money one has to spend. Thus, a prospective buyer who wants to know the value of a four-unit apartment building (fourplex) would probably select an appraisal letter. An out-of-state investor considering a 200-unit apartment building would probably want a narrative report. Eminent domain actions almost always require full narrative reports.

CHARACTERISTICS OF VALUE

Up to this point we have been primarily concerned with value based on evidence found in the marketplace and how we report it. Before concluding this chapter, let us briefly touch on what creates value, the principles of real property valuation, and appraisal for purposes other than market value.

For a good or service to have value in the marketplace, it must possess four characteristics: demand, utility, scarcity, and transferability. **Demand** is a need or desire coupled with the purchasing power to fill it, whereas **utility** is the ability of a good or service to fill that need. **Scarcity** means there must be a short supply relative to demand. Air, for example, has utility and is in demand, but it is not scarce. Finally, a good or service must be **transferable** to have value to anyone other than the person possessing it.

PRINCIPLES OF VALUE

The **principle of anticipation** reflects the fact that what a person will pay for a property depends on the benefits that he/she expects to receive from it in the future. Thus, the buyer of a home anticipates receiving shelter plus the investment and psychic benefits of home ownership. The investor buys property now in anticipation of future income.

The **principle of substitution** states that the maximum value of a property in the marketplace tends to be set by the cost of purchasing an equally desirable substitute property provided no costly delay is encountered in making the substitution. In other words, substitution sets an upper limit on price. Thus, if there are two similar houses for sale, or two similar apartments for rent, the lowest priced one will generally be purchased or rented first. In the same manner, the cost of buying land and constructing a new building sets a limit on the value of existing buildings.

Principle of Highest and Best Use

The **highest and best use** of a property is that use which will give the property its greatest current value. Therefore, in valuing a property, one must be alert to the possibility that the present use of a parcel of land may not be the use that makes the land the most valuable. Take, for instance, a 30-year-old house located at a busy intersection in a shopping area. To place a value on that property based on its continued use as a residence would be misleading if, in fact, the property would be worth more with the house removed and shopping or commercial facilities built on the land instead.

The **principle of competition** recognizes that where substantial profits are being made competition will be encouraged. For example, if apartment rents increase to the point where owners of existing apartment buildings are making substantial profits, builders and investors will be encouraged to build more apartment buildings.

Supply and Demand

Applied to real estate, the **principle of supply and demand** refers to the ability of people to pay for land coupled with the relative scarcity of land. Thus, in evaluating a property's potential worth, attention must be given to such matters on the demand side as population growth, personal income, and the tastes and preferences of people. On the supply side, one must look at the available supply of land and its relative scarcity. When the supply of land is limited and demand is great, the result is rising land prices. Conversely, where land is abundant and there are relatively few buyers, supply and demand will be in balance at only a few cents per square foot.

The **principle of change** serves as a reminder that real property uses are always in a state of change. Although it may be imperceptible on a day-to-day basis, change can easily be seen when longer periods of time are considered. Because the present value of a property is related to its future uses, the more potential changes that can be identified, the more accurate the estimate of its present worth.

Diminishing Marginal Returns

The principle of **diminishing marginal returns,** also called the **principle of contribution,** refers to the relationship between added cost and the value it returns. It tells us that we should invest dollars whenever they will return to us more than $1 of value and should stop when each dollar invested returns less than $1 in value.

The **principle of conformity** holds that despite varying construction costs, properties in the same neighborhood will tend to conform in price. This was illustrated earlier with the example of the $160,000 house built in the $80,000 neighborhood.

MULTIPLE MEANINGS OF THE WORD "VALUE"

When we hear the word "value," we tend to think of market value. However, at any given moment in time, a single property can have other values too. This is because value or worth is very much affected by the purpose for which the valuation was performed. For example, **assessed value** is the value given a property by the county tax assessor for purposes of property taxation. **Estate tax value** is the value that federal and state taxation authorities establish for a dead person's property; it is used to calculate the amount of estate taxes that must be paid. **Insurance value** is concerned with the cost of replacing damaged property. It differs from market value in two major respects: (1) the value of the land is not included, as it is presumed only the structures are destructible, and (2) the amount of coverage is based on the replacement cost of the structures. **Loan value** is the value set on a property for the purpose of making a loan.

Plottage Value

Plottage value results from the combination of two or more parcels of land to form one large parcel that has more usefulness, and hence a greater market value, than the sum of the individual parcels. For example, local zoning laws may permit a six-unit apartment building on a single 10,000-square-foot lot. However, if two of these lots can be combined, zoning laws permit 15 units. This makes the lots more valuable if sold together.

Rental value is the value of a property expressed in terms of the right to its use for a specific period of time. The fee simple interest in a house may have a market value of $80,000, whereas the market value of 1 month's occupancy might be $600. **Replacement value** is value as measured by the current cost of building a structure of equivalent utility. **Salvage value** is the price that can be expected for an improvement for purposes of removal and use elsewhere. Because of the high amount of labor necessary to recover salvageable parts, the salvage value of most buildings is usually very low.

This list of values is not exhaustive, but it points out that the word value has many meanings. The key, when reading an appraisal report, is to read the first paragraph to see why the appraisal was prepared.

BUYER'S AND SELLER'S MARKETS

Whenever supply and demand are unbalanced because of excess supply, a **buyer's market** exists. This means a buyer can negotiate prices and terms more to his liking and a seller, if he wants to sell, must accept them. When the imbalance occurs because demand exceeds supply, it is a **seller's market,** and sellers are able to negotiate prices and terms more to their liking as buyers compete for the available merchandise.

A **broad market** means that many buyers and sellers are in the market at the same time. This makes it relatively easy to establish the price of a property, and for a seller to find a buyer quickly, and vice versa. A **thin market** is said to exist when there are only a few buyers and a few sellers in the market at the same time. It is oftentimes difficult to appraise a property in a thin market because there are so few sales to use as comparables.

PROFESSIONAL APPRAISAL SOCIETIES

During the 1930s, two well-known professional appraisal societies were organized: The American Institute of Real Estate Appraisers (AIREA) and the Society of Real Estate Appraisers.

Although a person offering his services as a real estate appraiser need not be associated with either of these groups, there are advantages in membership. Both organizations have developed designation systems that are intended to recognize appraisal education, experience, and competence. Within the AIREA, the highest-level designation is the MAI (Member of the Appraisal Institute). To be an MAI requires a 4-year college degree or equivalent education, 16 hours of examinations, a variety of demonstration appraisals, and at least 5 years of appraisal experience, including 3 years in non-single-family real estate. There are about 5,000 MAI's in the United States. Also available is the RM (Residential Member) designation for those who have a high school education, a passing appraisal examination score, three demonstration appraisal reports, and 3 years of experience in residential real estate.

The highest designations offered by the Society of Real Estate Appraisers are the SREA (Senior Real Estate Analyst) and SRPA (Senior Real Property Appraiser). For members specializing in residential appraisal, the professional designation is SRA (Senior Residential Appraiser). The SRA designation requires completion of basic courses in real estate appraisal, economics and statistics, an examination on appraising and a residential appraisal demonstration report. To this the SRPA designation adds requirements for advanced course work in real estate appraisal, plus an income property demonstration appraisal. For the SREA designation further advanced course work and an analytical demonstration appraisal are necessary. For all designations the applicant must have field experience and submit, for review by the Society, actual appraisals he or she has completed.

VOCABULARY REVIEW

Match terms **a-q** *with statements* **1–17.**

a. *Adjustments*
b. *Capitalize*
c. *Comparables*
d. *Competitive market analysis*
e. *Cost approach*
f. *Economic obsolescence*
g. *Functional obsolescence*
h. *Market approach*
i. *Net operating income*
j. *Operating expenses*
k. *Physical deterioration*
l. *Plottage value*
m. *Principle of substitution*
n. *Replacement cost*
o. *Reproduction cost*
p. *Scheduled gross*
q. *Subject property*

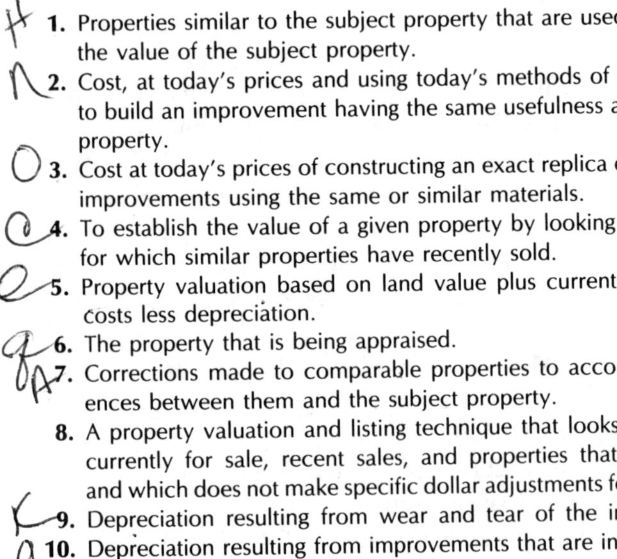

1. Properties similar to the subject property that are used to establish the value of the subject property.
2. Cost, at today's prices and using today's methods of construction, to build an improvement having the same usefulness as the subject property.
3. Cost at today's prices of constructing an exact replica of the subject improvements using the same or similar materials.
4. To establish the value of a given property by looking at the prices for which similar properties have recently sold.
5. Property valuation based on land value plus current construction costs less depreciation.
6. The property that is being appraised.
7. Corrections made to comparable properties to account for differences between them and the subject property.
8. A property valuation and listing technique that looks at properties currently for sale, recent sales, and properties that did not sell, and which does not make specific dollar adjustments for differences.
9. Depreciation resulting from wear and tear of the improvements.
10. Depreciation resulting from improvements that are inadequate, overly adequate, or improperly designed for today's needs.
11. Loss of value due to external forces or events.
12. Estimated rent that a fully occupied property can be expected to produce on an annual basis.
13. To convert future income to current value.
14. Income available from a rental property for those who provide the capital.
15. Expenses necessary to maintain the production of income.
16. Acts as an upper limit on prices; the lower priced of two similar properties will usually sell first.
17. Value resulting from the joining of two or more adjacent parcels of land to form a single large parcel.

QUESTIONS AND PROBLEMS

1. What is meant by the phrase "fair market value"?
2. In Minnesota, is the amount of documentary transfer tax shown on a deed a good indicator of the sale price? Why or why not?
3. When making a market comparison appraisal, how many comparable properties should be used?
4. How useful are asking prices and offers to buy when making a market comparison appraisal?
5. In the market approach, are the adjustments made to the subject property or to the comparables? Why?
6. Why is it important when valuing vacant land that comparable properties have similar zoning, neighborhoods, size, and usefulness?
7. Explain the use of gross rent multipliers in valuing real properties. What are the strengths and the weaknesses of this method?
8. What are the five steps used in valuing an improved property by the cost approach?

9. Explain briefly the square-foot method of estimating construction costs.
10. Briefly explain the concept of the income approach to valuing real property.
11. As the rate of return on investment demanded by investors rises, should property values rise or fall?
12. Explain how the competitive market analysis method differs from the standard market approach method. Which method is better? And for what?
13. What is the purpose of reconciling the three approaches to value?
14. Why is transferability necessary before something can have value in the marketplace?
15. What precaution does the principle of diminishing marginal returns suggest to a real estate owner?
16. With regard to appraising a single-family house, what type of appraisal format would most likely be requested by a lender? A prospective buyer? An executor of an estate? A highway department?

ADDITIONAL READINGS

American Institute of Real Estate Appraisers. *The Appraisal of Real Estate,* 8th ed. Chicago: American Institute of Real Estate Appraisers, 1983, 750 pages. Covers the fundamental concepts of real estate value and its appraisal by the market, cost, and income approaches.

Bloom, George F., and **Harrison, Henry S.** *Appraising the Single Family Residence.* Chicago: American Institute of Real Estate Appraisers, 1978, 510 pages. A textbook for the novice in real estate appraisal and a reference book for the real estate veteran. Provides a thorough discussion of house appraisal from the standpoints of buyers, sellers, builders, lenders, government, etc.

Boyce, Byrl N. *Real Estate Terminology,* rev. ed. Cambridge, Mass.: Ballinger, 1981, 367 pages. Excellent reference book that contains definitions and explanations of hundreds of real estate and appraisal terms.

Friedman, Edith J. *Encyclopedia of Real Estate Appraising,* 3rd ed. Englewood Cliffs, N.J.: Prentice-Hall, 1978, 1,283 pages. Contains practical information on a wide variety of appraisal problems and situations. Includes theory, practice, and specific applications.

Harrison, Henry S. *Houses,* rev. ed. Chicago: National Institute of Real Estate Brokers, 1976, 435 pages. Teaches the reader about architectural styles, basic construction, building materials, interior design, and mechanical systems as they relate to both old and new houses.

Harrison, Henry S. *Illustrated Dictionary of Real Estate Appraisal.* Reston, Va.: Reston Publishing Co., 1981, 304 pages. Contains definitions of real estate and appraisal terms plus over 1,000 illustrations, drawings and photographs.

Maes, Marrin A. "Appraisal Value vs. Contract Price." *Real Estate Today,* February, 1977, pages 10–14. Article explains why there is often a difference between the appraised value of a property and its ultimate selling price.

Shenkel, William M. *Modern Real Estate Appraisal.* New York: McGraw-Hill, 1978, 579 pages. A readable book that contains appraisal principles, procedures, and applications for valuing both residential and commercial properties.

17

The Owner-Broker Relationship

KEY TERMS

Agent: the person empowered to act by and on behalf of the principal

Commingling: the mixing of clients' funds with an agent's personal funds

Dual agency, Divided agency: representation of two or more parties in a transaction by the same agent

Exclusive right to sell: a listing that gives the broker the right to collect a commission no matter who sells the property during the listing period

Middleman: a person who brings two or more parties together but does not conduct negotiations

Principal: a person who authorizes another to act for him; also refers to a property owner

Puffing: nonfactual or extravagant statements a reasonable person would recognize as such

Ready, willing, and able buyer: a buyer who is ready to buy now without further coaxing, and who has the financial capability to do so

Third parties: persons who are not parties to a contract but who may be affected by it

AGENCY

When a property owner gives a real estate broker a listing authorizing the broker to find a buyer or a tenant and promising compensation if he does, an **agency relationship** is created. For an agency to exist, there must be a principal and an agent. The **principal** is the person who empowers another to act as his representative; the **agent** is the person who is empowered to act. When someone speaks about the "laws of agency," he refers to those laws that govern the rights and duties of the principal, agent, and the persons (called **third parties)** with whom they deal.

Agencies are divided into three categories: universal, general, and specific. A **universal agency** is very broad in scope, as the principal gives his agent the legal power to transact matters of all types for him. A **general agency** gives the agent the power to bind his principal in a particular trade or business. For example, the relationship between a real estate broker (principal) and his salesperson (agent) is considered a general agency. With a **special agency** the principal empowers his agent to perform only specific acts and no others. Applications of special agency include (1) written power of attorney whereby a principal can empower another person to convey, mortgage, or lease his real property, and (2) real estate listings, the topic we shall discuss next.

LISTING AGREEMENT

A **real estate listing** is an employment contract between a property owner and a real estate broker. By it the property owner appoints the broker as the owner's agent for the specific purpose of finding a buyer or tenant for his property who is willing to meet the conditions set forth in the listing. It does not authorize the broker to actually sell or convey title to the property.

When a property owner signs a listing, all the essential elements of a valid contract must be present. The owner and broker must be legally capable of contracting, there must be mutual assent, and the agreement must be for a lawful purpose. Minnesota tends to view most listing contracts as unilateral. The owner promises to pay a commission if a buyer is found but the broker need not promise to find one. However, it is presumed that when a Minnesota broker takes a listing, he intends to work on it for the seller's benefit. Accordingly, we will include mutual consideration as a listing contract requirement.

Although some states still do not require that listing agreements be in writing to be valid, the trend is to require that they be written and signed to be enforceable in a court of law. Minnesota follows this trend and requires that listings for the sale or lease of real property be in writing and signed to be enforceable.

Figure 17:1 illustrates a simplified exclusive right-to-sell listing agreement. Beginning at ①, there is a description of the property plus the price and terms at which the broker is instructed to find a buyer. At ②, the broker promises to make a reasonable effort to find a buyer. This is the broker's part of mutual consideration. The period of time that the listing is to be in effect is shown at ③. In Minnesota there must be a specific expiration date on a listing in order to be enforceable.

At ④, the owner agrees not to list the property with any other brokers, permit other brokers to have a sign on the property, or advertise it during the listing period. Also, the owner agrees not to revoke the broker's exclusive right to find a buyer as set forth by this contract.

The broker recognizes that the owner may later accept a price and terms that are different from those in the listing. The wording at ⑤ states that the broker will earn a commission no matter what price and terms the owner ultimately accepts.

Brokerage Commissions

At ⑥, the amount of compensation the owner agrees to pay the broker is established. The usual arrangement is to express the amount as a percentage of the sale or exchange price, although a stated dollar amount could be used if the owner and broker agreed. In any event, the amount of the fee is negotiable between the owner and the broker.

To emphasize the fact that commissions are negotiable, Minnesota requires that the following wording be inserted in not less than 10 point boldface type immediately preceding any provision of the listing relating to compensation of the broker:

Notice: The commission rate for the sale, lease, rental, or management of real property shall be determined between each individual broker and its client.

If the owner feels the fee is too high, he can list with someone who charges less or sell the property himself. The broker recognizes that if the fee is too low it will not be worthwhile spending time and effort finding a buyer. The typical commission fee in the United States at present is 5% to 7% of the selling price for houses, condominiums, and small apartment buildings, and 6% to 10% on farms, ranches, and vacant land. On multimillion dollar improved properties, commissions usually drop to the 2% to 4% range. Brokerage commissions are not set by a state regulatory agency or by local real estate boards. In fact, any effort by brokers to set commission rates among themselves is a violation of federal anti-trust laws. The penalty can be as much as triple damages, criminal liability and suspension or revocation of the broker's license.

The conditions under which a commission must be paid by the owner to the broker appear next. At ⑦, a commission is deemed to be earned if the owner agrees to a sale or exchange of the property, no matter who finds the buyer. In other words, even if the owner finds his own buyer, or a friend of the owner finds a buyer, the broker is entitled to a full commission fee. If the owner disregards his promise at ④ and lists with

Figure 17:1

EXCLUSIVE RIGHT TO SELL LISTING CONTRACT

① *Property Description:* A single-family house at 2424 E. Main Street, City, State. Legally described as Lot 17, Tract 191, County, State.

Price: $105,000

Terms: Cash

② *In consideration of the services of* ABZ Realty Company *(herein called the "Broker"), to be rendered to* Roger and Mary Leeving *(herein called the "Owner"), and the promise of said Broker to make reasonable efforts to obtain a purchaser, therefore, the Owner hereby grants to the Broker*

③ *for the period of time from noon on* April 1, 19xx, *to noon on* July 1, 19xx *(herein called the "listing period")*

④ *the exclusive and irrevocable right to advertise and find a purchaser for the above described property at the price and terms shown*

⑤ *or for such sum and terms or exchange as the owner later agrees to accept.*

⑥ ***Notice: The commission rate for the sale, lease, rental, or management of real property shall be determined between each individual broker and its client.*** *The Owner hereby agrees to pay Broker a cash fee of* 7% *of the selling or exchange price:*

⑦ *(A) in case of any sale or exchange of the above property within the listing period either by the Broker, the Owner or any person, or*

⑧ *(B) upon the Broker finding a purchaser who is ready, willing, and able to complete the purchase as proposed by the owner, or*

⑨ *(C) in the event of a sale or exchange within 60 days of the expiration of the listing period to any party shown the above property during the listing period by the Broker or his representative and where the name was disclosed to the Owner.*

⑩ *The Owner agrees to give the Broker access to the buildings on the property for the purposes of showing them at reasonable hours and allows the Broker to post a "For Sale" sign on the premises.*

Figure 17:1 *continued*

⑪ *The Owner agrees to allow the Broker to place this listing information in any multiple listing organization of which he is a member and to engage the cooperation of other brokers to bring about a sale.*

⑫ *The Owner agrees to refer to the Broker all inquiries regarding this property during the listing period.*

⑬ *Accepted:* ABZ Realty Company

By: Kurt Kwiklister *Owner:* Roger Leeving

Owner: Mary Leeving

Date: April 1, 19xx

another broker who then sells the property, the owner is liable for two full commissions.

Protecting the Broker

The wording at ⑧ is included to protect the broker against the possibility that the owner may refuse to sell after the broker has expended time and effort to find a buyer at the price and terms of the listing contract. The listing itself is not an offer to sell property. It is strictly a contract whereby the owner employs the broker to find a buyer. Thus, even though a buyer offers to pay the exact price and terms shown in the listing, the buyer does not have a binding sales contract until the offer is accepted in writing by the owner. However, if the owner refuses to sell at the listed price and terms, the broker is still entitled to a commission. If the owner does not pay the broker voluntarily, the broker can file a lawsuit against the owner to collect.

Protecting the Owner

At ⑨, the broker protects himself against the possibility that the listing period will expire while still working with a prospective purchaser. Thus, the broker will still earn a commission if the property is sold, after the listing expires, to anyone the broker was negotiating with prior to the listing's expiration. In fairness to the owner, however, two limitations are placed on the broker. First, a sales contract must be concluded within a reasonable time after the listing expires. Minnesota refers to a clause such as ⑨ as an "override clause" and by rule prohibits it from being more than six months. Second, Minnesota's rules require that a "protective list" of the names and addresses of all prospective purchasers with whom a licensee has negotiated during the term of the listing be supplied to the owner within 72 hours of the expiration of the contract. If such a list is not furnished, the licensee waives any right to a commission for a sale made after expiration of the listing.

Continuing at ⑩, the owner agrees to let the broker enter the property at reasonable hours to show it and put a "For Sale" sign on the property. Note that in Minnesota, the broker must have specific permission from the property owner in order to place a "For Sale" sign on the property. At ⑪ the property owner gives the broker specific permission to enter the property into a multiple listing service and to engage the cooperation of other brokers to bring about a sale.

At ⑫, the owner agrees to refer all inquiries regarding the availability of the property to the broker. The purpose is to discourage the owner from thinking that he might be able to save a commission by selling it himself during the listing period, and to increase the broker's chances of generating a sale of the property. Finally, at ⑬, the owner and the broker (or the broker's salespersons if authorized to do so) sign and date the agreement.

EXCLUSIVE RIGHT TO SELL LISTING

The listing illustrated in Figure 17:1 is called an **exclusive right to sell,** or an **exclusive authority to sell,** listing. Its distinguishing characteristic is that no matter who sells the property during the listing period, the listing broker is entitled to a commission. This is the most widely used type of listing in Minnesota. Once signed by the owner and accepted by the broker, the primary advantage to the broker is that the money and effort the broker expends on advertising and showing the property will be to the broker's benefit. The advantage to the owner is that the broker will usually put more effort into selling a property on which the broker holds an exclusive right to sell than on one for which the broker has only an exclusive agency or an open listing.

EXCLUSIVE AGENCY LISTING

The **exclusive agency listing** is similar to the listing shown in Figure 17:1, except that the owner may sell the property himself during the listing period and not owe a commission to the broker. The broker, however, is the only broker who can act as an agent during the listing period; hence the term exclusive agency. For an owner, this may seem like the best of two worlds: the owner has a broker looking for a buyer, but if the owner finds a buyer first, he can save a commission fee. The broker is less enthusiastic, because the broker's efforts can too easily be undermined by the owner. Consequently, the broker may not expend as much effort on advertising and showing the property as with an exclusive right to sell.

OPEN LISTING

Open listings carry no exclusive rights. An owner can give an open listing to any number of brokers at the same time, and the owner can still find a buyer himself and avoid a commission. This gives the owner the greatest freedom of any listing form, but there is little incentive for the broker to expend time and money showing the property as the broker has little control over who will be compensated if the property is sold. The broker's only protection is that, if he does find a buyer at the listing price and terms, he is entitled to a commission. This reluctance to develop a sales effort usually means few, if any, offers will be received and may result in no sale or a sale below market price. Yet, if a broker does find a buyer, the commission earned may be the same as with an exclusive right to sell.

NET LISTING

A **net listing** is created when an owner states the price he wants for his property and then agrees to pay the broker anything he can get above that price as his commission. It can be written in the form of an exclusive right to sell, an exclusive agency, or an open listing. If a homeowner asks for a "net $60,000" and the broker sells the home for $75,000, the commission would be $15,000. By using the net listing method, many owners feel that they are forcing the broker to look to the buyer for the commission by marking up the price of the property. In reality though, a buyer will rarely pay $75,000 for a home that, compared to similar properties for sale, is worth only $60,000 or $65,000. Consequently, we must conclude that the home is actually worth $75,000 and the $15,000 (in effect a 20% commission) came from the seller. If other brokers in the area are charging 4% to 7% of the sales price, a 20% commission invites both public criticism and a lawsuit questioning the broker's loyalty to his seller for accepting such a low listing price.

Because of widespread misunderstanding regarding net listings and because they provide such fertile ground for questionable commission practices they are strongly discouraged in Minnesota. Most brokers strenuously avoid them even though requested by property owners and some states prohibit them outright. There is no law that says a broker must accept a listing; a broker is free to accept only those listings for which the broker can perform a valuable service and earn an honest profit.

MULTIPLE LISTING SERVICE

Multiple listing service (MLS) organizations enable brokers in a given geographical area to exchange information on listings. The purpose is to inform other brokers and their clients of listings held by each member, thus broadening the market exposure for a given property. Member brokers are permitted to show each others' properties to their clients and, if a sale results, the commission is divided between the broker who found the buyer and the broker who obtained the listing, less a small deduction for the cost of operating the multiple listing service. The exact division of the commission is either established by an agreement held at the MLS office and signed by all members of the MLS, or it is stated on each listing submitted to the MLS.

Market Exposure

A property listed with a broker who is a multiple listing service member receives the advantage of greater sales exposure, which, in turn, means a better price and a quicker sale. For the buyer, it means learning about what is for sale at many offices without having to visit each individually. For the salesman and broker, it means that, if his own office does not have a suitable property for a prospect, the opportunity to make a sale is not lost, because the prospect can be shown the listings of other brokers.

To give a property the widest possible market exposure and to maintain fairness among its members, most multiple listing organizations obligate each member broker to provide information to the organization on each of his listings within three to seven days after the listing is taken. To facilitate the exchange of information, multiple listing organizations have developed customized listing forms. These forms are a combination of an exclusive right-to-sell listing agreement (with authority to place the listing into multiple) plus a data sheet on the property. The data sheet, which describes all the physical and financial characteristics of the property, and a photograph of the property are published weekly in a multiple listing book which is distributed to MLS members. Then, if Broker B has a client interested in a property listed by Broker A, Broker B telephones Broker A and arranges to show the property to his client. If Broker B's client makes an offer on the property, Broker B contacts Broker A and together they call on the seller with the offer.

Listing Period

It is to the broker's advantage to make the listing period for as long as possible, as it provides more time to find a buyer. Sometimes, even an overpriced property will become salable if the listing period is long enough and prices rise fast enough. From a legal standpoint, an owner and a broker can agree to a listing period of several years if they wish. However, most owners are reluctant to be committed for that long and prefer a better balance between their flexibility and the amount of time needed for a broker to conduct a sales campaign. In residential sales, 3 to 4 months is a popular compromise; farm, ranch, commercial, and industrial listings are usually made for 6 months to 1 year.

HOLDOVER CLAUSE

Problems can result from listings that appear on the surface to last for only a few months but, in the fine print, commit the owner to a much longer period. Particularly troublesome is the **holdover clause** or **automatic renewal clause** that allows a listing to renew itself indefinitely after its expiration date unless canceled in writing by the owner. What often happens is that, after several months pass without a sale of the property, the expiration date arrives and the owner lists with another broker who produces a sale. Then the first broker steps forward to demand "his" commission in addition to the one being paid to the broker who produced the sale. Alternatively, the expiration date arrives without a sale and the owner forgets the matter, only to find the broker on his doorstep a year later with a buyer and a demand for a commission. Because of these

recurring problems, many states (including Minnesota) now outlaw automatic renewals and require definite expiration dates.

AGENT'S AUTHORITY

A written listing agreement is an example of an expressed contract. It outlines on paper the extent of the agent's authority to act on behalf of the principal and the principal's obligations to the agent.

Agency authority may also arise from custom in the industry, common usage, and conduct of the parties involved. For example, in some other states the right of an agent to post a "For Sale" sign on the listed property is implied although it may not be expressly stated in the listing. In those states, if it is the custom in the industry to do so, and presuming there are no deed covenants or city ordinances to the contrary, the agent has **implied authority** to post the sign. In Minnesota, a broker does not have an implied authority to post a "For Sale" sign. If the broker wants to post a "For Sale" sign, the broker must get expressed permission from the property owner to do so.

Ostensible authority (apparent authority) is conferred when a principal gives a third party reason to believe that another person is his agent even though that person is unaware of the appointment. If the third party accepts this as true, the principal may well be bound by the acts of his agent. For example, you give your house key to a plumber with instructions that when he has finished unstopping the waste lines he is to lock the house and give the key to your next door neighbor. Even though you do not call and expressly appoint your neighbor as your agent to receive your key, once the plumber gives the key to your neighbor, your neighbor becomes your agent with regard to that key. Since you told the plumber to leave the key there, he has every reason to believe that you appointed your neighbor as your agent to receive the key.

An **agency by ratification** is one established after the fact. For example, if an agent secures a contract on behalf of a principal and the principal subsequently ratifies or agrees to it, a court may hold that an agency was created at the time the initial negotiations started. An **agency by estoppel** can result when a principal fails to maintain due diligence over his agent and the agent exercises powers not granted to him. If this causes a third party to believe the agent has these powers, an agency by estoppel has been created. An **agency coupled with an interest** is said to exist when the agent holds an interest in the property he is representing. Any time this occurs, the agent must disclose that fact to those with whom he is negotiating.

BROKER'S OBLIGATIONS TO HIS PRINCIPAL

When a real estate broker accepts a listing, a **fiduciary relationship** is created. This requires that the broker exhibit trust and honesty and exercise good business judgment when working on behalf of his principal. Specifically, the broker must faithfully perform the agency agreement, be loyal to his principal, exercise competence, and account for all funds handled by him in performing the agency. The broker also has certain obligations toward the third parties he deals with. Let us look at these requirements more closely.

Faithful Performance

Faithful performance (also referred to as **obedience**) means that the agent is to obey all legal instructions given to him by his principal and apply his best efforts and diligence to carry out the objectives of the agency. For a real estate broker this means he must perform as promised in the listing contract. A broker who promises to make a "reasonable effort" or apply "diligence" in finding a buyer, and who then does nothing to promote the listing, gives the owner legal grounds for terminating the listing. Faithful performance also means not departing from the principal's instructions. If the agent does so (except in extreme emergencies not foreseen by the principal), it is at his own risk. If the principal thereby suffers a loss, the agent is responsible for that loss. For example, a broker accepts a personal note from a buyer as an earnest money deposit, but fails to tell the seller that the deposit is not in cash. If the seller accepts the offer and the note is later found to be worthless, the broker is liable for the amount of the note.

Another aspect of faithful performance is that the agent must personally perform the tasks delegated to him. This protects the principal who has selected an agent on the basis of trust and confidence from finding that the agent has delegated that responsibility to another person. However, a major question arises on this point in real estate brokerage, as a large part of the success in finding a buyer for a property results from the cooperative efforts of other brokers and their salesmen. To eliminate the possibility of the owner refusing to pay a commission if a cooperating broker finds a buyer, listing agreements often include a statement that the listing broker is authorized to secure the cooperation of other brokers for the purpose of bringing about a sale.

Loyalty to Principal

Probably no other area of agency is as fertile ground for lawsuits as the requirement that, once an agency is created, the agent must be loyal to his principal. The law is clear in all states that in a listing agreement the broker (and the broker's sales staff) occupy a position of trust, confidence, and responsibility. As such, the agent is legally bound to keep the property owner fully informed as to all matters that might affect the sale of the listed property and to promote and protect the owner's interests.

Unfortunately, greed and expediency sometimes get in the way. As a result, numerous laws have been enacted for the purpose of protecting the principal and threatening the agent with court action for misplaced loyalty. For example, an out-of-town landowner who is not fully up to date on the value of his land visits a local broker and asks him to list it for $30,000. The broker is much more knowledgeable of local land prices and is aware of a recent city council decision to extend roads and utilities to the area of this property. As a result, he knows that the land is now worth $50,000. The broker remains silent on the matter and the property is listed for sale at $30,000. At this price, the broker can find a buyer before the day is over and have a commission on the sale. However, the opportunity for a quick $20,000 is too tempting to let pass. He buys the property himself or, to hide his identity, in his wife's name or that of a friend and shortly thereafter resells it for $50,000. Whether he sold the property to a client for $30,000 or bought it himself and sold it for $50,000, the broker did not exhibit loyalty to the principal. Laws and penalties for breach of loyalty are stiff: the broker can be sued for recovery of the price difference and the commission paid, his real estate license can be suspended or revoked, and he may be required to pay additional fines and money damages.

If a licensee intends to purchase a property listed for sale by his agency or through a cooperating broker, he is under both a moral and a legal obligation to make certain that the price paid is the fair market value and that the seller knows who the buyer is. In Minnesota a licensee has a legal obligation to inform the seller if the licensee intends to acquire, either directly or indirectly through a third party, any interest in the listed property. This disclosure should be made in writing and signed by the seller in the event the licensee later has to defend himself in court on the issue.

Protecting the Owner's Interest

Loyalty to the principal also means that, when seeking a buyer or negotiating a sale, the broker must continue to protect the owner's financial interests. Suppose that an owner lists his home at $82,000 but confides in the broker, "If I cannot get $82,000, anything over $79,000 will be fine." The broker shows the home to a prospect who says, "Eighty-two thousand is too much. What will the owner really take?" or "Will he take seventy-nine thousand?" Loyalty to the principal requires the broker to say that the owner will take $82,000, for that is the price in the listing agreement. If the buyer balks, the broker can suggest that the buyer submit an offer for the seller's consideration. State laws require that all written offers be submitted to the owner, no matter what the offering price and terms. This prevents the agent from rejecting an offer that the owner might have accepted if he had known about it. If the seller really intends for the broker to quote $79,000 as an acceptable price, the listing price should be changed; then the broker can say, "The property was previously listed for $82,000, but is now priced at $79,000."

A broker's loyalty to his principal includes keeping him informed of changes in market conditions during the listing period. If, after a listing is taken for example, an adjacent landowner is successful in rezoning his land to a higher use and the listed property becomes more valuable, the broker's responsibility is to inform the seller. Similarly, if a buyer is looking at a property priced at $30,000 and tells the broker, "I'll offer $27,000 and come up if need be," it is the duty of the broker to report this to the owner. The owner can then decide if he wants to accept the $27,000 offer or try for more. If the broker does not keep the owner fully informed, he is not properly fulfilling his duties as the owner's agent.

Although the law is clear in requiring the broker to report

to the owner all facts that may have a bearing on the property's ultimate sale, it is less clear about the broker-buyer relationship. This ambiguity sometimes places the broker in a difficult position if a prospective buyer is not fully aware of this and thinks instead that the broker is *his* agent in the transaction. It is true that the broker owes the buyer honesty, integrity and fair business dealings, but the broker must also make it clear to the buyer that he is the agent of the owner, and therefore loyal to the owner. Otherwise the broker becomes a dual agent, in which case the law requires that he make this known to everyone concerned.

Dual Agency

If a broker represents a seller, it is his duty to obtain the highest price and the best terms possible for the seller. If a broker represents a buyer, the broker's duty is to obtain the lowest price and terms for the buyer. When the same broker represents two or more principals in the same transaction, it is a **dual or divided agency,** and a conflict of interest results. If the broker represents both principals in the same transaction, to whom does he owe his loyalty? Does he work equally hard for each principal? This is an unanswerable question; therefore, the law requires that each principal be informed that he cannot expect the agent's full allegiance and thus each is responsible for looking after his own interest personally. If a broker represents more than one principal and does not obtain their consent, he cannot claim a commission and the defrauded principal(s) may be able to rescind the transaction itself. Moreover, his real estate license may be suspended or revoked. This is true even though the broker does his best to be equally fair to each principal.

Dual agency automatically results when one broker represents two or more parties in a real estate exchange. Consequently, the broker must take care to inform his principals of his dual agency in writing before an offer is made.

A dual agency also develops when a buyer agrees to pay a broker a fee for finding a property that suits his needs, and the broker finds one, lists it, and earns a fee from the seller as well as the buyer. Again, both the buyer and seller must be informed of the dual agency in advance of negotiations. If either principal does not approve of the dual agency, he can refuse to participate.

Middleman

A **middleman** is a person who brings two or more parties together who conduct negotiations between themselves without the help of the middleman. If it is clearly understood by all parties involved that the middleman's only purpose was to bring them together, no one expects the middleman's loyalty. If, however, the middleman assists or influences the negotiations, he becomes an agent and is subject to the rules of agency. It is nearly impossible for a real estate licensee to be classified as a middleman in Minnesota.

Reasonable Care

The duty of **reasonable care** implies competence and expertise on the part of the broker. It is the broker's responsibility to disclose all knowledge and material facts concerning a property to his principal. Also, the broker must not become a party to any fraud or misrepresentation likely to affect the sound judgment of the principal.

Although the broker has a duty to disclose all material facts of a transaction to his principal, he may not give legal interpretations. Giving legal interpretations of documents involved in a transaction can be construed as practicing law without a license, an act specifically prohibited by real estate licensing acts. Moreover, the broker can be held financially responsible for any wrong legal information he gives to a client.

The duty of reasonable care also requires an agent to take proper care of property entrusted to him by his principal. For example, if a broker is entrusted with a key to an owner's building to show it to prospects, it is the broker's responsibility to see that it is used for only that purpose and that the building is locked when he leaves. Similarly, if a broker receives a check as an earnest money deposit, the check must be deposited into the broker's trust account within one business day.

Accounting for Funds Received

When a broker obtains an offer on a property, the earnest money that accompanies it belongs to the buyer until the offer is accepted, and upon acceptance, to the seller subject to completion of the transaction. The money does not belong to the broker, even though he possesses a check made out to him. For the purpose of holding clients' money, laws in nearly all states require a broker to maintain a special trust or escrow account. Minnesota's trust account requirements are set forth in §§82.17, subds. 6–7, and §82.24, and in Rules 4 MCAR

1.41505–1.41507. The full text of these rules appears in Chapter 18. All monies received by a broker as agent for his principal are to be promptly deposited in this account. Minnesota requires that this account be a demand deposit (checking account) at a bank or a trust account at a trust company. There is a new trend underway to allow brokers to deposit trust funds in savings accounts where the money can earn interest. Minnesota permits trust funds to be deposited in an interest bearing account, provided that the agreement of both buyer and seller is secured.

The broker's **trust account** must be separate from his personal bank account, and the broker is required by law to accurately account for all funds received into and paid out of the trust account. State-conducted surprise audits are made on brokers' trust accounts to ensure compliance with the law. One trust account is adequate for all the monies received on behalf of all principals. Failure to comply with trust fund requirements can result in the loss of one's real estate license.

Commingling

If a broker places a client's money in his own personal account, it is called **commingling** and is grounds for suspension or revocation of the broker's real estate license. The reason for such severe action is that in the past some brokers have used clients' money for short-term loans to themselves and then have been unable to replace the money. Also, clients' money placed in a personal bank account can be attached by a court of law to pay personal claims against the broker.

If a broker receives a check as an earnest money deposit, along with instructions from the buyer that it remain uncashed, the broker may comply with the buyer's request as long as the seller is informed of this fact when the offer is presented. Similarly, the broker can accept a promissory note, if he informs the seller. The objective is to disclose all material facts to the seller that might influence his decision to accept or reject the offer. The fact that the deposit accompanying the offer is not cash is a material fact. If the broker withholds this information, he violates the laws of agency.

Minnesota also prohibits the commingling of personal funds with trust funds. However, it is specifically provided that a licensee may maintain up to $100 of personal funds in the trust account to absorb bank service charges. In addition, nondepositable items, such as notes or stocks, must be immediately placed with an escrow agent who is under written agreement with the buyer. The broker may act as the escrow agent only when he has the written authorization of both buyer and seller (see §82.24, subd. 3, and 4 MCAR 1.41507 in Chapter 18).

BROKER'S OBLIGATIONS TO THIRD PARTIES

A broker's obligations are primarily to the principal who has employed him. Minnesota laws nonetheless make certain demands on the broker in relation to the third parties the broker deals with on behalf of the principal. Foremost among these are honesty, integrity, and fair business dealing. This includes the proper care of deposit money and offers, and the responsibility for written or verbal statements made by the broker or his sales staff or any impression made by withholding information. Misrepresenting a property by omitting vital information is as wrong as giving false information. Disclosure of such misconduct usually results in a broker losing his right to a commission. He may also lose his real estate license, and can be sued by any party to the transaction who suffered a financial loss because of the misrepresentation.

In guarding against misrepresentation, a licensee must be careful not to make statements about which he does not know the answer. For example, a prospect looks at a house listed for sale and asks if it is connected to the city sewer system. The agent does not know the answer, but sensing it is important to making a sale, says, "Yes." This is fraud. If the prospect relies on this statement, purchases the house, and finds out that there is no sewer connection, the agent may find himself the center of litigation regarding sale cancellation, commission loss, damage lawsuit, and state license discipline. The answer should be, "I don't know, but I will find out for you."

Suppose instead, that the property owner has told the broker that the house is connected to the city sewer system, and the broker, having no reason to doubt the statement, accepts it in good faith and gives that information to prospective buyers. If this statement is not true, the owner is at fault, owes the broker a commission, and is subject to legal action from the buyer for sale cancellation and money damages. In addition, the broker has committed a fraud, is liable to the buyer for damages, and is entitled to recover from the owner. Therefore, relying on the owner for information does not completely relieve the broker's responsibility to third parites. When a broker must rely on information supplied by the owner, it is best to have it in writing.

Disclosure

Lawsuits against brokers and their clients are becoming more frequent. A recent case that typifies current legal thinking held that facts not known by the buyer must be disclosed to him by the seller, or the broker representing him, if they materially affect the desirability of the property. Even the use of an "as is" clause in the purchase contract does not excuse a broker from disclosing material facts regarding a property. The court went on to say that a buyer of real estate has every right to rescind a contract when the agent by his silence has allowed the transaction to proceed without informing the buyer of all facts relevant to the property. In Minnesota an agent's license can be revoked for failure to disclose.

In another case, the buyers of a home built on filled land sued the seller because the lot settled and damaged the house. Their complaint against the seller was that they had not been told of the filled land. The seller in turn sued the broker because the broker had made no mention of that fact to the buyers. In court, the buyers were able to rescind their deal with the seller. In turn the seller successfully sued the broker and recovered the real estate commission, attorney fees and earnings lost while defending the buyer's suit. The court said the broker violated his duty to his principal by not informing the purchasers that the house was on filled land.

In another case, Mrs. Widow was interested in buying an income property. She visited a broker who showed her a number of income and expense statements from listed properties. He recommended one in particular that he claimed would yield a monthly income to her of $700 to $900. This estimate was based on unverified statements made by the current owner. She bought the property only to learn that, in fact, the property's income was insufficient to meet fixed expenses. Subsequently she lost the property through foreclosure. In years past, she would have been simply called foolish for not personally investigating and verifying the income and expenses of the property herself and would have had to bear the loss herself. Today, however, courts look upon real estate licensees as professionals who possess superior knowledge or special information regarding real property and to which their clients are legally entitled. (This is especially significant in that "professional" status is what the real estate industry has been working hard to achieve in recent years.) Mrs. Widow sued the broker for withholding information that should have been disclosed and won. As a result, the broker is responsible for reimbursing her loss. In Minnesota buyers have been very successful in suing real estate agents for damages.

Puffing

Puffing (or **puffery**) refers to nonfactual or extravagant statements that a reasonable person would recognize as such. Thus, a buyer may have no legal complaint against a broker who told him that a certain hillside lot had the most beautiful view in the world, or that a listed property had the finest landscaping in the county. Usually, a reasonable buyer can see these things for himself and make up his own mind. However, if a broker in showing a rural property says it has "fantastic" well water, there had better be plenty of good water when the buyer moves in. If a consumer believes the broker and relies on the representation, the broker may have a potential liability. The line between puffery and misrepresentation is subjective, but it can be more easily defined by placing oneself in the position of the prospect about to pay a substantial amount of hard-earned money for a property.

OWNER-BROKER OVERVIEW

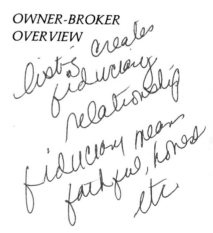

Because the owner-broker relationship is so important, let us stop for an overview of it. When a seller and a broker enter into a listing agreement, a contract is created that appoints the broker as the special agent of the seller for the purpose of finding a purchaser who is ready, willing, and able to buy at the price and terms set forth in the listing. The listing creates a fiduciary relationship between the broker and the owner. The term fiduciary describes the faithful relationship owed by an agent to his principal. Specifically these are the duties of faithful performance, loyalty, competence, accounting, and disclosure. When an agent breaches his fiduciary responsibilities, the principal can bring a civil suit to recover losses, and the agent's license to operate may be revoked or suspended by the state.

Principal's Obligations

The principal or owner also has certain obligations to the agent. Although these do not receive much statutory attention in most states, they are important when the principal fails to live up to his obligations. The principal's primary obligation from the agent's standpoint is **compensation.** However, the agent is also eligible for **reimbursement** for expenses not related to the sale itself. For example, if an agent had to pay a plumber to fix a broken pipe for the owner, he could expect reimbursement from the owner over and above the sales commission.

The other two obligations of the principal are indemnification and performance. An agent is entitled to **indemnification** when he suffers a loss through no fault of his own; for example, because a misrepresentation by the principal to the agent was passed on in good faith to the buyer. The duty of **performance** means the principal is expected to do whatever he reasonably can to accomplish the purpose of the agency, for instance, referring inquiries by prospective buyers to the broker.

Third Parties

Although the broker has no contracts with third parties, the broker is nonetheless responsible for honesty, integrity and fairness of business dealings with them. In fact, courts today (including Minnesota's) are bending over backwards to protect buyers from misleading or missing information, undisclosed fees, and hidden broker identity.

BROKER'S SUBAGENTS

The salespersons associated with a broker are general agents of the broker. This agency is created by way of a contract between the broker and each salesperson. The salesperson owes the broker the duties of competence, obedience, accounting, loyalty, and disclosure. The broker's obligations to the salesperson as a subagent are compensation, reimbursement, indemnification and performance. In addition, the employment contract will state the extent to which the salesperson can bind the broker. For example, is the salesman's signature by itself sufficient to bind the broker to a listing or must the broker also sign it? With regard to third parties, the salesperson also owes them honesty, integrity, and fair business dealings.

Cooperating Brokers

When a cooperating broker (or one of his or her salespersons) finds a buyer for a property listed by another broker, who does the cooperating broker represent? There are three schools of thought on this matter. The first holds that the cooperating broker represents the buyer by virtue of the fact that he is trying to locate a suitable property for the buyer. The second sees the cooperating broker as a subagent of the seller because the seller is paying the commission and the agency line must follow the money line. The third school of thought holds that since the cooperating broker has no contract with the seller (only an agreement to share with the listing broker) and none with the buyer, he is the agent of neither.

Whereas the principal-agent concept has existed for centuries and considerable statutory and case law has been developed about it, large-scale cooperation among brokers is a product of only the past three decades. Thus the question of who represents whom in a cooperative sale is something Minnesota courts and the state legislature will undoubtedly wrestle with in the future.

BROKER COMPENSATION

To be legally eligible for compensation, the broker must be able to clearly show that he was employed. Usually, this requirement is fulfilled by using a preprinted listing form approved for use by the local multiple listing service or the state Realtor's association. The broker fills in the blank spaces with the information that applies to the property he is listing. If listings come in the form of letters or verbal requests from property owners, the broker must make certain that all the essential requirements of a valid listing are present and clearly stated. If they are not, the broker may expend time and money finding a buyer only to be denied a commission because he was not properly employed. To guard against this, the broker should transfer the owner's request to the preprinted listing form that he uses and have the owner sign it.

"Ready, Willing, and Able"

The broker earns his commission at whatever point in the transaction he and the owner agree upon. In nearly all listing contracts, this point occurs when the broker produces a **"ready, willing, and able buyer"** at the price and terms acceptable to the owner. "Ready and willing" means a buyer who is ready to buy now and needs no further coaxing. "Able" means financially capable of completing the transaction. An alternative arrangement is for the broker and owner to agree to a "no sale, no commission" arrangement whereby the broker is not entitled to a commission until the transaction is closed.

The difference between the two arrangements becomes important when a buyer is found at the price and terms acceptable to the owner, but no sale results. The "ready, willing, and able" contract provides more protection for the broker as his commission does not depend on the deal reaching settlement. The "no sale, no commission" approach is to the owner's advantage, for he is not required to pay a commission unless there is a completed sale. However, with the passage of time, court decisions have tended to blur the clear-cut distinction between the two. For example, if the owner has a "no sale, no commission" agreement, it would appear that, if the broker brought a ready, willing, and able buyer at the listing price and terms and the owner refused to sell, the owner would owe no commission, for there was no sale. However, a court of law would find in favor of the broker for the full amount of the commission if the refusal to sell was arbitrary and without reasonable cause or in bad faith. Under a "ready, willing, and able" listing, traditionally, if a broker produced a buyer, it was up to the owner to decide if the buyer was, in fact, financially able to buy. If the owner accepted the buyer's offer and subsequently the buyer did not have the money to complete the deal, the owner still owed the broker a commission. The legal thinking today is that the broker should be responsible, because he is in a much better position to analyze the buyer's financial ability than the owner.

PROCURING CAUSE

A broker who possesses an open listing or an exclusive agency listing is entitled to a commission if he can prove that the resulting sale was primarily due to his efforts. That is, he was the **procuring cause,** the one whose efforts originated procurement of the sale. Suppose that a broker shows an open-listed property to a client and, during the listing period or an extension, the client goes directly to the owner and concludes a deal. Even though the owner negotiates his own transaction and prepares his own sales contract, the broker is entitled to a full commission for finding the buyer. This would also be true if the owner and the client used a subterfuge or strawman to purchase the property to avoid paying a commission.

State laws protect the broker who in good faith has produced a buyer at the request of an owner.

When an open listing is given to two or more brokers, the first one who produces a buyer is entitled to the commission. For example, Broker 1 shows a property to Client C, but no sale is made. Later C goes to Broker 2 and makes an offer, which is accepted by the owner. Although two brokers have attempted to sell the property, only one has succeeded, and he is the one entitled to a commission. The fact that Broker 1 receives nothing, even though he may have expended considerable effort, is an important reason why brokers dislike open listings.

TERMINATING THE LISTING CONTRACT

The usual situation in a listing contract is that the broker finds a buyer acceptable to the owner. Thus, in most listing contracts the agency terminates because the objective of the contract has been completed. In the bulk of the listings for which a buyer is not found, the agency is terminated because the listing period expires.

Even when a listing calls for mutual consideration and has a specific termination date, it is still possible to revoke the agency aspect of the listing before the termination date. However, liability for breach of contract still remains, and money damages may result. Thus, an owner who has listed his property may tell the broker not to bring any more offers, but the owner still remains liable to the broker for payment for the effort expended by the broker up to that time. Depending how far advanced the broker is at that point, the amount could be as much as a full commission.

Mutual Agreement

A listing can be terminated by mutual agreement of both the owner and broker without money damages. Because listings are the stock in trade of the brokerage business, brokers do not like to lose listings, but sometimes this is the only logical alternative open, as the time and effort in setting and collecting damages can be very expensive. Suppose, however, that a broker has an exclusive right-to-sell listing and suspects that the owner wants to cancel because he has found a buyer and wants to avoid paying a commission. The broker can stop showing the property, but the owner is still obligated to pay a commission if the property is sold before the listing period expires. Whatever the broker and seller decide, it is best to put the agreement into writing and sign it.

With regard to open listings, once the property is sold by anyone, broker or owner, all listing agreements pertaining to the property are automatically terminated; the objective has been completed, there is no further need for the agency to exist. Similarly, with an exclusive agency listing, if the owner sells the property himself, the agency with the exclusive broker is terminated.

Abandonment, etc.

Agency can also be terminated by improper performance or abandonment by the agent. Thus, if a broker acts counter to his principal's best financial interests, the agency is terminated, no commission is payable, and the broker may be subject to a lawsuit for any damages suffered by the principal. If a broker takes a listing and then does nothing to promote it, the owner can assume that the broker abandoned it and has grounds for revocation. The owner should keep written documentation in the event the matter ever goes to court.

An agency is automatically terminated by the death of either the principal or the agent, or if either is judged legally incompetent by virtue of insanity or if either becomes bankrupt. Destruction of the listed property also terminates the agency because the object of the agency no longer exists.

DEPOSIT MONEY DISPOSITION

When an earnest money deposit accompanies an offer to buy, the normal procedure is to apply it to the purchase price if the offer is accepted or to return it to the buyer if the offer is rejected. Suppose, however, that the offer is accepted and subsequently the buyer does not fulfill his obligations and forfeits the deposit to the seller as liquidated damages. If the broker is to share in any part of that money, there must be an agreement between the seller and the broker. Such an arrangement is usually made on the listing agreement or earnest money contract. One that would protect the broker is to agree with the owner to split the deposit equally, but with the limitation that the broker's portion not exceed the amount of the commission he would have earned if the transaction had been completed. Not to have such an agreement may leave the broker with nothing for his efforts and the owner with all the forfeited deposit.

BARGAIN BROKERS

The full-service real estate broker who takes a listing and places it in multiple, advertises the property at his expense, holds open house, qualifies prospects, shows property, obtains offers, negotiates, opens escrow and follows through until closing is the mainstay of the real estate selling industry. Approximately 90% of today's sales are handled that way. The remaining 10% are sold by owners, some handling everything themselves and some using flat-fee brokers who oversee the transaction but do not do the actual showing and selling.

Flat-Fee Brokers

For a fee that typically ranges from $400 to $1,500, a **flat-fee broker** will list a property, suggest a market price, write advertising, assist with negotiations, draw up a sales contract, and turn the signed papers over to an escrow company for closing. The homeowner is responsible for paying for advertising, answering inquiries, setting appointments with prospects, showing the property, and applying whatever salesmanship is necessary to induce the prospect to make an offer.

In the seller's market that existed in the latter half of the 1970 decade, homes sold quickly as buyers scoured newspaper ads and drove through neighborhoods in search of "For Sale" signs. Finding buyers was relatively easy and flat-fee brokers gained in popularity. For a person with a $100,000 house to sell, the difference between a full-service fee of $5,000 to $7,000 and a flat-fee of $1,000 can make the effort of showing their own property well worth their time.

The future popularity of this type of brokerage service will greatly depend on whether home resales are in a buyer's market or a seller's market. In a seller's market it is relatively easy to find buyers. In a buyer's market, the effort that a full service broker expends on finding a buyer becomes much more valuable. Additionally, a full-service broker is paid only if a sale results. A flat-fee broker earns his fee whether the property sells or not.

Discount Broker

A **discount broker** is a full-service broker who charges less than the prevailing commission rates in his community.

In a seller's market a real estate agent's major problem is finding salable property to list, not finding buyers. The discount broker attracts sellers to his agency by offering to do the job for less money, for example, 3% or 4% instead of 5% to 7%. Charging less means a discount broker must sell more properties to be successful. Consequently, most discount brokers are careful to take listings only on property that will sell quickly, and to reject those that won't. Discounting tends to prevail more in a seller's market than in a buyer's market. This is because the broker is competing harder to find sellers than to find buyers.

PROPERTY DISCLOSURE STATEMENTS

The federal government through the Department of Housing and Urban Development (HUD) has enacted legislation to protect purchasers of property in new subdivisions from misrepresentation, fraud, and deceit. The HUD requirements, administered by the Office of Interstate Land Sales Registration (OILSR), apply primarily to subdivisions containing 100 or more vacant lots and which are sold across state lines. The purpose of this law, which took effect in 1969 and was amended in 1979, is to require that developers give prospective purchasers more information regarding the property that they are being asked to buy. In passing this law, Congress recognized that all too often subdivision salesmen tell prospects untruths or withhold important information regarding the subdivisions that they are promoting. A color brochure might be handed to prospects picturing an artificial lake and boat marina within the subdivision, yet the developer has not obtained the necessary permits to build either and may never do so. Or, a developer, through his sales force, implies that the lots being offered for sale are ready for building when in fact there is no sewer system and the soil cannot handle septic tanks. Or prospects are not told that many roads in the subdivision will not be built for several years, and, when they are, lot owners will face a hefty paving assessment followed by annual maintenance fees, because the county has no intention of maintaining them as public roads.

Property Report

To give the prospective purchaser more information, OILSR requires developers to file a property report that meets HUD specifications before any lots can be sold. A copy of this report must be given to each purchaser before a contract to purchase is signed. If one is not received, the buyer may cancel the contract at anytime within two years from the date of signing. The report deals with the following questions.

What is the name and address of the developer? How far is the development from the nearest established city via paved and unpaved roads? Will the sales contract be recorded with the public recorder in the county where the land is located? If not, could the developer's creditors acquire title to the property free of any obligation to deliver a deed to the buyer, even though the buyer has made all his payments? What happens to a lot buyer's interest if he fails to make a payment on time as called for by his sales contract? Does the land present any special soil conditions that could cause problems in laying foundations? If so, what extra costs would the buyer incur?

Are schools, shopping, medical, and public transportation facilities available at or near the site of the development? How many homes and commercial-use buildings have already been built at the development site? Are all lots accessible by public automobile road and are they paved? If not, when will this occur and at what additional cost to the lot buyer? Are lots surveyed and staked so that the buyer can find his? Under what conditions will money paid by the buyer be returned to him if he is not satisfied with his purchase? Are there or will there be recreational facilities at the development? If so, who will pay to build and maintain them? What guarantee is there that these recreational facilities will actually be built? And when will they be built?

Is there a mandatory property owner's association with mandatory dues? What arrangements have been made for sewage and trash disposal and for water, gas, electricity, and telephone services to each lot? Are the cost of these in addition to the lot price? Is there an adequate water supply to service the lots once they are developed with buildings? What mortgage or other encumbrances are presently against the property that are senior to the buyer's land contract? What restrictive easements, covenants, reservations and building codes must the buyer observe if and when he builds on his lot? Who owns the oil and mineral rights and the surface right of entry to explore for them?

The developer is also required to provide a summary of

costs associated with purchasing the lot, including cash price, finance charges, installation charges of utilities, annual taxes, dues and assessments. The buyer also has a right for three business days after signing the purchase contract to revoke it.

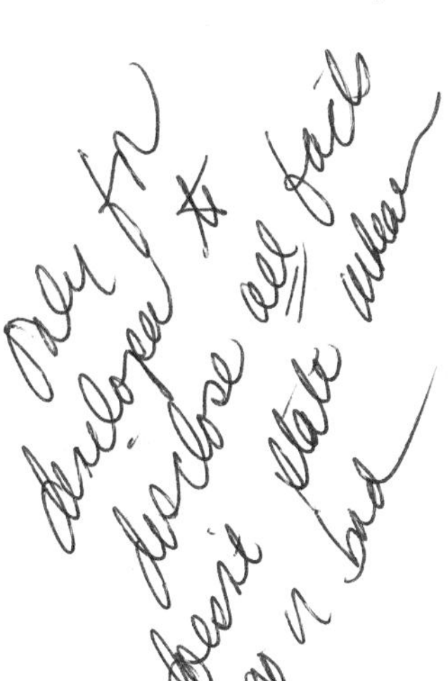

Government's Position

In enforcing disclosure requirements, neither HUD nor OILSR takes a position as to whether a particular subdivision is a good investment or a bad one, and a statement to this effect is printed on the first page of every property report given to a prospective buyer. The statement also urges the prospective buyer to read the property report before signing anything. The primary purpose of the property report is to ensure that the developer and his sales agents disclose to third parties pertinent facts regarding the property before a sale is made.

Minnesota also enacted its own disclosure laws. These apply to developers of house subdivisions, condominiums, cooperatives, and vacant lots, whereas the federal laws are primarily concerned with vacant land sales. Also, state disclosure laws deal with developments sold entirely within a state and in some cases with developments in other states sold to their residents, whereas HUD and OILSR deal only with lots in one state sold to residents of another state.

FAIR HOUSING LAWS

There are two major federal laws that prohibit discrimination in housing. The first is the Civil Rights Act of 1866. It states that, "All citizens of the United States shall have the same right in every State and Territory, as is enjoyed by the white citizens thereof to inherit, purchase, lease, sell, hold, and convey real and personal property." In 1968, the Supreme Court affirmed that the 1866 Act prohibits "all racial discrimination, private as well as public, in the sale of real property." The second is the Federal Fair Housing Law, officially known as Title VIII of the Civil Rights Act of 1968. This law makes it illegal to discriminate based on race, color, religion, sex, or national origin in connection with the sale or rental of housing.

With regard to the sale or rental of housing, the 1968 Civil Rights Act makes it illegal (1) to refuse to rent to, negotiate, or deal with any competent person, (2) to offer different terms or conditions for buying or renting depending on a person's race, color, religion, sex or national origin, (3) to advertise housing as available only to persons of a certain race, color, religion, sex or national origin, (4) to make false statements regarding the availability of housing for rent or sale, (5) to induce panic selling in a neighborhood; i.e., blockbusting, (6) to deny credit or set different loan terms or conditions because of race, color, religion, sex or national origin, or (7) to exclude any qualified person from membership in a real estate board, multiple listing organization or other facility related to the sale or rental of housing.

A real estate agent also violates fair housing laws if he or she gives a minority buyer or seller less than favorable treatment by ignoring the customer or referring him to an agent of the same minority, fails to use best efforts, does not submit an offer, delays submitting an offer, or induces a seller to reject an offer because of race, color, religion, sex or national origin.

Steering

Preventing a minority member from obtaining housing in a community of his choice is a violation of the law. Called **steering,** this includes efforts to exclude minority members from one community as well as efforts to direct them to minority or changing communities. Examples include showing only certain neighborhoods, slanting property descriptions, downgrading non-integrated neighborhoods to minority buyers and vice versa.

Blockbusting

Blockbusting is the illegal practice of inducing panic selling in a neighborhood for financial gain. Blockbusting typically starts when one person induces another to sell his property cheaply by stating that an impending change in the racial or religious composition of the neighborhood will cause property values to fall, school quality to decline, and crime to increase. The first home thus acquired is sold (at a mark-up) to a minority member. This event is used to reinforce fears that the neighborhood is indeed changing. The process quickly snowballs as residents panic and sell at progressively lower prices. The homes are then resold at higher prices to incoming residents.

Note that blockbusting is not limited to fears over people moving into a neighborhood. In a Virginia case, a real estate firm attempted to gain listings in a certain neighborhood by playing upon residents' fears regarding an upcoming expressway project. Blockbusting in any form is outlawed by the 1968 Civil Rights Act.

Differences

The differences between the 1968 Act and the 1866 Act are more theoretical than real. For example, the 1968 Act contains certain exemptions for single-family houses owned by a private individual who owns three or less houses and offers them for sale or rent without the use of a broker and without the use of discriminatory advertising, and for rooms or units offered for rent in 1 to 4 dwelling-unit, owner-occupied buildings. However, the 1866 Act contains no such exceptions. In 1965 a Negro from St. Louis, Joseph L. Jones, brought suit in federal court complaining that the Alfred H. Mayer Company had refused to sell him a home for the sole reason that he was black. The case went to the U.S. Supreme Court where in 1968 it was decided in Jones' favor. With that decision the Supreme Court substantially nullified the two exemptions just mentioned. In other words, whereas the 1968 Act allowed small property owners some latitude in choosing to whom they sold or rented, the 1866 Act and *Jones* v. *Mayer* state that if the discrimination is on racial grounds, it is unlawful—no exceptions! Theoretically this leaves religion and national origin as legitimate grounds for discrimination by owners. However, it is unlikely that the courts will be receptive to distinctions of this kind.

Minnesota Human Rights Act

Minnesota's Human Rights Act, §363.01, *et seq.*, is even broader in its coverage than the Federal Fair Housing Act. Section 363.03, sets forth the conduct determined by the legislature to constitute unfair discriminatory practices. It is important to note that individual property owners, as well as agents and financial institutions, are specifically prohibited from discriminating against those within a protected class. In addition, Minnesota prohibits discrimination not only on the federal grounds of race, color, religion, sex, and national origin, but also on the grounds of marital status, children, disability or status with regard to public assistance. Violation of the Minnesota Human Rights Act constitutes a misdemeanor.

There are only three exceptions recognized in the Minnesota Human Rights Act. These are found in §363.02, subd. 2. First, discrimination on the basis of sex is permitted in the renting or leasing of rooms in residence homes operated by nonprofit organizations such as the YWCA. Second, the resident of a one-family unit may discriminate in renting a room or rooms within that unit, but only on the basis of sex, marital status, children, disability or status with regard to public assistance. Third, there can be restrictions regarding the presence and age of minor children in buildings occupied by the owner and containing four or fewer units, in the rental or sale of condominiums (other than conversions), and in rental units within buildings that have been exempted from these provisions by the Commissioner of Human Rights.

Also, certain Minnesota municipalities have local ordinances prohibiting discrimination on additional grounds. As an example, Minneapolis prohibits discrimination in housing on the basis of affectional preference. It is important to be aware of all human rights laws in your area. Violation of any of these laws can result in revocation or suspension of a real estate agent's license.

To summarize Minnesota and federal fair housing laws: no one, owner or agent, may refuse to sell, lease, or rent to another because of race, color, creed, religion, sex, national origin, marital status, children, disability or status with regard to public assistance. Should a property owner ask a real estate agent to so discriminate, the agent must refuse to accept the listing or convince the owner to abandon his discriminatory course.

If a person has a discrimination complaint based on the Civil Rights Act of 1866, he/she should take that complaint directly to a federal court. A complaint to enforce compliance with the Federal Fair Housing Act of 1968 can be filed with the Department of Housing and Urban Development (HUD), a U.S. District Court, or the Attorney General.

If a person claims discrimination under Minnesota's Human Rights Act, he may file a charge with the Department of Human Rights. This must be done within six months of the alleged discriminatory conduct. The Department will then conduct an impartial investigation and make a finding of whether there is probable cause to support the charge. If probable cause is found, the Commissioner may attempt to have the parties conciliate their differences, or he may order a formal hearing of the matter. After a full hearing, the hearing examiner may order the payment of compensatory damages together with punitive damages of up to $6,000. In addition, the examiner may order the lease, sale or rental of the property to the complainant according to the terms as listed with the broker or as advertised or offered by the owner. The hearing examiner's final decision is, of course, subject to judicial review. Minnesota can also take direct action against the alleged discriminating party. In addition, local and state fair housing agencies as well as civil rights organizations stand ready to help.

The burden of proving illegal discrimination is the responsibility of the complainant. If successful, the complainant can also ask for the following federal remedies: (1) an injunction to stop the sale or rental of the desired property to someone else and make it available to the complainant, (2) actual damages, (3) punitive damages up to $1,000, and (4) court costs. Criminal penalties are provided for those who coerce, intimidate, threaten, or interfere with a person's buying, renting, or selling of housing.

VOCABULARY REVIEW

Match Terms **a-n** *with statements* **1–14.**

a. *Agent*
b. *Commingling*
c. *Dual agency*
d. *Exclusive agency*
e. *Exclusive right to sell*
f. *Middleman*
g. *Multiple listing service*
h. *Net listing*
i. *Open listing*
j. *Principal*
k. *Procuring cause*
l. *Puffing*
m. *Special agency*
n. *Third parties*

1. A person who authorizes another to act for him.
2. Listing giving a broker a nonexclusive right to find a purchaser.
3. Persons who are not parties to a contract but who may be affected by it.
4. An agency created for the performance of specific acts only.
5. A person who brings two or more parties together but does not assist in conducting negotiations.
6. Listing giving the broker the right to collect a commission no matter who sells the property during the listing period.
7. A listing wherein the owner reserves the right to sell the property himself, but agrees to list with no other broker during the listing period.
8. Person empowered to act by and on behalf of the principal.
9. A listing for which the commission is the difference between the sales price and a minimum price set by the seller.

10. An organization of real estate brokers that exists for the purpose of exchanging listing information.
11. One broker representing two or more parties in a transaction.
12. Mixing of clients' funds with an agent's personal funds.
13. Broker who is the primary cause of a real estate transaction.
14. Nonfactual or extravagant statements that a reasonable person would recognize as such.

QUESTIONS AND PROBLEMS

1. When we speak of an agency relationship, to what are we referring?
2. How does a universal agency differ from a general agency?
3. What does broker cooperation refer to? How is it achieved?
4. Why do brokers strongly prefer to take exclusive right-to-sell listings rather than exclusive agency or open listings?
5. What advantages and disadvantages does the open listing offer a property owner?
6. The laws of agency require that the agent be faithful and loyal to the principal. What does this mean to a real estate broker who has just taken a listing?
7. What does the phrase "ready, willing, and able buyer" mean in a real estate contract?
8. If a person holds a real estate license in Minnesota, is he or she required to disclose that fact when acting as a principal?
9. How are listings terminated?
10. What is the purpose of HUD property disclosure statements?
11. Briefly define the terms steering and blockbusting.
12. What impact did the *Jones* v. *Mayer* case have on fair housing laws?

ADDITIONAL READINGS

California Association of Realtors. *How to Negotiate in Listing and Selling Homes.* Los Angeles: California Association of Realtors, 1977. This is one of a series of books published by the CAR that deal with listing and selling real property.

Gale, Jack. *Listing Real Estate Successfully.* Reston, Va.: Reston Publishing Co., 1982. This is an up-to-date version of a classic, comprehensive handbook for residential salespeople.

Lank, Edith. *Selling Your Home With An Agent.* Reston, Va.: Reston Publishing Co., 1982. Contains how to choose an agent, listing, pricing, showing, financing, negotiating, tax consequences, and applicable law.

Scaro, Janet. *The Condominium Home: A Special Marketing Challenge.* Chicago: Realtors National Marketing Institute, 1981, 253 pages. Looks at condominium listing, marketing, selling, and opportunities for agents.

Sklar, Stanley P. "The Liability of Brokers for Misrepresentation," *Real Estate Today,* September, 1980, pages 38–41. A very informative article that focuses on what a broker says or does not say about a listing to a buyer. Includes actual court cases plus a list of helpful guidelines.

United States Department of Housing and Urban Development. "Buying Lots From Developers." Washington, D.C.: U.S. Government Printing Office, 1975, 26 pages. This is must reading for anyone planning to buy a vacant lot. Contains what to watch out for, what questions to ask, and HUD property report requirements.

18

Licensing Laws and Professional Affiliation

KEY TERMS

Broker: a natural or legal person licensed to act independently in conducting a real estate brokerage business

Independent contractor: one who contracts to do work according to his own methods and is responsible to his employer only as to the results of that work

License revocation: to recall and make void a license

License suspension: to temporarily make a license ineffective

Principal broker: the broker in charge of a real estate office

Realtor: a term copyrighted by the National Association of Realtors for use by its members

Reciprocity: an arrangement whereby one state honors licenses issued by another state and vice versa

Recovery fund: a state-operated fund that can be tapped to pay for uncollectible judgments against real estate licensees

Salesman or Salesperson: a person employed by a broker to list, negotiate, sell or lease real property for others

The first attempt in the United States to license persons acting as agents in real estate transactions was in the year 1917 in California. Opponents claimed that the new law was an unreasonable interference with the right of every citizen to engage in a useful and legitimate occupation and were successful in having the law declared unconstitutional by the courts on a technicality. Two years later, in 1919, the California legislature passed a second real estate licensing act; this time it was upheld by the Supreme Court. That same year, Michigan, Oregon, and Tennessee also passed real estate licensing acts. Today all 50 states and the District of Columbia require that persons who offer their services as real estate agents be licensed.

Minnesota's License Law Act, formally known as *Chapter 82, Real Estate Brokers and Salespersons,* was originally enacted in 1955. Since that time, it has undergone constant changes and amendments reflecting the development of the real estate industry in Minnesota. The entire License Law Act was replaced and redrafted in 1973. The *Real Estate Rules for Minnesota Statute Chapter 82,* also called the *Minnesota Code of Agency,* was last revised in 1982. The Code contains standards of conduct for real estate brokers, further definitions of rules and regulations defining actions and omissions which constitute fraudulent, dishonest or deceptive practices, and other rules and procedures necessary to carry out the provisions of Chapter 82. The Statute and Code, in their current form, are printed at the end of this chapter. (For purposes of taking the Minnesota real estate examination, it is very important to be familiar with the precise language of the Statute and Code.)

PURPOSE OF LICENSING

Although licensing laws often appear as stumbling blocks to persons wishing to become real estate agents, the public has a vested interest in seeing that salesmen and brokers have the qualifications of honesty, truthfulness, and good reputation. This was the intent of the first license laws. Some years later the additional requirements of license examinations and real estate education were added in the belief that a person who wants to be a real estate agent should meet special knowledge qualifications.

Experience to date clearly indicates that license laws have helped to upgrade technical competency and have increased public confidence in brokers and salesmen. Moreover, license laws are an important and powerful tool in reducing fraudulent real estate practices because a state can suspend or revoke a person's license to operate.

PERSONS REQUIRED TO BE LICENSED

A person who for compensation or the promise of compensation lists or offers to list, sells or offers to sell, buys or offers to buy, negotiates or offers to negotiate either directly or indirectly for the purpose of bringing about a sale, purchase or option to purchase, exchange, auction, lease, or rental of real estate, or any interest in real estate, is required to hold a valid real estate license. Some states also require persons offering their services as real estate appraisers, property managers, mortgage bankers, or rent collectors to hold real estate licenses.

Generally, owners dealing with their own property and licensed attorneys conducting a real estate transaction as an incidental part of their duties as an attorney for a client are exempt from holding a license. Also exempt are trustees and receivers in bankruptcy, legal guardians, administrators and executors handling a deceased's estate, officers and employees of a government agency dealing in real estate. In addition, Section 82.18 of the Minnesota License Law Act exempts (1) individuals selling burial plots in cemeteries; (2) janitors, custodians and others leasing residential units on behalf of the building's owner or manager, but not property managers; (3) state or federally-chartered lending institutions when engaging in the lending or banking business; (4) bonded auctioneers; (5) construction contractors, provided no more than 25 buildings are sold per year; and (6) sellers of registered securities and registered franchises. However, the law does not permit a person to use the exemptions as a means of conducting a brokerage business without the proper license.

BROKER

The licensing procedure in use in nearly all states calls for two types of licenses: real estate broker and real estate salesperson. A **real estate broker** is a person licensed to act independently in conducting a real estate brokerage business. He (she) brings together those with real estate to be marketed and those seeking real estate and negotiates a transaction. For his services he receives a fee, usually in the form of a commission based on the selling price or lease rent. The broker may represent the buyer or the seller, or, if he makes full disclosure, both at the same time. His role is more than that of a middleman who puts two interested parties in contact with each other, for the broker usually takes an active role in negotiating price and terms acceptable to both the buyer and seller. A broker can be an actual person or a business firm owned and operated by an actual broker. The laws of all states permit a real estate broker to hire licensed salespeople to work for him for the purpose of bringing about real estate transactions.

Minnesota's definition for a "broker" is quite detailed. It is found in §82.17, subd. 4(a)–4(f). Minnesota specifically includes within its definition of "broker" property managers, business opportunity brokers, subdivided land brokers, and even private investors if they sell five or more properties per year without using a broker.

SALESPERSON

A **real estate salesperson,** within the meaning of the license laws, is a person working on behalf of a real estate broker to list and negotiate the sale, exchange, lease, or rental of real property for others for compensation, under the direction, guidance, and responsibility of the broker. Only an actual person can be licensed as a salesperson (a business firm cannot be licensed as a salesperson), and a salesperson must be affiliated with a broker; he cannot operate independently. Thus, a salesperson who takes a listing on a property does so in the name of his broker. In the event of a legal dispute caused by a salesperson, the dispute would be between the principal and the broker. Thus, brokers must take considerable care to oversee the documents that their salespeople prepare and sign.

The salesperson is a means by which a broker can expand his sales force. Presumably, the more salespeople a broker has, the more listings and sales generated, and thus the more commissions earned by the broker. Against this, the broker must pay enough out of these commissions to keep his sales force from leaving, provide sales facilities and personnel management, and take ultimate responsibility for any mistakes.

QUALIFICATIONS FOR LICENSING

Of the two license levels, the salesperson's license is regarded as the entry-level license and, as such, requires no previous real estate sales experience. By comparison, the broker's license in Minnesota requires 2 years of experience as a real estate salesperson. An applicant for either license in Minnesota must be at least 18 years of age. Additionally, the applicant is expected to have a past record of trustworthiness and honest business dealings.

Examination

Examination of the license applicant's knowledge of real estate law and practices, mathematics, valuation, finance, and the like, is now an accepted prerequisite for license granting in all states. The Minnesota salesperson exam is 4½ hours in length. The broker exam is also 4½ hours long. Salesperson exams cover the basic aspects of state license law, contracts and agency, real property interests, subdivision map reading, fair housing laws, real estate mathematics, and the ability to follow written instructions. Broker exams cover the same topics in more depth and test the applicant's knowledge of listings, offer and acceptance contracts, leasing contracts, closing statements, real estate finance and appraisal.

Education Requirements

In recent years education has also become an increasingly important part of license qualification requirements. Nearly all states require that applicants take real estate education courses at community colleges, private real estate schools, or through adult education programs at high schools. Education requirements are usually structured so that the least rigorous requirements are for salesmen and the most rigorous are for brokers.

Table 18:1 shows the education and experience requirements in effect in the United States at the time this book was printed. The table is included to give you an overview of the emphasis currently being placed on education and experience by the various states. Minnesota currently requires each applicant for a salesperson's license to complete a total of 90 hours of classroom education. The first 30 hours must be taken before a license applicant takes his examination. The next 30 hours must be taken before the license is issued. The final 30 hours must be completed within one year of the time the salesperson's license is first issued and before any application for a broker's license is made.

Licensing authorities in a number of states now feel that in addition to meeting the original education requirement to obtain a license, a real estate licensee should continue to take courses in order to renew his license. States that require continued education for license renewal are identified in Table 18:1. Minnesota requires all licensees, brokers and salespeople alike, to take 45 hours of continuing education every three years. Other states are considering the matter and will undoubtedly require continuing education before long.

LICENSING PROCEDURE

When a license applicant has completed or is close to completing the education and experience requirements, he begins his formal application for licensure by filling out a license application form. Applications may be secured either in person or by mail from his state's real estate licensing department. When the application is completed, it is returned to the department along with a fee to cover application processing and the examination charge. On this application, the applicant is required to furnish personal identification and the names of character references. These are for the threefold purpose of verifying the applicant's identity, obtaining an indication of the applicant's honesty in past business dealings, and locating any criminal record the applicant may have that might disqualify him from being licensed.

Table 18:1 REAL ESTATE EDUCATION AND EXPERIENCE REQUIREMENTS

STATE	SALESPERSON LICENSE		BROKER LICENSE			
	Education Requirement	Continuing Education	Education Requirement		Experience Requirement	Continuing Education
Alabama	45 hours	No	45 hours		2 years	No
Alaska	None	No	None		2 years	No
Arizona	45 hours	Yes	90 hours		3 years	Yes
Arkansas	30 hours	No	90 hours	*or*	2 years	No
California	None	Yes	270 hours		2 years	Yes
Colorado	48 hours	No	96 hours		2 years	No
Connecticut	30 hours	No	90 hours		2 years	No
Delaware	75 hours	No	30 hours		5 years	No
District of Columbia	None	No	None		None	No
Florida	51 hours	Yes	48 hours		1 year	Yes
Georgia	24 hours	Yes	60 hours		3 years	Yes
Hawaii	40 hours	No	46 hours		2 years	No
Idaho	45 hours	No	90 hours		2 years	No
Illinois	30 hours	No	90 hours		1 year	No
Indiana	40 hours	No	64 hours		1 year	No
Iowa	30 hours	Yes	No addt'l.		1 year	Yes
Kansas	30 hours	Yes	No addt'l.		2 years	Yes
Kentucky	96 hours	No	336 hours		2 years	No
Louisiana	90 hours	Yes	150 hours		2 years	Yes
Maine	High school	Yes	90 hours	*or*	1 year	Yes
Maryland	60 hours	Yes	135 hours		3 years	Yes
Massachusetts	24 hours	No	30 hours		1 year	No
Michigan	30 hours if fails exam	No	90 hours		3 years	No
Minnesota	90 hours	Yes	90 hours		2 years	Yes

Explanation: Hours are clock-hours in the classroom; experience requirement is experience as a licensed real estate salesperson; continuing education refers to education required for license renewal. Some states credit completed salesperson education toward the broker education requirement.

Examination Next, the department schedules a written examination for the applicant. Exams are held in various parts of the state so the applicant need not travel to the state capital. The same exam is given at each examining center on the same day and at the same time. The applicant is not allowed to bring any books or notes into the testing room. However, forty-four states (including Minnesota) allow the use of battery-operated calculators. Exams are machine scored and applicants should bring pencils and an eraser. By law, Minnesota must offer the exam at least every 45 days.

Table 18:1 *continued*

STATE	SALESPERSON LICENSE		BROKER LICENSE		
	Education Requirement	Continuing Education	Education Requirement	Experience Requirement	Continuing Education
Mississippi	60 hours	No	90 hours	1 year	No
Missouri	54 hours	No	94 hours	None	No
Montana	Tenth grade	No	High school	2 years	No
Nebraska	60 hours	No	120 hours	2 years	No
Nevada	90 hours	Yes	360 hours	2 years	Yes
New Hampshire	None	Yes	None	1 year	Yes
New Jersey	45 hours	No	90 hours	2 years + 12 transactions	No
New Mexico	60 hours	No	90 hours	2 years	No
New York	45 hours	Yes	90 hours	2 years	Yes
North Carolina	30 hours	No	90 hours	2 years	No
North Dakota	30 hours	Yes	90 hours	2 years	Yes
Ohio	60 + 60 hours	Yes	180 hours	2 years + 20 transactions	Yes
Oklahoma	45 hours	Yes	45 hours	1 year	Yes
Oregon	90 hours	Yes	150 hours	3 years	Yes
Pennsylvania	60 hours	No	240 hours	3 years	No
Rhode Island	None	No	90 hours *or*	1 year	No
South Carolina	60 hours	No	90 hours	2 years	No
South Dakota	30 hours	Yes	90 hours	3 years	Yes
Tennessee	30 hours	Yes	90 hours	2 years	Yes
Texas	180 hours	Yes	720 hours	2 years	No
Utah	90 hours	No	120 hours	3 years	No
Vermont	High school	No	High school	1 year	No
Virginia	45 hours	No	180 hours	3 years	No
Washington	None	Yes	90 hours	2 years	No
West Virginia	90 hours	No	180 hours	2 years	No
Wisconsin	30 hours	Yes	60 hours	None	Yes
Wyoming	None	No	None	2 years	No

Source: National Association of Real Estate License Law Officials. Check with your state for any changes that may have occurred since this book was printed.

The applicant is notified of the results within 6 weeks. If a passing score was achieved, the applicant pays a fee for the license itself. Also, a salesperson applicant must name the broker he will be working for. This information is provided on a form signed by the employing broker. A broker applicant must give the address where he plans to operate his brokerage business. These forms are processed by the department and a license is mailed to the applicant in the case of a broker, or to the employing broker in the case of a salesperson. Upon receipt, the licensee can operate as a real estate salesperson or broker, as the case may be.

If the applicant fails the written examination, the usual procedure is to allow the applicant to repeat it until he passes. A fee is charged to retake the exam and the applicant must wait until the next testing date.

Renewal

Once licensed, as long as a person remains active in real estate and meets any post-license education requirements, he may renew his license by paying the required renewal fee. No additional exam is required. If a license is not renewed before it expires, Minnesota allows a grace period of one year and charges the normal renewal fee, but does not require re-examination. Once the grace period is passed, all license rights lapse and the individual must meet current application requirements and take another written exam.

EXAMINATION SERVICES

Real estate license examinations in approximately three-quarters of the states are administered by either the Educational Testing Service (ETS), the American College Testing Program (ACT) or Assessment Systems Incorporated (ASI). The remaining states write and grade their own exams.

Educational Testing Service

ETS, headquartered in Princeton, New Jersey, developed its real estate license examination program in 1970 under the sponsorship of four licensing jurisdictions. By mid-1983 ETS had expanded to 28. They were Alaska, Bermuda, Colorado, Connecticut, Delaware, Guam, Hawaii, Indiana, Kansas, Kentucky, Louisiana, Maryland, Michigan, Minnesota, Missouri, Montana, Nebraska, New Hampshire, New Mexico, North Carolina, North Dakota, Pennsylvania, Rhode Island, South Dakota, Tennessee, Virgin Islands, Virginia and Wyoming.

The ETS broker and salesperson exams are each divided into two parts. Part 1, called the **uniform test,** contains questions that are revelant to the general principles and practices of real estate that are common or uniform across the country. Part 2, called the **state test,** contains questions regarding the laws, rules, regulations and practices of the jurisdiction where the examination is being given.

The tests are composed entirely of objective, multiple-choice questions which are constantly being revised and updated to keep them current with the changing practices and laws of real estate. There are many different versions of the tests, but all are equal in difficulty.

Applicants must pass both the uniform test and the state test. Minimum passing scores are set by the individual jurisdictions using the tests, not by ETS. In Minnesota the minimum passing score is 75%. If the applicant passes the test, he or she will receive a score report showing only that the test was passed. Scores are not indicated so as to avoid the possibility of their misuse in hiring practices. If the applicant fails, separate scores will be reported for the individual parts of the examination. This helps the applicant to know in what areas he needs more study.

The ETS salesperson examination contains 120 questions: 80 in the uniform test and 40 in the state test. In the uniform test, 13% of the questions deal with real estate contracts, 24% with financing, 22% with ownership, 24% with brokerage and 17% with appraisal. Approximately 20% of the uniform questions will involve arithmetic. The state test is not subdivided into categories.

The ETS broker examination is made up of 130 questions: 80 in the uniform test and 50 in the state test. In the uniform test, 35% of the questions deal with real estate brokerage, 27% with contracts and law, 15% with appraisal, and 23% with finance and investment. Approximately 20% of the uniform questions deal with arithmetic problems related to real estate. The state portion is not subdivided into categories.

Sample questions of the type asked on ETS salesperson and broker tests can be found in Appendix B at the back of this book.

American College Testing

The American College Testing Program, headquartered in Iowa City, Iowa, prepares and administers real estate license examinations for several states. These states presently are Alabama, Georgia, Idaho, Illinois, Iowa, Nevada, Oregon, Utah, Washington, and Wisconsin.

To address basic real estate concerns, plus information specific to a given state, the ACT examinations are divided into two parts: Multistate and Local Supplement. The Multistate, salesperson and broker examinations, each contains 100 objective, multiple-choice questions. The Local Supplement, salesperson and broker examinations, varies from 20 to 50 questions each, depending on the type of examination and the state.

ACT questions are designed to measure the candidates' ability to understand and apply the fundamental principles of real estate. There are two general types of questions: (1) those based on general background information about real estate, and (2) those which test the candidates' ability to apply fundamental real estate laws, principles and methods to familiar as well as to new problems. Separate item banks are maintained for the salesperson and broker examinations, and a different form of the examination is assembled every month.

In the ACT Multistate salesperson examination, 50% of the questions are concerned with real estate law, 5% with public control, 17% with real estate valuation, 15% with real estate finance, and 13% with special fields. In the Multistate broker examination, 50% of the questions are concerned with real estate law, 10% with public control, 15% with real estate valuation, 10% with real estate finance, and 15% with special fields.

Minimum passing scores are set by individual states using the examinations. Score reports sent to passing applicants give only a PASS designation, while score reports sent to failing candidates include separate scores for the individual parts of the examination in addition to a FAIL designation.

Assessment Systems Incorporated

Organized in 1981 and located in Philadelphia, Assessment Systems Incorporated develops and administers real estate exams for Arkansas, Massachusetts, New Jersey, Vermont, and Washington, D.C. Each state can customize its own exam, picking the number and types of questions desired from the ASI examination question pool. To this, each state adds its own questions based on local law, custom and practice. In addition to testing services, ASI offers states a computerized license management system.

NONRESIDENT LICENSING

The general rule regarding license requirements is that a person must be licensed in the state within which he negotiates. Thus, if a broker or one of his salesmen sells an out-of-state property, but conducts the negotiations entirely within the borders of his own state, he does not need to be licensed to sell in the state where the land is actually located. State laws also permit the broker of one state to split a commission with the broker of another state provided each conducts negotiations only within the state where he is licensed. Therefore, if Broker B, licensed in State B, takes a listing at his office on a parcel of land located in State B, and Broker C in State C sells it to one of his clients, conducting the sale negotiations within State C, then Brokers B and C can split the commission. If, however, Broker C comes to State B to negotiate a contract, then a license in State B is necessary. The standard practice has been to apply for a license and meet substantially the same exam and experience requirements as demanded of resident brokers.

License Reciprocity

In recent years, there has been considerable effort to design real estate licensing systems that permit a broker and his sales staff to conduct negotiations in other states without having to obtain nonresident licenses. The result is **license reciprocity** and it results when one state honors another's license. In permitting reciprocity, state officials are primarily concerned with the nonresident's knowledge of real estate law and practice as it applies to the state in which he wishes to operate.

A few states accept real estate licenses issued by other states. This is called **full reciprocity** and means that a licensee can operate in another state without having to take that state's examination and meet its education and experience requirements. More commonly found is **partial reciprocity** where one state will allow licensees of another state credit for experience, education and the uniform portion of the ETS, ACT or ASI Exam. Minnesota provides for reciprocity by written agreement with other states under the terms of §82.22, subd. 12.

Nonresident Service

Minnesota requires all nonresident licensees to appoint the Commissioner of Commerce as their lawful attorney for the purpose of receiving any legal papers which could not otherwise be served on the nonresident (see §82.31). This provides an avenue by which a state resident can sue a nonresident broker.

LICENSING THE BUSINESS FIRM

When a real estate broker wishes to establish a brokerage business of his own, the simplest method is a sole proprietorship under his own name, such as, John B. Jones, Real Estate

Broker. Some states (including Minnesota) permit a broker to operate out of his residence. However, operating a business in a residential neighborhood can be bothersome to neighbors, and most states require brokers to maintain a place of business in a location that is zoned for businesses.

Fictitious Business Name

When a person operates under a name other than his own, he must register that name by filing a **fictitious business name statement** with his county clerk and the state real estate licensing authority. This statement must also be published in a local newspaper. Thus, if John B. Jones wishes to call his brokerage business Great Lakes Realty, his business certificate would show "John B. Jones, doing business as Great Lakes Realty." (Sometimes "doing business as" is shortened to dba or d/b/a.)

A sole proprietorship, whether operated under the broker's name or a fictitious name, offers a broker advantages in the form of absolute control, flexibility, ease of organization, personal independence, ownership of all the profits and losses, and the freedom to expand by hiring all the salespeople and staff he can manage and afford. Against this the sole proprietor must recognize that he is the sole source of capital for the business and the only owner available to manage it.

Recognizing the need to accumulate capital and management expertise within a single brokerage operation, states also permit corporations and partnerships to be licensed. Since a corporation is an artificial being (not an actual person), it cannot take a real estate examination. Therefore, laws require that the chief executive officer (usually the president) be a licensed real estate broker and be responsible for the management of the firm. Minnesota requires that at least one corporate officer be licensed as a broker in order for the corporation to secure its license. However, every officer performing activities requiring a license must have a broker's license. No corporate officer may hold a salesperson's license in Minnesota.

In most states when a brokerage firm is formed as a partnership, the law requires each partner to be licensed as a real estate broker. However, Minnesota requires only that a single partner be licensed as a broker in order for the partnership to secure its license. As with corporate officers, no partner can hold a salesperson's license. The partnership must also file a fictitious business name statement showing the names of the partners and the name of the partnership.

Branch Offices

A broker may expand by establishing branch offices that are geographically separate from the main or home office. The person in charge of a branch office can be a partner, a corporate owner who is a broker, or an employee who has a broker's license. Minnesota also allows a branch office to operate without a broker on the premises. However, there must be a broker licensee within the organization who is personally responsible for the activities of the branch office. The responsible broker is called a **primary broker** in Minnesota.

REAL ESTATE REGULATION

The legislature of each state has established a government agency for the purpose of regulating real estate licensing procedures and real estate practices within its state. These regulatory agencies are variously known as real estate commissions, or departments or divisions of real estate, or they may be a part of the state's business and vocational licensing and regulation departments. In Minnesota it is the Department of Commerce.

Legislature

The role of the **legislature** is to enact laws within constitutional limits for the purpose of promoting the safety, health, morals, order, and general welfare of the population. Laws so enacted must not be unreasonable or unnecessary and they must be applied evenhandedly. Acting under the right of police power, legislatures of all the states have deemed it in the public interest that persons offering their services as real estate brokers and salesmen have the qualifications of good reputation, honesty, truthfulness, and knowledge of the field. If an applicant meets the requirements, he must be issued a license.

Commissioner of Commerce

In Minnesota, the legislature has created a Department of Commerce to oversee the banking, insurance, real estate, and securities industries. The Department of Commerce is headed by a **Commissioner of Commerce,** appointed by the governor. The Commissioner of Commerce has, in turn, appointed four Deputy Commissioners, one each for banking, insurance, licensing and registration, and enforcement.

The Commissioner, Deputy Commissioners, and the Department of Commerce are responsible for carrying out the laws enacted by the legislature. With regard to real estate, this includes screening and qualifying of applicants for licenses, investigating complaints against license holders and persons without licenses, and regulating subdivisions and real estate syndicates.

Real Estate Advisory Council

Minnesota has established a **Real Estate Advisory Council** to assist and advise the Commissioner. The Minnesota Real Estate Advisory Council is composed of seven members appointed by the Commissioner of Commerce. Five of the members must be real estate brokers with at least five years experience in Minnesota. The other two members are selected from the general public. The Council meets publicly on a quarterly basis around the state, and more often if requested by the Commissioner. The Council's task is to advise the Commissioner on all major policy matters involving the Minnesota License Law Act, particularly education and pre-license requirements.

Department of Commerce

The day-to-day responsibility of real estate regulation rests with the **Minnesota Department of Commerce.** Staffed by full-time civil service employees, the Department answers correspondence, sends out application forms, arranges for examinations, collects fees, issues licenses, approves subdivision reports, and so forth. Manpower is also available for the investigation of alleged malpractices and for audits of broker trust fund accounts. Additionally, the Department publishes a periodic newsletter or magazine to keep licensees informed about changes in real estate law and prints books or leaflets describing the state's license and subdivision laws. In short, it is the Department with which licensees have the most contact, but it is the Council, the Commissioner, and the legislature that set license requirements and tell a licensee what can and cannot be done in real estate transactions.

LICENSE SUSPENSION AND REVOCATION

The most important control mechanism a state has over its real estate salesmen and brokers is that it can **suspend** (temporarily make ineffective) or **revoke** (recall and make void) a real estate license. Without one, it is unlawful for a person to engage in real estate activities for the purpose of earning a commission or fee. Unless an agent has a valid license, a court of law will not uphold his claim for a commission from a client.

Reasons for license suspension and revocation include any violation of the state's real estate act, misrepresentation or false promises, undisclosed dual agency, commingling, and acting as an undisclosed principal. Licenses can also be revoked or suspended for false advertising, obtaining a license by fraud, negligence or incompetence, failure to supervise salesmen, failure to properly account for clients' funds, practicing law without a license, paying commissions to unlicensed persons, conviction of a felony or certain types of misdemeanors, dishonest conduct in general, and failure to have a fixed termination date on an exclusive listing.

Complaint Procedure

When the Commissioner of Commerce receives a complaint from someone who feels he was wronged by a licensee, an investigation is conducted by the enforcement staff. Statements are received from witnesses. Title company records, public records, and the licensee's bank records are checked as necessary. The Commissioner, or someone authorized by the Commissioner, may call an informal conference and invite all parties involved to attend. If it appears the complaint is serious enough and that a violation of the law has occurred, a formal hearing is scheduled. At this hearing the Commissioner becomes the **complainant** and brings charges against the licensee. The person who originally brought the matter to the Commissioner's attention is a **witness.** The licensee, called the **respondent,** may appear with or without legal counsel. Testimony is taken under oath and a written record is made of the proceedings. A hearing officer is appointed by the Commissioner to hear the case and make a recommendation, which the Commissioner may accept, reject, or modify. If the Commissioner's decision is to suspend or revoke the respondent's license, the respondent has the right of appeal to the district court. In Minnesota, this procedure is governed by the Administrative Procedures Act and §82.27. In addition, Minnesota's Commissioner of Commerce has established extensive regulations outlining general standards of conduct and specific fraudulent, deceptive or dishonest practices. These are contained in 4 MCAR 1.41515 through 1.41526 and 1.41528, and are printed at the end of this Chapter.

BONDS AND RECOVERY FUNDS

The fact that a salesman or broker can lose his or her license for a wrongdoing strongly encourages licensees to operate within the law. However, the threat and loss of a license do nothing to provide financial compensation for any losses suffered by a wronged party. This must be recovered from the licensee or his employer, either through a mutually agreed upon monetary settlement or a court judgment resulting from a civil lawsuit brought by the wronged party. But even with a court-ordered settlement in his favor, all too often court judgments turn out to be uncollectible because the defendant has no money.

Two solutions to the uncollectible judgment problem are in common use. Some states require that a person post a **surety bond** with the state before a salesman's or broker's license will be issued. In the event of an otherwise uncollectible court judgment against a licensee, the bond money is used to provide payment. Bond requirements vary from $1,000 to $10,000, with $2,000 to $5,000 being the most popular range. Licensees either can obtain these bonds from bonding companies for an annual fee, or they can themselves post the required amount of cash or securities with the state.*

The second method of protecting the public is through a state sponsored **recovery fund.** A portion of the money that each licensee pays for his real estate license is set aside in a fund which is made available for the payment of otherwise uncollectible judgments. The number of states that use such recovery funds is growing rapidly.†

Minnesota's recovery fund is established in §82.34 and

---

* Bonds are used in Alabama, Arizona, District of Columbia, Kentucky, Massachusetts, Montana, Tennessee, West Virginia, and Wyoming.

† Recovery funds are used in Alabama, Alaska, Arizona, Arkansas, California, Colorado, Connecticut, Delaware, Florida, Georgia, Hawaii, Idaho, Illinois, Kansas, Kentucky, Louisiana, Maryland, Minnesota, Nevada, New Jersey, New Mexico, North Carolina, North Dakota, Ohio, Oklahoma, Pennsylvania, Rhode Island, South Dakota, Texas, Utah, and Virginia.

provides funds for use in real estate education and research, as well as maintaining a minimum of $400,000 for recovery purposes. Every licensee in Minnesota contributes $40 to the fund when his license is first issued. Additional fees of up to $40 can be charged each licensee at renewal time if the fund has been depleted. The maximum payment the fund can make to aggrieved members of the public is limited to $20,000 per transaction and $25,000 per licensee. Also, a Minnesota licensee's license is automatically suspended if payment is made from the fund on his behalf. To become actively licensed again, the licensee must (1) serve out any disciplinary action taken against the licensee by the Commissioner, (2) repay to the recovery fund twice the amount paid out plus interest of 12% per year, and (3) obtain a surety bond in the amount of $40,000.

The requirement for bonds and the establishment of recovery funds are not perfect solutions to the problem of uncollectible judgments because the wronged party must expend considerable effort to recover his loss, and it is quite possible that the maximum amount available per transaction or licensee will not fully compensate for the losses suffered. However, either system is better than none at all, which is still the case in some states.

AFFILIATING WITH A BROKER

If you plan to enter real estate sales, selecting a broker to work for is one of the most important decisions you must make. The best way to approach it is to stop and carefully consider what you have to offer the real estate business and what you expect in return. And look at it in that order! It is easy to become captivated by the big commission income you visualize coming your way. But if that is your only perspective, you will meet with disappointment. The reason is that people are willing to pay you money because they expect to receive some product or service in return. That is their viewpoint and it would be yours if you were in their position. Your clients are not concerned with your income goal, it is only incidental to their goals. If you help them attain their goals, you will reach yours.

Before applying for a real estate license ask yourself if the working hours and conditions of a real estate agent are suitable to you. Specifically, are you prepared to work on a commission-only basis? Evenings and weekends? On your own? With people you've never met before? If you can comfortably answer "Yes" to these questions, then start looking for a broker to sponsor you. (Salesperson license educational requirements can be completed and the examination taken without broker sponsorship, but a salesperson must have a broker to work for before the license application is submitted.)

Training

Your next step is to look for those features and qualities in a broker that will complement, enhance, and encourage your personal development in real estate. If you are new to the industry, training and education will most likely be at the top of your list. Therefore, in looking for a broker you will want to find one that will in one fashion or another teach you the trade. (What you have learned to date from books, classes and license examination preparation will be helpful, but you will need additional specific training.) Real estate franchise operations and large brokerage offices usually offer extensive training. In smaller offices, the broker in charge is usually responsible for seeing that newcomers receive training. An office that offers no training to a newcomer should be avoided.

Compensation

Another question high on your list will be compensation. Very few offices provide a newcomer with a guaranteed minimum wage or even a draw against future commissions. Most brokers feel that one must produce to be paid and the hungrier the salesperson, the quicker he will produce. A broker who pays salespersons regardless of sales produced simply must siphon the money from those who are producing. The old saying, "There's no such thing as a free lunch" applies to sales commissions.

Compensation for salespersons is usually a percentage of the commissions they earn for the broker. How much each receives is open to negotiation between the broker and each salesperson working for him. A broker who offers his sales staff office space, extensive secretarial help, a large advertising budget, a mailing program, and generous long-distance telephone privileges might take 40% to 50% of each incoming commission dollar for office overhead. A broker who provides fewer services might take 25% or 30%.

Salespersons with proven sales records can usually reduce the portion of each commission dollar they earn that must go to the broker. This is because the broker feels that with an outstanding sales performer, a high volume of sales will offset a smaller house cut. Conversely, a new and untried salesperson, or one with a mediocre past sales record, may have to give up a larger portion of each dollar for the broker's overhead.

When one brokerage agency lists a property and another locates the buyer, the commission is split according to any agreement the two brokers wish to make. A common arrangement is a fifty-fifty split. After splitting, each broker pays a portion of the money he receives to the salesperson involved in accordance with his commission agreements. If the sale is through a multiple listing service, the MLS fee is deducted before brokers and salesmen are paid.

While investigating commission arrangements, one should also inquire about incentive and bonus plans, automobile expense reimbursement, health insurance, life insurance, and retirement plans.

An alternative commission arrangement is the **100% commission** wherein the salesperson does not share his commission with the broker. Instead the salesperson is charged for office space, advertising, telephone, multiple listing and any other expenses the broker incurs on behalf of the salesperson. Generally speaking, 100% arrangements are more popular with proven performers than with newcomers.

Broker Support

Broker support will have an impact on any salesperson's success. Specifically: Will you have your own desk to work from? Are office facilities efficient and modern? Does the broker provide secretarial services? What is the broker's advertising policy and who pays for ads? Does the broker have sources of secondary financing for clients? Does the broker allow his salespersons to invest in real estate? Does the broker have a good reputation in the community? Who pays for signs, business cards, franchise fees, and realty board dues?

Finding a Broker

Many salespersons associate with a particular broker as a result of a friendship or word-of-mouth information. However, there are other ways to find a suitable position. An excellent way to start your search is to decide what geographical area you want to work in. With higher gasoline prices, location becomes a very important factor in selecting a broker. Moreover, a salesperson who works in the same community or neighborhood in which he lives will already possess a valuable sense and feel for that area.

Having selected a geographical area to specialize in, look in the Sunday newspaper real estate advertisements section and the telephone book Yellow Pages for names of brokers. Plan to interview with several brokers and as you do, remember that you are interviewing them just as intensively as they are interviewing you. At your visits with brokers be particularly alert for your feelings. Intuition can be as valuable a guide to a sound working relationship as can a list of questions and answers regarding the job.

As you narrow your choices, revisit the offices of brokers who particularly impressed you. Talk with some of the salespersons who have worked or are working there. They can be very candid and valuable sources of information. Be wary of individuals who are extreme in their opinions: rely instead on the consensus of opinion. Locate clients who have used the firm's services and ask them their opinions of the firm. You might also talk to local appraisers, lenders, and escrow agents for candid opinions. If you do all this advance work, the benefits to you will be greater enjoyment of your work, more money in your pocket, and less likelihood of wanting to quit or move to another office.

Employment Contract

Having selected a broker with whom to associate, your next step is to make an employment contract. An **employment contract** formalizes the working arrangement between the broker and his salespersons. An oral contract may be satisfactory, but a written one is preferred because it sets forth the relationship with a higher degree of precision. This greatly reduces the potential for future controversy and litigation.

The employment contract will cover such matters as compensation (how much and under what circumstances), training (how often and if required), hours of work (including assigned office hours and open houses), company identification (distinctive articles of clothing and name tags), fees and dues (license and realty board), expenses (automobile, advertising, telephone), fringe benefits (health and life insurance, pension and profit-sharing plans), withholding (income taxes and social security), territory (assigned area of the community), termination of employment (quitting and firing), and general office policies and procedures (office manual).

INDEPENDENT CONTRACTOR ISSUE

Is a real estate salesperson an employee of the broker or an independent contractor? At issue is the federal tax status of salespersons (whether licensed as salesmen or brokers) who work for real estate firms. If an employee, the firm is required to withold income taxes and social security from the salesperson's commission checks. If an independent contractor, the salesperson is responsible for paying his/her own income taxes and social security.

The Internal Revenue Service (IRS) has favored employee status because it is easier to collect taxes from an employer than an employee and because the combined social security contributions of employee and employer is greater than that paid by a self-employed agent earning the same amount. Brokers prefer independent contractor status for their salespeople because the broker does not have the paperwork and responsibility of withholding taxes and does not have to pay social security taxes on the salesperson's earnings.

Brokers have argued that since salespersons work for commissions, not a salary, a salesperson is an independent contractor and should be treated as such by the IRS. The IRS has argued that the broker exerts enough control on its salespeople to qualify them as employees and therefore are subject to withholding.

The Tax Equity and Fiscal Responsibility Act of 1982 has resolved the question. Effective January 1, 1983, real estate salespersons will not be treated as employees for federal tax purposes if they meet all of the following three requirements. First, the salesperson must be a licensed real estate agent. Second, substantially all of the salesperson's payment for services as a real estate agent must be directly related to sales and not to hours worked. Third, a written agreement must exist between the salesperson and the firm stating that the salesperson will not be considered an employee for federal tax purposes. The agreement must also state that the salesperson is responsible for paying his/her own income taxes and social security contributions.

These are only highlights of the issue. If you plan to be

a real estate agent, you should consult an attorney regarding the specifics of your employment situation. You may, in fact, find it valuable to have your entire employment contract reviewed at the same time.

PROFESSIONAL REAL ESTATE ASSOCIATIONS

Even before laws required real estate agents to have licenses, there were professional real estate organizations. Called real estate boards, they joined together agents within a city or county on a voluntary basis. The push to organize came from real estate people who saw the need for some sort of controlling organization that could supervise the activities of individual agents and elevate the profession's status in the public's mind. Next came the gradual grouping of local boards into state associations, and finally, in 1908, the National Association of Real Estate Boards (NAREB) was formed. In 1914, NAREB developed a model license law that became the basis for real estate license laws in many states.

Today the local boards are still the fundamental units of the National Association of Realtors (NAR; the name was changed from NAREB on January 1, 1974). Local board membership is open to anyone holding a real estate license. Called boards of Realtors, real estate boards, and realty boards, they promote fair dealing among their members and with the public, and protect members from dishonest and irresponsible licensees. They also promote legislation that protects property rights, offer short seminars to keep members up to date with current laws and practices, and, in general, do whatever is necessary to build the dignity, stability, and professionalization of the industry. Local boards often operate the local multiple listing service, although in some communities it is a privately owned and operated business.

The Minnesota Association of Realtors is composed of the members of local boards plus salesmen and brokers who live in areas where no local board exists. The purposes of the state association are to unite members statewide, to encourage legislation that benefits and protects the real estate industry and safeguards the public in their real estate transactions, and to promote economic growth and development in the state. Also, the Minnesota Association of Realtors holds conventions to educate members and foster friendships among them, offers group insurance plans, and sponsors work–pleasure travel trips.

Realtor

The NAR is made up of local boards and state associations in the United States. The term **"Realtor"** is a copyrighted and registered term that belongs to NAR. Realtor is not synonymous with real estate agent. It is reserved for the exclusive use of members of the National Association of Realtors, who as part of their membership pledge themselves to abide by the Association's Code of Ethics. The term Realtor cannot be used by nonmembers and in Minnesota the unauthorized use of the term is a violation of the real estate law. Prior to 1974, the use of the term Realtor was primarily reserved for principal brokers. Then in November of that year, by a national membership vote, the decision was made to create an additional membership class, the **Realtor-Associate,** for salespersons working for member Realtors.

In the minds of many persons familiar with NAREB and later NAR, the single greatest contribution of the Association was the development of a strict code of ethics in the year 1913. Prior to that time, dealing with real estate agents was hazardous. Cutthroat competition prevailed, and the general spirit of the real estate business was "let the buyer beware." NAREB introduced a code of ethics that members agreed to abide by, and which it was hoped would generate public confidence and attract business to members.

Code of Ethics

The Code of Ethics has been revised several times since then and now contains 23 Articles that pertain to the Realtor's relation to his clients, to other real estate agents, and to the public as a whole. The full Code is reproduced in Figure 18:1.

Although a complete review of each article is beyond the scope of this chapter, it can be seen in the Code that some articles parallel existing laws. For example, Article 10 speaks against racial discrimination and Article 12 speaks for full disclosure. However, the bulk of the Code addresses itself to the obligations of a Realtor that are beyond the written law. For example, in Article 2, the Realtor agrees to keep himself informed regarding laws and regulations, proposed legislation, and current market conditions so that he may be in a position to advise his clients properly. In Article 5, the Realtor agrees to willingly share with other Realtors the lessons of his own experience. In other words, to be recognized as a Realtor, one must not only comply with the letter of the law, but also observe the ethical standards by which the industry operates.

Figure 18:1

Preamble . . .

Under all is the land. Upon its wise utilization and widely allocated ownership depend the survival and growth of free institutions and of our civilization. The REALTOR® should recognize that the interests of the nation and its citizens require the highest and best use of the land and the widest distribution of land ownership. They require the creation of adequate housing, the building of functioning cities, the development of productive industries and farms, and the preservation of a healthful environment.

Such interests impose obligations beyond those of ordinary commerce. They impose grave social responsibility and a patriotic duty to which the REALTOR® should dedicate himself, and for which he should be diligent in preparing himself. The REALTOR®, therefore, is zealous to maintain and improve the standards of his calling and shares with his fellow-REALTORS® a common responsibility for its integrity and honor. The term REALTOR® has come to connote competency, fairness, and high integrity resulting from adherence to a lofty ideal of moral conduct in business relations. No inducement of profit and no instruction from clients ever can justify departure from this ideal.

In the interpretation of his obligation, a REALTOR® can take no safer guide than that which has been handed down through the centuries, embodied in the Golden Rule, "Whatsoever ye would that men should do to you, do ye even so to them."

Accepting this standard as his own, every REALTOR® pledges himself to observe its spirit in all of his activities and to conduct his business in accordance with the tenets set forth below.

ARTICLE 1

The REALTOR® should keep himself informed on matters affecting real estate in his community, the state, and nation so that he may be able to contribute responsibly to public thinking on such matters.

ARTICLE 2

In justice to those who place their interests in his care, the REALTOR® should endeavor always to be informed regarding laws, proposed legislation, governmental regulations, public policies, and current market conditions in order to be in a position to advise his clients properly.

ARTICLE 3

It is the duty of the REALTOR® to protect the public against fraud, misrepresentation, and unethical practices in real estate transactions. He should endeavor to eliminate in his community any practices which could be damaging to the public or bring discredit to the real estate profession. The REALTOR® should assist the governmental agency charged with regulating the practices of brokers and salesmen in his state.

ARTICLE 4

The REALTOR® should seek no unfair advantage over other REALTORS® and should conduct his business so as to avoid controversies with other REALTORS®.

ARTICLE 5

In the best interests of society, of his associates, and his own business, the REALTOR® should willingly share with other REALTORS® the lessons of his experience and study for the benefit of the public, and should be loyal to the Board of REALTORS® of his community and active in its work.

ARTICLE 6

To prevent dissension and misunderstanding and to assure better service to the owner, the REALTOR® should urge the exclusive listing of property unless contrary to the best interest of the owner.

ARTICLE 7

In accepting employment as an agent, the REALTOR® pledges himself to protect and promote the interests of the client. This obligation of absolute fidelity to the client's interests is primary, but it does not relieve the REALTOR® of the obligation to treat fairly all parties to the transaction.

Figure 18:1 *continued*

ARTICLE 8

The REALTOR® shall not accept compensation from more than one party, even if permitted by law, without the full knowledge of all parties to the transaction.

ARTICLE 9

The REALTOR® shall avoid exaggeration, misrepresentation, or concealment of pertinent facts. He has an affirmative obligation to discover adverse factors that a reasonably competent and diligent investigation would disclose.

ARTICLE 10

The REALTOR® shall not deny equal professional services to any person for reasons of race, creed, sex, or country of national origin. The REALTOR® shall not be a party to any plan or agreement to discriminate against a person or persons on the basis of race, creed, sex, or country of national origin.

ARTICLE 11

A REALTOR® is expected to provide a level of competent service in keeping with the Standards of Practice in those fields in which the REALTOR® customarily engages.

The REALTOR® shall not undertake to provide specialized professional services concerning a type of property or service that is outside his field of competence unless he engages the assistance of one who is competent on such types of property or service, or unless the facts are fully disclosed to the client. Any person engaged to provide such assistance shall be so identified to the client and his contribution to the assignment should be set forth.

The REALTOR® shall refer to the Standards of Practice of the National Association as to the degree of competence that a client has a right to expect the REALTOR® to possess, taking into consideration the complexity of the problem, the availability of expert assistance, and the opportunities for experience available to the REALTOR®.

ARTICLE 12

The REALTOR® shall not undertake to provide professional services concerning a property or its value where he has a present or contemplated interest unless such interest is specifically disclosed to all affected parties.

ARTICLE 13

The REALTOR® shall not acquire an interest in or buy for himself, any member of his immediate family, his firm or any member thereof, or any entity in which he has a substantial ownership interest, property listed with him, without making the true position known to the listing owner. In selling property owned by himself, or in which he has any interest, the REALTOR® shall reveal the facts of his ownership or interest to the purchaser.

ARTICLE 14

In the event of a controversy between REALTORS® associated with different firms, arising out of their relationship as REALTORS®, the REALTORS® shall submit the dispute to arbitration in accordance with the regulations of their board or boards rather than litigate the matter.

ARTICLE 15

If a REALTOR® is charged with unethical practice or is asked to present evidence in any disciplinary proceeding or investigation, he shall place all pertinent facts before the proper tribunal of the member board or affiliated institute, society, or council of which he is a member.

ARTICLE 16

When acting as agent, the REALTOR® shall not accept any commission, rebate, or profit on expenditures made for his principal-owner, without the principal's knowledge and consent.

Figure 18:1 *continued*

ARTICLE 17

The REALTOR® shall not engage in activities that constitute the unauthorized practice of law and shall recommend that legal counsel be obtained when the interest of any party to the transaction requires it.

ARTICLE 18

The REALTOR® shall keep in a special account in an appropriate financial institution, separated from his own funds, monies coming into his possession in trust for other persons, such as escrows, trust funds, clients' monies, and other like items.

ARTICLE 19

The REALTOR® shall be careful at all times to present a true picture in his advertising and representations to the public. He shall neither advertise without disclosing his name nor permit any person associated with him to use individual names or telephone numbers, unless such person's connection with the REALTOR® is obvious in the advertisement.

ARTICLE 20

The REALTOR®, for the protection of all parties, shall see that financial obligations and commitments regarding real estate transactions are in writing, expressing the exact agreement of the parties. A copy of each agreement shall be furnished to each party upon his signing such agreement.

ARTICLE 21

The REALTOR® shall not engage in any practice or take any action inconsistent with the agency of another REALTOR®.

ARTICLE 22

In the sale of property which is exclusively listed with a REALTOR®, the REALTOR® shall utilize the services of other brokers upon mutually agreed upon terms when it is in the best interests of the client.

Negotiations concerning property which is listed exclusively shall be carried on with the listing broker, not with the owner, except with the consent of the listing broker.

ARTICLE 23

The REALTOR® shall not publicly disparage the business practice of a competitor nor volunteer an opinion of a competitor's transaction. If his opinion is sought and if the REALTOR® deems it appropriate to respond, such opinion shall be rendered with strict professional integrity and courtesy.

Where the word REALTOR® is used in this Code and Preamble, it shall be deemed to include REALTOR®-ASSOCIATE. Pronouns shall be considered to include REALTORS® and REALTOR®-ASSOCIATES of both genders.

The Code of Ethics was adopted in 1913. Amended at the Annual Convention in 1924, 1928, 1950, 1951, 1952, 1955, 1956, 1961, 1962, 1974 and 1982.

In some states, ethical standards such as those in the NAR Code of Ethics have been legislated into law. Called **canons,** their intent is to promote ethical practices by all brokers and salesmen, not just by those who join the National Association of Realtors.

In addition to its emphasis on real estate brokerage, the National Association of Realtors also contains a number of specialized professional groups within itself. These include the American Institute of Real Estate Appraisers, the Farm and Land Institute, the Institute of Real Estate Management, the Realtors National Marketing Institute, the Society of Industrial Realtors, the Real Estate Securities and Syndication Institute, the American Society of Real Estate Counselors, the American Chapter of the International Real Estate Federation, and the Women's Council of Realtors. Membership is open to Realtors interested in these specialties.

Realtist

The National Association of Real Estate Brokers, Inc. is a national trade association representing minority real estate professionals actively engaged in the industry. Its members have adopted the designation **Realtist** as their trade name and the organization extends through 14 regions across the country with more than 40 active local boards.

GRI Designation

To help encourage and recognize professionalism in the real estate industry, state Boards of Realtors sponsor education courses leading to the GRI designation. Course offerings typically include real estate law, finance, appraisal, investments, office management, and salesmanship. Upon completion of the prescribed curriculum, the designation, Graduate Realtor's Institute is awarded. GRI courses are offered under the guidance of the Minnesota Association of Realtors and satisfy the state's 90-hour education requirement.

Minnesota License Law Act

CHAPTER 82. REAL ESTATE BROKERS AND SALESPERSONS

82.17 Definitions

Subdivision 1. *For the purposes of this chapter the terms defined in this section have the meanings given to them.*

Subd. 2. *"Person" means a natural person, firm, partnership, corporation or association, and the officers, directors, employees and agents thereof.*

Subd. 3. *"Commissioner" means the commissioner of commerce or his designee.*

Subd. 4. *"Real estate broker" or "broker" means any person who:*

(a) *For another and for commission, fee or other valuable consideration or with the intention or expectation of receiving the same directly or indirectly lists, sells, exchanges, buys or rents, manages, or offers or attempts to negotiate a sale, option, exchange, purchase or rental of an interest or estate in real estate, or advertises or holds himself, herself, or itself out as engaged in these activities;*

(b) *For another and for commission, fee or other valuable consideration or with the intention or expectation of receiving the same directly or indirectly negotiates or offers or attempts to negotiate a loan, secured or to be secured by a mortgage or other encumbrance on real estate;*

(c) *For another and for commission, fee or other valuable consideration or with the intention or expectation of receiving the same directly or indirectly lists, sells, exchanges, buys, rents, manages, offers or attempts to negotiate a sale, option, exchange, purchase or rental of any business opportunity or business, or its goodwill, inventory, or fixtures, or any interest therein;*

(d) *For another and for commission, fee or other valuable consideration or with the intention or expectation of receiving the same directly or indirectly offers, sells or attempts to negotiate the sale of property that is subject to the registration requirements of chapter 83, concerning subdivided land;*

(e) *Engages in the business of charging an advance fee or contracting for collection of a fee in connection with any contract whereby he or she undertakes to promote the sale of real estate through its listing in a publication issued primarily for this purpose;*

(f) *Engages wholly or in part in the business of selling real estate to the extent that a pattern of real estate sales is established, whether or not the real estate is owned by such person. A person shall be presumed to be engaged in the business of selling real estate if the person engages as principal in five or more transactions during any 12 month period, unless represented by a licensed real estate broker or salesperson.*

Subd. 5. *"Real estate salesperson" means one who acts on behalf of a real estate broker in performing any act authorized by this chapter to be performed by the broker.*

Subd. 6. *"Trust account" means, for the purposes of this chapter, a demand deposit or checking account maintained for the purpose of segregating trust funds from other funds. A trust account shall not be an interest bearing account except by agreement of the parties and subject to rules of the commissioner, and shall not allow the financial institution a right to set off money owed it by the licensee.*

Subd. 7. *"Trust funds" means funds received by a broker or salesperson in a fiduciary capacity as a part of a real estate or business opportunity transaction, pending the consummation or termination of a transaction, and includes all down payments, earnest money deposits, rents for clients, tax and insurance escrow payments, damage deposits, and any funds received on behalf of any person.*

Subd. 8. *For purposes of sections 82.17 to 82.34, real estate shall also include, a manufactured home, when such manufactured home is affixed to land. Manufactured home means any factory built structure or structures equipped with the necessary service connections and made so as to be readily movable as a unit or units and designed to be used as a dwelling unit or units.*

Subd. 9. *"Public member" means a person who is not, or never was, a real estate broker or real estate salesperson or the spouse of such person, or a person who has no, or never has had a material financial interest in acting as a real estate broker or real estate salesperson or a directly related activity.*

82.18 Exceptions

Unless a person is licensed or otherwise required to be licensed under this chapter, the term real estate broker does not include:

(a) *A licensed practicing attorney acting solely as an incident to the practice of law, provided, however, that the attorney complies in all respects with the trust account provisions of this chapter;*

(b) *A receiver, trustee, administrator, guardian, executor, or other person appointed by or acting under the judgment or order of any court;*

(c) *Any person owning and operating a cemetery and selling lots therein solely for use as burial plots;*

(d) *Any custodian, janitor, or employee of the owner or manager of a residential building who leases residential units in the building;*

(e) *Any bank, trust company, savings and loan association, public utility, or any land mortgage or farm loan association organized under the laws of this state or the United States, when engaged in the transaction of business within the scope of its corporate powers as provided by law;*

(f) *Public officers while performing their official duties;*

(g) *Employees of persons enumerated in clauses (b), (e) and (f), when engaged in the specific performance of their duties;*

(h) *Any person who acts as an auctioneer bonded in conformity with section 330.02, when that person is engaged in the specific performance of his or her duties as an auctioneer;*

(i) *Any person who acquires such real estate for the purpose of engaging in and does engage in, or who is engaged in the business of constructing residential, commercial or industrial buildings for the purpose of resale, if no more than 25 such transactions occur in any 12 month period and the person complies with section 82.24;*

(j) *Any person who offers to sell or sells an interest or estate in real estate which is a security registered pursuant to chapter 80A, when acting solely as an incident to the sale of these securities;*

(k) *Any person who offers to sell or sells a business opportunity which is a franchise registered pursuant to chapter 80C, when acting solely to sell the franchise;*

(l) *Any person who contracts with or solicits on behalf of a provider a contract with a resident or prospective resident to provide continuing care in a facility, pursuant to the continuing care facility disclosure and rehabilitation act (chapter 80D), when acting solely as incident to the contract;*

(m) *Any broker-dealer or agent of a broker-dealer when participating in a transaction in which all or part of a business opportunity or business, including any interest therein, is conveyed or acquired pursuant to an asset purchase, merger, exchange of securities or other business combination, if the agent or broker-dealer is licensed pursuant to chapter 80A.*

82.19 Prohibitions

Subdivision 1. *No person shall act as a real estate broker or salesperson unless he is licensed as herein provided.*

Subd. 2. *No person shall advertise or represent himself to be a real estate broker or salesperson unless licensed as herein provided.*

Subd. 3. *No real estate broker or salesperson shall offer, pay or give, and no person shall accept, any compensation or other thing of value from any real estate broker or salesperson by way of commission-splitting, rebate, finder's fees or otherwise, in connection with any real estate or business opportunity transaction; provided this subdivision does not apply to transactions (1) between a licensed real estate broker or salesperson and the person by whom he is engaged to purchase or sell real estate or business opportunity, (2) among persons licensed as provided herein, and (3) between a licensed real estate broker or salesperson and persons from other jurisdictions similarly licensed in that jurisdiction.*

Subd. 4. *No real estate broker or salesperson shall engage or authorize any person, except one licensed as provided herein, to act as a real estate broker or salesperson on his behalf.*

82.20 Licensing requirements

Subdivision 1. Generally. (a) *The commissioner shall issue a license as a real estate broker or real estate salesperson to any person who qualifies for such license under the terms of this chapter:*

(b) *The commissioner is authorized to establish by rule a special license for real estate brokers and real estate salespersons engaged solely in the rental or management of an interest or estate in real estate, to prescribe qualifications for the license, and to issue the license consistent with the terms of this chapter. This clause shall not be construed to require those owners or managers or their agents or employees who are excluded by section 82.18, clause (d) from the definition of real estate broker, to obtain the special license.*

Subd. 2. Qualification of applicants. *Every applicant for a real estate broker or real estate salesperson license shall be at least 18 years of age at the time of making application for said license.*

Subd. 3. Application for license; contents. (a) *Every applicant for a license as a real estate broker or real estate salesperson shall make his application in writing upon forms prepared and furnished by the commissioner. Each application shall be signed* *and sworn to by the applicant and shall be accompanied by the license fee required by this chapter;*

(b) *Each application for a real estate broker license and real estate salesperson license shall contain such information as required by the commissioner consistent with the administration of the provisions and purposes of this chapter;*

(c) *Each application for a real estate salesperson license shall give the applicant's name, age, residence address and the name and place of business of the real estate broker on whose behalf said salesperson is to be acting;*

(d) *The commissioner may require such further information as he deems appropriate to administer the provisions and further the purposes of this chapter.*

Subd. 4. Corporate and partnership licenses. **(a)** *A corporation applying for a license shall have at least one officer individually licensed to act as broker for the corporation. The corporation broker's license shall extend no authority to act as broker to any person other than the corporate entity. Each officer who intends to act as a broker shall obtain a license;*

(b) *A partnership applying for a license shall have at least one partner individually licensed to act as broker for the partnership. Each partner who intends to act as a broker shall obtain a license;*

(c) *Applications for a license made by a corporation shall be verified by the president and secretary. Applications made by a partnership shall be verified by at least two partners;*

(d) *Any partner or officer who ceases to act as broker for a partnership or corporation shall notify the commissioner upon said termination. The individual licenses of all salespersons acting on behalf of a corporation or partnership, are automatically ineffective upon the revocation or suspension of the license of the partnership or corporation. The commissioner may suspend or revoke the license of an officer or partner without suspending or revoking the license of the corporation or partnership;*

(e) *The application of all officers of a corporation or partners in a partnership who intend to act as a broker on behalf of a corporation or partnership shall accompany the initial license application of the corporation or partnership. Officers or partners intending to act as brokers subsequent to the licensing of the corporation or partnership shall procure an individual real estate broker's license prior to acting in the capacity of a broker. No license as a real estate salesperson* *shall be issued to any officer of a corporation or member of a partnership to which a license was issued as a broker;*

(f) *The corporation or partnership applicant shall make available upon request, such records and data required by the commissioner for enforcement of this chapter.*

Subd. 5. Responsibility. *Each broker shall be responsible for the acts of any and all of his sales people while acting on his behalf as his agents. Each officer of a corporation or partner in a partnership licensed as a broker shall have the same responsibility under this chapter as a corporate or partnership broker with regard to the acts of the salespersons acting on behalf of the corporation or partnership.*

Subd. 6. Issuance of license; salesperson. *A salesperson must be licensed to act on behalf of a licensed broker and may not be licensed to act on behalf of more than one broker in this state during the same period of time. The license of each real estate salesperson shall be mailed to and remain in the possession of the licensed broker with whom he is or is to be associated until canceled or until such licensee leaves such broker.*

Subd. 7. Effective date of license. *Every license issued pursuant to this chapter shall expire on the June 30 next following the issuance of said license.*

Subd. 8. Renewals. (a) *Persons whose applications have been properly and timely filed who have not received notice of denial of renewal are deemed to have been approved for renewal and may continue to transact business either as a real estate broker or salesperson whether or not the renewed license has been received on or before July 1. Application for renewal of a license shall be deemed to have been timely filed if received by the commissioner on or before June 15 in each year. Applications for renewal shall be deemed properly filed if made upon forms duly executed and sworn to, accompanied by fees prescribed by this chapter and contain any information which the commissioner may require. An application mailed shall be deemed proper and timely received if addressed to the commissioner and postmarked prior to 12:01 A.M. on June 14;*

(b) *Persons who have failed to make a timely application for renewal of a license and who have not received the renewal license as of July 1, shall be unlicensed until such time as the license has been issued by the commissioner and is received.*

Subd. 9. Terminations; transfers. (a) *Except as pro-*

vided in paragraph (b), when a salesperson terminates his activity on behalf of a broker, the salesperson's license shall be ineffective. Within ten days of the termination the broker shall notify the commissioner in writing, and shall return to the commissioner the license of the salesperson. The salesperson may apply for transfer of the license to another broker at any time during the remainder of the license period, on forms provided by the commissioner. If the application for transfer qualifies, the commissioner shall grant the application. Upon receipt of a transfer application and payment of the transfer fee, the commissioner may issue a 45 day temporary license. If an application for transfer is not made within the license period, the commissioner shall require that an application for a new license be filed.

(b) *When a salesperson terminates his activity on behalf of a broker in order to begin association immediately with another broker, the commissioner shall permit the automatic transfer of the salesperson's license. The transfer shall be effective either upon the mailing of the required fee and the executed documents by certified mail or upon personal delivery of the fee and documents to the commissioner's office. The commissioner may adopt rules and prescribe forms as necessary to implement this paragraph.*

Subd. 10. Effect of suspension or revocation. *The license of a salesperson is not effective during any period for which the license of the broker on whose behalf he is acting is suspended or revoked. The salesperson may apply for transfer to some other licensed broker by complying with subdivision 9.*

Subd. 11. Notice. *Notice in writing shall be given to the commissioner by each licensee of any change in personal name, trade name, address or business location not later than ten days after such change. The commissioner shall issue a new license if required for the unexpired period.*

Subd. 12. Nonresidents. *A nonresident of Minnesota may be licensed as a real estate broker or real estate salesperson upon compliance with all provisions of this chapter.*

Subd. 13. Limited broker's license. *The commissioner shall have the authority to issue a limited real estate broker's license authorizing the licensee to engage in transactions as principal only. Such license shall be issued only after receipt of the application described in subdivision 3 and payment of the fee prescribed by section 82.21, subdivision 1. No salesperson may be licensed to act on behalf of an individual holding a limited broker's license. An officer of a* *corporation or partner of a partnership licensed as a limited broker may act on behalf of that corporation or partnership without being subject to the licensing requirements.*

Subd. 14. Licenses; extending duration. *Notwithstanding the provisions of subdivisions 7 and 8, the commissioner may institute a system by rule pursuant to chapter 14 to provide three year licenses from the date of issuance for any license prescribed by this section.*

82.21 Fees

Subdivision 1. Amounts. *The following fees shall be paid to the commissioner:*

(a) *A fee of $50 for each initial individual broker's license, and a fee of $25 for each annual renewal thereof;*

(b) *A fee of $25 for each initial salesperson's license, and a fee of $10 for each annual renewal thereof;*

(c) *A fee of $50 for each initial corporate or partnership license, and a fee of $25 for each annual renewal thereof;*

(d) *A fee not to exceed $40 per year for payment to the education, research and recovery fund in accordance with section 82.34;*

(e) *A fee of $10 for each transfer.*

Subd. 2. Forfeiture. *All fees shall be retained by the commissioner and shall be nonreturnable, except that an overpayment of any fee shall be the subject of a refund upon proper application.*

Subd. 3. Deposit of fees. *Unless otherwise provided by this chapter, all fees collected under this chapter shall be deposited in the state treasury.*

82.22 Examinations

Subdivision 1. Generally. *Each applicant for a license must pass an examination conducted by the commissioner. The examinations shall be of sufficient scope to establish the competency of the applicant to act as a real estate broker or as a real estate salesperson.*

Subd. 2. Broker's examination. (a) *The examination for a real estate broker's license shall be more exacting than that for a real estate salesperson, and shall require a higher degree of knowledge of the fundamentals of real estate practice and law.*

(b) *Every application for a broker's examination shall be accompanied by proof that the applicant has had a minimum of two years of actual experience as a licensed real estate salesperson in this or in another state having comparable requirements or is, in the opinion* *of the commissioner, otherwise or similarly qualified by reason of education or practical experience. An applicant for a limited broker's license pursuant to section 82.20, subdivision 13, shall not be required to have a minimum of two years of actual experience as a real estate person in order to obtain a limited broker's license to act as principal only.*

Subd. 3. Re-examinations. *An examination may be required before the renewal of any license which has been suspended, or before the issuance of a license to any person whose license has been ineffective for a period of one year, except no re-examination shall be required of any individual who has failed to cause renewal of an existing license because of absence from the state while on active duty with the armed services of the United States of America.*

Subd. 4. Examination frequency. *The commissioner shall hold examinations at such times and places as he may determine, except that said examinations will be held at least every 45 days.*

Subd. 5. Period for application. *An applicant who obtains an acceptable score on a salesperson's examination must file an application for the license within one year of the date of successful completion of the examination or a second examination must be taken to qualify for the license.*

Subd. 6. Instruction; new licenses. (a) *Every salesperson, licensed after July 1, 1973 and before July 1, 1976 shall, within two years of the date his license was first granted be required to successfully complete a course of study in the real estate field consisting of not less than 60 hours of instruction, approved by the commissioner. Upon appropriate showing of hardship by the licensee, or for persons licensed pursuant to section 82.20, subdivision 1, clause (b), the commissioner may waive or modify the requirements of this subdivision. Every salesperson licensed after July 1, 1976 and before July 1, 1978 shall, within three years of the date his license was first issued, be required to successfully complete a course of study in the real estate field consisting of not less than 90 hours of instruction, approved by the commissioner;*

(b) *After July 1, 1978, and before January 1, 1984, every applicant for a salesperson's license shall be required to successfully complete a course of study in the real estate field consisting of 30 hours of instruction approved by the commissioner before taking the examination specified in subdivision 1. Every salesperson licensed after July 1, 1978, and before January 1, 1984, shall, within one year of the date his license was first issued, be required to successfully* *complete a course of study in the real estate field consisting of 60 hours of instruction approved by the commissioner.*

(c) *After December 31, 1983, every applicant for a salesperson's license shall be required to successfully complete a course of study in the real estate field consisting of 30 hours of instruction approved by the commissioner before taking the examination specified in subdivision 1. After December 31, 1983, every applicant for a salesperson's license shall be required to successfully complete an additional course of study in the real estate field consisting of 30 hours of instruction approved by the commissioner before filing an application for the license. Every salesperson licensed after December 31, 1983, shall, within one year of the date his license was first issued, be required to successfully complete a course of study in the real estate field consisting of 30 hours of instruction approved by the commissioner.*

(d) *The commissioner may approve courses of study in the real estate field offered in educational institutions of higher learning in this state or courses of study in the real estate field developed by and offered under the auspices of the national association of realtors, its affiliates, or private real estate schools licensed by the state department of education. The commissioner may by rule prescribe the curriculum and qualification of those employed as instructors.*

Subd. 7. Instruction; licensees subsequent to July 1, 1969. *Every salesperson licensed prior to July 1, 1973, but subsequent to July 1, 1969, within two years of the date his license was first granted, shall be required to successfully complete a course of study in the real estate field consisting of not less than 30 hours of instruction, approved by the commissioner. Upon the failure of a licensee covered by this subdivision to complete the required 30 hours of instruction, the licensee must pass a second examination more difficult in degree than the one required for granting of his salesman's license.*

Subd. 8. Duration. *No renewal of a salesperson's license shall be effective beyond a date two years after the granting of such salesperson's license unless the salesperson has furnished evidence of compliance with either subdivision 6 or 7. The commissioner shall cancel the license of any salesperson who fails to comply with subdivision 6 or 7.*

Subd. 9. Application. *Subdivisions 6 to 8 shall not apply to salespersons licensed in Minnesota prior to July 1, 1969.*

Subd. 10. Renewal; examination. *Except as provided in subdivisions 3 and 7, no examination shall be required for the renewal of any license, provided, however, any licensee having been* *licensed as a broker or salesperson in the state of Minnesota and who shall fail to renew the license for a period of one year shall be required by the commissioner to again take an examination.*

Subd. 11. Examination eligibility; revocation. *No applicant shall be eligible to take any examination if his license as a real estate broker or salesperson has been revoked in this or any other state within two years of the date of the application.*

Subd. 12. Reciprocity. *The requirements of this section may be waived for individuals of other jurisdictions, provided: (1) a written reciprocal licensing agreement is in effect between the commissioner and the licensing officials of that jurisdiction, (2) the individual is licensed in that jurisdiction, and (3) the licensing requirements of that jurisdiction are substantially similar to the provisions of this chapter.*

Subd. 13. Continuing education. (a) *After July 1, 1978, all real estate salespersons not subject to or who have completed the educational requirements contained in subdivision 6 and all real estate brokers shall be required to successfully complete 45 hours of real estate education, either as a student or a lecturer, in courses of study approved by the commissioner, within three years after their annual renewal date.*

(b) *For the purposes of administration, the commissioner shall classify by lot, the real estate brokers and salespersons subject to (a) above, in three classifications of substantially equal size. The first class shall complete 15 hours of approved real estate study between July 1, 1978 and June 30, 1979 inclusive. The second class shall complete 30 hours of approved real estate study between the dates of July 1, 1978 and June 30, 1980 inclusive. The third class shall complete 45 hours of approved real estate study between the dates of July 1, 1978 and June 30, 1981. After the first period, each class shall complete the prescribed educational requirements during successive three year periods.*

(c) *The commissioner shall adopt rules defining the standards for course and instructor approval, and may adopt rules for the proper administration of this subdivision.*

82.23 Broker's records

Subdivision 1. Retention. *A licensed real estate broker shall retain for three years copies of all listings, deposit receipts, purchase money contracts, cancelled checks, trust account records, and such other documents as may reasonably be related to carrying on* *a real estate brokerage business. The retention period shall run from the date of the closing of the transaction, or from the date of the listing if the transaction is not consummated.*

Subd. 2. Delivery. *Each real estate broker or real estate salesperson shall furnish parties to a transaction a true and accurate copy of any document pertaining to their interests as the commissioner through appropriate rules may require.*

Subd. 3. Examination of records. *The commissioner may make examinations within or without this state of each broker's records at such reasonable time and in such scope as is necessary to enforce the provisions of this chapter.*

82.24 Trust account requirements

Subdivision 1. Generally. *All trust funds received by a broker or his salespersons shall be deposited forthwith upon receipt in a trust account, maintained by the broker for such purpose in a bank designated by the broker, except as such moneys may be paid to one of the parties pursuant to express written agreement between the parties to a transaction. The depository bank shall be a Minnesota bank or trust company or any foreign bank and shall authorize the commissioner to examine its records of such deposits upon demand by the commissioner.*

Subd. 2. Licensee acting as principal. *Any licensed real estate broker or salesperson acting in the capacity of principal in the sale of interests in real estate owned by him shall deposit in a Minnesota bank or trust company, or any foreign bank which authorizes the commissioner to examine its records of such deposits, in a trust account, those parts of all payments received on contracts which are necessary to meet any amounts concurrently due and payable on any existing mortgages, contracts for deed or other conveyancing instruments, and reserve for taxes and insurance or any other encumbrance on such receipts. Such deposits shall be maintained until disbursement is made under the terms of the encumbrance pertaining thereto and proper accounting on such property made to the parties entitled thereto.*

Subd. 3. Nondepositable items. *Any instrument or equity or thing of value received by a broker or salesperson in lieu of cash as earnest money or down payment in a real estate transaction shall be held by an authorized escrow agent, whose authority is evidenced by a written agreement executed by the offeror and the escrow agent.*

Subd. 4. Commingling funds. *A broker or salesperson shall deposit only trust funds in a trust account and shall not commingle personal funds or other funds in a trust account, except that a broker or salesperson may deposit and maintain a sum not to exceed $100 in a trust account from his personal funds, which sum shall be specifically identified and used to pay service charges relating to the trust account.*

Subd. 5. Trust account records. *Each broker shall maintain and retain records of all trust funds and trust accounts. The commissioner may prescribe information to be included in the records by appropriate rules and regulations.*

Subd. 6. Notice of trust account status. *The names of the banks and the trust account numbers used by a broker shall be provided to the commissioner at the time of application for the broker's license. The broker shall immediately report to the commissioner any change of trust account status including changes in banks, account numbers, or additional accounts in the same or other banks. A broker shall not close an existing trust account without giving ten days written notice to the commissioner.*

Subd. 7. Interest bearing accounts. *Notwithstanding the provisions of sections 82.17 to 82.31, a real estate broker may establish and maintain interest bearing accounts for the purpose of receiving deposits in accordance with the provisions of section 504.20.*

82.25 Investigation and subpoenas

Subdivision 1. *When it appears by reasonable evidence that any provision of this chapter or any rule or order hereunder has been violated or is about to be violated, the commissioner may make necessary public or private investigations within or outside this state to aid in the enforcement of this chapter. The commissioner may also make necessary investigation incident to the promulgation of rules hereunder.*

Subd. 2. *The commissioner may require or permit any person to file a statement in writing, under oath or otherwise as the commissioner determines, as to all the facts and circumstances concerning the matter to be investigated.*

Subd. 3. *For the purpose of any investigation hearing or proceeding under this chapter, the commissioner or any person designated by him may administer oaths or affirmations, and may subpoena witnesses, compel their attendance, take evidence, and compel the pro-*

duction of documents or other tangible items which the commissioner deems relevant or material to the inquiry.

Subd. 4. *Upon failure to obey a subpoena or to answer questions propounded by the investigating officer and upon reasonable notice to all persons affected thereby, the commissioner may apply to the district court for an order for contempt.*

82.26 Legal actions; injunctions

Whenever it appears to the commissioner that any person has engaged or is about to engage in any act or practice constituting a violation of this chapter or any rule or order hereunder, he may bring an action in the name of the state in the district court of the appropriate county to enjoin the acts or practices and to enforce compliance with this chapter or any rule or order hereunder, or he may refer the matter to the attorney general. Upon a proper showing, a permanent or temporary injunction, restraining order, or other appropriate relief shall be granted.

82.27 Denial, suspension and revocation of licenses

Subdivision 1. *The commissioner may by order deny, suspend or revoke any license or may censure a licensee if he finds (1) that the order is in the public interest, and (2) that the applicant or licensee or, in the case of a broker, any officer, director, partner, employee or agent or any person occupying a similar status or performing similar functions, or any person directly or indirectly controlling the broker or controlled by the broker:*

(a) *Has filed an application for a license which is incomplete in any material respect or contains any statement which, in light of the circumstances under which it is made, is false or misleading with respect to any material fact;*

(b) *Has engaged in a fraudulent, deceptive or dishonest practice;*

(c) *Is permanently or temporarily enjoined by any court of competent jurisdiction from engaging in or continuing any conduct or practice involving any aspect of the real estate business;*

(d) *Has failed to reasonably supervise his brokers or salesperson so as to cause injury or harm to the public; or*

(e) *Has violated or failed to comply with any provision of this chapter or any rule or order under this chapter.*

Subd. 2. *The commissioner may promulgate rules and regulations further specifying and defining those actions and omissions which* *constitute fraudulent, deceptive or dishonest practices, and establishing standards of conduct for real estate brokers and salespersons.*

Subd. 3. *The commissioner shall issue an order requiring a licensee or applicant for a license to show cause why the license should not be revoked or suspended, or the licensee censured, or the application denied. The order shall be calculated to give reasonable notice of the time and place for hearing thereon, and shall state the reasons for the entry of the order. The commissioner may by order summarily suspend a license pending final determination of any order to show cause. If a license is suspended pending final determination of an order to show cause, a hearing on the merits shall be held within 30 days of the issuance of the order of suspension. All hearings shall be conducted in accordance with the provisions of chapter 14. After the hearing, the commissioner shall enter an order making such disposition of the matter as the facts require. If the licensee or applicant fails to appear at a hearing of which he has been duly notified, such person shall be deemed in default, and the proceeding may be determined against him upon consideration of the order to show cause, the allegations of which may be deemed to be true.*

Subd. 4. *The commissioner may delegate to a hearing examiner his authority to conduct a hearing. The examiner shall make proposed findings of fact and submit them to the commissioner. The examiner shall have the same power as the commissioner to compel the attendance of witnesses, to examine them under oath, to require the production of books, papers and other evidence, and to issue subpoenas and cause the same to be served and executed in any part of the state.*

Subd. 5. *Orders of the commissioner shall be subject to judicial review pursuant to chapter 14.*

Subd. 6. *The commissioner may promulgate rules of procedure concerning all hearings and other proceedings conducted pursuant to this chapter.*

82.28 Rule making powers

The commissioner may promulgate such rules and regulations as are reasonably necessary to carry out and make effective the provisions and purposes of this chapter.

82.29 Publication of information

The commissioner may publish by newspaper, news letter or otherwise information to assist in the administration of sections 82.17 to 82.34, or to educate and protect the public regarding fraudulent, deceptive or dishonest practices. The commissioner may also publish materials for the benefit of license applicants.

82.30 Advisory council

Subdivision 1. *There shall be a real estate advisory council of seven members to be appointed by the commissioner of securities. Five members shall be real estate brokers with at least five years experience as licensed real estate brokers in Minnesota and two members shall be public members. They shall meet at the call of the commissioner on a quarterly basis at publicized sessions and at such other times as the commissioner may deem necessary and advise and consult with him on all matters relating to education of licensees, prelicensing requirements, and such other major policy matters relating to the administration of sections 82.17 to 82.34. The council shall expire and the terms, compensation, and removal of members shall be as provided in section 15.059. No member of the real estate advisory council may establish, own, operate, invest in a course designed to fulfill any requirement of Minnesota law pertaining to licenses for real estate sales persons or brokers.*

82.31 Nonresident service of process

Subdivision 1. *Every nonresident, before being licensed as a real estate broker or real estate salesman, shall appoint the commissioner and his successor or successors in office as true and lawful attorney, upon whom may be served all legal process in any action or proceedings against such person, or in which such person may be a party, in relation to or involving any transaction covered by this chapter or any rule or order hereunder, which appointment shall be irrevocable. Service upon such attorney shall be as valid and binding as if due and personal service had been made upon such person. Any such appointment shall be effective upon the issuance of the license in connection with which the appointment was filed.*

Subd. 2. *The commission of any act which constitutes a violation of this chapter or rule or order hereunder by any nonresident person who has not theretofore appointed the commissioner his attorney in compliance with subdivision 1 shall be conclusively deemed an irrevocable appointment by such person of the commissioner and his successor or successors in any action or proceedings against him or in which he may be a party in relation to or involving such violation; and such violation shall be a signification of his agreement that all* *such legal process which is so served shall be as valid and binding upon him as if due and personal service thereof had been made upon him.*

Subd. 3. *Service of process under this section may be made by filing a copy of the process with the commissioner or his representative, but is not effective unless:*

(a) *The plaintiff, who may be the commissioner in an action or proceeding instituted by him, sends notice of the service and a copy of the process by certified mail to the defendant or respondent at his address as shown by the records at the office of the commissioner in the case of service made on the commissioner as attorney pursuant to appointment in compliance with subdivision 1, and at his last known address in the case of service on the commissioner as attorney pursuant to appointment by virtue of subdivision 2; and*

(b) *The plaintiff's affidavit of compliance with this subdivision is filed in the action or proceeding on or before the return day of the process, if any, or within such further time as the court or hearing examiner allows.*

82.32–Penalty

Any person who violates any provision of this chapter, or any rule or order of the commissioner, shall be guilty of a gross misdemeanor.

82.33 Civil actions

Subdivision 1. *No person shall bring or maintain any action in the courts of this state for the collection of compensation for the performance of any of the acts for which a license is required under this chapter without alleging and proving that he was a duly licensed real estate broker or salesperson at the time the alleged cause of action arose.*

Subd. 2. *No person required by this chapter to be licensed shall bring or maintain any action in the courts for any commission, fee or other compensation with respect to the sale, lease or other disposition or conveyance of real property, or with respect to the negotiation or attempt to negotiate any sale, lease or other disposition or conveyance of real property unless such property was first listed in writing for sale, lease or other disposition with the person bringing or maintaining the action.*

82.34 Real estate education, research and recovery fund

Subdivision 1. *There is established a "real estate education, research and recovery fund" to be administered by the commissioner of securities. The state treasurer shall be the custodian of the fund and shall operate under the direction of the commissioner.*

Subd. 2. *There is hereby created in the state treasury a real estate education, research and recovery fund which shall be administered by the commissioner in the manner and for the purposes prescribed in this section.*

Subd. 3. *Each real estate broker and real estate salesperson entitled under this chapter to renew his license, when renewing for the first time after July 1, 1973, shall pay in addition to the appropriate renewal fee a further fee of $20 which shall be credited to the real estate education, research and recovery fund. Any person who receives a new real estate broker's or real estate salesperson's license after July 1, 1973 shall pay said fee of $20 in addition to all other fees payable, provided that in no case shall any real estate broker or real estate salesperson be required under this subdivision to pay said fee of $20 more than once. The one time fee shall increase to $40 for any person who receives a new real estate broker's or real estate salesperson's license after July 1, 1980. In addition each real estate broker or real estate salesperson when renewing his license after July 1, 1980, shall each time pay a fee of $5 to be credited to the real estate education, research and recovery fund.*

Subd. 4. *If at the end of any fiscal year prior to calendar year 1981 following the establishment of the real estate education, research and recovery fund, the amount remaining in the fund is less than $200,000, every licensed real estate broker and real estate salesperson, when renewing his license, shall pay in addition to the annual renewal fee, a sum not to exceed $20 said sum having been determined by the commissioner to be sufficient to restore the balance in the fund to at least $200,000.*

Commencing with calendar year 1981, not to exceed $400,000 of the fund shall be available for recovery purposes to satisfy all claims authorized for payment each calendar year. This shall be designated as the recovery portion of the fund. Commencing in calendar year 1981, if the amount remaining in the fund after payment of all amounts authorized during the preceding calendar year for payment to claimants is less than $400,000 plus the amount appropriated pursuant to subdivision 6, every licensed real estate broker and real estate salesperson, when renewing his license, shall pay, in addition *to the annual renewal fee and the $5 fee set forth in subdivision 3, a sum not to exceed $35, said sum having been reasonably determined by the commissioner to be necessary to restore the balance in the fund.*

Subd. 5. *Any funds shall, upon request of the commissioner, be invested by the state board of investment in the class of securities specified in section 11A.24 and acts amendatory thereto. All interest and profits from such investments shall be credited to the real estate education, research and recovery fund. The state treasurer shall be the custodian of securities purchased under the provisions of this section.*

Subd. 6. *The commissioner may expend moneys as appropriated for the following purposes:*

(a) *To promote the advancement of education and research in the field of real estate for the benefit of those licensed under this chapter;*

(b) *To underwrite educational seminars and other forms of educational projects for the benefit of real estate licensees;*

(c) *To establish a real estate chair or courses at Minnesota state institutions of higher learning for the purpose of making such courses available to licensees and the general public;*

(d) *To contract for a particular educational or research project in the field of real estate to further the purposes of this chapter;*

(e) *To pay the costs of the real estate advisory council established under section 82.30;*

(f) *To pay any reasonable costs and disbursements, excluding attorney's fees, incurred in defending actions against the real estate education, research and recovery fund including the cost of mailing or publication of notice pursuant to subdivisions 12 and 14.*

Subd. 7. *When any aggrieved person obtains a final judgment in any court of competent jurisdiction against any person licensed under this chapter, on grounds of fraudulent, deceptive or dishonest practices, or conversion of trust funds arising directly out of any transaction when the judgment debtor was licensed and performed acts for which a license is required under this chapter, or performed acts permitted by section 327.55, subdivision 1a, and which cause of action occurred on or after July 1, 1973, the aggrieved person may, upon the judgment becoming final, and upon termination of all proceedings, including reviews and appeals, file a verified application in the court in which the judgment was entered for an order directing payment out of the recovery portion of the fund of the amount of actual and direct out of pocket loss in such transaction, but excluding* *interest on the loss and on any judgment obtained as a result of such loss, up to the sum of $20,000 of the amount unpaid upon the judgment, provided that nothing in this chapter shall be construed to obligate the fund for more than $20,000 per transaction, subject to the limitations set forth in subdivisions 12 and 14, regardless of the number of persons aggrieved or parcels of real estate involved in such transaction. A copy of the verified application shall be served upon the commissioner and upon the judgment debtor, and a certificate or affidavit of such service filed with the court.*

20,000 per transaction

Subd. 8. *The court shall conduct a hearing upon such application 30 days after service of the application upon the commissioner. Upon petition of the commissioner, the court shall continue the hearing up to 60 days further; and upon a showing of good cause may continue the hearing for such further period as the court deems appropriate. At the hearing the aggrieved person shall be required to show that:*

(a) *He is not a spouse of debtor, or the personal representative of such spouse;*

(b) *He has complied with all the requirements of this section;*

(c) *He has obtained a judgment as set out in subdivision 7, stating the amount thereof and the amount owing thereon at the date of the application;*

(d) *He has made all reasonable searches and inquiries to ascertain whether the judgment debtor is possessed of real or personal property or other assets, liable to be sold or applied in satisfaction of the judgment;*

(e) *By such search he has discovered no personal or real property or other assets liable to be sold or applied, or that he has discovered certain of them, describing them, owned by the judgment debtor and liable to be so applied, and that he has taken all necessary action and proceedings for the realization thereof, and that the amount thereby realized was insufficient to satisfy the judgment, stating the amount so realized and the balance remaining due on the judgment after application of the amount realized;*

(f) *He has diligently pursued his remedies against all the judgment debtors and all other persons liable to him in the transaction for which he seeks recovery from the real estate education, research and recovery fund;*

(g) *He is making said application no more than one year after the judgment becomes final, or no more than one year after the termination of any review or appeal of the judgment.*

Subd. 9. *Whenever the court proceeds upon an application* *as set forth in subdivision 7, it shall order payment out of the recovery portion of the fund only upon a determination that the aggrieved party has a valid cause of action within the purview of subdivision 7 and has complied with the provisions of subdivision 8. The judgment shall be only prima facie evidence of such cause of action and for the purposes of this section shall not be conclusive. The commissioner may defend any such action on behalf of the fund and shall have recourse to all appropriate means of defense and review including examination of witnesses. The commissioner may move the court at any time to dismiss the application when it appears there are not triable issues and the petition is without merit. The motion may be supported by affidavit of any person or persons having knowledge of the facts, and may be made on the basis that the petition, and the judgment referred to therein, does not form the basis for a meritorious recovery claim within the purview of subdivision 7; provided, however, the commissioner shall give written notice at least ten days before such motion. The commissioner may, subject to court approval, compromise a claim based upon the application of an aggrieved party. He shall not be bound by any prior compromise or stipulation of the judgment debtor.*

Subd. 10. *The commissioner may defend any such action on behalf of the fund and shall have recourse to all appropriate means of defense and review, including examination of witnesses. The judgment debtor may defend any such action on his own behalf and shall have recourse to all appropriate means of defense and review, including examination of witnesses. Whenever an applicant's judgment is by default, stipulation, or consent, or whenever the action against the licensee was defended by a trustee in bankruptcy, the applicant shall have the burden of proving his cause of action for fraudulent, deceptive or dishonest practices, or conversion of trust funds. Otherwise, the judgment shall create a rebuttable presumption of the fraudulent, deceptive or dishonest practices, or conversion of trust funds. This presumption is a presumption affecting the burden of producing evidence.*

Subd. 11. *If the court finds after the hearing that said claim should be levied against the recovery portion of the fund, the court shall enter an order directed to the commissioner requiring payment from the recovery portion of the fund of whatever sum it shall find to be payable upon the claim pursuant to the provisions of and in accordance with the limitations contained in this section.*

Subd. 12. **(a)** *Notwithstanding any other provision of this* *section, the liability of the recovery portion of the fund to all persons for losses shall not exceed $25,000 for any one licensee;*

(b) *If the $25,000 liability of the recovery portion of the fund is insufficient to pay in full the valid claims of all aggrieved persons by whom claims have been filed against any one licensee, such $25,000 shall be distributed among them in the ratio that their respective claims bear to the aggregate of such valid claims or in such other manner as the court deems equitable. Distribution of such moneys shall be among the persons entitled to share therein, without regard to the order of priority in which their respective judgments may have been obtained or their claims have been filed. Upon petition of the commissioner, the court may require all claimants and prospective claimants against one licensee to be joined in one action, to the end that the respective rights of all such claimants to the recovery portion of the fund may be equitably adjudicated and settled.*

Subd. 13. *Should the commissioner pay from the recovery portion of the fund any amount in settlement of a claim or toward satisfaction of a judgment against a licensed broker or salesperson, the license of the broker or salesperson shall be automatically suspended upon the effective date of an order by the court as set forth herein authorizing payment from the recovery portion of the fund. No such broker or salesperson shall be granted reinstatement until he has repaid in full, plus interest at the rate of 12 percent a year, twice the amount paid from the recovery portion of the fund on his account, and has obtained a surety bond issued by an insurer authorized to transact business in this state in the amount of $40,000. The bond shall be filed with the commissioner, with the state of Minnesota as obligee, conditioned for the prompt payment to any aggrieved person entitled thereto, of any amounts received by the real estate broker or salesperson or to protect any aggrieved person from loss resulting from fraudulent, deceptive or dishonest practices or conversion of trust funds arising out of any transaction when the real estate broker or salesperson was licensed and performed acts for which a license is required under this chapter. The bond shall remain operative for as long as that real estate broker or salesperson is licensed. No payment shall be made from the recovery portion of the fund based upon claims against any broker or salesperson who is granted reinstatement pursuant to this subdivision. A discharge in bankruptcy shall not relieve a person from the penalties and disabilities provided in this section.*

Subd. 14. *The commissioner shall satisfy all claims against licensees for which an order pursuant to subdivision 11 directing* *payment from the recovery portion of the fund has become final during the calendar year. Each claim shall be satisfied by the commissioner in not less than 30 and not more than 90 days following the end of the calendar year in which the order directing payment of the claim becomes final, commencing with calendar year 1981. If, at the end of any calendar year, the commissioner determines that the courts have issued orders that have become final during the year directing payment out of the recovery portion of the fund in a total amount in excess of $400,000, the commissioner shall allocate the $400,000 available for recovery purposes among all claimants in the ratio that the amount ordered paid to each claimant bears to the aggregate of all amounts ordered paid. The commissioner shall mail notice of the allocation to all claimants not less than 45 days following the end of the calendar year. Any claimant who objects to the plan of allocation shall file a petition in the district court of Ramsey or Hennepin County within 20 days of the mailing of notice setting forth the grounds for objection. Upon motion of the commissioner the court shall summarily dismiss the petition and order distribution in accordance with the proposed plan of allocation unless it finds substantial reason to believe that the distribution would be in violation of the provisions of this section. If a petition is filed, no distribution shall be made except in accordance with a final order of the court. In the event no petition is filed within 20 days of the mailing of notice, the commissioner shall make a distribution in accordance with the plan of allocation. Any distribution made by the commissioner in accordance with this subdivision shall be deemed to satisfy and extinguish the claims of any claimant receiving a distribution against the recovery portion of the fund.*

Subd. 15. *Any sums received by the commissioner pursuant to any provisions of this section shall be deposited in the state treasury, and credited to the real estate education, research and recovery fund, and said sums shall be allocated exclusively for the purposes provided in this section. All moneys in the fund are appropriated annually to the commissioner for the purposes of this section.*

Subd. 16. *It shall be unlawful for any person or the agent of any person to knowingly file with the commissioner any notice, statement, or other document required under the provisions of this section which is false or untrue or contains any material misstatement of fact. Such conduct shall constitute a gross misdemeanor.*

Subd. 17. *When, upon the order of the court, the commissioner has paid from the recovery portion of the fund any sum to the judgment* *creditor, the commissioner shall be subrogated to all of the rights of the judgment creditor to the extent of the amount so paid and the judgment creditor shall assign all his right, title and interest in the judgment to the extent of the amount so paid to the commissioner and any amount and interest so recovered by the commissioner on the judgment shall be deposited to the fund.*

Subd. 18. *Nothing contained in this section shall limit the authority of the commissioner to take disciplinary action against any licensee under other provisions of this chapter; nor shall the repayment in full of all obligations to the recovery portion of the fund by any licensee nullify or modify the effect of any other disciplinary proceeding brought pursuant to the provisions of this chapter.*

Subd. 19. *The commissioner shall include in the annual report of the commerce commission pursuant to section 45.033, a report on the activities of the real estate education, research and recovery fund; noting the amount of money received by the fund, the amount of money expended and the purposes therefor.*

Subd. 20. *Claims for which orders for payment have become final prior to January 1, 1981 shall be paid in accordance with Minnesota Statutes 1978, Section 82.34, but shall be subject to the limitations set forth in subdivisions 7 and 12. If at any time the amount deposited in the recovery portion of the fund is insufficient to satisfy any duly authorized claim or portion thereof for which an order directing payment has become final prior to January 1, 1981, the commissioner shall treat the unpaid claims or portions thereof as if entered pursuant to orders which become final in the calendar year 1981. Those claims shall be paid in accordance with the procedure set forth in subdivision 14 and shall be subject to the limitations set forth in subdivisions 4 and 14.*

MINNESOTA CODE OF AGENCY RULES

Note: The following are key excerpts from the Minnesota Code of Agency Rules and are current at the time of printing. You can obtain the complete Code of Agency with any subsequent changes from the State of Minnesota, Documents Division, 117 University Avenue, St. Paul, MN 55155.

§ 1.41500

A. *For the purposes of these rules, the terms defined in this section shall have the meanings given to them.*

1. *"Commissioner" means the Commissioner of Commerce.*

2. *"Licensee" shall mean any person duly licensed under Minnesota Statutes, chapter 82.*

3. *"Override clause" shall mean a provision in a listing agreement or similar instrument allowing the broker to receive a commission when the property is sold, after the listing agreement has expired, to persons with whom a broker or salesperson had negotiated or exhibited the property prior to the expiration of the listing agreement.*

4. *"Primary broker" means the broker on whose behalf salespersons are licensed to act pursuant to Minnesota Statutes, section 82.20, subdivision 6. In the case of a corporation licensed as a broker, "primary broker" means each officer of the corporation who is individually licensed to act as a broker for the corporation. In the case of a partnership, "primary broker" means each partner licensed to act as a broker for the partnership.*

5. *"Protective list" shall refer to the written list of names and addresses of prospective purchasers with whom a broker or salesperson had negotiated or exhibited the property prior to the expiration of the listing agreement.*

6. *"Rental service" means a person who gathers and catalogs information concerning apartments or other units of real estate available for rent, and who, for a fee, provides information intended to meet the individual needs of specifically identified lessors or prospective lessees. This term shall not apply to newspapers or other periodicals with a general circulation or individual listing contracts between an owner or lessor of property and a licensee.*

§ 1.41502

Passing grade. A passing grade for a salesperson's and broker's examination shall be a score of 75 percent or higher on the uniform portion and a score of 75 percent or higher on the state portion of the examination. The commissioner shall not accept the scores of a person who has cheated on an examination. Cheating on a real estate examination shall be grounds for denying an application for a broker's or salesperson's license.

§ 1.41503

A. *Application for broker's license. After successful completion of the real estate broker's examination, an individual shall have one year from the date of the examination to apply for a broker's license, unless the individual is a salesperson who remains continuously active in the real estate field as a licensee. Failure to apply for the broker's license or to remain continuously active in the real estate field will necessitate a reexamination.*

B. *Cancellation of a salesperson's or broker's license. A salesperson's or broker's license which has been cancelled for failure of a licensee to complete post-licensing education requirements must be returned to the commissioner by the licensee's broker within ten days of receipt of notice of cancellation. The license shall be reinstated without reexamination by completing the required instruction, filing an application, and paying the fee for a salesperson's or broker's license within one year of the cancellation date.*

C. *Waivers. The commissioner may waive the real estate licensing experience requirement for the broker's examination.*

1. *Qualifications. An applicant for a waiver shall provide evidence of either:*

a. *successful completion of a minimum of ninety (90) quarter credits or two hundred seventy (270) classroom hours of real estate related studies; or*

b. *a minimum of five (5) consecutive years of practical experience in real estate related areas; or*

c. *successful completion of thirty (30) credits or ninety (90) classroom hours and three (3) consecutive years of practical experience in real estate related areas.*

2. *Requests. A request for a waiver shall be submitted to the commissioner in writing and be accompanied by such documents as necessary to evidence qualification as set forth in 1.*

3. *The waiver will lapse if the applicant fails to successfully complete the broker's examination within one year from the date of the granting of the waiver.*

§ 1.41505 Trust funds

A. *Listing broker. Unless otherwise agreed upon in writing by the parties to a transaction, the broker with whom trust funds are to be deposited in satisfaction of Minnesota Statutes, section 82.24, subdivision 1 shall be the listing broker.*

B. *Maintenance.* *Trust funds shall be maintained in a trust account until disbursement is made in accordance with the terms of the applicable agreements and proper accounting is made to the parties entitled to an accounting. Disbursement shall be made within a reasonable time following the consummation or termination of a transaction if the applicable agreements are silent as to the time of disbursement.*

C. *Consent to place in special account.* *Trust funds may be placed by the broker in a special account, which may be an interest bearing account or certificate of deposit if the buyer and the seller consent in writing to the special account and to the disposition of the trust funds, including any interest thereon.*

D. *Licensee as principal.* *Funds which would constitute trust funds if received by a licensee acting as an agent must, if received by a licensee acting as principal, be placed in a trust account unless a written agreement signed by all parties to the transaction specifies a different disposition of the funds. The written agreement shall state that the funds would otherwise be placed in a real estate trust account.*

§ 1.41506

A. *Trust account records.*

1. *Every broker shall keep a record of all trust funds received, including notes, savings certificates, uncashed or uncollected checks, or other similar instruments. Said records shall set forth:*

a. *date funds received;*

b. *from whom received;*

c. *amount received;*

d. *with respect to funds deposited in a trust account, the date of said deposit;*

e. *with respect to funds previously deposited in a trust account, the check number or date of related disbursements;*

f. *a monthly balance of the trust account.*

Each broker shall maintain a formal trust cash receipts journal and a formal cash disbursement journal, or similar records, in accordance with generally accepted accounting principles. All records and funds shall be subject to inspection by the commissioner or his agent at any time.

2. *Each broker shall keep a separate record for each beneficiary or transaction, accounting for all funds therein which have been deposited in the broker's trust bank account. These records shall set forth information sufficient to identify the transaction and the parties thereto. At a minimum, each such record shall set forth:*

a. *the date funds are deposited;*
b. *the amount deposited;*
c. *the date of each related disbursement;*
d. *the check number of each related disbursement;*
e. *the amount of each related disbursement;*
f. *a description of each disbursement.*

3. *A check received from the potential buyer shall be deposited into the listing broker's trust account not later than the next business day after delivery of the check to the broker except that the check may be held by the listing broker until acceptance or rejection of the offer if:*

a. *the check by its terms is not negotiable by the broker or if the potential buyer has given written instructions that the check shall not be deposited nor cashed until acceptance or shall be immediately returned if the offer is rejected; and*

b. *the potential seller is informed that the check is being so held before or at the time the offer is presented to him for acceptance.*

If the offer is accepted, the check shall be deposited in a neutral escrow depository or the trust fund account of the listing broker not later than the next business day following acceptance of the offer unless said broker has received written authorization from all parties to the transaction to continue to hold the check. If the offer is rejected, the check shall be returned to the potential buyer not later than the next business day after rejection.

§ 1.41507

A. *Non-depositable items. In the event earnest money or other down payments are received by the broker or salesman in the form of a non-depositable item such as a note, bond, stock certificate, treasury bill or any other item of value taken in lieu of cash, a receipt shall be issued to the buyer for the value thereof and such items shall be deposited immediately with an authorized escrow agent.*

In the event the broker acts as the escrow agent, he shall obtain written authority from the buyer and seller to hold such items in escrow. In all cases the parties shall be advised of the details relative to the non-depositable item, including the nature of the item, the amount, and in whose custody such item is being held. The fact that such an item is being held by the broker shall be duly recorded in the broker's trust account records.

§ 1.41515 Standards of conduct.

The methods, acts, or practices set forth in 4 MCAR §§ 1.41516–1.41526 are standards of conduct governing the activities of real estate brokers and salespersons under Minnesota Statutes, chapter 82. Failure to comply with these standards shall constitute grounds for license denial, suspension, or revocation or for censure of the licensee.

§ 1.41516 Responsibilities of brokers.

A. *Supervision of personnel. Brokers shall adequately supervise the activities of their salespersons and employees. Supervision includes the on-going monitoring of listing agreements, purchase agreements, other real estate-related documents which are prepared or drafted by the broker's salespersons or employees or which are otherwise received by the broker's office, and the review of all trust account books and records. If an individual broker maintains more than one place of business, each place of business shall be under the broker's direction and supervision. If a partnership or corporate broker maintains more than one place of business, each place of business shall be under the direction and supervision of an individual broker licensed to act on behalf of the partnership or corporation.*

The primary broker shall maintain records specifying the name of each broker responsible for the direction and supervision of each place of business. If an individual broker, who may be the primary broker, is responsible for supervising more than one place of business, the primary broker shall, upon written request of the commissioner, file a written statement specifying the procedures which have been established to assure that all salespersons and employees are adequately supervised. Designation of another broker to supervise a place of business does not relieve the primary broker of the ultimate responsibility for the actions of licensees.

B. *Preparation and safekeeping of documents. Brokers shall be responsible for the preparation, custody, safety, and accuracy of all real estate contracts, documents and records, even though another person may be assigned these duties by the broker.*

C. *Documentation and resolution of complaints. Brokers shall investigate and attempt to resolve complaints made regarding the practices of any individual licensed to them and shall maintain, with respect to each individual licensed to them, a complaint file containing all material relating to any complaints received in writing for a period of three years.*

D. *Disclosure of listed property information.* *No broker shall allow any unlicensed person to disclose any information regarding a listed property except to state the address of the property and whether it is available for sale or lease.*

§ 1.41517 Temporary broker's permit.

In the event of death or incapacity of a broker, the commissioner may issue a 45-day temporary permit to an individual who has had a minimum of two years actual experience as a licensed real estate salesperson and who is otherwise reasonably qualified to act as a broker. Upon application prior to its expiration, the 45-day temporary permit shall be renewed once by the commissioner if the applicant demonstrates that he or she has made a good faith effort to obtain a broker's license within the preceding 45 days and an extension of time will not harm the public interest.

Only those salespersons licensed to the deceased or incapacitated broker at the time of death or incapacity may conduct business for or on behalf of the person to whom the temporary broker's license was issued.

§ 1.41518 Licensee as agent of broker; disclosure.

A salesperson shall only conduct business under the licensed name of and on behalf of the broker to whom he or she is licensed. An individual broker shall only conduct business under his or her licensed name. A broker licensed to a corporation or partnership shall only conduct business under the licensed corporate or partnership name. A licensee shall affirmatively disclose prior to the negotiation or consummation of any transaction the licensed name of the broker under whom he or she is authorized to conduct business in accordance with this rule.

§ 1.41519 Listing agreements.

A. *Requirement.* *Licensees shall obtain a signed listing agreement, or other written authorization, from the owner of real property or from another person authorized to offer the property for sale or lease prior to advertising to the general public that the real property is available for sale or lease.*

For the purposes of this rule "advertising" shall include placing a sign on the owner's property which indicates that the property is being offered for sale or lease.

B. *Contents.* *All listing agreements shall be in writing and shall include:*

1. *A definite expiration date;*

2. *A description of the real property involved;*

3. *The list price and any terms required by the seller;*

4. *The amount of any compensation or commission or the basis for computing the commission;*

5. *A clear statement explaining the events or conditions which will entitle a broker to a commission;*

6. *Information regarding an override clause, if applicable, including a statement to the effect that the override clause will not be effective unless the licensee supplies the seller with a protective list within 72 hours after the expiration of the listing agreement; and*

7. *The following notice in not less than ten point boldface type immediately preceding any provision of the listing agreement relating to compensation of the licensee:*

"Notice: The commission rate for the sale, lease, rental, or management of real property shall be determined between each individual broker and its client."

C. *Prohibited provisions. Licensees shall not include in a listing agreement a holdover clause, automatic extension, or any similar provision, or an override clause the length of which is more than six months after the expiration of the listing agreement.*

D. *Override clauses. Licensees shall not seek to enforce an override clause unless a protective list has been furnished to the seller within 72 hours after the expiration of the listing agreement.*

E. *Protective lists. A broker or salesperson has the burden of demonstrating that each person on the protective list has, during the period of the listing agreement, either made an affirmative showing of interest in the property by responding to an advertisement or by contacting the broker or salesperson involved or has been physically shown the property by the broker or salesperson. For the purpose of this rule the mere mailing or other distribution by a licensee of literature setting forth information about the property in question does not, of itself, constitute an affirmative showing of interest in the property on the part of a subsequent purchaser.*

The protective list shall contain the following notice in boldface type:

"If you relist with another broker within the override period and then sell your property to anyone whose name appears on this list, you could be liable for full commissions to both brokers. If this notice is not fully understood, seek competent advice."

The protective list need not contain this notice if the written listing agreement specifically states that after its expiration the seller will not be obligated to pay the licensee a fee or commission if the seller has executed another valid listing agreement pursuant to which the seller is obligated to pay a fee or commission to another licensee for the sale, lease, or exchange of the real property in question.

§ 1.41520 Guaranteed sale programs.

If a broker advertises or offers a guaranteed sale program, or other program whereby the broker undertakes to purchase real property in the event he or she is unable to effectuate a sale to a third party within a specified period of time, a written disclosure which sets forth clearly and completely the general terms and conditions under which the broker agrees to purchase the property and the disposition of any profit at the time of resale by the broker must be provided to the seller prior to the execution of a listing agreement.

§ 1.41521 Disclosure requirements.

A. *Advertising. Each licensee shall identify himself or herself as either a broker or an agent in any advertising for the purchase, sale, lease, exchange, mortgaging, transfer, or other disposition of real property, whether the advertising pertains to his or her own property or the property of others.*

B. *Financial interests of licensee. Prior to the negotiation or consummation of any transaction, a licensee shall affirmatively disclose to the owner of real property that the licensee is a real estate broker or agent, and in what capacity the licensee is acting, if the licensee directly, or indirectly through a third party, purchases for himself or herself or acquires, or intends to acquire, any interest in, or any option to purchase, the owner's property.*

C. *Material facts. Licensees shall disclose to any prospective purchaser all material facts pertaining to the property, of which the licensee is aware, which could adversely and significantly affect an ordinary purchaser's use or enjoyment of the property, or any intended use of the property of which the licensee is aware.*

D. *Nonperformance of any party. If a licensee is put on notice by any party to a real estate transaction that the party will not perform in accordance with the terms of a purchase agreement or other similar written agreement to convey real estate, the licensee shall immediately disclose the fact of that party's intent not to perform to the other party or parties to the transaction. Whenever reasonably possible, the licensee shall inform the party who will not perform of* *the licensee's obligation to disclose this fact to the other party or parties to the transaction prior to making the disclosure. The obligation required by this rule shall not apply to notice of a party's inability to keep or fulfill any contingency to which the real estate transaction has been made subject.*

§ 1.41522 Prohibition on guaranteeing future profits.

Licensees shall not, with respect to the sale or lease of real property, guarantee or affirmatively encourage another person to guarantee future profits or earnings which may result from the purchase or lease of the real property in question unless the guarantee and the assumptions upon which it is based are fully disclosed and contained in the contract, purchase agreement, or other instrument of sale or lease.

§ 1.41523 Negotiations.

A. *Written offers. All written offers to purchase or lease shall be promptly submitted in writing to the seller or lessor.*

B. *Nondisclosure of terms of offer. A licensee shall not disclose the terms of an offer to another prospective buyer or the buyer's agent prior to the presentation of the offer to the seller.*

C. *Closing costs. Licensees shall disclose to a buyer or a seller at or before the time an offer is written or presented that the buyer or seller may be required to pay certain closing costs, which may effectively reduce the proceeds from the sale or increase the cash outlay at closing.*

D. *Required documents. Licensees shall furnish to the parties to the transaction at the time the documents are signed or become available a true and accurate copy of listing agreements, earnest money receipts, purchase agreements, contracts for deed, option agreements, closing statements, truth-in-housing forms, energy audits, and any other record, instrument, or document which is material to the transaction and which is in the licensee's possession.*

E. *Closing statement. The listing broker or his or her designee shall deliver to the seller at the time of closing a complete and detailed closing statement setting forth all of the receipts and disbursements handled by the broker for the seller. The listing broker shall also deliver to the buyer at the time of closing a complete and detailed statement setting forth the disposition of all moneys received in the transaction from the buyer.*

F. *Exclusive agency agreements. A licensee shall not negotiate the sale, exchange, lease, or listing of any real property directly with* *the owner or lessor knowing that the owner or lessor has executed a written contract granting exclusive agency in connection with the property to another real estate broker. The licensee shall inquire of the owner or lessor whether such a contract exists.*

G. *Prohibition against interference with contractual relationships of others. Licensees shall not induce any party to a contract of sale or lease, option, or exclusive listing agreement, to breach the contract, option, or agreement.*

H. *Prohibition against discouraging use of attorney. Licensees shall not discourage prospective parties to a real estate transaction from seeking the services of an attorney.*

§ 1.41524 Compensation.

A. *Licensee to receive only from broker. A licensee shall not accept a commission or other valuable consideration for the performance of any acts requiring a real estate license from any person except the real estate broker to whom he is licensed or to whom he was licensed at the time of the transaction.*

B. *Undisclosed compensation. A licensee shall not accept, give, or charge any undisclosed commission or realize any direct or indirect remuneration which inures to the benefit of the licensee on an expenditure made for a principal.*

C. *Limitation on broker when transaction not completed. When the owner fails or is unable to consummate a real estate transaction, through no fault of the purchaser, the listing broker may not claim any portion of any trust funds deposited with the broker by the purchaser, absent a separate agreement with the purchaser.*

§ 1.41525 Notice to the commissioner.

Licensees shall notify the commissioner of the facts in A.-D.

A. *Change of application information. The commissioner shall be notified in writing of a change of information contained in the license application on file with the commissioner within ten days of the change.*

B. *Civil judgment. The commissioner shall be notified in writing within ten days of a final adverse decision or order of a court, whether or not the decision or order is appealed, regarding any proceeding in which the licensee was named as a defendant, and which alleged fraud, misrepresentation, or the conversion of funds, if the final adverse decision relates to the allegations of fraud, misrepresentation, or the conversion of funds.*

C. *Disciplinary action. The commissioner shall be notified in writing within ten days of the suspension or revocation of a licensee's real estate or other occupational license issued by this state or another jurisdiction.*

D. *Criminal offense. The commissioner shall be notified in writing within ten days if a licensee is charged with, adjudged guilty of, or enters a plea of guilty or nolo contendere to a charge of any felony, or of any gross misdemeanor alleging fraud, misrepresentation, conversion of funds or a similar violation of any real estate licensing law.*

§ 1.41526 Access to governing statutes and rules.

Every real estate office and branch office shall have a current copy of Minnesota Statutes, chapters 82 and 83 and the rules adopted thereunder available for the use of licensees.

§ 1.41527 Rental services.

A. *License. A rental service shall obtain a real estate broker's license prior to engaging in business or holding itself out as being engaged in business. No person shall act as a real estate salesperson on behalf of a rental service without first obtaining a real estate salesperson's license on behalf of the rental service.*

B. *Dissemination of unit information. A rental service shall not provide information regarding a rental unit without the express authority of the owner of the unit.*

C. *Availability of unit. A rental service shall not represent a unit as currently available unless its availability has been verified within 72 hours preceding the representation.*

D. *Advertising. A rental service shall not advertise in a manner which is misleading with regard to fees charged, services provided, the availability of rental units or rental terms or conditions.*

§ 1.41528 Fraudulent, deceptive, and dishonest practices.

For the purposes of Minnesota Statutes, section 82.27, subdivision 1, clause (b), the following acts and practices constitute fraudulent, deceptive, or dishonest practices:

A. *Act on behalf of more than one party to a transaction without the knowledge and consent of all parties;*

B. *Act in the dual capacity of licensee and undisclosed principal in any transaction;*

C. *Receive funds while acting as principal which funds would constitute trust funds if received by a licensee acting as an agent, unless the funds are placed in a trust account. Funds need not be placed in a trust account if a written agreement signed by all parties to the transaction specifies a different disposition of the funds, in accordance with 4 MCAR § 1.41505 D.;*

D. *Violate any state or federal law concerning discrimination intended to protect the rights of purchasers or renters of real estate;*

E. *Make a material misstatement in an application for a license or in any information furnished to the commissioner;*

F. *Procure or attempt to procure a real estate license for himself or herself for any person by fraud, misrepresentation, or deceit;*

G. *Represent membership in any real-estate-related organization in which the licensee is not a member;*

H. *Advertise in any manner which is misleading or inaccurate with respect to properties, terms, values, policies, or services conducted by the licensee;*

I. *Make any material misrepresentation or permit or allow another to make any material misrepresentation;*

J. *Make any false or misleading statements, or permit or allow another to make any flase or misleading statements of a character likely to influence, persuade, or induce the consummation of a transaction contemplated by Minnesota Statutes, ch. 82;*

K. *Fail within a reasonable time to account for or to remit any money coming into the licensee's possession which belongs to another;*

L. *Commingle with his or her own money or property trust funds or any other money or property of another held by the licensee;*

M. *Demand from a seller a commission to which the licensee is not entitled, knowing that he or she is not entitled thereto;*

N. *Pay or give money or goods of value to an unlicensed person for any assistance or information relating to the procurement by a licensee of a listing of a property or of a prospective buyer of a property. This paragraph does not apply to money or goods paid or given to the parties to the transaction;*

O. *Fail to maintain a trust account at all times, as provided by law;*

P. *Engage, with respect to the offer, sale, or rental of real estate, in an anticompetitive activity.*

A licensee shall be deemed to have violated this provision if he has been found to have violated the Minnesota Antitrust Law of 1971, Minnesota Statutes, sections 325D.49 to 325D.66 by a final decision or order of a court of competent jurisdiction.

Nothing in 4 MCAR § 1.41528 limits the authority of the commissioner to take actions against a licensee for fraudulent, deceptive, or dishonest practices not specifically described in this rule.

§ 1.41529 Salespersons; initial real estate education requirements.

A. *Generally.* *An approved 90-hour course of initial education shall consist of three 30-classroom-hour courses to be designated as Course I, Course II, and Course III. Pursuant to Minnesota Statutes, section 82.22, subdivision 6, each applicant for a salesperson's license or salesperson is required to complete all courses successfully. Courses I, II, and III must be taken in sequence and may not be taken concurrently.*

B. *Salesperson's examination.* *Applicants must successfully complete the salesperson's examination within one year after the successful completion of Course I. After this date, credit for Course I will expire and successful completion of the first 30-hour course must be repeated before taking the salesperson's examination.*

An exception will be made for students pursuing a full-time course of study in either a two-year or four-year real estate education program. The burden of demonstrating full-time status is on the student. Applicants must successfully complete the salesperson's examination within one year after the successful completion of the two-year or four-year course of study.

C. *Application for salesperson's license.* *Applicants must apply for a salesperson's license within one year after successful completion of the licensing examination. Applicants who fail to apply for a license within the one-year period must retake Course I and successfully complete the examination.*

G. *Limitation on use of certain education courses.* *Courses I and II may not be taken for credit towards a licensee's continuing education requirements.*

Any Course III may be taken for credit towards a licensee's continuing education requirements if the licensee has not previously received credit for that course or a substantially similar course.

J. Course I.

1. *Hours.* *Course I shall incorporate the following number of hours for each of the following topics, for a total of 30 hours:*

(a) *Introduction to real estate, one hour;*
(b) *Real estate licensing law (Minnesota Statutes, chapters 82 and 83), four hours;*
(c) *Law of agency, four hours;*
(d) *Law of contracts, five hours;*
(e) *Real estate financing, six hours;*
(f) *Types and classifications of property, three hours;*
(g) *Examination of title, one hour; and*
(h) *Title closing, six hours.*

K. Course II.

1. *Hours. Course II shall incorporate the following number of hours for each of the following topics, for a total of 30 hours:*

(a) *Deeds, three hours;*
(b) *Search and examination of title, one hour;*
(c) *Residential appraisal, six hours;*
(d) *Residential construction, two hours;*
(e) *Land development and use, three hours;*
(f) *Condominiums, cooperatives, planned unit developments, and manufactured housing, three hours;*
(g) *Taxation, four hours;*
(h) *Investment and appraisal, four hours;*
(i) *Real property management, two hours; and*
(j) *Leases and leasing, two hours.*

L. Course III.

1. Hours. *Course III shall be a 30-hour course consisting of one of the following:*

(a) *Real estate appraisal, 30 hours;*
(b) *Closing procedures, 30 hours;*
(c) *Farm and ranch brokerage, 30 hours;*
(d) *Real estate finance, 30 hours;*
(e) *Real estate investment, 30 hours;*
(f) *Real estate law, 30 hours;*
(g) *Real estate management, 30 hours;*
(h) *Real estate mathematics, 30 hours;*
(i) *Business brokerage, 30 hours; or*
(j) *A combination course of no more than three of the subjects set forth in (a)-(i), 30 hours. A combination course shall consist of no more than three of the preceding nine subjects and shall devote at least ten hours to each subject. A school which proposes to offer a combination Course III shall sub-*

mit to the commissioner, as part of the application for approval, an outline setting forth the subjects to be addressed and the number of hours proposed to be devoted to each topic.

§ 1.41530 Continuing education.

A. *Generally. Continuing education shall consist of approved courses which impart substantive and procedural knowledge in the real estate field.*

B. *Attendance. Courses must be attended in their entirety in order for a licensee to obtain credit. No credit will be given for partial attendance at a course.*

§ 1.41537 Extensions.

Upon appropriate showing of a bona fide financial or medical hardship, the commissioner may extend the time period during which post-licensing or continuing education instruction must be successfully completed. Loss of income resulting from cancellation of a license is not a bona fide hardship. Requests for extensions must be submitted in writing no later than 45 days prior to the date of license cancellation and shall include an explanation and verification of the hardship, and a verification of enrollment in an approved course of study and the dates during which the course will be held.

§ 1.41538 Waivers.

Required real estate education shall not be waived for any licensee or applicant for a license.

§ 1.41547 Course completion certificates.

Applicants for a salesperson's license shall submit to the commissioner, along with their application for licensure, a copy of the Course Completion Certificate, 4 MCAR S 1.41553 (RE-1), for Course I, and for Courses II and III if completed prior to being licensed.

Students are responsible for maintaining copies of Course Completion Certificates.

§ 1.41548 Reports to commissioner.

Continuing education credits shall be reported by the licensee on the form in 4 MCAR § 1.41561 (RE-9).

Forms will not be accepted unless they reflect the entire 45 required hours. Incomplete forms will be returned to the licensee.

Forms must be received by the commissioner no later than June 15 of the year in which the credits are due. Forms which are mailed shall be deemed timely received if addressed to: Real Estate Licensing, 500 Metro Square Building, Saint Paul, MN 55101, and postmarked prior to 12:01 a.m. on June 14. Licensees are encouraged to submit the form as soon as they have completed the 45 hours of continuing education credit.

§ 1.41549 Automatic transfer of salesperson's license.

A. *Applicability. A salesperson may utilize the automatic license transfer provisions of Laws 1982, chapter 478, section 1, subdivision 9, clause (b) if the salesperson commences his or her association with the broker to whom he or she is transferring, as evidenced by the dates of the signatures of both brokers on the form in 4 MCAR S 1.41562 (RE-10), within five days after terminating his or her association with the broker from whom he or she is transferring, provided the salesperson's educational requirements are not past due.*

A salesperson may not utilize the automatic license transfer provisions of Laws 1982, chapter 478, section 1, subdivision 9, clause (b) if he or she has failed to notify the commissioner within ten days of any change of information contained in his or her license application on file with the commissioner or of a civil judgment, disciplinary action, or criminal offense, which notice is required pursuant to 4 MCAR S 1.41525.

B. *Procedure. An application for automatic transfer shall be made only on the form in 4 MCAR S 1.41562 (RE-10). The transfer is ineffective if the form is not completed in its entirety.*

The form in 4 MCAR S 1.41562 (RE-10) shall be accompanied by a $10 transfer fee, and the license renewal fee, if applicable, plus an additional $10 if the salesperson holds a subdivided land license. Cash will not be accepted. If the licensee holds a subdivided land license it must be transferred at the same time as the salesperson's license. In order for the transfer of the subdivided land license to be effective the broker to whom the salesperson is transferring must also hold a subdivided land license.

The signature on the form in 4 MCAR S 1.41562 (RE-10) of the broker from whom the salesperson is transferring must predate the signature of the broker to whom the salesperson is transferring. The salesperson is unlicensed for the period of time between the times and dates of both signatures. The broker from whom the salesperson is transferring shall sign and date the transfer application upon the request of the salesperson and shall destroy the salesperson's license immediately.

C. *Effective date.*

1. *The transfer is effective when the broker to whom the salesperson is transferring signs and dates the transfer application form in 4 MCAR S 1.41562 (RE-10), provided the commissioner receives the form and fee within 72 hours after the date and time of the new broker's signature, either by certified mail or personal delivery to the commissioner's office. In the event of a delay in mail delivery, an application postmarked within 24 hours of the date of the signature of the new broker shall be deemed timely received.*

2. *The transfer is ineffective if the fee is paid by means of a check, draft or other negotiable or non-negotiable instrument or order of withdrawal drawn on an account with insufficient funds.*

3. *The salesperson shall retain the certified mail return receipt, if the transfer application is delivered to the commissioner by mail, retain a photocopy of the executed transfer application, and provide a photocopy of the executed transfer application to the broker from whom he or she is transferring.*

§ 1.41550 Approved lender is not a broker.

The definition of "real estate broker" or "broker" set forth in Minnesota Statutes, section 82.17, subdivision 4, clause (b) shall not apply to the originating, making, processing, selling, or servicing of a loan in connection with his or her ordinary business activities by a mortgagee, lender or servicer approved or certified by the secretary of housing and urban development, or approved or certified by the administrator of veterans affairs, or approved or certified by the administrator of the farmers home administration, or approved or certified by the federal home loan mortgage corporation, or approved or certified by the federal national mortgage association.

§ 1.41552 Withdrawal of license or application.

A. *Request to commissioner. A licensee or license applicant may at any time file with the commissioner a request to withdraw from the status of licensee or to withdraw a pending license application. Withdrawal from the status of licensee or withdrawal of the license application becomes effective 30 days after receipt of a request to withdraw or within a shorter period the commissioner determines unless a revocation, suspension, or denial proceeding is pending when the request to withdraw is filed or a proceeding to revoke, suspend, deny,* *or to impose conditions upon the withdrawal is instituted within 30 days after the request to withdraw is filed. If a proceeding is pending or instituted, withdrawal becomes effective at the time and upon the conditions the commissioner by order determines. If no proceeding is pending or instituted and withdrawal automatically becomes effective, the commissioner may institute a revocation or suspension proceeding within one year after withdrawal became effective and enter a revocation or suspension order as of the last date on which the license was in effect.*

B. *Failure to renew license. If a license lapses or becomes ineffective due to the licensee's failure to file a timely renewal application or otherwise, the commissioner may institute a revocation or suspension proceeding within one year after the license was last effective and enter a revocation or suspension order as of the last date on which the license was in effect.*

C. *Revocations. If the commissioner finds that any licensee or applicant is no longer in existence or has ceased to do business as a broker or salesperson or is subject to an adjudication of mental incompetence or to the control of a committee, conservator, or guardian, or cannot be located after reasonable search, the commissioner may by order revoke the license or deny the application.*

VOCABULARY REVIEW

Match terms **a–m** *with statements* **1–13.**

a. *Broker*
b. *Commissioner of Securities*
c. *ETS*
d. *Fictious business name*
e. *Licensee*
f. *Real estate salesperson*
g. *Realtor*
h. *Realty board*
i. *Reciprocity*
j. *Recovery fund*
k. *Respondent*
l. *Revoke*
m. *Suspend*

1. A company based in Princeton, New Jersey, that writes, administers, and grades real estate license exams.
2. A person who is licensed to bring about real estate transactions for a fee, but who must do so only in the employment of a real estate broker.
3. A copyrighted and registered term owned by the National Association of Realtors for exclusive use by its members.
4. Any person holding either a broker or salesperson license.
5. An arrangement whereby states honor each other's licenses.
6. A business operated under any name other than the owner's name.
7. An independent agent who negotiates transactions for a fee.

8. A person appointed by the governor to implement and carry out those laws enacted by the state legislature that pertain to real estate.
9. To temporarily make ineffective.
10. To recall and make void.
11. A real estate licensee against whom a complaint has been filed with the real estate commission.
12. A local trade organization for real estate licensees and other persons allied with the real estate industry.
13. A state-operated fund that can be tapped to pay for uncollectible judgments against real estate licensees.

QUESTIONS AND PROBLEMS

1. What was the purpose of early real estate license laws?
2. When is a person required to hold a real estate license?
3. What factors does a broker consider when deciding what percentage of commissions should be paid to the salespersons in his office?
4. Does Minnesota subscribe to the ETS or ACT exam services or does it write all its own questions? How often are the broker and the salesman exams given?
5. What trends are apparent in Minnesota with regard to real estate education requirements?
6. In Minnesota, what requirements must be met to obtain the GRI designation?
7. Name the four Deputy Commissioner positions appointed by the Minnesota Commissioner of Commerce.
8. How is the real estate advisory council selected in Minnesota? What are its duties and responsibilities?
9. Under what circumstances are real estate licenses suspended or revoked in Minnesota?
10. What is the purpose of a bond or recovery fund? What does Minnesota require?
11. What is the purpose of the National Association of Realtors?
12. An employment contract between a broker and a salesperson would cover what items?
13. If you were seeking employment as a salesperson for a brokerage firm, how would you decide what firm to associate with?

ADDITIONAL READINGS

Bove, Richard X. "Franchised Real Estate Brokerage: The Giant Fledgling." *Real Estate Review,* Summer, 1979, pages 46–52. Article deals with two questions: What makes franchising so popular? and will its attraction endure?

Liniger, Dave. "The 100 Percent Commission Concept." *Real Estate Today,* February, 1977, pages 46–51. Article presents the case for 100% commissions. Advantages and disadvantages for the broker and his sales staff are cited.

"Making the Switch to Employees." *Real Estate Today,* February, 1978, pages 4–9. Changing from independent contractor to employee status is easier than it sounds, states this article.

National Association of Real Estate License Law Officials. *Guide to Examinations and Careers in Real Estate.* Reston, Va.: Reston Publishing Co., 1979, 192 pages. First half of this book looks at real estate career opportunities. The second half presents study methods designed to produce high scores on license exams.

"The Choice is Yours." *Real Estate Today,* July, 1977, pages 48–51. Which firm to go with and why? Article helps make the choice.

Tosh, Dennis S., and **Ordway, Nicholas.** *Real Estate Principles for License Preparation,* 2nd ed. Reston, Va.: Reston Publishing Co., 1981, 400 pages. Contains a comprehensive treatment of the subject matter which is tested by the Educational Testing Service on its real estate exams.

19

Condominiums, Cooperatives, and Planned Unit Developments

KEY TERMS

Bylaws: rules that govern how an owners' association will be run

Common elements: those parts of a condominium in which each unit owner holds an undivided interest

Condominium: individual ownership of separate portions of a building plus common ownership of the common elements

Cooperative: land and building owned or leased by a corporation which in turn leases space to its shareholders

Declaration: a document that converts a given parcel of land into a condominium subdivision

Floor plan: architectural drawings that show the layout, location, dimensions, and number of a condominium unit

Limited common elements: common elements, the use of which is limited to certain owners; for example, walls and ceilings between individual units

Planned Unit Development or **PUD (Townhouse):** an individually owned house with association ownership of common areas

Proprietary lease: a lease issued by a cooperative corporation to its shareholders

Time-sharing: part ownership of a property coupled with a right to exclusive use of it for a specified number of days per year

The idea of combining community living with community ownership is not new. Two thousand years ago, the Roman Senate passed condominium laws that permitted Roman citizens to own individual dwelling units in multi-unit buildings. This form of ownership resulted because land was scarce and expensive in Rome. After the fall of the Roman Empire, condominium ownership was used in the walled cities of the Middle Ages. However, this was primarily a defensive measure as residing outside the walls was dangerous due to roving bands of raiders. With the stabilization of governments after the Middle Ages, the condominium concept became dormant until the early twentieth century, when in response to land scarcity in cities, the idea was revived in Western Europe. From there the concept spread to several Latin American countries and, in 1951, to Puerto Rico.

UNITED STATES

Puerto Rican laws and experience became the basis for the passage by the U.S. Congress in 1961 of Section 234 of the National Housing Act. This section provides a legal model for condominium ownership and makes available FHA mortgage loan insurance on condominium units. Currently, one in four new residences being built in the United States is a condominium. Additionally, many existing apartment buildings are being converted to condominium ownership.

Condominium ownership is not the only legal framework available that combines community living with community ownership, although it is currently the best known. Prior to the enactment of condominium legislation, cooperative ownership of multifamily residential buildings was popular in the United States, particularly in the states of Florida, New York, and Hawaii. A more recent variation is the individually owned house combined with community ownership of common areas in what is called a planned unit development or PUD.

Of the forces responsible for creating the need for condominiums, cooperatives and PUDs, the most important are land scarcity in desirable areas, continuing escalation in construction costs, disenchantment with the work of maintaining the grounds around a house, and the desire to own rather than rent.

Land-use Efficiency

When constructing single-family houses on separate lots, a builder can usually average four to five houses per acre of land. In a growing number of cities, the sheer physical space necessary to continue building detached houses either does not exist or, if it does, it is a long distance from employment centers or is so expensive as to eliminate all but a small portion of the population from building there. As in ancient Roman times, the solution is to build more dwellings on the same parcel of land. Instead of four or five dwellings, build 25 or 100 on an acre of land. That way not only is the land more efficiently used, but the cost is divided among more owners. From the standpoint of construction costs, the builder does not have the miles of streets, sewers, or utility lines that would be necessary to reach every house in a subdivision. Furthermore, the facts that there are shared walls, that one dwelling unit's ceiling is often another's floor, and that one roof can cover many vertically stacked units can produce savings in construction materials and labor.

Amenities

For some householders, the lure of "carefree living," wherein such chores as lawn mowing, watering, weeding, snow shoveling, and building maintenance are provided, is the major attraction. For others, it is the security often associated with clustered dwellings or the extensive recreational and social facilities that are not economically possible on a single-dwelling-unit basis. It is commonplace to find swimming pools, recreation halls, tennis and volleyball courts, gymnasiums, and even social directors at some condominium, cooperative, and PUD projects.

A large rental apartment project can also produce the same advantages of land and construction economy and amenities. Nevertheless, we cannot overlook the preference of most American households to own rather than rent their dwellings. This preference is typically based on a desire for a savings program, observation of inflation in real estate prices, and advantageous income tax laws that allow owners, but not renters, to deduct property taxes and mortgage interest.

DIVIDING THE LAND

Figure 19:1 illustrates the estate in land created by a condominium, cooperative, and planned unit development and compares each with the estate held by the owner of a house. Notice in Figure 19:1 that the ownership of house A extends from lot line B across to lot line C. Except where limited by zoning or other legal restrictions, the owner of house A has full control over and full right to use the land between his lot lines from the center of the earth to the limits of the sky. Within the law, he can choose how to use his land, what to build on it or add to it, what color to paint his house and garage, how many people and animals will live there, what type of landscaping to have, from whom to purchase property insurance, and so on. The owner of house D has the same control over the land between lot lines C and E.

The owner of A cannot dictate to his neighbor what color to paint his house, what kind of shrubs and trees to grow, or from whom to buy hazard insurance if he buys it at all.

Figure 19:1 **COMPARISON OF ESTATES**

(Presume fee simple ownership in each case)

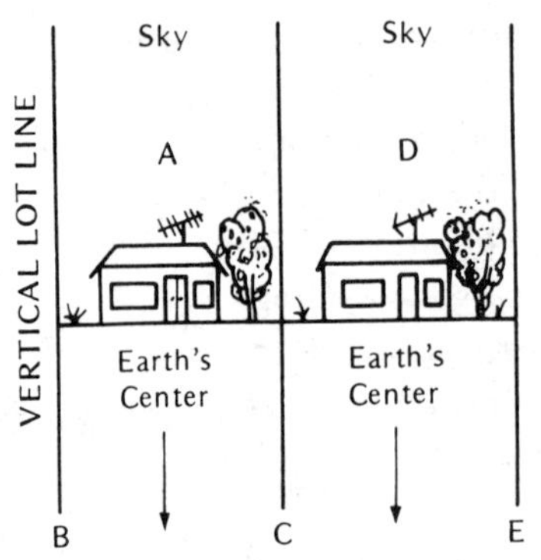

1. HOUSE

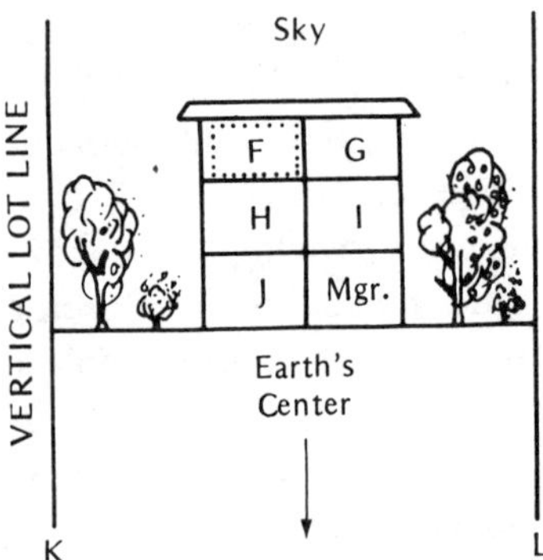

2. CONDOMINIUM

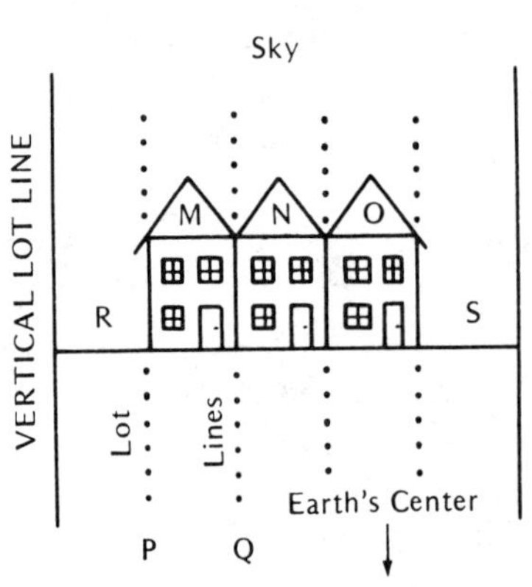

3. PLANNED UNIT DEVELOPMENT

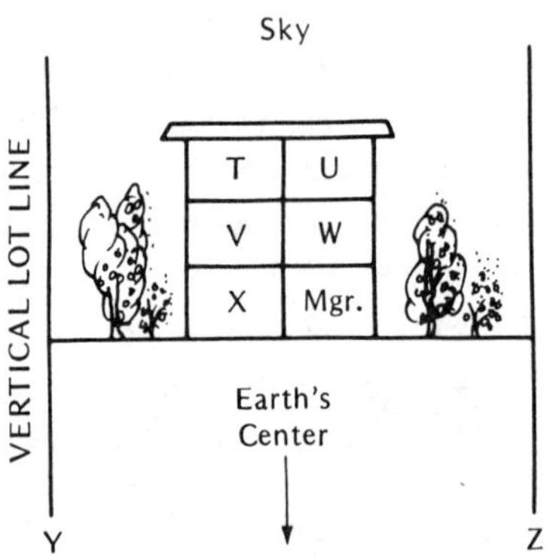

4. COOPERATIVE

(Occasionally, one will find deed restrictions in housing subdivisions that give the owners a limited amount of control over each other's land uses in the subdivision.)

Condominium

In a **condominium,** each dwelling unit owner owns as his **separate property** the cubicle of air space that his unit occupies. This is the space lying between the interior surfaces of the unit sides and between the floor and the ceiling. The remainder of the building and the land are called the **common elements** or common areas. Each unit owner holds an undivided interest in the common elements.

In Figure 19:1, the owner of dwelling unit F owns as his separate property the air space enclosed by the dotted lines. Except for the individual unit owners' air spaces, F, G, H, I, and J each owns an undivided interest in everything between lot lines K and L. This includes the land and the shell of the building, plus such things as the manager's apartment, lobby, hallways, stairways, elevators, and recreation facilities. In some states the walls and ceilings between individual units are called **limited common elements.** The word "limited" means that their use is limited to the abutting units.

Planned Unit Development (PUD)

In a **planned unit development** (PUD), also called a **townhouse** in Minnesota, each owner owns as his separate property the land that his dwelling unit occupies. For example, the owner of house M in Figure 19:1 owns the land between lot lines P and Q from the center of the earth skyward. A homeowners' association consisting of M, N, and O owns the land at R and S and any improvements thereon, such as recreation facilities or parking lots.

Cooperative

In a **cooperative** there is no separate property at all. Rather, the owners hold shares of stock in a cooperative corporation, which, in turn, owns the land and building and issues proprietary leases to the owners to use specific apartments. A **proprietary lease** differs from the usual landlord–tenant lease in that the "tenant" is also an owner of the building. In the cooperative in Figure 19:1, all the land and building lying between lot lines Y and Z are owned by a corporation that is owned by shareholders T, U, V, W, and X. Ownership of the corporation's shares carries the right to occupy apartment units in the building.

Having now briefly illustrated the estates created by the condominium, townhouse, and PUD forms of real estate ownership, let us take a closer look at their organization, financing, and management.

CONDOMINIUM

A condominium is created when a person, usually a real estate developer, files a **declaration** with the county recorder or registrar of titles that converts a parcel of land held under a single deed into a number of individual condominium estates, plus an estate that includes the common elements. Included in the declaration is a description of the location of each individual unit with respect to the land, identification of the common elements to be shared, and the percentage interest each unit owner will have in the common elements. Also in the declaration are the floor plans of the building, the percentage of expenses and number of votes for each unit, and any restrictions on the use, occupancy or sale of the units. If the condominium is to be on leasehold land, the declaration converts the single leasehold interest into individual leases or subleases. The right of a person to file a declaration is outlined in the Minnesota Uniform Condominium Act. Basically, it follows the model FHA legislation.

The developer must file a set of floor plans of the building showing the layout, location, apartment numbers and dimensions of the apartments, stating the name of the building or that it has no name, and bearing the verified statement of a registered architect, engineer or surveyor.

Owners' Association

In addition to filing the declaration (also known as the master deed, plan of condominium ownership, or condominium subdivision), the developer must provide a legal framework by which the unit owners can govern themselves. Minnesota requires the formation of a nonprofit condominium **homeowners' association** which is incorporated. Each unit purchaser automatically becomes a member. The main purpose of the owners' association is to control, regulate, and maintain the common elements.

Bylaws

Bylaws must also be recorded with the declaration. They provide the rules by which the association's board of directors is elected from among the association members and set the standards by which the board must rule. They also set forth how association dues (maintenance fees) will be established and collected, how contracts will be let for maintenance, management, and repair work, and how personnel will be hired. Sale, rental, and transfer restrictions are also found in the bylaws, as well as restrictions regarding the use and maintenance of the apartments and common elements.

House Rules

Additional regulations may be embodied in a set of **house rules.** Typically, these govern such things as when the swimming pool and other recreation facilities will be open for use and when quiet hours will be observed in the building.

Unit Deed

Each purchaser of a condominium unit receives a deed to his or her unit from the developer. The deed describes the unit number and the legal description of the land. The deed will also recite the percentage interest in the common elements that the grantee is receiving. The deed is recorded upon closing just as one would record a deed to a house.

When the owner sells, he has a new deed prepared that describes the unit and the common element interest, and delivers it to the purchaser at closing. If the condominium is on leased land, the developer will deliver a lease (or sublease) to the unit buyer. When he later sells, he assigns that lease to the buyer.

Voting Rules

Once the units in the building have been sold and the association turned over to the unit owners, the unit owners can change the rules. The bylaws will set forth the number of votes required to make a change.

Votes are weighted in accordance with the bylaws, and two variations are presently used in Minnesota. The most straightforward method is to give each unit owner one vote without regard to the size of each unit. In other associations, the weight of one's vote depends on the percentage of the building he owns. Thus, in a condominium composed of 1,000- and 1,500-square-foot apartments, the owners of the 1,500-square-foot units would have one and one-half times the vote of those with 1,000-square-foot units. Interests in the common elements and liability for the expenses of the association can also be allocated per unit or per square foot. The prevailing method in Minnesota is to allocate on a square foot basis, i.e., a weighted basis.

CONDOMINIUM MANAGEMENT

For condominium owners to enjoy maintenance-free living, the association must employ the services of a building manager. If the project contains only a few units, the association may elect to employ one of its members on a part-time basis to take care of the landscaping, hallways, trash, and the like and to keep records of his expenses. For major maintenance items such as painting, roof repairs, and pool refurbishing, independent contractors are hired.

In larger projects, the association can either hire a full-time manager or a professional management firm. A management firm supplies a management package that combines an on-site resident manager plus off-site services, such as accounting for the building's expenses and handling the payroll. The management firm will also contract for gardening, trash hauling, and janitorial services. Each month the firm bills the association for the package of services rendered.

Whether hired directly by the association or by the management firm, the resident manager is usually responsible for enforcing the house rules, handling complaints or problems regarding maintenance, and supervising such matters as the handling of the mail and the use of the swimming pool and recreation areas. The extent of his duties and responsibilities is set by the owners' association. The association should also retain the right to fire the resident manager and the management firm if their services are not satisfactory.

MAINTENANCE FEES

The costs of maintaining the common elements in a condominium are allocated among the unit owners in accordance with percentages set forth in the declaration. These **maintenance fees** or **association dues** are collected monthly. Failure to pay creates a lien against the delinquent owner's unit. The amount collected is based on the association's budget. This in turn is based on the association's estimate of the cost of month-to-month maintenance, insurance, legal counsel, and accounting services, plus reserves for expenses that do not occur monthly.

The importance of setting aside reserves each month is illustrated by the following example. Suppose it is estimated that the exterior of a 100-unit building will have to be painted every 5 years, and that the cost, allowing for inflation, will be $18,000. The association has two choices: the members can either wait until the paint job is needed and then divide the $18,000 cost among the 100 owners, or they can pay a small amount each month into a reserve fund so that in 5 years there will be $18,000 available. The first choice means a special assessment averaging $180 per owner at the time the job needs to be done. The second choice requires an average of $3 per month from each owner for 60 months. If the reserves are kept in an interest-bearing savings account, as they should be, less than $3 per month would need to be collected.

PROPERTY TAXES AND INSURANCE

Since condominium law recognizes each condominium dwelling unit as a separate legal ownership, property taxes are assessed on each unit separately. Property taxes are based on the assessed value of the unit, which is based on its market value. As a rule, it is not necessary for the taxing authority to assess and tax the common elements separately. The reason is that the market value of each unit reflects not only the value of the unit itself, but also the value of the fractional ownership in the common elements that accompanies the unit.

The association is responsible for purchasing hazard and liability insurance covering the common elements. Each dwelling unit owner is responsible for purchasing hazard and liability insurance for the interior of his dwelling.

Thus, if a visitor slips on a banana peel in the lobby or a hallway of the building, the association is responsible. If the accident occurs in an individual's unit, the unit owner is responsible. In a high-rise condominium, if the roof breaks during a heavy rainstorm and floods several apartments below, the association is responsible. If an apartment owner's dishwasher overflows and soaks the apartments below him, he is responsible.

If the condominium unit is being rented, the owner will want to have landlord insurance, and the tenant, for his own protection, will want a tenant's hazard and liability policy.

CONDOMINIUM FINANCING

Because each condominium unit can be separately owned, each can be separately financed. Thus, a condominium purchaser can choose whether or not to borrow against his unit. If he borrows, he can choose a large or small down payment and a long or short amortization period. Once in his unit, if he wants to repay early or refinance, that is his option too. When he sells, the buyer can elect to assume the loan, pay it off, or obtain new financing. In other words, while association bylaws, restrictions, and house rules may regulate how an owner may use his unit, in no way does the association control how a unit may be financed.

Since each unit is a separate ownership, if a lender needs

to foreclose against a delinquent borrower in the building, the remaining unit owners are not involved. They are neither responsible for the delinquent borrower's mortgage debt, nor are they parties to the foreclosure.

Loan Terms

Loan terms offered condominium buyers are quite similar to those offered on houses. Typically, lenders will make conventional, uninsured loans for up to 80% of value. With private mortgage insurance, this can be raised to 90% or 95%. On FHA-approved buildings, the FHA will insure on terms similar to single-family dwellings. Amortization periods typically run 25 to 30 years. Financing can also be in the form of an installment contract or a purchase money mortgage.

When a condominium is being sold by a developer to private buyers for the first time, the usual procedure is for the developer to find a lender who will advance the money the developer needs to build and offer to finance the unit purchasers. As purchasers sign their mortgage papers, the lender is credited on his loan. Although a buyer can still pay cash or obtain his own lender, having a loan package ready for the buyer is a valuable marketing tool.

Deposit Practices

If a project is not already completed and ready for occupancy when it is offered for sale, it is common for the developer to require a substantial deposit. The best practice is to place this in an escrow account payable to the developer upon completion. However, some developers use deposits to help pay the expenses of construction while the building is being built. Unfortunately, if such deposits are spent by a developer who goes bankrupt before the project is completed, the buyer receives neither a finished unit nor the return of his deposit. If the deposits are held in escrow, the buyers do not receive a unit but they do get their deposits back.

CONDOMINIUM CONVERSIONS

During the late 1970s the idea of condominium ownership became very popular in the United States. Builders constructed new condominiums at a rapid pace, but there were not enough to fill demand. Soon enterprising developers found that existing apartment buildings could be converted to condominiums and sold to the waiting public. Compared to new construction, a condominium conversion is often simpler, faster and more profitable for the developer. The procedure involves finding an attractively built existing building that is well-located and has good floor plans. The developer does a facelift on the outside, adds more landscaping, paints the interior, and replaces carpets and appliances. The developer also files the necessary legal paperwork to convert the building and land into condominium units and common elements.

There are, however, some significant problems which have surfaced. One of these is the plight of the tenants who are forced to move when a building is converted. Initially, they could find other rentals available. But as more and more buildings were converted there were progressively more evicted tenants looking for progressively fewer remaining rentals. This caused rents to rise and worked a particular hardship on the elderly and the handicapped. Tenants prevailed upon their political representatives and numerous laws were passed at state and local levels. Rent control laws were enacted. Developers were required to give tenants more time to move, for example, 120 days and up to a year in some cases. Some jurisdictions passed laws requiring developers to help tenants find new quarters. Others require developers to set aside 20% of their units at below-market prices for the elderly and handicapped. Some cities require that one-third to one-half of the tenants in a building approve of the conversion before it can proceed. And in a few cities, there have been outright moratoriums on conversions. Minnesota has dealt with the problem by requiring that notice of conversion must be given to each tenant 120 days prior to forcing them to vacate. Also, for 60 days after delivery of the notice, tenants have an option to purchase the unit. Interestingly though, it was the real estate market itself that put the brakes on conversions. Rising real estate prices coupled with rising interest rates slowed conversions to a trickle by 1982.

Another potential problem area with condominium conversions, and one that a prospective buyer should be aware of, is that converted buildings are used buildings that were not intended as condominiums when built. As used buildings, there may be considerable deferred maintenance and the building may have thermal insulation suitable to a time when energy costs were lower. If the building was originally built for rental purposes, sound-deadening insulation in the walls, floors and ceilings may be inadequate. Fire protection between units may also be less than satisfactory. In contrast, newly built condominiums must meet current building code requirements regarding thermal and sound insulation, fire-wall construction, and so forth.

Lastly, it is worth noting that not all condominium conversions are carried out by developers. Enterprising tenants have successfully converted their own buildings and saved considerable sums of money. It is not uncommon for the value of a building to double when it is converted to a condominium. Tenants who are willing to hire the legal, architectural, and construction help they need can create valuable condominium homes for themselves in the same building where they were previously renters.

DISCLOSURE STATEMENT

Minnesota requires that the following disclosures must be provided to purchasers not later than the date of signing a purchase agreement.

1. A general description of the condominium.
2. A copy of the declarations, floor plans for that unit, bylaws, articles of incorporation, rules and regulations, and copies of contracts and leases which will be charged to the association.
3. A budget for the association, including current and expected common expense assessments.
4. A description of insurance coverage.

Right to Cancel

Purchasers in Minnesota have 15 days after receipt of disclosure to rescind (cancel) and receive a refund of earnest money. However, if the purchaser received the disclosures more than 15 days before signing a purchase agreement, the purchaser cannot rescind.

The purpose of having laws that require disclosures and then giving a purchaser 15 days to read them is so that the purchaser is better informed before being committed. A condominium buyer is bound by far more complex agreements than the buyer of a house. It is not uncommon for the master deed, bylaws, and restrictions of a condominium to total 100 or more pages of legal language. It is in the interest of the buyer to read all of these documents or have them read and explained by an attorney before buying. The benefit of having disclosure statement laws is of no avail if a buyer refuses to read them or obtain legal counsel.

PHYSICAL APPEARANCE OF A CONDOMINIUM

Before we turn our attention from condominiums, let it be reemphasized that a condominium is first and foremost a legal concept. It tells how title to real property is owned. It does not, by itself, tell us what a condominium looks like. Physically, a condominium can take the shape of a two-story garden apartment building, a 20-story tower, or houses sharing a single parcel of land. You will hear them called low-rise and high-rise condominiums, town-homes, and garden-rises.

Condominiums are not restricted to residential uses. In recent years, a number of developers across the nation have built office buildings and sold individual suites to doctors, dentists, and lawyers. The same idea has been applied to shopping centers and industrial space. A condominium does not have to be a new building. Starting in the late 1960s, many existing apartment houses were converted from rental status to condominium ownership with only a few physical changes to the building.

COOPERATIVE APARTMENTS

non-profit organization

Prior to the availability of condominium enabling legislation in the United States, owner-occupied community housing took the form of the cooperative housing corporation. Although the condominium is dominant today, there are still substantial numbers of cooperative apartments in New York City, Miami, the Twin Cities, Chicago, San Francisco, and Honolulu.

A **cooperative apartment** is organized by forming a nonprofit corporation. This is usually done by a developer who is planning to convert an existing rental building to cooperative ownership or build a new structure. Sometimes, the tenants in a rental building will organize a cooperative corporation to buy their building from the owner. To raise the funds necessary to pay for the building, the corporation borrows as much as it can by mortgaging the building. The balance is raised by selling shares of stock in the corporation.

The Cooperator

The shareholder, or **cooperator,** receives a **proprietary lease** from the corporation to occupy a certain apartment in the building. The more desirable apartments require the purchase of more shares than the less desirable ones.

In return for this lease, the cooperator does not pay rent; instead, he agrees to pay to the corporation his share of the cost of maintaining the building and his share of the monthly mortgage payments and annual property taxes. This sharing of expenses is a unique and crucial feature of this form of ownership. If one or more cooperators fail to pay their pro rata share, the remaining cooperators must make up the difference. Suppose that the monthly loan payment on a 10-unit cooperative building is $4,000 and it is shared equally by its 10 cooperators, each contributing $400 per month. If one shareholder fails to contribute his $400, only $3,600 is available for the required payment. If the lender is paid $3,600 rather than $4,000, the loan is delinquent and subject to foreclosure. The lender does not take the position that, since 9 of the 10 cooperators made their payments, nine-tenths of the building is free from foreclosure threat. Therefore, it is the responsibility of the remaining nine to continue making the $4,000 monthly payments or lose the building. They can seek voluntary reimbursement by the tardy cooperator, or, if that does not work, terminate him as a shareholder.

In most cooperative leases written today, shareholder termination is the worst that can happen to a nonpaying cooperator, because under American corporation law a shareholder is not liable for the debts of the corporation. Thus, even if the cooperative corporation owes more than it owns and is in foreclosure or bankruptcy, the shareholders cannot be dunned for deficiency payments. The lender can look only to the value of the corporation's property for recovery of its loan. In view of this, lenders are especially cautious when making loans to cooperatives, and this has made it difficult for cooperatives to raise money. To counteract this situation, the FHA, under Section 213 of the National Housing Act, will insure lenders against losses on loans made to nonprofit housing cooperatives.

Refinancing Methods

As the entire building serves as collateral for the loan, obtaining new financing on an individual apartment unit in the building is impossible. If there is to be new mortgage financing, it must be on the entire building. When the original mortgage loan is substantially reduced and/or apartment prices have risen, as evidenced by a rise in the value of shares, this can be a severe handicap if a cooperator wants to sell. To illustrate, suppose that a family buys into a cooperative for \$5,000. Several years later the family wants to sell, and is offered \$40,000 for its shares. Unlike the purchaser of a house or a condominium who can obtain most of the money he needs by mortgaging the dwelling he is buying, the cooperative purchaser cannot mortgage his unit. Consequently, if the buyer does not have \$40,000 in cash, he has been forced to mortgage other assets or seek an unsecured personal loan at an interest rate higher than for regular home mortgage loans. Lender reluctance has stemmed from the feeling that a loan against cooperative stock is, in effect, a second mortgage and second mortgages are not acceptable as collateral. In addition, it has been difficult to convince lenders that ownership in a cooperative apartment is as tangible as ownership of a house. An alternative to institutional lenders is seller financing. If the seller is willing to help the buyer with financing, the shares can be sold on an installment contract.

Board of Directors

How a cooperative will be run is set forth in its articles of incorporation, bylaws, covenants and restrictions, and house rules. The governing body is a board of directors elected by a vote of the cooperators and voting can either be based on shares held or on a one-vote-per-apartment basis. The board hires the services needed to maintain and operate the building and decides on how cooperative facilities will be used by shareholders. The annual budget and other matters of importance are submitted to all shareholders for a vote. Between shareholder meetings, normally scheduled annually, unhappy cooperators can approach board members and ask that a desired change be made. Or, at election time, they can vote for more sympathetic contenders for board membership or can run for board positions themselves.

Owners' Association

In two very significant areas, the authority of a cooperative owners' association and its board differs from that found in a condominium. First, as the interior of a cooperator's apartment is not his separate property, the association can control how he uses it. This right is based on the principle that the entire building is owned jointly by all cooperators for their mutual benefit. Thus, if a cooperator damages his apartment or is a constant nuisance, his lease can be terminated. As a rule, this requires at least a two-thirds vote of the shareholders and return of the cooperator's investment.

Second, in a cooperative, the owners' association has the right to accept or reject new shareholders and sublessees. (The latter occurs when a shareholder rents his apartment to another.) If there is much turnover in the building, the association will delegate this right to the board. Thus, whenever a shareholder wishes to sell or rent, the transaction is subject to approval by the board. Except in cases of unlawful discrimination, this feature has been upheld by the courts. The legal basis is that cooperators share not only mutual ownership in their building, but also a joint financial responsibility. However, the board cannot be capricious or inconsistent.

From a social standpoint, the right to approve purchasers and renters helps to foster and maintain the economic and social status of residents, which some persons find attractive. It is also a very useful feature when a person wants to own in a building that excludes children and/or pets.

Tax Treatment

Although owners of houses and condominium units have always enjoyed deductions for mortgage interest and property taxes on their federal income tax returns, such was not always the case with cooperatives. Originally, cooperators were excluded because it was the corporation, not the shareholder, that was liable for interest and taxes. Now, however, if 80% of a cooperative's income is derived from tenant–owner rentals, the individual cooperators may deduct their proportionate share of property taxes and loan interest. If the land or building is leased to the corporation and the fee owner pays the taxes, he is entitled to the deduction, not the cooperators. In Minnesota, the homestead exemption is available to resident owners of cooperative apartments.

Low-Cost Cooperatives

Low-cost cooperatives can be found in a number of United States cities. Sponsored by the FHA or by the city itself, these cooperatives are subsidized by public tax revenues and provide low- and moderate-income families with an opportunity for home ownership. Leases in these buildings are usually written for only 1 to 3 years and are not automatically renewable by the cooperator. This feature reflects the possibility that public funds may be cut back in the future. Also, when a cooperator sells, he is not permitted to retain any profits made upon resale. Rather, he is restricted to recovering only the money he has actually invested (that is, his down payment, mortgage amortization, and improvements).

PLANNED UNIT DEVELOPMENT

As illustrated in Figure 19:1, each owner in a planned unit development (PUD), also called a **townhouse,** owns as separate property the land beneath his or her dwelling. In addition, each unit owner is a shareholder in a nonprofit, incorporated owners' association that holds title to the common areas surrounding the dwelling units. The common areas can be as minimal as a few green spaces or might include parks, pools, golf courses, clubhouses, and jogging trails.

Since each owner in a planned unit development owns his land and dwelling as separate property, presumably he may use and maintain it as he wishes. However, there may be mutual restrictions upon all separately owned lots and dwellings. The right to establish and enforce these restrictions is usually vested in the owners' association. The association can dictate what color an owner can paint his window shutters, how he can landscape the front of his lot, and how many children and pets can reside in his dwelling. Additionally, the association maintains the common areas and governs how these areas shall be used by the residents and their guests.

From a structural standpoint, the dwellings in a residential planned unit development typically look more like houses than apartment buildings and generally contain more living area than apartment units. Because vertical stacking is limited to one owner, densities are usually limited to eight or ten units per acre. Even though this is twice the density of a typical detached house subdivision, by careful planning, a developer can give each owner the feeling of more spaciousness. One way is by taking advantage of uneven terrain. If a parcel contains some flat land, some hilly land, some land covered with trees, and a running stream, the dwellings can be clustered on the land best suited for building and thus preserve the stream, woods, and steep slopes in their natural state. With a standard subdivision layout the developer would have to remove the groves of trees, fill in the stream, and terrace the slopes, and would still be able to provide homes for only half the number of families.

Such thoughtful planning is not limited to single-family PUDs. Some of the most attractive planned residential developments in the United States combine natural surroundings with detached houses, row houses, clustered houses, apartment buildings, condominiums, and stores for shopping. So skillfully has this been done that residents are far more aware of the project's green vistas and lakes than they are of neighboring buildings. Reston, Virginia and Columbia, Maryland are city-sized examples of the planned unit development concept. A PUD can also consist of just one or two dozen homes on six acres in surburbia.

Comparison

When comparing a PUD to a condominium, note that a condominium is a creature of state statute, whereas a PUD is a creature of local zoning. Typically a PUD is an overlay zoning (that is, a zoning that overlays an existing residential zoning) that allows a developer to increase the dwelling density of one part of his development if he leaves another part as open space. Also note that in a condominium the owners own an undivided interest in all the common elements in the project. The owners' association owns nothing but is responsible for seeing the project is managed properly. In a PUD, the owners' association has title to the common areas. In both the condominium and the planned unit development, membership in the owners' association is automatic upon purchasing a unit in the project. PUDs are regulated under Minnesota condominium laws.

TIME-SHARING OWNERSHIP

Thus far, we have been concerned only with the three-dimensional utilization of real estate (that is, the sharing of land and air space). Since 1970, a fourth dimension, time ownership, has received increasing attention in the United States. Used primarily in resort areas, the principle of time-sharing ownership is that a person buys the right to the exclusive use of real estate for a specified length of time each year, such as a week or a month.

Two systems are described here. One is the long-term lease wherein a promoter purchases a motel, hotel, or apartment building in a resort area and for each unit in the building, sells 25 two-weeks-a-year leases for 30 years. (The remaining two weeks are generally reserved for maintenance work.) The sale of these leases pays for the building, and the lessee is charged only his share of the cost of managing, servicing, and maintaining the building. The lessee may be assigned to a specific unit to be used each year or allowed to use any unit in the building that is available when he wishes to visit. To obtain his 2 weeks each year, the lessee makes a reservation through the on-site manager, often on a first-come first-served basis. As 30 years at the same resort is a long time, the lease should permit the lessee the right to sell his lease to another person.

The second system is to establish a condominium and sell each unit to several owners in common ownership. With ownership, each owner obtains the right to use the unit for a certain period each year. For example, a unit might be sold to 10 or 12 buyers as tenants in common, each of whom obtains the right to the exclusive use of the unit for 2 weeks in the winter and 2 weeks in the summer. The ownership agreement should also state how user priorities are set, who is responsible for maintenance, what procedures must be followed if an owner wants to sell his interest, and what happens if one or more owners fail to pay their share of expenses and the mortgage.

If you plan to buy, sell or broker time-shares, you should be familiar with the time-share regulations contained in Chapter 83 of the Minnesota Statutes.

VOCABULARY REVIEW

Match terms **a–m** *with statements* **1–13.**

a. *Bylaws*
b. *Common elements*
c. *Condominium*
d. *Cooperative*
e. *Cooperator*
f. *Declaration*
g. *Floor plan*
h. *House rules*
i. *Limited common elements*
j. *Maintenance fees*
k. *Owners' association*
l. *Proprietary lease*
m. *Townhouse*

1. Individual ownership of separate portions of a building plus undivided ownership of the common elements.
2. Land and building owned or leased by a corporation which in turn leases space to its shareholders.
3. Roof, stairs, elevator, lobby, etc., in a condominium.

4. An organization composed of unit owners in which membership is automatic upon purchase of a unit.
5. Walls and ceilings between two condominium units.
6. Type of lease issued by a cooperative corporation to its shareholders.
7. Architectural drawings that show the layout, location, dimensions and number of a condominium unit.
8. A document that converts a given parcel of land into a vertical subdivision; also called a master deed.
9. Rules that govern how the owners' association will be run.
10. Rules that govern the day-to-day use of condominium and cooperative facilities by owners and tenants.
11. A shareholder in a cooperative apartment.
12. Charges levied against unit owners to cover the costs of maintaining the common areas. Also called association dues.
13. Form of community ownership where the building sites are privately owned but title to common areas is held by an owners' association.

QUESTIONS AND PROBLEMS

1. What has caused the explosive growth in condominium construction since the late 1960s?
2. Who owns the land in a fee simple condominium project? In a cooperative?
3. What is the key difference between a proprietary lease in a cooperative and a landlord–tenant lease?
4. What is the purpose of the enabling declaration in a condominium project?
5. To whom does the wall between two condominium units belong?
6. What are CC&Rs and how do they affect a condominium owner?
7. What are condominium maintenance fees? What happens if they are not paid?
8. If the condominium owners' association carries hazard and liability insurance, why is it also advisable for each unit owner to purchase a hazard and liability policy?
9. Briefly explain the concept of time-sharing condominiums.
10. Briefly explain how title to land in a PUD is held.

ADDITIONAL READINGS

Fletcher, David R. *Condominium Sales and Listings.* Reston, Va.: Reston Publishing Co., 1982, 256 pages. Topics include listing and selling condominiums, conversions, time-sharing, pricing strategy, prospecting, and qualifying buyers.

Hart, Christopher W. "A Method for Valuing Time-Share Intervals." *Real Estate Review,* Summer, 1980, pages 107–113. Reviews history and concept of time-sharing recreational facilities. Points out benefits and pitfalls to buyers as well as methods of estimating the value of a time-share interval.

Holeman, Jack R. *Condominium Management.* Englewood Cliffs, N.J.: Prentice-Hall, Inc., 1980, 356 pages. This book focuses on the organization and management of a condominium. Topics include budget making, fiscal responsibility, insurance, association meetings, elections, directors, committees, rules, security, and employee standards.

Jackson, F. Scott. "How Homeowner Associations Solve Their Enforcement Problems." *Real Estate Review,* Spring, 1978, pages 80–86. Enforcing regulations and restrictions in a condominium or PUD is key to smooth operations. Article discusses methods short of litigation.

Lee, Steven James, Jr. *Buyer's Handbook for Cooperatives and Condominiums.* New York: Van Nostrand-Reinhold, 1978, 325 pages. Topics include the decision to buy, looking for property, inspecting property, negotiating, and closing.

Richardson, Dennis M. "The Creative Art of Condominium Conversion." *Real Estate Review,* Summer, 1979, pages 53–58. Article looks at the decision and development process in converting an existing building to a condominium.

Untermann, Richard, and **Small, Robert.** *Site Planning for Cluster Housing.* New York: Van Nostrand-Reinhold, 1977, 306 pages. Book deals with the layout and design of housing environments. Heavily illustrated with photographs and illustrations.

20

Property Insurance

KEY TERMS

All-risks policy: all perils, except those excluded in writing, are covered

Broad-form: an insurance term that describes a policy that covers a large number of named perils

Endorsement: an agreement by the insurer to extend coverage to perils not covered by the basic policy; also called a rider or an attachment

Homeowner policy: a packaged insurance policy designed for homeowners and tenants. Includes property damage and public liability coverage

Insurance premium: the amount of money one must pay for insurance coverage

Perils: hazards or risks

Public liability: the financial responsibility one has toward others as a result of one's actions or failure to take action

As an owner of real estate, one takes the risk that his property may be damaged due to fire or other catastrophe. Additionally there is the possibility that someone may injure himself while on the property and hold the owner responsible. Insurance to cover losses from either of these sources is available.

The basic property damage policy is the New York fire form developed by the New York State Legislature and now used throughout the United States. Its 165 lines of court-tested language cover (1) loss by fire, (2) loss by lightning, and (3) losses sustained while removing property from endangered premises. Coverage can be on real property improvements, personal property, or both. Let us briefly discuss these **perils** (also called hazards or risks).

PROPERTY DAMAGE

To be covered for loss by fire, there must be flames. Smoke or heat damage or damage by explosion, no matter how severe, does not qualify unless preceded by flames. Also, the fire must be hostile as opposed to friendly. A **hostile fire** is a fire where it is not intended to be. A **friendly fire** is a fire burning in a place designed for it, such as a furnace, fireplace, gas stove, or water heater. However, if a friendly fire gets out of control, it is then classed as hostile and losses are covered. Insurers are required to pay whether the fire was purely accidental or the result of negligence by the insured or some other person. For example, suppose that you have a fire in the fireplace of your home and do not bother to close the fireplace screen. If, while you have left the room, the fire throws out a live ember onto a rug and starts a fire, you are covered even though you were negligent in not closing the screen. However, if the insured intentionally starts a hostile fire, the insurer is excused from paying for the damage.

Damage caused by lightning is covered whether or not an actual fire develops. However, man-made electrical discharges are not covered. For example, melted wires caused by an electrical short circuit are not covered unless the cause was lightning or a fire on the premises.

To encourage the removal of personal property from an endangered building, the New York form also covers certain types of loss or damage resulting from removal and storage elsewhere. Coverage is good for 5 days at a new location, after which a new policy must be obtained.

Endorsements

Although fire is the single most important cause of property damage in the United States, a property owner is also exposed to many other perils, including hail, tornado, earthquake, riot, windstorm, smoke damage, explosion, glass breakage, water-pipe leaks, vandalism, freezing, and building collapse. Coverage for each peril can be purchased with a separate policy or it can be added to the fire form as an **endorsement.** An endorsement, also called a **rider** or **attachment,** is an agreement by the insurer to extend coverage to losses by perils not included in the basic policy. Using endorsements, a policyholder can create a single policy that covers only the perils he is exposed to and not pay for coverage he does not need. The amount of money the policyholder pays for coverage is called the **insurance premium.**

PUBLIC LIABILITY

Public liability is the financial responsibility one has toward others as a result of one's actions or failure to take action. For example, if you are trimming the limbs from a tall tree in your backyard and a limb falls on your neighbor's roof and damages it, you are liable to your neighbor for damages. Or, if you have a swimming pool in your backyard and a neighbor child drowns in it, the child's parents may be able to successfully sue you for money damages.

Generally, you are liable when there exists a legal duty to exercise reasonable care and you fail to do so, thereby causing injury to an innocent party. Even though you did not intend for the limb to fall on your neighbor's roof or the child to drown in your pool, you are not excused from liability. You can be held accountable, in money, for the amount of damage caused.

HOMEOWNER PACKAGE POLICIES

For major commercial and industrial property owners and users, carefully identifying each risk exposure and then insuring for it is a logical and economic approach to purchasing insurance. But for the majority of homeowners, owners of small apartment and business properties, and their tenants, purchasing insurance piecemeal is a confusing process. As a result, package policies designed for owners and tenants of specific kinds of properties have been developed.

Of these, the best known and most widely used is the **homeowner's package policy,** which contains the coverages deemed by insurance experts to be most useful to persons who own or rent the home in which they live. Not only does this approach avoid overlaps and lessen the opportunity for gaps in coverage, but the cost is less than purchasing separate individual policies with the same total coverage. Moreover, homeowner policies go beyond covering only damage and public liability directly connected with the insured property. They also include coverage for theft of the insured's real and personal property and public liability arising from the personal activities of the insured. Let us take a closer look.

Policy Formats

There are six standardized homeowner policy forms in use in the United States. Each contains two sections. **Section I** deals with property insurance and includes a standard fire policy with a wide variety of endorsements, plus a theft policy. Buildings and their contents and, to a certain extent, personal property when it is taken off the insured premises are covered. **Section II** deals with liability on the premises, plus personal liability.

Form HO-2

Form HO-2 covers damage and loss to buildings and contents caused by such perils are fire, lightning, hail, windstorm, explosion, riot, smoke, vandalism, theft, sonic boom, falling objects, weight of ice, snow, or sleet, building cracking or collapse, accidental plumbing leakage or overflow, freezing of pipes, artificial electrical discharge, and hot-water-system malfunction. If damage to the premises requires the insured to live elsewhere while repairs are being made, HO-2 coverage pays for additional living costs up to a limit equaling 20% of the dwelling insurance.

Major HO-2 exceptions are loss or damage caused by an enemy attack, insurrection, rebellion, revolution, civil war, or usurped power. As a group, these exceptions are sometimes referred to as a **war clause exemption.** Also excepted are the perils of earthquake, flood, landslide, mudflow, tidal waves, or underground seepage. If a property owner is exposed to these perils, he must buy additional insurance. With regard to theft, major exceptions to coverage are motorized vehicles, business property, and animals. These require separate policies or endorsements.

Section II of the policy includes liability insurance, medical payments coverage for injuries to others, and insurance for physical damage to the property of others. This section covers such incidents as a tree falling onto a neighbor's house, the family dog biting a visitor, a guest slipping on a freshly waxed kitchen floor, and the insured or the insured's child kicking a football through someone's window. Not covered is damage to, or damage caused by the homeowner's automobile.

HO-1

Form HO-1 is a homeowner policy that covers fewer perils and has more restrictions than HO-2. These limitations deal with aircraft and vehicle damage to the insured property, smoke damage, glass breakage, and theft.

HO-3

Form HO-3 covers more perils to the building structure than HO-2 and is sometimes referred to as an **all-risks** policy. However, property damage by flood, earthquake, war, termites, rodents, wear and tear, marring and scratching, rust, mold, and contamination (nuclear, for example) are still excluded. The difference between an all-risks policy and a **named-peril** policy, such as HO-1 or HO-2, is that in a named-peril policy each peril must be named in the policy in order to be covered. In an all-risks policy, all perils except those excluded are covered. The term **broad-form** is used to describe policies that cover a large number of named perils. Form HO-2, for example, is a broad-form policy.

HO-4 Tenant's Policy

Form HO-4, often referred to as a **tenant's policy,** provides the same coverages as HO-2 except that there is no coverage on building structures. It is designed for renters.

HO-5

Form HO-5 is the most liberal of the six forms from the standpoint of the insured. It extends the all-risk coverage described in Form HO-3 to personal property and increases the amount of dollar coverage.

HO-6

Form HO-6 is designed for condominium and cooperative owners where the owners' association carries property damage and public liability insurance on the common elements. Form HO-6 covers the same perils as the tenant's form, but increases the additional living expense limit and puts addition and alteration coverage on a replacement cost basis with a maximum recovery of $1,000. Endorsements can be added to increase these coverages, cover appurtenant structures on the premises that are solely owned by the insured, and pay for special assessments levied against the policyholder for uninsured property or liability losses of the association.

Homeowner Endorsements

Any of the six homeowner policies can be endorsed for additional coverage. For example, **inflation guard** endorsements are available that automatically increase property damage coverage by 1½%, 2% or 2½% per quarter, as selected by the insured. If the property is to be rented out, tenant coverage can also be added. Alternatively, a policy specifically designed for rental property can be purchased.

NEW FOR OLD

A special problem in recovering from damage to a building is that, although the building may not be new, any repairs are made new. For example, if a 20-year-old house burns to the ground, it is absurd to think we can put back a used house, even though a used house is exactly what the insured lost. Thus, the question is whether insurance should pay for the full cost of fixing the damage, in effect replace "new for old," or simply pay the actual cash value of the loss. **Actual cash value** is the new price minus accumulated depreciation and is, in effect, "old for old." Under "old for old," if the owner rebuilds, he pays the difference between actual cash value and the cost of the repairs. As this can be quite costly to the insured, the alternative is to purchase a policy that replaces "new for old."

For the owner of an apartment building, store, or other property operated on a business basis, obtaining "new for old" coverage is a matter of substituting the term "replacement cost" for "actual cash value" wherever it appears in the policy. Also, the policyholder must agree to carry coverage amounting to at least 80% of current replacement cost and to use the insurance proceeds to repair or replace the damaged property within a reasonable time.

Under a homeowner's policy, if the amount of insurance carried is 80% or more of the cost to replace the house today, the full cost of repair will be paid by the insurer, up to the face amount of the policy. If the face amount is less than 80% of replacement costs, the insured is entitled to the higher of (1) the actual cash value of the loss or (2) the amount calculated as follows:

$$\frac{\text{Insurance carried}}{\left(\begin{array}{c}\text{80\% of today's cost}\\ \text{to replace whole structure}\end{array}\right)} \times \left(\begin{array}{l}\text{Today's cost to replace}\\ \text{the damaged portion}\end{array}\right) = \text{Recovery}$$

FLOOD INSURANCE

In 1968 Congress created the National Flood Insurance Program. This program is a joint effort of the nation's insurance industry and the federal government to offer property owners coverage for losses to real and personal property resulting from the inundation of normally dry areas from (1) the overflow of inland or tidal waters, (2) the unusual and rapid accumulation or runoff of surface waters, (3) mudslides resulting from accumulations of water on or under the ground, and (4) erosion losses caused by abnormal water runoff.

All mortgages in which the federal government is involved (FDIC and FSLIC insured lenders and FHA, VA, FNMA, FHLMC, and GNMA loans) require either a certificate that the mortgaged property is not in a flood zone or a policy of flood insurance. Flood insurance is available through private insurance agents.

POLICY CANCELLATION

A property damage or public liability policy can be canceled at anytime by the insured. Since the policy is billed in advance, the insured is entitled to a refund for unused coverage. This refund is computed at short rates, which are somewhat higher than a simple pro rata charge. For example, the holder of a 1-year policy who cancels one-third of the way through the year is charged 44% of the 1-year price, not $33\frac{1}{3}$%.

The insurer also has the right to cancel a policy. However, unlike the policyholder, who can cancel on immediate notice, the New York fire form requires the insurer to give the policyholder 5-day notice. Also, the cost of the policy, and hence the refund of unused premium, must be calculated on a pro rata basis. For example, the insured would be charged one-half the annual premium for 6 months of coverage.

Policy Suspension

Certain acts of the policyholder will suspend his coverage without the necessity of a written notice from the insurer. Suspension automatically occurs if the insured allows the hazard exposure to the insurer to increase beyond the risks normally associated with the type of property being insured, for example, converting a dwelling to a restaurant. Suspension also occurs if the insured building is left unoccupied for more than 30 days because unoccupied buildings are more attractive to thieves, vandals, and arsonists. If the condition causing the suspension is corrected (returning the restaurant to a dwelling or reoccupying the building) before a loss occurs, the policy becomes effective again.

Willful concealment or misrepresentation by the insured of any material fact or circumstance concerning the policy, the property, or the insured, either before or after a loss, will make the policy void. Thus, if a person operates a business in the basement of his house and conceals this from the insurer for fear of being charged more for insurance, the money he pays for insurance could be wasted.

POLICY TAKEOVERS

Often in a real estate transaction the buyer will ask to assume the seller's existing insurance policy for the property. This way the buyer avoids having to pay a full year's premium in advance and the seller benefits by avoiding a short-rate cancellation charge. To avoid a break in coverage, the insurer must accept the buyer as the new policyholder before the closing takes place. This is done with an endorsement issued by the insurer naming the buyer as the insured party. The reason for this requirement is that an insurance policy does not protect the property, but the insured's financial interest in the property. This is called an **insurable interest.**

Suppose the property is destroyed by fire immediately after the closing. Once title has passed, the seller no longer has an insurable interest in the property. If the insurance company has not endorsed the policy over to the buyer, the company is under no obligation to pay for the damage. If there is doubt that the endorsement to the buyer can be obtained in time for the closing, the buyer should purchase a new policy in his/her own name.

Note, that anyone holding a mortgage on an improved property has an insurable interest and should require the borrower to carry a policy that names both the borrower and lender as insured parties. This is a standard requirement of institutional lenders.

HOME BUYER'S INSURANCE

A long-standing concern of home buyers has been the possibility of finding structural or mechanical defects in a home after buying it. In Minnesota, in every sale of a new dwelling, and in every contract for the sale of a dwelling to be completed, and every home improvement contract, the builder/contractor must warrant that:

1. for 1 year from taking ownership, the dwelling will be free from defects caused by faulty workmanship and defective materials;
2. for 2 years the dwelling will be free from defects caused by faulty installation of plumbing, electrical, heating, and cooling systems; and
3. for 10 years the dwelling will be free from major construction defects.

A number of builders in Minnesota have chosen to associate with the Home Owners Warranty Corporation (HOW) in order to comply with the law. This way if the builder cannot or will not honor this warranty, the HOW program underwriter will do so.

In a growing number of cities, the purchaser of a used house can obtain a warranty for 12 to 18 months to cover most things that can go wrong. Available through real estate brokers, this coverage is sold through two plans. Under one plan, the insurer makes an inspection of the home and issues a policy covering all defects not identified by the inspection.

Under the second plan, there is no inspection. However, a participating broker must agree to insure all homes he sells.

Ongoing insurance can also be purchased annually. For an annual fee of approximately $250, the insurer will repair or replace defective systems in pre-owned homes including electrical, plumbing, heating, air conditioning, and built-in appliances.

VOCABULARY REVIEW

Match terms **a–k** *with statements* **1–11.**

a. *Actual cash value*
b. *Friendly fire*
c. *Homeowner's policy*
d. *Hostile fire*
e. *Inflation guard*
f. *Liability*
g. *Perils*
h. *Premium*
i. *Replacement cost*
j. *Tenant's policy*
k. *War clause*

1. A fire that is burning in a place intended for it.
2. A fire that is burning in a place not intended for it.
3. A policy endorsement that automatically increases the amount of insurance coverage periodically during the life of the policy.
4. Also called hazards or risks.
5. Words inserted in an insurance policy to limit the extent of coverage for damages caused by warfare, insurrection, etc.
6. A combined property and liability policy designed for persons who do not own the dwelling in which they live.
7. Current cost of replacing damaged property less depreciation; in effect, "old for old."
8. Cost of replacing damaged property at current prices; in effect, "new for old."
9. A combined property and liability policy designed for residential owner–occupants.
10. The financial responsibility one has toward others.
11. The amount of money paid for insurance coverage.

QUESTIONS AND PROBLEMS

1. Do fire policies cover losses caused by negligence? Losses intentionally caused by the insured?
2. What role does an endorsement or rider play in an insurance policy?
3. What is the purpose of public liability insurance?
4. In a homeowner's policy, what type of loss does Section I deal with? Section II?
5. How do all-risk insurance policies differ from broad-form policies?
6. What does the phrase "new for old" refer to when talking about insurance policies that cover property damage?

7. Why will an insurer suspend coverage if a property is left vacant too long?

ADDITIONAL READINGS

Huebner, S. S., Black, Kenneth, Jr., and **Cline, Robert S.** *Property and Liability Insurance,* 3rd ed. New York: Appleton-Century-Crofts, 1982, 608 pages. A college-level text that deals with fire, marine, inland marine (personal property), public liability, and workers' compensation insurance. It also covers package policies, rate making and government regulations affecting insurers.

"New Twist to Home Protection Program." *Real Estate Today,* February, 1979, pages 36–39. Article explains various insurance plans designed to pay in the event of a failure of a home component.

Riegel, Robert T., Miller, Jerome S., and **Williams, C. Arthur, Jr.** *Insurance Principles and Practices,* 6th ed. Englewood Cliffs, N.J. Prentice-Hall, 1976, 619 pages. A very readable textbook that deals with risk management, property insurance, liability insurance, package policies, and government insurance programs.

Williams, Chester Arthur, and **Heins, Richard M.** *Risk Management and Insurance,* 3rd ed. New York: McGraw-Hill, 1976, 678 pages. Book looks at insurance from the standpoint of risk identification, risk management and insurance contracts.

21

Land-Use Control

KEY TERMS

Building codes: local and state laws that set minimum construction standards

Certificate of occupancy: a government issued document that states a structure meets local zoning and building code requirements and is ready for use

Comprehensive plan: a guide for the physical growth of a community

Environmental impact statement: a report that contains information regarding the effect of a proposed project on the environment of an area

Land-use control: a broad term that describes any legal restriction that controls how a parcel of land may be used

Nonconforming use: an improvement that is inconsistent with current zoning regulations

Restrictive covenants: clauses placed in deeds to control how future landowners may or may not use the property; also used in leases

Transferable development right (TDR): a legal means by which the right to develop a particular parcel of land can be transferred to another parcel

Variance: a permit granted to an individual property owner to vary slightly from strict compliance with zoning requirements

Zoning: public regulations that control the specific use of land in a given district

ZONING

No other aspect of land-use control affects the American public to a greater degree than **zoning.** Since the first zoning law went into effect in 1916 in New York City, nearly every town and city in the United States, plus a large number of counties, has adopted zoning ordinances. (The original purpose for adopting zoning in New York City was to keep the expanding garment industry out of the fashionable Fifth Avenue business and residential areas.) Zoning laws divide land into zones (districts) and within each zone regulate the purpose for which buildings may be constructed, the height and bulk of the buildings, the area of the lot that they may occupy, and the number of persons that they can accommodate. Through zoning, a community can protect existing land users from encroachment by undesirable uses, ensure that future land uses in the community will be compatible with each other, and control development so that each parcel of land will be adequately serviced by streets, sanitary and storm sewers, schools, parks, and utilities.

The authority to control land use is derived from the basic police power of each state to protect the public health, safety, morals, and general welfare of its citizens. Through an enabling act passed by the state legislature, the authority to control land use is also given to individual towns, cities, and counties. These local government units then pass zoning ordinances that establish the boundaries of the various land-use zones and determine the type of development that will be permitted in each of them. By going to his local government offices, a landowner can see on a map how his land is zoned. Once he knows the zoning for his land, he can consult the zoning ordinance to see how he will be allowed to use it.

Zoning Symbols

For convenience, zones are usually identified by code abbreviations such as R (residential), C (commercial), I or M (industrial-manufacturing), and A (agriculture). Within each general category there are subcategories, such as R-1 (single-family residence), R-2 (two-family residence), R-3 (low-density, garden-type apartments), R-4 (high-density, high-rise apartments), and PUD (mixed or multiple use). Similarly, there are usually three or four manufacturing zones ranging from light, smoke-free industry (I-1 or M-1) to heavy industry (I-4 or M-4). However, there is no uniformity in zoning classifications in the United States or in Minnesota. One city may use R-4 to designate high-rise apartments, while another uses R-4 to designate single-family homes on 4,000-square-foot lots and the letter A to designate apartments.

Land-Use Restrictions

Besides telling a landowner the use to which he may put his land, the zoning ordinance imposes additional rules. For example, land zoned for low-density apartments may require 1,500 square feet of land per living unit, a minimum of 600 square feet of living space per unit for one bedroom, 800 square feet for two bedrooms, and 1,000 square feet for three bedrooms. The zoning ordinance may also contain a set-back requirement which states that a building must be placed at least 25 feet back from the street, 10 feet from the sides of the lot, and 15 feet from the rear lot line. The ordinance may also limit the building's height to 2½ stories and require that the lot be a minimum of 10,000 square feet in size. As can be seen, zoning encourages uniformity.

Apart from local zoning ordinances, Minnesota has passed extensive legislation governing lot size and set-back requirements in shoreland areas. Also, the State Department of Natural Resources (DNR) works closely with municipalities to establish watershed districts and rules and regulations to prevent developments which would adversely impact the environment. In addition, Minnesota law provides for the establishment of regional commissions to oversee development according to comprehensive plans drafted by individual cities within each region. These comprehensive plans may eventually supersede local zoning ordinances.

Enforcement of Zoning Laws

Zoning laws are enforced by virtue of the fact that in order to build upon his land a person must obtain a building permit from his city or county government. Before a permit is issued, the proposed structure must conform with government-imposed structural standards and comply with the zoning on the land. If a landowner builds without a permit, he can be forced to tear down his building.

When an existing structure does not conform with a new zoning law, it is "grandfathered-in" as a **nonconforming use.** Thus, the owner can continue to use the structure even though it does not conform to the new zoning. However, the owner is not permitted to enlarge or remodel the structure or to extend its life. When the structure is ultimately demolished, any new use of the land must be in accordance with the zoning law. If you are driving through a residential neighborhood and see an old store or service station that looks very much out of place, it is probably a nonconforming use that was allowed to stay because it was built before the current zoning on the property went into effect.

Zoning Changes

Once an area has been zoned for a specific land use, changes are made by **amending the zoning ordinance** or by obtaining a variance. The amendment approach is taken when a change in zoning is necessary. An amendment can be initiated by a property owner in the area to be rezoned or by local government. Either way, notice of the proposed change must be given to all property owners in and around the affected area, and a public hearing must be held so that property owners and the public at large may voice their opinions on the matter. By comparison, **variances** allow an individual landowner to deviate somewhat from zoning code requirements and do not involve a zoning change. For example, a variance might be granted to the owner of an odd-shaped lot to reduce the setback requirements slightly so that he can fit a building on it. Variances usually are granted where strict compliance with the zoning ordinance or code would cause undue hardship. However, the variance must not change the basic character of the neighborhood, and it must be consistent with the general objectives of zoning as they apply to that neighborhood.

Spot zoning, another term you will frequently encounter in real estate, refers to the rezoning of a small area of land in an existing neighborhood. For example, a neighborhood convenience center (grocery, laundry, barbershop) might be allowed in a residential neighborhood provided it serves a useful purpose for neighborhood residents and is not a nuisance.

A close relative to spot zoning is the conditional use permit. A **conditional use permit** allows a nonconforming use of land provided the use is within that granted by the permit. For example, whereas local commercial zoning might allow for a variety of commercial structures, a conditional use permit would specify the use to which the structure can be put. Thus a conditional use permit is quite restrictive and if the conditions of the permit are violated, the permit is no longer valid. For example, a neighborhood grocery store operating under a conditional use permit can only be a neighborhood grocery. The structure could not be used as an auto parts store.

A zoning law can be changed or struck down if it can be proved in court that it is unclear, discriminatory, unreasonable, not for the protection of the public health, safety, and general welfare, or not applied to all property in a similar manner.

It must be recognized that zoning alone does not create land value. For example, zoning a hundred square miles of lonely desert or mountain land for stores and offices would not appreciably change its value. Value is created by the number of people who want to use a particular parcel of land for a specific purpose. To the extent that zoning channels that demand to certain parcels of land and away from others, zoning does have an important impact on property value.

PLANNING AHEAD FOR DEVELOPMENT

When a community first adopts a zoning ordinance, the usual procedure is to recognize existing land uses by zoning according to what already exists. Thus, a neighborhood that is already developed with houses is zoned for houses. Undeveloped land may be zoned for agriculture or simply left unzoned. As a community expands, undeveloped land is zoned for urban uses in a pattern that typically follows the availability of new roads, the aggressiveness of developers, and the willingness of landowners to sell. All too often this results in a hodgepodge of land-use districts, all conforming internally because of tightly enforced zoning, but with little or no relationship among them. This happens because they were created over a period of years without the aid of a land-use plan that took a comprehensive view of the entire growth pattern of the city. Since uncoordinated land use can have a negative impact on both the quality of life and economic vitality of a community, more attention is now being directed toward comprehensive plans to guide the development of towns and cities, districts, and even whole states.

Comprehensive Plans

To prepare a **comprehensive plan** (or **general plan**), a city or regional planning commission is usually created. The first step should be a physical and economic survey of the area to be planned. The physical survey involves mapping existing roads, utility lines, and developed and undeveloped land. The economic survey looks at the present and anticipated economic base of the region, its population, and its retail trade facilities. Together the two surveys provide the information upon which a comprehensive plan is built. The key is to view the region as a unified entity that provides its residents with jobs and housing, as well as social, recreational, and cultural opportunities. In doing so, the plan uses existing patterns of transportation and land use and directs future growth so as to achieve balanced development. For example, if agriculture is important to the area's economy, special attention is given to retaining the best soils for farming. Waterfront property may also receive special planning protection. Similarly, if houses in an older residential area of town are being converted to rooming houses and apartments, that transition can be encouraged by planning apartment usage for the area. In doing this, the plan guides those who must make day-to-day decisions regarding zoning changes and gives the individual property owner a long-range idea of what his property may be used for in the future.

To assure long-run continuity, a plan should look at least 15 years into the future and preferably 25 years or more. It must also include provisions for flexibility in the event that the city or region does not develop as expected, such as when population grows faster or slower than anticipated. Most importantly, the plan must provide for a balance between the economic and social functions of the community. For example, to emphasize culture and recreation at the expense of adequate housing and the area's economic base will result in the slow decay of the community, because people must leave to find housing and jobs.

SUBDIVISION REGULATIONS

Before a building lot can be sold, a subdivider must comply with government regulations concerning street construction, curbs, sidewalks, street lighting, fire hydrants, storm and sanitary sewers, grading and compacting of soil, water and utility lines, minimum lot size, and so on. In addition, the subdivider may be required to either set aside land for schools and parks or provide money so that land for that purpose may be purchased nearby. Until he has complied with all state and local regulations, the subdivider cannot receive his subdivision approval. Without approval he cannot record his plat map, which in turn means he cannot sell his lots to the public. If he tries to sell his lots without approval, he can be stopped by a government court order and in some states fined. Moreover, permits to build will be refused to lot owners, and anyone who bought from the subdivider is entitled to a refund.

BUILDING CODES

Recognizing the need to protect public health and safety against slipshod construction practices, state and local governments have enacted building codes. These establish minimum acceptable material and construction standards for such things as structural load and stress, windows and ventilation, size and location of rooms, fire protection, exits, electrical installation, plumbing, heating, lighting, and so forth.

Before a building permit is granted, the design of a proposed structure must meet the building-code requirements. During construction, local building department inspectors visit the construction site to make certain that the codes are being observed. Finally, when the building is completed, a **certificate of occupancy** is issued to the building owner to show that the structure meets the code. Without this certificate, the building cannot be legally occupied.

W/O certificate cannot move in—

DEED RESTRICTIONS

Although property owners tend to think of land-use controls as being strictly a product of government, it is possible to achieve land-use control through private means. In fact, Houston, Texas, with a population of more than 2 million persons, operates without zoning and relies almost entirely upon private land-use controls to achieve a similar effect.

Private land-use controls take the form of deed and lease restrictions. In the United States, it has long been recognized that the ownership of land includes the right to sell or lease it on whatever legally acceptable conditions the owner wishes, including the right to dictate to the buyer or lessee how he shall or shall not use it. For example, a developer can sell the lots in his subdivision subject to a restriction written into each deed that the land cannot be used for anything but a single-family residence containing at least 1,200 square feet of living area. The legal theory is that, if the buyer or lessee agrees to the restrictions, he is bound by them. If they are not obeyed, any lot owner in the subdivision can obtain a court order to enforce compliance. The only limit to the number of restrictions that an owner may place on his land is economic. If there are too many restrictions, the landowner may find that no one wants his land.

Deed restrictions, also known as **restrictive covenants,** can be used to dictate such matters as the purpose of the structure to be built, architectural requirements, set-backs, size of the structure, and aesthetics. In neighborhoods with view lots, they are often used to limit the height to which trees may be permitted to grow. Deed restrictions cannot be used to discriminate on the basis of sex, race, color, or creed; if they do they are unenforceable by the courts.

ENVIRONMENTAL IMPACT STATEMENTS

The purpose of an **environmental impact statement** (EIS) is to gather into one document enough information about the effect of a proposed project on the total environment so that a neutral decision maker can judge the environmental benefits and costs of the project. For example, a city zoning commission that has been asked to approve a zone change can request an EIS that will show the expected impact of the change on such things as population density, automobile traffic, noise, air quality, water and sewage facilities, drainage, energy consumption, school enrollments, employment, public health and safety, recreation facilities, wildlife, and vegetation. The idea is that with this information at hand better decisions regarding land uses can be made. When problems can be anticipated in advance, it is easier to make modifications or explore alternatives.

At the city and county level, where the EIS requirement has the greatest effect on private development, the EIS usually accompanies the development application that is submitted to the planning or zoning commission. Where applicable, copies are also sent to affected school districts, water and sanitation districts, and highway and flood control departments. The EIS is then made available for public inspection as part of the hearing process on the development application. This gives concerned civic groups and the public at large an opportunity to voice their opinions regarding the anticipated benefits and costs of the proposed development. If the proposed development is partially or wholly funded by state or federal funds, state or federal hearings are also held.

Content of an EIS

Typically an EIS will contain a description of present conditions at the proposed development site, plus information on the following five points: (1) the probable impact of the proposed project on the physical, economic, and social environment of the area, (2) any unavoidable adverse environmental effects, (3) any alternatives to the proposed project, (4) the short-term versus long-term effects of the proposed project on the environment, and (5) a listing of any irreversible commitment of resources if the project is implemented. For a government-initiated project, the EIS is prepared by a government agency, sometimes with the help of private consultants. In the case of a private development, it may be prepared by the developer, a local government agency for a fee, or by a private firm specializing in the preparation of impact statements.

Costs

Although the concept of examining the environmental impact of a proposed action is now considered an important part of good planning, EIS laws have a cost. From the public at large, tax money must be collected to pay for the additional government employees who must be hired to accept and review impact statements. For the developer there is the cost of preparing the statement, a cost that can easily run from $5,000 to $20,000 for a modest-sized tract of homes. This must ultimately be passed on to the home buyer. There is also the cost of delays caused by the EIS requirement. For example, for each month of delay a developer incurs in constructing an $80,000 house, interest and inflation add $800 to the price the purchaser must pay. Before 1970, housing developers usually estimated 3 months between land purchase and the start of grading and construction. By 1980, it took from 9 to 18 months and the EIS requirement was a major contributor to the extra delay.

WINDFALLS AND WIPE-OUTS

Planning and zoning tend to provide windfall gains for the owners of land that has been authorized for development, while landowners who are prohibited from developing their land suffer financial wipe-outs. This has been a major stumbling block to the orderly utilization of land in America. It is only natural that a landowner will want his land to be zoned for a use that will make it more valuable; however, not all land can be zoned for housing, stores, and offices. Some land must be reserved for agriculture and open spaces. If local and state governments embark upon bold land planning programs, how will these financial inequities be resolved?

The past and current position of government and the courts is that, if land-use restrictions are for the health, safety, and general welfare of the community at large, then under the rules of police power the individual landowner is not compensated for any resulting loss in value. Only when there is an actual physical taking of land is the owner entitled to compensation under the rules of eminent domain. In today's environmentally conscious society, this often results in pitting the landowner who wants to develop his land against those who want to prevent development without compensation. For example, a government planning agency in one state stretched the limits of police power to deny an urban landowner a permit to build on his property and instead told him he should grow flowers for the public's enjoyment. Many decisions like this could ultimately undermine planning efforts. Yet, government planning agencies do not have the money to buy all the land that they would like to see remain undeveloped.

TRANSFERABLE DEVELOPMENT RIGHTS

The solution may come from some radical new thinking about land and the rights to use it. The new planning idea is to eliminate windfalls and wipe-outs by creating **transferable development rights** (TDRs). Previously, the right to develop a parcel of land could not be separated from the land itself. Now planners are exploring the idea of separating the two so that development rights can be transferred to land where greater density will not be objectionable. For example, suppose that within a given planning district there is an area of high-quality farmland that planners feel should be retained for agriculture and not be paved over with streets and covered with buildings. Also in the district is an area deemed more suitable for urban uses and hence an area where government will concentrate on constructing streets, schools, parks, waterlines, and other public facilities. To direct growth to the urban area, it is planned and zoned for urban uses. Meanwhile, areas designated for agriculture are forced to remain as farmland. Ordinarily, this would result in windfall gains for the owner of the urban land and a loss in land value for the owner of the farmland.

With the TDR concept in effect owners of farmland are allowed to sell development rights to the owners of urban land. By purchasing development rights, the urban landowner is permitted to develop his land more intensely than he otherwise could. This compensates the farmer for the loss of his right to develop his land. For the TDR concept to work, there must be a comprehensive regional master plan and an environmental impact statement.

TDRs could be traded on the open market like stocks and bonds. Alternatively, a government agency could pay cash for the value of rights lost. This would be financed by selling those rights to owners in districts to be developed.

Where Used

To date, Chicago and New York City have made use of TDRs for the purpose of protecting historical buildings not owned by the government. Under this system, an owner who agrees not to tear down his building is given TDRs, which can be sold to other nearby landowners. Additionally, TDRs are presently being used to protect open spaces, as well as agricultural and environmentally sensitive lands in parts of Pennsylvania, Virginia, Florida, Vermont, New Jersey, Maryland and Puerto Rico. In a number of states, the TDR concept is still being tested in court cases. It appears that much of the legal debate centers on the concept of separating the right to develop land from the land itself. The idea is new and has little legal precedence. But, for that matter, neither did zoning before 1916.

VOCABULARY REVIEW

Match terms **a–j** *with statements* **1–10.**

a. *Certificate of occupancy*
b. *Comprehensive plan*
c. *EIS*
d. *Land-use control*
e. *Nonconforming use*
f. *Restrictive covenants*
g. *TDR*
h. *Windfall gain*
i. *Wipe-out*
j. *Zoning*

1. A broad term used to describe any legal restriction (such as zoning) that controls how a parcel of land may be used.
2. Public regulations that control the specific use to which land in a given district may be put.
3. An improvement that is inconsistent with current zoning regulations.
4. A comprehensive guide for a community's physical growth.
5. Clauses placed in deeds to control how future landowners may or may not use the property.
6. A document issued by a building department stating that a structure meets local zoning and building code requirements and is ready for use.
7. A report that contains information regarding the effect of a proposed project on the environment.
8. An increase in property value resulting from a publicly made decision; i.e., a zoning change from agricultural to residential use.
9. A decrease in property value resulting from a publicly made decision, such as a change in zoning from urban uses to open space.
10. A means by which the rights to develop a given parcel of land can be conveyed to another parcel of land.

QUESTIONS AND PROBLEMS

1. For land-use control to be successful, why is it necessary to consider the rights of individual property owners as well as the public as a whole?
2. Explain how a city obtains its power to control land use through zoning.
3. What is the purpose of a variance? How does it differ from a zoning ordinance amendment?
4. In your community, what are the letter/number designations for the following: high-rise apartments, low-rise apartments, single-family houses, stores, duplexes, industrial sites?

5. What is the difference between comprehensive planning and zoning?
6. What is the purpose of an environmental impact statement?
7. What are the pros and cons of requiring an EIS before a housing subdivision can be built?
8. How would the use of transferable development rights reduce windfalls and wipe-outs for land owners?
9. Does any city or county in your state currently use transferable development rights? What have been the results?

ADDITIONAL READINGS

Bellandi, Robert M. L., and **Hennigan, Robert D.** "The Why and How of Transferable Development Rights." *Real Estate Review,* Summer, 1977, pages 60–64. Article contains discussion and examples of the TDR concept.

Campbell, Carlos C. *New Towns: Another Way to Live.* Reston, Va.: Reston Publishing Co., 1976, 283 pages. The new town concept features land planning on a city-wide scale and offers an alternative to uncontrolled urban growth. Author discusses new towns in America and contrasts them with those in Europe.

Hagman, Donald G. and **Misczynski, Dean J.** *Windfalls for Wipeouts.* Chicago: American Society of Planning Officials, 1978, 660 pages. Book discusses how present systems of land planning and zoning produce financial windfalls and wipeouts for property owners. Author suggests alternatives that would achieve more desirable land-use patterns and be more equitable to property owners.

Nelson, Robert H. *Zoning and Property Rights.* Cambridge, Mass.: MIT Press, 1977, 259 pages. Author discusses purposes and problems of present zoning and planning laws and makes suggestions for improvements that take into consideration private property rights.

Netter, Edith, ed. *Land Use Law: Issues for the Eighties.* Chicago: Planners Press, 1981, 232 pages. Contains a collection of articles on current land-use planning challenges.

Seidel, Stephen R. *Housing Costs and Government Regulations.* New Brunswick, N.J.: The Center for Urban Policy Research, 1978, 434 pages. Book deals with the topic of government regulation of residential development and points out that although aimed at positive objectives (environment, sprawl, safety, etc.) regulations result in higher housing prices and restricted supply.

Simko, Patricia. "Trends in Land-Use Regulation." *Real Estate Today,* November, 1978, pages 20–25. Article points out that land development today faces more restrictions than ever before due to efforts to protect the environment.

22

Real Estate and the Economy

KEY TERMS

Acceleration principle: states that an event has a greater impact on demand or prices than can be traced to that event alone
Base industry: an industry that produces goods or services for export from the region
Cost-push inflation: higher prices due to increased costs of labor and supplies
Demand-pull inflation: higher prices due to buyers bidding against each other
Economic base: the ability of a region to export goods and services to other regions and receive money in return
Illiquidity: a lack of cash or assets that can be converted to cash quickly
Real-cost inflation: higher prices due to greater effort needed to produce the same product today versus several years ago
Service industry: an industry that produces goods and services to sell to local residents
Short cycles: economic cycles averaging about four years

Economic concepts and ideas are interwoven throughout this book, but the objective of this chapter is to discuss several vital relationships between the economy and real estate that are not covered elsewhere.

ECONOMIC BASE

Just as one nation must equalize its imports and exports with the rest of the world to maintain a stable balance of trade, regions and cities must export goods and services so that their residents may purchase goods and services not produced locally. To illustrate, Hollywood produces motion pictures for theaters and television stations across the country. The income earned from these films permits residents in Hollywood to send money to Detroit to purchase automobiles. The money Detroit receives is used to buy farm products and other needed goods and services produced outside Detroit. A farming region produces farm products that are sold outside the region to generate income with which to buy farm machinery, gasoline, fertilizer, clothing, vacations, and so forth. In turn, the economy of a resort area is kept alive with the money spent there by vacationers, and so on.

The ability of a city or region to produce a commodity or service that has exchange value outside its area is its **economic base.** Industries that produce goods and services for export are called **base, export,** or **primary industries.** Thus, film making is a base industry for Hollywood, automobile manufacturing is a base industry for Detroit, and agriculture is a base industry in the Midwest. Producers of goods and services that are not exported are called **service, filler** or **secondary industries.** This category includes local school systems, supermarkets, doctors, dentists, drugstores, and real estate agents.

Effect on Real Estate

Because land is immovable, the existence of base industries is absolutely essential to maintaining local real estate values. Unless a region or city exports, it will die economically, and the value of local real estate will fall. An extreme example of this can be found in the abandoned mining towns of yesteryear. Before the discovery of mineral riches, land was often worth but a few dollars an acre for grazing purposes. With the discovery of minerals and subsequent mine development, land that was suitable for townsites zoomed in value. A new and far richer economic base industry than grazing was bringing wealth and people into the area, and land that had been used for strictly agricultural purposes was now in demand for homesites, stores, and offices. Years later, when the mines played out and mineral wealth could no longer be exported from the area, outside money ceased to flow into the town. As a result, miners were laid off and left for other towns where jobs could be found. Without the miners' money, service industries folded and their employees left. The demand for real estate dropped and, in turn, real estate prices fell, often all the way back to their value for grazing purposes.

The extent to which regions and cities are vulnerable to changes in economic base depends on how many different kinds of base industries are present and their ability to consistently export their products. Thus, a city that relies extensively on one base industry for support is much more economically vulnerable than one with a diversified group of base industries. For example, a city or town that has grown up around a military base will suffer extensively if that base is cut back in size or closed down. In Seattle, real estate prices were adversely affected in the early 1970s by layoffs at Boeing Aircraft due to a lack of airplane orders. Several years later, a combination of increased aircraft orders at Boeing plus local industrial expansion helped real estate prices to recover. Then again in 1982, Boeing experienced another lack of aircraft orders and began laying off employees. Agriculturally oriented communities often experience ups and downs in farmland prices that correspond with the rise and fall of farm product prices.

Employment Ratios

Through the application of employment ratios, an economic base study can also tell us what effect a change in base industry employment will have on the local population and economy. Generally, for each additional person employed in a base industry, two persons will be employed in service and intermediate industries. Thus, if an electronics firm moves into a community and creates 100 new base industry jobs, opportunities will be created for another 200 persons in jobs such as retail store clerks, restaurant services, gas station operators, gardeners, bankers, doctors, dentists, lawyers, police and firemen, school teaching, and local government, to name a few.

With economic base data, one can also calculate the total impact on local population and the need for land and housing. For example, the 100 base industry jobs created by the electronics firm result in 200 service jobs, for a total of 300 new job opportunities in the community. If every three jobs require two households (more than one person working in some families) and each household averages 2.9 persons, then 300 jobs will provide income for 200 households containing a total of 580 persons. The ultimate effect of the 300 new jobs on local employment and housing demand will depend on what portion of the jobs can be filled from within the community and the extent of vacant housing. If the community is already operating at full employment and has no vacant housing to speak of, the addition of 100 base jobs will result in a demand for land, building materials, and labor necessary to provide 200 new housing units. From the standpoint of local government, 580 more people must be supplied with schools, parks, water, sewage treatment, street maintenance, police and fire protection, and so forth.

SHORT-RUN DEMAND FOR HOUSING

Because it takes time to develop raw land into homes, offices, and stores, the supply of developed real estate is not immediately responsive to sudden changes in demand. Furthermore, because of the high entry and holding costs of developed real estate and the possibility of making improvements to land where they may not be needed, considerable risk is involved in developing land in advance of a known demand. As a result, price changes for developed real property can be rapid and dramatic over short periods of time. Let us explore this economic phenomenon more closely with the use of an example.

Increase in Demand

Suppose that in a given community there are presently 5,000 single-family houses, and their average value is $82,000. A new industry moves into the community and increases the demand for houses by 100. Local builders, recognizing the new demand, set to work adding 100 houses to the available housing stock. However, it will take time to acquire land, file subdivision maps, acquire building permits, grade the land, and construct the houses. The entire process typically takes 10 to 36 months. Meanwhile, despite increased demand, the available supply of houses remains fixed. The result will be an increase in house prices as the newly arriving employees bid against each other for a place to live in the existing housing stock. The result is diagrammed in Figure 22:1. Demand Curve 1 represents the demand for houses at various prices before the new industry's employees arrive. More units would be purchased at lower prices and fewer at higher prices. Prior to the arrival of the new industry, supply and demand are in balance at $82,000 per house, as shown at A.

Now the new industry moves in. Adding new employees to the housing market produces Demand Curve 2. Prices rise owing to competition for the existing houses. This increase literally rations the existing stock of 5,000 houses among 5,100 households. Prices rise until enough existing owners decide to sell and enough new buyers are priced out of the market. Once again, supply and demand are in balance with 5,000 houses occupied by 5,000 families. This is point B at $86,000.

Increase in Supply

At last, the 100 new houses that were started in response to the new demand are completed and are on the market. At what price must these be offered in order to sell them all? It would appear that $86,000 is the answer, as that is what houses are now selling for. However, the supply-demand relationship

Figure 22:1

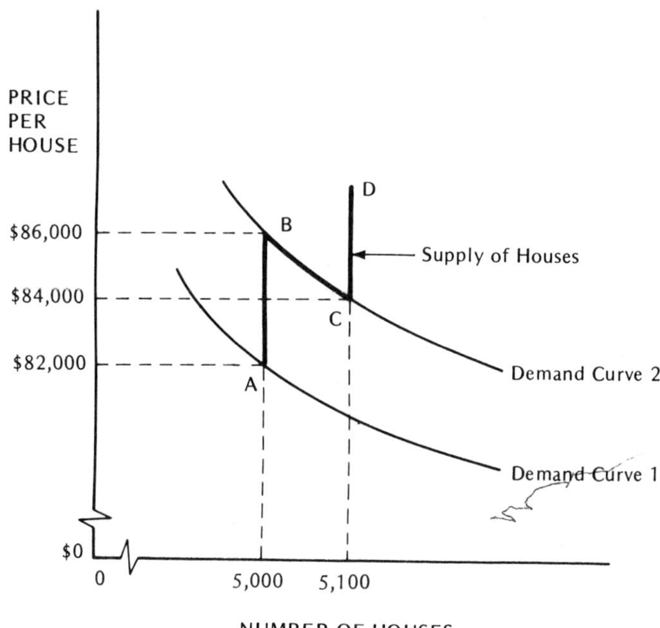

in Figure 22:1 shows that only 5,000 houses are in demand at $86,000, not 5,100 houses. To find out at what price the additional 100 houses will be absorbed by the market, we must travel along Demand Curve 2 to 5,100 houses. At point C, the market will absorb 5,100 houses if they are priced at $84,000 each. Thus, a temporary glut of homes causes prices to be reduced slightly. This price softening applies not only to the builders of the 100 new houses, but also to the owners of the other 5,000 homes if they wish to sell during this temporary oversupply situation.

Aware of the oversupply of houses on the market, builders will react by halting building activity until those units are sold and demand starts pushing prices upward again to D, at which time the process repeats itself. Over a period of years, the supply pattern for houses takes on a stair-step appearance as temporary shortages and temporary excesses alternate.

Decrease in Demand

Just as a short-run increase in demand can cause a quick run-up in prices, a short-run decrease in demand can have the opposite effect, because supply cannot be decreased as fast

Figure 22:2

SHORT-RUN DROP IN DEMAND

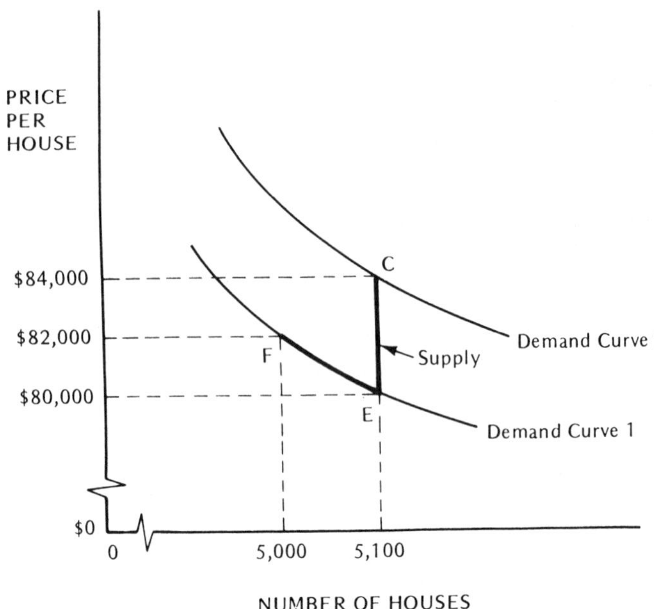

as demand falls. This situation is diagrammed in Figure 22:2 with supply and demand in balance at 5,100 houses at $84,000 each. Suppose that there was an overnight cutback of jobs and, as a result, 100 house owners decided to sell and move out of the community. This would cause demand to shift downward from Demand Curve 2 to Demand Curve 1. To sell all 100 houses, it will be necessary for prices to fall from $84,000 at point C to $80,000 at point E. Presuming no increase in the economic base of the community, only a reduction in the supply of existing houses through demolition, disasters, and conversions to other uses will push prices back up along Demand Curve 1. If supply falls to 5,000 houses, prices will go to $82,000 at point F.

Effect of Inflation

The presence of inflation will cushion the drop in dollar values when demand shifts to Demand Curve 1 in Figure 22:2. Similarly, the drop in prices from B to C in Figure 22:1 will be milder in the presence of moderate inflation. In the presence of high inflation prices may not drop, but actually rise. However, if you strip away the masking effect of inflation, Figures 22:1 and 22:2 accurately portray what actually happens when demand suddenly changes and supply cannot react fast enough. Although we have been talking in terms of houses, the same concept applies to vacant lots, apartment buildings, townhouses, condominiums, office buildings, factories, hotels and motels, store space, and so forth.

LONG-RUN DEMAND FOR HOUSING

Future demand for housing in the United States can be seen by looking at the population in terms of age distribution, and the ability of people to obtain income at various age levels. As shown in Figure 22:3, during the first 10 years of life a person earns no income and is dependent on others, usually parents, for sustenance. During junior high school, high school, and college (if any) a person has part-time jobs but usually is still dependent on others for financial support.

Upon leaving school and entering the labor market on a full-time basis, a person's income rises quickly, reflecting increased productive capacity in society. As skills increase, income continues to rise rapidly. In another decade the rise stops increasing as rapidly, although it still advances. Then, somewhere between the ages of 40 and 60, depending on a person's skills and the usefulness of those skills in society, health and/

Figure 22:3

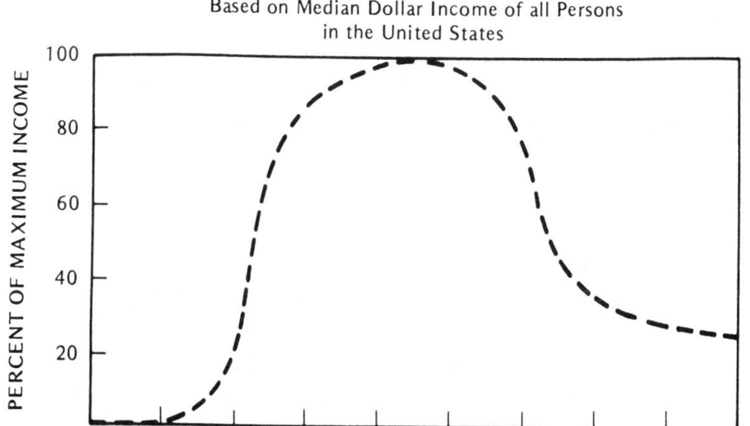

or the desire to slow down, the peak earning year occurs. For those with 4 years of college or the equivalent, this occurs around age 55. For the nation as a whole, it occurs in the mid-forties. The peak earning year is followed at first by mild decreases in income, and then by more rapid decreases as retirement occurs.

Buying Pattern

With this earning pattern in mind, it can be seen how the progression of housing demand must follow. When a person is young and setting up a household for the first time, income is low and so are accumulated assets. Thus, housing that requires no equity investment at a minimum cost is needed; that is, an inexpensive rental with no frills. During the next decade income increases, enabling the household to increase the quality of its rental unit. Also, savings accumulate, which, coupled with the ability to make mortgage payments, enable the household to meet the down payment and mortgage requirements for a modest housing purchase. As the family grows and income increases, the household can move to larger, more expensive quarters. Typically, this occurs between the ages of 35 and 45. Another upward move in house size and price usually occurs between 45 and 55 when the family reaches its maximum income.

As the children move out and income peaks and then begins to recede, the household begins to consider a smaller and less expensive dwelling unit. The need for less expensive housing becomes even more compelling upon retirement and a further reduction in income. Retirement income typically is not sufficient to carry mortgage payments on the large home bought during the peak earning years. However, the household has an equity that it can now consolidate into a smaller residence, which is fully or nearly fully paid for.

AGE DISTRIBUTION

With this information in mind, let us now turn our attention to Figure 22:4 in which the population of the United States is graphed according to its age distribution. The lines labeled 1970 and 1980 are based on the U.S. census; the 1990 and 2000 lines are government-prepared population projections. These are based on the fact that persons on the 1980 line will be 10 and 20 years older, respectively, minus losses due to deaths and additions due to immigration.

Figure 22:4

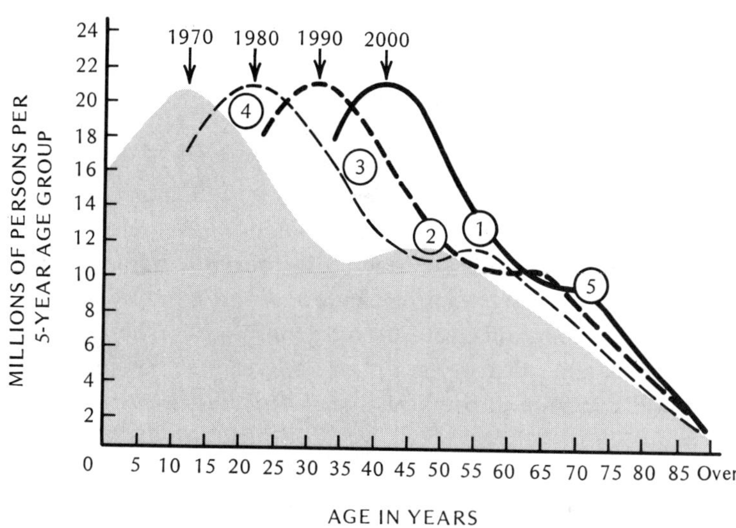

There are two peaks in the 1980 age distribution line. The smaller of the two, identified as ①, represents persons aged 50 to 60 years in 1980. These persons were born during the decade of the 1920s, a period of economic prosperity in most parts of the United States. Moving to the left, the dip at ② represents children born during the economic depression that spanned the 1930s. By 1980, they were 40 to 50 years old. Moving again to the left, a substantial upward rise is encountered at ③. This is the famed World War II and postwar "baby boom." It started in 1940 and lasted until 1960. In 1960, the number of births per year began to decline and continued to decline in each subsequent year through 1978. This is shown at ④.

Housing Demand

As the two waves in the 1980 line grow older and move to the right across the graph, the impact on housing demand in the United States will be substantial. A wave of demand has been created for more expensive housing accommodations by those born between 1920 and 1930. In contrast, those born during the 1930s will have many opportunities to move into housing vacated by the 1920 to 1930 group. However, substantial amounts of additional housing will have to be built in order to accommodate the children who were born from 1940 to 1960. How does the 1940–1960 "wave" translate into demand? Since the early 1960s, the United States has been experiencing a growing demand for inexpensive rentals by persons under 25 years of age. By 1985, that demand will peak as all children born from 1940 to 1960 will be 25 years or older. Between 1965 and 1975, the number of persons in the United States aged 25 through 34 increased by 9 million and resulted in the formation of 5 million households. Each household required a housing unit suitable to its income characteristics. Between 1975 and 1985, this age group will grow by another 9 million persons and create an additional 5 million households, each of which will require a place to live. This has produced and will continue to produce an upward pressure on housing demand.

More Homeowners

As the population wave caused by the 1940–1960 baby boom continues to move to the right in Figure 22:4, the United States will continue to experience increasing demand by this group for better and more expensive housing. Also, owner-occupants will predominate. Government statistics show that 60% of the households aged 35 through 44 are homeowners, and among those 45 through 54 years old, 75% are owners. (The percentages are even higher if there are children present.) This upgrading process will continue until the year 2015, at which time persons born in 1960 will reach the age of 55. Because personal income patterns decline after that age, a retrenchment into more modest housing will then be observed.

Although the dominant factor in housing demand in the next several decades will be the maturing members of the 1940–1960 baby boom, we must not overlook the present steady growth in households over the age of 65 years and the dramatic drop in children born since 1960. Households aged 65 and above are growing in numbers and, as may be seen at ⑤, will continue to do so until 1995. At that time there will be a 10-year pause in growth due to persons born during the 1930 decade reaching the age of 65. Following that, this age group will again grow in numbers as those born between 1940 and 1960 reach this age level. As less than 20% of the population over the age of 65 remains in the labor force, the housing demand created by these age groups will primarily be the result of investments, pensions, social security income, public welfare, and assets accumulated earlier in life, including the family home.

When the children born after 1960 reach the age at which they want to have a residence of their own (usually 18 to 25 years of age), they will find large amounts of housing available as the persons born between 1940 and 1960 climb the lifetime income curve and upgrade their housing. Unless some of the housing being abandoned by the 1940–1960 group can be used to accommodate households over the age of 65, this situation will probably cause a slowdown in new housing construction. The United States has already seen a virtual halt in new elementary school construction because of the drop in births after 1960. And this came after a 15-year-long frantic effort to build enough schoolrooms.

By 1982, the drop in births that began in 1960 was reversing itself. If this continues, we may expect the formation of a third wave in the age distribution of the U.S. population, and, with it, a new surge in housing demand when those children form households.

REAL ESTATE CYCLES

When viewed over time, do prices for real estate follow a recurring order or interval, that is, a cyclical pattern? If so, is the pattern predictable in advance with enough accuracy that one can predict when real estate prices will rise and fall in the future? As this section will show, cycles can be found in real estate activity and prices. However, whether the passage of time alone is responsible for these ups and downs is debatable. Let us explore the matter further.

Whether one looks at construction activity, land prices, or deed recordings, over a long enough period of time cyclical patterns appear to repeat themselves every 15 to 20 years. These are called **long cycles.** An excellent example is shown in Figure 22:5. This graph shows how land prices in the United States have alternately risen and fallen since the early 1800s.

Glancing at Figure 22:5, it would appear that a land speculator need only look at a calendar to determine the next upswing. However, although the cycles seem to average 18 years in length, there is no reliability in judging how long the up or down leg of a cycle will last, nor precisely how high prices will go before peaking. For example, the first drop in prices

Figure 22:5 LONG CYCLES IN UNITED STATES LAND PRICES

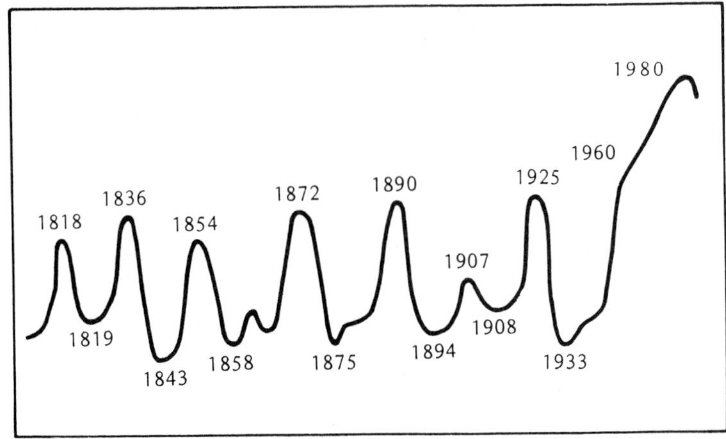

Sources: Graph through 1960 reprinted with permission from ULI—The Urban Land Institute, 1200 8th Street N.W., Washington, D.C. 20036, Technical Bulletin 38, © 1960. From 1961 through 1982 based on HUD statistics.

shown took just 1 year: 1818 to 1819. Then it took 17 years to reach the next peak. The next cycle took 7 years to reach bottom and then lasted 11 years on the upswing. If a person had bought in 1837, he would have experienced 6 more years of falling prices. If he kept his land in anticipation of prices returning to the 1836 level, he would have waited until 1872. In more recent years, relying on past cycles would have signaled a reverse in land prices sometime in the 1950s, or certainly by 1960. But the next peak did not occur until 1980.

Causes

In looking for the causes of real estate cycles, researchers have found that although cycles sometimes appear to be calendar oriented, in reality they have been caused by events such as the general state of the nation's economy, immigration into the United States, the westward movement, railroad construction, birth-rate changes, the increased use of debt financing to purchase real estate, and government encouragement of home ownership. For example, the low point in real estate prices in 1933 coincided with the depths of the Great Depression. Subsequently, government programs such as the FHA and VA, general economic prosperity, the 1940–1960 baby boom, easy credit, and various federal policies that encouraged inflation and real estate ownership produced a strong upward influence on real estate prices.

Events such as changes in the birth rate, immigration, railway construction and creation of the FHA and VA, are called **secular events.** Scarcer and costlier energy is a current example of a secular event that will have a major impact on real estate values.

Secular events often last several decades and are not by themselves cyclical in nature. However, when different types of secular events follow each other, a cyclical pattern can be produced. The fact that a given event can produce a dramatic change in real estate prices is often due to what is called the **acceleration principle.** For example, the completion of railway lines through unsettled areas in the United States resulted in the establishment of thousands of American towns. Many have grown to major cities today, not because everyone works for the railroad, but because the railroad was the catalyst that attracted trade, business, and industry to a given location. The acceleration principle is a well-accepted one, for many land booms have been started on the strength of one railway station. Unfortunately, the psychology of the human mind often tends to exaggerate the effects of acceleration and soon overbidding occurs. When overbidding is finally recognized, prices drop dramatically, and more often than not people become overly pessimistic. This is what tends to give cycles such long, steep sides.

SENSITIVITY TO CREDIT

Superimposed on the long cycles are also real estate **short cycles,** with an average length of about 4 years. These cycles have been particularly apparent since the end of World War II, and it is generally agreed among economists that they result from the ease or difficulty of borrowing money to finance residential real estate. Few home buyers can afford to pay all cash for a place to live; most must borrow. As a result, the housing industry is very sensitive to the price and availability of loan money. Not only does this affect contractors and construction workers, but also appliance and furniture manufacturers, lumber mills, cement factories, real estate appraisers, and real estate agents. Anyone connected with the manufacture, sale or resale of housing is directly affected by the availability of mortgage money to home buyers.

To attract deposits, banks, mutual savings banks, and savings and loan associations now offer money market certificates to savers. These carry interest rates comparable to those on U.S. Treasury obligations. This has kept money flowing into savings institutions, but the cost of the borrower has gone up in the process. In 1981 and 1982, these certificates were paying savers between 13½% and 15½% interest. Adding overhead expenses, this meant home buyers had to pay 16% to 18% to borrow. At those prices, many stopped borrowing and as a result, houses went unsold, developers were hurt financially, and real estate commissions were lost. By mid-1983, rates paid to savers on certificates had dropped to 10% and lenders were offering loans at 12%.

SECONDARY MORTGAGE MARKET

A very important influence on residential real estate activity and prices in the United States has been the secondary mortgage market. Prior to the 1970 decade, home loan money came mostly from savings and loan associations, mutual savings banks, commercial banks and life insurance companies. In each case the lender would make loans that the lender was prepared to carry on its books until it was repaid. The lender also established a mortgage loan department to process applications and make loans, and a mortgage service department to collect loan payments. (Life insurance companies usually paid correspondents or mortgage bankers to do these tasks.) Compared to government or corporate bonds, home mortgages involved considerably more work on the part of the lender.

A major purpose in establishing a secondary market for home mortgage loans was to attract loan money that would otherwise go into corporate or government bonds. By 1983, the Federal National Mortgage Corporation, the Government National Mortgage Corporation, the Federal Home Loan Mortgage Corporation, and the Mortgage Guaranty Insurance Corporation all had developed methods for channeling money into home loans. All have plans that save investors from the work of making and servicing loans. Individuals and pension funds that previously had never invested in mortgages because of the work involved now invest with ease.

In addition, a secondary market provides a place to sell a mortgage that a lender does not want to hold until the last payment is made by the borrower. This feature has been very successful in attracting lenders who previously avoided mortgage lending. An immense amount of loan money became available to mortgage borrowers in the 1970's due to the secondary mortgage market.

GOVERNMENT SUPPORT

To enable home buyers to bid more for housing, the federal government has a number of very supportive policies, programs and laws. Best known among these is the deductibility of property taxes and mortgage interest for homeowners—but not renters. For a household in a combined state and federal income tax bracket of 40%, a 10% interest rate does not look expensive, especially if the general rate of inflation is 8%. Likewise, 12% interest does not look expensive if inflation is running 10%. And 15% looks cheap if inflation is 13%. In fact, if one looks at the after-tax cost of interest, one may be money ahead to borrow all he or she can. For example, in a 40% bracket, the after-tax cost of a 12% mortgage loan is 7.2%. In the 30% bracket it is 8.4%, and in the 20% bracket it is 9.6%. In all three of these cases, the homebuyer is ahead of a 10% inflation rate. Thus it comes as no surprise that the phrase, "Sure it's expensive, but it's deductible" was heard so often from home buyers and real estate agents during the inflationary period of the late 1970s. In addition, a home has been, in most years, one of the few mass investments that has actually beaten inflation.

To further aid borrowers in their quest for larger mortgage loans, FHA loan insurance limits are raised regularly and required down payments reduced. The VA guarantee is also raised frequently, as are lending limits for federally chartered and supervised lenders. Moreover, the FHA now offers a graduated payment mortgage to squeeze the last ounce of borrowing power out of a loan applicant's income.

New Laws

Higher loan limits and deductibility of interest and taxes by themselves are not enough to allow prices to shoot up as they did between 1970 and 1980. Loan applicants must also have income in order to qualify for a loan in the first place. In this respect, the federal Equal Credit Opportunity Act of 1974 (ECOA), equal pay for equal work laws, female job opportunities, two wage-earner households, and wage increases in general have all played key roles.

Prior to the ECOA, it was commonplace for lenders to refuse to count the wife's income if she was pregnant, and to discount it by 50% if she was not pregnant but in the prime child-bearing years. Moreover, her income was likely to be only half of what her husband was earning. As a result, the size of the loan they could get was pretty much limited by the husband's income. Additionally, widows, divorcees, and singles were considered high risk borrowers and either did not get credit or did so only in small amounts.

This has all changed. Today, by law, all income of a woman must be counted in full regardless of her marital status or whether she is (or might become) pregnant.

For millions of households, the ECOA suddenly created borrowing power that did not exist before. Husband-wife families could combine their incomes to qualify for bigger loans. Mothers and daughters living together, brothers owning together, single persons, divorced and widowed persons all suddenly found themselves with new and greater borrowing power. And with it, the ability to bid up prices.

In addition to being able to count all their income for a loan application, during the 1970s women began to earn more money because of laws that required equal pay for equal work and laws prohibiting sex discrimination in hiring. The 1970s also saw more women who wanted to go to work.

INFLATION

Each of us is aware of the almost uninterrupted upward march in prices of nearly all goods and services offered for sale since the end of World War II. Why has this happened, and why might it continue to happen? The explanations fill volumes. However, for our purposes here, there are four concepts with which you should be familiar: cost-push inflation, demand-pull inflation, monetary inflation, and real-cost inflation.

Cost-push Inflation

The increasing cost of inputs necessary to manufacture a product or offer a service results in what is called **cost-push inflation.** To illustrate, an automobile manufacturer increases the price of cars because labor and materials cost more. A major reason for higher new home prices in the 1970s was the increase in prices of lumber, bricks, concrete, metal, construction labor, construction loans, and government permits.

Many of these items were more expensive because the price of energy to produce them rose so rapidly between 1970 and 1979. The cost of oil, for example, became a major cost-push factor in the 1970s.

Demand-pull Inflation

When buyers bid against each other to buy something that has been offered for sale, **demand-pull inflation** results. For example, three buyers for a single available residence may bid $75,000, $76,000, and $77,000, respectively, in an effort to buy that particular home. Demand-pull inflation is basically the result of too much money chasing too few goods. This type of inflation usually has little to do with the actual cost of producing the particular goods or services being sought. Thus, from the standpoint of the seller who may have paid $30,000 for the home some years back, the offers of $75,000 $76,000 and $77,000 are a reflection of what the three buyers feel they would pay elsewhere to obtain similar housing rather than what the house originally cost the seller.

Monetary Inflation

Monetary inflation results from the creation of excessive amounts of money by government. The classic example of this was in Germany during the first 5 years after World War I. In an effort to provide money to solve all the war-torn country's problems at once, the German government created and spent money on a grand scale. However, there was no parallel increase in goods and services to be purchased with that money. The result was demand-pull inflation as millions of people with pockets, and later wheelbarrows, stuffed with newly printed currency fought to buy everything from bread and vegetables to real estate. Within the space of a few short years, prices rose on the order of 1 million percent before the printing presses were finally shut down.

Much economic arguing over prices in the United States revolves around how much the money supply should be allowed to grow. Allowing the money supply to grow faster than the available supply of goods and services causes a temporary economic stimulus by placing more money in peoples' hands. But the ultimate result is a reduction in the purchasing power of the dollar. The alternative, according to many economists, is for the growth in the money supply to more closely parallel the nation's long-run ability to produce goods and services. Productivity in the United States has grown at the average rate of 3.1% during 1955–65, 2.3% during 1965–73, and 1% since then. Any increase in the money supply over that amount each year will show up as increased prices.

Beginning in the fall of 1979, the Federal Reserve Board slowed the growth of money supply expansion in the United States. This action, together with a marketplace already crowded with more borrowers than lenders, caused interest rates to rise. The higher interest rates began to discourage borrowing which, in turn, caused a softening in demand, and hence prices, for most goods and services, including real estate. This produced substantial unemployment in the construction industry and its suppliers, such as the lumber industry. Then in the summer of 1982 the "Fed" began increasing the growth of money supply expansion. Interest rates fell and by early 1983 homebuilders were cautiously increasing the number of housing starts.

Real-cost Inflation

Real-cost inflation is inflation caused by the increased effort necessary to produce the same quantity of a good or service. The Alaskan pipeline and North Slope oil wells are excellent examples of real-cost inflation. In 1960, all oil produced in the United States came from within the 48 contiguous states and consequently was near the American markets in which it was consumed. Today, at great expense, oil fields are being developed in the frozen North Slope of Alaska. Added to this is a costly transportation network to get the oil to the lower 48 states. Thus, although a gallon of gasoline or fuel oil is chemically the same whether it comes from Oklahoma or Alaska, the one from Alaska involves much more work to get it to the consumer.

Another good example of real-cost inflation can be found in the iron mining areas of northern Minnesota. For decades, the richest areas of these fields have been tapped to feed America's steelmaking industry and provide steel-containing products to American consumers. Today the rich fields have been depleted, and steel companies are forced to mine a lower-grade ore. This ore requires an extra processing step to make it suitable for steelmaking. The cost of this step must be built into the finished product—an automobile, refrigerator, or the steel frame for a high-rise building.

Real-cost inflation also affects the cost of developing land around cities. Much easy-to-develop land has already been built upon, forcing developers to utilize land that requires more effort to bulldoze into usable lots. To provide water service to new lots, local water districts that once could supply the town's population from a few wells or a nearby lake or river must travel many miles to find water. The additional cost of the water system and pumping charges must be added to the user's water bill. Also, we cannot overlook the nation's efforts to clean up pollution. The generation of electrical power is an excellent example. At one time, our primary concern was the end product—kilowatt hours of electricity produced. Today, we still want electricity, but we also want the smoke emitted by the generating plant to be clean. The cost to do this must be added to the cost of each kilowatt of electricity produced.

PYRAMIDING

A phenomenon that was observed between 1975 and 1980 was pyramiding. For example, the family that bought a house for $40,000 is offered $60,000 by a young two-income household that is trying to get into the housing market. So the family sells and with the profit makes a down payment on an $80,000 house. The seller of that home takes his profit and puts it down on a $110,000 house. That seller then moves up to a $150,000 house, and so on. Tax laws encourage this whole process because a home seller can postpone taxes on his gain whenever he buys a more expensive house. The upward push to higher-priced homes slows when people can no longer qualify for the ever-increasing loan payments, or loans are difficult to find at any price, or because the general home buying mood becomes negative.

ILLIQUIDITY

The decade of the 1970s will be remembered for relatively easy mortgage credit and rising real estate prices. In contrast, the decade of the 1980s began with illiquidity and falling real estate prices. What caused this?

From 1970 through 1978, mortgage money was available at rates ranging from 7½% to 9¾%. At the same time, household incomes climbed rapidly as a result of wage increases and a rise in two-income households. In addition, millions of baby boom children were reaching the age at which they wanted homes of their own. Meanwhile, the secondary mortgage market was efficiently channelling funds into mortgages, the Equal Credit Opportunity Act made it easier to qualify for loans, and savings institutions were offering more attractive interest rates than Treasury bills. With a plentiful supply of loan money available, homes were bought and refinanced with increasingly larger mortgage loans. Real estate prices rose and fortunes were made in cash and on paper, often with as little as 10% down. After selling, sellers would take their profits and buy more property. In turn, those sellers would take their profits and buy still more property, in a pyramid fashion, with prices increasing at each sale along the way. Even though mortgage interest rates started rising toward the end of the decade, inflation was climbing faster. Thus it was still relatively cheap to borrow and the fashionable thing to do was to own tangible assets as inflation hedges. The saving of money was considered unrealistic because rates paid savers did not keep up with inflation. Ironically, this is what brought an end to rising prices.

Reversal

From a market standpoint, the lack of people who wanted to save resulted in a lack of credit availability for those who wanted to borrow. And without borrowed money, most people cannot buy real estate. From a political standpoint stopping inflation became the nation's most important domestic issue at the end of the 1970 decade. The Federal Reserve responded with a restrictive policy toward monetary growth that also reduced credit availability. Lastly, federal deficits began to climb adding more demand for available credit. By 1982, the federal government was absorbing 80% of available savings to finance its deficits. Housing, business, and consumer borrowers fought for the remainder. As they did, home mortgage rates increased to the 16% to 18% range, a price that eliminated most buyers. Real estate agents found that whereas in the 1975–79 period there were more buyers than sellers, by 1980 the number of buyers was dwindling. Houses that once sold in 30 to 60 days were now on the market for a year or more and still unsold. The ones that did sell were usually sold because the seller had an assumable loan at an old, lower interest rate and/or the seller was willing to finance the buyer at a below-market interest rate, say 10% or 12% rather than 16% or 18%.

Deflation Psychology

When prices stopped rising and started to soften, another interesting thing happened. The inflation anticipation psychology that had persisted for so many years began to disappear. The inflation rate that had reached 18% at one point in 1979 dropped to less than half that three years later. By 1982, unemployment was up sharply and for the first time in several decades people were accepting wage cuts instead of wage increases. As a result of these factors, housing starts tumbled to new lows and resales of existing properties nearly stopped. Property owners who wanted to sell badly enough began reducing their asking prices. This created a deflation psychology. Prospective homeowners began to sense that they could buy cheaper by waiting. Many chose to rent, oftentimes renting the same homes that sellers took off the market because they did not sell.

Seller Financing

A change from institutionally-financed sales to ones that are seller-financed significantly impacts the real estate sales market. The reason is that if the seller receives only part of his or her equity in cash rather than all of it, the seller has less purchasing power as a buyer.

To illustrate, suppose a home that was originally purchased for $40,000 is resold for $80,000 and the loan balance at the time of sale is $30,000. If institutional financing is available to the buyer, the seller will leave the closing table with $44,000 in cash after deducting $6,000 in selling costs. If the seller has to finance the buyer and the buyer puts 20% down, the seller will leave the closing table with only $10,000 in cash after allowing $6,000 for selling costs. As you can now visualize, when the seller goes out to buy another home, the difference between having $44,000 and having $10,000 makes a lot of difference in how aggressively he or she can bid for another property. Multiply this event by all the sellers in the nation who are taking notes rather than cash and you can begin to see why seller financing is a deterrent to increasing prices.

The Outlook

As this material is being written, there are two probable economic scenarios pending. The first possibility is that the political pressure of the 1982 recession will result in monetary and fiscal pump priming. This has been the case in previous recessions. The Federal Reserve Bank adds money to the banking system thereby driving down interest rates. Simultaneously, the federal government adds programs to its budget that put people to work. The new programs produce larger deficits which must be financed by printing more money lest interest rates go up. Unfortunately, the amount of pump priming necessary to produce relief will, in the long run, produce inflation far worse than the 18% rate reached at 1979.

The other scenario is for the Federal Reserve to let the credit markets work out their own problems. This means that credit will remain expensive and scarce for some time. In turn, this will discourage borrowing and encourage saving. Without easy credit, prices stop rising and instead stagnate and fall. How far prices will fall will depend on several factors: people's incomes, people's expectations, and the cost and availability of credit in the future.

There is no lack of household formation potential in the United States. What is in short supply is people who can make the necessary down payments and monthly payments to buy a home. Either personal incomes must rise, interest rates must fall, or prices must fall before significant increases in real estate sales activity can occur.

VOCABULARY REVIEW

Match terms **a–l** *with statements* **1–12.**

a. *Acceleration principle*
b. *Base industry*
c. *Cost-push inflation*
d. *Demand-pull inflation*
e. *Economic base*
f. *Illiquidity*
g. *Long cycles*
h. *Money market certificate*
i. *Real-cost inflation*
j. *Secular event*
k. *Service industry*
l. *Short cycle*

1. An industry that produces goods or services for export from the region.
2. An industry that produces goods or services to sell to local residents.
3. The ability of a region to export goods and services to other regions.
4. A shortage of cash or assets that can be quickly converted to cash.
5. Six-month savings certificates that pay interest based on prevailing U.S. Treasury bill rates.
6. Economic patterns that tend to repeat every 15 to 20 years.
7. A long-lasting and noncyclical event.
8. Economic cycles averaging about 4 years in length.
9. Higher prices due to buyers bidding against each other.

10. Higher prices due to greater effort needed to produce the same product today.
11. Higher prices due to increased costs of labor and supplies.
12. An event results in a greater impact on demand or prices than can be traced to that event alone.

QUESTIONS AND PROBLEMS

1. List and rank in order of importance the base industries that support your community. How stable are they? Are any new ones coming? Are any existing ones leaving?
2. What would be the effect of a new industry creating 500 new jobs in your community? Is there sufficient vacant housing available? What would be the effect of a loss of 500 jobs?
3. Why do savings institutions issue money market certificates?
4. Does the population age distribution of your community differ from the United States as a whole? How would this affect demand for housing in your area?
5. What is the after-tax cost of an 11% mortgage loan to a person in a 40% income tax bracket?
6. What was the intent of government in passing the Equal Credit Opportunity Act?
7. What is the purpose of the secondary mortgage market?
8. What secular events currently appear to be affecting real estate prices in the United States? Do any of these suggest that a drop in real estate prices will occur soon?
9. Identify three specific examples of cost-push inflation that you have personally observed or read about during the past 12 months.

ADDITIONAL READINGS

Barlowe, Raleigh. *Land Resource Economics,* 3rd ed. Englewood Cliffs, N.J.: Prentice-Hall, 1978, 653 pages. Deals with the economic relationship between man and land, with emphasis on the supply of and demand for land resources, land economics, institutional and social conditions.

Case, Fred E. *Real Estate Economics.* Sacramento: California Association of Realtors, 1974, 289 pages. Written especially for the real estate salesman and broker who is seeking a logical and easy to read introduction to real estate economics.

Davis, Jerry C. "Government Over-Regulation: It's Costing All of Us Money." *Real Estate Today,* June, 1979, pages 26–31. Article points out that government regulation accounts for 20% to 25% of the cost of a new home. Author suggests how to reduce these costs.

Klepper, Martin. "The National Energy Act: Its Impact on Real Estate and Real Estate Financing." *Real Estate Review,* Spring, 1979, pages 40–49. Discusses the carrot and stick provisions of the Act as they affect the cost of owning, constructing, financing, and operating buildings.

Shafer, Thomas W. *Urban Growth and Economics.* Reston, Va.: Reston Publishing Co., 1977, 256 pages. Looks at how and why cities grow, land-use patterns, the role of government, current trends and beyond.

United States Bureau of the Census. *Statistical Abstract of the United States.* Washington, D.C.: U.S. Government Printing Office, 1982. Includes U.S. statistics on a wide variety of topics including real estate, mortgage finance, population growth, employment, manufacturing, etc. Published annually.

23

Investing in Real Estate

KEY TERMS

Accelerated depreciation: any method of depreciation that achieves a faster rate of depreciation than straight-line

Cash flow: the number of dollars remaining each year after collecting rents and paying operating expenses and mortgage payments

Cash-on-cash: the cash flow produced by a property divided by the amount of cash necessary to purchase it

Downside risk: the possibility that an investor will lose his money in an investment

Equity build-up: the increase of one's equity in a property due to mortgage balance reduction and price appreciation

Investment strategy: a plan that balances returns available with risks that must be taken in order to enhance the investor's overall welfare

Negative cash flow: a condition wherein the cash paid out exceeds the cash received

Prospectus: a disclosure statement that describes an investment opportunity

Straight-line depreciation: depreciation in equal amounts each year over the life of the asset

Tax shelter: the income tax savings that an investment can produce for its owner

The monetary returns that are possible from real estate ownership make it a very attractive investment. However, at the same time the real estate investor takes two risks: he may never obtain a return on his investment and he may never recover his investment. There are no simple answers as to what is a "sure-fire" real estate investment. Rather, success depends on intelligently made decisions. With that in mind, we shall consider investment benefits, property selection, investment timing, investment strategy, and limited partnerships.

BENEFITS OF REAL ESTATE INVESTING

The monetary benefits of investing in real estate come from cash flow, tax shelter, mortgage reduction, and appreciation. Let us look at each of these more closely.

CASH FLOW

Cash flow refers to the number of dollars remaining each year after you collect rents and pay operating expenses and mortgage payments. For example, suppose you own an apartment building that generates $30,000 per year in rents when fully occupied. Against this you have an allowance of 5% for vacancies and collection losses, operating expenses (including reserves) of $9,000 per year, and mortgage payments of $19,000. Given these facts, your cash flow picture would be as shown in Figure 23:1.

The purpose of calculating cash flow is to show the investor the cash-in-the-pocket effect of owning a particular property. In the Figure 23:1 example, $500 per year is going into the investor's pocket. When money is flowing to the investor, it is called a **positive cash flow.** If the investor must dip into his pocketbook to keep the property going, he has a **negative cash flow,** also called an "alligator." For example, if in Figure 23:1, the mortgage payments were $21,000 per year, or the owner decided to make improvements to the property and pay cash for them, there would be a negative cash flow.

A negative cash flow does not mean a property is a poor investment. There may be tax benefits and appreciation that more than offset this. Note also that cash flow analysis adds mortgage reduction to the expenses of a property when, in fact, the owner will recover that money if he sells for more than he paid.

Two terms that are related to cash flow are net spendable and cash-on-cash. **Net spendable** is the same thing as cash flow and refers to the amount of spendable income a property produces for its owner. **Cash-on-cash** is the cash flow (or net spendable) that a property produces in a given year divided by the amount of cash required to buy the property. For example, if a property has a cash flow of $5,000 per year and can be purchased with a $50,000 down payment (including closing costs), the cash-on-cash figure for that property is 10%. For many real estate investors, this is the heart of the investment

Figure 23:1

Scheduled gross income	**$30,000**
Less allowance for vacancies and collection losses	1,500
Equals effective gross income	28,500
Less operating expenses	9,000
Less mortgage payments	19,000
Equals cash flow	**$ 500**

decision, namely, "How much do I have to put down and how much will I have in my pocket at the end of each year?"

TAX SHELTER

Tax shelter refers to the income tax savings that an investor can realize. This is possible because depreciation is deductible as a cost of doing business when computing income taxes, although it is not an out-of-pocket expense. This usually means that part or all of the income from the property is not subject to taxation. In fact, sometimes it is possible to generate tax shelter in excess of that needed to shelter the income from the property itself. Income tax laws in effect at this writing permit the taxpayer to use these tax losses to offset gains in other investments, business profits, and salaries.

To illustrate the benefits of tax shelter, let us continue with the example started in Figure 23:1. Suppose that the investor is in a combined state and federal income tax bracket of 40%. Suppose further that he can claim depreciation of $10,000 per year on the improvements. Figure 23:2 illustrates the property from the standpoint of income tax consequences.

Comparing Figures 23:1 and 23:2, we see two important differences. First, mortgage balance reduction is an out-of-pocket expense, but not a deduction for income tax purposes. Second, depreciation is a deduction against income taxes, but not an out-of-pocket expense. Where does that leave our hypothetical investor? The $10,000 depreciation deduction shelters $1,000 of rental income that goes toward principal reduction, $500 in positive cash flow, and $8,500 of income the investor has from other sources.

The value of $10,000 worth of depreciation to someone in the 40% bracket is $4,000. In other words, our investor

Figure 23:2

Scheduled gross income	**$30,000**
Less allowance for vacancies and collection losses	1,500
Equals effective gross income	28,500
Less operating expenses	9,000
Less interest	18,000
Less depreciation	10,000
Equals taxable income	**($ 8,500)***

* In accounting language, parentheses indicate a negative or minus amount.

saves $4,000 in income taxes by owning this property. Now, if we look at cash flow on an after-tax basis, our investor actually enjoys a cash flow of $4,500. This makes the property a much more appealing investment, especially if the investor can also look forward to appreciation. Note that the higher the investor's tax bracket, the more valuable depreciation becomes. For a person in the 50% bracket, $10,000 of depreciation is worth $5,000. For someone in the 20% bracket, it is worth only $2,000.

CALCULATING DEPRECIATION

There are a number of methods of calculating depreciation for income tax purposes. The simplest is to take the price paid for the improvements and divide by the number of years of anticipated remaining economic life. (Land is not included as it cannot be depreciated for tax purposes.) For example, a $150,000 structure depreciated over 15 years and having no scrap value would be depreciated at the rate of $10,000 per year. This is called **straight-line depreciation** because the same amount of depreciation is taken each year.

To encourage the ownership of improved real estate, the government permits accelerated depreciation methods. These allow depreciation at a faster rate than straight line during the first several years of ownership. Although an owner cannot depreciate more than the price paid for the improvements, if depreciation can be taken sooner rather than later, it is more valuable.

Accelerated Depreciation

Accelerated depreciation can be illustrated with two examples: double-declining balance and sum-of-the-years' digits. To illustrate **double-declining balance** suppose that a new apartment building has an expected useful life of 40 years. Using straight-line depreciation, this would permit the taxpayer to depreciate 2½% of the price he paid for the improvements each year. But by using double-declining balance he can take 5% of the undepreciated balance each year. For example, if the improvements cost $800,000, straight line depreciation would result in depreciation of $20,000 per year in each of the 40 years. Using the double-declining balance method gives a first year depreciation of 5% × $800,000 = $40,000. Depreciation the second year would be 5% × ($800,000 − $40,000) = $38,000. Depreciation the third year would be

5% × ($800,000 − $40,000 − $38,000) = $36,100. Depreciation the fourth year would be 5% × ($800,000 − $40,000 − $38,000 − $36,100) = $34,295. The amount that can be taken drops each year, approaching zero by the 40th year. In addition to double-declining balance, the tax codes also permit 175%, 150% and 125% declining balance on certain types of property. For example, on a 40-year building using 150% declining balance, the annual depreciation would be 2½% × 150% = 3.75% per year.

The **sum-of-the-years' digits** approach involves adding together the number of years of remaining life and dividing that number into the remaining economic life. For example, if an asset has a remaining useful life of 5 years, depreciation in the first year would be 5 ÷ (5 + 4 + 3 + 2 + 1) = 33%. The second year it would be 4 ÷ (5 + 4 + 3 + 2 + 1) = 27%, and so forth.

Recapture

Accelerated depreciation methods lose some of their advantages because they are subject to **recapture** (taxation) at ordinary income tax rates when the property is sold. This can be quite costly to the investor in view of the fact that any gain that can otherwise be classed as a long-term capital gain will be taxed at only 40% of ordinary rates.

To illustrate, suppose an investment property is purchased for $100,000 and resold several years later for $150,000. If during the holding period the investor takes straight-line depreciation totaling $20,000, he will enjoy a tax shelter in that amount that can be used to shelter income from that property or other income he may have. However, the $20,000 in depreciation reduces his basis in the property to $80,000. When he sells, he is subject to long-term capital gains treatment on the difference between $150,000 and his $80,000 basis in the property. In other words, one of the benefits of real estate investing is taking depreciation now at ordinary rates and paying it back later at lower, long-term capital gains rates.

The government places a practical limitation on this benefit. If an investor elects to use an accelerated depreciation method, he gets faster write-off in the beginning, but pays for it later. For example, if the just mentioned investor had used an accelerated depreciation method to boost his depreciation to $30,000 during the holding period, and then sold, he would be taxed at ordinary rates on $10,000 and at long-term capital gain rates on $70,000. If the investor wishes to avoid ordinary rates on the $10,000, he could hold the property for its full useful life, in which case accelerated depreciation and straight-line depreciation will be about equal. If he wishes to dispose of the property without an immediate tax liability, he can enter into a tax-deferred exchange.

TAX ACT OF 1981

The Economic Recovery Tax Act of 1981 allows investors to depreciate real estate improvements faster than previously possible. Under the old law, which affects buildings acquired before January 1, 1981, the investor was required to estimate the building's useful life and then apply one of the depreciation methods just described. A typical residential structure might be assigned a useful life in the range of 20 to 40 years depending on its age and condition. The 1981 Tax Act provides for a 15-year depreciable life for buildings acquired on or after January 1, 1981. This effectively doubles tax shelter benefits attainable from depreciable property.

To illustrate, suppose a building valued at $300,000 was assigned a useful life of 30 years under the old law. Then using straight-line depreciation, one-thirtieth of the $300,000 would be depreciated each year, in other words, $10,000 per year. Under the 1981 law, the $300,000 building would be depreciated over 15 years for a deduction of $20,000 per year. At the end of the fifteenth year, the property is sold, another property bought, and the 15-year depreciation process started over again.

Under the 1981 law, an investor can use straight-line depreciation, or depending on the property, an **accelerated cost recovery** method. The accelerated methods produce larger write-offs than straight-line in the first few years. However, they are also subject to recapture. In contrast, if straight-line depreciation is used and the property has been held for more than one year, there is no depreciation recapture and all the gain is capital gain.

The major purpose of the Tax Act of 1981 was to encourage investment in depreciable property by shortening the depreciation period. It sets forth depreciation periods for various classes of real and personal property that are, for the most part, considerably shorter than their actual lives. A second purpose of the Act was to simplify the estimation of depreciation. In the past, taxpayers tended to estimate short lives in order to maximize tax shelter benefits while the Internal Revenue Service preferred longer depreciable lives for the opposite reason. With the Tax Act of 1981, nearly all types of real property improvements may be depreciated over 15 years and no distinction is made as to whether the property is new or used. Additionally, it is no longer necessary to estimate scrap value and deduct it before calculating depreciation. Remember, however, these new rules apply only to property purchased on or after January 1, 1981. Property purchased before that date is still subject to the old depreciation rules.

MORTGAGE REDUCTION

Mortgage reduction occurs because the investor uses a portion of the property's rental income to reduce the balance owing on the mortgage, thus increasing his equity. At first the reduction may be almost imperceptible because most of the monthly payments are going to interest. But eventually the balance owing begins to fall at a more rapid rate. Some investors invest with the idea that if they hold a rental property for the entire life of the loan, the tenants will have paid for the property. That is to say, the investor acquires the property free and clear of debt for only the cost of the down payment. This presumes the investor is patient and the property does not generate a negative cash flow.

APPRECIATION

Appreciation refers to the increase in property value that the owner hopes will occur while he owns it. Appreciation is the wonder-cure of investing. It can overcome a negative cash flow, overestimated income, underestimated expenses, and a variable rate mortgage that seems to vary only upward. Without appreciation, real estate becomes less attractive as an investment and people will take their investment money elsewhere, such as into stocks and bonds.

EQUITY BUILD-UP

An owner's **equity** in a property is defined as the market value of the property less all liens or other charges against the property. Thus, if you own a property worth $125,000 and owe $75,000, your equity is $50,000. If you own that property with your brother or sister, each with a one-half interest, your equity is $25,000 and his/her equity is $25,000.

Figure 23:3 CALCULATING EQUITY BUILD-UP

Equity at Time of Purchase		Equity 5 Years Later		Equity Build-up	
Purchase price	$200,000	Market value	$220,000	Current equity	$100,000
Mortgage loan	−140,000	Less loan balance	−120,000	Less beginning equity	−60,000
Down payment (equity)	$ 60,000	Equals current equity	$100,000	Equals equity build-up	$ 40,000

Equity build-up is the change in your equity over a period of time. Suppose you purchase a small apartment building for $200,000, placing $60,000 down and borrowing the balance. Your beginning equity is your down payment of $60,000. If after 5 years you have paid the loan down to $120,000 and you can sell the property for $220,000, your equity is now $100,000. Since you started with $60,000, your equity build-up is $40,000. Figure 23:3 recaps this calculation.

PROPERTY SELECTION

The real estate market offers a wide selection of properties for investments, including vacant land, houses, condominiums, small, medium, and large apartment buildings, office buildings, stores, industrial property, and so forth. Selecting a suitable type of property is a matter of matching an investor's capital with his attitudes toward risk taking and the amount of time he is willing to spend on management. Let us begin by looking at the ownership of vacant land.

Vacant Land

The major risk of owning vacant land as an investment is that one will have to wait too long for an increase in value. Vacant land produces no income, yet it consumes the investor's dollars in the form of interest, property taxes, insurance, and eventually selling costs. The rule of thumb is that the market value of vacant land must double every 5 years for the investor to break even. If this increase does not occur, the owner will find he has spent more on interest, insurance, property taxes, brokerage fees, and closing costs than he has made on the price increase.

Income tax laws currently in effect improve land speculation benefits somewhat, since insurance, interest, and property taxes plus any other costs of holding the investment are tax deductible at ordinary rates in the year paid. Yet the increase in property value is taxed only after the property is sold, and then at much lower long-term capital gains rates, provided the property was owned more than one year.

The key to successful land speculating is in outguessing the general public. If the public feels that development of a vacant parcel to a higher use is 10 years in the future, the market price will reflect the discounted cost at current interest rates and property taxes for that waiting period. If the land speculator buys at these prices, and the higher use occurs in 5 years, there is a good chance his purchase will be profitable. However, the speculator will lose money if the public expects the higher use to occur in 5 years and it actually takes 10 years.

Finally, land speculators expose themselves to an extra risk that owners of improved property can usually avoid: when it comes time to sell, unless buildings will immediately be placed upon the land by the purchaser, very few lenders will loan the purchaser money to buy the land. This may force the seller to accept the purchase price in the form of a down payment plus periodic payments for the balance. If the interest rate on the balance is below prevailing mortgage rates, as often happens in land sales, the seller is effectively subsidizing the buyer. Furthermore, if the payments are made over several years, the seller takes the risk that the money he receives will buy less because of inflation.

Houses and Condominiums

Houses and condominiums are the smallest properties available in income-producing real estate and as such are within the financial reach of more prospective investors than apartment buildings, stores, or offices. Moreover, they can usually be purchased with lower down payments and interest rates, because lenders feel that loans on houses and condominiums are less prone to default than on larger buildings. With a small property, the investor can fall back upon his salary and other income to meet loan payments in the event rents fall short. With larger buildings, the lender knows he must rely more on the rental success of the property and less on the owner's other sources of income.

Houses and condominiums are usually overpriced in relation to the monthly rent they can generate. This is because their prices are influenced both by the value of the shelter they provide and the amenity value of home ownership. Thus, an investor must pay what prospective owner-occupants are willing to pay, yet when the property is rented, a tenant will pay only for the shelter value. However, when the investor sells, he will be able to sell at a higher price than would be justified by rents alone. What this means to the investor is that he can usually expect a negative cash flow while he owns the property. Consequently, there must be a substantial increase in property value to offset the monthly negative cash flow, and give the investor a good return on his investment.

From time-to-time substantial appreciation has occurred. During parts of the 1970 decade, house prices rose very rapidly and produced excellent returns to those with single-family houses as investments. This rise can be traced to the relatively low number of new housing starts compared to the demand for new homes. In contrast, during the early 1960s, houses were poorer investments because sufficient new construction kept the prices of existing houses from rising rapidly. In many cities of the United States, condominiums were overbuilt in the early 1970s resulting in unsold new units. Consequently, investors in existing units could not get the appreciation needed to provide a decent return on investment. Later in the decade the supply-demand picture for condominiums changed and more appreciation occurred. Then during the tight money periods of the early 1980s, houses and condominiums again became poor investment performers because of the lack of appreciation.

Small Apartment Buildings

Because considerable appreciation must occur to make house and condominium investments profitable, many investors who start with these move to more income-oriented properties as their capital grows. This reduces investment risk because returns from rental income can be more reliably forecast than changes in prices. Particularly popular with investors who have modest amounts of investment capital are duplexes (two units), triplexes (three units), and four- and five-unit apartment buildings.

If it were necessary to hire professional management, such small buildings would be uneconomical to own. However, for most owners of two- to five-unit apartment buildings, management is on a do-it-yourself basis. Moreover, it is possible for the owner to live on the premises. This eliminates a cash outlay for management and allows the owner to reduce repair and maintenance expenses by handling them himself. Also, with the owner living on the property, tenants are encouraged to take better care of the premises and discouraged from moving out without paying their rent. Finally, the ownership of a residential rental property provides the owner with a wealth of experience and education in property management.

Medium-size Buildings

Apartment buildings containing 6 to 24 units also present good investment opportunities for those with sufficient down payment. However, in addition to analyzing the building, rents, and neighborhood, thought must be given to the matter of property management before a purchase is made. An apartment building of this size is not large enough for a full-time manager; therefore, the owner must either do the job or hire a part-time manager to live on the property. If the owner does the job, he should be willing to live on the property and devote a substantial amount of his time to management, maintenance, and upkeep activities. If a part-time manager is hired, the task is to find one who is knowledgeable and capable of maintaining property, showing vacant units, interviewing tenants, collecting rents on time, and handling landlord-tenant relations in accordance with local landlord-tenant laws. As the size of an apartment building increases, so does its efficiency. As a rule of thumb, when a building reaches 25 units, it will generate enough rent so that a full-time professional manager can be hired to live on the premises. With a live-in manager, the property owner need not reside on the property nor be involved in day-to-day management chores. This is very advantageous if the owner has another occupation where his time is better spent.

Larger Apartment Buildings

As the number of apartment units increases, the cost of management per unit drops. Beyond 60 units, assistant managers can be hired. This makes it possible to have a representative of the owner on the premises more hours of the day to look after the investment and keep the tenants happy. Size also means it is possible to add recreational facilities and other amenities that are not possible on a small scale. The cost of having a swimming pool in a 10-unit building might add so much to apartment rents that they would be priced out of the market. The same pool in a 50- or 100-unit building would make relatively little difference in rent. As buildings reach 200 or more units in size, it becomes economical to add such things as a children's pool, gymnasium, game room, lounge, and a social director.

Since larger apartment buildings cost less to manage per unit and compete very effectively in the market for tenants, they tend to produce larger cash flows per invested dollar. However, errors in location selection, building design, and management policy are magnified as the building grows in size. Also, many lenders, particularly small- and medium-sized banks and savings associations, are simply not large enough to lend on big projects. Finally, the number of investors who can single-handedly invest a down payment of $500,000 or more is limited. This has caused the widespread growth of the limited partnership as a means of making the economies of large-scale ownership available to investors with as little as $2,500 to invest.

Office Buildings

Office buildings offer the prospective investor not only a higher rent per square foot of floor space than any of the investments discussed thus far, but also larger cash flows per dollar of property worth. This is because office buildings are costlier to build and operate than residential structures, and because they expose the owner to more risk.

The higher construction and operating costs of an office building are due to the amenities and services office users demand. To be competitive today, an office building must offer air-conditioning to all tenants on a room-by-room basis thus adding to construction and operating costs. Office users also expect and pay for daily office housecleaning services, such as emptying waste baskets, cleaning ashtrays, dusting, and vacuuming. Apartment dwellers neither expect these services nor pay for them.

Tenant turnover is more expensive in an office building than an apartment building because a change in office tenants usually requires more extensive remodeling. To offset this, building owners include the cost of remodeling in the tenant's rent. Another consideration is that it is not unusual for office space to remain vacant for long periods of time. Also, if a building is rented to a single tenant, a single vacancy means there is no income at all. To reduce tenant turnover, incentives such as lower rent may be offered if a tenant agrees to sign a longer lease, such as 5 years instead of 1 or 2 years. Care, however, must be taken on longer leases so that the owner does not become locked into a fixed monthly rent while operating costs escalate rapidly due to inflation.

The risk in properly locating an office building is greater than with a residential property since office users are very particular about where they locate. If a residential building is not well located, the owner can usually drop rents a little and still fill the building. To do the same with an office building may require a much larger drop; then, even with the building full, it may not generate enough rent to pay the operating expenses and mortgage payments. Finally, the tax shelter benefits available from offices may not be as attractive as comparably priced apartments. This is because compared to office buildings, residential properties tend to have a higher percentage of their value in depreciable improvements and less in nondepreciable land.

INVESTMENT TIMING

The potential risks and rewards available from owning improved real estate depend to a great extent on the point in the life of a property at which an investment is made. Should one invest while a project is still an idea? Or is it better to wait until it is finished and fully rented? That depends on the risks one can afford and the potential rewards.

Land Purchase

The riskiest point to invest in a project is when it is still an idea in someone's head. At this point, money is needed to purchase land. But beyond the cost of the land, there are many unknowns, including the geological suitability of the land to support buildings, the ability to obtain the needed zoning and building permits, the cost of construction, the availability of a loan, the rents the market will pay, how quickly the property will find tenants, the expenses of operating the property, and finally the return the investor will obtain. Even though the investor may have a feasibility study that predicts success for the project, such a report is still only an educated guess. Therefore, the anticipated returns to an investor entering a project at this point must be high to offset the risks he takes. As the project clears such hurdles as zoning approval, building permits, obtaining construction cost bids, and finding a lender, it becomes less risky. Therefore, a person who invests after these hurdles are cleared would expect somewhat less potential reward. Nonetheless, the investor is buying into the project at a relatively low price; if it is successful, he will enjoy a developer's profit upon which no income tax must be paid until the property is finally sold. Against this, he takes the risk that the project may stall along the way or that, once completed, it will lose money.

Project Completion

Another major milestone is reached when the project is completed and opens its doors for business. At this point, the finished cost of the building is known, and during the first 12 months of operation the property owners learn what rents the market will pay, what level of occupancy will be achieved and what actual operating expenses will be. As estimates are replaced with actual operating experience, the risk to the investor decreases. As a result, the investor entering at this stage receives a smaller dollar return on his investment, but is more certain of his return than if he had invested earlier. The tax benefits at this stage are very attractive, but not quite as rewarding as in the earlier stages.

First Decade

A building is new only once, and after its first year it begins to face competition from newer buildings. However, in an inflationary economy that forces up the construction cost of newer buildings, existing buildings will be able to charge less rent. Furthermore, newer buildings may be forced to use less desirable sites. During the first 10 years, occupancy rates are stable, operating expenses are well established, tax benefits are good, and the building is relatively free of major repairs or replacements.

Second Decade

As a building passes its tenth birthday, the costs and risks it presents to a prospective investor change. He must ask whether the neighborhood is still expected to remain desirable to tenants and whether the building's location will increase in value enough to offset wear and tear and obsolescence. A careful inspection must be made of the structure to determine whether poor construction quality will soon result in costly repairs. Also, the buyer must be prepared for normal replacements and expenses such as new appliances, water heaters, and a fresh coat of paint. As a result, an investor buying a 10-year-old building will seek a larger return than when the building was younger.

Third & Fourth Decades

Larger returns are particularly important as a building reaches its twentieth year and major expense items such as a new roof, replacement of plumbing fixtures, repair of parking areas, and remodeling become necessary. As a building approaches and passes its thirtieth year, investors must consider carefully the remaining economic life of the property and whether rents permit a return on investment as well as a return of investment. Also, maintenance costs climb as a building becomes older, and decisions will be necessary regarding whether or not major restoration and remodeling should be undertaken. If it is, the cost must be recovered during the balance of the building's life. The alternative is to add little or no money to the building, a decision the surrounding neighborhood may already be forcing upon the property owner. Older properties have been a strong magnet to real estate investors who hope to find attractive buys that can be fixed up for a profit. However, care must be taken not to overpay for this privilege in light of the foregoing discussion.

Building Recycling

More buildings are torn down than fall down, and this phase in a building's life also represents an investment opportunity. However, like the first stage in the development cycle, raw land, the risks are high. In effect, when the decision is made to purchase a structure with the intention of demolishing it, the investor is counting on the value of the land being worth more in another use. That use may be a government-sponsored renewal program, or the investor may be accumulating adjoining properties with the ultimate intention of creating plottage value by demolishing the structures and joining the lots. Because the risks of capital loss in this phase are high, the potential returns should be too.

GLITAMAD

The acronym GLITAMAD, developed by Maury Seldin and Richard Swesnick, is a helpful way to remember the various phases in the life cycle of improved real estate investments. (See Figure 23:4.)

Figure 23:4

"GLITAMAD"

G = Ground (the raw land stage)	↑	Increasing risk, Increasing returns
L = Loan (long-term loan commitment)		
I = Interim (short-term loan and construction)		
T = Tenancy (building filled with tenants)	}	Least risk, Least returns
A = Absorption (second through tenth year)	}	
M = Maturity (eleventh through thirtieth year)		
A = Aging (more than 30 years)		Increasing risk, Increasing returns
D = Demise (demolition, reuse of the land)	↓	

As the risk that an investor will suffer a loss increases, the expected returns must increase.

Source: Maury Seldin and Richard H. Swesnik, *Real Estate Investment Strategy,* copyright © 1970, John Wiley & Sons, Inc., New York. Used by permission.

DEVELOPING A PERSONAL INVESTMENT STRATEGY

The objective in developing a personal investment strategy is to balance the returns available with the risks that must be taken so that the overall welfare of the investor is enhanced. To accomplish this, it is very helpful to look at lifetime income and consumption patterns.

In Figure 23:5 the broken line represents the income that a person can typically expect to receive at various ages during his or her life. It includes income from wages, pensions, and investments, and is the same income curve that was discussed in Chapter 22. The solid line represents a person's lifetime consumption pattern. Taken together, the two lines show that, during the first 20 to 25 years, consumption exceeds income. Then the situation reverses itself and income outpaces consumption. If one is planning an investment program, these are the years to carry it out.

Figure 23:5

LIFETIME INCOME AND CONSUMPTION PATTERNS

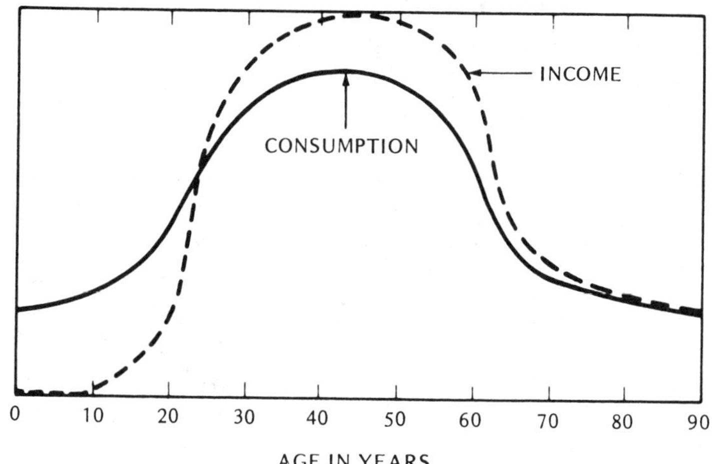

Risk Taking

The graph shows that an investment opportunity that offers a high risk of loss is better suited for a person under the age of 45. Then, even if the investment does turn sour, the investor still has a substantial amount of working life remaining to recover financially. An investor between 45 and 55 years of age should be somewhat more cautious in terms of risk taking, since there is less time to make a financial recovery if the need arises. Above the age of 55, high-risk investments are even less appropriate for the same reason. Therefore, as a person reaches 55, 60, and 65, there should be a program of moving toward relatively risk-free investments, even though the returns will be smaller. Upon retirement, the investor can live off the investments he or she made when younger.

Debt Repayment

Mortgage debt commitments that require a portion of the investor's personal income should also be considered in light of one's position on the lifetime income and consumption curves. This is done to ascertain whether there will be sufficient income in the future to meet the loan payments. Not to consider the future may force a premature sale, perhaps in the midst of a very sluggish market at a distressed price. For the investor who has passed his income peak, financing with less debt and more equity means a higher probability that his properties will generate enough income to meet monthly loan payments.

Also, with fewer dollars going to debt repayment, more can be kept by the investor for living expenses. By comparison, a relatively young investor may be handicapped by the lack of starting capital; however, he has the advantages of time and increasing income on his side.

Tax Planning

The income curve in Figure 23:5 provides us insight with regard to tax planning using tax shelter investments. During the peak income years, a person is in the highest tax brackets of life; a larger portion of each dollar of income is paid out as income taxes than later in life. Thus, a strategy to minimize taxes calls for sound investments that emphasize tax shelter during the peak income years. Later in life when income falls and the investor moves to successively lower tax brackets, there is less concern with finding investments that shelter income or selling properties in which there is a taxable gain. Developing a workable tax strategy requires thoughtful advance planning. If a person aged 40 purchases a real estate investment that offers excellent tax shelter for 5 years and then is to be resold at a profit, the income curve shows that, while his short-run tax picture will be improved, his tax problems 5 years hence will be made worse. To solve that problem, the investor must either trade for another property in the fifth year or, if he sells, be prepared to invest in another tax shelter investment large enough to shelter the taxable gain from the first.

The same points made here in connection with investments can also be applied to one's home. If a homeowner can purchase a home with a mortgage and then pay down the mortgage during those years in life when income substantially exceeds consumption, the home can be carried debt free into retirement to provide a place to live without mortgage payments. The home then becomes an investment in every sense of the word.

VALUING AN INVESTMENT

In Chapter 16, "Real Estate Appraisal," we discussed value from the standpoint of someone who was looking at available facts in the marketplace in order to make an estimate of the value of a property. The investor's valuation problem is somewhat different. He knows as a fact what the seller's asking price is. He can find information relating to the current income and expenses of a property and can make a projection of future income based on these. Additionally, he will have information

Figure 23:6

Appraiser's Viewpoint	**Investor's Viewpoint**
$\text{Value} = \dfrac{\text{Net Income}}{\text{Return}}$	$\text{Return} = \dfrac{\text{Net Income}}{\text{Price}}$

The appraiser solves for value. The investor solves for return.

relating to how the property can be financed and he will have some figure in mind as to how much appreciation he expects will take place in the future. From these he calculates the return the property will give him on his investment. If this return is more appealing than alternative investments he is considering, he will purchase the property. If it is not, he will pass it by. Figure 23:6 illustrates the different viewpoints of the appraiser and the investor.

If an investor makes his investment decision based on cash-on-cash, he is solving for the annual cash return he can expect on his cash investment. Suppose that for a particular property offered to him it is 10%. He will use that figure to compare with the cash-on-cash figures he has determined for other properties presently offered for sale. He will select the property with the highest cash-on-cash figure commensurate with the risks that he is willing to accept.

If an investor uses a more sophisticated method of valuation, such as the mortgage equity technique discussed in Chapter 16, the emphasis will still be the same. Of the possible eight variables in a mortgage equity problem, the investor will provide these seven: the price of the property, net operating income, loan ratio, loan term, loan interest, holding period, and anticipated appreciation. The factor he will solve for is the equity yield rate; that is, the annual return on his investment. This figure is compared with other properties currently for sale and together with an analysis of tax consequences and investment risk, a decision is made as to whether or not to invest.

LIMITED PARTNERSHIPS

As discussed earlier in this chapter, large investment properties have a number of economic advantages over small ones. Yet the vast majority of investors in the United States do not have the capital to buy a large project single-handedly. Moreover, many persons who would like to own real estate for its yield and tax benefits do not do so because they wish to avoid the work and responsibilities of property management. As a result, the United States has witnessed the widespread use of limited partnerships for real estate investment. This popular form of investment offers investors the following advantages:

1. Management of the property and financial affairs of the partnership by the general partner.
2. Financial liability limited to the amount invested.
3. The opportunity for a small investor to own a part of large projects and to diversify.
4. The same tax benefits as enjoyed by sole owners.

The organizers of a limited partnership are responsible for selecting properties, putting them into a financial package, and making it available to investors. As a rule, the organizers are the general partners and the investors are the limited partners. For their efforts in organizing the partnership, the general partners receive a cash fee from the limited partners or a promotional interest in the partnership or both.

Property Purchase Methods

Property is purchased by one of two methods. The organizers can either buy properties first and then seek limited partners, or they can find limited partners first and then buy properties. The first approach is a **specific property offering.** The second is a **blind pool.** The advantage of the specific property offering is that the prospective limited partner knows in advance precisely what properties he will own. However, this approach requires the organizers either to find a seller who is willing to wait for a partnership to be formed or to buy the property in their own names using their own capital. If they use their own capital, the organizers risk the chance of financial loss if limited partners cannot be found.

The advantage of the blind pool is that the organizers do not buy until money has been raised from the limited partners. This requires less capital from the organizers, and avoids the problem of holding property but not being able to find sufficient investors. Also, the organizers can negotiate better prices from sellers when they have cash in hand. However, if the organizers are poor judges of property, the investors may wind up owning property that they would not have otherwise purchased.

Property Management

Once property is purchased, the general partners are responsible for managing the property themselves or selecting a management firm to do the job. In addition, the general partners must maintain the accounting books and at least once a year remit to each investor his portion of the cash flow, an accounting of the partnership's performance for the year, and profit or loss data for income tax purposes. With regard to selling partnership property, the partnership agreement usually gives the limited partners the right to vote on when to sell, to whom to sell, and for how much. In practice, the general partners decide when to put the matter up to a vote, and the limited partners usually follow their advice.

Financial Liability

The word "limited" in limited partnership refers to the limited financial liability of the limited partner. In a properly drawn agreement, limited partners cannot lose more than they have invested. By comparison, the general partners are legally liable for all the debts of the partnership, up to the full extent of their entire personal worth. Being a limited partner does not eliminate the possibility of being asked at a later date for more investment money if the properties in the partnership are not financially successful. When this happens, each limited partner must decide between adding more money in hopes the partnership will soon make a financial turnaround, or refusing to do so and being eliminated from the partnership. By way of comparison, an individual investor who buys real estate in his own name takes the risks of both the limited and general partner, since he is exposed to all the risks of ownership.

Investment Diversification

Investment groups provide the means for an investor to diversify. For example, a limited partnership of 200 members each contributing $5,000 would raise $1,000,000. This could be used as a down payment on one property worth $4,000,000 or on four different properties priced at $1,000,000 each. If the $4,000,000 property is purchased, the entire success or failure of the partnership rides on that one property. With four $1,000,000 properties, the failure of one can be balanced by the success of the others. Even greater diversification can be achieved by purchasing properties in different rental price ranges, in different parts of the same city, and in different cities in the country. Regarding income tax benefits, a very important advantage of the limited partnership is that it allows the investor to be taxed as though he was the sole owner of the property, because the partnership itself is not subject to taxation. All income and loss items, including any tax shelter generated by the property, are proportioned to each investor directly.

Service Fees

The prospective investor should carefully look at the price the organizers are charging for their services. Is it adequate, but not excessive? To expect good performance from capable people, they must be compensated adequately, but to overpay reduces the returns from the investment that properly belong to those who provide the capital. When is the compensation to be paid? If management fees are paid in advance, there is less incentive for the organizers to provide quality management for the limited partners after the partnership is formed. The preferred arrangement is to pay for management services as they are received, and for the limited partners to reserve the right to vote for new management. Similarly, it is preferable to base a substantial portion of the fee for organizing the partnership on the success of the investment. By giving the organizers a percentage of the partnership's profits instead of a fixed fee, the organizers have a direct stake in the success of the partnership.

Pitfalls

Although the limited partnership form of real estate ownership offers investors many advantages, experience has shown that there are numerous pitfalls that can separate investors from their money. Most importantly, a limited partner should recognize that the success or failure of a limited partnership is dependent on the organizers. Do they have a good record in selecting, organizing, and managing real estate investments in the past? Are they respected in the community for prompt and honest dealings? Will local banks and building suppliers offer them credit? What is their rating with credit bureaus? Are they permanent residents of the community in which they operate? Do the county court records show lawsuits or other legal complaints against them?

With reference to the properties in the partnership, are the income projections reasonable and have adequate allowances been made for vacancies, maintenance, and management?

Overoptimism, sloppy income and expense projections, and outright shading of the truth will ultimately be costly to the investor. Unless the investor has extreme confidence in the promoters, he will personally visit the properties in the partnership and verify the rent schedules, vacancy levels, operating expenses, and physical condition of the improvements. He will also want to make an estimate of the partnership's **downside risk** (that is, the risk that he will lose his money).

The careful investor will consult with a lawyer to make certain that the partnership agreement does limit his liability and that the tax benefits will be as advertised. He will also want to know what to expect if the partnership suffers financial setbacks. Are the partnership's properties to be sold at a loss or at a foreclosure sale, or do the general partners stand ready to provide the needed money? Will the limited partners be asked to contribute? The prospective investor should also investigate to see if the properties are overpriced. Far too many partnerships organized to date have placed so much emphasis on tax shelter benefits that the entire matter of whether the investment was economically feasible has been overlooked. Even to a 50% bracket taxpayer, a dollar wasted before taxes is still 50¢ wasted after taxes.

Finally, to receive maximum benefits from his investment, the investor must be prepared to stay with the partnership until the properties are refinanced or sold. The resale market for limited partnership interests is almost nonexistent, and when a buyer is found, the price is usually below the proportional worth of the investor's interest in the partnership. Moreover, the partnership agreement may place restrictions on limited partners who want to sell their interests.

DISCLOSURE LAWS

Because investors are vulnerable to unsound investments and exploitation at the hands of limited partnership organizers, state and federal disclosure laws have been passed to protect them. Administered by the Securities & Exchange Commission at the federal level and by real estate regulatory departments and commissions at state levels, these laws require organizers and salesmen to disclose all pertinent facts surrounding their partnership offerings. Prospective investors must be told how much money the organizers wish to raise, what portion will go for promotional expenses and organizers' fees, what properties have been (or will be) purchased, from whom they were bought, and for how much. Also, prospective investors must be provided with a copy of the partnership agreement and given property income and expense records for past years. They must be told how long the partnership expects to hold its properties until selling, the partnership's policy on cash flow distribution, the right of limited partners to a voice in management, the names of those responsible for managing the partnership properties, and how profits (or losses) will be split when the properties are sold.

The Prospectus

The amount of disclosure detail required by state and federal laws varies with the number of properties and the partners' relationship. For a handful of friends forming a partnership among themselves, there would be little in the way of formal disclosure requirements. However, as the number of investors increases and the partnership is offered to investors across state lines, disclosure requirements increase dramatically. It is not unusual for a disclosure statement, called a **prospectus,** to be 50 to 100 pages long.

Blue-Sky Laws

The philosophy of disclosure laws is to make information available to prospective investors and let them make their own decisions. Thus, an investor is free to invest in an unsound investment as long as the facts are explained to him in advance. An alternative point of view is that many investors do not read nor understand disclosure statements; therefore, it is the duty of government to pass on the economic soundness of an investment before it can be offered to the public. The result has been the passage of **blue-sky laws** in several states. The first of these was passed by the Kansas legislature in 1911 to protect purchasers from buying into dubious investment schemes that sold them nothing more than a piece of the blue sky. Some states retain these laws and apply them to limited partnerships and other securities offered within their borders.

VOCABULARY REVIEW

Match terms **a–j** *with statements* **1–10.**

a. *Accelerated depreciation*
b. *Blind pool*
c. *Cash flow*
d. *Downside risk*
e. *Equity build up*
f. *GLITAMAD*
g. *Negative cash flow*
h. *Prospectus*
i. *Straight-line*
j. *Tax shelter*

1. Number of dollars remaining each year after collecting rents and paying operating expenses and mortgage payments.
2. Requires the investor to dip into his own pocket.
3. Income tax savings that an investment can produce for its owner.
4. Results from mortgage balance reduction and price appreciation.
5. An acronym that refers to the various phases in the life cycle of an improved property.
6. A method of calculating depreciation that takes equal amounts of depreciation each year.
7. Any method of depreciation that achieves a faster rate of depreciation than the straight-line method.
8. A limited partnership wherein properties are purchased after the limited partners have invested their money.
9. The possibility that an investor will lose his money in an investment.
10. A disclosure statement that describes an investment opportunity.

QUESTIONS AND PROBLEMS

1. What is a tax-sheltered real estate investment?
2. What monetary benefits do investors expect to receive by investing in real estate?
3. What is the major risk that a vacant land speculator takes?
4. What advantages and disadvantages do duplexes and triplexes offer to a prospective investor?
5. Is an investor better off investing in a project before it is built or after it is completed and occupied? Explain.
6. As a building grows older, why should an investor demand a higher return per dollar invested?
7. How does a person's age affect his or her investment goals and the amount of investment risk that may be taken?
8. An investor is looking at a property that produces a net operating income of $22,000 per year. He expects the property to appreciate 50% in ten years and plans to finance it with a 25-year, 11% interest, 75% loan-to-value loan. If the property is priced to produce an 18% return on the investor's equity, how much is the seller asking? (Use Table 16:5 in Chapter 16.)
9. Another investor looks at the property described in Problem 8, but feels it will appreciate only 25% in value. How much would he offer to pay the seller?
10. All facts same as in Problem 8 except the interest rate jumps to 12%. To keep the same investor return of 18%, how much should the investor offer the seller for the property?

11. What advantages does the limited partnership form of ownership offer to real estate investors?
12. What can a prospective investor do to increase his chances of joining a limited partnership that will be successful?

ADDITIONAL READINGS

Carless, Daniel G. "More Than Rents and Repairs." *Real Estate Today,* April, 1978, pages 22–29. Analyzing an apartment complex as an investment takes more than a quick look at rents and repairs. The little things count too.

Case, Frederick E. *Investing in Real Estate.* Englewood Cliffs, N.J.: Prentice-Hall, 1978, 243 pages. Book contains discussion plus a series of checklists to help investors evaluate raw land, houses, apartment buildings, second homes, and recreational property as investments.

Lyons, Paul. *Investing in Real Estate.* Reston, Va.: Reston Publishing Co., 1981, 288 pages. A guide to residential real estate investment that assumes no previous investment knowledge.

Royster, Michael J. "The Six-Flat: Tax Haven for Middle America." *Real Estate Review,* Winter, 1979, pages 71–76. Article focuses on the realities of real estate investment as seen by the man in the street.

Seldin, Maury, and **Swesnik, Richard H.** *Real Estate Investment Strategy,* 2nd ed. New York: John Wiley & Sons, 1979, 345 pages. A very readable and thoughtful book designed to aid the prospective real estate investor in choosing the type of property to invest in. Emphasizes risks versus returns.

Swesnik, Richard H. *Acquiring and Developing Income-Producing Real Estate.* Reston, Va.: Reston Publishing Co., 1979, 240 pages. Author provides concrete advice on setting up ownership, protecting one's interests, and handling financing. This is an advanced book, however the author's writing style makes it very readable.

Wiedemer, John P. *Real Estate Investment,* 2nd ed. Reston, Va.: Reston Publishing Co., 1982, 288 pages. Book provides a general background of information essential to successful real estate investment. Topics include property analysis, taxation, depreciation, forms of ownership, land use, financing, and types of property available.

APPENDIX A

Answers to Q

UNIFORM TEST

EXA...

REAL ESTATE CONTRACTS

1. **B**

FINANCING

1. **C** 2. **A**

REAL ESTATE OWNERSHIP

1. **D** 2. **C** 3. **D** 4. **C**

REAL ESTATE BROKERAGE

1. **C** 2. **D** 3. **A**

REAL ESTATE VALUATION

1. **D** 2. **C** 3. **B** 4. **B**

STATE TEST

1. **B** 2. **Local answer** 3. **D**

UNIFORM TEST

ETS BROKER EXAMINATION

REAL ESTATE BROKERAGE

1. **C** 2. **A**

CONTRACTS AND OTHER LEGAL ASPECTS

1. **C** 2. **B** 3. **B**

PRICING AND VALUATION

1. **C** 2. **A** 3. **B**

FINANCE AND INVESTMENT

1. **B** 2. **C** 3. **A**

ANSWERS TO CHAPTER QUESTIONS AND PROBLEMS

CHAPTER 2
Nature and Description of Real Estate

VOCABULARY REVIEW

a. 17	**e.** 9	**i.** 16	**l.** 7	**o.** 5
b. 4	**f.** 11	**j.** 8	**m.** 18	**p.** 14
c. 15	**g.** 1	**k.** 12	**n.** 6	**q.** 2
d. 10	**h.** 13			**r.** 3

QUESTIONS AND PROBLEMS

1. Requires local answer.

2.

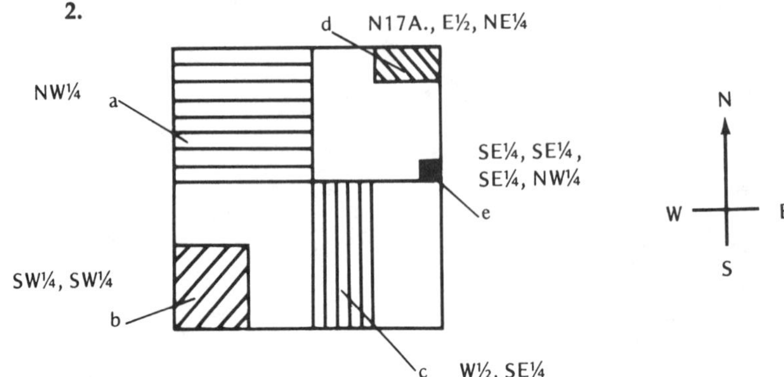

3. (a) 160 acres
(b) 40 acres
(c) 80 acres
(d) 17 acres
(e) 2 1/2 acres

4. (a) NE$\frac{1}{4}$
(160 acres)
(b) E$\frac{1}{2}$ of the SE$\frac{1}{4}$
(80 acres)
(c) SW$\frac{1}{4}$ of the NW$\frac{1}{4}$
(40 acres)
(d) W$\frac{1}{2}$ of the SE$\frac{1}{4}$ of the NW$\frac{1}{4}$
(20 acres)
(e) NE$\frac{1}{4}$ of the SE$\frac{1}{4}$ of the NW$\frac{1}{4}$
(10 acres)

5.

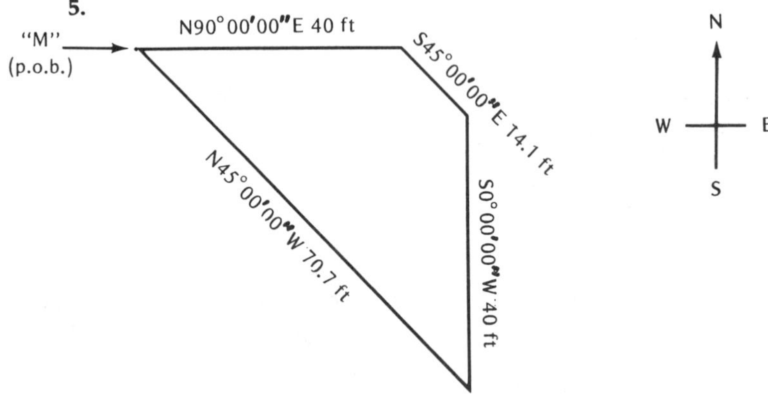

6. No. In the general public interest, laws have been passed that give aircraft the right to pass over land provided they fly above certain altitudes.

7. The key to a door, although highly portable, is adapted to the door and as such is real property.

8. Requires individualized answer. However, as a general rule, anything that is permanently attached is real property and anything that is not attached is personal property.

9. Requires local answer. Right of reasonable value.
10. Unless corrections are made (and they usually are) survey inaccuracies would result. Could cause bench mark to move.

CHAPTER 3
Rights and Interests in Land

VOCABULARY REVIEW

a. 8	e. 17	i. 13	m. 10	q. 3
b. 12	f. 19	j. 14	n. 16	r. 9
c. 4	g. 7	k. 1	o. 15	s. 20
d. 18	h. 5	l. 6	p. 2	t. 11

QUESTIONS AND PROBLEMS

1. For a freehold estate to exist, there must be actual possession of the land (that is, ownership) and the estate must be of unpredictable duration. Leasehold estates do not involve ownership of the land and are of determinate length. Freehold estate cases are tried under real property laws. Leasehold cases are tried under personal property laws.
2. An easement is created when a landowner fronting on a public byway deeds or leases a landlocked portion of his land to another person. This would be an easement by necessity. A second method is by prolonged use and is called an easement by prescription.
3. Dower, curtesy and homestead are referred to as statutory estates because they are created by state laws and not by the landowner.
4. The holder of an easement coexists side-by-side with the landowner; that is, both have a shared use of the land in question. The holder of a lease obtains exclusive right of occupancy and the landowner is excluded during the term of the lease.
5. An encumbrance is any impediment to clear title. Examples are: lien, lease, easement, deed restriction, and encroachment.
6. Requires local answer. (Answers will likely center around zoning, building codes, general land planning, rent control, property taxation, eminent domain, and escheat.)
7. The entire home (No monetary limitation. Limited to 80 acres in the country or ½ acre in town.) is protected except from liens for work on the home or purchase money mortgage. Own the home and live there.
8. It is considered both.

CHAPTER 4
Holding Title

VOCABULARY REVIEW

a. 8	e. 5	h. 17	k. 13	n. 3
b. 1	f. 12	i. 14	l. 15	o. 2
c. 16	g. 11	j. 4	m. 9	p. 6
d. 10				q. 7

QUESTIONS AND PROBLEMS

1. The key advantage of sole ownership is flexibility—the owner can make all decisions without approval of co-owners. The key disadvantages are responsibility and the high entry cost.
2. Undivided interest means that each co-owner has a right to use the entire property.
3. The four unities are—
   Time: each joint tenant must acquire his or her ownership at the same moment.
   Title: all joint tenants acquire their interests from the same source.
   Interest: each joint tenant owns an undivided whole of the property.
   Possession: all joint tenants have the right to use the whole property.
4. Right of survivorship means that upon the death of a joint tenant, his interest in the property is extinguished and the remaining joint tenants are automatically left as the owners.
5. Tenancy in common.
6. Yes.
7. The three women would be considered to be tenants in common with each owning an undivided one-third interest.
8. No assumption can safely be made based on name only. Inquiry must be made into whether the land in question was separate or community property.
9. The key differences are in the financial liability of the limited partners, the limited management role of the limited partners, and the fact that limited partners are not found in a general partnership.
10. REITs offer investors single taxation, built-in management, small minimum investment, and liquidity.

CHAPTER 5 · Transferring Title

VOCABULARY REVIEW

a. 15	**e.** 14	**i.** 20	**m.** 3	**q.** 13
b. 9	**f.** 16	**j.** 1	**n.** 12	**r.** 10
c. 18	**g.** 5	**k.** 17	**o.** 11	**s.** 2
d. 7	**h.** 6	**l.** 4	**p.** 19	**t.** 8

QUESTIONS AND PROBLEMS

1. Yes. The fact that a document is a deed depends on the wording it contains, not what it is labeled or not labeled.
2. Title passes upon delivery of the deed by the grantor to the grantee and its willing acceptance by the grantee.
3. The full covenant and warranty deed offers the grantee protection in the form of the grantor's assurances that he is the owner and possessor, that the grantee will not be disturbed after taking possession by someone else claiming ownership, that the title is not

encumbered except as stated in the deed, and that the grantor will procure and deliver to the grantee any subsequent documents necessary to make good the title being conveyed.

4. Warranty deed. It provides the grantee with the maximum title protection available from a deed.
5. No.
6. The hazards of preparing one's own deeds are that any errors made will cause confusion and may make the deed legally invalid. Preprinted deeds may not be suitable for the state where the land is located or for the grantor's purpose. An improperly prepared deed, once recorded, creates errors in the public records.
7. Dower right, curtesy right, community property right, mortgage right of redemption, tax lien, judgment lien, mechanic's lien, undivided interest held by another, inheritance rights, and easements are all examples of title clouds.
8. When a person dies without leaving a will, state law directs how his assets are to be distributed.
9. An executor is named by the deceased in his will to carry out its terms. In the absence of a will, the state appoints an administrator to settle the deceased's estate.
10. No. Two.
11. No. Occupancy on a rental basis is not hostile to the property owner, but rather is by his permission.
12. Requires local answer.

CHAPTER 6
Recordation, Abstracts, and Title Insurance

VOCABULARY REVIEW

a. 10	**e.** 2	**h.** 14	**k.** 13	**n.** 5
b. 3	**f.** 6	**i.** 16	**l.** 4	**o.** 15
c. 1	**g.** 8	**j.** 9	**m.** 11	**p.** 12
d. 7				**q.** 17

QUESTIONS AND PROBLEMS

1. By visibly occupying a parcel of land or by recording a document in the public records a person gives constructive notice that he is claiming a right or interest in that parcel of land. Actual notice is knowledge that one has actually gained, based on what he has seen, heard, read, or observed.
2. Requires local answer.
3. Requires local answer.
4. The grantor and grantee indexes are used to locate documents filed in the public recorder's office.
5. Although the bulk of the information necessary to conduct a title search can be found in the public recorder's office, it may also be necessary to inspect documents not kept there, for example, marriage records, judgment lien files, probate records, and the U.S. Tax Court.

6. A title opinion issued by an attorney is his opinion of ownership, whereas a Torrens certificate of title shows ownership as determined by a court of law.
7. A title opinion shows the condition of title at a specific moment in time. An abstract provides a complete historical summary of all recorded documents affecting title. From this an attorney renders an opinion as to the current condition of title.
8. The purpose of title insurance is to protect owners and lenders from monetary loss due to errors in title report preparation and inaccuracies in the public records.
9. Although Williams did not record his deed, his occupancy of the house constitutes legal notice. The out-of-state investor who probably felt safe because he bought a title insurance policy apparently did not read the fine print which, in most owner's policies, does not insure against facts, rights, interests or claims that could be ascertained by an on-site inspection or by making inquiry of persons in possession. The out-of-state investor is the loser unless he can recover his money from Thorsen.
10. Requires local answer.

CHAPTER 7 Contract Law

VOCABULARY REVIEW

a. 12	**e.** 8	**h.** 3	**k.** 13	**n.** 15
b. 14	**f.** 10	**i.** 16	**l.** 7	**o.** 17
c. 4	**g.** 11	**j.** 5	**m.** 9	**p.** 2
d. 1				**q.** 6

QUESTIONS AND PROBLEMS

1. An expressed contract is the result of a written or oral agreement. An implied contract is one that is apparent from the actions of the parties involved. (Examples will vary with personal experiences.)
2. A legally valid contract requires: (a) legally competent parties, (b) mutual agreement, (c) lawful objective, (d) sufficient consideration or cause, and (e) a writing when required by law.
3. A void contract has no legal effect on any party to the contract and may be ignored at the pleasure of any party to it. A voidable contract binds one party but gives the other the right to withdraw.
4. Examples of legal incompetents include: minors, insane persons, drunks, and felons. (Exceptions are possible in the latter two.)
5. An offer can be terminated by the passage of time and by withdrawal prior to its acceptance. Passage of time can be in the form of a fixed termination date for the offer or, lacking that, a reasonable amount of time to accept, as fixed by a court of law.
6. Mistake as applied to contract law arises from ambiguity in negotiations and mistake of material fact.
7. Consideration is one of the legal requirements of a binding con-

tract. The concept of one party doing something and receiving nothing in return is foreign to contract law. Examples generally fall into four categories: money, goods, services, and forbearance.

8. The parties to a legally unenforceable contract can still voluntarily carry out its terms. However, compliance could not be enforced by a court of law.
9. Alternatives include: mutual rescission, assignment, novation, partial performance, money damages, unilateral rescission, specific performance suit, or liquidated damages.
10. His primary concern would be whether money damages would suitably restore his position or whether actual performance is necessary.

CHAPTER 8
Real Estate Sales Contracts

VOCABULARY REVIEW

a. 7
b. 2
c. 6
d. 9
e. 4
f. 3
g. 5
h. 1
i. 8
j. 10
k. 11

QUESTIONS AND PROBLEMS

1. The purchase contract provides time to ascertain that the seller is capable of conveying title, time to arrange financing, and time to carry out the various terms and conditions of the contract.
2. Anything left to be "ironed out" later is an area for potential disagreement and possibly a lost deal. Moreover, the basic contract requirement of a meeting of the minds may be missing.
3. The advantages are convenience (the bulk of the contract is already written) and time (it is faster to fill out a form than construct a contract from scratch). The disadvantages are that a preprinted contract may not adequately fit a given transaction and the blank spaces still leave room for errors.
4. A seller can accept an offer with or without a deposit. (An exception is that some court-ordered sales require a specified deposit.)
5. Most fixtures are considered by law to be a part of the land and therefore do not need separate mention. However, mention is made of any fixture that might be open to differences of opinion.
6. If a seller is not under pressure to sell quickly and/or there are plenty of buyers in the marketplace, he can hold out for price and terms to his liking. If a buyer is aware of other buyers competing for the same property, he will act quickly and meet (or offer close to) the seller's price and terms. If the seller is in a rush to sell or is afraid that there are few buyers for his property in the market, he will negotiate terms more to the buyer's liking rather than risk not making the sale. If the buyer is aware of this he can hold out for price and terms to his liking.

7. The advantages to the seller of holding title in a contract for deed sale are that the seller already has title in the event of the buyer's default and where nonrecording provisions are valid and used, the seller can pledge the property as collateral for a loan.
8. They are permitted subject to Minnesota's contract for deed cancellation statute.
9. The key advantages of trading are the tax-free exchange possibility and the need for little or no cash to complete the transaction. The disadvantages are in finding suitable trade property for all parties involved and in the fact that there are more transaction details in a trade (compared to a cash sale) that can go awry and ruin the trade.
10. A letter of intent is a mutual expression of interest to carry out some business objective. No firm, legal obligation is created.

CHAPTER 9 *Mortgage Theory and Law*

VOCABULARY REVIEW

a. 9	**e.** 2	**i.** 4	**m.** 16	**q.** 11
b. 13	**f.** 18	**j.** 15	**n.** 12	**r.** 19
c. 6	**g.** 5	**k.** 1	**o.** 17	**s.** 14
d. 10	**h.** 3	**l.** 8	**p.** 7	**t.** 20

QUESTIONS AND PROBLEMS

1. A prepayment privilege is to the advantage of the borrower. Without it he cannot repay his debt ahead of schedule.
2. Lien theory sees a mortgage as creating only a lien against a property whereas title theory sees a mortgage as conveying title to the lender subject to defeat by the borrower.
3. Strict foreclosure gives title to the lender whereas foreclosure by sale requires that the foreclosed property be sold at public auction and the proceeds used to repay the lender. Foreclosure by sale.
4. The first mortgage is the senior mortgage while the second and third mortgages are classed as junior mortgages.
5. Foreclosure by advertisement is most commonly used.
6. Minnesota allows both, including a 6 or 12 months statutory redemption period.
7. Yes. No.
8. The obligor is the party making the obligation, that is, the borrower. The obligee is the party to whom the obligation is owed, that is, the lender.
9. The lender includes mortgage covenants pertaining to insurance, property taxes, and removal in order to protect the value of the collateral pledged under the mortgage.
10. A certificate of reduction is prepared by the lender and shows how much remains to be paid on the loan. An estoppel certificate provides for a borrower's verification of the amount still owed and the rate of interest.

CHAPTER 10
Deed of Trust

VOCABULARY REVIEW

a. 3 **c.** 5 **d.** 1 **e.** 4 **f.** 2
b. 6

QUESTIONS AND PROBLEMS

1. Under a deed of trust the borrower gives the trustee title and the lender a promissory note. When the debt is paid, the lender instructs the trustee to reconvey title back to the borrower. With a mortgage, the lender acquires both the note and title (or lien rights) under the mortgage. Upon repayment the lender releases the mortgage directly. In the event of default under a deed of trust, the trustee conducts the sale and delivers title to the buyer. With a mortgage, the lender is responsible for conducting the sale (if power of sale is present) or carrying out foreclosure proceedings.
2. The trustee's title lies dormant and there is no right of entry or use as long as the promissory note secured by the trust deed is not in default.
3. A request for reconveyance is notification from the beneficiary to the trustee to reconvey (release) the trustee's title to the trustor.
4. The power of sale clause gives the trustee the right to foreclose the borrower's rights, sell the property and convey title to a purchaser without having to go to court.
5. An assignment of rents clause gives the lender the right to operate the property and collect any rents or income generated by it if the borrower is delinquent.
6. In the automatic form, the trustee is not notified of his appointment as trustee and is usually unaware of it until called to perform in the event of default or to reconvey title when the note is paid. In the accepted form, the trustee agrees to his position as trustee at the time the deed of trust is prepared and signed.
7. The deed of trust is not recognized in Minnesota.

CHAPTER 11
Lending Practices

VOCABULARY REVIEW

a. 16 **e.** 12 **h.** 8 **k.** 11 **n.** 6
b. 5 **f.** 4 **i.** 3 **l.** 1 **o.** 2
c. 15 **g.** 14 **j.** 10 **m.** 7 **p.** 13
d. 9

QUESTIONS AND PROBLEMS

1. The major risk is that when the final payment is due, the borrower will not have the cash to pay it and will not be able to find a lender to refinance it.

2. An amortized loan requires equal, periodic payments of principal and interest such that the loan balance owing will be zero at maturity. During the life of the loan, payments are first applied to interest owing and then to principal. As the balance owed is reduced, less of each monthly payment is taken for interest and more applied to principal reduction until finally the loan is repaid.
3. 65 × $9.91 = $644.15 per month
4. $60,000
5. $55,900
6. $81,180
7. The purpose of Section 203b insurance is to qualify buyers of modest-priced homes for low down-payment loans. This is done by insuring lenders against loan default and charging borrowers a small insurance premium.
8. The VA offers a qualified veteran the opportunity of purchasing a home with no cash down payment and no mortgage insurance fee.
9. A point is one percent. It is a method of expressing loan origination fees and discounts in connection with lending. Discount points are used to increase the effective rate of interest (yield) to the lender without changing the quoted interest rate (also called the face rate or coupon rate.)
10. The basic purpose of truth in lending legislation is to show the borrower how much he will be paying for credit in percentage terms and in total dollars.
11. With a reverse mortgage the lender makes monthly payments to the borrower and is repaid in a lump sum at a later time. The transaction is secured by a mortgage against the borrower's home.

CHAPTER 12 *Sources of Financing*

VOCABULARY REVIEW

a. 6	d. 11	g. 5	i. 3	k. 9
b. 7	e. 12	h. 1	j. 2	l. 10
c. 8	f. 4			m. 13

QUESTIONS AND PROBLEMS

1. The FSLIC and FDIC have made loans more available by insuring savings and checking accounts thus encouraging deposits by savers which in turn can be loaned out.
2. Savings certificates offer savers a greater return than passbook accounts. For savings institutions, time deposits reduce volatility in savings account balances.
3. Loan servicing refers to the care and upkeep of a loan once it is made. This includes payment collection and accounting, handling

defaults, borrower questions, loan payoff processing, and mortgage releasing.

4. An adjustable rate mortgage is a loan on which the interest rate can be adjusted up or down as current interest rates change.
5. An owner occupant is less likely to default than an investor. This reflects a homeowner's pride of ownership coupled with the fact that default means loss of a roof over his head. Investors tend to look more at the numbers—if a project is not doing well financially, it is likely to be dumped.
6. As a rule, it is from the borrower's monthly income that monthly loan payments will be made. The assets, although substantial in size may not be available for monthly payments.
7. FNMA buys, by auction, mortgage loans. These purchases are financed by the sale of FNMA stock and bonds as well as the sale of these loans to investors. GNMA buys FHA and VA mortgage loans and packages them into blocks for investors.
8. A loan dollar that is the result of real savings won't cause inflation. That is because the borrower is using goods and services the saver has foregone. But a fiat money dollar does not represent available goods and services; instead it competes with real savings dollars and pushes prices up.
9. Variable rate loans share the risk of changing interest rates between the borrower and the lender. The lender feels more comfortable knowing the interest rate charged will change with the cost of money to the lender.
10. Rentals and leases are considered financing forms as they allow a person the use of something without having to first pay the full purchase price.
11. Above all, the investor should make certain that the realistic market value of the property is well in excess of the loans against it.

CHAPTER 13
Taxes and Assessments

VOCABULARY REVIEW

a. 10 **b.** 2 **c.** 4 **d.** 7 **e.** 5 **f.** 11 **g.** 9 **h.** 12 **i.** 1 **j.** 8 **k.** 3 **l.** 6

QUESTIONS AND PROBLEMS

1. Sources of funds other than property taxes are subtracted from the district budget. The remainder is then divided by the total assessed valuation of property in the district to obtain the tax rate.

2. $960,000 divided by $120,000,000 equals 8 mills
3. $40,000 times $.008 equals $320
4. $10,000 times $0.05 divided by $100 equals $5
5. He would first appeal to his city board of equalization and review and then to the county board.
6. Requires local interpretation. However, the point is that the assessor does not set the tax rate. He only applies it. If the complaint regards assessment procedures, the assessment appeal process is taken. If it regards the tax rate, the city, county, or state budget makers are responsible.
7. The greater the amount of tax-exempt property in a taxation district, the less taxable property is available to bear the burden of taxation.
8. A certificate of real estate value is to be filed with each conveyance. Also there are field reappraisals made.
9. $68,000 − $5,000 − ($21,000 + $2,000 + $5,000) = $35,000
10. $68,000 − $5,000 − $58,000 = $5,000
    It will be a long-term capital gain.
11. $1.10 per $500, or fraction thereof, with a minimum tax of $2.20.

CHAPTER 14
Title Closing and Escrow

VOCABULARY REVIEW

a. 2 **b.** 1 **c.** 5 **d.** 3 **e.** 6 **f.** 4 **g.** 7

QUESTIONS AND PROBLEMS

1. The closer's duties include arranging the closing, ordering the abstract continuation, preparing documents, making prorations, loan payoffs, loan disbursement, closing statements, and handling papers and paperwork relative to the transaction.
2. The key difference is that an escrow holder is a common agent of the parties to the transaction. This eliminates the need for each party to attend the closing and personally represent himself.
3. The escrow agent is an agent of the buyer with respect to the buyer's role in the transaction and an agent of the seller with respect to the seller's role. The same holds true for the lender, title company, etc.
4. $180 divided by 12 equals $15 per month or 50¢ per day. Using standard 30-day months and presuming the buyer is the owner commencing with the settlement date, there are one month and 26 days used and 10 months and 4 days remaining. For this remaining coverage, the buyer pays the seller 10 times $15 plus 4 times $.50 equals $152.00.
5. Daily rate equals $45,000 times 8% divided by 360 equals $10. The buyer is credited 11 days times $10 equals $110. The seller is debited the same amount.

6. **Buyer:**
lender's title policy
loan appraisal fee
mortgage recording

Seller:
deed stamps
deed preparation
mortgage release

CHAPTER 15
Real Estate Leases

VOCABULARY REVIEW

a. 4 **b.** 8 **c.** 5 **d.** 2 **e.** 1 **f.** 6 **g.** 11 **h.** 10 **i.** 12 **j.** 7 **k.** 9 **l.** 3

QUESTIONS AND PROBLEMS

1. From the tenant's standpoint, the lease assures him of space and the rent stated in the lease. But it also requires him to pay for it. The month-to-month arrangement commits him to a maximum of one month at a time; however, it also commits the landlord for only one month at a time.
2. He may bring an action for forcible entry and unlawful detainer.
3. Yes. See Figure 15:2 for the major provisions of the act. Requires local answer.
4. Contract rent is the amount of rent the tenant must pay the landlord. Economic rent is market value rent.
5. The tenant's basis would be that the premises is unfit to occupy as intended in the lease. The tenant's purpose is to terminate the lease and be relieved of liability to pay rent.
6. An option to renew is to the advantage of the lessee.
7. Real estate licensees are not to accept sole or rental listings where they are asked to discriminate, nor are they permitted to make, print, or publish any statement or advertisement with respect to a sale or rental of a dwelling which suggests discrimination because of race, color, religion, or national origin.
8. Requires local answer.
9. Questions asked will center on the ability of the prospective tenant to pay the rent each month, his or her willingness to abide by the house rules and on the general compatibility of the prospect with the existing tenants. Names and addresses of the prospect's current employer and previous landlord would be requested and checked to verify information supplied by the tenant.

CHAPTER 16
Real Estate Appraisal

VOCABULARY REVIEW

a. 7 **b.** 13 **c.** 1 **d.** 8 **e.** 5 **f.** 11 **g.** 10 **h.** 4 **i.** 14 **j.** 15 **k.** 9 **l.** 17 **m.** 16 **n.** 2 **o.** 3 **p.** 12 **q.** 6

QUESTIONS AND PROBLEMS

1. Fair market value refers to the expected cash price that a willing seller and a willing buyer would agree upon, given reasonable exposure of the property to the marketplace, full information as to the uses of the property, and no undue compulsion to act.
2. No, unless you know the amount of "old money" in the transaction.
3. Enough comparables should be used so that the appraiser feels reasonably certain he can establish fair market value but not so many as to involve more time and expense than is gained in added information. For a single-family house, 3 to 5 good comparables are usually adequate but not excessive.
4. Asking prices are useful in that they set an upper limit on value whereas offering prices are useful in that they set a lower limit on value.
5. Adjustments are made to the comparable properties. This is because it is impossible to adjust the value of something for which one does not yet know the value.
6. Using comparables that are not similar to the subject property with respect to zoning, neighborhood characteristics, size or usefulness, requires adjustments that are likely to be very inaccurate or impossible to make.
7. Gross rent times gross rent multiplier equals indicated property value. The strength of this approach is in its simplicity. Its weakness is also in its simplicity as it overlooks anything other than gross rents.
8. The five steps are (1) estimate land value as though vacant (2) estimate new construction cost of a similar building (3) subtract estimated depreciation from construction cost to obtain (4) the indicated value of the structure (5) add this to the land value.
9. The square-foot method involves dividing the cost to construct a given building by the number of square feet it has. The resulting cost per square foot is applied to similar buildings. Refinements are then made either on a square-foot or lump-sum adjustment basis.
10. The income approach values a property based on its expected monetary returns in light of current rates of return being demanded by investors.
11. All other things being equal, if the rate of return demanded by investors rises, the value of an asset will fall.
12. In the standard market comparison approach a specific dollar adjustment is made for each item of difference between the comparables and the subject property. With competitive market analysis, adjustments are made in a generalized fashion in the minds of the agent and the seller. The CMA approach is usually preferred for listing property for sale because there is less room for disagreement. The standard market approach is preferred for appraisal

reports as it shows exactly how the appraiser valued his adjustments.

13. In the reconciliation process the appraiser assigns to each approach a weighting factor based on his judgement as to which of the approaches used are the most relevant for the property being appraised.
14. Unless someone else can receive the services or benefits of something, it will be of no value to him.
15. The principle of diminishing marginal returns warns against investing more than the capitalized value of the anticipated net returns.
16. **Lender:** form report.
    Buyer: oral or letter report.
    Executor: letter or narrative report.
    Highway department: narrative report.

CHAPTER 17
The Owner-Broker Relationship

VOCABULARY REVIEW

a. 8
b. 12
c. 11
d. 7
e. 6
f. 5
g. 10
h. 9
i. 2
j. 1
k. 13
l. 14
m. 4
n. 3

QUESTIONS AND PROBLEMS

1. An agency is created when one person (called the principal) empowers another (the agent) to act as his representative.
2. A universal agency is very broad in scope in that the principal gives his agent the legal power to transact matters of all types for him. A general agency gives the agent the power to transact the principal's affairs in a particular trade or business.
3. Broker cooperation refers to the sharing of a single commission fee among the various brokers who brought about a sale. It is achieved by an agreement between the listing broker and the cooperating brokers.
4. An exclusive right to sell listing protects the broker by entitling him to a commission no matter who sells the property. The exclusive agency listing puts the broker in competition with the owner by allowing the owner to find a buyer and owe no commission. The open listing adds other brokers to the competition as any number of brokers can have the listing simultaneously and the owner can still sell it himself and pay no commission.
5. The open listing allows the owner to employ any number of brokers simultaneously and to sell the property himself and owe no commission. However, this arrangement usually results in no broker being willing to put much effort into finding a buyer—

which is presumably why the property was listed in the first place.

6. **Faithful:** the broker must perform as promised in the listing contract and not depart from the principal's instructions.
   Loyal: the broker owes his allegiance to the principal and as such works for the benefit of the principal. This means promoting and protecting the principal's best interests and keeping him informed of all matters that might affect the sale of the listed property.
7. "Ready, willing, and able buyer" means a buyer who is ready to buy now, with no further coaxing, and who has the financial capacity to do so.
8. Yes.
9. Listings are usually terminated with the completion of the agency objective, namely finding a buyer or a tenant. Lacking a buyer, termination usually results when the listing period expires. A listing can also be terminated if the broker fails to perform as agreed in the listing.
10. The purpose of the HUD property disclosure statement is to require that sellers of subdivisions of 50 or more lots sold across state lines provide prospective purchasers a standardized property report with information regarding the property they are being asked to buy.
11. Steering means to guide a client away from one neighborhood and/or to another based on the client's race, color, religion, sex, or national origin. Blockbusting is the illegal practice of inducing panic selling in a neighborhood for financial gain.
12. The case of *Jones* v. *Mayer* nullified the exemptions for race discrimination allowed to owners of small income properties by the 1968 Civil Rights Act.

CHAPTER 18
Licensing Laws and Professional Affiliation

VOCABULARY REVIEW

a. 7 **b.** 8 **c.** 1 **d.** 6 **e.** 4 **f.** 2 **g.** 3 **h.** 12 **i.** 5 **j.** 13 **k.** 11 **l.** 10 **m.** 9

QUESTIONS AND PROBLEMS

1. Early license laws were primarily aimed at protecting the public by qualifying license applicants based on their honesty, truthfulness and good reputation. Real estate examinations and education requirements were added later.
2. Generally speaking, a real estate license is required when a person, who for compensation or the promise of compensation, lists or offers to list, sells or offers to sell, buys or offers to buy, negotiates

or offers to negotiate, either directly or indirectly, for the purpose of bringing about a sale, purchase, option to purchase, exchange, auction, lease or rental of real estate. Some states also require that real estate appraisers, property managers, mortgage bankers and rent collectors hold real estate licenses.

3. In deciding on a compensation schedule for his salespersons, a broker must consider office overhead, employee retention, and the emphasis he wishes to place on listing versus selling.
4. ETS. At least every 45 days.
5. The trend is to increase the educational requirements to obtain and keep a license.
6. 90 hours of instruction.
7. Banking, insurance, licensing and regulation, and enforcement.
8. Five experienced brokers and 2 public members are appointed by the commissioner. Its members advise the commissioner on licensing and education requirements.
9. Section 82.27 and the rules promulgated by the commissioner set forth the procedures and standards for disciplining licensees.
10. The purpose of a bond requirement or a recovery fund is to have funds available that can be drawn upon in the event a court judgement against a licensee, resulting from a license-related wrongdoing, is uncollectible. Minnesota uses a recovery fund.
11. The purpose of the National Association of Realtors is to promote the general welfare of the real estate industry by encouraging fair dealing among Realtors and the public, supporting legislation to protect property rights, offering education for members, and in general doing whatever is necessary to build the dignity, stability and professionalization of the industry.
12. An employment contract will cover such matters as compensation, training, hours of work, company identification, fees and dues, expenses, use of automobile, fringe benefits, withholding of taxes, termination of employment, and general office policies and procedures.
13. You would want to consider location, compensation, broker's reputation, working hours, broker support, training opportunities, advertising policy, expense reimbursement, and fringe benefits.

CHAPTER 19
Condominiums, Cooperatives, and Planned Unit Developments

VOCABULARY REVIEW

a. 9	**d.** 2	**g.** 7	**i.** 5	**k.** 4
b. 3	**e.** 11	**h.** 10	**j.** 12	**l.** 6
c. 1	**f.** 8			**m.** 13

QUESTIONS AND PROBLEMS

1. Condominiums have become popular because they are usually cheaper to buy than a single-family house, are often better located, offer security and maintenance, and can be individually financed.

2. Each condominium unit owner holds an undivided interest in the land in a fee simple condominium project. The corporation owns the land in a cooperative.
3. A proprietary lease is a lease issued by a corporation to its stockholders; that is, the lessees are the owners. The lease "rent" is actually the stockholder's share of the cost of operating the building and repaying the debt against it. In a standard landlord-tenant lease, the tenant pays a cash rent for use of the premises, is not responsible for the operating expenses of the premises nor debt repayment, and does not have an ownership interest in the premises.
4. The enabling declaration converts a given parcel of land into a condominium subdivision.
5. The wall between two condominium apartments belongs to the condominium owners as a group.
6. CC&Rs are the covenants, conditions, and restrictions by which a property owner agrees to abide. They are established for the harmony and well-being of the owners as a group.
7. Maintenance fees (association dues) are the operating costs of a condominium, spread among the unit owners. Failure to pay creates a lien against the delinquent owner's unit.
8. The owners' association hazard and liability policy covers only the common elements. To be protected against property loss and accident liability within a dwelling unit, the owner must have his own hazard and liability policy.
9. Two time-sharing methods that are currently in use are (1) the long-term lease that gives a lessee the exclusive right to use the same premises at different specified periods of time each year, and (2) co-ownership of a fee property with each owner taking exclusive occupancy for a specified period of time each year.
10. In a PUD, the unit owner holds title to the land occupied by his unit and an owners' association (of which each unit owner is a member) holds title to the common areas.

CHAPTER 20 Property Insurance

VOCABULARY REVIEW

a. 7
b. 1
c. 9
d. 2
e. 3
f. 10
g. 4
h. 11
i. 8
j. 6
k. 5

QUESTIONS AND PROBLEMS

1. Fire policies cover losses resulting from negligence but not damage intentionally caused by the insured.
2. An endorsement or rider is an agreement by the insurer and the insured to modify the coverage in the basic policy.
3. Public liability insurance is concerned with insuring against finan-

cial losses resulting from the responsibility of one person to another with regard to one's actions or failure to take action.

4. Section I in a homeowner's policy covers loss of and damage to the insured's property. Section II deals with the public liability of the insured.
5. All-risk insurance policies cover loss or damage resulting from any cause not excluded by the policy. A broad-form policy is one that covers a large number of perils that are specifically named in the policy.
6. "New for old" means that the insurer will pay for replacement at today's costs. Thus, although the property lost by the insured was used; that is, old, he will receive a new replacement from the insurer.
7. Coverage is suspended on vacant buildings because they are more attractive to thieves, vandals, and arsonists than are occupied buildings.

CHAPTER 21
Land-Use Control

VOCABULARY REVIEW

a. 6	**c.** 7	**e.** 3	**g.** 10	**i.** 9
b. 4	**d.** 1	**f.** 5	**h.** 8	**j.** 2

QUESTIONS AND PROBLEMS

1. The individual property owner does not consider his property to be a community resource. Thus, any substantial progress in land planning and control in the future must also consider the right of the individual to develop his land.
2. The authority of government to control land use is derived from the state's right of police power. Through enabling acts, this authority is passed on to the counties, cities, and towns in the state.
3. A variance allows an individual landowner to deviate slightly from strict compliance with zoning requirements for his land. A variance must be consistent with the character of the neighborhood and general objectives of zoning as they apply to that neighborhood.
4. Requires local answer.
5. A master plan takes a broad look at the entire land-use picture in a community, county or region. The object is to view the area as a unified entity that provides its residents with jobs and housing as well as social, recreational and cultural activities. In contrast, zoning laws tell a property owner specifically how he may use his land and what type and size structures he may place on it.
6. The purpose of an EIS is to gather information about the effect of a proposed project on the environment so that the anticipated

environmental costs and benefits of the project may be considered along with the economic and humanitarian aspects.

7. On the plus side, an EIS can show in advance areas where a project might do irreparable damage to the environment out of proportion to its other benefits. The project can either be modified or abandoned. On the minus side is the cost in terms of time and money to both the taxpayer and the applicant.
8. Transferable development rights would equalize financial windfalls and wipe-outs by requiring those whose land is approved for urban uses to purchase development rights from those whose land is prohibited from development.
9. Yes. The preservation of a natural deer habit and the development of a subdivision.

CHAPTER 22 *Real Estate and The Economy*

VOCABULARY REVIEW

a. 12	**d.** 9	**f.** 4	**h.** 5	**j.** 7
b. 1	**e.** 3	**g.** 6	**i.** 10	**k.** 2
c. 11				**l.** 8

QUESTIONS AND PROBLEMS

1. Requires local answer.
2. Requires local answer.
3. The reason for creating money market certificates was to remain competitive for savers' dollars.
4. Requires local answer.
5. $11\% \times (100\% - 40\%) = 6.6\%$
6. The purpose of the Equal Credit Opportunity Act is to require lenders to make credit available without regard to sex or marital status.
7. The secondary mortgage market permits lenders and investors to buy and sell mortgage loans. This makes more money available for real estate loans.
8. Requires an answer based on prevailing economic conditions. Your list should contain reference to the cost and supply of mortgage loan money.
9. Requires personal answer. However, it should contain reference to the cost of gasoline, heating oil, electricity, and other forms of energy.

CHAPTER 23 *Investing in Real Estate*

VOCABULARY REVIEW

a. 7	**c.** 1	**e.** 4	**g.** 2	**i.** 6
b. 8	**d.** 9	**f.** 5	**h.** 10	**j.** 3

QUESTIONS AND PROBLEMS

1. A tax-sheltered investment is one where part or all of the return from a property is not subject to income taxes. The primary source is depreciation, which, although shown as an expense for calculating income taxes, is not an out-of-pocket (cash) expense.
2. Investors in real estate look for cash flow, tax shelter, mortgage reduction, and appreciation.
3. The major risk of owning vacant land is having to wait too long for an increase in value.
4. The advantages of duplexes and triplexes are that, compared to larger buildings, the investor's capital, management, and risk are on a smaller scale. These buildings are not, however, as efficient to manage and rents are often relatively low per dollar of purchase price.
5. "Better off" must be considered in light of the investor's objectives and ability to take risks. The earlier he invests, the bigger the risks and potential rewards. By waiting he can lower the risks and the rewards.
6. Higher returns are necessary in an older building to compensate for major replacement, repair, and refurbishing costs; for increasing maintenance expenses; for the risk that the neighborhood may be in, or about to enter into, a decline in popularity; and that the building itself may have a limited remaining economic usefulness.
7. A person who has a number of high income years remaining in life can more comfortably take risks as there is time to recover financially if losses should result. An older person without the time and energy to recover financially would seek to avoid risky investments.
8. \$22,000 ÷ .10756 = \$204,537. Round to \$205,000.
9. \$22,000 ÷ .11819 = \$186,141. Round to \$186,000.
10. \$22,000 ÷ .11463 = \$191,921. Round to \$192,000.
11. Limited partnerships offer the investor the advantages of relatively small minimum investment, built-in property management, limited financial liability, the opportunity to diversify, and the same tax benefits as sole owners.
12. A careful investor will check out both the properties and the general partners. Do the general partners have a good record in selecting, organizing and managing real estate investments? Are they honest and creditworthy? Are there lawsuits or other legal complaints against them? Regarding the properties, are the income and expense projections accurate and reasonable? Are the properties in sound physical and financial condition? Are they well located? Are they priced right? Are the tax benefits realistic? Is there financial responsibility or liability for the limited partner in the future? Is the limited partner willing and able to stay in the partnership for its full lifespan?

APPENDIX B

Construction Illustrations and Terminology

Figure B:1 **COMBINED SLAB AND FOUNDATION (thickened edge slab)**

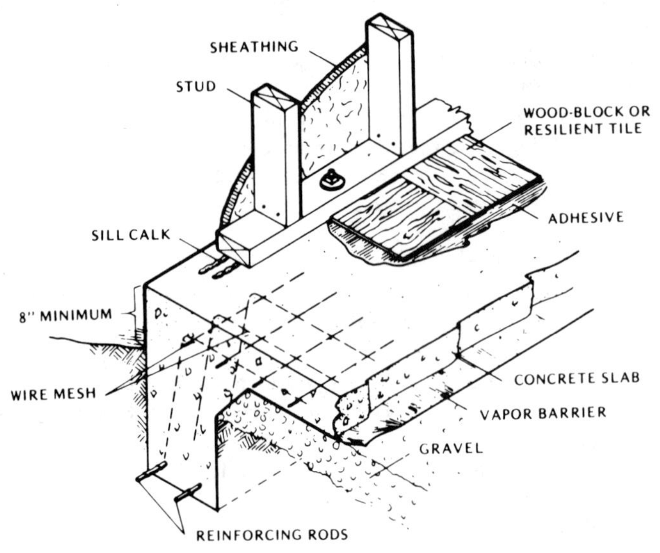

Figure B:2 **BASEMENT DETAILS**

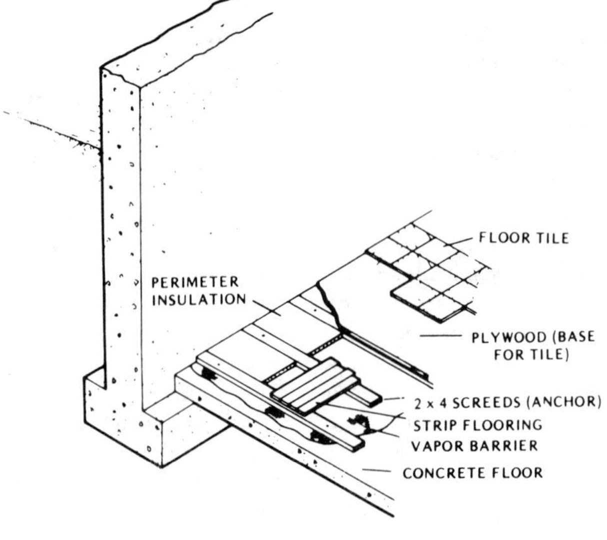

FLOOR FRAMING

Figure B:3

1. nailing bridging to joists; 2. nailing board subfloor to joists; 3. nailing header to joists; 4. toenailing header to sill

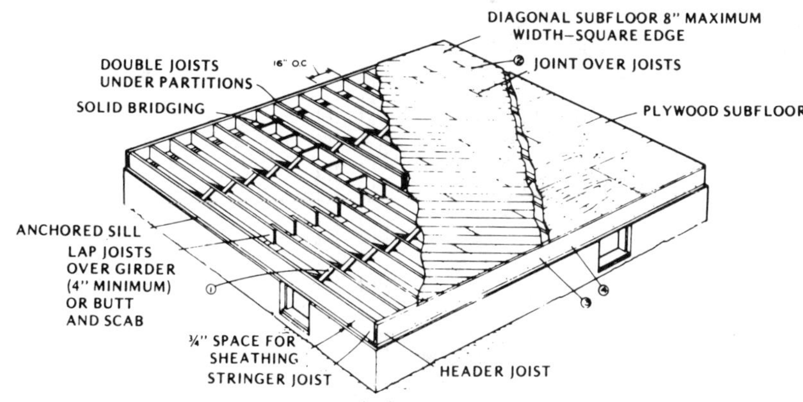

WALL FRAMING USED WITH PLATFORM CONSTRUCTION

Figure B:4

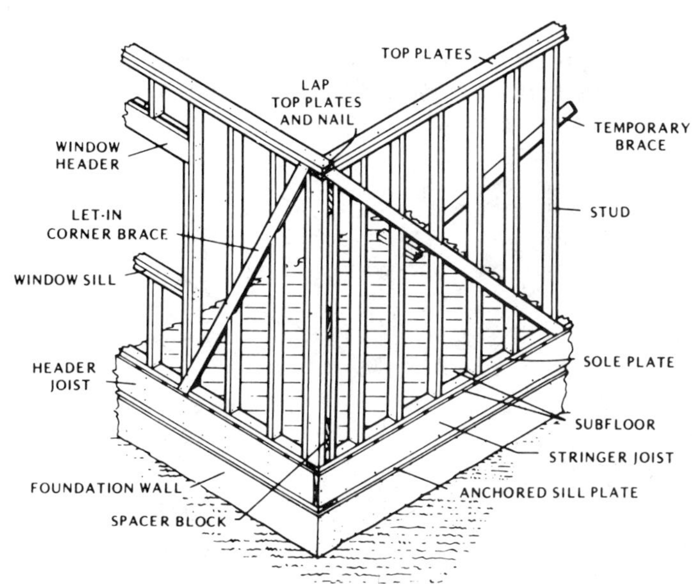

Figure B:5 **HEADERS FOR WINDOWS AND DOOR OPENINGS**

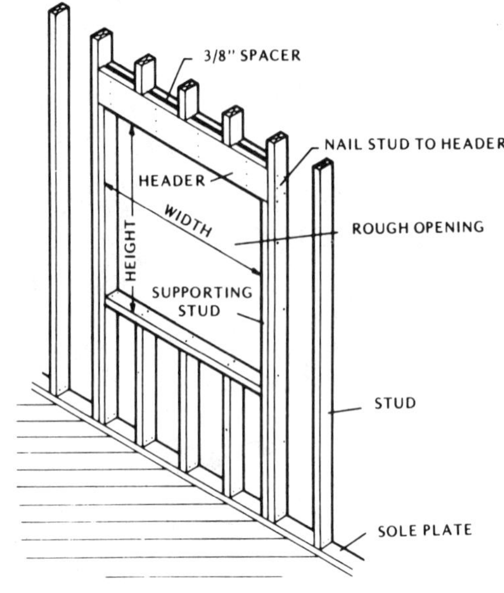

Figure B:6 **VERTICAL APPLICATION OF PLYWOOD OR STRUCTURAL INSULATING BOARD SHEATHING**

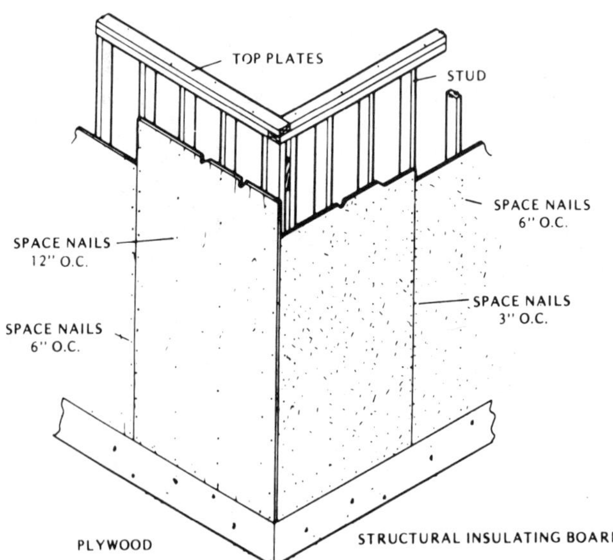

EXTERIOR SIDING

Figure B:7

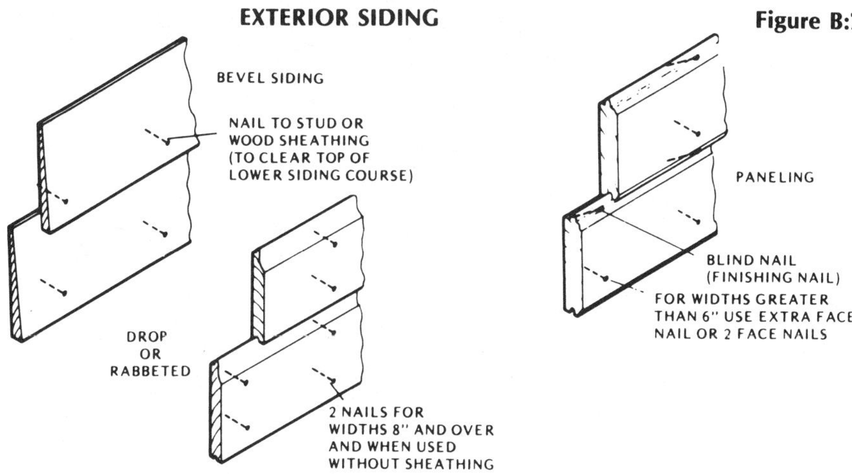

VERTICAL BOARD SIDING

Figure B:8

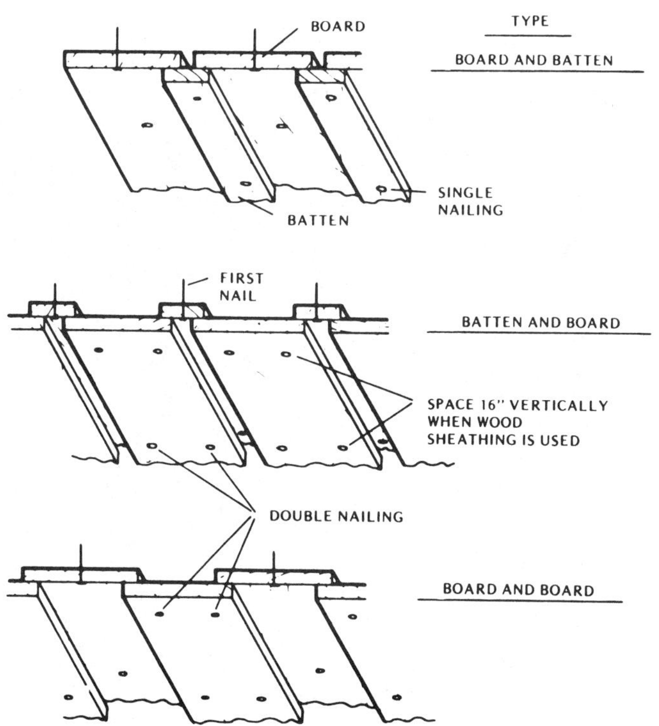

Figure B:9 **APPLICATION OF GYPSUM BOARD FINISH**
A: vertical application; B: horizontal application

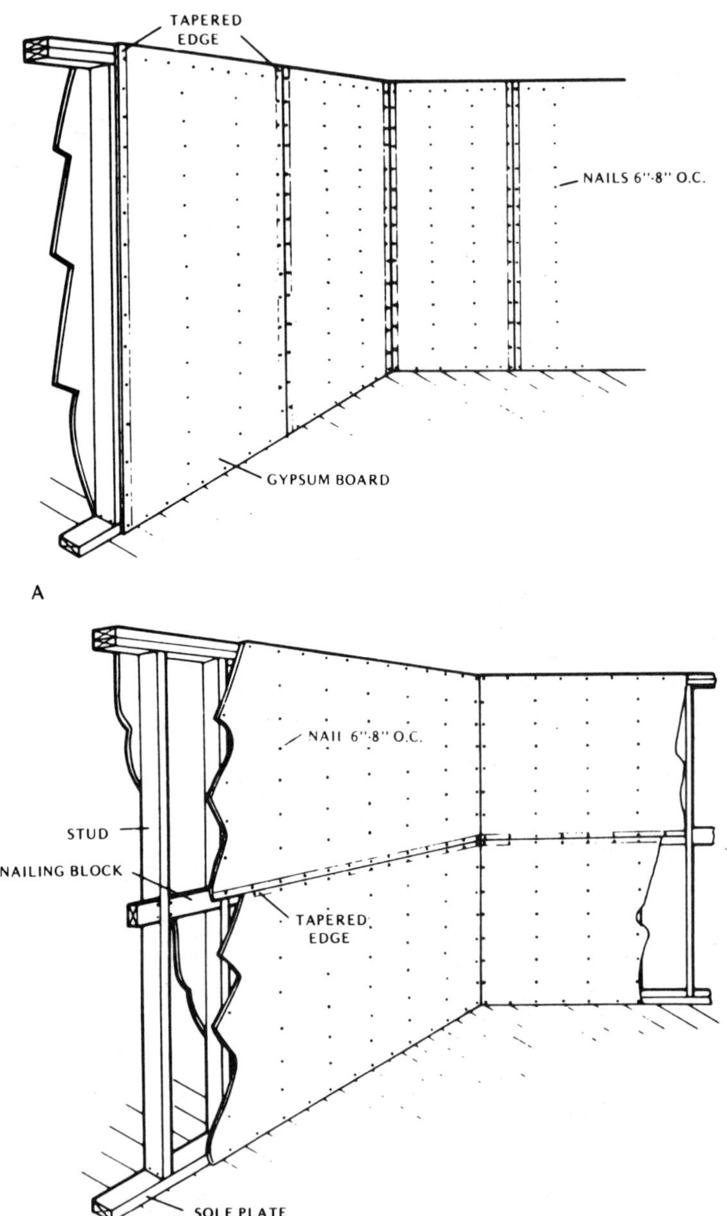

APPLICATION OF INSULATION

A: wall section with blanket type; B: wall section with "press-fit" insulation; C: ceiling with full insulation

Figure B:10

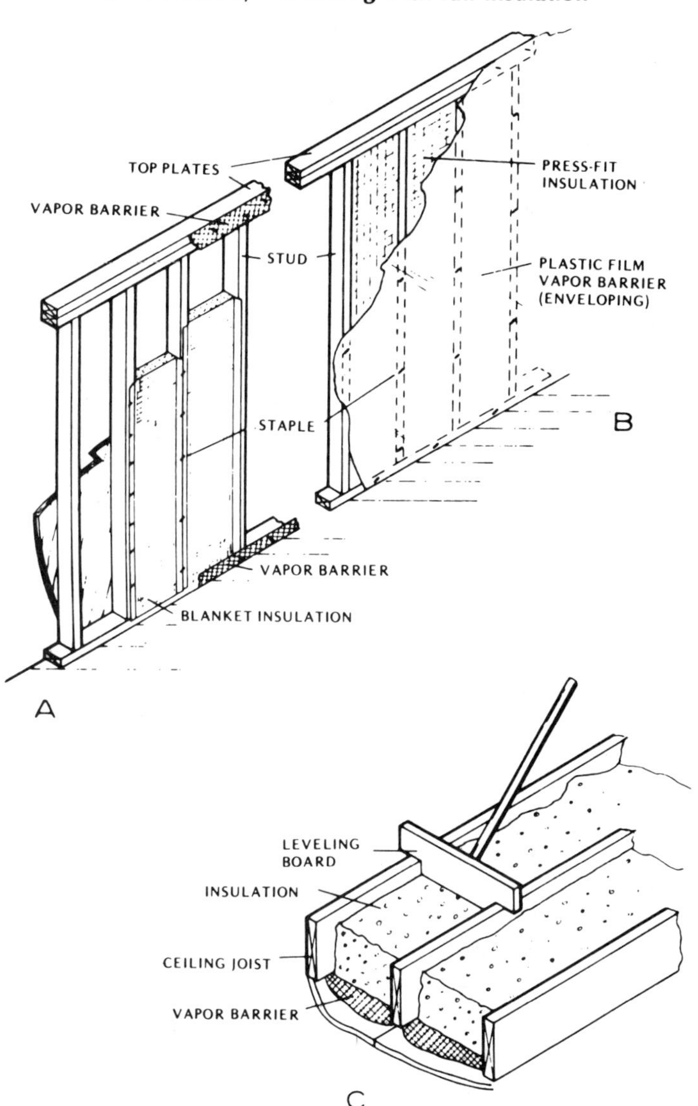

Figure B:11 **PLACEMENT OF INSULATION**

A: in walls, floor, and ceiling; B. in 1-1/2 story house; C: at attic door; D: in flat roof

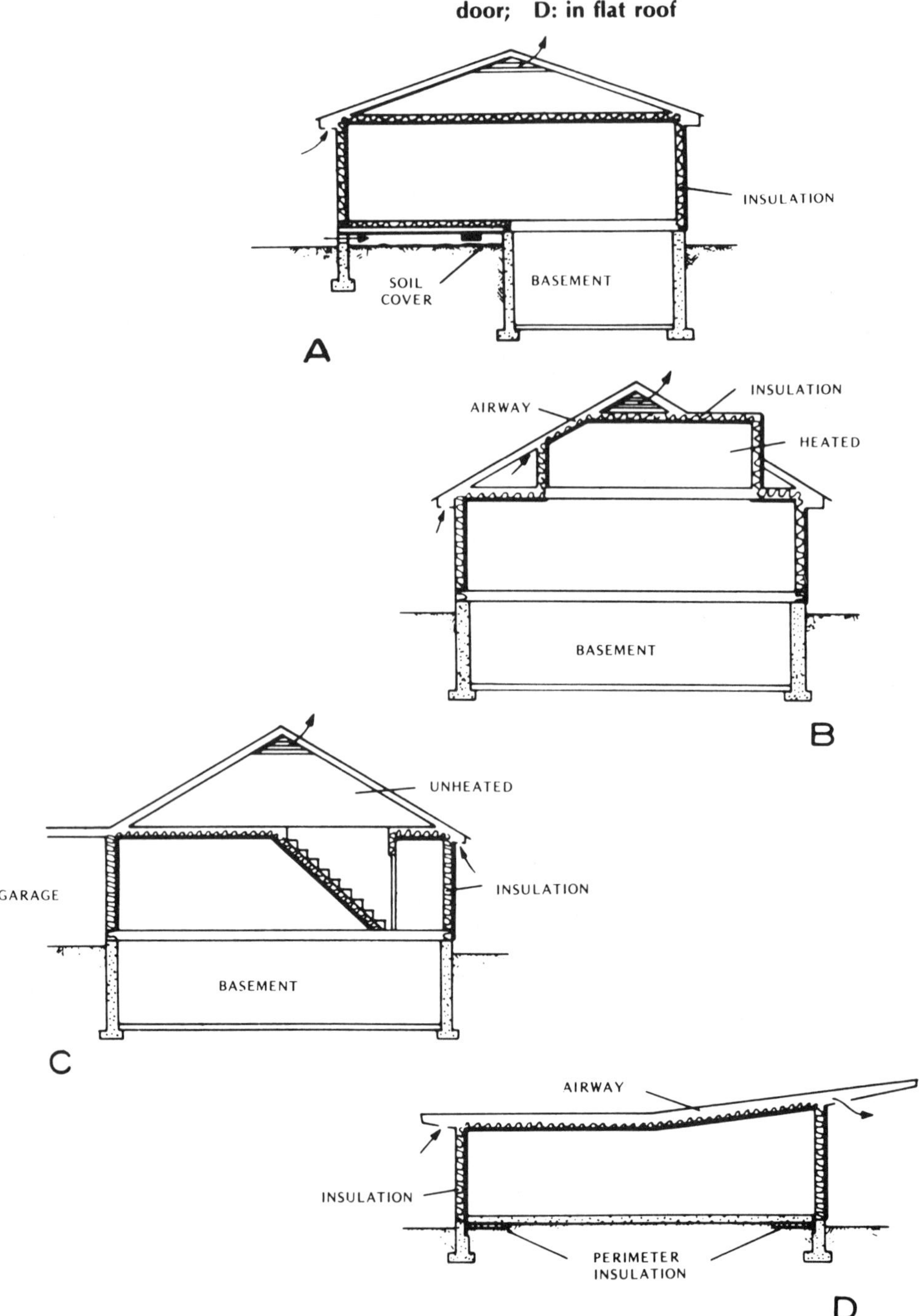

MASONRY FIREPLACE

Figure B:12

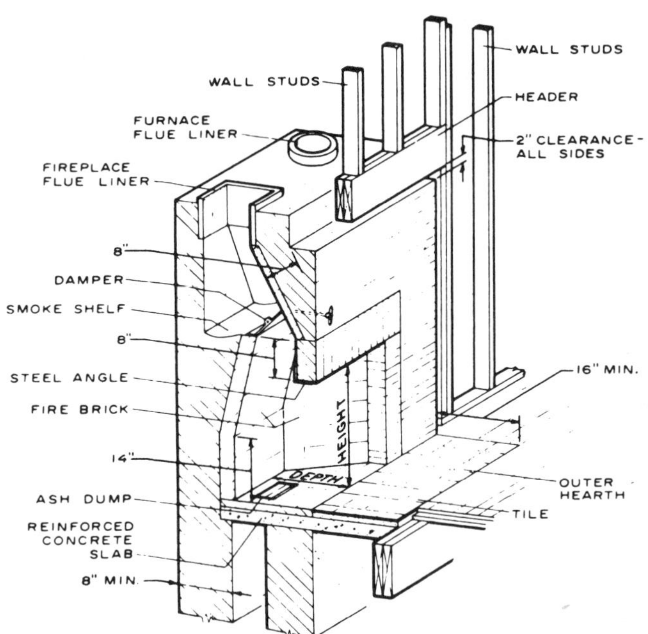

STAIRWAY DETAILS

Figure B:13

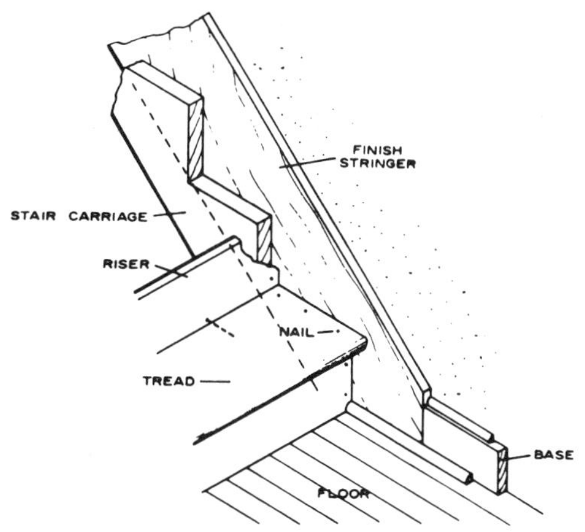

Figure B:14 **DOOR DETAILS**

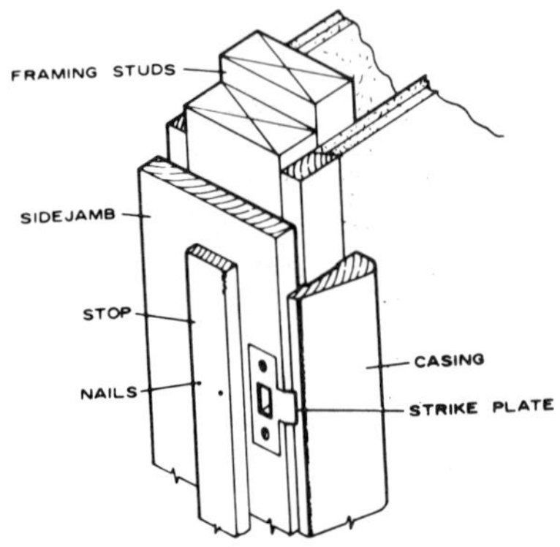

Figure B:15 **SOUND INSULATION**

WALL DETAIL	DESCRIPTION	STC RATING
16" 2 x 4	1/2" GYPSUM WALLBOARD 5/8" GYPSUM WALLBOARD	32 37
2 x 4	5/8" GYPSUM WALLBOARD (DOUBLE LAYER EACH SIDE)	45
2 x 4 BETWEEN OR "WOVEN"	1/2" GYPSUM WALLBOARD 1 1/2" FIBROUS INSULATION	49
16" 2 x 4	RESILIENT CLIPS TO 3/8" GYPSUM BACKER BOARD 1/2" FIBERBOARD (LAMINATED) (EACH SIDE)	52

CEILING AND ROOF FRAMING

Figure B:16

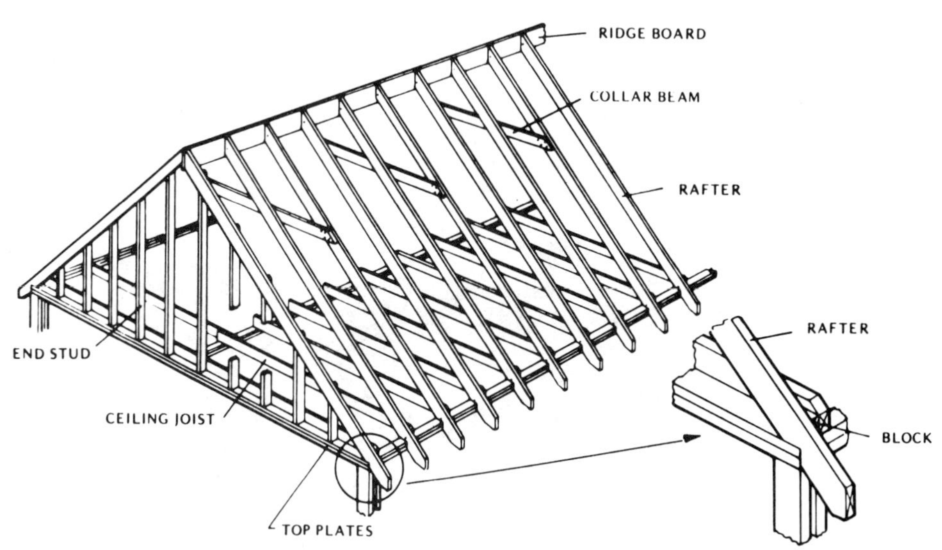

INSTALLATION OF BOARD ROOF SHEATHING, SHOWING BOTH CLOSED AND SPACED TYPES

Figure B:17

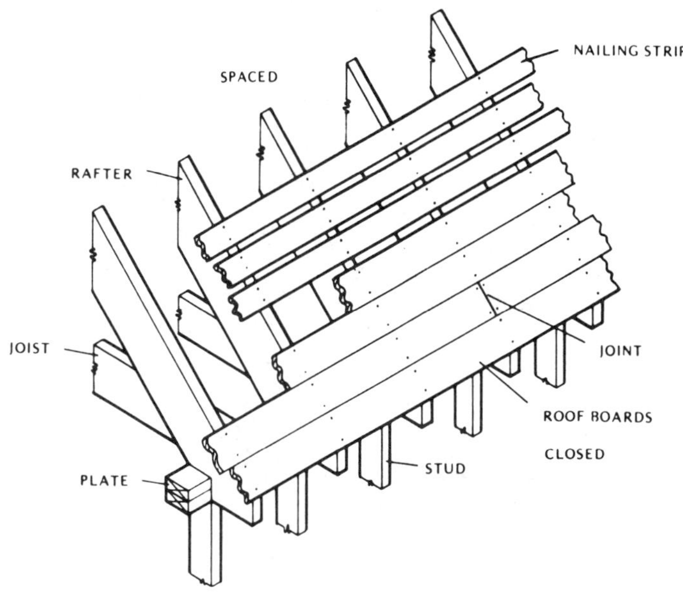

Figure B:18 **BUILT-UP ROOF**

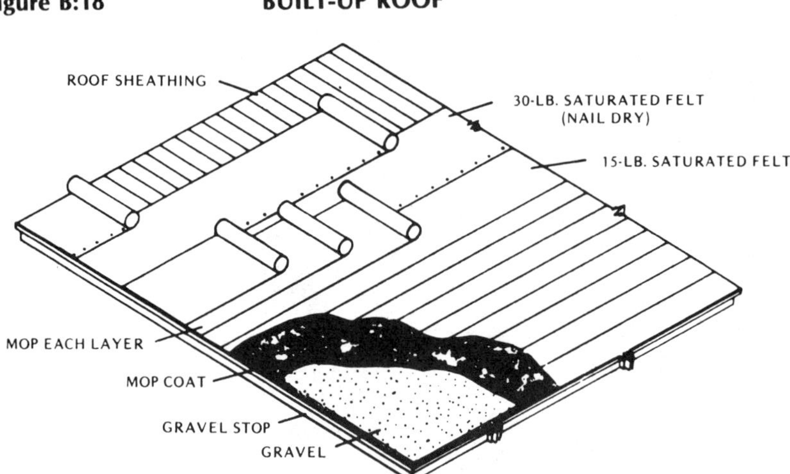

Figure B:19 **APPLICATION OF ASPHALT SHINGLES**

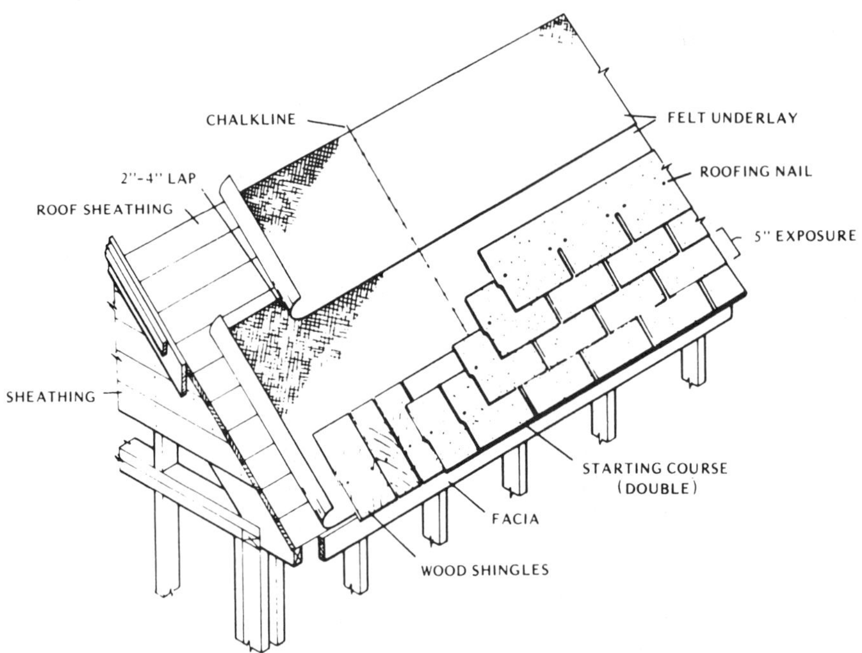

ROOFS USING SINGLE ROOF CONSTRUCTION **Figure B:20**

A: flat roof; B: low-pitched roof

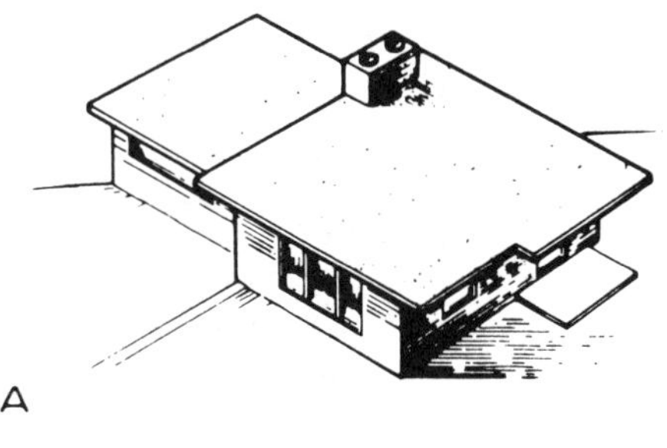

TYPES OF PITCHED ROOFS

A: gable; B: gable with dormers; C: hip

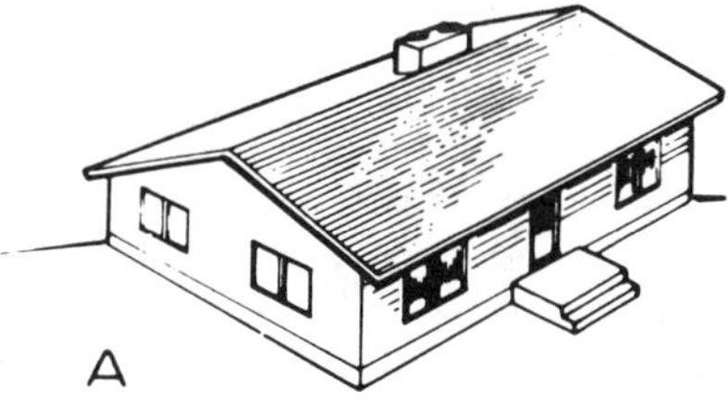

APPENDIX C

Sample ETS-Type Test Questions

ETS SALESPERSON EXAMINATION

The ETS examination for real estate salespersons in Minnesota is four and a half hours long and is made up of 120 questions. It is divided into two separate tests, the uniform test and the state test.

The Uniform Test (80 questions) contains questions in the subject areas described below. Approximately 20 percent of the uniform test consists of questions dealing with arithmetic functions. These questions are distributed throughout the test.

1. *Real Estate Contracts:* (13% of uniform test)

Questions in this area cover the general definition and essential elements of a contract and specific contracts used in real estate, including leases, listing agreements, sales contracts (offer to purchase agreements), and options. Applicants are required to interpret a completed listing contract and a completed sales contract (offer to purchase agreement); they are expected to answer the questions dealing with listing and sales contracts solely on the basis of the completed sample instruments.

2. *Financing:* (24% of uniform test)

These questions deal with two major aspects of real estate financing: financing instruments and means of financing.

Questions in these areas will cover such topics as sources of financing; governmental agencies and acts pertaining to financing (e.g., Federal Housing Administration, Veterans Administration, Truth-in-Lending Act); basic definitions of the major financing instruments; anatomy of a mortgage loan (including types of mortgages, loan fees, loan placement procedures, and term loans); junior finance; default; and foreclosure.

3. *Real Estate Ownership:* (22% of uniform test)

The questions in this subject area cover the following topics:

a. Deeds: the definition of necessary elements for recordation and acknowledgment of various types of deeds.

b. Interests in Real Property: estates (extent of title), private rights to real property (ownership), public powers over real property, and special interests in real property (easements, etc.).

c. Condominiums: general information about condominiums, ownership of common and separate elements, and the duties and responsibilities of a condominium owners' association.

d. Federal Fair Housing Act: grievances, penalties, practices, and procedures with regard to the federal Fair Housing Act.

4. *Real Estate Brokerage:* (24% of uniform test)

The questions in this area of the test cover the following topics:

a. Law of Agency: definitions, rights, responsibilities, and functions of a principal and an agent.

b. Property Management: general scope and functions of property management.

c. Settlement Procedures: title validity, conveyance, settlement charges, credits, adjustments, and prorating.

5. *Real Estate Valuation:* (17% of uniform test)
The questions in this area cover the following topics:

a. Appraisal: definition of value, approaches to value, the appraisal process, the valuation of partial interests, and appraisal terminology.

b. Planning and Zoning: public land-use control, public planning and zoning, and private subdividing and developing.

c. Property Description: kinds of property description, plat reading, and related terms and concepts.

d. Taxes and Assessments: real property taxes, special assessments, liens, and other tax factors.

The State Test (40 questions) contains questions dealing with the real estate laws, rules, and regulations and other aspects of real estate practice appropriate to the jurisdiction in which the test is being given. Aspects of real estate practice that may be covered in this section include state statutes dealing with condominiums, subdivisions, fair housing, and administrative hearing procedures. Other aspects of real estate practice, which are not uniform, may also be included. Be sure to check with your state real estate commission for more details regarding coverage in this section.

License applicants in ETS examination states should send for the free "Bulletin of Information for Applicants for Real Estate Licensing Examinations." Write to: Educational Testing Service, Box 2837, Princeton, N.J. 08540. A Sample Salesperson's Uniform Test can be purchased from ETS at this address.

The following **Sample Questions** illustrate the types of questions in the examination for real estate salespersons. They do not, however, represent the full range of content or the levels of difficulty found in the test. An answer key is provided in Appendix A.

Uniform Test

REAL ESTATE CONTRACTS

1. The party who makes an offer to another is known as the
A. offeree. **B.** offeror. **C.** major. **D.** minor.

FINANCING

1. When a loan insured by a private insurance company goes into default the insuror
I. may buy the property from the lender.
II. may let the lender foreclose and compensate the lender for his loss.
(A) I only **(B)** II only **(C)** Both I and II **(D)** Neither I nor II

When answering this kind of multiple-choice question, read the question and the two statements or possibilities carefully. Determine whether statement (possibility) I is right or wrong; then determine whether statement (possibility) II is right or wrong.

Next, look at the four choices, (A), (B), (C), and (D). Choice (A) is always "I only." You should pick (A) if you believe statement (possibility) I is right and statement (possibility) II is wrong. Choice (B) is always "II only," and you should pick (B) if you believe statement (possibility) I is wrong and statement (possibility) II is right. Choice (C) is "Both I and II." You should pick (C) when you believe both statements (possibilities) are right, whether or not they happen at the same time. Choice (D) is always "Neither I nor II." You should pick (D) when you believe neither of the two statements (possibilities) is correct.

2. As used in real estate finance, the term "point" means
I. 1 percent of the loan.
II. 1 percent of the price of the property.
(A) I only **(B)** II only **(C)** Both I and II **(D)** Neither I nor II

REAL ESTATE OWNERSHIP

1. All of the following are essential elements in a valid deed EXCEPT
A. consideration
B. property description
C. seller's signature
D. buyer's signature

2. CHARACTERISTIC(s) of ownership as tenants by the entireties is (are)
I. the right of survivorship of a surviving spouse.
II. any transfer of title requires the signature of husband and wife.
(A) I only **(B)** II only **(C)** Both I and II **(D)** Neither I nor II

3. A change made to an existing will is known as
A. an addendum.
B. an amendment.
C. a supplement.
D. a codicil.

4. The law which requires that transfers of real property ownership be in writing is known as the
A. Law of Evidence.
B. Statute of Liberties.
C. Statute of Frauds.
D. Statute of Limitations.

REAL ESTATE BROKERAGE

1. Which of the following will result in the termination of an agency?
I. Insanity
II. Bankruptcy
(A) I only **(B)** II only **(C)** Both I and II **(D)** Neither I nor II

2. Which of the following would not normally be handled by an escrow agent?
A. Ordering title insurance
B. Ordering title examinations

C. Proration of tax and/or insurance
D. Negotiations for and preparation of sales contracts

3. Brown sold his home to Green, and closing took place on July 18. Green agreed to assume Brown's hazard insurance policy, which was effective as of December 13 of the previous year. The premium had been paid in advance for one year from the effective date of the policy. Prorations are made on the basis of 30-day months, with the buyer responsible for the day of closing. The annual premium on the policy was $194.40. Which of the following statements is true?
   A. Green would be charged $78.30.
   B. Brown would be credited $116.10.
   C. Green would be credited $78.30.
   D. Green would be charged $194.40.

REAL ESTATE VALUATION

1. The lot diagrammed here is sold for $20,800. What is the price per square foot?
   (A) $1.00 (B) $1.30 (C) $1.625 (D) $2.00

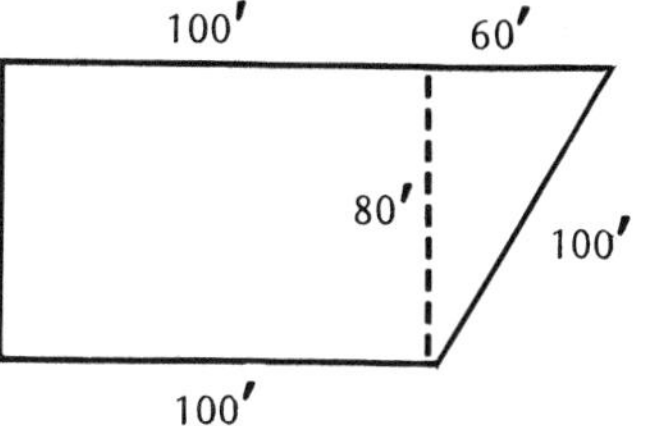

2. In applying the income approach to real property, the appraiser considers which of the following?
   I. The amount of income produced by the property
   II. The rate of return demanded by investors
   (A) I only (B) II only (C) Both I and II (D) Neither I nor II

3. Valuing a certain property, an appraiser finds that the market, cost, and income approaches indicate $65,000, $62,000, and $64,000, respectively. If he weights these 40%, 20%, and 40%, respectively, his reconciliation would result in a final indicated value of (select closest answer)
   A. $65,000 B. $64,000 C. $63,000 D. $62,000

4. All of the following are real estate appraisal approaches EXCEPT
   A. cost B. anticipation C. income D. market

State Test

Note: The following questions are samples of the *type* of question asked in this part of the examination, which is different for each jurisdiction.

1. Which persons are specifically exempt from the real estate licensing act?
   A. War veterans
   B. Executors
   C. Part-time salesman
   D. Listers of real estate

2. A Real Estate Salesperson license issued on May 15 is valid until
   A. May 15 the following year
   B. the end of current license term.
   C. January 15 of the following year.
   D. the salesman's next birthday.

3. An unlicensed secretary in a broker's office may do which of the following?
I. Give information to a caller about listings available
II. Take a listing by telephone
(A) I only **(B)** II only **(C)** Both I and II **(D)** Neither I nor II

BROKER EXAMINATION

The ETS examination for real estate brokers, four and a half hours long, is made up of 130 questions. It is divided into two separate tests, the uniform test and the state test.

The Uniform Test (80 questions) contains questions in the subject areas outlined below. Approximately 20 percent of the test consists of questions requiring arithmetic calculations. These questions are distributed throughout the test.

1. *Real Estate Brokerage* (35% of uniform test)
The questions in this area cover the following topics:

a. Listing and Showing Property: the responsibilities of a broker when contracting to list, advertise, and show property for sale, lease, trade, or exchange; including responsibilities under the law of agency, compliance with federal Fair Housing Act, and obligations when entering into written listing agreements.

b. Settlement Procedures: the responsibilities of a broker in arranging settlement or closing, including recordation procedures; closing costs, charges, credits, adjustments, and prorations; and compliance with the Real Estate Settlement Procedures Act.

c. Property Management: the responsibilities of a broker managing property on behalf of an owner, including property maintenance; collecting rents and security deposits in accordance with terms of leases and legal agreements; negotiating leases; and advising on current market conditions.

2. *Contracts and Other Legal Aspects* (27% of uniform test)
The questions in this area cover the following topics:

a. Contracts: general aspects of contract law; familiarity with listing contracts, contracts for sales, options, leases, installment land contracts, and escrow agreements; the referring of clients to legal counsel.

b. Land Use Controls: zoning; private restrictions; requirements for subdividing and developing; deed restrictions and covenants.

c. Deeds: the general characteristics of various types of deeds and the circumstances under which specific deeds are appropriate.

d. Property Ownership: the rights and interests which may affect ownership of real property; characteristics of various types of ownership (joint tenancy, time-sharing, etc.).

e. Condominiums and Cooperatives: the requirements for certification of real property as a condominium or cooperative; types of ownership (individual and common); aspects of property conversion to condominium or cooperative.

f. Other Legal Aspects: the legal implications of public powers over real property (eminent domain, escheat, police power, taxation, etc.); and special interests in real property (easements, party walls, etc.).

3. *Pricing and Valuation* (15% of uniform test)

a. Appraising: the principles of value and approaches to estimating value.

b. Pricing by Comparative Market Analysis: the pricing of real estate for sale, rent, or exchange in the absence of an appraisal report.

4. *Finance and Investment* (23% of uniform test)

a. Financing Arrangements: costs involved in placement of loans; governmental agencies which guarantee or insure mortgages; requirements of the Truth in Lending Act regarding advertising financial aspects of a sale.

b. Financing Instruments: characteristics of notes and mortgages, deeds of trust, installment land contracts, and other financing instruments.

c. Loans and Mortgages: characteristics of different types of loans or mortgages (amortizing, term, blanket, package, etc.); essential elements and special clauses of mortgages (prepayment, due on sale clause, variable payment, etc.); sources of junior or secondary loans; conditions and procedures involved in default and foreclosure.

d. Tax Ramifications: the tax ramifications of home ownership, including interest and property tax deductions, deferred capital gains, etc.; also, the tax ramifications of real estate investments, including depreciation, capital gains and losses, refinancing, etc.

The State Test (50 questions) contains questions dealing with the real estate laws, rules, and regulations and other aspects of real estate practice appropriate to the jurisdiction in which the test is being given. Aspects of real estate practice that may be covered in this section include state statutes dealing with condominiums, subdivisions, fair housing practices, and administrative hearing procedures. Other aspects of real estate practice, which are not uniform from state to state, may also be included. Be sure to check with your state real estate commission for more details regarding coverage in this section.

The following **Sample Questions** illustrate the types of questions in the examination for real estate brokers. They do not, however, represent the full range of content or levels of difficulty found in the test. An answer key is provided in Appendix A. A Sample Uniform Broker's Test is available from ETS for a fee.

Uniform Test

REAL ESTATE BROKERAGE

1. A property management contract generally contains which of the following?
   I. A description of the property
   II. An agreement that the property manager will render periodic statements to the owner
   (A) I only **(B)** II only **(C)** Both I and II **(D)** Neither I nor II

2. Which of the following would be classified as off-site management?
   A. Accounting
   B. Handling tenant complaints
   C. Showing vacant space to prospective tenants
   D. Maintenance work

CONTRACTS AND OTHER LEGAL ASPECTS

1. A person who is without heirs may avoid having his property pass to the state by
   I. leaving a valid will containing instructions as to the disposition of his property.
   II. giving it to a charity prior to death.
   (A) I only **(B)** II only **(C)** Both I and II **(D)** Neither I nor II

2. Gift deeds usually take the form of
   A. sheriff's deeds. **C.** warranty deeds.
   B. bargain and sale deeds. **D.** grant deeds.

3. A contract entered into by a competent and an incompetent may be disaffirmed by which of the following?
   I. The competent party
   II. The incompetent party
   (A) I only **(B)** II only **(C)** Both I and II **(D)** Neither I nor II

PRICING AND VALUATION

1. A quarterly tax payment is $657 on a property assessed at 90 percent of market value. If the annual tax rate is $0.02 per $1 of assessed valuation, then the market value of the property is
   A. $146,000 **C.** $36,500
   B. $87,600 **D.** $18,250

2. Which of the following would ordinarily be included in the reserves for replacement?
   I. Replacement cost for refrigerators in an apartment unit
   II. Depreciation on the apartment building
   (A) I only **(B)** II only **(C)** Both I and II **(D)** Neither I nor II

3. A contractor estimates he can build a 5,800 square foot structure for $232,000. Due to inflation, this is 10% more than he estimated last year for the same job. How much per square foot did he estimate last year?

A. $36.00
B. $36.36
C. $40.00
D. $44.00

FINANCE AND INVESTMENT

1. An owner's agreement to finance personally the sale of a house for a buyer is known as a
   A. conventional loan
   B. purchase money mortgage
   C. secured transaction
   D. bill of sale

2. FHA mortgage insurance programs are available for
   I. private, single-family residences.
   II. multi-family residential buildings.
   (A) I only (B) II only (C) Both I and II (D) Neither I nor II

3. Calculate the balance owing after two $100 monthly payments have been made on a 10-year, $10,000 loan that carries 12% annual interest.
   A. $10,000
   B. $ 9,800
   C. $10,200
   D. $ 9,833.33

State Test

Questions for the state test are the same as those for the salespersons' state test.

Real Estate Math Review

PERCENT

Percent (%) means parts per hundred. For example, 25% means 25 parts per hundred; 10% means 10 parts per hundred. Percentages are related to common and decimal fractions as follows:

5% = .05 = 1/20
10% = .10 = 1/10
25% = .25 = 1/4
75% = .75 = 3/4
99% = .99 = 99/100

A percentage greater than 100% is greater than 1. For example:

110% = 1.10 = 1 1/10
150% = 1.50 = 1 1/2
200% = 2.00 = 2
1,000% = 10.0 = 10

To change a decimal fraction to a percentage, move the decimal point two places to the right and add the % sign. For example:

.0001 = .01%
.01 = 1%
.06 = 6%
.35 = 35%
.356 = 35.6%
1.15 = 115%

A percentage can be changed to a common fraction by writing it as hundredths and then reducing it to its lowest common denominator. For example:

20% = 20/100 = 1/5
90% = 90/100 = 9/10
225% = 2 25/100 = 2 1/4

ADDING AND SUBTRACTING DECIMALS

To add decimals, place the decimal points directly over one another. Then place the decimal point for the solutions in the same column and add. For example:

$$\begin{array}{r} 6.25 \\ 1.10 \\ \underline{10.277} \\ 17.627 \end{array}$$

If you are working with percentages, there is no need to convert to decimal fractions; just line up the decimal points and add. For example:

```
 68.8%
  6.0%
 25.2%
------
100.0%
```

When subtracting, the same methods apply. For example:

```
  1.00     100%
 - .80    - 80%
 -----    -----
   .20      20%
```

When there is a mixture of decimal fractions and percentages, first convert them all either to percentage or to decimal fractions.

MULTIPLYING AND DIVIDING DECIMALS

Multiplying decimals is like multiplying whole numbers except that the decimal point must be correctly placed. This is done by counting the total number of places to the right of the decimal point in the numbers to be multiplied. Then count off the same number of places in the answer. The following examples illustrate this:

```
 .6     .2    1.01    6     6      .03
×.3    ×.2   ×   2   ×.1   ×.11  ×  .02
----   ----  -----   ---   ----  -----
 .18    .04   2.02   .6    .66   .0006
```

When dividing, the process starts with properly placing the decimal point. A normal division then follows. When a decimal number is divided by a whole number, place the decimal point in the answer directly above the decimal point in the problem. For example:

```
  1.03     .033
3)3.09   3).099
```

To divide by a decimal number, you must first change the divisor to a whole number. Then you must make a corresponding change in the dividend. This is done by simply moving both decimal points the same number of places to the right. For example, to divide .06 by .02, move the decimal point of each to the right two places.

.02).06 becomes 2)6

.5)3 becomes 5)30

.05)30 becomes 5)3,000

When multiplying or dividing with percentages, first convert them to decimal form. Thus 6% of 200 is

```
  200
×  .06
------
 12.00
```

PROBLEMS INVOLVING RATES

The basic equation for solving rate problems is:
Percent times **Base amount** equals **Result**

$$P \times B = R$$

If you know the result and the percent and you want the base amount, then divide both sides of the equation by P to get:

$$B = \frac{R}{P}$$

If you know the result and the base amount and you want to know the percentage, divide both sides of the equation by B to get:

$$P = \frac{R}{B}$$

> **Note:** An equation will remain an equation as long as you make the same change on both sides of the equal sign. If you add the same number to both sides, it is still an equation. If you subtract the same amount from each side, it is still equal. If you multiply both sides by the same thing, it remains equal. If you divide both sides by the same thing, it remains equal.

One way to remember the basic equation for solving rate problems is to think of a campaign button that looks like this:

$R = P \times B \qquad P = \frac{R}{B} \qquad B = \frac{R}{P}$

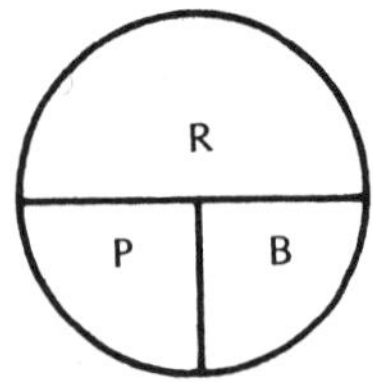

Another useful tool in solving rate problems is to think of
the word **is** as = (an equal sign).
the word **of** as × (a multiplication sign).
the word **per** as ÷ (a division sign).

for example:
"7% of $50,000 is $3,500"
translates:
7% × $50,000 = $3,500

Problem 1

Beverly Broker sells a house for $60,000. Her share of the commission is to be 2.5% of the sales price. How much does she earn?

Her commission is 2.5% of $60,000
Her commission = .025 × $60,000
Her commission = $1,500
This is an example of Result = Percent × Base.

Problem 2

Sam Salesman works in an office which will pay him 70% of the commission on each home he lists and sells. With a 6% commission, how much would he earn on a $50,000 sale?

His commission is 70% of 6% of $50,000
His commission = .70 × .06 × $50,000
His commission = $2,100
This is an example of Result = Percent × Base

Problem 3

Newt Newcommer wants to earn $21,000 during his first 12 months as a salesman. He feels he can average 3% on each sale. How much property must he sell?

3% of sales is $21,000
.03 × sales = $21,000
sales = $21,000 ÷ .03
sales = $700,000
This is an example of Base = Result ÷ Percent

Problem 4

An apartment building nets the owners $12,000 per year on their investment of $100,000. What percent return are they receiving on their investment?

$12,000 is __% of $100,000

$12,000 = __% × $100,000

$$\frac{\$12,000}{\$100,000} = 12\%$$

This is an example of Percent = Result ÷ Base

Problem 5

Smith wants to sell his property and have $47,000 after paying a 6% brokerage commission on the sales price. What price must Smith get?

$47,000 is 94% of selling price
$47,000 = .94 × selling price

$$\frac{\$47,000}{.94} = \text{selling price}$$

$50,000 = selling price

Problem 6

Miller sold his home for \$75,000, paid off an existing loan of \$35,000 and paid closing costs of \$500. The brokerage commission was 6% of the sales price. How much money did Miller receive?
The amount he received is 94% of \$75,000 less \$35,500

amount = .94 × \$75,000 − \$35,500
amount = \$70,500 − \$35,500
amount = \$35,000

Problem 7

The assessed valuation of the Kelly home is \$10,000. If the property tax rate is \$12.50 per \$100 of assessed valuation, what is the tax?

$$\text{The tax is } \frac{\$12.50}{100} \text{ of } \$10{,}000$$

$$\text{tax} = \frac{\$12.50}{100} \times \$10{,}000$$

$$\text{tax} = \$1{,}250$$

Problem 8

Property in Clark County is assessed at 75% of market value. What should the assessed valuation of a \$40,000 property be?

Assessed valuation is 75% of market value
Assessed valuation = .75 × \$40,000
Assessed valuation = \$30,000

Problem 9

An insurance company charges \$.24 per \$100 of coverage for a one-year fire insurance policy. How much would a \$40,000 policy cost?

$$\text{Cost is } \frac{\$.24}{\$100} \text{ of } \$40{,}000$$

$$\text{Cost} = \frac{\$.24}{\$100} \times \$40{,}000$$

$$\text{Cost} = \$96$$

AREA MEASUREMENT

The measurement of the distance from one point to another is called *linear* measurement. Usually this is along a straight line, but it can also be along a curved line. Distance is measured in inches, feet, yards, and miles. Less commonly used are chains (66 feet) and rods ($16\frac{1}{2}$ feet). Surface areas are measured in square feet, square yards, acres (43,560 square feet), and square miles. In the metric system, the standard unit of linear measurement is the meter (39.37 inches). Land area is measured in square meters and hectares. A hectare contains 10,000 square meters or 2.471 acres.

To determine the area of a square or rectangle, multiply its length times its width. The formula is:

Area = Length × Width
A = L × W

Problem 10

A parcel of land measures 660 feet by 330 feet. How many square feet is this?

Area = 660 feet × 330 feet
Area = 217,800 square feet

How many acres does this parcel contain?

Acres = 217,800 ÷ 43,560
Acres = 5

If a buyer offers $42,500 for this parcel, how much is the offering per acre?

$42,500 ÷ 5 = $8,500

To determine the area of a right triangle, multiply one-half of the base times the height:

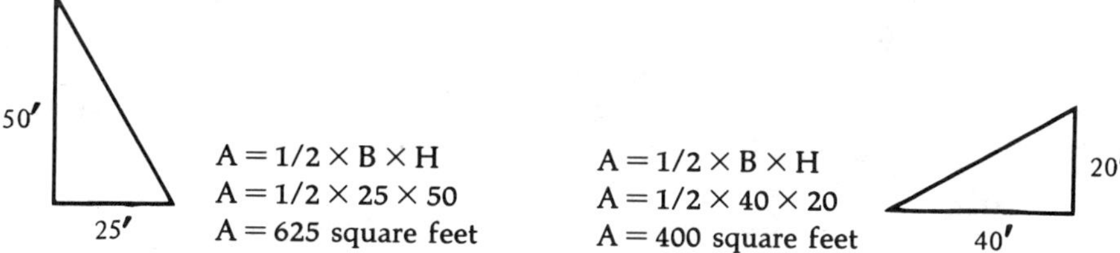

A = 1/2 × B × H
A = 1/2 × 25 × 50
A = 625 square feet

A = 1/2 × B × H
A = 1/2 × 40 × 20
A = 400 square feet

To determine the area of a circle, multiply 3.14 (π) times the square of the radius:

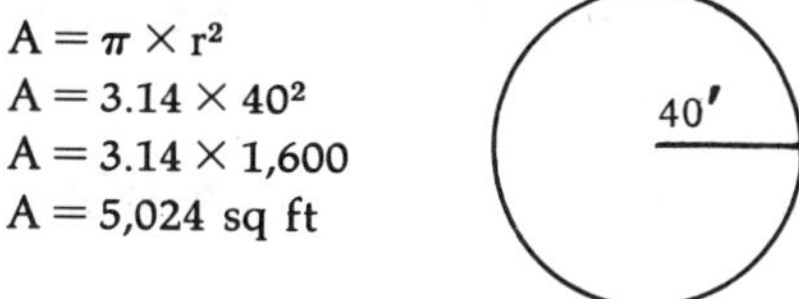

$A = \pi \times r^2$
$A = 3.14 \times 40^2$
$A = 3.14 \times 1{,}600$
A = 5,024 sq ft

> **Note:** where the diameter of a circle is given, divide by two to get the radius.

To determine the area of composite figures, separate them into their various components. Thus:

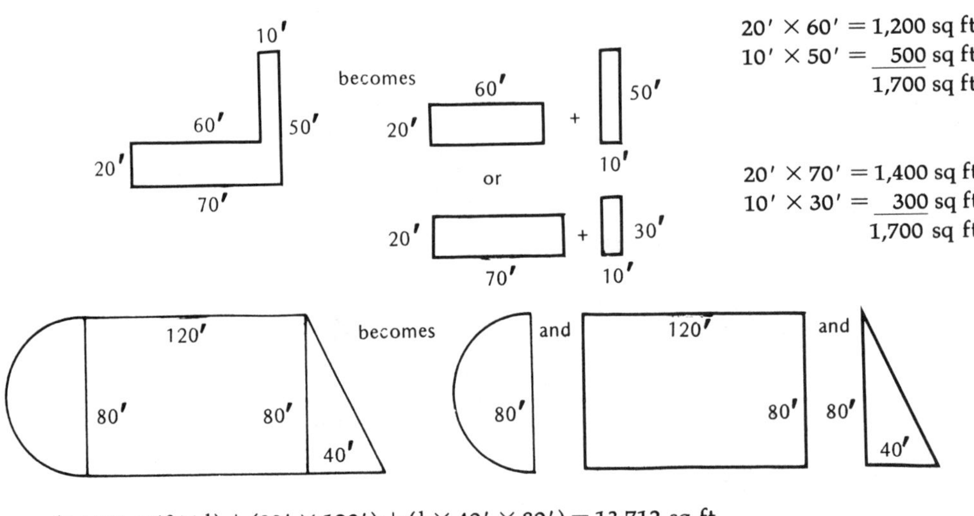

$(3.14 \times 40'^2 \times \frac{1}{2}) + (80' \times 120') + (\frac{1}{2} \times 40' \times 80') = 13{,}712$ sq ft

VOLUME MEASUREMENT

Volume is measured in cubic units. The formula is:

Volume = Length × Width × Height

$V = L \times W \times H$

For example, what is the volume of a room that is 10 ft by 15 ft with an 8 ft ceiling?

$V = 10' \times 15' \times 8'$

$V = 1{,}200$ cu ft

> **Caution:** When solving area and volume problems, make certain that all the units are the same. For example, if a parcel of land is one-half mile long and 200 ft wide, convert one measurement so that both are expressed in the same unit; thus the answer will be either in square feet or in square miles. There is no such area measurement as a mile-foot. If a building is 100 yards long by 100 feet wide by 16′ 6″ high, convert to 300 ft by 100 ft by 16.5 ft before multiplying.

RATIOS & PROPORTIONS

If the label on a five-gallon can of paint says it will cover 2,000 square feet, how many gallons are necessary to cover 3,600 sq ft?

A problem like this can be solved two ways:

One way is to find out what area one gallon will cover. In this case 2,000 sq ft ÷ 5 gallons = 400 sq ft per gallon. Then divide 400 sq ft/gal into 3,600 sq ft and the result is 9 gallons.

The other method is to set up a proportion:

$$\frac{5 \text{ gal}}{2{,}000 \text{ sq ft}} = \frac{\text{Y gal}}{3{,}600 \text{ sq ft}}$$

This reads, "5 gallons is to 2,000 sq ft as 'Y' gallons is to 3,600 sq ft." To solve for "Y," multiply both sides of the proportion by 3,600 sq ft. Thus:

$$\frac{5 \text{ gal} \times 3{,}600 \text{ sq ft}}{2{,}000 \text{ sq ft}} = \text{Y gal}$$

Divide 2,000 sq ft into 3,600 sq ft and multiply the result by 5 gallons to get the answer.

FRONT-FOOT CALCULATIONS

When land is sold on a front-foot basis, the price is the number of feet fronting on the street times the price per front foot.

Price = front footage × rate per front foot

Thus a 50 ft × 150 ft lot priced at $1,000 per front foot would sell for $50,000. Note that in giving the dimensions of a lot, the first dimension given is the street frontage. The second dimension is the depth of the lot.

Compound Sum of Single Dollar

Year	2%	4%	6%	8%	10%	12%	14%	16%	18%	20%	22%	25%	30%	40%
1	1.020	1.040	1.060	1.080	1.100	1.120	1.140	1.160	1.180	1.200	1.220	1.250	1.300	1.400
2	1.040	1.082	1.124	1.166	1.210	1.254	1.300	1.346	1.392	1.440	1.488	1.563	1.690	1.960
3	1.061	1.125	1.191	1.260	1.331	1.405	1.482	1.561	1.643	1.728	1.816	1.953	2.197	2.744
4	1.082	1.170	1.262	1.360	1.464	1.574	1.689	1.811	1.939	2.074	2.215	2.441	2.856	3.842
5	1.104	1.217	1.338	1.469	1.611	1.762	1.925	2.100	2.288	2.488	2.703	3.052	3.713	5.378
6	1.126	1.265	1.419	1.587	1.772	1.974	2.195	2.436	2.700	2.986	3.297	3.851	4.827	7.530
7	1.149	1.316	1.504	1.714	1.949	2.211	2.502	2.826	3.185	3.583	4.023	4.768	6.275	10.541
8	1.172	1.369	1.594	1.851	2.144	2.476	2.853	3.278	3.759	4.300	4.908	5.960	8.157	14.758
9	1.195	1.423	1.689	1.999	2.358	2.773	3.252	3.803	4.435	5.160	5.987	7.451	10.604	20.661
10	1.219	1.480	1.791	2.159	2.594	3.106	3.707	4.411	5.234	6.192	7.305	9.313	13.786	28.925
11	1.243	1.539	1.898	2.332	2.853	3.479	4.226	5.117	6.176	7.430	8.912	11.642	17.921	40.496
12	1.268	1.601	2.012	2.518	3.138	3.896	4.818	5.936	7.288	8.916	10.872	14.552	23.298	56.694
13	1.294	1.665	2.133	2.720	3.452	4.363	5.492	6.886	8.599	10.699	13.264	18.190	30.287	79.371
14	1.319	1.732	2.261	2.937	3.797	4.887	6.261	7.988	10.147	12.839	16.182	22.737	39.373	
15	1.346	1.801	2.397	3.172	4.177	5.474	7.138	9.266	11.974	15.407	19.742	28.422	51.185	
16	1.373	1.873	2.540	3.426	4.595	6.130	8.137	10.748	14.129	18.488	24.085	35.527	66.541	
17	1.400	1.948	2.693	3.700	5.054	6.866	9.276	12.468	16.672	22.186	29.384	44.409	86.503	
18	1.428	2.026	2.854	3.996	5.560	7.690	10.575	14.462	19.673	26.623	35.849	55.511		
19	1.457	2.107	3.026	4.316	6.116	8.613	12.056	16.776	23.214	31.948	43.735	69.389		
20	1.486	2.191	3.207	4.661	6.727	9.646	13.743	19.461	27.393	38.337	53.357	86.736		
21	1.516	2.279	3.400	5.034	7.400	10.804	15.667	22.574	32.323	46.005	65.096			
22	1.546	2.370	3.603	5.437	8.140	12.100	17.861	26.186	38.142	55.206	79.417			
23	1.577	2.465	3.820	5.871	8.954	13.552	20.361	30.376	45.007	66.247	96.888			
24	1.608	2.563	4.049	6.341	9.850	15.179	23.212	35.236	53.108	79.497				
25	1.641	2.666	4.292	6.848	10.835	17.000	26.462	40.874	62.668	95.396				

Source: John J. Hampton, *Handbook for Financial Decision Makers*, Reston Publishing Company, Reston, Virginia, 1979.

APPENDIX E–2

Compound Sum of Annuity of $1

Year	2%	4%	6%	8%	10%	12%	14%	16%	18%	20%	22%	25%	30%	40%
1	1.000	1.000	1.000	1.000	1.000	1.000	1.000	1.000	1.000	1.000	1.000	1.000	1.000	1.000
2	2.020	2.040	2.060	2.080	2.100	2.120	2.140	2.160	2.180	2.200	2.220	2.250	2.300	2.400
3	3.060	3.122	3.184	3.246	3.310	3.374	3.440	3.506	3.572	3.640	3.708	3.813	3.990	4.360
4	4.121	4.246	4.375	4.506	4.641	4.779	4.921	5.066	5.215	5.368	5.524	5.766	6.187	7.104
5	5.204	5.416	5.637	5.867	6.105	6.353	6.610	6.877	7.154	7.442	7.740	8.207	9.043	10.846
6	6.308	6.633	6.975	7.336	7.716	8.115	8.535	8.977	9.442	9.930	10.442	11.259	12.756	16.324
7	7.434	7.898	8.394	8.923	9.487	10.089	10.730	11.414	12.141	12.916	13.740	15.073	17.583	23.853
8	8.583	9.214	9.897	10.637	11.436	12.300	13.233	14.240	15.327	16.499	17.762	19.842	23.858	34.395
9	9.754	10.583	11.491	12.488	13.579	14.776	16.085	17.518	19.086	20.799	22.670	25.802	32.015	49.153
10	10.949	12.006	13.181	14.487	15.937	17.549	19.337	21.321	23.521	25.959	28.657	33.253	42.619	69.814
11	12.168	13.486	14.971	16.645	18.531	20.655	23.044	25.733	28.755	32.150	35.962	42.566	56.405	98.739
12	13.412	15.026	16.870	18.977	21.384	24.133	27.271	30.850	34.931	39.580	44.873	54.208	74.326	
13	14.680	16.627	18.882	21.495	24.522	28.029	32.088	36.786	42.218	48.496	55.745	68.760	97.624	
14	15.973	18.292	21.015	24.215	27.975	32.393	37.581	43.672	50.818	59.196	69.009	86.949		
15	17.293	20.024	23.276	27.152	31.772	37.280	43.842	51.659	60.965	72.035	85.191			
16	18.639	21.824	25.672	30.324	35.949	42.753	50.980	60.925	72.938	87.442				
17	20.011	23.697	28.212	33.750	40.544	48.884	59.117	71.673	87.067					
18	21.412	25.645	30.905	37.450	45.599	55.750	68.393	84.141						
19	22.840	27.671	33.759	41.446	51.158	63.440	78.968	98.603						
20	24.297	29.778	36.785	45.762	57.274	72.052	91.024							
21	25.783	31.969	39.992	50.423	64.002	81.699								
22	27.298	34.248	43.392	55.457	71.402	92.502								
23	28.844	36.618	46.995	60.893	79.542									
24	30.421	39.083	50.815	66.765	88.496									
25	32.029	41.646	54.864	73.106	98.346									

Source: John J. Hampton, *Handbook for Financial Decision Makers*, Reston Publishing Company, Reston, Virginia, 1979.

Present Value of Single Dollar

Year	2%	4%	6%	8%	10%	12%	14%	16%	18%	20%	22%	24%	25%	30%	40%
1	0.980	0.962	0.943	0.926	0.909	0.893	0.877	0.862	0.847	0.833	0.820	0.806	0.800	0.769	0.714
2	0.961	0.925	0.890	0.857	0.826	0.797	0.769	0.743	0.718	0.694	0.672	0.650	0.640	0.592	0.510
3	0.942	0.889	0.840	0.794	0.751	0.712	0.675	0.641	0.609	0.579	0.551	0.524	0.512	0.455	0.364
4	0.924	0.855	0.792	0.735	0.683	0.636	0.592	0.552	0.516	0.482	0.451	0.423	0.410	0.350	0.260
5	0.906	0.822	0.747	0.681	0.621	0.567	0.519	0.476	0.437	0.402	0.370	0.341	0.328	0.269	0.186
6	0.888	0.790	0.705	0.630	0.564	0.507	0.456	0.410	0.370	0.335	0.303	0.275	0.262	0.207	0.133
7	0.871	0.760	0.665	0.583	0.513	0.452	0.400	0.354	0.314	0.279	0.249	0.222	0.210	0.159	0.095
8	0.853	0.731	0.627	0.540	0.467	0.404	0.351	0.305	0.266	0.233	0.204	0.179	0.168	0.123	0.068
9	0.837	0.703	0.592	0.500	0.424	0.361	0.308	0.263	0.225	0.194	0.167	0.144	0.134	0.094	0.048
10	0.820	0.676	0.558	0.463	0.386	0.322	0.270	0.227	0.191	0.162	0.137	0.116	0.107	0.073	0.035
11	0.804	0.650	0.527	0.429	0.350	0.287	0.237	0.195	0.162	0.135	0.112	0.094	0.086	0.056	0.025
12	0.788	0.625	0.497	0.397	0.319	0.257	0.208	0.168	0.137	0.112	0.092	0.076	0.069	0.043	0.018
13	0.773	0.601	0.469	0.368	0.290	0.229	0.182	0.145	0.116	0.093	0.075	0.061	0.055	0.033	0.013
14	0.758	0.577	0.442	0.340	0.263	0.205	0.160	0.125	0.099	0.078	0.062	0.049	0.044	0.025	0.009
15	0.743	0.555	0.417	0.315	0.239	0.183	0.140	0.108	0.084	0.065	0.051	0.040	0.035	0.020	0.006
16	0.728	0.534	0.394	0.292	0.218	0.163	0.123	0.093	0.071	0.054	0.042	0.032	0.028	0.015	0.005
17	0.714	0.513	0.371	0.270	0.198	0.146	0.108	0.080	0.060	0.045	0.034	0.026	0.023	0.012	0.003
18	0.700	0.494	0.350	0.250	0.180	0.130	0.095	0.069	0.051	0.038	0.028	0.021	0.018	0.009	0.002
19	0.686	0.475	0.331	0.232	0.164	0.116	0.083	0.060	0.043	0.031	0.023	0.017	0.014	0.007	0.002
20	0.673	0.456	0.312	0.215	0.149	0.104	0.073	0.051	0.037	0.026	0.019	0.014	0.012	0.005	0.001
25	0.610	0.375	0.233	0.146	0.092	0.059	0.038	0.024	0.016	0.010	0.007	0.005	0.004	0.001	
30	0.552	0.308	0.174	0.099	0.057	0.033	0.020	0.012	0.007	0.004	0.003	0.002	0.001		
40	0.453	0.208	0.097	0.046	0.022	0.011	0.005	0.003	0.001	0.001					
50	0.372	0.141	0.054	0.021	0.009	0.003	0.001	0.001							

Source: John J. Hampton, *Handbook for Financial Decision Makers,* Reston Publishing Company, Reston, Virginia, 1979.

APPENDIX F–2

Present Value of Annuity of $1

Year	2%	4%	6%	8%	10%	12%	14%	16%	18%	20%	22%	24%	25%	30%	40%
1	0.980	0.962	0.943	0.926	0.909	0.893	0.877	0.862	0.847	0.833	0.820	0.806	0.800	0.769	0.714
2	1.942	1.886	1.833	1.783	1.736	1.690	1.647	1.605	1.566	1.528	1.492	1.457	1.440	1.361	1.224
3	2.884	2.775	2.673	2.577	2.487	2.402	2.322	2.246	2.174	2.106	2.042	1.981	1.952	1.816	1.589
4	3.808	3.630	3.645	3.312	3.170	3.037	2.914	2.798	2.690	2.589	2.494	2.404	2.362	2.166	1.849
5	4.713	4.452	4.212	3.993	3.791	3.605	3.433	3.274	3.127	2.991	2.864	2.745	2.689	2.436	2.035
6	5.601	5.242	4.917	4.623	4.355	4.111	3.889	3.685	3.498	3.326	3.167	3.020	2.951	2.643	2.168
7	6.472	6.002	5.582	5.206	4.868	4.564	4.288	4.039	3.812	3.605	3.416	3.242	3.161	2.802	2.263
8	7.325	6.733	6.210	5.747	5.335	4.968	4.639	4.344	4.078	3.837	3.619	3.421	3.329	2.925	2.331
9	8.162	7.435	6.802	6.247	5.759	5.328	4.946	4.607	4.303	4.031	3.786	3.566	3.463	3.019	2.379
10	8.983	8.111	7.360	6.710	6.145	5.650	5.216	4.833	4.494	4.192	3.923	3.682	3.571	3.092	2.414
11	9.787	8.760	7.887	7.139	6.495	5.937	5.453	5.029	4.656	4.327	4.035	3.776	3.656	3.147	2.438
12	10.58	9.385	8.384	7.536	6.814	6.194	5.660	5.197	4.793	4.439	4.127	3.851	3.725	3.190	2.456
13	11.34	9.986	8.853	7.904	7.103	6.424	5.842	5.342	4.910	4.533	4.203	3.912	3.780	3.223	2.468
14	12.11	10.56	9.295	8.244	7.367	6.628	6.002	5.468	5.008	4.611	4.265	3.962	3.824	3.249	2.477
15	12.85	11.12	9.712	8.559	7.606	6.811	6.142	5.575	5.092	4.675	4.315	4.001	3.859	3.268	2.484
16	13.58	11.65	10.11	8.851	7.824	6.974	6.265	5.669	5.162	4.730	4.357	4.033	3.887	3.283	2.489
17	14.29	12.17	10.48	9.122	8.022	7.120	6.373	5.749	5.222	4.775	4.391	4.059	3.910	3.295	2.492
18	14.99	12.66	10.83	9.372	8.201	7.250	6.467	5.818	5.273	4.812	4.419	4.080	3.928	3.304	2.494
19	15.68	13.13	11.16	9.604	8.365	7.366	6.550	5.877	5.316	4.844	4.442	4.097	3.942	3.311	2.496
20	16.35	13.59	11.47	9.818	8.514	7.469	6.623	5.929	5.353	4.870	4.460	4.110	3.954	3.316	2.497
25	19.52	15.62	12.78	10.68	9.077	7.843	6.873	6.097	5.467	4.948	4.514	4.147	3.985	3.329	2.499
30	22.40	17.29	13.77	11.26	9.427	8.055	7.003	6.177	5.517	4.979	4.534	4.160	3.995	3.332	2.500
40	27.36	19.79	15.05	11.93	9.779	8 244	7.105	6.234	5.548	4.997	4.544	4.166	3.999	3.333	2.500
50	31.42	21.48	15.76	12.23	9.915	8.304	7.133	6.246	5.554	4.999	4.545	4.167	4.000	3.333	2.500

Source: John J. Hampton, *Handbook for Financial Decision Makers*, Reston Publishing Company, Reston, Virginia, 1979.

APPENDIX G

Measurement Conversion Table

Mile =
5,280 feet
1,760 yards
320 rods
80 chains
= 1.609 kilometers

Square mile =
0 acres
= 2.590 sq kilometers

Acre =
43,560 sq ft
4,840 sq yds
160 sq rods
= 4,047 sq meters

Rod =
16.5 feet
= 5.029 meters

Chain =
66 feet
4 rods
100 links
= 20.117 meters

Meter =
39.37 inches
= 1,000 millimeters
3.281 feet
= 100 centimeters
1.094 yards
= 10 decimeters

Kilometer =
0.6214 miles
3,281 feet
1,094 yards
= 1,000 meters

Square meter =
10.765 sq ft
1.196 sq yds
= 10,000 sq centimeters

Hectare =
2.47 acres
107,600 sq ft
11,960 sq yds
= 10,000 sq meters

Square kilometer =
.3861 sq miles
247 acres
= 1,000,000 sq meters

Kilogram =
2.205 pounds
= 1,000 grams

Liter =
1.053 quarts
.263 gallons
= 1,000 milliliters

Metric ton =
(tonne)
2,205 pounds
1.102 tons
= 1,000 kilograms

Minnesota Subdivided Land Sales Practices Act

The following are key excerpts from the Minnesota Subdivided Land Sales Practices Act and are current at the time of printing. You can obtain the complete Act with any subsequent changes from the State of Minnesota, Documents Division, 117 University Avenue, St. Paul, MN 55105.

83.20 Definitions

Subdivision 1. (a) "Advertising" shall include the publication or causing to be published of any information offering for sale or for the purpose of causing or inducing any other person to purchase or to acquire an interest in the title to subdivided lands, including the land sales contract to be used and any photographs or drawings or artist's representations of physical conditions or facilities on the property existing or to exist by means of any:

(1) Newspaper or periodical;

(2) Radio or television broadcast;

(3) Written, printed or photographic matter; or

(4) Material used in connection with the disposition or offer of subdivided lands by radio, television, telephone or any other electronic means.

(b) "Advertising" shall further include material used by subdividers to induce prospective purchasers to visit a subdivision, or travel to this state or elsewhere, including vacation certificates which require the holders of such certificates to attend or submit to a sales presentation by a subdivider or its agents.

(c) "Advertising" shall further include the entire promotional plan for the disposition of the subdivided lands including promotional displays at public or private events, and parties, dinners or other meetings at which prospective purchasers may be shown or presented with other advertising as defined in (a) and (b) above.

(d) "Advertising" shall not be deemed to include: Stockholder communications such as annual reports and interim financial reports, proxy materials, registration statements, securities prospectuses, applications for listing securities on stock exchanges, and the like; prospectuses, property reports, offering statements, or other documents required to be delivered to a prospective purchaser by an agency of any other state or the federal government; communications addressed to and relating to the account of any persons who have previously executed a contract for the purchase of the subdivider's lands except when directed to the sale of additional lands.

Subd. 2. "Agent" means any person who represents, or acts for or on behalf of, a subdivider in disposing of subdivided lands or lots in a subdivision, and includes a real estate salesman or broker, but does not include an attorney at law whose representation of another person consists solely of rendering legal services.

Subd. 11. "Subdivision" and "subdivided land" means any land wherever located, improved or unimproved, whether adjacent or not, which is divided or proposed to be divided for the purpose of disposition pursuant to a common promotional scheme or plan of advertising and disposition by a single subdivider or a group of subdividers. If the land is designated or advertised as a common unit or by a common name, the land shall be presumed, without regard to the number of lots covered by each individual offering, as being offered for disposition as part of a common promotional plan.

83.21 Commissioner of commerce to administer

Sections 83.20 to 83.42 shall be administered by the commissioner of commerce of the Minnesota department of commerce.

83.23 Application for registration; filing fee

Subdivision 1. Unless the subdivided land or the transaction is exempt by sections 83.20 to 83.42, a person may not offer or dispose in this state of any interest in subdivided lands unless the subdivided lands are registered in accordance with sections 83.20 to 83.42.

Subd. 2. A filing fee of $250 shall accompany the application for registration plus an additional $1 for each lot unit, parcel or interest included in the offering. The maximum filing fee shall in no event be more than $2,500.

Subd. 3. The application for registration of subdivided lands shall be filed with the commissioner as prescribed by rule.

83.24 Public offering statement

Subdivision 1. A person may not dispose of any interest in subdivided lands unless a current public offering statement is delivered to the purchaser at the expense of the subdivider or his agent, and the purchaser is afforded a reasonable opportunity to examine, and is permitted to retain the public offering statement prior to the offer or disposition. The subdivider or his agent shall obtain a receipt, signed by the purchaser, acknowledging that he has received a copy of the public offering statement prior to the execution by the purchaser of a contract or agreement for the disposition of any lot or parcel in a subdivision, which receipt shall be kept in files in possession of the subdivider or his agent subject to inspection by the commissioner for a period of three years from the date the receipt is taken.

Subd. 2. A public offering statement shall disclose fully and accurately the physical and climatic characteristics of the subdivided lands offered and shall make known to prospective purchasers all unusual and material circumstances or features affecting the subdivided lands. A proposed public offering statement submitted to the commissioner shall be in a form prescribed by rule and shall include the following:

(1) The name, principal address and telephone number of the subdivider and of its offices and agents in this state;

(2) A general description of the subdivided lands stating the total number of lots, parcels, units or interests to be offered;

(3) A statement whether the subdivider holds any options to purchase adjacent properties, and if so, a description of such options and the location and zoning of the adjacent properties;

(4) A statement of the assistance, if any, that the subdivider or his agent will provide to the purchaser in the resale of the property and whether or not the subdivider or his agent will be in competition in the event of resale;

(5) The material terms of any encumbrances, easements, liens, and restrictions including zoning and other regulations affecting the subdivided lands and each unit or lot, a statement of the subdivider's efforts to remove such lien or encumbrance, and a statement of all existing taxes and existing or proposed special taxes or assessments which affect the subdivided lands;

(6) A statement of the use for which the property is to be offered;

(7) Information concerning existing or proposed improvements, including but not limited to streets, water supply, levees, drainage control systems, irrigation systems, sewage disposal systems and customary utilities and the estimated cost, date of completion, and responsibility for construction and maintenance of existing and proposed improvements which are referred to in connection with the offering or disposition of any lot, unit, parcel or interest in subdivided lands;

(8) A financial statement of the subdivider as of the end of the subdivider's most recent fiscal year, audited by an independent certified public accountant; and, if the fiscal year end of the subdivider is in excess of 90 days prior to the date of filing the application, a financial statement, which may be unaudited, as of a date within 90 days of the date of application;

(9) Such additional information as may be required by the commissioner to assure full and fair disclosure to prospective purchasers.

Subd. 3. The public offering statement shall not be used for any promotional purpose before registration of the subdivided lands and afterwards it shall be used only in its entirety. A person may not advertise or represent that the commissioner has approved or recommended the subdivided lands or disposition thereof. A portion of the public offering statement may not be underscored, italicized or printed in larger or heavier or different color type than the remainder of the statement unless required or approved by the commissioner.

Subd. 4. The commissioner may require the subdivider or his agent to alter or amend the proposed public offering statement in order to assure full and fair disclosure to prospective purchasers.

83.25 License required

Subdivision 1. No person shall offer or dispose in this state of any interest in subdivided lands until:

(1) He has obtained a license under chapter 82; and

(2) He has obtained an additional license to offer or dispose of subdivided lands. This license may be obtained by submitting an application in writing to the commissioner upon forms prepared and furnished by the commissioner. Each application shall be signed and sworn to by the applicant and accompanied by a license fee of $10. The commissioner may also require an additional examination for this license.

Subd. 2. Every license issued pursuant to this section expires on June 30 following the date of issuance. It may be renewed, transferred, suspended, revoked or denied in the same manner as provided in chapter 82 for licenses issued pursuant to that chapter.

Subd. 3. This section does not apply to persons offering or disposing of interests in subdivided lands which are registered as securities pursuant to chapter 80A.

83.26 Exemptions

Subdivision 1. Unless the method of disposition is adopted for the purpose of evasion of sections 83.20 to 83.42, sections 83.20 to 83.42 do not apply to offers or dispositions of interests in land:

(a) By a purchaser of subdivided lands for his own account in a single or isolated transaction;

(b) To any person who acquires such land for the purpose of engaging in and who does use such land to engage in the business of constructing residential, commercial or industrial buildings thereon for the purpose of resale or constructing commercial or industrial buildings for his own use;

(c) Pursuant to an order of a court of competent jurisdiction of this state;

(d) As cemetery lots or interests;

(e) If they are leases of apartments, stores, offices, or similar space in a building;

(f) If they are mortgages or deeds of trust of real estate securing evidences of indebtedness;

(g) If the land is located within the corporate limits of a municipality as defined in section 462.352, subdivision 2, or within any subdivision located within a town or municipality located within 20 miles of the city limits of a city of the first class or within three miles of the city limits of a city of the second class, or within two miles of the city limits of a city of the third or fourth class in this state. The commissioner may, by written rule or order, suspend, wholly revoke, or further condition this exemption, or may require, prior to the first disposition of subdivided lands, such further information with respect thereto as may be necessary for the protection of purchasers consistent with the provisions hereof.

Subd. 2. The provisions of sections 83.23 and 83.24 with respect to the registration of subdivided lands and the public offering statement, shall not apply to offers or dispositions of interests in land:

(a) If fewer than ten separate lots, parcels, units or interests in subdivided lands are offered or to be offered in any period of 12 consecutive months;

(b) Involving the offering of not more than 50 separate lots, parcels, units or interests within any period of 12 consecutive months, if the subdivider or his agent shall have furnished to the commissioner, not less than 20 days prior to the consummation of any such disposition, a filing fee of $10 and a statement of the subdivider on forms prescribed by the commissioner containing the following information:

(1) The subdivider's name and address, and the form, date of organization and jurisdiction of its organization; and the name and address of each of its offices and agents in this state;

(2) A general description of the subdivided lands stating the total number of lots, parcels, units or interests to be offered;

(3) A statement in a form acceptable to the commissioner of the condition of the title to the subdivided lands including all encumbrances, deed restrictions and covenants applicable thereto;

(4) Copies of instruments which will be delivered to a purchaser to evidence his interest in the subdivided lands and of the contracts or other agreements which a purchaser will be required to agree to or sign, together with the range of selling prices, rates or rentals at which it is proposed to dispose of the lots, units, parcels or interests in the subdivisions, and a list of mandatory fees the purchaser may be required to pay for membership in groups including but not limited to home owners' associations, country clubs, golf courses and other community organizations;

(5) A statement of and evidence showing compliance with zoning and other governmental laws, ordinances and regulations affecting the use of the subdivided lands and adjacent properties;

(6) A statement asserting that the subdivision is in compliance with federal, state and local environmental quality standards. If the subdivision is not in compliance, a listing of the steps to be taken, if any, to insure compliance;

(7) A statement of the permits required to be obtained from various federal, state and local agencies stating which have been obtained and which have been applied for. If any permit has been refused, the reasons for the refusal and the effect such refusal will have on subsequent development of the subdivision;

(8) A statement of the existing provisions of access to the subdivision, the availability of sewage disposal facilities and other public utilities including but not limited to water, electricity, gas and telephone facilities in the subdivision, the proximity in miles of the subdivision to nearby municipalities, the availability and scope of community fire and police protection, and the location of primary and secondary schools; a statement of the improvements to be installed, including off-site and on-site community and recreational facilities, by whom they are to be installed, maintained and paid and an estimated schedule for completion;

Provided, however, that the commissioner may by rule or order, as to the offer or disposition of any subdivided lands, withdraw or further condition this exemption, or require additional information, or increase or decrease the number of lots, parcels, units or interests in subdivided lands permitted.

Subd. 3. The commissioner may by order exempt from the provisions of sections 83.20 to 83.42 interests in subdivided lands which are registered as securities pursuant to the provisions of chapter 80.

83.28 Sales contract; rescission

Subdivision 1. Every contract for disposition relating to subdivided land shall state clearly the legal description of the lot, unit, parcel or interest disposed of and shall contain the disclosure substantially similar to that required by the federal truth in lending act, and the rules promulgated thereunder.

Subd. 2. Any contract or agreement for the disposition of a lot, parcel, unit or interest in a subdivision not exempt under section 83.26, is voidable at the discretion of the purchaser, if the subdivision was not registered under sections

83.20 to 83.42 at the time of the offer or disposition, or if a current public offering statement was not given to the purchaser in accordance with section 83.24.

Subd. 3. A purchaser has an unconditional right to rescind any contract, agreement or other evidence of indebtedness, or revoke any offer, at any time prior to or within five days after the date the purchaser actually receives a legible copy of the binding contract, agreement or other evidence of indebtedness or offer and the public offering statement as provided in section 83.24. Predating of a document does not affect the time in which the right to rescind may be exercised. The burden of proving that the document was not predated is upon the subdivider or lender.

Subd. 4. Each contract, agreement or other evidence of indebtedness shall be prominently labeled and captioned that it is a document taken in connection with a sale or other disposition of lands under sections 83.20 to 83.42.

Subd. 5. Each such contract, agreement or other evidence of indebtedness shall prominently contain upon its face the following notice printed in at least 16 point bold type, which shall be at least 4 point type larger than the body of the document, stating:

"Notice to Purchaser

You are entitled to rescind this agreement at any time if you have not received the public offering statement in advance of your signing of this agreement. In addition, you are entitled to rescind this agreement for any reason within five days from the day you actually receive a legible copy of this document signed by all parties. Such rescission must be in writing, and mailed to the subdivider or his agent or the lender at the address stated in this document. Upon rescission, you will receive a refund of all moneys paid."

The contract, agreement or other evidence of indebtedness shall contain sufficient space upon its face in immediate proximity to the above notice for the signature of each purchaser obligated under such instrument, acknowledging that such purchaser has read the notice.

Subd. 6. Rescission occurs when the purchaser gives written notice of rescission to the subdivider or his agent or the lender at the address stated in the contract, agreement or other evidence of indebtedness. Notice of rescission, if given by mail, is effective when it is deposited in a mailbox properly addressed and postage prepaid. A notice of rescission given by the purchaser need not take a particular form and is sufficient if it indicates by any form of written expression the intention of the purchaser not to be bound by the contract, agreement or other evidence of indebtedness.

Subd. 7. No act of a purchaser shall be effective to waive the right to rescind as provided in this section.

83.30 Annual report

Subdivision 1. Within 120 days after the fiscal year end of the subdivider, the subdivider shall file a report in the form prescribed by rule of the commissioner. Every annual report shall be accompanied by a fee of $100.

Subd. 2. The commissioner may permit the filing of annual reports within 30 days after the annual anniversary date of a consolidated registration in lieu of the annual anniversary date of the original registration.

Subd. 3. Failure to file the annual report shall constitute cause for cancellation of the registration. In the event of such cancellation, registration may be reinstated at a subsequent date following a filing of the report.

83.31 Changes subsequent to registration

Subdivision 1. All advertising not accompanying the original application shall be submitted to and approved by the commissioner prior to its use in this state.

Subd. 2. The subdivider or his agent shall immediately report any material changes in the information contained in an application for registration or the exhibits appended thereto.

83.32 Inspection of records

All records of a subdivider and his agents pertaining to the advertising or disposition of subdivided lands shall be maintained by the subdivider and his agents and be subject to inspection by the commissioner. The commissioner shall be promptly notified of any change of address affecting the location of the records of the subdivider and his agents.

83.34 Investigation and proceedings

Subdivision 1. The commissioner may make necessary public or private investigations within or outside of this state to determine whether any person has violated or is about to violate sections 83.20 to 83.42 or any rule or order hereunder or to aid in the enforcement of sections 83.20 to 83.42 or in the prescribing of rules and forms hereunder.

Subd. 2. For the purpose of any investigation or proceeding under sections 83.20 to 83.42, the commissioner or any person designated by him may require or permit any person to file a statement in writing, under oath or otherwise as the commissioner determines, setting forth the facts and circumstances concerning the matter to be investigated; administer oaths or affirmations, and upon his own motion or upon request of any party may subpoena witnesses, compel their attendance, take evidence, and require the production of any matter which is relevant to the investigation, including the existence, description, nature, custody, condition and location of any books, documents or other tangible things and the identity and location of persons having knowledge of relevant facts, or any other matter reasonably calculated to lead to the discovery of material evidence.

Subd. 3. Upon failure to obey a subpoena or to answer questions propounded by the investigating officer and upon reasonable notice to all persons affected thereby, the commissioner may apply to the district court for an order for contempt.

83.35 Enforcement; powers of commissioner

Subdivision 1. After notice and hearing, the commissioner may suspend or revoke a registration, and may issue a cease and desist order to any subdivider or other person if he finds that the subdivider or person has:

(1) Violated any provision of sections 83.20 to 83.42 or any lawful order or rule of the commissioner;

(2) Directly or through an agent or employee knowingly engaged in any false, deceptive or misleading advertising, promotional or sales methods to offer to dispose of an interest in subdivided lands;

(3) Made any material change in the advertising, plan of disposition or development of the subdivided lands subsequent to the order of registration without obtaining prior approval from the commissioner;

(4) Offered or disposed of any subdivided lands which have not been registered with the commissioner unless the subdivided lands or dispositions thereof are exempt from registration pursuant to section 83.26;

(5) Been convicted, or if any of the subdivider's officers, directors, partners, principals or agents has been convicted, of a crime involving fraud, deception, false pretenses, misrepresentation, false advertising or dishonest dealing in real estate transactions, subsequent to the time of the filing of the application for registration;

(6) Disposed of, concealed or diverted any funds or assets of any person so as to defeat the rights of subdivision purchasers;

(7) Failed faithfully to perform any stipulation or agreement made with the commissioner as an inducement to grant any registration, to reinstate any registration, or to permit any promotional plan or public offering statement;

(8) Made misrepresentations or concealed material facts in an application for registration;

(9) Permanently or temporarily been enjoined by any court of competent jurisdiction from engaging in or continuing any conduct or practice involving any aspect of land sales; or

(10) Failed to pay any filing or inspection fee required by sections 83.20 to 83.42.

Subd. 2. When initiating a proceeding under subdivision 1, the commissioner shall serve upon the subdivider or other person by personal service or by certified mail, a written notice of hearing setting the date, time and place of the hearing and a statement of the allegations upon which the cease and desist order, suspension or revocation will be based.

83.36 Injunctions; receivers

If it appears that a person has engaged or is about to engage in an act or practice constituting a violation of sections 83.20 to 83.42 or a rule or order hereunder, the commissioner, with or without prior administrative proceedings, may bring an action in district court to enjoin the acts or practices and to enforce compliance with sections 83.20 to 83.42 or any rule or order hereunder. Upon proper showing, injunctive relief or temporary restraining orders shall be granted and a receiver or conservator may be appointed. The commissioner is not required to post a bond in any court proceedings.

83.37 Penalties; civil remedies

Subdivision 1. Any person who knowingly authorizes, directs, or aids in the publication, advertisement, distribution, or circularization of any false statement or representation concerning any subdivided lands required to be registered under sections 83.20 to 83.42 and every such person who, with knowledge that any advertisement, pamphlet, prospectus, or letter concerning any such lands contains any written statement that is false or fraudulent, issues, circulates, publishes, or distributes the same, or shall cause the same to be issued, circulated, published or distributed, shall be guilty of a gross misdemeanor.

Subd. 2. Any violation of sections 83.20 to 83.42 and any failure to comply with any provisions of sections 83.20 to 83.42 not enumerated in subdivision 1 shall be a misdemeanor.

Subd. 3. Any person who fails to pay the filing or inspection fees required by sections 83.20 to 83.42, and continues to dispose of or offers to dispose of subdivided lands, is liable civilly in an action brought by the attorney general on behalf of the commissioner for a penalty in an amount equal to treble the unpaid fees.

Subd. 4. In the event of any fraud, false pretense, false promise, misrepresentation, unfair or deceptive acts, in addition to any other remedies, and whether or not the purchaser has in fact been misled, deceived or damaged thereby, the purchaser may recover the consideration paid for the lot, parcel, unit or interest in subdivided lands together with interest at the rate of six percent per year from the date of payment, property taxes paid, costs and reasonable attorneys' fees, less the amount of any income received from the subdivided lands, upon tender of appropriate instruments of reconveyance. If the purchaser no longer owns the lot, parcel, unit or interest in subdivided lands, he may recover the amount that would be recoverable upon a tender of a reconveyance, less the value of the land when disposed of and less interest at the rate of six percent per year on that amount from the date of disposition.

83.40 Scope of sections 83.20 to 83.42

Subdivision 1. The provisions of sections 83.20 to 83.42 concerning offers and dispositions of subdivided lands apply when an offer or disposition is made in this state.

Subd. 2. For the purpose of sections 83.20 to 83.42, an

offer or disposition is made in this state, whether or not either party is then present in this state, when:

(a) The offer originates from this state, or

(b) The offer is directed by the offeror to this state and received by the offeree in this state, or

(c) The subdivided lands are located in this state.

Subd. 3. An offer or disposition is not made in this state when the publisher circulates or there is circulated in his behalf in this state any bona fide newspaper or other publication of general, regular and paid circulation which is not published in this state, or a radio or television program originating outside this state is received in this state.

Subd. 4. Notwithstanding any provision of sections 83.20 to 83.42 to the contrary, sections 83.20 to 83.42 do not apply to or invalidate the lien of a mortgagee, nonaffiliated with the subdivider, when said lien attaches to land pledged as collateral in a transaction negotiated directly with the purchaser.

Minnesota's Mechanic's Lien Law

Following are major provisions of Chapter 514 of the Minnesota Statutes as they pertain to the protections offered to suppliers of labor and materials by Minnesota's Mechanic's Lien Law. Note that the information here applies to residential buildings of four or less units. If you are concerned with larger residential properties or with commercial properties, you should consult the full text of the Statute for differences.

Anyone who furnishes labor, skill, material, or machinery (including engineering or land surveying services) to improve real estate has a lien upon the improvement and the land on which it is located. Each lienholder has the right to foreclose on his lien for up to **one year** from the date of furnishing the last item of the claim, as long as the following notice and recording requirements are met.

Notice Requirements

Contractors Any person with whom the owner has contracted to provide labor, skill, or materials must personally deliver or send by certified mail the following notice within **10 days** after the contract is agreed upon. The notice shall be in at least 10-point bold type, if printed, or in capital letters if typewritten, and shall state as follows:

(a) Persons or companies furnishing labor or materials for the improvement of real property may enforce a lien upon the improved land if they are not paid for their contributions, even if such parties have no direct contractual relationship with the owner;

(b) Minnesota law permits the owner to withhold from his contractor as much of the contract price as may be necessary to meet the demands of all other lien claimants, pay directly such liens and deduct the cost thereof from the contract price, or withhold amounts from his contractor until the expiration of 90 days from the completion of such improvement unless the contractor furnishes to the owner waivers of claims for mechanics' liens signed by persons who furnished any labor or material for the improvement and who provided the owner with timely notice.

Subcontractors Any person who contributes to the improvement but is not under direct contract with the owner must serve the following notice to the owner within 45 days after the claimant has first furnished labor, skill, or materials in at least 10-point bold type, if printed, or in capital letters if typewritten:

"NOTICE TO OWNER"

TO: (name and address of owner)

We are authorized by law to provide you with this NOTICE. Your failure to read it carefully could result in unnecessary expense to you or in the loss of your (type of property) **at** (address of property).

We, (name & address of subcontractor) **, have been hired by your CONTRACTOR,** (name & address of contractor) **, to provide** (type of service or material) **for use in improving your property. We estimate our charges will be** (value of service or material). **If we are not paid by your CONTRACTOR, we can file a claim against your property for the price of our services. ENFORCEMENT OF OUR CLAIM COULD MEAN THE LOSS OF YOUR PROPERTY IF YOU ARE UNABLE TO PAY US FOR OUR SERVICES.**

To protect yourself, Minnesota law allows you to either:

1. Withhold payment to your CONTRACTOR for 90 days from the completion of the improvement or until he provides you with a waiver of claim from us which states that we will not file a claim against your property; or

2. Pay us directly and deduct the amount paid from the amount you owe your CONTRACTOR.

Recorded Statement The lien ceases *90 days* after the last item of labor, skill, material, or machinery is furnished unless it is preserved (perfected) by filing a statement in the county recorder's office that indicates:

(a) the intent to hold a lien
(b) the amount of the lien
(c) the items for which the lien is claimed

(d) the date of the first and last contributions
(e) a description of the premises
(f) the name of the owner
(g) the address of the claimant
(h) and proof that the required notice was given

INDEX AND GLOSSARY

Default: failure to perform a legal duty, such as failure to carry out the terms of a contract, 139–41, 154
Defeasance clause: a mortgage clause that states the mortgage is defeated if the accompanying note is repaid on time, 178, 186
Deficiency judgment: a judgment against a borrower if the sale of pledged property at foreclosure does not bring in enough to pay the balance owed, 194
de La Cuesta case: alienation clause enforcement allowed, 255–56
Delayed exchange: a nonsimultaneous tax-deferred trade, 173–74
Delinquent loan: a loan wherein the borrower is behind in his payments, 191
Delivery and acceptance of deed, 85
Demand for housing, long-run, 543–44; short-run, 539–43
Demand-pull inflation: higher prices due to buyers bidding against each other, 553
Department of Commerce: the Minnesota state department that regulates real estate licensees, 434
Department of Housing and Urban Development (HUD), GNMA, 250, 276; OILSR, 412–14; RESPA, 319–24
Deposit certificates: accounts wherein savers agree to leave their money on deposit for a specific period of time, 244
Deposit receipt: a receipt given for a deposit that accompanies an offer to purchase; also refers to a purchase contract that includes a deposit receipt, 146–49
Depreciation: loss of usefulness and value, 368–70; economic obsolescence, 370; functional obsolescence, 370; physical deterioration, 370; tax calculations, 563–66
Dereliction: the process whereby dry land is permanently exposed by a gradually receding waterline, 100
Descent of title, 94–96
Devise: a transfer of real property by means of a will, 95
Devisee: one who receives real property under a will, 95
Discharge of contracts, 138–39
Disclosure to third parties, 404–405
Discount broker: a full-service broker who charges less than the prevailing commission rates in his community, 411–12
Discount points: charges made by lenders to adjust the effective rate of interest on a loan, 231
Discrimination, Equal Credit Opportunity Act, 268, 551–52; fair housing laws, 338–39, 414–16
Disintermediation: the movement of money out of savings accounts into corporate and government debt instruments, 244–45
Distance and direction, 19–20
Distributees: those designated by law to receive the property of the deceased if he leaves no will, 94
Divorce, effect on ownership, as community property, 73
Doctrine of prior appropriation: a legal philosophy that allows a first user to continue diverting water, 17
Documentary tax: a fee or tax on deeds and other documents payable at the time of recordation, 298
Documents other than maps, 31
Dominant estate: the parcel of land which benefits from an easement, 47
Double declining balance: depreciation at twice normal rates for income tax purposes, 564
Dower: the legal right of a widow to a portion of her deceased husband's real property, 53, 58; by state, *table,* 55
Downside risk: the possibility that an investor will lose his money in an investment, 583
Drilling rights, 31, 59–60
Dry closing: a closing that is essentially complete except for disbursement of funds and delivery of documents, 305
Dual agency (divided agency): representation of two or more parties in a transaction by the same agent, 400
Due-on-sale: a clause in a note or mortgage that gives the lender the right to call the entire loan balance due if the property is sold or otherwise conveyed, 187, 255–56
Duration of estates, 53–57
Duress: the application of force to obtain an agreement, 134

Maggie Mae: a real estate industry nickname for the MGIC Investment Corporation, 252
MAI: Member of the American Institute of Real Estate Appraisers, 383
Maintenance fees: fees paid by a condominium or PUD unit owner to the owners' association for upkeep of the common elements, 500
Majority: the minimum age required for legal competency (in most states 18 years), 129
Maker: the person who signs a promissory note, 183
Management, condominium, 499–500; opportunities, 348–50; partnership, 73–75, 581; property, 342–48
Manner of attachment, 15
Map books, 28–30
Mapping a curve, 21
Market approach: a method of valuing a property based on the prices of recent sales of similar properties, 353–66; adjustment process, 356–60; comparables, 354–61; *illustrated* example, 357
Market value: the cash price that a willing buyer and a willing seller would agree upon, given reasonable exposure of the property to the marketplace, full information as to the potential uses of the property, and no undue compulsion to act, 354
Marketable title: title that is free from reasonable doubt as to who the owner is, 119–20
Marketable title acts: state laws aimed at cutting off rights and interests in land that have been inactive for long periods, 122–23
Married persons, community property, 71–73; as joint tenants, 70; as tenants by the entirety, 70–71
Master deed: a document that converts a parcel of land into a condominium subdivision, 497
Master plan: a comprehensive guide for the physical growth of a community, 529–30
Math review, Appendix D
Maturity: the end of the life of a loan, 209, 213; *also called* the maturity date
Measurement conversion table, Appendix G
Mechanic's lien: a claim placed against property by unpaid workmen or material suppliers, 50–51, 114
Meeting of the minds, mutual agreement: means that there must be agreement to the provisions of a contract by all parties involved, 131–34
Menace: threat of violence to obtain a contract, 134
Meridians: imaginary lines running north and south, used as references in mapping land, 22–26
Metes and bounds: a method of land description that identifies a parcel by specifying its shape and boundaries, 18–22, 28; monuments, 19–20; bench marks, 21–22; *illustrations,* 18–19, 21
Metric conversion table, Appendix G
MGIC: Mortgage Guaranty Insurance Corporation, 228–29, 252
Middleman: a person who brings two or more parties together but does not conduct negotiations, 401
Mile: 5,280 feet or 1,760 yards, 26–27
Mill rate: property tax rate that is expressed in tenths of a cent per dollar of assessed valuation, 283
Mineral rights, 31, 60
Minnesota Code of Agency, 471–89 (*excerpts*)
Minnesota Human Rights Act, 339, 416–18
Minnesota Landlord-Tenant Act, 335
Minnesota License Law Act, 448–89 (*excerpts*)
Minnesota Subdivided Land Sales Practices Act, 641–56 (*excerpts*)
Minnesota Uniform Condominium Act, 498
Minor or **Infant:** a person under the age of legal competence, in most states, under 18 years, 129
Mistake: refers to ambiguity in contract negotiations and mistake of material fact, 133–34
Modification: the influence on land use and value resulting from improvements made by man to surrounding parcels, 35
Monetary inflation: price rises due to the creation of excessive amounts of money by government, 553–54
Money damages: compensation paid in lieu of contract performance, 140
Money market accounts: interest bearing accounts with yields that rise and fall with current money market conditions, 244
Monument: an iron pipe, stone, tree, or other fixed point used in making a survey, 19–20
Mortgage: a pledge of property to secure the repayment of a debt, 177–96; amortized mortgage, 210–15; chattel mortgage, 180, 191; com-

north-south in the rectangular survey system, 23–26

Ready, willing, and able buyer: a buyer who is ready to buy now without further coaxing, and who has the financial capability to do so, 407–408

Real chattel: an interest in real estate that is personal property such as leasehold estate, 59

Real-cost inflation: higher prices due to greater effort needed to produce the same product today versus several years ago, 554–55

Real estate: land and improvements in a physical sense as well as the rights to own or use them, 17, 32–36

Real estate advisory council: in Minnesota, a board appointed by the Commissioner of Securities to advise and set policies regarding real estate licensees and transaction procedures, 434

Real estate cycles, long cycles, 547–49; sensitivity to credit, 549–50; short cycles, 549–50

Real estate investing, benefits, 561–64; investment timing, 573–75; limited partnership, 74–75, 579–84; personal strategy, 576–78; property selection, 568–73; risk taking, 561, 576; tax planning, 578; tax shelter, 563–64

Real estate investment trust (REIT): a method of pooling investor money using the trust form of ownership and featuring single taxation of profits, 77

Real estate license, application, 425, 451; branch office, 433; broker, 423; education requirements, 424–25, 458, 484–86; examination, 424, 426–30, 455–58; examination questions in Appendix C; history, 421–22; nonresident, 430–31, 454; procedure, 425–28; qualifications, 424–25; reciprocity, 431, 458; regulation, 433–34; renewal, 428; revocation and suspension, 133, 402–404, 434–36, 461–62; salesperson, 423–24; by state, *table,* 426–27; when required for transactions, 422–23

Real estate regulation, 433–34; license procedure, 425–28; real estate advisory council, 434; revocation and suspension of license, 133, 402–404, 434–36, 461–62; *see also* **Real estate license**

Real estate math review, Appendix D

Real Estate Resource Book, 2

Real estate sales contracts, 145–70

Real Estate Settlement Procedures Act: a federal law that deals with procedures to be followed in certain types of real estate closings, 319–24

Real property: ownership rights in land and its improvements, 17

Real savings: savings by persons and businesses that result from spending less than is earned, 253

Realtist: a member of the National Association of Real Estate Brokers, Inc., 447

Realtor: a term copyrighted by the National Association of Realtors for use by its members, 443; Code of Ethics, 443; Realtor-Associate, 443

Realtor-Associate: a membership designation for salespersons working for Realtors, 443

Realty: land and buildings and other improvements to land, 17

Reasonable care: a requirement that an agent exhibit competence and expertise, keep his client informed, and take proper care of property entrusted to him, 401

Recapture: depreciation in excess of straight-line rates is subject to recapture at ordinary income tax rates when the property is sold, 565–66

Reciprocity: an arrangement whereby one state honors licenses issued by another state and vice versa, 431, 458

Reconciliation: an appraisal technique whereby the appraiser weighs the cost, market, and income approaches to arrive at the final indicated value, 376–77

Reconveyance: the return to the borrower of legal title to his property upon repayment of the debt against it, 200–201

Recorded plat: a subdivision map filed in the county recorder's office that shows the location and boundaries of individual parcels of land, 28–30

Recorded survey: (same as recorded map or plat), 28–30

Recording acts: laws that provide for the placing of documents in the public records, 106–107

Recovery fund: a state-operated fund that can be tapped to pay for uncollectible judgments against real estate licensees, 436–37

Rectangular survey system: a government system for surveying land that uses latitude and longitude lines as references, 22–28; base line, 22–